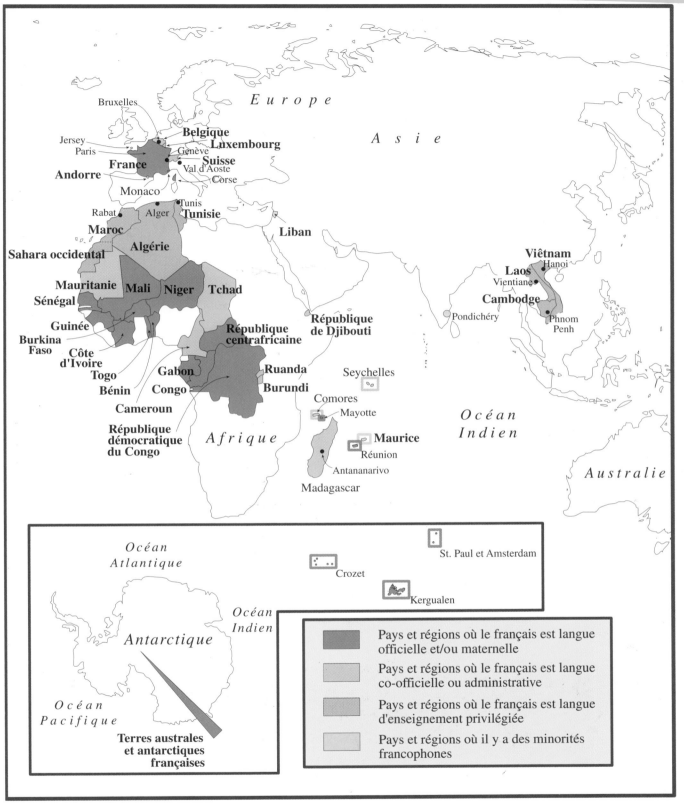

P9-AFZ-004

Europe

Asie

Bruxelles
Belgique
Jersey
Luxembourg
Paris
Genève
Suisse
France
Val d'Aoste
Andorre
Corse
Monaco

Tunis
Rabat
Alger
Tunisie
Maroc
Liban
Algérie
Sahara occidental
Viêtnam
Hanoi
Laos
Vientiane
Mauritanie
Mali
Niger
Tchad
Cambodge
Sénégal
Pondichéry
Guinée
Phnom
Penh
Burkina
Faso
République
centrafricaine
République
de Djibouti
Côte
d'Ivoire
Togo
Gabon
Ruanda
Seychelles
Bénin
Congo
Burundi
Cameroun
Comores
Mayotte
Océan
Indien
République
démocratique
du Congo
Afrique
Maurice
Réunion
Antananarivo
Australie
Madagascar

St. Paul et Amsterdam
Océan
Atlantique
Crozet
Océan
Indien
Kergualen
Antarctique

Océan
Pacifique
Terres australes
et antarctiques
françaises

Pays et régions où le français est langue
officielle et/ou maternelle

Pays et régions où le français est langue
co-officielle ou administrative

Pays et régions où le français est langue
d'enseignement privilégiée

Pays et régions où il y a des minorités
francophones

From the francophone world to the multimedia world . . . *Horizons* keeps you connected

Log on to the Book Companion Website
for more interactive practice opportunities!
academic.cengage.com/french/horizons

The **Companion Website** features cultural activities that prompt you to gather materials and information from authentic French websites. Self-correcting grammar and vocabulary activities as well as interactive flashcards provide additional practice and instant feedback for each chapter. The website also links you to **YouTube** video clips, **Google Earth**™ coordinates, and **Heinle iRadio** as well as an **iTunes playlist** featuring the songs from the text's new *Sélections musicales*.

NICE
NOMBRE D'HABITANTS: 347 100 (avec ses agglomérations *[metropolitan region]*: 933 080) (les Niçois)
DÉPARTEMENT: Alpes-Maritimes
RÉGION: Provence-Alpes-Côte d'Azur

Visit it live on Google Earth!

www Visit it live on Google Earth!

La rue et **la place** Masséna.

You can virtually visit each of the geographic locations featured in the text through **Google Earth**! Icons in the text indicate where you can access **Google Earth** coordinates that take you abroad to exciting francophone destinations. These coordinates can be found on the *Horizons* **Companion Website**.

Each *Comparaison culturelles* includes **new**, suggested **YouTube** video correlations that allow you to explore the diverse cultures of the French-speaking world through film.

Grammar
Le verbe aller
Le verbe avoir
Compréhension
Les adjectifs de couleur
Consonants
Les articles définis
Le verbe être
Final Consonants
Les articles indéfinis et définis
Les verbes –er

Le verbe aller

Structure grammaticale: The verb *aller*. Listen to the dialogue.

Les questions de papa
Papa: Où est-ce que vous allez, vous deux?
Laure: Nous allons au café, papa.
Papa: Et toi, Georges? Tu vas où?
Georges: Moi, je vais à l'université.
Laure: C'est pas vrai! Il va à la Fnac acheter des CD!

Explication: Now repeat the forms of the verb *aller*. Je vais. Tu vas. Il va. Elle va. On va. Nous allons. Vous allez. Ils vont. Elles vont. Did you notice anything about the *nous* and *vous* forms? That's right: The *s* was pronounced because *allez* and *allons* begin with a vowel. Now repeat the following sentences. Je vais à Paris. Elle va à Rome. Nous allons à Londres. Où est-ce que vous allez? Ils vont à Moscou. Tu vas à la Fnac? Elles vont au McDo. On va à Madrid?

aller	
je vais	nous allons
tu vas	vous allez
il/elle/on va	ils/elles vont

Tell Us What You Think – Win an iPod!   What is Podcasting/RSS?   RSS Podcast Feed

Heinle iRadio features MP3-ready grammar and pronunciation tutorials. Icons in the text indicate where you can turn to **Heinle iRadio** for mini-lessons on difficult grammar points and pronunciation to supplement your learning. With these downloadable audio lessons, you have the freedom to choose when, where, and how you practice.

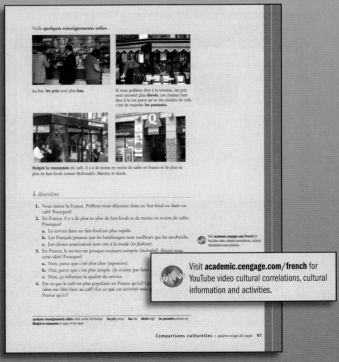

Voilà quelques renseignements utiles.

Au bar, **les prix** sont plus **bas**.

Si vous préférez être à la terrasse, les prix sont souvent plus **élevés**. Les chaises font face à la rue parce qu'un des plaisirs du café, c'est de regarder **les passants**.

Malgré la renommée du café, il y a de moins en moins de cafés en France et de plus en plus de fast-foods comme McDonald's (Macdo) et Quick.

À discuter
1. Vous visitez la France. Préférez-vous déjeuner dans un fast-food ou dans un café? Pourquoi?
2. En France, il y a de plus en plus de fast-foods et de moins en moins de cafés. Pourquoi?
   a. Le service dans un fast-food est plus rapide.
   b. Les Français pensent que les hamburgers sont meilleurs que les sandwichs.
   c. Les choses américaines sont très à la mode *(in fashion)*.
3. En France, le service est presque toujours compris *(included)*. Aimez-vous cette idée? Pourquoi?
   a. Non, parce que c'est plus cher *(expensive)*.
   b. Oui, parce que c'est plus simple. (Je n'aime pas faire ...)
   c. Non, ça influence la qualité du service.
4. Est-ce que le café est plus populaire en France qu'ici? Qu... *(does one like)* faire au café? Est-ce que ces activités sont ... France qu'ici?

Visit **academic.cengage.com/french** for YouTube video cultural correlations, cultural information and activities.

www Visit **academic.cengage.com/french** for YouTube video cultural correlations, cultural information and activities.

quelques renseignements utiles *some useful information* les prix *prices* bas *low* élevés *high* les passants *passers-by*
Malgré la renommée *in spite of the fame*

HORIZONS

Fourth Edition

Joan H. Manley
University of Texas—El Paso

Stuart Smith
Austin Community College

John T. McMinn
Austin Community College

Marc A. Prévost
Austin Community College

HEINLE
CENGAGE Learning™

Australia • Brazil • Japan • Korea • Mexico • Singapore • Spain • United Kingdom • United States

Horizons
Fourth Edition
Manley | Smith | McMinn | Prévost

Executive Editor: Lara Semones

Acquisitions Editor: Nicole Morinon

Senior Content Project Manager: Esther Marshall

Assistant Editor: Catharine Thomson

Associate Technology Project Manager:
  Morgen Murphy

Senior Marketing Manager: Lindsey Richardson

Marketing Assistant: Denise Bousquet

Senior Marketing Communications Manager:
  Stacey Purviance

Creative Director: Rob Hugel

Senior Art Director: Cate Rickard Barr

Senior Print Buyer: Elizabeth Donaghey

Text Designer: Brian Salisbury

Photo Researcher: Jill Engebretson

Permissions Editor: Sylvie Pittet

Cover Designer: Diane Lévy

Compositor: Pre-Press PMG

Cover image: ©Getty Images, Inc.

Photographers: Michael Brusselle, PureStock,
  David Hughes

For product information and technology assistance, contact us at
Cengage Learning Academic Resource Center, 1-800-423-0563

For permission to use material from this text or product,
submit all requests online at **cengage.com/permissions**
Further permissions questions can be e-mailed to
permissionrequest@cengage.com

Library of Congress Control Number: 2007943557

Student Edition:
ISBN-13: 978-1-4130-3307-6
ISBN-10: 1-4130-3307-5

Heinle Cengage Learning
25 Thomson Place
Boston, MA 02210
USA

Cengage Learning products are represented in Canada by Nelson Education, Ltd.

For your course and learning solutions, visit **academic.cengage.com**

Purchase any of our products at your local college store or at our preferred online store **www.ichapters.com**

Printed in Canada
1 2 3 4 5 6 7 12 11 10 09 08

Do you have a gift for languages?

Have you ever heard people say that they know someone who has a gift for languages? What does that mean? Are some people born with a special ability to learn languages? How do you know if you have a gift for languages? If you understood the sentence you just read, then you have a gift for languages. After all, you have already learned to speak and understand at least one language well—English. Everybody is born with a natural ability to learn languages, but some individuals seem to learn languages more quickly than others do. This is because, over time, we develop different learning styles.

The process individuals use to learn languages depends a great deal on their personality. As with any other process, such as learning a new computer program or writing a composition for English class, individuals can attain similar results, although they approach the task differently. Some language learners like to plan each step before beginning. Others prefer to jump in as soon as they know enough to get started, and continue from there using a hit-or-miss method. Some language learners like to understand in detail why a language works the way it does before they try to use it, whereas others are ready to try speaking as soon as they know only the most basic rules, making educated guesses about how to express themselves.

Both methods have advantages and disadvantages. Some people become so bogged down in details that they lose sight of their main purpose—communication. Others pay so little attention to details that what they say is unintelligible. No matter what sort of learner you are, the most important part of the language-learning process is to constantly try to use the language to express yourself. Always alternate study of vocabulary and structures with attempts to communicate.

Since you now know that you have a gift for languages, you might think of the following pages as a user's manual that suggests how to use your language-learning capacity to learn French efficiently. Some of the learning techniques will work for you, others may not fit your learning style. Read through the following three sections before beginning your French studies, and refer to them later to develop the language-learning process that works best for you.

- **Goals and expectations:** How much French should you expect to learn in your first year of study and how much time and effort will be required of you?
- **Motivation:** How do you motivate yourself to study and practice the language?
- **Learning techniques:** What are some study tips that will facilitate learning French?

Goals and Expectations

Who can learn a language?

Many people believe that, as an adult, you cannot learn a language as well as you might have when you were a child. It is true that children are good language learners, but there is no reason why adults cannot learn to speak a language with near-native fluency. Children learn languages well because they can adapt very easily and they do it willingly. Being able to adapt is very important in language learning. Children are not afraid to try something new, and they are not easily embarrassed if things do not turn out as they expect. Adults, on the other hand, are often afraid of doing something wrong or looking ridiculous. Don't be afraid to experiment, using what you already know to guess at how to express yourself in French. It does no harm if you try to say something and you do not get the expected response. Just try again.

By the time people become adults, they generally learn by analyzing, rather than by doing. They have also grown so accustomed to their own way of doing things that they are reluctant to change. Similarly, adult language learners often feel that the way English works is the natural way. They try to force the language they are learning into the same mold. In fact, languages work in a variety of ways, all equally natural. Learn to accept that the French way of doing things is just as natural and valid as the English way.

Another difference in the way that children and adults learn languages is that children spend a lot more time focused on what they are doing. When children learn languages, they spend almost every hour they are awake for several years doing nothing but learning the language. Learning to communicate is their principal objective in life. Most adults, on the other hand, spend just a few hours a week studying a new language, and during this time they are often distracted by many other aspects of their lives. In a classroom setting where small children have contact with a foreign language for just a few hours per week, children do not learn better than adults. In fact, adults have several advantages over children, such as their ability to organize and their longer attention spans. Your ability to develop fluency in French depends mainly on three things: the amount of time you spend with the language, how focused you are, and how willing you are to try to communicate using it.

How well will you speak after a year?

Those of you who are new to foreign language study probably have a variety of ideas about what you will be doing in this course. People who become frustrated in foreign language study generally do so because they start off with the wrong expectations. Some people begin a foreign language course with a negative attitude, thinking that it is impossible to really learn a language without going to a country where it is spoken. Although it is indeed usually easier to learn French in a French-speaking region, you can learn to speak French very fluently here as well. Once again, it is a question of spending time with the language, while focusing on how to communicate with it.

There are also some students who begin foreign language classes with expectations that are too high, thinking that they will begin speaking French with complete fluency nearly overnight. Learning a language takes time. Even after two years of concentrated study, it is reasonable to have achieved only basic fluency. If you set a goal for yourself to have everyday conversation skills after your second year of study, and if you work hard toward this goal, you will be able to function in most everyday conversation settings; however, you will still frequently have to look for words, you will probably still speak in short simple sentences, and you will often have to use circumlocution to get your meaning across. In *Horizons,* you will learn how to function in the most common situations in which you are likely to find yourself in a francophone region. To illustrate how much you will learn during the first few weeks of study, take out a sheet of paper, and list, in English, the first eight questions you would probably ask in the following situation: Before the first day of class, you sit down next to a student you have never seen before and you begin to chat.

In this situation, students generally ask questions like the following:

- How are you doing?
- What's your name?
- What are you studying?

- Where are you from?
- Where do you live? / Do you live on campus?
- Do you like it there?
- Do you work? Where?
- When are you graduating?

This is the extent of the conversation that you have with many people you will meet, and you will be able to do this in French after only a few weeks.

How much time and effort must you invest to be a successful language learner?

There are three P's involved in learning a language: patience, practice, and persistence. We have already said that success in learning a foreign language depends on how much time you spend studying and practicing it. You might wonder how time-consuming French class will be. The amount of time required depends on your study skills and attention span. However, nobody can be successful without devoting many hours to studying and using the language. Generally, to make steady progress at the rate that material is presented in most college or university classes, you should expect to spend two to three hours on the language outside of class, for every hour that you are in class.

What is involved in learning to express yourself in another language?

Students studying a foreign language for the first time may have false expectations about what is involved in learning to speak another language. Many people think that you just substitute a French word for the equivalent word in English. Most of the time, you cannot translate word for word from one language to another. For example, if a French speaker substituted the equivalent English word for each French word in the following sentence, it would create a very unusual sentence.

Nous ne l'avons pas encore fait.

We not it have not still done.

You might be able to figure out that this sentence means, "We haven't done it yet," but sometimes translating word for word can give a completely wrong meaning. For example, if you translate the following sentence word for word, you would think that it has the first meaning that follows it, whereas it really has the second. This is because the indirect object pronoun **vous** *([to] you)* precedes the verb in French.

Je voudrais vous parler demain, s'il vous plaît.

I would like you to speak tomorrow, if it you pleases.

I would like to speak to you tomorrow, please.

You probably noticed in this last example that one word in English may be translated by several words in French and vice versa (**voudrais** = *would like*, **vous** = *to you*, **parler** = *to speak*, **s'il vous plaît** = *please*).

Differences in languages are not due simply to a lack of one-to-one correspondence between words and structures. Cultural differences also strongly affect how we communicate. Culture and language are so interrelated that it is impossible to learn a language fluently without becoming familiar with the culture(s) where it is spoken. For example, in French, a cultural difference that affects the spoken language is that French society is not as informal as ours. Adults generally do not call each other by their first names, and the words for *sir* and *madam* are used much more frequently than in English. For example, it is normal to say **Bonjour, monsieur** *(Hello, sir),* whereas English speakers say *Hello.*

Cultural differences affect the spoken language and also nonverbal communication. For instance, when the French speak to each other, they generally stand closer than we do. When we are talking to a French-speaker, we may feel that our space is invaded and back away. The French interpret this as standoffishness. As you can see, learning to communicate in French entails a lot more than substituting French words for English words in a sentence.

Does practice make perfect?

Your goal in learning French should not be to say everything perfectly. If you set this goal for yourself, you will probably be afraid to open your mouth, fearing mistakes. Your goal should be to communicate clearly, but you should expect to make mistakes when speaking. If you make a mistake that impedes communication, those you are speaking to will ask for clarification or repeat what you have said to be sure of what you mean. Listen carefully to how they express themselves, and make adjustments the next time you need to convey a similar message.

Although perfection is not the goal of language learners, practice is vital to success. (Remember the three P's of language learning: patience, practice, and persistence.) You can learn every vocabulary word and rule in the book, but unless you practice regularly, listening to French and attempting to speak it, you will not learn the language. Practicing a language is just as necessary for success as practicing a sport or a musical instrument. Imagine that you are a football player or pianist. You might know every play in the book, or you might understand music theory completely, but unless you practice, you will never be able to perform. It is important to learn the rules of French, but you must also practice it regularly.

What do you do if foreign languages make you panic?

Most individuals feel nervous when they have to speak to strangers. This is true when you speak your own language, and it's even truer when speaking a foreign language. There is no reason to be nervous, yet fear of looking ridiculous is often difficult to control. It is normal to experience some anxiety in class. If you suffer extreme anxiety in language class—to such a degree that it impedes your ability to concentrate—it is best to recognize that you fear having to perform in class. Go see your instructor and discuss your anxiety. In order to conquer it, you must acknowledge it.

Motivation

How can learning a foreign language help you?

Learning a foreign language should be fun. After all, you will spend a lot of class time chatting with classmates, which most of us find enjoyable. However, learning French takes time and effort. No matter how much you enjoy it, there will be times when you need to motivate yourself to study or practice. You can use motivation techniques for practicing a language similar to those musicians or athletes use to practice an instrument or a sport.

Many musicians and athletes have a personal goal. They imagine themselves playing a great concert at Carnegie Hall or winning a big game, receiving applause and praise. Similarly, each time you start to practice French, imagine yourself speaking French fluently with a beautiful accent. In this mental image, you might be a diplomat, or you might be talking to the waiter at a French restaurant, impressing your friends.

Some people who practice an instrument or a sport do so for personal growth. Many people feel that learning a new language helps them discover a new side of their personality. By learning to appreciate another culture, you learn to understand your own better. You also come to know yourself better and you broaden your horizons.

Of course, a lot of people are motivated to practice an instrument or a sport because they make their living from it. This is good motivation for learning a language too. In today's international economy, the best jobs are going

How can you learn to enjoy studying?

As with any accomplishment, learning a foreign language requires a lot of work. You will enjoy it more if you think of it as a hobby or a pastime and as an opportunity to develop a skill. Here are some training techniques that can help you learn a new language.

- Get into a routine. Devote a particular time of day to studying French. It is best to find a time when you are fresh and free of distractions, so you can concentrate on what you are doing. If you study at the same time every day, getting started will become habitual, and you will have won half the battle. Once you are settled working and learning, it becomes fun.

- Make sure that the place where you study is inviting and that you enjoy being there.

- Study frequently for short periods of time, rather than having marathon sessions. After about two hours of study, the ability of the brain to retain information is greatly reduced. You tend to remember what you learn at the beginning of each study session and at the end. What you study in the middle tends to become blurred. To illustrate this, read the following words one time, then turn the page and see how many you remember.

  dog, house, sofa, cat, rooster, room, telephone, mouse, book, pencil, television

  Most people can remember the first word and the last. The longer the list, the harder it is to remember the words in the middle. The same is true with studying. Study smaller "chunks" of material more frequently, and set reasonable goals for yourself. Don't try to learn it all at once.

- Study with a classmate or a friend. It is much easier to practice talking with someone else, and it is easier to spend more time working with the language if you are interacting with another person. Also, by studying with classmates, you will feel more comfortable speaking in front of them, which eliminates some of the embarrassment some adults feel when trying to pronounce foreign words in front of the whole class.

- Play games with the language. It is fun to learn how to say things in a new language. For instance, ask yourself how you would say things you hear on the radio or television in French. If you do know how to say something in French that you hear, your knowledge will become more certain. If you don't know how to say something in French, that's normal if you are a beginner. When you finally learn the word or expression you were wondering about, you will remember it more easily, because you have already thought about it.

- Surround yourself by French. Rent French movies or watch DVDs of American movies in the French-language track, listen to French music, and read French comic books and magazines. Magazines with a lot of pictures are the best, because the pictures give you clues to the meaning of unfamiliar words. You probably will not understand very much at first in movies and songs, but they will motivate you to learn more. They teach you about cultural differences, and they help give you a sense of good pronunciation.

- Don't let yourself get frustrated. If you are frustrated each time you sit down to study, ask yourself why. First of all, make sure that you are not studying when you are too tired or hungry. Also, make sure that you clearly understand your assignment and its purpose. Learn to distinguish a language-learning problem from a problem understanding instructions. If you are confused about what you are to do or why, see your instructor during office hours or contact another student. (This is another reason to study with a classmate!)

Learning Techniques

How can you spend your study time most efficiently?

Individuals organize material differently as they learn it. Some people learn better by seeing something; others learn better by hearing it. The following are some study tips for how to go about learning French. You may find that some of these methods work for you and others do not. Be creative in practicing your French, using a variety of study techniques.

General study tips

- Learn not to translate word for word. Learn to read and listen to whole sentences at a time.

- Keep a log of your study time in a small spiral notebook. This will help you learn to study more efficiently.

Each time you sit down to study new material, write down the time you begin. When you finish, write down the time you stop, and two or three sentences summarizing what you studied. Students often feel frustrated that they spend a lot of time studying, but they do not retain much. By keeping a log, you will know exactly how much time you spend on French. Writing one or two sentences summarizing what you studied helps you check your retention.

- Alternate speaking, listening, reading, and writing activities. By changing tasks frequently, you will be able to study longer without losing your concentration.

Vocabulary-learning techniques

- Use your senses. Pronounce words aloud as you study them. Close your eyes as you pronounce the word and picture the thing or activity represented by nouns or verbs.

- Use flashcards. When possible, draw a simple picture instead of the English word. Also, write a sentence using the word on the card, trying to remember it each time you look at the card. Use different colored inks to help you visualize the meaning of words. For example, when studying colors, write them on the flashcard in that color. When learning food items, write the words for red foods, such as strawberries and tomatoes, in red, the words for green foods in green, etc. Write words that can be associated with shapes, such as tall, short, big, small, round, or square, with letters having similar shapes.

- Learn useful common phrases such as "What time is it?" or "How are you?" as a whole.

- Label household items in French on masking tape.

- Tape lists of vocabulary in places where you spend time doing routine tasks.

- Study vocabulary in manageable "chunks." Each morning, write out a list of 20 new words and carry it in your pocket. A few times during the day, spend two minutes trying to remember the words on the list. Take out the list and review the words you forgot for two minutes. By the end of the day, you will have spent just a few minutes and you will have learned the 20 words.

- Learn 10 useful phrases every day.

- The end-of-chapter vocabulary words are recorded on the *Text Audio CDs*. Play them at home, while you jog, or in your car.

- Make tests for yourself. At the end of a study session, write the English words or phrases on a sheet of paper. Put the sheet of paper away for a few hours. Later, take it out and see how many of the French equivalents of these words or phrases you remember.

- Group words in logical categories. For example, learn words for fruits together, words for animals together, sports-related vocabulary together, etc.

- Make flashcards with antonyms on each side such as hot/cold, near/far, to go to sleep/to wake up, etc.

- Use related English words to help you remember the French. For example, the French word for *to begin* is **commencer.** Associate it with *to commence.* Be creative in finding associations. For example, the word for *open* is **ouvert.** You can associate it with *overture,* which is the opening part of a musical piece, or an *overt* action, which is one that is done in the open. Write related English words on flashcards.

- Learn to say **"Comment dit-on... ?"** (*"How do you say . . . ?"*) when you do not know a word or phrase.

- Remember that we cannot say everything even in our own language. If you do not know a word, try to think of another way to say what you want. Use circumlocution. For example, if you do not know how to say "to drive," say "to take the car" instead.

Grammar-learning techniques

- Play teacher. Try to guess what your instructor would ask you to do if he or she were giving a quiz the next day.

- Do the **Pour vérifier** self-checks in the margins next to explanations of structures.

- Use color coding to help you remember grammatical information. For example, all nouns in French are categorized either as masculine or feminine, and you must memorize in which category each noun belongs. When you make the flashcards, write feminine nouns on pink cards or with pink ink and use blue for masculine nouns. Use an eye-catching color on flashcards to indicate points you want to remember, such as irregular plurals or verbs that take **être** in the **passé composé.**

- If you like to use lists to study, organize them so that they help you remember information about words. For example, to remember noun gender, write masculine words in a column on the left and feminine words in a column on the right. If you can visualize where the word is on the list, you can remember its gender.

- Learn to accept ambiguity. Sometimes, as soon as you learn a new rule, you find out that it doesn't always work the way you expect it to.

Pronunciation-learning techniques

- Repeat everything you hear in French under your breath or in your head, even if you have no idea what it means. This will not only help your pronunciation, it will help your listening comprehension and your ability to learn vocabulary. For instance, if you keep repeating an unfamiliar word you hear in your head, when you finally find out what it means, you will remember it very easily.
- Read French words aloud as you study.
- Listen to the CDs that go with the book and the *Cahier d'activités orales* (Lab Manual) several times. It is impossible to concentrate both on meaning and pronunciation the first time you listen to them. Listen to them at least once focusing on pronunciation only.
- Make tapes of yourself and compare them to those of native speakers.
- Exaggerate as you practice at home. Any pronunciation that is not English will seem like exaggeration. Psychologically, it is very difficult to listen to yourself speaking another language. Pretend you are a French actor playing a role as you practice pronunciation.

Using the Text Audio CDs and the Lab Audio CDs

There are two distinct CDs that go with each chapter of the **Horizons** program: the *Text Audio CD* and the *Lab Audio CD*. The activities on the *Text Audio CDs* correspond to the listening sections marked with an audio icon in the textbook. These CDs are provided so that you can review material covered in class on your own, or prepare for the next day's class. The activities corresponding to the *Lab Audio CDs* are found in the *Cahier,* in the *Activités orales* section. These activities give you extra practice listening to and pronouncing French. When you are preparing to do a listening activity in the textbook or the *Activités orales* section of the *Cahier,* it is important to make sure that you have the right CD.

In order to get maximum benefit from the CDs, approach listening activities with the right attitude. It takes time, patience, and practice to understand French spoken at a normal conversational speed. Do not be surprised if you find it difficult at first. Relax and listen to passages more than once. You will understand a little more each time. Remember that you will not understand everything and that, for some exercises, you are only expected to understand enough to answer specific questions. Read through exercises prior to starting the CD, so that you know what to listen for.

If you find you do not have enough time to process and respond to a question before the next one, take advantage of the pause or stop button on your CD player to give yourself more time. Most importantly, be patient and remember that you can always listen again.

Be willing to listen to the CDs several times. It is important to listen to them at least one separate time focusing solely on pronunciation. Practice, patience, and persistence pay!

We hope that the preceding suggestions on how to go about learning French will serve you well, helping you to become a successful language learner. Good luck with your French studies, and most of all, enjoy yourself!

Acknowledgments

We are grateful to a great many people for helping us transform our collective classroom experience into this text. Principal among these are Lara Semones and Nicole Morinon for the opportunity to work with Heinle and for their support; Esther Marshall with the help of Sev Champeny and Melissa Mattson from Pre-Press PMG, for their support and hard work down the home stretch; to the marketing and technology people and in particular Lindsey Richardson, Stacey Purviance, Cat Thomson, and Morgen Murphy; and to the other freelancers: interior designer, Brian Salisbury; cover designer, Diane Lévy; and native reader of the Companion Website, Dianne Harwood.

We would particularly like to thank our reviewers of the current and previous editions:

John Angell, *University of Louisiana at Lafayette*
Patricia Black, *California State University, Chico*
Guylene Deasy, *University of North Carolina, Greensboro*
Nicole Denner, *Stetson University*
Angela Elsey, *University of California, Santa Cruz*
Catherine H. Fraley, *University of Evansville*
Janette Funaro, *Johnson County Community College*
Gary Godfrey, *Weber State University*
Marvin Gordon, *University of Illinois at Chicago*
Patricia Gravatt, *Ithaca College*
Kristin Halling, *Wright State University*

Margaret Harp, *University of Nevada, Las Vegas*

Suzanne Hendrickson, *University of St. Louis, Missouri*

Susan Hennessy, *Missouri Western State University*

Caren Kindel, *Kent State University*

Mike Ledgerwood, *Samford University*

Leah Lyons, *Middle Tennesse State University*

Chantal Maher, *Palomer College*

Berenice V. Le Marchand, *San Francisco State University*

Matilde Mésavage, *Rollins College*

Stamos Metzidakis, *Washington University in St. Louis*

Kristina Watkins Mormino, *Georgia Gwinett College*

Shawn Morrison, *College of Charlestown*

Kathryn Murphy-Judy, *Virginia Commonwealth University*

Linda Nodjimbadem, *University of Texas – El Paso*

Pamela F. Paine, *Auburn University*

Mariagrazia Novelli Spina, *University of Central Florida*

Kimberly Swanson, *University of Kansas*

Kelle Truby, *University of California, Riverside*

Lawrence Williams, *University of North Texas*

List of Supplements Authors

Lara Mangiafico, *University of Michigan* (Revised testing program for the PowerLecture CD-ROM)

Heather McCoy, *The Pennsylvania State University* (Companion website cultural activities)

Tara Foster, *University of Missouri – Columbia* (Lesson plans for the PowerLecture CD-ROM)

Kelle Truby, *University of California, Riverside* (YouTube guide and correlations)

Joan Debrah, *University of Hawaii* (Companion website grammar quizzes)

Christine Wilson (iLrn Heinle Learning Center – Diagnostics portion)

Suzanne Hendrickson (iLrn Heinle Learning Center – Enrichment activities)

A special thanks to both Jims, Laura, Andrew, Annick, Daniel, and Joel.

Last, but obviously not least, we thank each other for the tolerance, mutual encouragement, and strengthened bonds of friendship such an endeavor requires.

Merci mille fois!

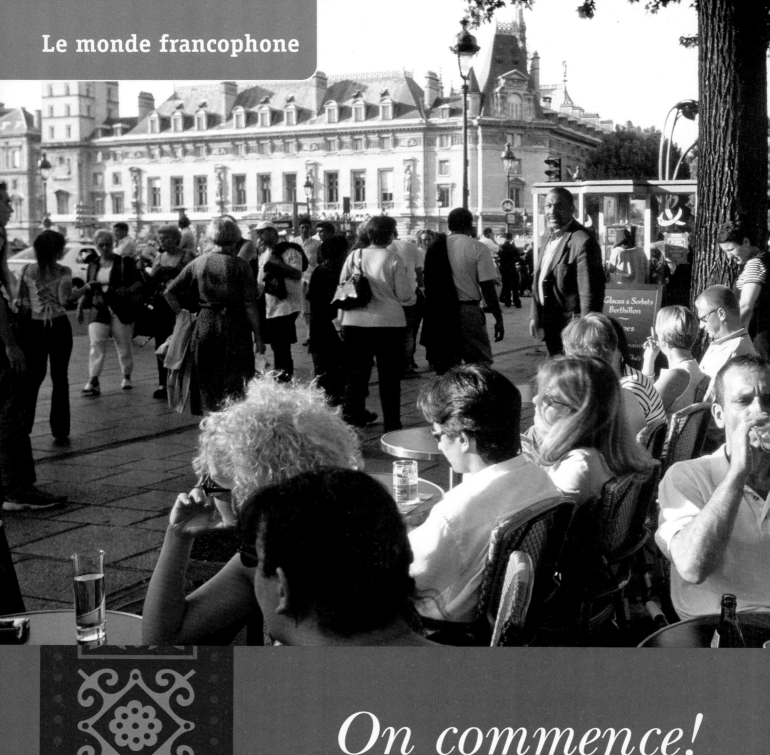

On commence!

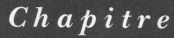

Compétence

iLrn iLrn Heinle Learning Center

academic.cengage.com/french/horizons

Système-D

Audio   iRadio

 Look inside the front cover of your book at the map of the countries and regions where French is spoken. Are you surprised that some of these countries and regions are francophone? Pick one of them and research its history on the Web to find out why people speak French there, and if they speak any other languages. If so, what percentage of the population speaks each language?

NOTE
Boldfaced words are glossed at the bottom of the page. Try to guess their meaning from the context before looking at the glosses.

Bienvenue dans le monde francophone!
Spoken in 44 countries, French plays an important role in international business and diplomacy. It is one of the official languages of the United Nations. How many French-speaking countries can you name? When talking about French culture, what are the first ten words or names that come to your mind?

Connaissez-vous...

la cuisine et le vin français: le pâté, la quiche, la soupe à l'oignon, le champagne?

la littérature francophone: Colette, Jules Verne, Jean-Paul Sartre, Léopold Senghor, Albert Camus, Victor Hugo?

le cinéma français: Louis Malle, François Truffaut, Catherine Deneuve, Gérard Depardieu, Juliette Binoche, Audrey Tautou?

la mode et les parfums français: Cartier, Chanel, Dior, Vuitton, Yves Saint Laurent?

Bienvenue dans le monde francophone! *Welcome to the French-speaking world!*   **Connaissez-vous... ?** *Are you familiar with . . . ?*

les peintres et les sculpteurs: Pierre Auguste Renoir, Camille Claudel, Auguste Rodin?

la musique de Claude Debussy, d'Édith Piaf, de Jacques Brel? la musique **cadienne**? la musique zouk?

la science et la technologie françaises: Pierre et Marie Curie, Descartes, Louis Pasteur, la **fusée** Ariane, le TGV?

les produits français: Bic, Danone, Yoplait, Michelin, Thomson, Lancôme, Perrier, Renault?

cadienne *Cajun* **la fusée** *the rocket*

❈ Qu'en savez-vous?

Test your knowledge of the francophone world. Before you look at the map inside the front cover, see how many of these questions you can answer.

1. In how many countries is French spoken: about 5, about 25, about 40, or about 100?
2. There are several places in the Americas where French is spoken. Name two.
3. In which three of these places in the Caribbean is French an important language: the Dominican Republic, Haiti, Guadeloupe, the Virgin Islands, the Bahamas, Martinique, the Cayman Islands?
4. True or false? French is not spoken in any areas of the South Pacific.
5. True or false? Some people in Laos, Cambodia, and Vietnam speak French.
6. True or false? The existence of French-speaking people in the Americas, Africa, Asia, and the Pacific is largely due to the history of French colonialism.
7. French is spoken in several other countries of Europe besides France. Name two.
8. French is spoken in many countries in Africa. Are most of them found in the north, west, east, or south?
9. French developed from a Latin base, whereas English developed from a Germanic base. However, English was greatly influenced by French largely due to what historical event?
10. Where in South America is French spoken?

Greeting people

Les formules de politesse

Use these expressions to greet adult strangers and those to whom you show respect.

CD 1-2

— Bonjour, madame.
— Bonjour, monsieur. Je suis Hélène Cauvin. Et vous, comment vous appelez-vous?
— Je m'appelle Jean-Marc Bertin.

— Bonsoir, mademoiselle.
— Bonsoir, monsieur. **Comment allez-vous?**
— **Je vais très bien, merci.** Et vous?
— **Assez** bien.

Use these expressions to say how you are doing.

CD 1-3 Comment allez-vous?

Je vais très bien. Et vous?

Assez bien. / **Pas mal.**

Pas très bien.

Comment allez-vous? *How are you?*   **Je vais très bien, merci.** *I'm doing very well, thank you.*   **Assez** *Fairly, Rather*
Pas mal. *Not badly.*

CD 1-4

Prononciation

Les consonnes muettes et la liaison

In French, consonants at the end of words are often silent. And **h** is always silent, as it is in some English words such as *hour* and *honest*. As you hear these greetings, note which consonants are not pronounced.

— Bonjour, monsieur. Je m'appelle Paul Richard. Et vous, comment vous appelez-vous?

— Je m'appelle Henri Dulac.

— Comment allez-vous?

— Très bien, et vous, monsieur?

— Très bien, merci.

The consonants **c, r, f,** and **l** (CaReFuL) are the only consonants that are generally pronounced at the end of a word. The final **r** of **monsieur,** however, is not pronounced.

Marc   bonjour   actif   Chantal

If a consonant at the end of a word is followed by a word beginning with a vowel sound (**a, e, i, o, u, y**) or a mute **h,** the final consonant sound is often pronounced and is linked to the beginning of the next word. This linking is called **liaison.** In liaison, a single **s** is pronounced like a **z.**

Commen*t* vous *z* appele*z*-vou*s*? Comment *t* alle*z*-vou*s*?

A. Prononcez bien. Copy these sentences, crossing out the consonants that should not be pronounced and marking where liaison would occur.

EXEMPLE   Comment alle*z*-vou*s*, monsieu*r*?

1. Je suis Chantal Hubert.
2. Bonjour, madame. Comment allez-vous?
3. Très bien, monsieur. Comment vous appelez-vous?
4. Je m'appelle Henri Dufour. Et vous?

Now go back and reorder the four sentences to create a logical conversation to read with a partner.

B. Que dit-on? Complete the conversations.

1.
2.
3.

C. Bonsoir! Imagine that you are at a formal reception. Greet three people, exchange names, and find out how they are doing. Be sure to shake hands.

To greet or exchange names with classmates, friends, family members, or children, say:

Vocabulaire supplémentaire

Comment t'appelles-tu? / Comment tu t'appelles?
  What's your name? (familiar)
Comment vas-tu? *How are you?* (familiar)
Ciao! *Bye!* (familiar)
Salut! *Hi! Bye!* (familiar)
Bon week-end! *Have a good weekend!*
Bonne journée! *Have a good day!*

CD 1-5

— Salut, Jean-Pierre. **Ça va?**
— Salut, Micheline. **Ça va.** Et toi, **comment ça va?**
— Pas mal.

— Bonjour, je m'appelle Anne-Marie. Et toi, tu t'appelles comment?
— Moi, je m'appelle Robert.

CD 1-6

Here are several ways to say good-bye in either formal or familiar situations.
  Au revoir. *Good-bye.*
  À tout à l'heure. *See you in a little while.*
  À bientôt. *See you soon.*
  À demain. *See you tomorrow.*

Prononciation

CD 1-7

*Les voyelles **a, e, i, o, u***

When you pronounce vowels in English, your tongue or lips move as you say them, so that the position of your mouth is not the same at the end of a vowel as at the beginning. In French, you hold your tongue and mouth firmly in one place while pronouncing vowels. This gives vowels a tenser sound. Practice saying these sounds.

a [a]:	*à*	*ça*	*va*	*madame*	*mal*	*assez*
e [ə]:	*je*	*ne*	*que*	*de*	*demain*	*devoirs*
i [i]:	*quiche*	*idéal*	*Paris*	*Micheline*	*six*	*merci*
o [ɔ]:	*votre*	*notre*	*Hector*	*port*	*fort*	*optimiste*
u [y]:	*tu*	*salut*	*Luc*	*super*	*du*	*université*

The vowel **o** has two pronunciations, [ɔ] or [o], and the vowel **e** has three pronunciations, [ə], [e], or [ɛ] . You will learn more about this in **Chapitre 3.** Final unaccented **e** is not generally pronounced, unless it is the only vowel in a word, as in **je.**

France   madame   appelle   une   Anne

Ça va? *How's it going?*   **Ça va.** *It's going fine.*   **Comment ça va?** *How's it going?*

A. Dans quelle situation? Would you be more likely to hear these phrases in situation **A** or **B**?

A

B

1. Bonsoir, madame. *A*
2. Salut, Thomas. *B*
3. Très bien, merci. Et vous? *A*
4. Tu t'appelles comment? *B*

5. Ça va? *B*
6. Comment allez-vous? *A*
7. Ça va. Et toi? *B*
8. Comment vous appelez-vous? *A*

Now, go back and indicate how one might respond to each of the sentences above.

B. Conversations. Act out the following conversations with a partner. Then act them out again, making the suggested changes that follow.

1. — Salut! Comment ça va, André(e)?
   — Pas mal. Et toi, Gabriel(le)?
   — Ça va.
   — Bon, à demain!
   — À demain!

   a. André(e) is not having a very good day.
   b. The two friends plan to see each other later today.
   c. The conversation is between two business associates, Christian(e) Sankara and Denis(e) Mazet.

2. — Bonjour, monsieur. Je suis Cécilia Pastini. Et vous, comment vous appelez-vous?
   — Bonjour, madame. Je m'appelle André Cardin.

   a. The woman is young and unmarried.
   b. The conversation is between two students, Denis(e) and Adrien(ne).

C. Que disent-ils? Imagine what these people are saying. Prepare brief exchanges with a partner.

CD 1-8 You can find a list of the new words from this **Compétence** on page 26 and a recording of this list on track CD 1-8 of your *Text Audio CD*.

Counting and describing your week

Les chiffres de zéro à trente

Comptez de zéro à trente, **s'il vous plaît!**

0 zéro		
1 un	**11** onze	**21** vingt et un
2 deux	**12** douze	**22** vingt-deux
3 trois	**13** treize	**23** vingt-trois
4 quatre	**14** quatorze	**24** vingt-quatre
5 cinq	**15** quinze	**25** vingt-cinq
6 six	**16** seize	**26** vingt-six
7 sept	**17** dix-sept	**27** vingt-sept
8 huit	**18** dix-huit	**28** vingt-huit
9 neuf	**19** dix-neuf	**29** vingt-neuf
10 dix	**20** vingt	**30** trente

$2 + 2 = 4$ **Combien** font deux et deux?
Deux et deux font quatre.

$10 - 3 = 7$ Combien font dix moins trois?
Dix moins trois font sept.

Prononciation

CD 1-9   *Les chiffres et les voyelles nasales*

Although final consonants are generally silent in French, they are pronounced in the following numbers when counting. In **sept,** the **p** is silent, but the final **t** is pronounced. The final **x** in **six** and **dix** is pronounced like the *s* in *so*.

cinq   six   se*p*t   huit   neuf   dix

Many numbers also contain nasal vowels. In French, when a vowel is followed by the letter **m** or **n** in the same syllable, the **m** or **n** is silent and the vowel is nasal. Use the words below as models of how to pronounce each of the three nasal sounds. The letter combinations that are grouped together are all pronounced alike.

[ɛ̃]: in / im / ain / aim / un / um	cinq	quinze	vingt	un
[ɑ̃]: en / em / an / am	trente	Henri	Jean	comment
[ɔ̃]: on / om	onze	bonjour	bonsoir	Simon

Comptez *Count*   **de** *from*   **à** *to*   **s'il vous plaît** *please*   **Combien** *How much, How many*

A. C'est logique! Complete each list with the logical numbers.

1. 1, 3, 5, ?, 9, 11, ?, 15, 17, ?
2. 2, 4, ?, 8, 10, ?, 14, ?, 18, 20
3. 0, 5, 10, ?, 20, ?, 30
4. 3, 6, ?, 12, 15, 18, ?

5. 20, 19, 18, ?, 16, 15, ?
6. 10, 11, 12, ?, 14, 15, ?
7. 11, 13, 15, ?, 19, 21, 23, 25, ?
8. 0, 10, 20, ?

B. Messages secrets.
You will hear a series of numbers read by your instructor. Write the letter corresponding to each number and you will discover a secret message. When you hear **zéro**, start another word (**un autre mot**).

EXEMPLE   VOUS ENTENDEZ (YOU HEAR): 8, 30, 29, 9, 30, 6, 10, 0,
12, 18, 0, 15, 18
VOUS ÉCRIVEZ (YOU WRITE): **Bonjour, ça va?**

0 un autre mot

1 é	**6** u	**11** f	**16** ô	**21** l	**26** p
2 q	**7** z	**12** ç	**17** t	**22** w	**27** y
3 c	**8** b	**13** g	**18** a	**23** à	**28** è
4 i	**9** j	**14** x	**19** s	**24** m	**29** n
5 d	**10** r	**15** v	**20** h	**25** e	**30** o

C. Combien font... ?

1. $2 + 3 =$
2. $1 + 3 =$
3. $9 + 4 =$

4. $14 + 16 =$
5. $10 + 9 =$
6. $8 + 17 =$

7. $18 + 12 =$
8. $13 + 5 =$
9. $21 + 6 =$

D. En taxi.
You've taken a taxi in a francophone country. Tell the driver the address of your destination.

EXEMPLE   28, rue du Dragon
Vingt-huit rue du Dragon, s'il vous plaît.

1. 27, boulevard Diderot
2. 11, rue Petit
3. 16, place Saint-Denis
4. 25, rue d'Angleterre

5. 15, rue Sébastopol
6. 12, rue Garibaldi
7. 30, boulevard Gabriel
8. 7, rue du Temple

E. Populations.
Guess the populations of these francophone countries. Your instructor will give you cues by saying **plus que ça** (*more than that*) or **moins que ça** (*less than that*), until you guess the correct number.

1. la Suisse   4 millions
2. le Sénégal   18 millions
3. la Côte d'Ivoire   19 millions
4. la Belgique   12 millions
5. la République centrafricaine   6 millions
6. le Canada   11 millions
7. le Niger   13 millions
8. Madagascar   33 millions
9. le Togo   8 millions
10. le Burkina Faso   14 millions

Vocabulaire supplémentaire

pendant la semaine *during the week*
sauf *except*

To ask and tell the day of the week, say:

— **C'est quel jour aujourd'hui?**
— C'est lundi.

lundi	mardi	mercredi	jeudi	vendredi	samedi	dimanche
(17)	18	19	20	21	22	23
24	25	26	27	28	29	30

*Do not translate the word **on** to say that you do something **on** a certain day. To say that you do something **every** Monday (or another day), use* **le** *with the day of the week.*

| Je travaille **lundi.** | *I work on Monday.* (this Monday) |
| Je travaille **le lundi.** | *I work on Mondays.* (every Monday) |

*To say **from** what day **to** what day you do something every week, use* **du... au...** *Use* **tous les jours** *to say you do something every day.*

| Je travaille **du** lundi **au** vendredi. | *I work Mondays to Fridays.* (every week) |
| Je travaille **tous les jours.** | *I work every day.* |

Use **le matin, l'après-midi,** *or* **le soir** *to say you do something **in the morning, in the afternoon,** or **in the evening,** and* **le week-end** *to say **on the weekend.** Use* **avant** *to say **before** and* **après** *to say **after.***

Le matin, je suis **à la maison** avant **le cours de français.**

L'après-midi, **je ne suis pas** à la maison. Je suis **dans un autre cours** après le cours de français.

Le soir, je travaille.

Le week-end, je ne travaille pas. Je suis à la maison.

Les jours de la semaine *The days of the week*   **C'est quel jour aujourd'hui?** *It's what day today?*   **à la maison** *at home*
le cours de français *French class*   **je ne suis pas** *I am not*   **dans un autre cours** *in another class*

CD 1-10

Two friends are talking about their schedule this semester.

— **Tu es en cours** quels jours **ce semestre?**

— Je suis en cours le lundi, le mercredi et le vendredi.

— Tu travailles **aussi?**

— **Oui,** je travaille le mardi matin, le jeudi matin et le week-end.

A. Ciao! Say good-bye to a friend whom you will see again in two days.

EXEMPLE Aujourd'hui, c'est lundi. **Au revoir! À mercredi!**

Aujourd'hui, c'est...

1. dimanche
2. mercredi
3. jeudi
4. samedi
5. vendredi
6. mardi

B. C'est quel jour?

1. Aujourd'hui, c'est...
2. Demain, c'est...
3. Après demain, c'est...
4. Après le week-end, c'est...
5. Avant le week-end, c'est...
6. Les jours du week-end sont...
7. Les jours du cours de français sont...
8. Je suis en cours...
9. Je travaille...
10. Je suis souvent *(often)* à la maison...

C. Emploi du temps. A student is talking about her week. Select the option in parentheses that is logical in each sentence.

1. Aujourd'hui, c'est (jeudi, le jeudi) et demain, c'est (vendredi, le vendredi).
2. Ce semestre, je suis en cours tous les jours du lundi au jeudi. Je ne suis pas en cours (vendredi, le vendredi).
3. Je suis en cours de français (après-midi, l'après-midi).
4. Ce semestre, je suis à la maison le matin (avant, après) le cours de français et je travaille l'après-midi (avant, après) le cours.
5. Le week-end, je travaille (samedi, le samedi) ce semestre.
6. Ce week-end, je travaille (lundi, dimanche) aussi.

D. Quand? Change the words in italics so that each statement is true. If a statement is already true, read it as it is.

1. Je suis à l'université *du lundi au vendredi.*
2. Je travaille *le mardi matin, le jeudi matin et le week-end. (Je ne travaille pas.)*
3. Aujourd'hui, c'est *lundi* et après le cours de français, je *suis dans un autre cours.*
4. Je *suis à la maison tous les jours* avant le cours de français.
5. Je suis souvent *(often)* à la maison *le week-end.*
6. Je suis rarement *(rarely)* à la maison *le vendredi soir.*

E. Conversation. With a partner, read aloud the conversation at the top of this page, paying particular attention to the pronunciation. Then act it out, changing it to make it true for you. Switch roles and do it again.

CD 1-11 You can find a list of the new words from this **Compétence** on page 26 and a recording of this list on track CD 1–11 of your *Text Audio CD.*

Tu es en cours... ? *You are in class . . . ? (familiar)*   **ce semestre** *this semester*   **aussi** *too, also*   **Oui** *Yes*

Talking about yourself and your schedule

Un autoportrait

Use these expressions to talk about yourself. Include the ending in parentheses if you are female.

Je suis...	étudiant(e).
Je ne suis pas...	professeur.
	américain(e).
	canadien(ne).
	de Chicago.
	d'ici.
J'habite...	à Toronto.
Je n'habite pas...	avec **un ami / une amie.**
	avec deux amis / deux amies.
	seul(e).
	avec ma famille.
	avec **un camarade de chambre / une camarade de chambre.**
	avec **un colocataire / une colocataire.**
Je travaille...	**beaucoup.**
Je ne travaille pas...	à l'université.
	pour IBM.
Je parle...	anglais.
Je ne parle pas...	français.
	espagnol.
	beaucoup en cours.
Je pense que le français est...	assez **facile.**
	un peu difficile.
	intéressant.
	super!
	assez cool!

Je suis de Montréal, mais je suis étudiante à Paris maintenant. Je parle anglais et français.

CD 1-12

In the following conversation, two people meet at a Canadian-American cultural event in Montreal.

— **Vous êtes** canadien?

— Oui, je suis d'ici. Et vous, vous êtes canadienne aussi?

— Non, je suis de Cleveland.

— **Mais** vous parlez très bien français! Vous habitez ici **maintenant**?

— Oui, **parce que** je suis étudiante à l'université. Et vous, vous travaillez ici?

— Non, je suis étudiant aussi.

---

de (d') *from* ici *here* J'habite *I live* un ami *a friend (male)* une amie *a friend (female)* seul(e) *alone* un camarade de chambre *a roommate (male)* une camarade de chambre *a roommate (female)* un colocataire *a housemate (male)* une colocataire *a housemate (female)* beaucoup *a lot* pour *for* Je parle *I speak, I talk* Je pense que *I think that* facile *easy* un peu *a little* Vous êtes *You are (formal)* Mais *But* maintenant *now* parce que *because*

A. Moi, je... Choose the words in parentheses so that each sentence describes you.

1. (Je suis / Je ne suis pas) étudiant(e). *I am a student*
2. (Je suis / Je ne suis pas) en cours maintenant. *I am in the course now.*
3. (Je suis / Je ne suis pas) de Los Angeles. *I am not from LA.*
4. (Je suis / Je ne suis pas) canadien(ne). *I am not Canadian.*
5. (J'habite / Je n'habite pas) à Minneapolis. *I do not live in minneapolis*
6. (J'habite / Je n'habite pas) avec ma famille maintenant. *I do not live with my family now.*
7. (Je travaille / Je ne travaille pas) à l'université. *I do not work at the university.*
8. (Je parle / Je ne parle pas) très bien français. *I do not speak French well*

B. Nationalités. Some international students from different French-speaking countries are talking about themselves. Can you find the sentences from each column that go together?

EXEMPLE **Je suis français. Je suis de France. J'habite à Paris.**

Je suis français.	Je suis de Belgique.	J'habite à Alger.
Je suis algérienne.	Je suis du Canada.	J'habite à Genève.
Je suis canadien.	Je suis d'Algérie.	J'habite à Paris.
Je suis belge.	Je suis de Côte d'Ivoire.	J'habite à Québec.
Je suis ivoirienne.	Je suis de Suisse.	J'habite à Abidjan.
Je suis suisse.	Je suis de France.	J'habite à Bruxelles.

C. Descriptions. Change the words in italics so that each statement is true for you. If a statement already is true, read it as it is.

1. Je m'appelle *Chris Jones.*
2. Je suis de *Toronto.*
3. Je suis *canadien(ne).*
4. Maintenant, j'habite à *Chapel Hill.*
5. Je suis étudiant(e) à *l'université de Caroline du Nord.*
6. J'habite *avec un(e) camarade de chambre.*
7. Je parle *un peu* français.
8. Je parle *anglais et espagnol.*
9. Je pense que le français est *très facile.*

D. Et vous? Answer the following questions.

1. Comment vous appelez-vous?
2. Comment allez-vous?
3. Vous êtes étudiant(e)?
4. Vous travaillez aussi?
5. Vous êtes américain(e)?
6. Vous êtes d'ici?
7. Vous habitez à Denver maintenant?
8. Vous parlez espagnol?

E. Conversation. With a partner, read aloud the conversation at the bottom of the previous page, paying particular attention to the pronunciation. Then act it out, changing it to make it true for you. Afterward, switch roles and do it again.

Note *culturelle*

Traditionally, the French workday followed a particular pattern: breakfast in the early morning, work, a two-hour break for lunch, then work in the afternoon and into the evening. Most people went home for lunch to eat and be with their family. As France has become more urban, however, *la journée continue*, or a nine-to-five schedule, has become a way of life. There is a shorter lunch break, and people have lunch at work or in a nearby restaurant, fast-food chain, or café. How does this compare to a typical workday in your area?

Note *de vocabulaire*

1. **Heures** has an **-s** except in **une heure**.
2. There is an **e** at the end of **demi(e)** when it is used with the word **heure**, but not with **midi** and **minuit**.
3. Some people use **douze heures** for **midi**.
4. One may also tell time by telling the minutes after the hour, instead of using **et quart, et demie,** and **moins**... For example, one hears **Il est trois heures quinze** or **Il est cinq heures trente**.
5. Although *at* may be dropped in English, **à** cannot be omitted in French: *(At) What time is French class?* **À quelle heure est le cours de français?**
6. Use **du matin / de l'après-midi / du soir** only for indicating *A.M.* and *P.M.* when telling time. Use **le matin / l'après-midi / le soir** to say *in the morning / afternoon / evening* in other cases.

L'heure

Quelle heure est-il maintenant?

Il est une heure.

Il est une heure dix.

Il est une heure et quart.

Il est une heure et demie.

Il est deux heures moins vingt-cinq.

Il est deux heures moins le quart.

Il est deux heures moins cinq.

Il est deux heures.

Il est midi.

Il est midi et demi.

Il est minuit.

Il est minuit et demi.

The French do not use A.M. and P.M. to distinguish morning from afternoon and evening. Instead, they use:

du matin *(after midnight until noon)*   Il est huit heures **du matin.**
de l'après-midi *(after noon until 6 P.M.)*   Il est une heure **de l'après-midi.**
du soir *(6 P.M. until midnight)*   Il est neuf heures **du soir.**

Do not use these expressions with **midi** *or* **minuit**.

Use **à** *to ask or tell* **at** *what time something takes place.*

Le cours de français est **à quelle heure**?

Le cours de français **commence** à une heure.

Le cours de français **finit** à deux heures moins dix.

To say that you do something ***from*** *a certain time* ***to*** *another, use* **de... à.**

Le lundi, je suis en cours **de** neuf heures **à** une heure.

à quelle heure *at what time*   **commence** *begins*   **finit** *finishes, ends*

Prononciation

L'heure et la liaison

The pronunciation of some numbers changes in liaison with the word **heures.**

deux	**Il est deux ẓ heures dix.**
trois	**Il est trois ẓ heures et quart.**
six	**Il est six ẓ heures et demie.**
neuf	**Il est neuf ṿ heures.**
dix	**Il est dix ẓ heures moins cinq.**

A. En français! Complete these expressions to tell the time in French.

EXEMPLE   *4:30 A.M.*   **Il est quatre heures et demie du matin.**

1. *5:10 A.M.*   Il est cinq heures...
2. *5:15 A.M.*   Il est cinq heures...
3. *3:20 P.M.*   Il est trois heures...
4. *3:30 P.M.*   Il est trois heures...
5. *7:35 P.M.*   Il est huit heures...
6. *7:45 P.M.*   Il est huit heures...
7. *7:50 P.M.*   Il est huit heures...
8. *8:00 P.M.*   Il est...
9. *12:00 A.M.*   Il est...
10. *12:00 P.M.*   Il est...

Il est six heures moins vingt-cinq.

B. Quelle heure est-il?

EXEMPLE  — Quelle heure est-il?
— Il est une heure de l'après-midi.

1.  2.  3.

4.  5.

6.  7.

C. Où es-tu? Where are you generally at these times each week?

je suis à la maison
je travaille
je suis en cours
je suis avec un(e) ami(e)
je suis avec mes *(my)* amis
je suis avec ma famille
je vais *(I'm going to)* à la maison
je vais à l'université
je suis à l'université mais je ne suis pas en cours

EXEMPLE Le lundi à 9h15 du matin,...
Le lundi à neuf heures et quart du matin, je suis en cours.

1. Le lundi à 7h00 du matin,...
2. Le mardi à midi,...
3. Le mercredi à 2h30 de l'après-midi,...
4. Le jeudi à 5h20 de l'après-midi,...
5. Le vendredi à 10h45 du soir,...
6. Le samedi à minuit,...
7. Le dimanche à 7h30 du soir,...

D. Il est quelle heure? Write the times you hear dictated. Notice how the word **heure(s)** is abbreviated in French.

EXEMPLE Vous entendez *(you hear)*: Il est dix heures et quart.
Vous écrivez *(you write)*: **10h15**

E. Quand? Complete these sentences so that they are true for you the first day of the week you have your French class.

> **EXEMPLE**   Je suis à la maison **avant sept heures et demie.**
>   *before*   *[time]*

1. Je suis à la maison _____ _____.
                      before   *[time]*

2. Je suis à l'université _____ _____. (J'habite sur *[on]* le campus.)
                      after   *[time]*

3. Le cours de français commence _____ _____.
                                at   *[time]*

4. Le cours de français finit _____ _____.
                        at   *[time]*

5. Je suis en cours _____ _____ _____ _____.
                from   *[time]*   *to*   *[time]*

6. Je travaille _____ _____ _____ _____. (Je ne travaille pas.)
          from   *[time]*   *to*   *[time]*

7. Je suis à la maison _____ _____.
                      after   *[time]*

F. Votre emploi du temps. On a sheet of paper, copy the schedule below twice, changing it to describe your schedule on one copy and leaving the other one blank. You and your partner take turns describing your schedules to each other. On your second (blank) schedule, fill in your partner's schedule as he/she describes it to you.

> **EXEMPLE**   **Le lundi, je suis en cours de dix heures à une heure. Je travaille de deux heures à quatre heures. Je suis à la maison après cinq heures.**
> **Le mardi...**

CD 1-14 You can find a list of the new words from this **Compétence** on page 27 and a recording of this list on track CD 1-14 of your *Text Audio CD.*

Communicating in class

En cours

Le professeur **dit aux** étudiants:

EN COURS

Ouvrez votre livre à la page 23.

Fermez votre livre.

Écoutez la question.

Répondez à la question.

Allez au tableau.

Écrivez la réponse en phrases complètes.

Prenez une feuille de papier et un crayon ou un stylo.

Faites l'exercice A à la page 21.

Donnez-moi votre feuille de papier.

À LA MAISON

Lisez la page 17 et **apprenez** les mots de vocabulaire.

Préparez l'examen pour le **prochain** cours.

Faites **les devoirs** dans le cahier et écoutez le CD.

dit aux *says to the* **Faites** *Do* **apprenez** *learn* **prochain(e)** *next* **les devoirs** *the homework*

Prononciation

CD 1-15 *Les voyelles groupées*

Practice the pronunciation of the following vowel combinations. Notice that the combination **eu** has two different sounds, depending on whether it is followed by a pronounced consonant in the same syllable.

- a + u / e + u / o + u

au, eau [o]:	au	aussi	beaucoup	tableau
eu [ø]:	deux	peu	jeudi	monsieur
eu [œ]:	heure	neuf	professeur	seul(e)
ou [u]:	vous	douze	jour	pour

- a + i / e + i / o + i / u + i

ai [ɛ]:	français	je vais	je sais	vrai
ei [ɛ]:	treize	seize	beige	neige
oi [wa]:	moi	toi	trois	au revoir
ui [ɥi]:	huit	minuit	aujourd'hui	suis

A. Où? Is your professor telling you to do these things **en cours** or **à la maison**?

1. Fermez votre livre.
2. Apprenez les mots de vocabulaire.
3. Écoutez et répondez, s'il vous plaît.
4. Allez au tableau.
5. Prenez une feuille de papier.
6. Lisez les pages 12, 13 et 14.
7. Faites les devoirs dans le cahier.
8. Ouvrez votre livre à la page 23.

B. En cours. In groups, make up commands your instructor might give you by matching items from the two columns. Which group can come up with the most commands?

Fermez...	... les devoirs.
Allez...	... les mots de vocabulaire.
Lisez...	... le CD.
Apprenez...	... l'exercice A.
Comptez...	... de 0 à 30.
Écoutez...	... au tableau.
Prenez...	... une feuille de papier.
Écrivez...	... la phrase.
Faites...	... votre livre.

C. C'est logique? How many logical ways can you complete these commands?

1. Écrivez...
2. Lisez...
3. Apprenez...
4. Prenez...
5. Faites...
6. Écoutez...

Des expressions utiles et l'alphabet

When you hear new words, it may be helpful to see how they are spelled. You can ask:

Ça s'écrit comment? — *How is that written?*

Ça s'écrit avec un accent ou sans accent? — *Is that written with an accent or without an accent?*

Ça s'écrit avec un **s** ou deux **s** en français / en anglais? — *Is that written with one **s** or two in French / in English?*

Ça s'écrit...

a a	**i** i	**q** ku	**y** i grec
b bé	**j** ji	**r** erre	**z** zède
c cé	**k** ka	**s** esse	
d dé	**l** elle	**t** té	**é** = e accent aigu
e e	**m** emme	**u** u	**è** = e accent grave
f effe	**n** enne	**v** vé	**â** = a accent circonflexe
g gé	**o** o	**w** double vé	**ï** = i tréma
h hache	**p** pé	**x** iks	**ç** = c cédille

You may also need to use these expressions.

Comment? Répétez, s'il vous plaît. — *What? Please repeat.*

— Vous comprenez? — *Do you understand?*

— Oui, je comprends. / Non, je ne comprends pas. — *Yes, I understand. / No, I don't understand.*

— Comment dit-on *a pen* en français? — *How does one say **a pen** in French?*
— On dit **un stylo.** — *One says **un stylo.***

— Qu'est-ce que ça veut dire **votre**? — *What does **votre** mean?*
— Ça veut dire *your.* — *It means **your.***

— Je ne sais pas. — *I don't know.*

— Merci (bien). — *Thanks.*

— De rien. — *You're welcome.*

— Pardon. / Excusez-moi. — *Excuse me.*

A. Dans l'ordre logique.
Put the sentences of the following conversations in the logical order.

1. — Ça veut dire *pen.*
   — Non, qu'est-ce que ça veut dire?
   — Vous comprenez le mot **stylo**?

2. — Je ne sais pas.
   — Comment dit-on *hi* en français?
   — On dit **salut.**

3. — Comment? Répétez s'il vous plaît.
   — Qu'est-ce que ça veut dire **bientôt**?
   — Je ne sais pas.
   — Qu'est-ce que ça veut dire **bientôt**?

4. — Ça s'écrit B-E-A-U-C-O-U-P.
   — Comment dit-on *a lot* en français?
   — On dit **beaucoup.**
   — Ça s'écrit comment?

B. Réponses. Look back at the expressions above and below the alphabet box on the preceding page. What would you say in the following situations?

1. You understood the question, but you don't know the answer.
2. You want to know how to say *giraffe* in French.
3. You want to know if *giraffe* is written with one *f* or two in French.
4. You want to know what the word **fou** means in English.
5. You need to pass through a group of students.
6. You stepped on someone's foot.

C. La francophonie. Say what letter is missing at the beginning of the following names of francophone places. Can you locate each place on the map inside the front cover?

EXEMPLE   _Q_uébec

1. ___rance
2. ___lgérie
3. ___ôte d'Ivoire
4. ___aïti
5. ___ahiti
6. ___uadeloupe

7. ___aroc
8. ___elgique
9. ___énégal
10. ___ouisiane
11. ___uanda
12. ___uinée

Jemma el Fna, Marrakech, Maroc

D. Ça s'écrit comment? Here are some French words that are similar to their English equivalents but spelled slightly differently. Explain to a French friend how to spell them in English. Your friend already knows not to use accents.

EXEMPLES   indépendance   **En anglais, *independence,* ça s'écrit avec un *e.***
appartement   **En anglais, *apartment,* ça s'écrit avec un *p* et sans *e.***

1. littérature
2. activité
3. chocolat
4. symptôme
5. criminel

6. dîner
7. environnement
8. moderne
9. hôpital
10. responsable

E. Présentations. Introduce yourself to a classmate, who will ask you to spell your last name.

EXEMPLE   — **Bonjour, je suis Paul Wyndel.**
— **Wyndel? Ça s'écrit comment?**
— **W-Y-N-D-E-L. Et toi, tu t'appelles comment?**
— **Je m'appelle Lynn Phan.**
— **Phan? Ça s'écrit comment?**
— **P-H-A-N.**

CD 1-16 You can find a list of the new words from this **Compétence** on page 27 and a recording of this list on track CD 1-16 of your *Text Audio CD*.

Comparaisons culturelles

L'heure officielle

In official schedules and often in conversations, the French use the 24-hour clock rather than the conversational manner of telling time, which you have already learned. With the 24-hour clock, you continue counting 13 to 24, instead of beginning with 1 to 12 o'clock again during the P.M. hours.

When using the 24-hour clock, state the hour and the number of minutes after the hour with a number, instead of using **midi, minuit, et quart, et demie,** or **moins le quart.** You will need the numbers **quarante** (*forty*) and **cinquante** (*fifty*). To convert times after 13h00 from official time to conversational time, subtract twelve hours.

douze heures trente = midi et demi

treize heures quinze = une heure et quart de l'après-midi

treize heures quarante-cinq = deux heures moins le quart de l'après-midi

Il est quatorze heures six.

A. Horaire de train. You are flying into Paris to study for a month at a French language institute in Lyons. The institute's website lists the following TGV trains you can take daily from the station in Paris (**Gare de Lyon**) to the station in Lyons (**Le Creusot**). Explain at what time each train arrives in Lyons, using official time. The first one has been done as an example.

Paris - Le Creusot TGV	
Départ de Paris Gare de Lyon	Arrivée à Le Creusot TGV
6h10	7h32
7h30	8h54
13h00	14h27
16h00	17h22
18h	19h25
20h00	21h22

EXEMPLE 6h10

Le train de six heures dix arrive à Lyon à sept heures trente-deux.

B. À la télé. A friend wants to watch these shows today on TV5, the international French TV station. Tell him what time each one is on. First use official time, then convert it to conversational time.

> **EXEMPLE** *Télé la question*
> ***Télé la question*** est à seize heures quinze, c'est-à-dire *(that is to say)* à quatre heures et quart de l'après-midi.

1. *Le journal de la TSR*
2. *Des chiffres et des lettres*
3. *Mains et merveilles*
4. *Pin-pon*
5. *Le journal de France 2*
6. *Catherine*
7. *Questions pour un champion*
8. *Princesse Marie*
9. *Tsunami, vague mortelle*
10. *C'est la vie*

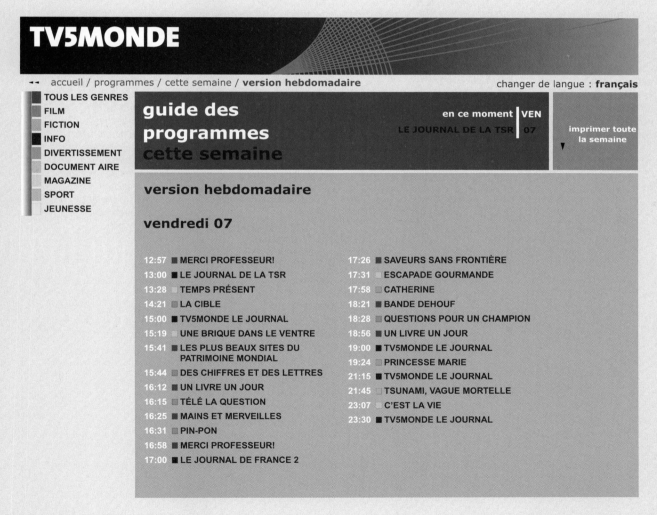

TV5MONDE

-- accueil / programmes / cette semaine / **version hebdomadaire**   changer de langue : **français**

- TOUS LES GENRES
- FILM
- FICTION
- INFO
- DIVERTISSEMENT
- DOCUMENT AIRE
- MAGAZINE
- SPORT
- JEUNESSE

guide des programmes cette semaine

en ce moment | VEN
LE JOURNAL DE LA TSR | 07

imprimer toute la semaine

version hebdomadaire

vendredi 07

12:57 ■ MERCI PROFESSEUR!	17:26 ■ SAVEURS SANS FRONTIÈRE
13:00 ■ LE JOURNAL DE LA TSR	17:31 □ ESCAPADE GOURMANDE
13:28 □ TEMPS PRÉSENT	17:58 □ CATHERINE
14:21 ■ LA CIBLE	18:21 ■ BANDE DEHOUF
15:00 ■ TV5MONDE LE JOURNAL	18:28 □ QUESTIONS POUR UN CHAMPION
15:19 □ UNE BRIQUE DANS LE VENTRE	18:56 ■ UN LIVRE UN JOUR
15:41 ■ LES PLUS BEAUX SITES DU PATRIMOINE MONDIAL	19:00 ■ TV5MONDE LE JOURNAL
15:44 □ DES CHIFFRES ET DES LETTRES	19:24 □ PRINCESSE MARIE
16:12 ■ UN LIVRE UN JOUR	21:15 ■ TV5MONDE LE JOURNAL
16:15 □ TÉLÉ LA QUESTION	21:45 □ TSUNAMI, VAGUE MORTELLE
16:25 ■ MAINS ET MERVEILLES	23:07 □ C'EST LA VIE
16:31 ■ PIN-PON	23:30 ■ TV5MONDE LE JOURNAL
16:58 ■ MERCI PROFESSEUR!	
17:00 ■ LE JOURNAL DE FRANCE 2	

C. À discuter

1. Is the 24-hour clock used in your country? In what circumstances?
2. Does using the 24-hour clock make things clearer or less clear to you? Why?

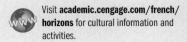

Visit **academic.cengage.com/french/ horizons** for cultural information and activities.

Vocabulaire

COMPÉTENCE 1 Track 8

Greeting people

À bientôt.	*See you soon.*
À demain.	*See you tomorrow.*
À tout à l'heure.	*See you in a little while.*
Au revoir.	*Good-bye.*
Bonjour.	*Hello., Good morning.*
Bonsoir.	*Good evening.*
Comment allez-vous?	*How are you?* (formal)
Je vais très bien.	*I'm doing very well.*
Assez bien.	*Fairly well.*
Pas mal.	*Not badly.*
Pas très bien.	*Not very well.*
Comment ça va/Ça va?	*How's it going?* (familiar)
Ça va.	*It's going fine.*
Comment vous appelez-vous?	*What's your name?* (formal)
Tu t'appelles comment?	*What's your name?* (familiar)
Je m'appelle...	*My name is . . .*
Je suis...	*I'm . . .*
et	*and*
Et toi?	*And you?* (familiar)
Et vous?	*And you?* (formal)
madame	*Mrs., madam*
mademoiselle	*Miss*
merci	*thank you, thanks*
moi	*me*
monsieur	*Mr., sir*
Salut!	*Hi!*

COMPÉTENCE 2 Track 11

Counting and describing your week

un chiffre	*a number, a numeral*
Combien font... et... ?	*How much is . . . plus . . . ?*
... et... font...	*. . . plus . . . equals . . .*
Combien font... moins... ?	*How much is . . . minus . . . ?*
... moins... font...	*. . . minus . . . equals . . .*
Comptez de... à...	*Count from . . . to . . .*
s'il vous plaît	*please (formal)*
les jours de la semaine	*the days of the week*
C'est quel jour aujourd'hui?	*What day is today?*
C'est...	*It's . . .*
lundi	*Monday*
mardi	*Tuesday*
mercredi	*Wednesday*
jeudi	*Thursday*
vendredi	*Friday*
samedi	*Saturday*
dimanche	*Sunday*
Tu es... ?	*Are you . . . ?*
Je suis... / Je ne suis pas...	*I'm . . . / I'm not . . .*
en cours	*in class*
à la maison	*at home*
dans un autre cours	*in another class*
le cours de français	*French class*
Tu travailles?	*Do you work?*
Je travaille /	*I work . . . /*
Je ne travaille pas...	*I don't work . . .*
le lundi	*on Mondays*
le lundi matin	*Monday morning*
le matin, l'après-midi, le soir	*in the morning, in the afternoon, in the evening*
le week-end	*weekends / on the weekend*
du lundi au vendredi	*from Monday to Friday (every week)*
tous les jours	*every day*
ce semestre	*this semester*
avant	*before*
après	*after*
aussi	*also*
oui	*yes*
Quels jours... ?	*What days . . . ?*

Pour les chiffres de zéro à trente, voir la page 10.

Talking about yourself and your schedule

Vous êtes... ?	*Are you . . . ?*
Je suis / Je ne suis pas...	*I am / I am not . . .*
américain(e)	*American*
canadien(ne)	*Canadian*
de (d')... (+ city)	*from . . . (+ city)*
d'ici	*from here*
étudiant(e)	*a student*
professeur	*a professor*
Vous habitez... ?	*Do you live . . . ?*
J'habite / Je n'habite pas...	*I live / I do not live . . .*
à... (+ city)	*in . . . (+ city)*
avec ma famille	*with my family*
avec un(e) ami(e)	*with a friend*
avec un(e) camarade de chambre	*with a roommate*
avec un(e) colocataire	*with a housemate*
seul(e)	*alone*
Vous parlez... ?	*Do you speak . . . ?*
Je parle / Je ne parle pas...	*I speak / I do not speak . . .*
anglais	*English*
espagnol	*Spanish*
français	*French*
beaucoup en cours	*a lot in class*
Je pense que...	*I think that . . .*
le français est...	*French is . . .*
un peu difficile	*a little difficult / hard*
assez facile	*fairly easy*
intéressant	*interesting*
super	*great*
assez cool	*pretty cool*
Vous travaillez...?	*Do you work . . . ?*
Je travaille / Je ne travaille pas...	*I work / I do not work . . .*
pour	*for*
à l'université	*at the university*
un autoportrait	*a self-portrait*
ici	*here*
mais	*but*
non	*no*
parce que	*because*
l'heure	*the time*
une heure	*an hour*
Quelle heure est-il?	*What time is it?*
Il est une heure /	*It's one o'clock /*
deux heures	*two o'clock*
et quart / et demi(e)	*a quarter past / half past*
moins le quart	*a quarter till*
midi	*noon*
minuit	*midnight*
À quelle heure?	*At what time?*
à... heure(s)	*at . . . o'clock*
du matin	*in the morning*
de l'après-midi	*in the afternoon*
du soir	*in the evening*
Le cours de français est / commence / finit à...	*French class is / starts / finishes at . . .*
de... à...	*from . . . to . . .*
maintenant	*now*

Communicating in class

Comment? Répétez, s'il vous plaît.	*What? Please repeat.*
Vous comprenez?	*Do you understand?*
Oui, je comprends. / Non, je ne comprends pas.	*Yes, I understand. / No, I don't understand.*
Comment dit-on...	*How does one say . . .*
en français / en anglais?	*in French / in English?*
On dit...	*One says . . .*
Qu'est-ce que ça veut dire?	*What does that mean?*
Ça veut dire...	*That means . . .*
Je ne sais pas.	*I don't know.*
Ça s'écrit comment?	*How is that written?*
Ça s'écrit...	*That's written . . .*
avec	*with*
ou	*or*
sans	*without*
un accent	*an accent*
Merci (bien).	*Thank you. / Thanks.*
De rien.	*You're welcome.*
Pardon. / Excusez-moi.	*Excuse me.*
Le professeur dit aux étudiants...	*The professor says to the students . . .*
Ouvrez votre livre à la page 23.	*Open your book to page 23.*
Fermez votre livre.	*Close your book.*
Écoutez la question.	*Listen to the question.*
Répondez à la question.	*Answer the question.*
Allez au tableau.	*Go to the board.*
Écrivez la réponse en phrases complètes.	*Write the answer in complete sentences.*
Prenez une feuille de papier et un crayon ou un stylo.	*Take out a piece of paper and a pencil or a pen.*
Faites l'exercice A à la page 21.	*Do exercise A on page 21.*
Donnez-moi votre feuille de papier.	*Give me your piece of paper.*
Lisez la page 17.	*Read page 17.*
Apprenez les mots de vocabulaire.	*Learn the vocabulary words.*
Préparez l'examen pour le prochain cours.	*Prepare for the exam for the next class.*
Faites les devoirs dans le cahier et écoutez le CD.	*Do the homework in the workbook and listen to the CD.*

Pour l'alphabet, voir la page 22.

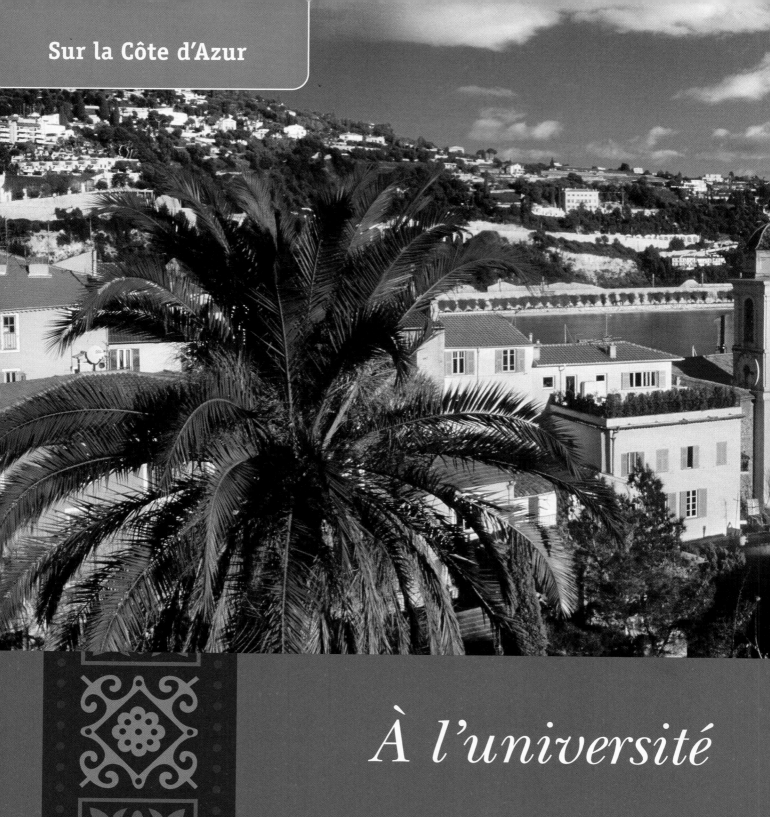

À l'université

 iLrn Heinle Learning Center

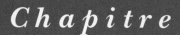 academic.cengage.com/french/horizons

 Système-D

 Audio   iRadio

There are many opportunities to study French in France. Find several possibilities on the Web and report on the two you like best: where and when they are, what the associated costs are, what courses and activities are involved, and what there is to see and do in the region.

Quelles régions françaises **connaissez-vous**? La Normandie? La Provence? La Champagne? **Voici** des photos de quatre régions pittoresques. **Laquelle voudriez-vous visiter?**

Le Pays-de-la-Loire / Le Centre

La Côte d'Azur

---

connaissez-vous *do you know*   **Voici** *Here are*   **Laquelle voudriez-vous visiter?** *Which one would you like to visit?*
Le Pays-de-la-Loire *The Loire Valley*   **La Côte d'Azur** *The Riviera*

LA FRANCE (LA RÉPUBLIQUE FRANÇAISE)

NOMBRE D'HABITANTS: 60 740 000 (les Français)

CAPITALE: Paris

 Visit it live on Google Earth!

La Bretagne

❀ Qu'en savez-vous?

Look at the map and photos and guess which province each sentence below describes.

la Côte d'Azur   **le Pays-de-la-Loire / le Centre**
la Bretagne   **l'Alsace**

1. This region shows both French and German influences in its architecture and culture because it was formerly part of Germany.
2. This province is known for its numerous castles and excellent wine.
3. Named for the color of the sky and water, this region is located along the Mediterranean sea.
4. The stone megaliths and tables reflect the traditions of the ancient Celtic people who inhabited this region from 3000 to 5000 years before our era.

La Bretagne *Brittany*

Identifying people and describing appearance

Les gens à l'université

Ce sont mes amis, David et Annette. Ils sont étudiants à l'université de Nice.

C'est David, **un jeune homme** français.
Il est étudiant.
Il est de Nice.

C'est Annette, **une jeune femme** américaine.
Elle est étudiante.
Elle est de Los Angeles.

C'est Jean, **le frère de** David.
Il n'est pas étudiant.
Il travaille.

C'est Yvette, **la sœur jumelle** d'Annette.
Elle n'est pas étudiante.
Elle travaille.

Yvette et Annette ne sont pas françaises. Elles sont américaines. Annette est à Nice **pour étudier.** Yvette est en France **pour voir sa** sœur et pour visiter la France.

Comment est David?

grand? petit?   gros? mince?   jeune? vieux?   beau? laid?

David est petit, mince et beau!

Comment est Annette?

grande? petite?   grosse? mince?   jeune? vieille?   belle? laide?

Annette est petite, mince et belle!

David et Annette sont **célibataires.** Et vous? Vous êtes célibataire, **comme** David et Annette, ou êtes-vous fiancé(e), marié(e) ou divorcé(e)?

Les gens *People*   **Ce sont...** *They are / These are / Those are . . .*   **mes ami(e)s** *my friends*   **C'est...** *He is / She is / It is / This is / That is . . .*   **un jeune homme** *a young man*   **une jeune femme** *a young woman*   **le frère de** *the brother of*   **la sœur de** *the sister of*   **jumeau (jumelle)** *twin*   **pour étudier** *in order to study*   **pour voir** *in order to see*   **sa (son, ses)** *his/her/its*   **Comment est... ?** *What is . . . like?*   **célibataire** *single*   **comme** *like, as*

🎧 David **rencontre** Annette **la première semaine des cours.**

CD 1-17 **DAVID:** Salut! Je suis David Cauvin. **Nous sommes** dans le **même** cours de littérature, non?

ANNETTE: Oui, c'est ça. **Alors,** bonjour! Moi, je m'appelle Annette Clark. Tu es d'ici?

DAVID: Oui, je suis de Nice. Et toi, **tu es d'où?**

ANNETTE: Je suis de Los Angeles, mais j'habite ici maintenant parce que je suis étudiante à l'université.

A. Identification. Qui est-ce? *(Who is it?)*

C'est…	David	Yvette	
Ce sont…	David et Annette	Annette et Yvette	David et Jean

1. Il est étudiant.
2. C'est le frère de Jean.
3. Elles sont de Los Angeles.
4. Ils sont français.
5. Elle est à Nice pour voir la France.
6. Ce sont des jeunes femmes.
7. C'est la sœur jumelle d'Annette.
8. Ils sont dans le même cours de littérature.

B. David et Annette. Relisez les descriptions de David et d'Annette en bas de *(at the bottom of)* la page précédente. C'est vrai *(true)* ou c'est faux *(false)*?

EXEMPLES David est grand. **C'est faux.**
Annette est petite. **C'est vrai.**

1. David est beau.
2. Annette est laide.
3. David est gros.
4. Annette est mince.
5. David est jeune.
6. Annette est vieille.
7. David est célibataire.
8. Annette est mariée.

C. Après les cours. Vous êtes dans un café et vous pensez reconnaître *(you think you recognize)* un(e) camarade de classe. Préparez une conversation avec les questions suivantes.

1. Tu es étudiant(e) à *[name of your school]*, non?
2. Tu es en cours de français *[days of your course]* à *[time of your course]*?
3. Le professeur, c'est un homme ou une femme?
4. Le professeur, c'est *[name of your professor]*?
5. Nous sommes dans le même cours, non?

D. Conversation. Avec un(e) partenaire, relisez à haute voix *(aloud)* la conversation entre David et Annette en haut de la page *(at the top of the page)*. Ensuite, changez la conversation pour décrire *(to describe)* votre propre *(your own)* situation.

CD 1-18 You can find a list of the new words from the vocabulary and grammar sections of this **Compétence** on page 62 and a recording of this list on track 1-18 of your *Text Audio CD.*

---

rencontre (rencontrer *to meet* [for the first time or by chance], *to run into*) **la première semaine des cours** *the first week of classes* **Nous sommes** *We are* **même** *same* **Alors** *So, Then, Therefore* **tu es d'où?** *where are you from?*

These self-check questions are provided throughout the book. Read the entire explanation before trying to answer the questions.

1. What two expressions are used to *identify* who someone is with *a noun*? What are the negative forms of these expressions?

2. When *describing* someone with an *adjective*, how do you say *he is*? *she is*? *they are* for a group of all females? *they are* for a group of all males or for a mixed group? What are the negative forms of these expressions?

3. What is the base form of an adjective? What do you usually do to make it feminine if it ends in **e**? in **é**? another vowel? a consonant?

4. What is the feminine form of **gros**? **canadien**? **beau**? **vieux**?

5. What do you usually do to make an adjective plural? What if it ends in **x** or **s**?

6. Is there a difference in pronunciation between **espagnol** and **espagnole**? between **petit** and **petite**? Is the final **s** of the plural form of an adjective pronounced?

Identifying and describing people

C'est et il est / elle est et les adjectifs

To *identify* people with *nouns*, use **c'est** and **ce sont.** Note their negative forms.

C'est (+ noun)	He is She is It is This/That is	**Ce n'est pas** (+ noun)	He isn't She isn't It isn't This/That isn't
Ce sont (+ noun)	They are These/Those are	**Ce ne sont pas** (+ noun)	They aren't These/Those aren't

To *describe* people with *adjectives*, use **il est, elle est, ils sont,** and **elles sont.** Use **ils** for a group of males or a mixed group and **elles** for a group of all females.

Il est **Elle est**	(+ adjective)	He is She is	**Il n'est pas** **Elle n'est pas**	(+ adjective)	He isn't She isn't
Ils sont **Elles sont**	(+ adjective)	They are They are	**Ils ne sont pas** **Elles ne sont pas**	(+ adjective)	They aren't They aren't

Adjective forms vary depending on whether they describe a male or a female and whether they describe one person or more than one. The masculine singular form of the adjective is the base form. Add an **e** to change this form to feminine, unless it already ends in *unaccented* **e.** If it ends in *accented* **é,** add another **e** to form the feminine. Add an **s** to make an adjective plural, unless it ends in **s** or **x.**

MASCULINE		FEMININE	
Singular	*Plural*	*Singular*	*Plural*
petit	petit**s**	petit**e**	petit**es**
jeune	jeune**s**	jeune	jeune**s**
marié	marié**s**	marié**e**	marié**es**
français	français	français**e**	français**es**

Gros doubles its final consonant before adding the **e** for the feminine form, as do adjectives ending in **-en,** like canadi**en.**

MASCULINE		FEMININE	
Singular	*Plural*	*Singular*	*Plural*
gros	gros	gros**se**	gros**ses**
canadien	canadien**s**	canadien**ne**	canadien**nes**

The adjectives **beau, jumeau,** and **vieux** are irregular.

MASCULINE		FEMININE	
Singular	*Plural*	*Singular*	*Plural*
beau	beaux	belle	belles
jumeau	jumeaux	jumelle	jumelles
vieux	vieux	vieille	vieilles

Prononciation

CD 1-19

Il est + *adjectif* / *Elle est* + *adjectif*

Since most final consonants are silent in French, you will not hear or say the final consonant of masculine adjective forms, unless they end in **c, r, f,** or **l.** When the **e** is added to make the feminine form, the consonant is no longer final and is pronounced.

> petit / petite   français / française

When a masculine adjective form ends in a pronounced final consonant, or in **e** or **é,** however, you will hear no difference between the masculine and feminine forms.

> espagnol / espagnole   jeune / jeune   marié / mariée

The final **s** of plurals is not pronounced, nor is a consonant that immediately precedes it, unless it is **c, r, f,** or **l.** The masculine plural forms sound like the masculine singular forms and the feminine plural forms sound like the feminine singular forms. You must pick up the plurality from the context.

> Il est petit. / Ils sont petits.   Elle est petite. / Elles sont petites.

Be careful to pronounce the vowels in **il/ils** and **elle/elles** distinctly. The letter **i** in French is pronounced similarly to the double *ee* in the English words *see* and *feed,* but it is said more quickly and the tongue is held more tensely. The letter **e** in **elle/elles** is pronounced somewhat like the *e* in the English word *bet.*

> Il est grand. Ils sont beaux.   Elle est grande. Elles sont belles.

A. Claude qui? Écoutez les phrases. C'est la phrase **a** pour Claude Bellon ou la phrase **b** pour Claude Lacoste?

1. **a.** Claude est grand.
   b. Claude est grande.
2. **a.** Claude n'est pas petit.
   b. Claude n'est pas petite.
3. **a.** Claude est français.
   b. Claude est française.
4. **a.** Claude n'est pas canadien.
   b. Claude n'est pas canadienne.
5. **a.** Claude n'est pas gros.
   b. Claude n'est pas grosse.

a. Claude Bellon   **b.** Claude Lacoste

B. Comment sont-ils? Décrivez David et Annette avec un antonyme.

> **EXEMPLE**   David n'est pas marié.   **Il est célibataire.**

1. David n'est pas gros.
2. David n'est pas vieux.
3. David n'est pas laid.
4. Annette n'est pas mariée.
5. Annette n'est pas laide.
6. Annette n'est pas vieille.

C. Gens célèbres. Répondez logiquement.

> **EXEMPLE**   Tom Cruise est grand?   **Non, il n'est pas grand. Il est petit.**

1. Cameron Diaz est grosse?
2. Rosie O'Donnell est mince?
3. Gwyneth Paltrow est célibataire?
4. Brad Pitt est laid?
5. Angelina Jolie est laide?
6. Shaquille O'Neal est petit?
7. Jennifer Lopez est vieille?
8. William Shatner est jeune?

Stratégies et Lecture

At first, it can seem overwhelming to read a lengthier text in French. However, there are certain strategies you can use to learn to read more easily. This section is designed to help you learn to apply these strategies.

> ### ⚘ Pour mieux lire: *Using cognates and familiar words to read for the gist*
>
> Cognates are words that look the same or similar in two languages and have the same meaning. Take advantage of cognates to help you read French more easily. There are some patterns in cognates. What three patterns do you see here? What do the last two words in each column mean?
>
> | | | |
> |---|---|---|
> | soudainement *suddenly* | obligé *obliged* | hôpital *hospital* |
> | décidément *decidedly* | décidé *decided* | île *isle, island* |
> | complètement *???* | compliqué *???* | honnête *???* |
> | généralement *???* | sauvé *???* | forêt *???* |
>
> Recognizing words you have already learned in different forms will also help you read. Use the phrases you already know on the left to guess the meaning of those on the right.
>
> | | |
> |---|---|
> | Comment dit-on *pen* en français? | Qu'est-ce que tu dis? |
> | Je ne sais pas la réponse. | Yvette ne sait pas quoi répondre. |
>
> You will run across many unknown words in reading French, but this should not prevent you from understanding. Be flexible, changing forms of words or word order if necessary, and skip over little words that may not be needed to get the message.

A. Avant de lire. Can you state the general idea of the following sentences? Do not try to read them word by word; rather, focus on the words that you can understand.

> Yvette hésite un moment avant de répondre.
>
> C'est juste à ce moment qu'Annette arrive.
>
> Annette sauve la pauvre Yvette.
>
> David voit Annette et Yvette et s'exclame: «Je vois double!»

B. Mots apparentés. Before reading the following text, ***Qui est-ce?,*** skim through it and list the cognates you see. You should find about twenty.

CD 1-20

Lecture: Qui est-ce?

Yvette Clark is visiting her twin sister, Annette, a student at the University of Nice. As she waits for her sister in front of the **musée des Beaux-Arts,** a young man approaches. Since she does not speak French very well, Yvette is unsure what to say when he speaks to her.

— Salut, Annette! Ça va?

Yvette hésite un moment avant de répondre.

— Non, non… euh, ça va, mais… euh… je regrette… je ne suis pas Annette. Je suis Yvette.

— Qu'est-ce que tu dis, Annette?

Yvette pense en elle-même: «*He thinks I'm Annette. How do I tell him . . . ?*»

— Non, non, répond Yvette. Vous ne comprenez pas. Je ne suis pas Annette.

— Comment ça, tu n'es pas Annette?

Décidément, ce jeune homme ne comprend rien! Yvette insiste encore une fois.

— Je ne suis pas Annette. Vous ne comprenez pas! Écoutez! Je ne suis pas Annette! Je ne suis pas étudiante.

— Mais qu'est-ce que tu dis? demande David. Tu es malade? C'est moi, David. Nous sommes dans le même cours de littérature.

Yvette pense: «*I'm never going to get this guy to understand. He's so sure I'm Annette.*»

C'est juste à ce moment qu'Annette arrive. La pauvre Yvette est sauvée.

— Salut, Yvette! Bonjour, David!

David, très surpris de voir les deux sœurs jumelles, s'exclame:

— Mais, ce n'est pas possible! Je vois double! Maintenant je comprends. C'est ta sœur jumelle, Annette.

— Mon pauvre David! Voilà, je te présente ma sœur, Yvette.

— Bonjour, Yvette. Désolé pour la confusion, mais quelle ressemblance!

A. Avez-vous compris? Qui parle: **David, Yvette** ou **Annette**?

1. Vous ne comprenez pas. Je ne suis pas Annette.
2. Mais nous sommes dans le même cours de littérature.
3. Je ne suis pas étudiante à l'université de Nice.
4. Je ne parle pas très bien français.
5. Je te présente ma sœur.

B. D'abord... Which happens first, **a** or **b**?

1. **a.** David dit bonjour à Yvette.
   b. Yvette arrive au musée des Beaux-Arts.
2. **a.** David dit: «Bonjour, Annette.»
   b. Yvette pense: «Il ne comprend pas.»
3. **a.** Yvette hésite à répondre parce qu'elle ne parle pas très bien français.
   b. Yvette répond: «Non, non, vous ne comprenez pas.»
4. **a.** David comprend qu'Annette et Yvette sont sœurs jumelles.
   b. Annette arrive.
5. **a.** David dit: «Désolé *(Sorry)* pour la confusion.»
   b. David comprend la situation.

Describing personality

Vocabulaire supplémentaire

excentrique	sérieux (sérieuse)
matérialiste	têtu(e) *stubborn*
énergique	brillant(e)
organisé(e)	imaginatif (imaginative)
désorganisé(e)	honnête *honest*
sociable	malhonnête *dishonest*

✹ Note *de vocabulaire*

1. Most people use the abbreviated form **sympa** for **sympathique**. Do not add an **e** to **sympa** to make it feminine, but do add an **s** in the plural.

2. Use **le football** for *soccer* and **le football américain** for *football.*

3. There are three ways to say *my* (**mon, ma, mes**) and *your* [singular familiar] (**ton, ta, tes**), depending on whether the possession you are identifying is masculine or feminine, singular or plural. You will learn about this in ***Chapitre 3.***

Les personnalités

Je suis très...   Je suis **plutôt**...   Je suis assez...   Je suis un peu...

Je **ne** suis **pas (du tout)**...

optimiste / pessimiste, idéaliste / réaliste

timide / extraverti(e)

sympathique (sympa), **gentil (gentille),** agréable / désagréable, méchant(e)

intelligent(e), intellectuel (intellectuelle) / **bête**

amusant(e), intéressant(e) / ennuyeux (ennuyeuse)

dynamique, sportif (sportive) / paresseux (paresseuse)

What are you like, compared to your best friend?

Je suis **plus** dynamique **que mon meilleur ami (ma meilleure amie).**

Je suis **aussi** sportif (sportive) **que** mon meilleur ami (ma meilleure amie).

Je suis **moins** timide **que** mon meilleur ami (ma meilleure amie).

Une **nouvelle** amie, Marie-Louise, parle avec David.

CD 1-21

MARIE-LOUISE: **Tes amis** et toi, vous êtes étudiants, non?

DAVID: Oui, nous sommes étudiants à l'université de Nice.

MARIE-LOUISE: Vous êtes plutôt intellectuels, alors?

DAVID: Mes amis sont assez intellectuels, mais moi, je ne suis pas très intellectuel. Et toi? Tu es étudiante aussi?

MARIE-LOUISE: Non, **les études, ce n'est pas mon truc.**

DAVID: Et le sport? **Tu aimes** le sport?

MARIE-LOUISE: Oui, j'aime bien le tennis, mais je n'aime pas beaucoup **le football.**

---

plutôt *rather*   **ne... pas du tout** *not at all*   **sympathique** *nice*   **gentil(le)** *nice*   **bête** *stupid, dumb*   **dynamique** *active*
plus... que *more . . . than*   **mon meilleur ami (ma meilleure amie)** *my best friend*   **aussi... que** *as . . . as*   **moins... que** *less . . . than*   **nouveau (nouvelle)** *new*   **Tes amis** *Your friends*   **les études** *studies, going to school*   **ce n'est pas mon truc** *it's not my thing*   **Tu aimes** *You like*   **le football** *soccer*

A. Ils sont comment? Complétez les phrases.

EXEMPLE Ben Affleck est (plus, moins, aussi) grand que Tom Cruise.
Ben Affleck est plus grand que Tom Cruise.

1. Johnny Depp est (plus, moins, aussi) beau que Tom Cruise.
2. Jon Stewart est (plus, moins, aussi) amusant que David Letterman.
3. Tiger Woods est (plus, moins, aussi) sportif que Sammy Sosa.
4. Paris Hilton est (plus, moins, aussi) belle que Gwyneth Paltrow.
5. Katie Couric est (plus, moins, aussi) intelligente qu'Oprah Winfrey.
6. Les Républicains sont (plus, moins, aussi) idéalistes que les Démocrates.

B. Comment sont-ils? Complétez les phrases.

1. Moi, *je suis / je ne suis pas* très extraverti(e).
2. *Je suis / Je ne suis pas* pessimiste.
3. Mon meilleur ami *est / n'est pas* bête. *Il est / Il n'est pas* intelligent.
4. Mes amis *sont / ne sont pas* sportifs. *Ils sont / Ils ne sont pas* paresseux.
5. Ma famille et moi, *nous sommes / nous ne sommes pas* très dynamiques. *Nous sommes / Nous ne sommes pas* gentils.
6. Et vous, *[name your professor],* vous êtes / vous n'êtes pas très méchant(e)!

C. Et vous? Comment êtes-vous?

très	plutôt	assez	un peu	ne... pas du tout

EXEMPLE optimistic
Je suis très / plutôt / assez / un peu optimiste.
Je ne suis pas (du tout) optimiste.

1. idealistic
2. mean
3. lazy
4. intellectual
5. shy
6. boring
7. athletic
8. married

D. Réponses. Quelle est la réponse logique?

1. Tu es étudiant(e)?
2. Tu aimes le sport?
3. Tes amis et toi, vous êtes sportifs?
4. Tes amis et toi, vous êtes intellectuels?
5. Tes amis sont extravertis?
6. Tes amis sont dynamiques?

a. Oui, nous sommes très sportifs.
b. Oui, nous sommes assez intellectuels.
c. Oui, je suis étudiant(e).
d. Non, ils sont plutôt paresseux.
e. Oui, j'aime beaucoup le football.
f. Non, ils sont plutôt timides.

E. Conversation. Avec un(e) partenaire, relisez à haute voix *(aloud)* la conversation entre Marie-Louise et David à la page précédente. Ensuite, changez la conversation pour décrire *(to describe)* votre propre *(own)* situation.

CD 1-22 You can find a list of the new words from the vocabulary and grammar sections of this **Compétence** on page 62 and a recording of this list on track 1-22 of your *Text Audio CD.*

Pour vérifier

1. What pronoun would you use to say *you* to a child? two children? a salesclerk?

2. How do you say *I* in French? When do words like **je, ne,** and **que** replace the final **e** with an apostrophe (**j', n', qu'**)? What is this called?

3. How do you say *he* in French? *she*? *they* for a group of all females? *they* for a group of all males? *they* for a mixed group?

4. What is an infinitive? How do you say *to be*?

5. What form of **être** do you use with each of the subject pronouns?

6. What do you place before a conjugated verb to negate it? What do you place after it? What happens to **ne** when it is followed by a vowel sound?

7. What are five irregular patterns of adjective agreement?

8. What is the feminine form of **gentil**? of **beau**? of **nouveau**?

✳ Note *de grammaire*

With noun subjects or compound subjects, use the verb form that goes with the corresponding subject pronoun.

David is = he is **(il est)** = **David est**

David and I are = we are **(nous sommes)** = **David et moi sommes**

Your friends and you = you (plural) are **(vous êtes)** = **tes ami(e)s et toi, vous êtes**

my friends are = they are **(ils/elles sont)** = **mes ami(e)s sont**

✳ Note *de grammaire*

For a review of all the patterns of adjective agreement you have seen, see the **Résumé de grammaire** section on page 61.

 To download a podcast on Plural Adjectives and Subject Pronouns, go to **academic.cengage.com/french.**

Describing people

*Les pronoms sujets, le verbe **être**, la négation et d'autres adjectifs*

Below are the subject pronouns *(I, you, he . . .)* and the forms of the verb **être** *(to be)*. To say *you* when speaking to a friend, family member, classmate, animal, or child, use **tu.** Use **vous** when speaking to an adult stranger, someone to whom you should show respect, or when talking to more than one person. For **je** and other words that consist of a consonant sound and **e (ne, que, me...)**, replace the **e** with an apostrophe before a vowel or mute **h.** This is called elision.

The word **être** is the infinitive, the verb form you will find in the dictionary. The chart below shows the conjugation, the forms you use with different subject pronouns.

ÊTRE (to be)					
je suis	*I am*		**nous**	**sommes**	*we are*
tu es	*you are*		**vous**	**êtes**	*you are*
il est	*he is, it is*		**ils**	**sont**	*they are*
elle est	*she is, it is*		**elles**	**sont**	*they are*

To negate a conjugated verb, place **ne... pas** around it. Remember to use **n'** before a vowel sound or mute **h.**

ne (n') + verbe + pas		
je **ne** travaille **pas**	je **n'**habite **pas**	je **n'**aime **pas**
je **ne** suis **pas**	tu **n'**es **pas**	il/elle **n'**est **pas**
nous **ne** sommes **pas**	vous **n'**êtes **pas**	ils/elles **ne** sont **pas**

Remember that adjectives agree in gender (masculine, feminine) and number (singular, plural) with what they describe. Review the forms of adjectives on page 34. Note the patterns of these common adjective endings when **-e** is added for the feminine form.

MASCULINE	FEMININE	MASCULINE		FEMININE	
		Singular	*Plural*	*Singular*	*Plural*
-eux	-euse	paresseux	paresseux	paresseuse	paresseuses
-en	-enne	canadien	canadiens	canadienne	canadiennes
-if	-ive	sportif	sportifs	sportive	sportives
-el	-elle	intellectuel	intellectuels	intellectuelle	intellectuelles
-er	-ère	premier	premiers	première	premières

Gentil doubles the final consonant before adding the **-e** for the feminine form (**gentil → gentille**).

The adjective **nouveau** follows the same pattern as **beau** and **jumeau**.

MASCULINE		FEMININE	
Singular	*Plural*	*Singular*	*Plural*
beau	beaux	belle	belles
nouveau	nouveaux	nouvelle	nouvelles

A. Tu ou vous? Demandez à ces personnes d'où ils sont *(where they are from)*.

EXEMPLES your classmate: **Tu es d'où?** your boss: **Vous êtes d'où?**

1. your roommate
2. your teacher
3. a salesclerk
4. two friends
5. your parents
6. an elderly neighbor

B. Quel pronom? Complétez les phrases avec le pronom personnel qui s'impose *(required subject pronoun)*: **je, tu, il, elle, nous, vous, ils, elles.**

1. David est étudiant à l'université mais _____ n'est pas très intellectuel. Marie-Louise n'est pas intellectuelle non plus *(either)*. _____ est plutôt sportive!

2. Annette et Yvette ne sont pas paresseuses. _____ sont dynamiques. David et Jean sont dynamiques aussi, mais _____ sont moins dynamiques qu'Annette et Yvette. Mes amis et moi, _____ sommes assez dynamiques aussi. Et tes amis et toi, _____ êtes dynamiques?

3. David et Annette ne sont pas mariés. _____ sont célibataires. Moi, _____ suis célibataire aussi. Et toi, _____ es célibataire ou marié(e)?

C. Au contraire! Complétez les descriptions avec le verbe **être.** Donnez le négatif si nécessaire.

EXEMPLE Les étudiants du cours de français... (bêtes, dynamiques, intelligents)
Les étudiants du cours de français ne sont pas bêtes. Ils sont dynamiques. Ils sont intelligents.

1. Moi, je... (extraverti[e], dynamique, timide, un peu paresseux [paresseuse])
2. En général, mes professeurs... (intéressants, intellectuels, bêtes, ennuyeux, intelligents)
3. Mes amis et moi, nous... (sportifs, intellectuels, paresseux, sympathiques)

D. Comment sont-ils? Dites si ces adjectifs décrivent *(describe)* bien ces personnes. Changez la forme de l'adjectif si nécessaire.

EXEMPLE Annette ... beau, laid **Annette est belle. Elle n'est pas laide.**

Annette...
intellectuel, gros,
paresseux, dynamique

Annette et Yvette...
américain, français,
gentil, méchant, beau

David et Jean...
laid, beau, vieux,
jeune

Moi, je...
dynamique, paresseux,
ennuyeux, sportif

E. Descriptions. Décrivez ces personnes. Faites attention à la forme du verbe **être** et aussi à l'accord *(agreement)* de l'adjectif!

moi, je	sommes / ne sommes pas	sportif
mon meilleur ami	suis / ne suis pas	sympathique
mes amis et moi	sont / ne sont pas	ennuyeux
les étudiants du cours de français	est / n'est pas	marié
les étudiantes du cours de français		extraverti
le professeur de français		???

Pour vérifier

1. What are three ways of asking a question that can be answered with **oui** or **non**? What happens to your intonation in each case? Which of these ways can you also use to ask a question that is answered with a choice?

2. What happens to **est-ce que** before a vowel sound?

Asking what someone is like

Les questions

There are several ways to ask a question that will be answered **oui** or **non.**

- You can ask a question with rising intonation, that is by raising the pitch of your voice at the end. A statement normally has falling intonation.

STATEMENT: Tu es extravertie.   QUESTION: Tu es extravertie?
You are outgoing.   *Are you outgoing?*

- You can also ask a question by adding **est-ce que** to the beginning of a statement and using rising intonation.

STATEMENT: Tu es sportif.   QUESTION: Est-ce que tu es sportif?
You are athletic.   *Are you athletic?*

Due to elision, **est-ce que** becomes **est-ce qu'** before vowel sounds.

     Est-ce qu'il est d'ici?   **Est-ce qu'**elles sont canadiennes?

- You can also use rising intonation or **est-ce que** to ask a question that is answered with a choice.

     Tu es marié ou célibataire?   Est-ce que tu es marié ou célibataire?
     Are you married or single?   *Are you married or single?*

- If you are presuming that someone will probably answer **oui** to a question, you can use either **n'est-ce pas?** *(isn't that right?)* or **non?** at the end of a question with rising intonation.

STATEMENT: Il est marié.   QUESTION: Il est marié, n'est-ce pas?
He's married.   Il est marié, non?
                                           He's married, isn't he?

A. C'est une question? Listen to your instructor make some statements and ask some questions about your class and university. If you hear a statement, don't write anything on your paper. If you hear a question, answer it with **oui** or **non** on your paper.

B. Et toi? Demandez à un(e) camarade de classe comment il/elle est. Faites attention à la forme de l'adjectif!

> **EXEMPLE**   sportif ou intellectuel
>   — **Est-ce que tu es sportif (sportive) ou intellectuel(le)?**
>   — **Je suis plutôt sportif (sportive) / plutôt intellectuel(le) / les deux** *(both).*

1. idéaliste ou réaliste   **5.** amusant ou ennuyeux
2. timide ou extraverti   **6.** dynamique ou paresseux
3. gentil ou méchant   **7.** optimiste ou pessimiste
4. intelligent ou bête   **8.** marié, célibataire, fiancé ou divorcé

Maintenant, présentez votre partenaire à la classe en suivant l'exemple.

> **EXEMPLE**   C'est Mario. Il est intellectuel...

C. Et le professeur? Posez ces questions à votre professeur. Utilisez **est-ce que, n'est-ce pas** ou **non.**

> **EXEMPLE** Vous êtes marié(e)?
> **Est-ce que vous êtes marié(e)?**
> **Vous êtes marié(e), n'est-ce pas / non?**

1. Vous êtes américain(e)?
2. Le français est facile pour vous?
3. Les examens de français sont très faciles?
4. Votre premier cours commence à huit heures?
5. Vous êtes à l'université le lundi matin?
6. Vous êtes en cours à trois heures?

D. Encore des questions! David pose des questions à Annette. Qu'est-ce qu'il dit? Formez des questions logiques avec le verbe **être.**

> **EXEMPLE** **Est-ce que tu es plus jeune que moi?**

Est-ce que	tes amis... nous... tu... ta sœur...	américaine de Los Angeles étudiante d'ici dans le même cours plus extravertis que toi plus jeune que moi en cours à une heure aussi intelligente que toi

E. Entretien. Interviewez votre partenaire.

1. Est-ce que tu es américain(e)? Ta famille et toi, vous êtes d'ici? Est-ce que vous êtes plutôt idéalistes ou plutôt réalistes?
2. Est-ce que les études sont faciles ou difficiles pour toi? Est-ce que les professeurs ici sont intéressants ou ennuyeux? Ton meilleur ami (Ta meilleure amie) est étudiant(e) aussi? Tes amis et toi, est-ce que vous êtes intellectuels? Est-ce que tes amis sont intelligents ou bêtes? Ils sont amusants ou ennuyeux?
3. Est-ce que tu aimes le sport? Tu es plutôt sportif (sportive)? Est-ce que tu es dynamique ou plutôt paresseux (paresseuse)?

Describing the university area

❈ Note *culturelle*

Le concept d'une université et d'un campus est très différent en France et aux USA. En France, l'université n'est pas un centre social. Il y a peu *(few)* d'activités extrascolaires ou de sport sur le campus. La majorité des étudiants vont *(go)* à l'université dans leur propre ville *(their own city)* et ils habitent avec leurs parents. Ils vont à l'université juste pour aller en cours. Dans une autre partie de la ville, il y a un quartier où se trouvent *(are located)* des résidences universitaires. Ce quartier s'appelle la cité universitaire. Préférez-vous habiter chez vos parents ou près de chez eux *(at or near your parents' house)*? Est-ce que les activités sociales sont importantes pour vous à l'université?

Le campus et le quartier

Qu'est-ce qu'il y a sur votre campus?

Sur le campus, **il y a…**

des salles *(f)* de classe *(f)*

un amphithéâtre

une bibliothèque

des résidences *(f)*

un stade avec des matchs *(m)* de football américain

une librairie

un parking

❈ Note *de vocabulaire*

The word **universitaire** is an adjective. It must be paired with a noun that it is describing; for example, *a university restaurant* (**un restaurant universitaire**), *a university bookstore* (**une librairie universitaire**), *university dorms* (**des résidences universitaires**). The word **université** is a noun: **J'habite près de l'université.**

Dans le quartier universitaire, près de l'université, il y a…

beaucoup de grands bâtiments *(m)* modernes avec **des bureaux** *(m)*

des maisons *(f)*

un parc avec beaucoup d'arbres *(m)*

des concerts *(m)* de rock *(m)* / de jazz *(m)* / de musique *(f)* populaire / de musique classique

---

Qu'est-ce qu'il y a… ? *What is there . . . ?*   **sur** *on*   **il y a** *there is, there are*   **un amphithéâtre** *a lecture hall*   **une résidence** *a dormitory*   **Dans le quartier universitaire** *In the university neighborhood*   **près de** *near*   **un bureau** *an office*

une boîte de nuit

un théâtre

un cinéma avec
des films
étrangers et des
films américains

un club de gym

Vocabulaire supplémentaire

un arrêt d'autobus *a bus stop*
un centre administratif *an administration building*
un centre d'étudiants *a student center*
un court de tennis *a tennis court*
une fontaine *a fountain*
un gymnase *a gym*
une infirmerie *a health center*
un laboratoire *a lab*
une piscine *a pool*
une statue

Annette et un ami parlent du campus et du quartier.

CD 1-23

MICHEL:	Comment est **ton** université? Tu aimes le campus?
ANNETTE:	Oui, il est très agréable. Les vieux bâtiments sont très **jolis.**
MICHEL:	Qu'est-ce qu'il y a sur le campus?
ANNETTE:	Il y a une grande bibliothèque et beaucoup d'arbres, mais **il n'y a pas assez de** parkings.
MICHEL:	Qu'est-ce qu'il y a dans le quartier?
ANNETTE:	Il y a de jolies maisons, des cafés, deux ou trois **bons** restaurants et beaucoup de **mauvais** fast-foods.

A. Chez nous. Décrivez votre université.

1. Le campus ici est *grand / petit / joli / laid / ???.*
2. Sur le campus il y a *plus de nouveaux bâtiments / plus de vieux bâtiments.*
3. La bibliothèque universitaire est *grande / petite / agréable / ???.*
4. *Il y a / Il n'y a pas* assez de résidences sur le campus.
5. *Il y a / Il n'y a pas* beaucoup d'arbres sur le campus.
6. Le restaurant universitaire, c'est un *bon / mauvais* restaurant. *(Il n'y a pas de restaurant sur le campus.)*
7. *Il y a / Il n'y a pas* assez de parkings.
8. Le week-end, il y a souvent *(often) des matchs de football américain / des concerts / des films / ???.*
9. Dans le quartier près de l'université, il y a *des restaurants / des cafés / des fast-foods / un joli parc / ???.*
10. *Barnes & Noble / BookPeople / ???* est une bonne librairie dans le quartier.

B. Qu'est-ce qu'il y a? Complétez ces phrases pour décrire votre quartier universitaire.

1. Sur le campus, il y a...
2. Dans le quartier universitaire, il y a...

C. Conversation. Avec un(e) partenaire, relisez la conversation entre Michel et Annette ci-dessus *(above).* Ensuite, changez la conversation pour décrire votre propre université.

CD 1-24 You can find a list of the new words
from the vocabulary and grammar sections of this
Compétence on page 63 and a recording of
this list on track 1-24 of your *Text Audio CD.*

étranger (étrangère) *foreign* **ton (ta, tes)** *your* **joli(e)** *pretty* **il n'y a pas** *there isn't, there aren't* **assez de** *enough*
bon(ne) *good* **mauvais(e)** *bad*

1. What are the two forms of the word for *a*? When do you use each? How do you say *some*?

2. How do you say *there is*? *there are*? *there isn't*? *there aren't*?

3. In what three circumstances do you use **de (d')** instead of **un, une,** or **des**? What is an exception to replacing **un, une,** or **des** with **de (d')** in a negative sentence?

 To download a podcast on the Indefinite Article and on Nouns, go to **academic. cengage.com/french.**

Saying what there is

*Le genre, l'article indéfini et l'expression **il y a***

All nouns in French have a gender (masculine or feminine). The categorization of most nouns as masculine or feminine cannot be guessed, unless they represent people.

The short word **un** *(a, an),* **une** *(a, an),* or **des** *(some)* before a noun is called the indefinite article. Use **un** with masculine singular nouns, **une** with feminine singular nouns, and **des** with all plural nouns.

Always learn a new noun as a unit with the article (**un, une**) in order to remember its gender!

	SINGULAR	PLURAL
MASCULINE	un théâtre	des théâtres
FEMININE	une bibliothèque	des bibliothèques

Un, une, and **des** change to **de (d')** in the following cases.

- After most negated verbs.

Il y a **un** stade.	Il **n'**y a **pas de** stade.
Il y a **une** résidence.	Il **n'**y a **pas de** résidence.
Il y a **des** matchs de football.	Il **n'**y a **pas de** matchs de football.
Écrivez **des** phrases complètes.	**N'**écrivez **pas de** phrases complètes.

But not after the verb **être:**

C'est **un** bon restaurant.	Ce **n'**est **pas un** bon restaurant.

- After expressions of quantity, such as **combien, beaucoup,** and **assez.**

Il y a **des** cinémas.	Il y a **beaucoup de** cinémas.
Il y a **un** parking.	Il y a **assez de** parkings.

- Directly before a plural adjective.

Il y a **des** bâtiments modernes.	Il y a **de jolis** bâtiments.

To say *there is* or *there are* in French, use the expression **il y a (un, une, des...).** To say *there isn't* or *there aren't,* use **il n'y a pas (de...).**

To make a noun plural, add an **s** to the end of it. Do not add an **s,** however, if the noun already ends in an **s, x,** or **z.** Nouns that end in **-eau (bureau)** form their plural with an **x (bureaux).**

Prononciation

CD 1-25

L'article indéfini

Be careful to pronounce **un** and **une** differently. Use the very tight sound **u** with lips pursed, as in **tu,** to say **une.** To pronounce the **u** sound, position your mouth to pronounce a French **i** with your tongue held high in your mouth. Then, purse your lips. The vowel sound of **un** is nasal. Pronounce the **n** in **un** only when there is **liaison** with a following noun beginning with a vowel sound.

une résidence	**un** bâtiment
une amie	**un** ami

A. Scènes. Complétez ces questions avec **un, une** ou **des.** Après, posez les questions à votre partenaire.

1. C'est _____ bibliothèque ou _____ restaurant?

   Ce sont _____ étudiants ou _____ professeurs?

2. C'est _____ cinéma ou _____ salle de classe?

   Ce sont _____ femmes ou _____ hommes?

3. C'est _____ concert ou _____ film?

   C'est _____ concert de jazz ou de musique classique?

4. C'est _____ librairie ou _____ boîte de nuit?

   Ce sont _____ gens timides ou _____ gens extravertis?

B. Qu'est-ce qu'il y a? Relisez la **Note culturelle** à la page 44. Sur le campus d'une université française, est-ce qu'il y a probablement ces choses?

EXEMPLES   un restaurant universitaire   des matchs de football

Oui, il y a un restaurant universitaire.   **Non, il n'y a pas de matchs de football.**

1. des amphithéâtres
2. un stade
3. des bureaux de profs
4. une bibliothèque
5. des résidences
6. des salles de classe
7. une boîte de nuit
8. des matchs de football américain

C. Dans le quartier. Complétez ces questions avec **un, une, des** ou **de (d').**
Ensuite *(Then),* posez-les à un(e) camarade de classe.

1. Est-ce qu'il y a _____ librairie sur le campus? Est-ce qu'il y a _____ grande bibliothèque? Est-ce qu'il y a _____ livres en français à la *(in the)* bibliothèque?

2. Est-ce qu'il y a _____ restaurant sur le campus? Est-ce qu'il y a _____ bons restaurants dans le quartier? Est-ce qu'il y a beaucoup _____ fast-foods près de l'université?

3. Est-ce qu'il y a _____ vieux bâtiments sur le campus? Il y a _____ bâtiments modernes? Il y a _____ jolis arbres? Est-ce qu'il y a assez _____ parkings?

4. Est-ce qu'il y a _____ grand stade sur le campus? Quels jours de la semaine est-ce qu'il y a _____ matchs de football américain?

Pour vérifier

1. Do you use **c'est** and **ce sont** or **il est / elle est** and **ils sont / elles sont** with a noun to identify or describe someone or something? with an adjective to describe? with a prepositional phrase? with nationalities, professions, and religions without the indefinite article?

2. Are most adjectives placed before or after the noun they describe? Which adjectives are placed before the noun they describe?

3. What are the alternate masculine singular forms of **beau, nouveau,** and **vieux**? When are they used?

✳ Note *de grammaire*

Remember to use **il y a** to say *there is / there are*. Use **c'est / ce sont** and **il est / elle est / ils sont / elles sont** to say *he is / she is / it is* and *they are*.

Sur le campus, **il y a** beaucoup de bâtiments. **Ils sont** beaux!

*On the campus, **there are** a lot of new buildings. **They are** pretty!*

 To download a podcast on Adjectives, go to **academic.cengage.com/french.**

Identifying and describing people and things

*C'est ou **il est / elle est** et la place de l'adjectif*

Since all nouns in French are masculine or feminine, there is no neuter *it*. Generally, use **il** or **elle** to say *it* and **ils** or **elles** to say *they* when talking about things, depending on the gender of the noun being referred to.

Le campus? Il est beau. Les parkings? Ils sont petits!
La bibliothèque? Elle est jolie. Les résidences? Elles sont très vieilles!

Note that **c'est,** as well as **il est / elle est,** can mean *he is / she is / it is* and **ce sont,** as well as **ils sont / elles sont,** can mean *they are.* These expressions are not interchangeable.

Use **c'est** and **ce sont:**

- with *nouns* to identify or describe
  C'est David. C'est un ami français.

Use **il est / elle est** and **ils sont / elles sont:**

- with *adjectives* to describe
  Il est beau et sympa.

- with *prepositional phrases*
  Il est de Nice. Il est en cours.

- with *nationalities, professions* (including **étudiant[e]**), and *religions* without the indefinite article
  Il est étudiant. Il est français. Il est catholique.

In French, most descriptive adjectives are placed *after* the noun they describe.

un campus moderne une boîte de nuit populaire des amis sympas

However, these 14 very common adjectives are placed *before* the noun.

beau (belle)	jeune	bon (bonne)	grand(e)	autre
joli(e)	vieux (vieille)	mauvais(e)	petit(e)	même
	nouveau (nouvelle)	gentil(le)	gros(se)	seul(e) *(only)*

un joli campus une grande boîte de nuit de bons amis

The adjectives **beau, nouveau,** and **vieux** have alternate masculine singular forms, **bel, nouvel,** and **vieil,** that are used before nouns beginning with a vowel sound.

MASCULINE SINGULAR (PLUS CONSONANT SOUND)	MASCULINE SINGULAR (PLUS VOWEL SOUND)	FEMININE SINGULAR
un beau quartier	un bel ami	une belle amie
un nouveau quartier	un nouvel ami	une nouvelle amie
un vieux quartier	un vieil ami	une vieille amie

A. Qu'est-ce que c'est? Identifiez ces personnes ou ces choses. Après, décrivez-les avec l'adjectif le plus logique.

EXEMPLES

café (grand / petit)
C'est un café.
Il est petit.

étudiantes (sympa / méchant)
Ce sont des étudiantes.
Elles sont sympas.

1.
maisons (nouveau / vieux)

2.
amphithéâtre (grand / petit)

3.
maison (grand / petit)

4.
femme (sportif / paresseux)

5.
parc (joli / laid)

6.
salle de classe (moderne / vieux)

B. C'est ou il est / elle est? Commencez chaque phrase avec **c'est, ce sont, il est, elle est, ils sont** ou **elles sont**.

EXEMPLE **C'est un jeune homme. Il est dynamique.**
Il n'est pas paresseux. Il est sportif. Il est beau.

un jeune homme, dynamique, paresseux, sportif, beau

1. des hommes, étudiants, jeunes, sympathiques

2. Yvette, française, en France, professeur, à l'université, à la maison

C. Compliments. Faites des compliments. Écrivez la forme correcte de l'adjectif logique dans la phrase pour faire un compliment.

EXEMPLE C'est une _____ femme _____. (intelligent / bête)
C'est une femme intelligente.

1. C'est un _bon_ restaurant _____. (bon / mauvais)
2. Ce sont de/des _gentil_ étudiantes _____. (gentil / méchant)
3. C'est un _beau_ campus _____. (beau / laid)
4. C'est une _jolie_ femme _____. (joli / laid)
5. C'est un _bel_ homme _____. (beau / laid)
6. C'est une _____ résidence _____. (nouveau / vieux)
7. Ce sont de/des _____ gens _____. (intéressant / désagréable)

Talking about your studies

L'université et les cours

Est-ce que vous aimez l'université?

J'aime beaucoup…	J'aime assez…	Je n'aime pas (du tout)…	Je préfère…
les professeurs	la bibliothèque	les devoirs	**les fêtes**
les étudiants	le laboratoire	les examens	le sport
le campus	de langues	le laboratoire	les matchs
		d'informatique	de basket

Qu'est-ce que vous étudiez?

J'étudie la philosophie.   Je n'étudie pas la littérature.

LES LANGUES *(f)*   LES SCIENCES HUMAINES *(f)*   LES BEAUX-ARTS *(m)*
l'allemand *(m)*   l'histoire *(f)*   le théâtre
l'anglais *(m)*   la psychologie   la musique
l'espagnol *(m)*   **les sciences politiques** *(f)*
le français

LES COURS DE COMMERCE   LES COURS TECHNIQUES   LES SCIENCES
la comptabilité   les mathématiques   la biologie
le marketing   (les maths) *(f)*   **la chimie**
                               l'informatique *(f)*   la physique

J'aime beaucoup le cours de… Il est facile / difficile / intéressant.

CD 1-26   David et Annette parlent de **leurs** études.

DAVID: Qu'est-ce que tu étudies ce semestre?
ANNETTE: J'étudie le français et la littérature classique. Et toi?
DAVID: J'étudie la philosophie et la littérature classique, comme toi.
ANNETTE: Comment sont tes cours?
DAVID: J'aime beaucoup le cours de philosophie. Il est très intéressant. Je n'aime pas du tout le cours de littérature parce que le prof est ennuyeux.

---

une fête *a party*   l'allemand *(m)* German   les sciences politiques *(f)* government, political science   les beaux-arts *(m)* the fine arts   la comptabilité *accounting*   l'informatique *(f)* computer science   la chimie *chemistry*   leur(s) *their*

A. Préférences. Interviewez votre partenaire sur ses préférences.

EXEMPLE le français / les mathématiques
— **Est-ce que tu préfères le français ou les mathématiques?**
— **Je préfère le français.**

1. la littérature / les sciences
2. les cours de commerce / les langues
3. les cours à huit heures du matin / les cours à deux heures de l'après-midi
4. les matchs de football américain / les matchs de basket
5. les cours dans les grands amphithéâtres / les cours dans les petites salles de classe / les cours dans le laboratoire de langues
6. les examens / les fêtes
7. les cours à huit heures du matin / les cours à sept heures du soir
8. le laboratoire de langues / la bibliothèque
9. la philosophie / l'informatique
10. la chimie / la physique
11. la chimie / la biologie
12. l'espagnol / l'allemand

B. Et vous? Changez les mots en italique pour parler de vous et de vos préférences.

1. J'étudie *le français, la biologie et les mathématiques.*
2. À l'université, j'aime *les étudiants.*
3. À l'université, je n'aime pas *les matchs de football américain.*
4. Je préfère les cours à *dix heures du matin.*
5. J'aime le cours de *français.* Il est intéressant.
6. Je n'aime pas le cours de *marketing.* Il est ennuyeux.

C. Entretien. Interviewez votre partenaire.

1. Qu'est-ce que tu étudies ce semestre?
2. Quels cours est-ce que tu préfères?
3. Pour toi, la chimie est plus facile ou plus difficile que la biologie?
4. Les maths sont plus intéressantes ou moins intéressantes que l'informatique?
5. L'histoire est plus ennuyeuse ou moins ennuyeuse que les sciences politiques?
6. La philosophie est plus intéressante ou moins intéressante que la littérature?

D. Conversation. Avec un(e) partenaire, relisez à haute voix la conversation entre David et Annette à la page précédente. Ensuite, changez la conversation pour décrire vos cours ce semestre.

CD 1-27 You can find a list of the new words from the vocabulary and grammar sections of this **Compétence** on page 63 and a recording of this list on track 1-27 of your *Text Audio CD*.

La cour de la Sorbonne

Pour vérifier

1. What are the four forms of the word for *the* in French? When do you use each?
2. Besides meaning *the,* what are two other uses of the definite article in French?
3. When is the **s** of the plural form **les** pronounced?

To download a podcast on the Definite Article, go to **academic.cengage.com/french.**

Identifying people and things

L'article défini

The short words **le, la, l', les** *(the)* before nouns are called the definite the article.

le campus   la bibliothèque   l'université   les cours

The form of the definite article you use depends on the noun's gender, whether it starts with a consonant or vowel sound, and whether it is singular or plural.

	SINGULAR BEFORE CONSONANT SOUND	SINGULAR BEFORE VOWEL SOUND	PLURAL
MASCULINE	**le** livre	**l'**homme	**les** livres, **les** hommes
FEMININE	**la** librairie	**l'**étudiante	**les** librairies, **les** étudiantes

Use the definite article before nouns:

- To specify items, as when using *the* in English.
  Apprenez **les** mots de vocabulaire.   *Learn **the** vocabulary words.*

- To say what you like, dislike, or prefer.
  Je n'aime pas **les** devoirs.   *I don't like homework.*

- To talk about something as a general category or an abstract noun.
  Les langues sont faciles pour moi.   *Languages are easy for me.*

In the last two cases, there is no article in English.

Prononciation

CD 1-28 *La voyelle **e** et l'article défini*

As you know, a *final* unaccented **e** is usually not pronounced, unless it is the only vowel, as in **le.**

grand**e**   histoire   langu**e**   bibliothèqu**e**   j'aim**e**

Otherwise, an unaccented **e** has three different pronunciations, depending on what follows it.

- In short words like **le** or **je,** or when **e** is followed by a single consonant within a word, pronounce it as in:
  je   ne   le   regarde   devoirs

- When, as in **les, e** is followed by an unpronounced consonant at the end of a word, pronounce it as in:
  les   mes   parlez   aimez   étudiez

- In words like **elle,** where **e** is followed by two consonants within a word, or by a single pronounced consonant at the end of a word, pronounce it as in:
  intellectuel   belle   quel   espagnol   basket

Since the final **s** of plural nouns is not pronounced, you must pronounce the article correctly to differentiate singular and plural nouns. Listen carefully as you repeat each of the following nouns. Notice the **z** sound of final **s** in liaison.

le livre   la science   l'étudiant   l'étudiante
les livres   les sciences   les ᶻétudiants   les ᶻétudiantes

A. Parlez bien. Listen as David talks about university life. In each sentence, you will hear the singular or plural form of one of the following nouns. Indicate which form you hear by writing the article on your paper.

1. le professeur — les professeurs
2. le cours — les cours
3. l'étudiant — les étudiants
4. l'examen — les examens
5. le livre — les livres
6. l'exercice — les exercices
7. le campus — les campus
8. la bibliothèque — les bibliothèques

B. Vos cours. Est-ce que vous étudiez les matières suivantes *(following subjects)*?

EXEMPLE   **Oui, j'étudie la chimie.**
          Non, je n'étudie pas la chimie.

1.   2.   3.

4.   5.   6.   7.

C. Et vous? Complétez les phrases pour parler de vos cours et de votre université.

1. J'étudie...
2. J'aime beaucoup...
3. J'aime assez...
4. Je n'aime pas beaucoup...
5. Je n'aime pas du tout...
6. Je ne comprends pas...
7. Je comprends bien...
8. Je pense que le cours de... est...

D. Entretien. Complétez les questions suivantes avec l'article défini **(le, la, l', les)** ou l'article indéfini **(un, une, des)**. Après, posez ces questions à votre partenaire.

1. Tu aimes _____ sport? Est-ce qu'il y a souvent _____ matchs de football américain sur _____ campus de cette *(this)* université le week-end? Tu préfères _____ football américain ou _____ basket?

2. Tu aimes _____ musique? Est-ce que tu préfères _____ rock, _____ jazz, _____ musique populaire ou _____ musique classique?

3. Tu comprends bien _____ français? _____ français est facile ou difficile pour toi? Tu aimes _____ cours de français? Est-ce qu'il y a _____ étudiants étrangers dans _____ classe? _____ cours est difficile? Est-ce qu'il y a _____ examen aujourd'hui?

Reprise

Talking about the university and your studies

In *Chapitre 1,* you practiced talking about your classes and identifying and describing the people, places, and things found at and around a university. Now you have a chance to review what you have learned.

See the ***Résumé de grammaire*** section at the end of each chapter for a review of all the grammar of the chapter.

A. Qui est-ce? Complétez les descriptions de ces célébrités francophones avec **c'est, il est** ou **elle est.**

Audrey Tatou

_____ Audrey Tautou.
_____ une femme.
_____ très belle.
_____ actrice.
_____ française.

Yannick Noah

_____ Yannick Noah.
_____ un homme.
_____ sportif.
_____ musicien.
_____ de France.

Maintenant, identifiez un(e) camarade de classe et parlez un peu de lui *(him)* ou d'elle.

B. Interview. Formez des questions logiques avec le verbe **être.** Interviewez votre partenaire avec les questions.

> **EXEMPLE**   Est-ce que tu / en cours le lundi?
> — **Est-ce que tu es en cours le lundi?**
> — **Oui, je suis en cours le lundi.**
>   **Non, je ne suis pas en cours le lundi.**

1. Est-ce que le cours de français / très facile?
2. Est-ce que le prof / méchant?
3. Est-ce que tu / timide en cours?
4. Est-ce que les devoirs / intéressants?
5. Est-ce que les examens / difficiles?
6. Est-ce que tu / dynamique en classe?
7. Est-ce que les autres étudiants / intelligents?
8. Tes amis et toi, est-ce que vous / intellectuels?
9. Tes amis et toi, est-ce que vous / sportifs?

C. Descriptions. Identifiez et décrivez les personnes et les objets suivants avec les adjectifs donnés.

EXEMPLE   maison (laid, petit)
             C'est une petite maison laide.

1. femme (joli, sportif)   **2.** homme (sympa, vieux)   **3.** homme (beau, sportif)

4. restaurant (mauvais, désagréable)   **5.** femme (intelligent, jeune)   **6.** boîte de nuit (grand, populaire)

D. Entretien. Complétez les questions suivantes avec l'article défini (**le, la, l', les**), l'article indéfini (**un, une, des**) ou avec **de (d')**. Après, posez ces questions à votre partenaire.

1. Est-ce qu'il y a beaucoup _____ vieux bâtiments sur le campus? Est-ce que tu aimes _____ vieux bâtiments? Est-ce qu'il y a beaucoup _____ arbres sur le campus? Est-ce qu'il y a assez _____ parkings?

2. Est-ce que tu aimes _____ sport? Est-ce qu'il y a _____ matchs de football américain à l'université? Est-ce que tu aimes _____ matchs de football américain? Tu préfères _____ football américain, _____ basket ou _____ tennis?

3. Est-ce qu'il y a _____ cinémas près de l'université? Est-ce qu'il y a _____ cinéma ici où on passe *(they show)* _____ films étrangers? Est-ce que tu aimes _____ films étrangers? Est-ce que tu préfères _____ films étrangers ou _____ films américains?

E. Vos cours. Avec un(e) partenaire, préparez la conversation suivante. Ensuite, changez de rôles.

Ask your partner:

- what he/she is studying this semester
- what his/her course(s) is (are) like
- if he/she likes the university
- what the students and professors are like
- what the campus is like
- what there is on campus and in the neighborhood

Lecture et Composition

Lecture

❀ Pour mieux lire: *Scanning to preview a text*

You are going to read a work by Jacques Prévert (1900–1977), one of the most popular poets of the last century, from his collection *Paroles* (1949). You have learned to use cognates to make reading easier. It can also help you read if you scan a text before reading it in order to anticipate its content.

On peut deviner! Scan the text *L'accent grave* and answer these questions to prepare yourself for understanding the text.

1. This is clearly a conversation. Who is it between? Where do you think it takes place?
2. What is the student's name? Where have you heard this name before? What was that character famous for saying?

L'accent grave

Le professeur
Élève Hamlet!

L'élève Hamlet (*sursautant*)
…Hein… Quoi… Pardon…
Qu'est-ce qui se passe… Qu'est-ce qu'il y a… Qu'est-ce que c'est?…

Le professeur (*mécontent*)
Vous ne pouvez pas répondre «présent» comme **tout le monde**? Pas possible, vous êtes **encore** dans **les nuages.**

Élève Hamlet
Être ou ne pas être dans les nuages!

Le professeur
Suffit. Pas tant de manières. Et conjuguez-moi le verbe être, comme tout le monde, **c'est tout ce que je vous demande.**

Élève Hamlet
To be . . .

Le professeur
En français, s'il vous plaît, comme tout le monde.

Élève Hamlet
Bien, monsieur. *(Il conjugue:)*
Je suis ou je ne suis pas, tu es ou tu n'es pas, il est ou il n'est pas, nous sommes ou nous ne sommes pas…

Le professeur (*excessivement mécontent*)
Mais **c'est vous qui n'y êtes pas,** mon pauvre ami!

Élève Hamlet
C'est exact, monsieur le professeur, Je suis «où» je ne suis pas.
Et, **dans le fond,** hein, à la réflexion, être «où» ne pas être, c'est **peut-être** aussi la question.

Compréhension

1. Dans quel cours sont-ils? À votre avis (*In your opinion*), les élèves sont très jeunes, assez jeunes ou ils ne sont pas jeunes? Pourquoi?

2. Qu'est-ce que ça veut dire, **ou**? et **où**? Qu'est-ce que ça veut dire **être ou ne pas être**? et **être où ne pas être**?

3. Comment est l'élève Hamlet? Attentif ou inattentif? conformiste ou rebelle? bon ou mauvais? intelligent ou bête? intellectuel?

4. Comment est le professeur? Patient ou impatient? intéressant ou ennuyeux? sympathique ou méchant?

5. Comment est la lecture (*the reading*)? Intéressante ou ennuyeuse? amusante? facile ou difficile à comprendre?

---

un élève *a student, a pupil*   **sursautant** *looking up startled*   **Hein** *Huh*   **Quoi** *What*   **Qu'est-ce qui se passe?** *What's going on?*   **mécontent** *displeased*   **Vous ne pouvez pas répondre...?** *Can't you answer . . . ?*   **tout le monde** *everyone*   **encore** *still, again*   **les nuages** *the clouds*   **Suffit.** *Enough.* **Pas tant de manières.** *Don't make such a fuss.*   **c'est tout ce que je vous demande** *that's all I'm asking of you*   **c'est vous qui n'y êtes pas** *you're the one that's not with it*   **dans le fond** *really, basically* **peut-être** *perhaps*

Composition

⚙ Pour mieux écrire: *Using and combining what you know*

Certain strategies can help you learn to write better in a foreign language. When you write, avoid translating. It is very difficult to translate correctly. Use and combine what you already know in French instead. Link sentences with words like **et, mais, alors,** or **parce que** to make your writing flow better.

Organisez-vous. You will be writing a short description of yourself and your studies. First, organize your thoughts by completing these sentences in French.

1. Je m'appelle…
2. Je suis de (d')…
3. J'habite…
4. Du point de vue physique, je suis…
5. Du point de vue personnalité, je suis…
6. Je suis étudiant(e) à…
7. Sur le campus, il y a… mais il n'y a pas…
8. Dans le quartier universitaire, il y a… mais il n'y a pas…
9. En général, j'aime / je n'aime pas l'université parce que…
10. J'étudie…
11. J'aime / Je n'aime pas…

Un autoportrait

Write a short paragraph introducing yourself. Use the sentences you completed in *Organisez-vous* above to guide you. Remember to use words like **et, mais,** or **parce que** to make your paragraph flow better.

EXEMPLE   **Je m'appelle Daniel Reyna. Je suis de San Antonio mais maintenant j'habite à Austin…**

If you have access to SYSTÈME-D software, you will find the following phrases, vocabulary, grammar, and dictionary aids there.

Phrases: Introducing; Describing people
Vocabulary: Studies, courses; Personality
Grammar: Definite articles; Indefinite articles; Nouns after **c'est, il est;**
    Comparison with **que**
Dictionary: The verb **être**

Comparaisons culturelles

Les études

How similar (**semblable**) is the French education system to the education system in your area? Read these descriptions of secondary schools and universities in France and compare them to schools in your region, by saying one of the following.

C'est très semblable ici. / C'est assez semblable ici. / C'est très différent ici.

1. Students in high school (**le lycée**) already have a "major." They pursue their diploma, **le baccalauréat (le bac),** in a chosen field, such as **le bac littéraire, scientifique, économique et social, technologique,** or **professionnel.**

2. At the end of their secondary studies, French students must pass a series of difficult national exams, also called **le baccalauréat** or **le bac,** covering all the material they have studied, in order to receive the **baccalauréat** degree. The results of the exam are so important that the day of the exam is sometimes referred to as **le Jour J** *(D-Day)*. The failure rate of the **baccalauréat** in recent years has been around 20%. If students do not pass, they cannot go on to the university, unless they repeat the last year at the **lycée** and successfully retest.

3. Every high school student who has received the **bac** is eligible for a nearly free college education. Students generally only pay the equivalent of about $300 per year to attend French universities, because the government finances higher education. However, students are only accepted into certain specialized schools by competitive exam. For example, to be accepted at the most competitive French universities, the **grandes écoles,** which prepare students for high-level positions in the public and private sectors, students generally take two years of preparatory courses and must pass a highly competitive exam.

4. If you want to continue your education after receiving the **baccalauréat,** you have a wide range of choices, such as the following:

Une université:
Two-year degrees: **un DEUG (diplôme d'études universitaires générales)**
un DEUST (diplôme d'études universitaires scientifiques et techniques)
Three-year degree: **une licence**
Five-year degree: **un master**
Eight-year degree: **un doctorat**
Five- to eleven-year degree: **un diplôme de médecine, de chirurgie dentaire ou de pharmacie**

Un institut universitaire de technologie (IUT):
Two-year degree: **un DUT (diplôme universitaire de technologie)**

Un lycée:
Two-year certificate: **un BTS (brevet de technicien supérieur)**
Two years of preparatory school: **classes préparatoires aux grandes écoles**

Une grande école (GE):
Three- to five-year degree: **un diplôme d'ingénieur, de sciences, d'économie, de commerce ou de lettres**

Une école spécialisée:
Two- to five-year degree: **un diplôme d'art**
Three- to five-year degrees: **un diplôme de travail social ou de commerce**
Six-year degree: **un diplôme d'architecte**

5. University students enter directly into field-specific courses (including law and medical school). French universities are divided into divisions or schools called **facultés,** such as **la faculté des lettres, la faculté des sciences,** and **la faculté de médecine.** In France, most older universities do not have campuses. The **facultés** have buildings in various areas of town where their classes meet. They are often older buildings in the center of town. Some more modern universities, however, do have a campus that is more similar to universities in the United States and Canada.

6. Traditionally, most university classes in France took place in huge lecture halls in a lecture format. Grades were based almost entirely on one or two exams. There has been a movement toward smaller classes, working in groups, and more frequent assignments.

7. Most French students live at home with their parents and attend the university in their region. There are few student activities. Extracurricular events and sports are not generally a part of the university.

Compréhension

1. What is the French equivalent of a "high school diploma?" What do students have to do to earn it? What are the advantages and disadvantages of a system in which students must pass a rigorous cumulative exam in order to receive a secondary education diploma?

2. What are the general fields in which French high school students can earn their diploma? Would you have liked to pick your "major" while still in high school? What would be the advantages and disadvantages?

3. What are some of the options French students have for continuing their studies after the **lycée**? How do these compare to the options students have in your area?

4. Who is entitled to a college education? Is it expensive? Do French students generally attend college far from where they live? Should higher education be almost free in the United States as in France? Why or why not?

5. What is a division or school within a French university called? What are the older universities like? How much of a role do extracurricular activities and sports play in university life? Where do most students live? How does this compare to your university?

6. Where were classes traditionally held in French universities? What were course grades traditionally based on? What have been more recent trends? Which approach would you prefer? Why?

 Visit **academic.cengage.com/french** for YouTube video cultural correlations, cultural information and activities.

Résumé de grammaire

Subject pronouns, the verb *être*, and *il y a*

Je **suis** timide.
Tu **es** étudiant?
Le professeur **est** sympa.
Nous **sommes** d'ici.
Vous **êtes** français?
Ils **sont** en cours.

Conjugate verbs by changing their forms to correspond to each of the subject pronouns. Here is the conjugation of **être** *(to be)*.

ÊTRE *(to be)*					
je **suis**	*I am*		nous **sommes**	*we are*
tu **es**	*you are*		vous **êtes**	*you are*
il/elle **est**	*he/she/it is*		ils/elles **sont**	*they are*

Je **ne** suis **pas** optimiste.
Tu **n'**es **pas** bête!

To negate a verb, place **ne** before it and **pas** after. **Ne** elides to **n'** before vowels or silent **h.**

Il est sympathique.
Il est en cours.
Ce sont mes amis.
C'est un bon ami.

Use **il est / elle est** and **ils sont / elles sont** with *adjectives* or *prepositional phrases* to describe people or things. Use **c'est** and **ce sont** instead of **il est / elle est** and **ils sont / elles sont** to say *he/she/it is* or *they are* when identifying or describing someone *with a noun.*

Ils sont étudiants.
Il est professeur.

Use **il est / elle est** and **ils sont / elles sont** without the indefinite article to state professions, nationalities, or religions.

—**Il y a** un examen demain?
—Non, **il n'y a pas** d'examen.

Use **il y a** instead of **être** to say *there is* or *there are*. Its negated form is **il n'y a pas.**

Nouns and articles

Nouns in French are classified by gender as either masculine or feminine. The definite and indefinite articles have different forms, depending on a noun's gender and whether it is singular or plural.

DEFINITE ARTICLE *(the)*		
	Singular	*Plural*
MASCULINE	**le** cours, **l'**examen	**les** cours, **les** examens
FEMININE	**la** classe, **l'**étudiante	**les** classes, **les** étudiantes

Où sont **les** étudiants?
Ils sont à **la** bibliothèque.

Le and **la** elide to **l'** before vowel sounds.

Besides translating the word *the,* the definite article is also used where there is no article in English . . .

J'aime **la** musique classique.
Les concerts de rock sont amusants.

- to say what you like or prefer
- to make generalized statements

INDEFINITE ARTICLE *(a, an, some)*		
	Singular	*Plural*
MASCULINE	**un** cours, **un** examen	**des** cours, **des** examens
FEMININE	**une** classe, **une** étudiante	**des** classes, **des** étudiantes

Il y a **des** restaurants près d'ici?
Chez Pierre est **un** bon restaurant.
Tu as *(have)* **une** amie américaine?

The indefinite article changes to **de** (**d'** before vowel sounds) . . .

Il **n'**y a **pas de** librairie ici.
(Ce **n'**est **pas une** librairie.)

Il y a **beaucoup de** devoirs et d'examens.

Ce sont **de** bons amis.

- after negated verbs (except after **être**)
- after expressions of quantity like **beaucoup** or **assez**
- directly before plural adjectives

Adjectives

Adjectives have masculine and feminine, singular and plural forms, which correspond to the nouns they describe. Add an **e** to the masculine form of most adjectives to form the feminine, unless it already ends in an *unaccented* **e**. Add an **s** to make an adjective plural, unless it already ends in **s, x,** or **z.**

MASCULINE		FEMININE	
Singular	*Plural*	*Singular*	*Plural*
joli	jolis	jolie	jolies
divorcé	divorcés	divorcée	divorcées
français	français	française	françaises
bête	bêtes	bête	bêtes

Le parc est **joli.** / La maison est **jolie.**

Il est **divorcé.** / Elle est **divorcée.**

Mes amis sont **français.** / Mes amies sont **françaises.**

Il n'est pas **bête.** / Elle n'est pas **bête.**

The following adjective endings have consonant changes before adding the **e** for the feminine form.

	MASCULINE		FEMININE	
	Singular	*Plural*	*Singular*	*Plural*
-eux / -euse:	ennuyeux	ennuyeux	ennuyeuse	ennuyeuses
-en / -enne:	canadien	canadiens	canadienne	canadiennes
-if / -ive:	sportif	sportifs	sportive	sportives
-el / -elle:	intellectuel	intellectuels	intellectuelle	intellectuelles
-er / -ère:	étranger	étrangers	étrangère	étrangères

Le film est **ennuyeux.** / La fête est **ennuyeuse.**

Paul est **canadien.** / Marie est **canadienne.**

David est **sportif.** / Yvette est **sportive.**

Ils sont **intellectuels.** / Elles sont **intellectuelles.**

Il est **étranger.** / Elle est **étrangère.**

The adjectives **bon (bonne), gros (grosse),** and **gentil (gentille)** also double their final consonants.

Adjectives generally are placed after nouns they describe.

The following adjectives go before nouns.

beau (belle)	jeune	bon (bonne)	grand(e)	autre
joli(e)	vieux (vieille)	mauvais(e)	petit(e)	même
	nouveau (nouvelle)	gentil(le)	gros(se)	seul(e)

Il est **bon.** / Elle est **bonne.**
Il est **gros.** / Elle est **grosse.**
Il est **gentil.** / Elle est **gentille.**

C'est un **cours intéressant** mais il y a beaucoup **d'examens difficiles.**

Sur le campus il y a beaucoup de **nouveaux bâtiments** et une **grande bibliothèque.**

The adjectives **beau, nouveau,** and **vieux** have irregular forms. The alternate singular forms **bel, nouvel,** and **vieil** are used before masculine singular nouns beginning with a vowel sound.

MASCULINE		FEMININE	
Singular	*Plural*	*Singular*	*Plural*
beau (bel)	beaux	belle	belles
nouveau (nouvel)	nouveaux	nouvelle	nouvelles
vieux (vieil)	vieux	vieille	vieilles

un **beau** parc / un **bel** homme / une **belle** femme

un **nouveau** film / un **nouvel** ami / une **nouvelle** amie

un **vieux** bâtiment / un **vieil** homme / une **vieille** femme

Questions

Questions that are answered with **oui** or **non** or by a choice have rising intonation. You may just use rising intonation or you may begin the question with **est-ce que,** which elides to **est-ce qu'** before vowel sounds.

If you expect the answer to a question to be **oui,** use **n'est-ce pas?** or **non?** to translate tag questions like *right?, isn't he?, can't you?,* or *won't they?* in English.

Le professeur est bon?
Est-ce qu'il est sympa ou méchant?

Tu étudies le français, **n'est-ce pas?**
Nous sommes dans le même cours, **non?**

Vocabulaire

CD1

Identifying people and describing appearance

NOMS MASCULINS

mes amis	my friends
un cours de littérature	a literature class
un frère	a brother
les gens	people
un (jeune) homme	a (young) man

NOMS FÉMININS

mes amies	my friends
une (jeune) femme	a (young) woman
la France	France
une semaine	a week
une sœur	a sister
l'université	the university

ADJECTIFS

américain(e)	American
beau (belle)	handsome, beautiful
célibataire	single
divorcé(e)	divorced
fiancé(e)	engaged
français(e)	French
grand(e)	tall, big
gros(se)	fat
jeune	young
jumeau (jumelle)	twin
laid(e)	ugly
marié(e)	married
même	same
mince	thin
petit(e)	short, small
premier (première)	first
vieux (vieille)	old

EXPRESSIONS VERBALES

C'est...	He is / She is / It is / This is / That is . . .
Ce sont...	They are / These are / Those are . . .
Ce n'est pas...	He is not / She is not/ It is not / This is not / That is not . . .
Ce ne sont pas...	They are not / These are not / Those are not . . .
Comment est... ?	What is . . . like?
Il est / Elle est...	He is / She is / It is . . .
Ils sont / Elles sont...	They are . . .
Il n'est pas / Elle n'est pas...	He is not / She is not / It is not . . .
Ils ne sont pas / Elles ne sont pas...	They are not . . .
Nous sommes...	We are . . .
(pour) étudier	(in order) to study
(pour) visiter	(in order) to visit
(pour) voir	(in order) to see
rencontrer	to meet (for the first time or by chance), to run into
Tu es...	You are . . .

DIVERS

à	to, at, in
alors	so, then, therefore
comme	like, as, for
de	of, from, about
d'où	from where
non?	right?
son / sa / ses	his / her / its

Describing personality

NOMS MASCULINS

tes amis	your friends
le football	soccer
mon meilleur ami	my best friend
le sport	sports
le tennis	tennis

NOMS FÉMININS

tes amies	your friends
les études	studies, going to school
ma meilleure amie	my best friend
la personnalité	personality

ADJECTIFS

agréable	pleasant
amusant(e)	fun, amusing
bête	stupid, dumb
désagréable	unpleasant
dynamique	active
ennuyeux (ennuyeuse)	boring
extraverti(e)	extroverted, outgoing
gentil (gentille)	nice
idéaliste	idealistic
intellectuel(le)	intellectual
intelligent(e)	intelligent
intéressant(e)	interesting
méchant(e)	mean
nouveau (nouvelle)	new
optimiste	optimistic
paresseux (paresseuse)	lazy
pessimiste	pessimistic
réaliste	realistic
sportif (sportive)	athletic
sympathique (sympa)	nice
timide	timid, shy

EXPRESSIONS VERBALES

être	to be
je suis...	I am . . .
tu es...	you are . . .
il est...	he is / it is . . .
elle est...	she is / it is . . .
nous sommes...	we are . . .
vous êtes...	you are . . .
ils/elles sont...	they are . . .
j'aime / je n'aime pas	I like / I don't like
tu aimes	you like

DIVERS

assez	rather
aussi... que	as . . . as
Ce n'est pas mon truc.	That's not my thing.
Est-ce que...	(particle used in questions)
moins... que	less . . . than
ne... pas	not
ne... pas du tout	not at all
n'est-ce pas?	right?
plus... que	more . . . than
plutôt	rather
un peu	a little

Describing the university area

NOMS MASCULINS

un amphithéâtre	a lecture hall
un arbre	a tree
un bâtiment	a building
un bureau	an office
un café	a café
un campus	a campus
un cinéma	a movie theater
un club de gym	a gym, a fitness club
un concert (de jazz, de rock, de musique populaire, de musique classique)	a (jazz, rock, pop music, classical music) concert
un fast-food	a fast-food restaurant
un film	a movie, a film
un match de football américain	a football game
un parc	a park
un parking	a parking lot
un quartier (universitaire)	a (university) neighborhood
un restaurant	a restaurant
un stade	a stadium
un théâtre	a theater (for live performances)

NOMS FÉMININS

une bibliothèque	a library
une boîte de nuit	a nightclub
une classe	a class
une librairie	a bookstore
une maison	a house
une résidence	a dormitory
une salle de classe	a classroom

ADJECTIFS

bon(ne)	good
catholique	Catholic
étranger (étrangère)	foreign
joli(e)	pretty
mauvais(e)	bad
moderne	modern
populaire	popular
seul(e)	only
universitaire	university

EXPRESSIONS VERBALES

Comment est... ?	What is . . . like?
Il y a...	There is, There are . . .
Il n'y a pas (de)...	There isn't, There aren't . . .
Qu'est-ce qu'il y a... ?	What is there . . . ?

DIVERS

assez (de)	enough (of)
beaucoup (de)	a lot (of)
dans	in
des	some
près de	near
sur	on
ton, ta, tes	your
un(e)	a, an

Talking about your studies

NOMS MASCULINS

l'allemand	German
l'anglais	English
le basket	basketball
les beaux-arts	the fine arts
un cours de commerce	a business course
un cours technique	a technical course
les devoirs	homework
l'espagnol	Spanish
un examen	an exam
le français	French
un laboratoire de langues	a language lab
un laboratoire d'informatique	a computer lab
le marketing	marketing
le théâtre	theater, drama

NOMS FÉMININS

la biologie	biology
la chimie	chemistry
la comptabilité	accounting
une fête	a party
l'histoire	history
l'informatique	computer science
une langue	a language
la littérature classique	classical literature
les mathématiques (les maths)	mathematics (math)
la musique	music
la philosophie	philosophy
la physique	physics
la psychologie	psychology
les sciences (humaines)	the (social) sciences
les sciences politiques	political science, government

EXPRESSIONS VERBALES

Comment sont... ?	What are . . . like?
Est-ce que vous aimez... ?	Do you like . . . ?
J'aime beaucoup/assez...	I like a lot/somewhat . . .
Je n'aime pas (du tout)...	I don't like . . . (at all)
Je préfère...	I prefer . . .
Qu'est-ce que vous étudiez / tu étudies?	What are you studying?, What do you study?
J'étudie...	I study . . .
Je n'étudie pas...	I don't study . . .

DIVERS

leur(s)	their

Après les cours

Chapitre 2

C o m p é t e n c e

 iLrn Heinle Learning Center

academic.cengage.com/french/horizons

 Système-D

 Audio   iRadio

France is divided into regions and departments. Nice is in the region Provence-Alpes-Côte d'Azur and in the department Alpes-Maritimes. On the Web, find out what the ten largest cities in France are, and which region and department they are in. Then pick the city you would most like to visit besides Paris and find five interesting facts about it.

When you vis a new city, what do you preffer to do there.

Quand vous visitez une nouvelle **ville,** qu'est-ce que vous préférez **y faire**? Visiter les sites historiques et les musées? faire du shopping? dîner au restaurant? profiter des festivals? **sortir** en boîte de nuit? **faire une promenade**? apprécier des vues panoramiques? À Nice, il est difficile de **choisir**!

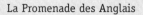

La Promenade des Anglais

Le quartier médiéval du Vieux Nice

Le Carnaval de Nice

Quand *When*   **ville** *city*   **y faire** *to do there*   **sortir** *to go out*   **faire une promenade** *to go for a stroll*   **choisir** *to choose*

NICE

NOMBRE D'HABITANTS: 347 100 (avec ses agglomérations
[metropolitan region]: 933 080) (les Niçois)
DÉPARTEMENT: Alpes-Maritimes
RÉGION: Provence-Alpes-Côte d'Azur

 Visit it live on Google Earth!

Le **marché** Saleya

La rue et **la place** Masséna

Les ruines romaines et le monastère du
quartier Cimiez

❀ Qu'en savez-vous?

Quel endroit *(place)* ou événement *(event)* à Nice correspond
à chaque description?

**la Promenade des Anglais   le Carnaval de Nice
le Vieux Nice   le marché Saleya   le quartier Cimiez
la rue et la place Masséna**

1. Dans ce quartier chic, il y a des ruines romaines, le musée
    Matisse et un monastère franciscain du XVIe siècle *(from
    de XVIth century)*. Les jardins *(gardens)* du monastère
    offrent une vue magnifique de Nice et de la mer
    Méditerranée.
2. Les touristes et les Niçois visitent cet endroit pour
    faire des promenades ou du roller *(to go for a walk or
    rollerblading)* ou pour contempler la Baie des Anges dans
    une des célèbres chaises bleues *(famous blue chairs)*.
3. Cette célébration date de 1294. Aujourd'hui, plus de
    1 200 000 personnes y participent durant deux semaines
    en février ou mars.
4. Il y a toujours beaucoup d'étudiants dans les restaurants
    et boîtes de nuit des rues étroites *(narrow streets)* de ce
    vieux quartier animé.
5. Cette rue est une zone piétonne *(pedestrian)* avec une
    grande variété de boutiques, restaurants et cafés. La place
    à l'extrémité de la rue est connue *(known)* pour ses
    bâtiments de couleur rose.
6. Les couleurs et le parfum des roses et des autres fleurs de
    ce marché enchantent les touristes et les Niçois.

---

marché *market*   **la rue** *street*   **la place** *square*

Saying what you like to do

✸ **Note** *culturelle*

Le passe-temps le plus populaire en France, c'est regarder la télé. En moyenne *(average)*, les Français regardent la télé trois heures et demie par jour. Les jeux d'ordinateur sont aussi très populaires. Quarante pour cent (40%) des foyers *(households)* avec un ordinateur l'utilisent *(use it)* pour jouer à des jeux d'ordinateur. Quels sont les passe-temps les plus populaires dans votre région?

✸ **Note** *de vocabulaire*

1. To say what you *like,* use **j'aime.** To say what you *would like,* or *want,* use **je voudrais.**
2. There are many ways to say *an e-mail:* **un mail, un e-mail, un email, un mel, un mèl, un mél, un courriel, un courrier électronique.**

Les passe-temps

— Qu'est-ce que vous aimez **faire** après les cours?

— J'aime...   — Je n'aime pas...   — Je préfère...

— Qu'est-ce que **vous voudriez** faire aujourd'hui après les cours?

— **Je voudrais...**

SORTIR AVEC DES AMIS

aller au cinéma
(aller) voir un film

aller au café
(aller) **prendre un verre**

aller en boîte
(aller) danser

dîner au restaurant

faire du sport
jouer au tennis / au basket /
au football / au volley

faire de l'exercice
faire du vélo
faire du jogging

RESTER À LA MAISON

lire

parler au téléphone

dormir

inviter des amis à
la maison

bricoler

jouer de la guitare / **de la
batterie** / du piano

---

faire *to do*   **vous voudriez** *you would like*   **Je voudrais** *I would like*   **sortir** *to go out*   **aller** *to go*   **prendre un verre** *to have a drink*   **faire du vélo** *to ride a bike*   **rester** *to stay, to remain*   **bricoler** *to do handiwork*   **de la batterie** *drums*

écouter la radio / de la musique / la chaîne hi-fi

regarder la télé(vision) / une vidéo / un DVD jouer à des jeux vidéo *(m)*

travailler sur l'ordinateur surfer le Net **écrire des mails** *(m)*

CD 1-29

David invite Annette à sortir.

DAVID: Tu es **libre ce soir**? Tu voudrais faire **quelque chose**?
ANNETTE: Je voudrais bien. Où est-ce que tu voudrais aller?
DAVID: Je ne sais pas. Tu voudrais aller en boîte?
ANNETTE: Non, **pas vraiment.** Je préfère aller au cinéma.
DAVID: Bon, **d'accord!** **On va** prendre un verre avant?
ANNETTE: **Pourquoi pas? Vers** quelle heure?
DAVID: Vers sept heures, sept heures et demie... au café La Martinique?
ANNETTE: D'accord. Alors, **à plus tard.**
DAVID: Au revoir, Annette. À ce soir!

A. Qu'est-ce que vous aimez faire? Complétez les phrases.

1. Après les cours, j'aime... mais je n'aime pas...
2. Aujourd'hui après les cours, je voudrais...
3. Le samedi matin, j'aime...
4. Le samedi soir, j'aime...
5. Le dimanche, je préfère...
6. Ce week-end, je voudrais...
7. À la maison, j'aime...
8. Je n'aime pas du tout...

B. Invitations. Invitez votre partenaire à faire les choses suivantes.

EXEMPLE   (demain) jouer au tennis
—**Tu es libre demain? Tu voudrais jouer au tennis avec moi?**
—**Oui, je voudrais bien. /**
  Pas vraiment. Je préfère aller au cinéma.
—**Vers quelle heure?**
—**Vers deux heures.**
—**Bon, d'accord. Alors, à demain.**
—**À demain. Au revoir!**

1. (ce soir) dîner au restaurant
2. (vendredi soir) aller voir un film
3. (aujourd'hui après les cours) faire les devoirs
4. (demain après-midi) aller prendre un verre

CD 1-30   You can find a list of the new words from the vocabulary and grammar sections of this **Compétence** on page 100 and a recording of this list on track 1-30 of your *Text Audio CD.*

écrire un mail *to write an e-mail*   **libre** *free*   **ce soir** *this evening*   **quelque chose** *something*   **pas vraiment** *not really*
d'accord *okay*   **On va... ?** *Shall we go . . . ?*   **Pourquoi pas?** *Why not?*   **Vers** *About, Around, Toward*   **à plus tard** *see you later*

Pour vérifier

1. What do you call the basic form of the verb that you find listed in the dictionary?

2. What are the four possible endings for infinitives in French?

3. When you have a sequence of more than one verb in a clause, which one is conjugated? Which ones are in the infinitive?

Vocabulaire supplémentaire

faire...
  du bateau *boating*
  du cheval *horseback riding*
  de l'escalade *rock climbing*
  des haltères *weightlifting*
  du ski
  du ski nautique
  du snowboarding
  de la voile *sailing*
  du yoga
jouer...
  au billard *pool*
  aux cartes *cards*
  au disc-golf
  au frisbee
  au golf
  au hockey
  au ping-pong
  au rugby
jouer...
  de la clarinette
  du clavier *keyboard*
  du cor d'harmonie *French horn*
  de la flûte
  de la guitare électrique
  du hautbois *oboe*
  de l'orgue *organ*
  du piccolo
  de la trompette
  du tuba
  du violon
  du violoncelle *cello*

Saying what you like to do

L'infinitif

To name an activity in French, use the verb in the infinitive. The infinitive is the basic form of the verb that you find listed in the dictionary. French infinitives are single words ending in **-er, -ir, -oir,** or **-re,** like **jouer** *(to play)*, **dormir** *(to sleep)*, **voir** *(to see)*, or **être** *(to be)*. In French, whenever there are two or more verbs together in a clause, the first verb is conjugated, but verbs that immediately follow are in the infinitive.

— Qu'est-ce que tu **aimes faire**?　　— Est-ce que tu **voudrais sortir**?

— J'**aime jouer** au football américain.　　— Je **préfère rester** à la maison.

Use **jouer** *au* to talk about playing most sports using balls or pucks. Many other sports use **faire** *du / de la / de l' / des.*

jouer **au** base-ball　　jouer **au** golf　　faire **du** ski　　faire **de l'**exercice

Use **jouer** *du / de la / de l' / des* to talk about playing most musical instruments.

jouer **du** piano　　　　　　jouer **de la** guitare

As with **un, une,** and **des; du, de la,** and **de l'** change to **de (d')** after a negative expression.

— Tu joues **de la** guitare?　　　— Tu fais **du** jogging le week-end?

— Non, je ne joue pas **de** guitare.　　— Non, je ne fais pas **de** jogging.

Prononciation

CD 1-31　*La consonne **r** et l'infinitif*

The consonant **r** is one of the few (CaReFuL) consonants that are often pronounced at the end of words. The final **r** of infinitives ending in **-er,** however, is not pronounced. The **-er** ending is pronounced [e], like the **é** in **café.**

parler	inviter	danser	aller
regarder	jouer	écouter	dîner

The **r** in infinitives ending in **-ir, -oir,** or **-re** is pronounced. To pronounce a French **r,** hold the back of your tongue firmly arched upward in the back of your mouth and pronounce a vocalized English *h* sound in your throat.

Pronounce the **-ir** verb ending as [iʀ], unless the verb ends in **-oir** [waʀ].

sortir　　　　dormir　　　　voir

The **e** in the infinitive ending of **-re** verbs is pronounced when this ending is preceded by a consonant, but not when it is preceded by a vowel.

faire　　　　lire　　　　être　　　　　　prendre

A. Préférences. Demandez à votre partenaire quelle activité il/elle préfère.

EXEMPLE lire / faire les devoirs
— **Tu préfères lire ou faire les devoirs?**
— **Je préfère lire.**

1. faire de l'exercice / dormir
2. sortir avec des amis / inviter des amis à la maison
3. prendre un verre au café / dîner au restaurant
4. jouer au tennis / regarder un match de tennis à la télé
5. regarder la télé / aller au cinéma
6. être à la maison / être en cours
7. parler à un ami au téléphone / inviter un ami à la maison
8. surfer le Net / écrire des mails
9. faire du jogging / faire du vélo

> ✳ **Note** *de vocabulaire*
>
> To say you don't like either activity, use **ne... ni... ni...** *(neither . . . nor . . .)*: **Je n'aime *ni* lire *ni* faire les devoirs.** To say that you like *both* activities, use **J'aime *les deux.***

B. Chacun ses goûts. Est-ce que vous aimez ces activités?

J'aime beaucoup...	J'aime assez...	Je n'aime pas beaucoup...
	Je n'aime pas du tout...	

EXEMPLE **J'aime assez bricoler.**

C. Entretien. Interviewez votre partenaire.

1. Qu'est-ce que tu aimes faire après les cours? Qu'est-ce que tu voudrais faire aujourd'hui après les cours?
2. Est-ce que tu aimes rester à la maison le week-end? Qu'est-ce que tu aimes faire le week-end? Qu'est-ce que tu voudrais faire ce week-end?
3. Est-ce que tu aimes travailler sur l'ordinateur? Tu aimes surfer le Net?
4. Est-ce que tu voudrais aller au cinéma ce week-end? Quel film est-ce que tu voudrais voir? Tu préfères aller voir un film au cinéma ou regarder un DVD à la maison?
5. Quel sport est-ce que tu préfères, le tennis, le golf ou le basket? Est-ce que tu préfères faire du sport ou regarder des matchs à la télévision?

Stratégies et Compréhension auditive

Pour mieux comprendre: *Listening for specific information*

It takes time and practice to understand a foreign language when you hear it. However, using listening strategies can help you learn to understand spoken French more quickly.

Often, you do not need to comprehend everything you hear. Practice listening for specific details, such as times, places, or prices. Do not worry about understanding every word.

CD 1-32

A. Quand? Écoutez ces trois scènes. Indiquez le jour et l'heure choisis *(chosen)*.

SCÈNE A: LE JOUR _____
      L'HEURE_____

SCÈNE B: LE JOUR _____
      L'HEURE _____

SCÈNE C: LE JOUR _____
      L'HEURE _____

CD 1-33

B. Qu'est-ce qu'elles font? Annette invite Yvette à sortir. Pour les trois scènes, indiquez ce qu'Yvette préfère faire.

SCÈNE A: _____

SCÈNE B: _____

SCÈNE C: _____

Comprehension auditive: On sort ensemble?

CD 1-34

David, Yvette, and Annette run into two of David's friends. Listen to their conversation. Do not try to understand every word. The first time, listen only for the leisure activities they mention. Each time you hear one mentioned, write it down.

A. Vous comprenez? Écoutez une seconde fois *(time)* la conversation entre David et ses amis et répondez à ces questions.

1. Est-ce que Thomas et Gisèle sont des amis d'Annette?
2. Faites une liste de trois choses que Thomas et Gisèle découvrent *(discover)* au sujet d'Annette et d'Yvette *(about Annette and Yvette)*.

B. Tu voudrais sortir? Invitez votre partenaire à faire les choses suivantes. Utilisez **B. *Invitations*** à la page 69 comme modèle.

voir un film

jouer au foot

faire du vélo

Saying how you spend your free time

Le week-end

Comment est-ce que vous aimez **passer le temps**? Qu'est-ce que **vous faites d'habitude** le samedi? Est-ce que vous passez **la matinée** à la maison?

(presque) toujours	souvent	quelquefois	rarement	ne... jamais
(almost) always	*often*	*sometimes*	*rarely*	*never*

Je reste souvent au lit **jusqu'à** 10 heures.

Le samedi matin, **d'abord** je mange quelque chose.

Quelquefois l'après-midi, je prépare les cours (j'étudie).

Le soir, je ne reste presque jamais **chez moi. Je vais** souvent au cinéma.

Est-ce que vous aimez faire du sport? de la musique? Est-ce que vous jouez bien?

très bien	assez bien	comme ci comme ça	assez mal	très mal
very well	*fairly well*	*so-so*	*fairly badly*	*very badly*

Je nage assez mal. Je joue **mieux** au hockey **que** je nage.

Je **gagne** souvent **quand** je joue au hockey.

Je joue du piano comme ci comme ça.

Je chante assez bien.

---

passer le temps *to spend time*　**vous faites (faire** *to do, to make)*　**d'habitude** *usually, generally*　**la matinée** *the morning*　**jusqu'à** *until*　**d'abord** *first*　**chez moi** *at home, at my house* **(chez...** = *to / at / in / by the house of . . .*)　**Je vais (aller** *to go)*　**mieux (que)** *better (than)*　**je gagne (gagner** *to win)*　**quand** *when*

Annette et David parlent de leurs activités *(f)* du week-end.

CD 1-35

ANNETTE: Qu'est-ce que **tu fais** d'habitude le week-end?

DAVID: Le samedi matin je reste au lit, le samedi après-midi je joue au tennis et le soir j'aime sortir. Et toi?

ANNETTE: Le matin je prépare mes cours, l'après-midi j'aime **faire du shopping** et le soir, moi aussi, j'aime sortir.

DAVID: Alors, tu es libre samedi soir? Tu voudrais sortir? Il y a un bon film au cinéclub **à la fac.** C'est un vieux classique de Truffaut.

ANNETTE: Oui, oui, je voudrais bien.

DAVID: Le film commence à huit heures. Je **passe** chez toi vers sept heures?

ANNETTE: D'accord! À samedi, alors.

A. Passe-temps. Complétez ces phrases pour parler de vous.

1. Le samedi matin, je passe *presque toujours / souvent / rarement* la matinée à la maison. *(Je ne passe jamais la matinée à la maison.)*
2. Le samedi matin, je reste au lit jusqu'à *sept heures / dix heures / ???.*
3. D'habitude, le samedi matin, je mange quelque chose *à la maison / dans un fast-food / au café / ???. (Je ne mange pas le samedi matin.)*
4. D'habitude je prépare les cours *à la maison / à la bibliothèque / chez un(e) ami(e) / au café / ???.*
5. Comme *(As)* exercice, je préfère *faire du sport / faire du jogging / nager / ???. (Je n'aime pas faire d'exercice.)*
6. Quand je joue *au tennis / au hockey / ???,* je gagne *toujours / souvent / rarement. (Je n'aime pas faire de sport.)*
7. Le samedi soir, le plus souvent *je reste à la maison / je travaille / j'invite des amis à la maison / je préfère sortir.*
8. Je vais plus souvent au cinéma *seul(e) / avec des amis / avec mon meilleur ami / avec ma meilleure amie / avec ma famille / ???.*
9. Je chante *très bien / assez bien / comme ci comme ça / ???.*
10. Je danse *très bien / assez bien / comme ci comme ça / ???.*
11. Je chante *mieux / aussi bien / moins bien* que je danse.
12. Je joue *du piano / de la guitare / de la batterie / ???. (Je ne joue pas d'un instrument de musique.)*

B. Conversation. Avec un(e) partenaire, relisez à haute voix la conversation entre Annette et David en haut de la page *(at the top of the page).* Ensuite, changez la conversation pour décrire vos activités du week-end et pour inviter votre partenaire à faire quelque chose que vous voudriez faire.

CD 1-36 You can find a list of the new words from the vocabulary and grammar sections of this ***Compétence*** on page 100 and a recording of this list on track 1-36 of your *Text Audio CD.*

tu fais (faire *to do, to make***)** **faire du shopping** *to go shopping* **à la fac** *at the university* **passer** *to pass (by)*

Telling what you do, how often, and how well

*Les verbes en **-er** et les adverbes*

Regular verbs are groups of verbs that follow a predictable pattern of conjugation. The largest group of regular verbs have infinitives ending in **-er.** Most verbs ending in **-er** that you have learned, *except* **aller,** are conjugated in the present tense by dropping the **-er** and adding the following endings: **-e, -es, -e, -ons, -ez, -ent.**

PARLER *(to speak, to talk)*	
je parl**e**	nous parl**ons**
tu parl**es**	vous parl**ez**
il/elle parl**e**	ils/elles parl**ent**

Note de grammaire

Verbs whose infinitives do not end in **-er,** and a few irregular verbs whose infinitives do, such as **aller,** do not follow the pattern of conjugation shown here. You will learn how to conjugate such verbs later. You may want to use these forms now to talk about your activities.

I go	**je vais**
I sleep	**je dors**
I do, I make	**je fais**
I read	**je lis**
I write	**j'écris**
I take	**je prends**
I go out	**je sors**

To download a podcast on Verbs and Adverbs, go to **academic.cengage.com/french.**

The present tense can be expressed in three ways in English. Express all three of the following English structures by a single verb in French.

I work.
I am working. } Je travaille.
I do work.

He studies.
He is studying. } Il étudie.
He does study.

Here are the regular **-er** verbs that you have seen so far.

aimer	*to like, to love*	jouer	*to play*
bricoler	*to do handiwork*	manger	*to eat*
chanter	*to sing*	nager	*to swim*
commencer	*to begin, to start*	parler	*to speak, to talk*
compter	*to count*	passer	*to pass (by), to spend* (time)
danser	*to dance*	penser	*to think*
dîner	*to have dinner*	préférer	*to prefer*
donner	*to give*	préparer	*to prepare*
écouter	*to listen (to)*	regarder	*to look (at), to watch*
étudier	*to study*	répéter	*to repeat*
fermer	*to close*	rester	*to stay, to remain*
habiter	*to live*	surfer	*to surf*
inviter	*to invite*	travailler	*to work, to study*

Remember that words such as **je, le, que,** and **ne** make elision before a vowel sound.

j'aime / je **n'**aime pas   **j'**habite / je **n'**habite pas

Adverbs such as **bien, souvent, rarement,** and **beaucoup** tell how well, how often, or how much you do something. In French, these adverbs are generally placed directly after the conjugated verb. However, **quelquefois** and **d'habitude** are often placed at the beginning or end of the clause and **comme ci comme ça** is placed at the end.

Thomas regarde **souvent** la télé.	*Thomas **often** watches T.V.*
Quelquefois, je joue **bien** du piano.	***Sometimes,** I play the piano **well.***
D'habitude, je travaille le week-end.	***Usually,** I work weekends.*
Je joue au tennis **comme ci comme ça.**	*I play tennis **so-so.***

Ne... jamais *(never)* follows the same placement rule as **ne... pas.**

Je **ne** joue **jamais** au golf.   *I **never** play golf.*

Prononciation

CD 1-37

*Les verbes en **-er***

All the present tense endings of **-er** verbs, except for the **nous (-ons)** and **vous (-ez)** forms, are silent.

je rest~~e~~	il rest~~e~~	ils rest~~ent~~
tu rest~~es~~	elle rest~~e~~	elles rest~~ent~~

Rely on context to distinguish between **il** and **ils,** or **elle** and **elles.** You will hear a difference only with verbs beginning with a vowel sound.

il travaill~~e~~ — il~~s~~ travaill~~ent~~   il aim~~e~~ — ils ^{z} aim~~ent~~

The **-ons** ending of the **nous** form rhymes with **maison** and the **-ez** of the **vous** form rhymes with **café** and sounds like the **-er** ending of the infinitive. There is liaison between the **s** of **nous** and **vous** and verbs beginning with vowel sounds.

nou~~s~~ parlons	nous ^{z} étudions
vou~~s~~ parlez	vous ^{z} étudiez

A. Activités. Complétez les phrases de la première colonne avec un choix logique de la deuxième colonne.

1. Le samedi soir, j'...
2. Et toi, qu'est-ce que tu...
3. Tes amis et toi, est-ce que vous...
4. Mes amis et moi, nous...
5. Mais mon meilleur ami...
6. Les étudiants...

   a. invitez souvent des amis à la maison?
   b. aimes faire?
   c. aime sortir avec des amis.
   d. préférons aller danser.
   e. aiment mieux sortir que travailler.
   f. préfère rester à la maison.

B. Opinions. Comment est le/la colocataire idéal(e)?

EXEMPLE   travailler beaucoup
Il/Elle travaille beaucoup.
Il/Elle ne travaille pas beaucoup.

1. aimer beaucoup aller en boîte
2. parler souvent au téléphone
3. bricoler bien
4. passer beaucoup de temps à la maison
5. inviter souvent des amis à la maison
6. regarder toujours la télé le week-end
7. chanter beaucoup et mal
8. écouter toujours du hip-hop

C. Et toi? Interviewez un(e) partenaire avec les verbes de l'exercice précédent.

EXEMPLE   — **Est-ce que tu travailles beaucoup?**
— **Oui, je travaille beaucoup.**
   Non, je ne travaille pas beaucoup.

Après, parlez de votre partenaire à la classe.

EXEMPLE   **Il/Elle travaille beaucoup et...**

D. Le samedi. Est-ce que vous faites toujours, souvent ou rarement ces choses le samedi? N'oubliez pas *(Don't forget)* de conjuguer le verbe!

(presque) toujours	souvent	quelquefois	rarement	ne... jamais

EXEMPLE le samedi matin: passer la matinée à la maison
Le samedi matin, je passe toujours (souvent...) la matinée à la maison. / Je ne passe jamais la matinée à la maison.

1. le samedi matin:
    rester à la maison
    manger à la maison
    travailler
    étudier
2. le samedi après-midi:
    nager
    jouer au foot
    regarder la télé
    surfer le Net

3. le samedi soir:
    dîner au restaurant
    manger dans un fast-food
    inviter des amis à la maison
    danser en boîte

Un restaurant dans le Vieux Nice

Maintenant, demandez à votre professeur s'il/si elle fait souvent les choses indiquées.

EXEMPLE le samedi matin: passer la matinée à la maison
Le samedi matin, est-ce que vous passez souvent la matinée à la maison?

E. C'est vrai? Formez des phrases pour décrire *(to describe)* votre classe.

EXEMPLE nous / parler beaucoup en cours
Nous parlons beaucoup en cours.
Nous ne parlons pas beaucoup en cours.

1. le professeur / parler quelquefois anglais en cours
2. les étudiants / commencer à parler très bien français
3. nous / travailler beaucoup en cours
4. je / aimer dormir en cours
5. les étudiants / travailler quelquefois ensemble *(together)*
6. nous / aimer travailler ensemble
7. je / écouter toujours les CD
8. les étudiants / manger quelquefois en cours

F. Talents. Dites si ces personnes font ces choses bien ou mal.

très bien	assez bien	comme ci comme ça	assez mal	très mal

EXEMPLE Ma sœur **joue très bien (assez mal) de la guitare.**
Ma sœur **ne joue pas de guitare.**
Je n'ai pas de sœur. *(I don't have a sister.)*

1. Mon meilleur ami (Ma meilleure amie)...
Mon frère...

2. Mes parents...
Moi, je...

3. Moi, je...
Mon ami _____ [name a friend]...

4. Mes ami(e)s _____ et _____ [name two friends]...
Mes amis et moi, nous...

G. Entretien. Interviewez votre partenaire.

1. Tu es musicien(ne)? Est-ce que tu danses bien ou mal? Est-ce que tu chantes bien? Tu préfères écouter la radio ou regarder la télé? Est-ce que tu regardes la télé quand tu manges? Tu écoutes de la musique quand tu étudies?

2. Est-ce que tu es sportif (sportive)? Est-ce que tu aimes le sport? Quel sport est-ce que tu préfères, le football américain, le basket, le golf ou le base-ball? Est-ce que tu joues au tennis? au golf? au volley? (Est-ce que tu gagnes souvent?)

3. Est-ce que tu restes souvent à la maison le week-end? Est-ce que tu bricoles quelquefois le week-end? Est-ce que tu prépares les cours à la maison? Est-ce que tu préfères bricoler ou préparer les cours?

H. Qu'est-ce qui se passe? Décrivez la scène chez la famille Li ce week-end. Dites au moins cinq choses.

Étienne   Monsieur Li   Madame Li

Audrey   Louise   Dominique   Georges   Antoine et le chien

Pour vérifier

1. In verbs like **préférer**, which forms have a spelling change in the stem in the present tense? What is the change? Which forms have stems like the infinitive?

2. What is special about the **nous** form of a verb with an infinitive ending in **-ger**? in **-cer**?

Telling what you do

Quelques verbes à changements orthographiques

A few **-er** verbs have spelling changes in their stems in the present tense.

- When the next-to-last syllable of an infinitive has an **e** or **é**, this letter often changes to **è** in all forms except **nous** and **vous.** The stem for the **nous** and **vous** forms is like the infinitive.

PRÉFÉRER *(to prefer)*		RÉPÉTER *(to repeat)*	
je préf**è**re	nous préférons	je rép**è**te	nous répétons
tu préf**è**res	vous préférez	tu rép**è**tes	vous répétez
il/elle préf**è**re	ils/elles préf**è**rent	il/elle rép**è**te	ils/elles rép**è**tent

- Verbs ending in **-cer** and **-ger** also have spelling changes. With verbs ending in **-ger,** like **manger, nager,** and **voyager** *(to travel),* you must insert an **e** before the **-ons** ending in the **nous** form. With verbs ending in **-cer,** like **commencer,** the **c** changes to a **ç** before the **-ons** ending in the **nous** form.

VOYAGER *(to travel)*		COMMENCER *(to start, to begin)*	
je voyage	nous voyag**e**ons	je commence	nous commen**ç**ons
tu voyages	vous voyagez	tu commences	vous commencez
il/elle voyage	ils/elles voyagent	il/elle commence	ils/elles commencent

Prononciation

CD 1-38 *Les verbes à changements orthographiques*

Spelling changes occur in verbs to reflect pronunciation. The letter **é (e accent aigu)** sounds like the vowel of **les.**

— Vous préférez passer la matinée à la maison?

— Non, nous préférons passer la matinée au café.

The letter **è (e accent grave)** often occurs in the final syllable of words ending in a silent **e (Michèle)** and sounds similar to the *e* in the English word *let.*

Je préfère aller à la bibliothèque avec Michèle.

In French, **c** and **g** are pronounced soft (the **c** like an **s** and the **g** like a French **j**) before an **e, i,** or **y.** They are pronounced hard (the **c** like **k** and the **g** similar to the *g* in the English word *go*) before an **a, o, u,** or a consonant.

Soft **g:** Georges, Gérard, Gilbert Hard **g:** Gabrielle, Hugo, Guillaume

Soft **c:** Cécile, Maurice Hard **c:** Catherine, Colette

The letter **ç** is used to indicate that a **c** is soft before **a, o,** or **u.** In verb endings, use **ç** to keep **c** soft before **o,** and introduce an **e** to keep **g** soft before **o.**

commen**ç**ons **ç**a va fran**ç**ais mang**e**ons voyag**e**ons nag**e**ons

A. Ça s'écrit comment? Dans les mots suivants, la lettre **c** est prononcée [s]. Lesquels de ces mots requièrent *(require)* une cédille?

1. mena**c**e / mena**c**ant
2. fa**c**ade / fa**c**ile
3. Ni**c**e / ni**c**ois
4. fa**c**e / fa**c**on
5. Fran**c**e / fran**c**ais
6. proven**c**al / Proven**c**e
7. prononciation / prononcons
8. **c**ela / **c**a

B. La lettre *g*. Dites si vous faites les choses suivantes. Faites attention à la prononciation de la lettre **g.**

> **EXEMPLE**   Je joue quelquefois / Je ne joue jamais (au golf, au backgammon).
> **Je joue quelquefois au golf.**
> **Je ne joue jamais au backgammon.**

1. Je voudrais / Je ne voudrais pas voyager (en Algérie, en Guyane, en Guadeloupe, à Genève, à Grenoble).
2. J'aime étudier / Je n'aime pas étudier (la géographie, l'algèbre, la géométrie, la géologie).
3. J'aime les gens / Je n'aime pas les gens (imaginatifs, organisés, généreux, égoïstes, courageux, arrogants).

C. Préférences. Complétez ces questions avec le verbe indiqué et interviewez votre partenaire.

1. Avec qui *(With whom)* est-ce que tu _____ (préférer) sortir?
2. Quel jour est-ce qu'il/elle _____ (préférer) sortir?
3. Vous _____ (manger) souvent ensemble *(together)*?
4. Est-ce que vous _____ (préférer) dîner ensemble à la maison ou au restaurant?
5. En général, est-ce que les étudiants _____ (préférer) dîner au restaurant ou étudier à la bibliothèque?
6. Tu _____ (aimer) le sport? Tu _____ (nager) bien?
7. Ton meilleur ami et toi, vous _____ (nager) souvent ensemble?
8. Ta famille et toi, vous _____ (voyager) souvent ensemble?

> ❋ **Note** *de vocabulaire*
>
> To say that someone likes *neither* of the activities, use **ne... ni... ni...**: Je n'aime *ni* danser *ni* chanter.
> To say that someone likes *both*, use **les deux**: J'aime *les deux.*

D. Et vous? Pour chaque paire d'activités, indiquez l'activité que chacun *(each one)* préfère et dites s'il/si elle la fait bien ou mal.

> **EXEMPLE**   Moi, je **préfère danser. Je danse très bien.**

1. Moi, je...
   Mon meilleur ami (Ma meilleure amie)...

3. Mes amis...
   Mon meilleur ami (Ma meilleure amie) et moi...

2. Mes amis...
   Ma famille et moi, nous...

Asking about someone's day

La journée

— Quand est-ce que vous êtes à l'université?
— Je suis à l'université...   le lundi, le mardi... de dix heures à quatre heures
le matin, l'après-midi, le soir
tous les jours, sauf le week-end
toute la journée

— Où est-ce que vous **déjeunez** d'habitude?
— Je déjeune...   chez moi / chez des amis / chez...
au restaurant universitaire
au café Trianon / dans un fast-food...

— Qu'est-ce que vous aimez faire après les cours?
— J'aime...   aller au parc / aller à la bibliothèque / aller chez un(e) ami(e)
rentrer à la maison
dormir...

— **Avec qui** est-ce que vous **aimez mieux** sortir?
— J'aime mieux sortir...   avec mon ami(e)...
avec **mon petit ami (ma petite amie)**
avec **mon mari (ma femme)**

— **Pourquoi** est-ce que vous préférez sortir avec... ?
— Parce qu'il/elle est...   amusant(e), sexy, riche, beau (belle)...
Parce qu'ils/elles sont...   sympas, intéressant(e)s, dynamiques...

— Quand est-ce que vous préférez sortir **ensemble**?
— Nous préférons sortir...   le vendredi soir
le samedi après-midi...

CD 1-39   Jean **demande** à Annette comment elle passe une journée typique.

JEAN: Quand est-ce que tu es en cours ce semestre?
ANNETTE: Je suis en cours tous les jours, sauf le week-end. Le lundi, par exemple, je suis en cours de midi à trois heures. Le matin, je prépare mes cours à la bibliothèque.
JEAN: Et après les cours, qu'est-ce que tu fais en général?
ANNETTE: Après les cours, je rentre à la maison. Je travaille ou **je dors** un peu.
JEAN: Et le soir?
ANNETTE: Le soir, je reste à la maison et je prépare les cours ou je surfe le Net.

---

tous les jours *every day*   **sauf** *except*   **toute la journée** *all day*   **déjeuner** *to eat lunch*   **rentrer** *to return, to go back (home)*   **Avec qui** *With whom*   **aimer mieux** *to like better, to prefer*   **mon petit ami (ma petite amie)** *my boyfriend (my girlfriend)*   **mon mari (ma femme)** *my husband (my wife)*   **Pourquoi** *Why*   **ensemble** *together*   **demander** *to ask (for)*   **je dors (dormir** *to sleep)*

A. Précisions.
Demain, David déjeune avec des amis au café Le Trapèze. Quelle est la réponse logique pour chaque question?

1. Quel jour est-ce que nous déjeunons ensemble?
2. À quelle heure?
3. Qui déjeune avec nous?
4. Pourquoi est-ce que tu n'invites pas Thomas?
5. Où est-ce que nous déjeunons?
6. Qu'est-ce que tu voudrais faire après?

    a. Au café Le Trapèze.
    b. Gisèle et Bruno.
    c. Vendredi.
    d. Aller au cinéma.
    e. Parce qu'il travaille.
    f. À midi et demi.

B. C'est vrai?
Lisez chaque phrase et dites si **c'est vrai** ou **ce n'est pas vrai** pour vous et votre cours de français.

1. Je suis à l'université tous les jours, sauf le dimanche.
2. Nous sommes en cours de français le matin, tous les jours sauf le week-end.
3. Le cours de français est de dix heures à onze heures.
4. Les autres étudiants et moi passons beaucoup de temps ensemble après les cours.
5. Nous déjeunons souvent ensemble.
6. Le samedi, je travaille toute la journée pour préparer le cours de français.
7. J'aime mieux aller en cours de français que de sortir avec des amis.

Maintenant, corrigez les phrases qui ne sont pas vraies.

C. Entretien.
Interviewez votre partenaire.

1. Quels jours est-ce que tu es à l'université? De quelle heure à quelle heure est-ce que tu es en cours? Est-ce que tu restes à l'université toute la journée? À quelle heure est-ce que tu rentres à la maison?
2. Quand est-ce que tu prépares les cours? Où est-ce que tu aimes mieux faire les devoirs: chez toi ou à la bibliothèque? Avec qui est-ce que tu préfères étudier?
3. Où est-ce que tu aimes mieux déjeuner? À quelle heure? Est-ce que tu déjeunes souvent chez toi? Où est-ce que tu préfères manger le soir? Est-ce que tu dînes plus souvent chez toi ou au restaurant? Est-ce que tu manges souvent dans un fast-food? Qu'est-ce que tu préfères: les hamburgers, la pizza ou les tacos?
4. Qu'est-ce que tu aimes faire le week-end? Où est-ce que tu aimes mieux aller avec des amis: au cinéma ou en boîte? Avec qui est-ce que tu préfères sortir? Quand est-ce que vous aimez mieux sortir?

D. Conversation.
Avec un(e) partenaire, relisez à haute voix la conversation entre Annette et Jean à la page précédente. Ensuite, changez la conversation pour décrire votre situation. Changez de rôles.

LE TRAPEZE
SALON DE THÉ • SNACK • BAR • GLACIER
17, Bd Delfino 06000 NICE
☎ **04 93 26 48 38**

PIZZAS
(Sauf le samedi)   **euros**

MARGUERITE: **5,00**
Tomate, fromage.

NAPOLITAINE: **5,20**
Tomate, fromage, anchois, olives.

POIVRONS: **5,80**
Tomate, fromage, champignons, poivrons.

REINE: **5,80**
Tomate, fromage, olives, champignons, jambon.

CALZONE: **6,00**
Tomate, champignons, œuf, crème fraîche.

Service continu de midi à 2h du matin

CD 1-40 You can find a list of the new words from the vocabulary and grammar sections of this ***Compétence*** on page 101 and a recording of this list on track 1-40 of your *Text Audio CD*.

Pour vérifier

1. How do you form an information question?
2. Which word becomes **qu'** before a vowel, **qui** or **que**?
3. When are three times you do not use **est-ce que**?
4. How do you say *Who is this/that? What is this/that?*

To download a podcast on Interrogatives, go to **academic.cengage.com/french**.

Asking for information

Les mots interrogatifs

You have learned to ask questions with **est-ce que.** To ask for information such as *what, when,* or *why,* add the appropriate question word before **est-ce que.**

où *where*	**Où est-ce que** vous étudiez?
que (qu') *what*	**Qu'est-ce que** vous étudiez?
pourquoi *why*	**Pourquoi est-ce que** vous étudiez le français?
quand *when*	**Quand est-ce que** vous préparez les cours?
avec qui *with whom*	**Avec qui est-ce que** vous préparez les cours?
comment *how*	**Comment est-ce que** vous passez la journée?
à quelle heure *at what time*	**À quelle heure est-ce que** vous êtes en cours?
quel(s) jour(s) *(on) what /* *which day(s)*	**Quels jours est-ce que** vous êtes en cours?

Note that **que** makes elision before a vowel sound, but **qui** does not.

   Qu'est-ce que vous aimez faire le soir? Avec **qui** est-ce que vous aimez sortir?

Do not use **est-ce que** with **qui** when it is the subject of the verb, or with **où** or **comment** when they are followed by **être.**

qui *who*	**Qui** travaille avec toi?
où *where*	**Où est** la bibliothèque?
comment *how*	**Comment est** l'université?

Use **Qui est-ce?** to ask *who* someone is. Use **Qu'est-ce que c'est?** to ask *what* something is.

— Qui est-ce?   — Qu'est-ce que c'est?
— C'est Jean.   — C'est un livre.

Prononciation

CD 1-41 *Les lettres **qu** et la prononciation du mot **quand** en liaison*

In French, **qu** is usually pronounced as in the word **quiche.** It is generally only pronounced with the *w* sound heard in the English word *quite* when it is followed by **oi,** as in **pourquoi.**

   qui   que   quand   quelle heure   pourquoi

Note that **d** in liaison is pronounced as a **t.**

   Quand *t* est-ce que tu travailles?

Où est-ce que vous aimez déjeuner?

A. Invitations. Des amis décident de déjeuner ensemble. Complétez les questions avec le mot convenable.

Qui	Que (Qu')	Quand	Où	Pourquoi	À quelle heure

— Tu voudrais déjeuner avec nous?
— (1) _____ ?
— Aujourd'hui.
— Je voudrais bien. (2) _____?
— Vers midi.
— (3) _____ est-ce que tu voudrais manger?
— Chez moi.
— (4) _____ est-ce que tu prépares?
— Une pizza.
— (5) _____ est-ce que tu invites?
— Jean-Luc et toi.
— (6) _____ est-ce que tu voudrais faire après?
— Aller au cinéma.
— (7) _____?
— Parce que je voudrais voir le nouveau film avec Audrey Tautou.

B. Beaucoup de questions. Formez des questions comme indiqué. Ensuite, posez-les à un(e) camarade de classe.

1. _____ est-ce que tu étudies? *(What? Where?)*
2. _____ est-ce que tu prépares les cours? *(When? With whom? Where?)*
3. _____ est-ce que tu aimes mieux déjeuner? *(At what time? With whom? Where?)*
4. _____ est-ce que tu dînes d'habitude le samedi soir? *(Where? With whom? At what time?)*

C. Un jeu. In teams, think of an appropriate question to elicit each answer, using a question word **(qui, que...)** based on the boldfaced word(s). Teams take turns selecting an item. A correct response earns the team the indicated points.

	A	B	C	D
5 points	Ça va **bien,** merci.	Je m'appelle **Annette Clark.**	Il est **5 heures.**	Aujourd'hui, c'est **lundi.**
10 points	C'est **Yvette.**	C'est **un parc.**	David est **sympa.**	Annette est **à la maison.**
15 points	Yvette aime **la musique.**	Thomas travaille **toute la journée.**	David aime sortir **avec Annette.**	Je rentre **à une heure.**
20 points	**Annette et David** étudient les maths.	Nous aimons mieux **aller au cinéma.**	**Parce que le prof est très intéressant.**	Annette parle **bien** français.

Pour vérifier

1. How would you invert the question **Il est ici?**
2. Do you ever use **est-ce que** and inversion in the same question?
3. When do you insert a **-t-** between a verb and an inverted subject pronoun?
4. Generally, can you invert nouns, or only pronouns? What do you do if the subject of the question is a noun? How would you invert the question: **Marie déjeune à midi?**
5. What is the inverted form of **il y a?** of **c'est?**
6. How would you invert **Où est-ce que vous déjeunez?**

Asking questions

Les questions par inversion

You can ask a question using rising intonation or **est-ce que.** You can also use inversion; that is, you can invert the subject pronoun and the verb. Add a hyphen when the subject and verb are inverted.

> Est-ce que tu travailles le lundi? = **Travailles-tu le lundi?**

- Inversion is the equivalent of **est-ce que.** Never use both inversion and **est-ce que** in the same question.

> **Est-ce que tu joues** de la guitare?   *OR*   **Joues-tu** de la guitare?

- You do not normally use inversion with **je.**

- When the inverted subject is **il** or **elle** and *the verb ends in a vowel,* place a **-t-** between the verb and the pronoun. Do not add **-t-** if the verb ends in a consonant.

> Parle-**t**-il anglais?   Est-il d'ici?
> Travaille-**t**-elle ici?   Est-elle d'ici?

- Invert the *conjugated* verb and the *subject pronoun.* Do not invert a following infinitive.

> Aimes-tu aller au cinéma?   Voudriez-vous aller danser?

- If the subject of the question is a *noun,* rather than a *pronoun,* state the noun first, then supply a matching pronoun for inversion. Be sure to choose the form (**il, elle, ils, elles**) that matches the subject noun.

> Le prof est-**il** français?   Marie parle-t-**elle** français?
> Les cours sont-**ils** difficiles?   Danielle et Antoinette étudient-**elles** ici?

- The inverted form of **il y a** is **y a-t-il. C'est** becomes **est-ce.**

> **Y a-t-il** un café dans le quartier? **Est-ce** un bon café?

- To ask information questions, place the question word before the inverted verb. **Qu'est-ce que** becomes **que (qu')** when using inversion.

> **Où** voudrais-tu aller? **Que** voudrais-tu faire? **Qu'**aimes-tu faire?

Prononciation

CD 1-42   *L'inversion et la liaison*

When the subject is **il, elle, ils,** or **elles,** there is liaison between the verb and its pronoun in inversion.

> Yvette est *t* elle américaine?
> David et Thomas parlent *t* ils anglais?

Thomas   Gisèle

A. Prononcez bien! D'abord, répétez ces questions après votre professeur. Ensuite, posez-les à un(e) camarade de classe. Faites attention à la prononciation!

Gisèle, où est-elle ce soir? Est-elle seule? Prépare-t-elle les cours? Thomas et Gisèle aiment-ils la musique? Dansent-ils bien? Et toi? Aimes-tu danser? Écoutes-tu souvent de la musique? Écoutons-nous de la musique française en cours quelquefois? Tes amis et toi, aimez-vous aller en boîte ensemble? Aimez-vous mieux aller au cinéma? Y a-t-il un bon cinéma dans le quartier universitaire?

B. Entretien. Changez ces phrases pour parler de vous. Après, posez une question logique à un(e) camarade de classe. Utilisez l'inversion.

> **EXEMPLE** Je travaille *le matin.* Et toi?...
> **Je travaille le soir. Et toi? Quand travailles-tu?**

1. Je suis en cours *le lundi, le mercredi et le jeudi.* Et toi?...
2. Je prépare les cours *chez moi.* Et toi?...
3. Je prépare les cours *avec des amis.* Et toi?...
4. Je préfère étudier *le français.* Et toi?...
5. Je préfère étudier *le français parce que le cours est intéressant.* Et toi?...

C. Notre classe. Utilisez l'inversion pour poser ces questions à un(e) camarade de classe.

> **EXEMPLE** Est-ce que tu aimes tes cours ce semestre / trimestre?
> **— Aimes-tu tes cours ce semestre?**
> **— Oui, ils sont intéressants.**
> **Non, je n'aime pas beaucoup mes cours ce semestre.**

1. Est-ce que le cours de français est facile ou difficile?
2. Est-ce que tu écoutes le CD tous les jours?
3. Est-ce que les étudiants aiment le cours?
4. Pourquoi est-ce qu'ils aiment le cours?
5. Est-ce que les examens sont faciles?
6. Est-ce que tu voudrais préparer le cours avec moi ce week-end?
7. Qu'est-ce que tu aimes faire le week-end?
8. Qu'est-ce que tu voudrais faire ce week-end?

D. Le samedi. Voilà un samedi typique pour Edgar, l'ami de David. Posez cinq questions à un(e) camarade de classe sur ce qu'Edgar fait *(on what Edgar does)* le samedi. Utilisez un mot interrogatif dans chaque question. Dites **il fait** pour *he does,* si nécessaire.

qui	que	où	quand	pourquoi	comment

ses copains *(his friends)*

Going to the café

Au café

Vous êtes au café. Qu'est-ce que vous allez prendre?

Je voudrais...

un expresso

Pour moi...

un café au lait

Je vais prendre...

un thé au citron

une eau minérale

un jus de fruit ou un jus d'orange

un coca (light)

un Orangina

un verre de vin rouge ou un verre de vin blanc

un demi

une bière

un sandwich au jambon

un sandwich au fromage

des frites

David et Annette **commandent une boisson** au café.

 CD 1-43

DAVID:	**Je n'ai pas très faim,** mais **j'ai soif.** Je vais prendre un demi. Et toi?
ANNETTE:	Moi, je voudrais un chocolat **chaud.**
DAVID:	Monsieur, s'il vous plaît.
LE GARÇON:	Bonjour, monsieur, mademoiselle. Vous désirez?
DAVID:	Pour moi, un demi. Et pour mademoiselle, un chocolat chaud.
LE GARÇON:	Très bien.

un coca (light) *a (diet) Coke, a (diet) cola*   **un demi** *a draft beer*   **commander** *to order*   **une boisson** *a drink, a beverage*
Je n'ai pas très faim (J'ai faim) *I am not very hungry (I'm hungry)*   **j'ai soif** *I'm thirsty*   **chaud(e)** *hot*   **un garçon** *a waiter*

Après, David et Annette **paient.**

DAVID: Ça fait combien, monsieur?
LE GARÇON: Ça fait sept euros cinquante.
DAVID: **Voilà** dix euros.
LE GARÇON: Et **voici** votre **monnaie.** Merci bien.

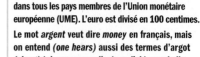

Note culturelle

La monnaie d'usage en France est l'euro, comme dans tous les pays membres de l'Union monétaire européenne (UME). L'euro est divisé en 100 centimes.

Le mot *argent* veut dire *money* en français, mais on entend *(one hears)* aussi des termes d'argot *(slang)* tels que: un radis *(a radish)*, une balle *(a bullet)* ou du blé *(wheat)* pour parler de l'argent. En anglais, est-ce qu'il y a une expression en argot qu'on utilise pour dire *a dollar?*

A. À votre santé. Quelle boisson est meilleure pour la santé *(health)*?

1. un café au lait / un jus d'orange
2. un Orangina / une eau minérale
3. un jus de fruit / un expresso
4. un thé / une bière
5. une eau minérale / un demi
6. un chocolat chaud / un jus d'orange

B. Préférences. Offrez les choses suivantes à un(e) camarade de classe.

EXEMPLE  —**Tu voudrais une eau minérale ou un coca?**
— **Je voudrais une eau minérale / un coca.**

1.

2.

3.

4.

5.

C. J'aime... Est-ce que vous aimez les choses indiquées dans l'exercice précédent? Utilisez **le, la, l'** ou **les** pour indiquer ce que vous aimez ou ce que vous n'aimez pas.

EXEMPLE **J'aime bien l'eau minérale. Je n'aime pas du tout le coca.**

D. Conversation. Avec deux autres étudiants, relisez à haute voix la conversation entre David et Annette qui commence à la page précédente. Le/La troisième étudiant(e) va jouer le rôle du serveur/de la serveuse *(server)*. Ensuite, changez la conversation pour commander ce que *(what)* vous voudriez. Changez de rôles.

You can find a list of the new words from CD 1-44 the vocabulary and grammar sections of this ***Compétence*** on page 101 and a recording of this list on track 1-44 of your *Text Audio CD.*

---

ils paient (payer *to pay)* **Voilà / Voici** *There is, There are / Here is, Here are* **la monnaie** *change*

Pour vérifier

1. How do you say **30**? **40**? **50**? **60**? **70**? **80**? **90**?

2. When do you use **et** with numbers? Do you use **et** with 81 and 91?

3. How do you say *one hundred*? Do you translate the word *one*?

4. What is the official currency of France?

Paying the bill

Les chiffres de trente à cent et l'argent

— Un café au lait, c'est combien?

— 3,50 € (trois euros cinquante).

30	trente	**70**	soixante-dix
31	trente et un	**71**	soixante et onze
32	trente-deux	**72**	soixante-douze
33	trente-trois...	**73**	soixante-treize...
40	quarante	**80**	quatre-vingts
41	quarante et un	**81**	quatre-vingt-un
42	quarante-deux	**82**	quatre-vingt-deux
43	quarante-trois...	**83**	quatre-vingt-trois...
50	cinquante	**90**	quatre-vingt-dix
51	cinquante et un	**91**	quatre-vingt-onze
52	cinquante-deux	**92**	quatre-vingt-douze
53	cinquante-trois...	**93**	quatre-vingt-treize...
60	soixante	**100**	cent
61	soixante et un		
62	soixante-deux		
63	soixante-trois...		

France uses the euro, the common currency of most of the European Union, of which France is a part. A euro is divided into 100 cents or **centimes.** € is the symbol for the euro.

Prononciation

CD 1-45   *Les chiffres*

Some French numbers are pronounced differently, depending on what follows them.

deux	deux cafés	deux ᶻeuros
trois	trois cafés	trois ᶻeuros
six	six cafés	six ᶻeuros
huit	huit cafés	huit ᵗeuros
dix	dix cafés	dix ᶻeuros

A. Prononcez bien. Commandez ces boissons.

EXEMPLES   trois demis   **Trois demis, s'il vous plaît.**
               trois expressos   **Trois expressos, s'il vous plaît.**

deux demis   trois demis   six demis   huit demis   dix demis
deux expressos trois expressos six expressos huit expressos dix expressos

Maintenant, lisez ces prix *(prices)*. N'oubliez pas *(Don't forget)* de faire la liaison avec le mot **euro** si *(if)* nécessaire.

  1 €   11 €   2 €   12 €   3 €   13 €   6 €   16 €   10 €   20 €
61 €   71 €   82 €   92 €   63 €   73 €   86 €   96 €   100 €   80 €

B. Prix indicatifs. Combien coûte chaque chose?

EXEMPLE   une baguette   **C'est 70 centimes.**

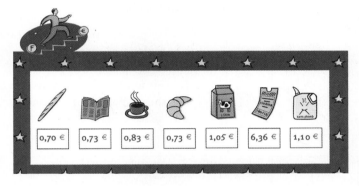

| 0,70 € | 0,73 € | 0,83 € | 0,73 € | 1,05 € | 6,36 € | 1,10 € |

1. un journal   **3.** un croissant   **5.** un billet de cinéma
2. un expresso   **4.** un litre de lait   **6.** un litre d'essence *(gasoline)*

C. Votre monnaie. Vous êtes au café et vous payez pour vos amis et vous. Suivez l'exemple.

EXEMPLE   6,85 € (10 €)
                — **C'est combien, monsieur?**
                — **Six euros quatre-vingt-cinq, mademoiselle.**
                — **Voilà dix euros.**
                — **Et voici votre monnaie.**

1. 12,98 € (15 €)   **4.** 14,88 € (15 €)   **7.** 2,50 € (5 €)
2. 32,45 € (40 €)   **5.** 36,75 € (40 €)   **8.** 16,80 € (20 €)
3. 23,68 € (30 €)   **6.** 7,75 € (10 €)

D. Ça fait combien? Écrivez les prix *(prices)* que vous entendez.

EXEMPLE   VOUS ENTENDEZ: C'est dix euros cinquante.
                VOUS ÉCRIVEZ: **10,50 €**

E. Au café. Préparez une conversation basée sur cette situation. Après, présentez la conversation à la classe.

In groups of three, prepare a scene in which you meet a friend at a café. One classmate plays the server and takes your orders. The two customers order, then decide what they would like to do after leaving the café. Finally, they call the server back and pay the bill.

Talking about how you spend your time

In **Chapitre 2,** you practiced saying what you like to do, asking about and telling how people spend their time, and ordering food and drink in a café. Now you have a chance to review what you learned.

A. Passe-temps préférés. Demandez à votre partenaire quelle activité il/elle préfère. Pour répondre *neither . . . nor . . .,* dites **ne... ni... ni...** comme dans l'exemple. Si vous aimez les deux *(both),* dites **J'aime les deux.**

EXEMPLE

— Est-ce que tu préfères inviter des amis à la maison ou parler au téléphone?
— Je préfère parler au téléphone.
Je n'aime ni inviter des amis à la maison ni parler au téléphone.
J'aime les deux.

1.   2.   3.   4.   5.

B. Qu'est-ce qu'elles font? Est-ce que ces personnes font les choses indiquées? Si oui *(If so),* est-ce qu'elles les font souvent, rarement, bien... ?

EXEMPLE   mon meilleur ami (ma meilleure amie) / jouer au tennis
Mon meilleur ami (Ma meilleure amie) joue assez bien au tennis.
Mon meilleur ami (Ma meilleure amie) ne joue jamais au tennis.

toujours	souvent	quelquefois	rarement	ne... jamais
	beaucoup	assez	(un) peu	ne... pas du tout
très bien	assez bien	comme ci comme ça	assez mal	très mal

1. moi, je / jouer au golf
2. mon meilleur ami (ma meilleure amie) / aimer le sport
3. nous / jouer au volley
4. je / manger à la maison
5. ma famille et moi / dîner ensemble
6. nous / manger au restaurant
7. mes amis / aimer voyager
8. nous / voyager ensemble

C. Au café. Complétez les phrases.

1. Quand j'ai très soif, j'aime prendre...
2. Le matin, j'aime bien prendre...
3. Maintenant, je voudrais...
4. Avec un hamburger, j'aime prendre...
5. Quand je dîne au restaurant, j'aime prendre... comme *(as a)* boisson.

D. C'est combien? Demandez à votre partenaire les prix des choses indiquées.

EXEMPLE un café express
— **Un café express, c'est combien?**
— **C'est deux euros quarante-cinq.**

1. un double express
2. un café au lait
3. un lait chaud
4. un café décaféiné
5. un chocolat
6. un cappuccino
7. un croissant
8. un vin chaud
9. un Irish Coffee

L'heure du thé

Prix Service Compris (15%)

Café express	2,45	Thé à la menthe	3,50
Double express	4,10	Thé au fruit de la passion	3,50
Café au lait	3,40	Thé à la framboise	3,50
Infusion	3,50	Cappuccino	4,30
(Tilleul, verveine, menthe, tilleul-		Croissants	1,60
menthe, verveine-menthe, camomille)		Confiture pot	1,40
Lait chaud	2,90	Tartines beurrées	2,80
Café décaféiné	2,60	Viandox	3,40
Double express avec pot de lait . .	3,60	Viandox avec vin	3,80
Chocolat	3,50	Grog au rhum	6,10
Café ou chocolat viennois	4,30	Vin chaud	3,75
Thé (avec lait ou citron)	3,50	Irish Coffee	7,80

E. Questions. Complétez la conversation comme indiqué. Utilisez **est-ce que** pour poser les questions.

— Je voudrais sortir ce soir.
— _____?
   What would you like to do?
— Je voudrais aller voir le film *Star Time*.
— _____?
   Why would you like to see Star Time?
— Parce qu'il y a beaucoup d'action. Et toi? _____?
                                             Would you like to see Star Time *too?*
— Oui, beaucoup!
— _____? _____?
   Are you free this evening?   *Would you like to go to the movies with me?*
— Bon, d'accord. _____?
                 What time does the movie start?
— À 8h55. Je passe chez toi vers 8 heures?
— D'accord.

Maintenant, recommencez la conversation. Utilisez l'inversion pour poser les questions.

F. Invitations. Avec un(e) partenaire, préparez une conversation basée sur cette situation. Après, présentez la conversation à la classe.

Ask your partner what he/she likes to do on the weekend. Ask for some details such as when, where, with whom, and why. Make plans to do something together and decide on a place and time.

Lecture et Composition

Lecture

By using cognates and what you already know about cafés, you should be able to make intelligent guesses about what is offered on this Parisian café menu. The following exercise will guide you.

Vous savez déjà... What you already know about cafés and restaurants will help you determine the following information.

1. Under **Buffet chaud,** what would **une omelette jambon** be? **une omelette fromage**? **une omelette nature**?
2. What you see at the bottom of the menu indicates that checks are accepted under one condition. What is usually the condition for accepting checks?
3. At the bottom of the menu, you see that the management claims it is not responsible for something. For what does management usually claim not to be responsible?

AUX TROIS OBUS
120, rue Michel-Ange
Paris

NOS SALADES

SALADE VERTE	2,60
SALADE NIÇOISE	7,00
(Tomate, œuf, thon, olives, salade, anchois, riz, poivron)	
SALADE 3 OBUS	7,00
(Salade, choux-fleur, foies de volaille, jambon, œuf dur)	
SALADE POULET	7,00
(Émincé de poulet, maïs, riz, tomates, poivron, salade)	
SALADE MIXTE	5,00
(Tomates, œuf dur, salade)	
SALADE CHEF	7,00
(Tomates, pommes à l'huile, jambon, gruyère, salade, œuf dur)	
SALADE DE CRUDITÉS	6,00
(Concombres, tomates, carottes, choux)	

BUFFET CHAUD

ŒUFS AU PLAT NATURE (3 œufs)	4,00	CROQUE-MONSIEUR	4,00
ŒUFS PLAT JAMBON (3 œufs)	4,50	CROQUE-MADAME	4,80
OMELETTE NATURE	4,00		
OMELETTE JAMBON	4,50	HOT-DOG	4,00
OMELETTE FROMAGE	4,50		
OMELETTE MIXTE (jambon, fromage)	6,50	FRANCFORTS FRITES	5,00
OMELETTE PARMENTIER	4,50	ASSIETTE DE FRITES	2,60

MOULES MARINIERES	7,00 €
FRISEE AUX LARDONS	7,00 €
ROTI DE BOEUF PUREE	7,50 €
CASSOULET AU CONFIT	11,00 €
ST JACQUES PROVENCALE	14,00 €

NOS SANDWICHES

		JAMBON DE PAYS	4,00
		PÂTÉ	2,20
JAMBON DE PARIS	2,20	TERRINE DU CHEF	4,00
SAUCISSON SEC	2,20	CLUB SANDWICH	6,00
SAUCISSON A L'AIL	2,20	(Pain de mie, poulet, jambon, tomates, œuf, laitue, mayonnaise)	
RILLETTES	2,20		
MIXTE (jambon, gruyère)	3,50	JAMBON A L'OS	4,00
SANDWICH CRUDITÉS	3,50	GRUYÈRE, CAMEMBERT	2,20

Suppl. Pain mie 0,50 Campagne 0,80

FROMAGES

Camembert	2,60		
Roquefort	3,00		
Brie	3,00		
Cantal	3,00	Gruyère	3,00
Chèvre	3,00	Assiette de fromages	5,00

PRIX SERVICE COMPRIS (15%)

Les chèques sont acceptés sur présentation d'une pièce d'identité.

La direction n'est pas responsable des objets oubliés dans l'établissement.

Compréhension

A. Mots apparentés. Read the menu and use cognates to identify:

1. Two kinds of sandwiches.
2. Three or four items used in the salads.
3. Two or three items you could order from the **buffet chaud.**

B. Lisez bien. Read the menu and answer these questions.

1. C'est combien pour une salade verte? pour une salade niçoise? pour une salade de crudités? pour une omelette jambon?
2. Le service est compris? Les chèques sont acceptés?

C. Bon appétit! Make a list of everything you can identify on this menu, then order something in French.

Composition

When writing about an activity that you have done often, such as ordering at a café or restaurant, it is useful to start by jotting down the usual sequence of events and typical phrases that are used at each step. This will provide you with a basic framework which you can flesh out with details.

Organisez-vous. You are going to prepare a scene in which two friends meet, talk, and order at a café. Before you begin, make sure you remember how to do these things in French.

- How do you greet a friend?
- How do you call the server over and order a drink?
- How do you talk about what you do on the weekend?
- How do you ask what your companion likes to do and say what you like or do not like to do?
- How do you invite a friend to do something?
- How do you pay the bill?
- How do you say good-bye?

Au café

Using your answers from the preceding activity, write a conversation in which two college students meet at a café. They greet each other, order a drink, and start to chat about what they have in common. Remember to add details, such as when they like to do some things or why they do not like to do other things. They finally make plans to do something later, they get the bill, and they pay.

SYSTÈME-D

If you have access to SYSTÈME-D software, you will find the following phrases, vocabulary, grammar, and dictionary aids there.

Phrases: Greetings; Introducing; Attracting attention; Asking for information; Inviting; Leaving

Vocabulary: Drinks; Time expressions; Time of day; Leisure; Sports; Numbers; Money

Dictionary: The verb **préférer**

Comparaisons culturelles

Le café et le fast-food

Le café en France est presque une institution sociale. Il y a des cafés **partout.** Les gens aiment aller au café pour...

prendre un café

déjeuner

passer du temps avec des amis

passer une heure tranquille

Dans un café-tabac, **on peut aussi acheter** des cigarettes, des **timbres,** des **cartes téléphoniques** et des cartes postales.

Il y a une grande variété de cafés.

Il y a des cafés élégants comme Les Deux Magots à Paris, fréquenté **autrefois** par des artistes et des écrivains **tels que** Cocteau et Hemingway.

Certains cafés servent une clientèle particulière: touristes, étudiants, travailleurs, **cadres.**

Il y a aussi **le café du coin** ou du village.

---

partout *everywhere*   **on peut aussi acheter** *one can also buy*   **timbres** *stamps*   **cartes téléphoniques** *phone cards*
autrefois *formerly*   **tels que** *such as*   **cadres** *business executives*   **le café du coin** *the neighborhood café*

Voilà **quelques renseignements utiles.**

Au bar, **les prix** sont plus **bas.**

Si vous préférez être à la terrasse, les prix sont souvent plus **élevés.** Les chaises font face à la rue parce qu'un des plaisirs du café, c'est de regarder **les passants.**

Malgré la renommée du café, il y a de moins en moins de cafés en France et de plus en plus de fast-foods comme McDonald's (Macdo) et Quick.

Compréhension

1. Vous visitez la France. Préférez-vous déjeuner dans un fast-food ou dans un café? Pourquoi?

2. En France, il y a de plus en plus de fast-foods et de moins en moins de cafés. Pourquoi?
   a. Le service dans un fast-food est plus rapide.
   b. Les Français pensent que les hamburgers sont meilleurs que les sandwichs.
   c. Les choses américaines sont très à la mode *(in fashion)*.

3. En France, le service est presque toujours compris *(included)*. Aimez-vous cette idée? Pourquoi?
   a. Non, parce que c'est plus cher *(expensive)*.
   b. Oui, parce que c'est plus simple. (Je n'aime pas faire de calculs.)
   c. Non, ça influence la qualité du service.

4. Est-ce que le café est plus populaire en France qu'ici? Qu'est-ce qu'on aime *(does one like)* faire au café? Est-ce que ces activités sont plus populaires en France qu'ici?

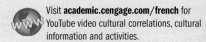
Visit **academic.cengage.com/french** for YouTube video cultural correlations, cultural information and activities.

---

quelques renseignements utiles *some useful information*   **les prix** *prices*   **bas** *low*   **élevés** *high*   **les passants** *passers-by*
Malgré la renommée *In spite of the fame*

Résumé de grammaire

The infinitive, *-er* verbs, and adverbs

Qu'est-ce que tu aimes **faire** le soir?
J'aime **rester** à la maison et **lire** ou
sortir pour **aller voir** un film.

The first verb in a clause is conjugated. Verbs after the first verb are in the infinitive (the base form of the verb). French infinitives end in **-er, -ir, -oir,** or **-re.**

écouter *to listen to*   **dormir** *to sleep*   **prendre** *to take*   **voir** *to see*

Here is the pattern of conjugation for verbs ending in **-er,** except **aller.**

Mes amis **aiment** sortir mais moi
j'**aime** rester à la maison.

PARLER *(to speak)*	
je parl**e**	nous parl**ons**
tu parl**es**	vous parl**ez**
il/elle parl**e**	ils/elles parl**ent**

Nous voyag**e**ons souvent ensemble.

With verbs ending in **-ger,** insert an **e** before the **-ons** ending in the **nous** form.

Nous commen**ç**ons l'examen.

With verbs ending in **-cer,** the **c** changes to a **ç** before the **-ons** ending in the **nous** form.

Après les cours, je **préfère** rentrer à
la maison. Mais le vendredi
après-midi, mes amis et moi
préférons aller prendre un
verre.

If the next-to-last syllable of an **-er** infinitive has an **e** or an **é,** this letter often changes to an **è** in all forms except **nous** and **vous.**

PRÉFÉRER *(to prefer)*	
je préf**è**re	nous préférons
tu préf**è**res	vous préférez
il/elle préf**è**re	ils/elles préf**è**rent

The present tense in French is the equivalent of three present tenses in English.

Je parle français. $\left\{ \begin{array}{l} \textit{I speak French.} \\ \textit{I am speaking French.} \\ \textit{I do speak French.} \end{array} \right.$

Je danse **souvent** le week-end.
Je joue **bien** au tennis.
Je vais au cinéma **quelquefois.**
Je travaille le soir **d'habitude.**
Je joue du piano **comme ci
comme ça.**
Je **ne** travaille **jamais** le samedi.

Adverbs that tell how much, how often, or how well you do something are generally placed immediately after the verb. However, **quelquefois** and **d'habitude** are normally placed at the beginning or end of the clause and **comme ci comme ça** is placed at the end. **Ne... jamais** surrounds the conjugated verb.

Information questions and inversion

To ask information questions, place the appropriate question word (**où, qui,** etc.) before **est-ce que.**

Où est-ce que tu travailles?	*(Where . . . ?)*
Qui est-ce que tu voudrais inviter?	*(Who . . . ?)*
Avec qui est-ce que tu déjeunes?	*(With whom . . . ?)*
Pourquoi est-ce que tu es ici?	*(Why . . . ?)*
Qu'est-ce que tu voudrais?	*(What . . . ?)*
Quand est-ce que tu déjeunes?	*(When . . . ?)*
À quelle heure est-ce que tu dînes?	*(At what time . . . ?)*
Quels jours est-ce que tu es en cours?	*(What / Which days . . . ?)*
Comment est-ce que tu aimes passer la matinée?	*(How . . . ?)*

Je suis en cours le mardi et le jeudi. Et toi? **Quand est-ce que** tu es en cours?

Do not use **est-ce que** with **qui** when it is the subject of the verb, or with **où** or **comment** when they are followed by **être.**

Comment sont tes cours?

You can also form questions by inverting the verb and its subject pronoun. Remember that:

- You do not normally use inversion with **je.**
- If the subject of the verb is a noun, state the noun, then insert the corresponding pronoun to invert with the verb.
- When the inverted subject is **il** or **elle** and the verb ends *in a vowel,* you place a **-t-** between the verb and the pronoun.
- The inverted forms of **il y a** and **c'est** are **y a-t-il** and **est-ce.**

Où **travaillez-vous**?
À quelle heure **êtes-vous** en cours?

Les cours **sont-ils** difficiles?

Marie **parle-t-elle** français?
Marie **est-elle** d'ici?
Y a-t-il un café dans le quartier?
Est-ce un bon café?

The numbers from 30 to 100 and money

The **euro** is the official currency of France. A euro is composed of 100 **centimes.** Read prices as:

    10 € 10 = dix euros dix
    84 € 35 = quatre-vingt-quatre euros trente-cinq
    65 € 75 = soixante-cinq euros soixante-quinze
  100 € 50 = cent euros cinquante

— C'est combien, un expresso?
— C'est **deux euros quarante.**

The numbers from 30 to 100 are based on:

  30 trente
  40 quarante
  50 cinquante
  60 soixante
  70 soixante-dix
  80 quatre-vingts
  90 quatre-vingt-dix
100 cent

COMPÉTENCE 1   Track 30

Saying what you like to do

EXPRESSIONS VERBALES

J'aime...	I like . . .
Je préfère...	I prefer . . .
Je voudrais (bien)...	I would like . . .
aller en boîte / au café / au cinéma	to go to a club / to the café / to the movies
bricoler	to do handiwork
danser	to dance
dîner au restaurant	to have dinner in a restaurant
dormir	to sleep
écouter la radio / la chaîne hi-fi / de la musique	to listen to the radio / the stereo / music
écrire des mails	to write e-mails
faire	to do, to make
faire de l'exercice	to exercise
faire du jogging	to jog, to go jogging
faire du ski	to ski, to go skiing
faire du sport	to play sports
faire du vélo	to ride a bike
faire quelque chose	to do something
inviter des amis à la maison	to invite friends to the house
jouer à des jeux vidéo	to play video games
jouer au base-ball / au basket / au football / au football américain / au golf / au tennis / au volley	to play baseball / basketball / soccer / football / golf / tennis / volleyball
jouer du piano / de la batterie / de la guitare	to play piano / drums / guitar
lire	to read
parler au téléphone	to talk on the phone
prendre un verre	to have a drink
regarder la télé(vision)	to watch TV
regarder une vidéo / un DVD	to watch a video / a DVD
rester à la maison	to stay home
sortir avec des ami(e)s	to go out with friends
surfer le Net	to surf the Net
travailler sur l'ordinateur	to work on the computer
voir un film	to see a movie
On va... ?	Shall we go . . .?
Qu'est-ce que vous aimez faire?	What do you like to do?
Qu'est-ce que vous voudriez faire?	What would you like to do?
Tu voudrais... ?	Would you like . . . ?

DIVERS

À ce soir!	See you tonight! / See you this evening!
À plus tard!	See you later!
après les cours	after class
D'accord!	Okay!
un passe-temps	a pastime
Pourquoi pas?	Why not?
quelque chose	something
Tu es libre ce soir?	Are you free this evening?
vers	about, around, toward
vraiment	really, truly

COMPÉTENCE 2   Track 36

Saying how you spend your free time

NOMS MASCULINS

le cinéclub	the cinema club
un classique	a classic

NOMS FÉMININS

une activité	an activity
la fac	the university, the campus

EXPRESSIONS VERBALES

Qu'est-ce que vous faites?	What are you doing? / What do you do?
Qu'est-ce que tu fais?	What are you doing? / What do you do?
chanter	to sing
commencer	to begin, to start
faire de la musique	to play music
faire du shopping	to go shopping
gagner	to win
jouer au hockey	to play hockey
manger	to eat
nager	to swim
passer chez...	to go by . . . 's house
passer le temps / la matinée	to spend one's time / the morning
préférer	to prefer
préparer les cours	to prepare for class, to study
répéter	to repeat
rester au lit	to stay in bed
je vais	I am going, I go
voyager	to travel

ADVERBES

(très / assez) bien	(very / fairly) well
comme ci comme ça	so-so
d'abord	first
d'habitude	usually
jusqu'à	until
(très / assez) mal	(very / fairly) badly
mieux (que)	better (than)
ne... jamais	never
presque	almost
quand	when
quelquefois	sometimes
rarement	rarely
souvent	often
toujours	always

DIVERS

chez...	to / at / in / by . . . 's house
le samedi matin / après-midi / soir	(on) Saturday mornings / afternoons / evenings
le week-end	the weekend, weekends, on the weekend

Asking about someone's day

NOMS MASCULINS

l'après-midi	the afternoon
un fast-food	a fast-food restaurant
un jour	a day
mon mari	my husband
le matin	the morning
un parc	a park
mon petit ami	my boyfriend
le soir	the evening

NOMS FÉMININS

ma femme	my wife
la journée	the day
ma petite amie	my girlfriend

EXPRESSIONS VERBALES

aimer mieux	to like better, to prefer
aller au parc	to go to the park
déjeuner	to have lunch, to eat lunch
demander	to ask (for)
je dors	I am sleeping, I sleep
manger dans un fast-food	to eat in a fast-food restaurant
rentrer	to return, to go back (home)

EXPRESSIONS ADVERBIALES

l'après-midi	in the afternoon, afternoons
de... heures à... heures	from . . . o'clock to . . . o'clock
ensemble	together
le matin	in the morning, mornings
le soir	in the evening, evenings
tous les jours	every day
toute la journée	all day

EXPRESSIONS INTERROGATIVES

à quelle heure	at what time
avec qui	with whom
comment	how
où	where
pourquoi (parce que)	why (because)
quand	when
quel(s) jour(s)	(on) what / which day(s)
que (qu'est-ce que)	what
Qu'est-ce que c'est?	What is this/that/it?, What are these/those/they?
qui	who(m)
Qui est-ce?	Who is he/she/it/this/that?, Who are they?

DIVERS

en général	in general
par exemple	for example
riche	rich
sauf	except
sexy	sexy
typique	typical

Going to the café

NOMS MASCULINS

l'argent	money, silver
un café (au lait)	a coffee (with milk)
un centime	a centime, a cent
un chocolat (chaud)	a (hot) chocolate
un coca (light)	a (diet) Coke, a (diet) cola
un demi	a draft beer
un euro	a euro
un expresso	an espresso
un garçon	a waiter
un jus de fruit / d'orange	a fruit / an orange juice
un Orangina	an Orangina
un sandwich au fromage / au jambon	a cheese / ham sandwich
un thé (au citron)	a tea (with lemon)
un verre de vin blanc / rouge	a glass of white / red wine

NOMS FÉMININS

une bière	a beer
une boisson	a drink, a beverage
une eau minérale	a mineral water
des frites	some fries
la monnaie	change

CHIFFRES

quarante, quarante et un...	forty, forty-one . . .
cinquante, cinquante et un...	fifty, fifty-one . . .
soixante, soixante et un...	sixty, sixty-one . . .
soixante-dix, soixante et onze...	seventy, seventy-one . . .
quatre-vingts, quatre-vingt-un...	eighty, eighty-one . . .
quatre-vingt-dix, quatre-vingt-onze...	ninety, ninety-one . . .
cent	one hundred

DIVERS

Ça fait combien? Ça fait... euros.	How much is it? That makes . . . euros.
C'est combien?	How much is it?
chaud(e)	hot
commander	to order (food and drink)
J'ai faim. / Je n'ai pas faim.	I'm hungry. / I'm not hungry.
J'ai soif. / Je n'ai pas soif.	I'm thirsty. / I'm not thirsty.
payer	to pay
Qu'est-ce que vous allez prendre?	What are you going to have?
Vous désirez?	What would you like?
Je vais prendre...	I'm going to have . . .
Je voudrais...	I would like . . .
Pour moi... s'il vous plaît.	For me . . . please.
voici	here is, here are
voilà	there is, there are
votre (vos)	your

Sélections musicales

Salut à toi

Le groupe électro-punk Kiemsa est de Mayenne, en France.

From Mayenne, France, the seven members of the electro-punk group Kiemsa have been playing together since the year 2000. Their high energy music often expresses a frenetic, unsettling anxiety. The following activities will help you understand better as you listen to the song.

A. Carrières. Dans la chanson *(song)* **Salut à toi,** le chanteur salue *(the singer greets)* des personnes et des choses liées à *(connected to)* une certaine industrie. Dans quelle industrie est-ce qu'on trouve les personnes et les choses mentionnées dans la chanson?

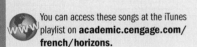

You can access these songs at the iTunes playlist on **academic.cengage.com/french/horizons.**

l'intermittent *seasonal worker*
le comédien *actor*
le jongleur *juggler*
le voltigeur *acrobat*
le plasticien *stage designer*
le régisseur *stage manager*
le chapiteau *big top*
les saltimbanques *street acrobats*
le perchiste *pole-vaulter*
le gréviste *striker*

le cadreur *camera person*
le réalisateur *movie director*
le monteur *film editor*
le camtar *van*
le sondier *sound person*
l'étalonneur *calibrator*
le circacien *circus worker*
les baladins *street artists*
le metteur en scène *theater director*
le larsen *audio feedback*

B. Mots apparentés. Voici d'autres mots de la chanson liés à l'industrie du spectacle. Qu'est-ce que chacun veut dire en anglais?

le musicien
le technicien
le créateur
le danseur
l'électro
le manageur
le percussionniste
le graphiste
le marionnettiste
le décorateur

le chorégraphe
le lighteux
l'accessoiriste
le roadie
le costumier
les employeurs
l'organisateur
les groupes
les compagnies
le comique

Chantez chantez

Amadou Bagayoko and Mariam Doumbia met at Mali's *Institute for the Young Blind.* Their shared interest in music brought them together and they married in 1980. In 1986, they moved from their home in francophone Mali to Abidjan, Côte d'Ivoire, to advance their career. Mixing rock guitar with traditional Malian sounds, their music is known as Afro-blues. Like many francophone Africans, they speak both French and an African language. The song **Chantez, chantez** is mainly in French, with a few lines in Bambara, another language spoken in Mali. The following activity will help you understand better as you listen to the song.

Amadou et Mariam sont du Mali.

Chérie *(Sweetheart).* Dans la chanson **Chantez, chantez**, Amadou parle de son amour *(love)* pour Mariam et de sa bonne volonté envers tout le monde *(goodwill toward everyone).* Quels mots sont logiques dans chaque phrase qui suit *(each sentence that follows)*? Il y a deux ou trois possibilités pour certaines phrases.

aime	donne	parle
voix *(voice)*	tiens *(hold)*	jure *(swear)*
adore	guitare	
préfère	chante	

1. Écoutez cette *(this)* _____ .
2. _____-moi ta main *(your hand)* / ton cœur *(your heart)*.
3. _____-moi dans tes bras *(your arms)*.
4. C'est toi que je (j') _____ .
5. Je ne _____ que pour toi. *(I only _____ for you.)*
6. Je ne _____ qu'avec toi. *(I only _____ with you.)*
7. Je ne _____ que par toi. *(I only _____ by you.)*

belle	du bonheur *(happiness)*	perdre *(to lose)*
reste	liberté	jolie
abandonner	jouer	de l'amour *(love)*
sauter *(to jump)*	gentille	
danser	chanter	

8. _____ à côté de *(beside)* moi.
9. Tu es la plus _____ .
10. Je ne veux pas te (t') _____ . *(I don't want to _____ you.)*
11. Nous allons *(We are going to)* _____ ensemble.
12. _____ pour tout le monde.

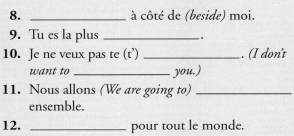

*Un nouvel
appartement*

Chapitre 3

Compétence

1 Talking about where you live
Le logement

Giving prices and other numerical information
Les chiffres au-dessus de 100 et les nombres ordinaux

Stratégies et Lecture
Pour mieux lire: *Guessing meaning from context*
Lecture: *Un nouvel appartement*

2 Talking about your possessions
Les effets personnels

Saying what you have
*Le verbe **avoir***

Saying where something is
Quelques prépositions

3 Describing your room
Les meubles et les couleurs

Identifying your belongings
*La possession et les adjectifs possessifs **mon**, **ton** et **son***

Indicating to whom something belongs
*Les adjectifs possessifs **notre**, **votre** et **leur***

4 Giving your address and phone number
Des renseignements

Telling which one
*Les adjectifs **quel** et **ce***

Reprise
Saying where you live and what you have

Lecture et Composition
    Pour mieux lire: *Previewing content*
    Lecture: *Les couleurs et leurs effets sur la nature humaine*
    Pour mieux écrire: *Brainstorming*
    Composition: *Une lettre*

Comparaisons culturelles *Le Québec d'aujourd'hui*

Résumé de grammaire

Vocabulaire

 iLrn Heinle Learning Center

 academic.cengage.com/french/horizons

 Système-D

 Audio   iRadio

Où est-ce qu'**on** parle français **aux Amériques**? **Laquelle** de ces régions voudriez-vous visiter? Quelle est la province francophone la plus importante du Canada? Voudriez-vous visiter cette province?

Do you know why there are so many francophones in Quebec? How would you characterize the linguistic situation in Canada today? Research online the history of French in Canada and the current linguistic situation there.

Plus vaste que l'Alaska, le Québec est **la plus grande** des provinces canadiennes et 25% de la population canadienne habite dans cette province.

---

on *one, people, they*   **aux Amériques** *in the Americas*   **Laquelle** *Which one*   **la plus grande** *the biggest*

Montréal, grand centre culturel et commercial, est la plus grande **ville** du Québec.

La ville de Québec est la capitale de la province de Québec. Fondée en 1608, c'est la plus vieille ville du Canada.

⚙ Qu'en savez-vous?

Complétez ces phrases.

1. Aux États-Unis, il y a des communautés francophones dans plusieurs états de (several states of) la Nouvelle-A_____ et dans l'état de la L_____. En Amérique du Sud, la G_____ française est francophone. On parle français dans plusieurs îles caraïbes: la M_____, la G_____, Saint-_____ et H_____.

2. Le _____ est la plus grande province du Canada et _____% de la population canadienne y habite (lives there). C'est la province francophone la plus importante du Canada!

3. _____ est la plus grande ville de la province de Québec, mais _____ est sa capitale. Québec est la plus _____ ville du Canada.

ville *city*

Talking about where you live

Le logement

J'habite... dans une maison
dans un appartement
dans **une chambre** à la
résidence universitaire
chez mes parents

Ma maison / Mon appartement /
Ma chambre est...
grand(e) / petit(e)
moderne / vieux (vieille)
joli(e) / laid(e)
(trop) cher (chère)
confortable

J'habite...

sur le campus / **(tout) près de** l'université / (très / assez) **loin de** l'université
au centre-ville (dans un grand **immeuble**) / **en ville** / **en banlieue** /
à la campagne

Le loyer est de...   550$ (cinq cent cinquante dollars)   **par mois.**
600$ (six cents dollars)
1 200$ (mille deux cents dollars)

Je n'ai pas de loyer!

Chez moi, il y a six **pièces** *(f).*

Vocabulaire supplémentaire

une caravane	a travel trailer
une cave	a cellar
un duplex	a split-level apartment
un emprunt-logement	a home loan
un garage	a garage
un grenier	an attic
un jardin	a yard, a garden
un mobile-home	a mobile home
une lingerie	a laundry room
une salle de séjour	a family room, a den
un W.-C.	a restroom

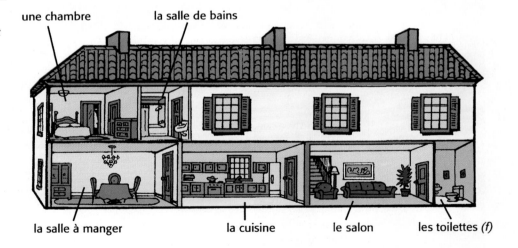

une chambre   la salle de bains

la salle à manger   la cuisine   le salon   les toilettes *(f)*

Le logement *Lodging, Housing*   **une chambre** *a bedroom*   **trop** *too*   **cher (chère)** *expensive*   **(tout) près (de)** *(very) near*
loin (de) *far (from)*   **au centre-ville** *downtown*   **un immeuble** *an apartment building*   **en ville** *in town* (**une ville** *a city*)
en banlieue *in the suburbs*   **à la campagne** *in the country*   **Le loyer** *The rent*   **par mois** *per month*   **Je n'ai pas** *I don't have*
une pièce *a room*

CD 2-2

Robert, un jeune Américain, **va** étudier à l'université Laval, au Québec. Il parle au téléphone à son ami Thomas, avec qui il pense habiter.

l'appartement de Thomas

l'ascenseur *(m)*

une fenêtre

la porte

au troisième étage (3e)

au deuxième étage (2e)

au premier étage (1er) *on the second floor*

au rez-de-chaussée (R.d.C.) *on the first / ground floor*

au sous-sol / *in the basement*

l'escalier *(m)*

ROBERT: Où est-ce que tu habites?
THOMAS: J'habite dans un immeuble au centre-ville.
ROBERT: **À quel étage?**
THOMAS: Mon appartement est au deuxième étage.
ROBERT: Tu habites seul?
THOMAS: Non, j'habite avec Claude, mon colocataire.
ROBERT: L'université est loin de chez toi?
THOMAS: Non, pas très loin. Et il y a **un arrêt d'autobus** tout près. C'est très **commode.**
ROBERT: Et l'appartement est agréable?
THOMAS: J'aime beaucoup mon appartement. Il est assez grand et pas trop cher.

⁂ Note *culturelle*

Dans les hôtels et les autres immeubles au Québec et en France, faites attention! Le premier étage est l'étage au-dessus du *(above the)* rez-de-chaussée. C'est-à-dire *(That is to say)* que le rez-de-chaussée est *the first floor / ground floor* et le premier étage est *the second floor*. À quel étage habitez-vous?

A. Et vous? Complétez les phrases avec les mots en italique qui vous correspondent le mieux.

1. J'habite dans *un appartement / une maison / une chambre.*
2. *Mon appartement / Ma chambre / Ma maison* est *sur le campus / (tout) près de l'université / (très / assez) loin de l'université.*
3. Il/Elle est *au centre-ville / en ville / en banlieue / à la campagne.*
4. Il/Elle est *joli(e) / grand(e) / moderne / confortable / ???.*
5. Il/Elle *est / n'est pas* trop cher (chère).
6. Le loyer est de *plus / moins* de cinq cents dollars par mois.
7. Chez moi, il y a *une / deux / trois / quatre / ???* chambre(s).
8. Je passe beaucoup de temps dans *la cuisine / le salon / ma chambre / ???.*
9. Ma chambre est *au rez-de-chaussée / au premier étage / ???.*
10. *Il y a un ascenseur / Il n'y a pas d'ascenseur* chez moi.

B. Entretien. Interviewez votre partenaire.
1. Est-ce que tu habites chez tes parents? Est-ce que tu habites dans une maison, dans un appartement ou dans une chambre à la résidence universitaire? Comment est la maison / la chambre / l'appartement? Est-ce qu'il est cher / elle est chère?
2. Tu habites près de l'université, loin de l'université ou sur le campus? Est-ce que c'est commode? Est-ce qu'il y a un arrêt d'autobus tout près?
3. Préfères-tu habiter au centre-ville, en ville, en banlieue ou à la campagne? Préfères-tu habiter au rez-de-chaussée ou au premier étage?
4. Quelles pièces est-ce qu'il y a chez toi? Dans quelle pièce aimes-tu passer beaucoup de temps? Dans quelle pièce préfères-tu faire tes devoirs? manger?

C. Conversation. Avec un(e) partenaire, relisez à haute voix la conversation entre Robert et Thomas en haut de la page. Ensuite, changez la conversation pour décrire votre propre situation.

CD 2-3 You can find a list of the new words from the vocabulary and grammar sections of this *Compétence* on page 138 and a recording of this list on track 2-3 of your *Text Audio CD.*

---

va (aller *to go)* **À quel étage?** *On what floor?* (**un étage** *a floor [of a building]*) **un arrêt d'autobus** *a bus stop* **commode** *convenient*

Pour vérifier

1. How do you say 100? 1,000? 1,000,000? Before which two of these numbers do you never put **un**?

2. How do you say 1 503? 12 612?

3. How do you say *first*? *fifth*? How do you say *on the* with a floor?

Giving prices and other numerical information

Les chiffres au-dessus de 100 et les nombres ordinaux

Here is how to say numbers over 100.

100 cent		**1 000** mille	
101 cent un		**1 001** mille un	
102 cent deux		**1 352** mille trois cent cinquante-deux	
199 cent quatre-vingt-dix-neuf		**2 000** deux mille	
200 deux cents		**1 000 000** un million	
201 deux cent un		**2 234 692** deux millions deux cent	
999 neuf cent quatre-vingt-dix-neuf		trente-quatre mille six cent quatre-vingt-douze	

Vocabulaire supplémentaire

un milliard	*one billion*
deux milliards	*two billion*

Note the following about numbers:

- **Cent** means *one hundred,* never say **un cent. Mille** means *one thousand,* never say **un mille.** On the other hand, do say **un million.** Use **de (d')** after the word **million(s)** whenever a noun follows it directly.

  cent habitants　　　**mille habitants**　　　**un million d'habitants**

- **Million** takes an **s** in the plural. **Cent** generally only takes an **s** when plural if not followed by another number. Never add an **s** to **mille.**

  deux **cents** habitants　　　deux **cent** cinquante habitants
  trois **millions** d'habitants　　　trois **millions** six **mille** habitants

- There is no hyphen between **cent, mille,** or **un million** and another number.

  un million deux cent cinquante-quatre mille habitants

- In France and in Quebec, commas are used to denote decimals, and a space (or a period) is used after thousands, millions, etc. Read a decimal as **virgule (1,5 = un virgule cinq).**

USA	FRANCE / QUÉBEC
1.5	1,5
1,000	1 000 *or* 1.000

Use **À quel étage?** to ask *On what floor?* To say *on the* with a floor, use **au.** When counting floors, use the ordinal numbers and remember that in a French-speaking country, the first floor (**le premier étage**) is the floor above the ground floor (**le rez-de-chaussée**).

　—**À quel étage habitez-vous?**　　　—*What floor do you live on?*
　—**J'habite au troisième étage**　　　—*I live on the fourth floor.*

In French, to convert cardinal numbers *(two, three, four . . .)* to ordinal numbers *(second, third, fourth . . .)*, add the suffix **-ième.** Drop a final **-e** from cardinal numbers before adding **-ième.**

　deux → deuxième　　　**quatre → quatrième**　　　**mille → millième**

These ordinal numbers are irregular: **premier (première), cinquième, neuvième.**

A. Le loyer. Quel est le loyer?

EXEMPLE 900$ **Le loyer est de neuf cents dollars par mois.**

1. 865$ **4.** 750$ **7.** 1 545$ **10.** 2 435$
2. 660$ **5.** 675$ **8.** 1 385$ **11.** 3 295$
3. 410$ **6.** 825$ **9.** 1 110$ **12.** 1 340$

B. Et vous? Décrivez l'endroit *(place)* où vous habitez en changeant les chiffres et les mots en italique.

1. La population de la ville où j'habite maintenant est de *150 000 / ???* habitants.
2. Il y a plus de *35 000 / ???* étudiants à notre *(our)* université.
3. Mon loyer est de *400$ / ???* par mois. *(Je n'ai pas de loyer.)*
4. Ma chambre est au *deuxième étage / ???.*
5. Je préfère habiter au *deuxième étage / ???.*
6. Maintenant, nous sommes au *troisième étage / ???.*
7. Le bureau du prof est *au rez-de-chaussée / au premier étage / ???.*

C. Statistiques. Lisez ces statistiques sur l'université Laval, le Québec et le Canada. Devinez *(Guess)* quel chiffre correspond à chaque description. Votre professeur dira *(will say)* **plus que ça** ou **moins que ça** jusqu'à ce que vous deviniez juste.

1. la population du Canada   **a.** 717 600
2. le nombre de francophones au Canada   **b.** 7 542 800
3. la population de la province de Québec   **c.** 32 799 100
4. la population de la ville de Québec   **d.** 249
5. la population de Montréal   **e.** 38 357
6. le nombre d'étudiants à l'université Laval   **f.** 3 720 000
7. le nombre d'étudiants étrangers à l'université Laval   **g.** 8 000 000
8. le loyer par mois dans les résidences à l'université Laval en dollars canadiens   **h.** 2 000

D. Chez Thomas. Regardez l'illustration et répondez aux questions.

l'appartement de Thomas

1. Il y a un ascenseur dans l'immeuble où habite Thomas? Il y a un escalier?
2. À quel étage habite le vieux monsieur? Qu'est-ce qu'il fait *(What is he doing)*?
3. À quel étage habitent Thomas et son colocataire? Qu'est-ce qu'ils font *(What are they doing)*?
4. À quel étage habite la jeune femme? Qu'est-ce qu'elle fait?
5. Où habitent les enfants? Qu'est-ce qu'ils font?

Stratégies et Lecture

⚜ Pour mieux lire: *Guessing meaning from context*

You can often guess the meaning of unknown words from context. Read this passage in its entirety, then guess the meaning of the boldfaced words.

L'immeuble de Thomas **se trouve** au centre-ville. Arrivé à l'immeuble, Robert **entre,** il **monte** l'escalier et il **sonne** à la porte de l'appartement de son ami. Une jeune femme **ouvre** la porte. Après un instant, elle **referme** la porte.

Some words may have different meanings in different contexts. For example, the word **bien** can mean *well* or it can also be used for emphasis, instead of **très** (*very*). Read the following sentences and use the context to decide if **bien** means *well* or *very*.

> Je comprends bien.
> C'est bien compliqué.
> Le prénom Claude est utilisé aussi bien pour une femme que pour un homme.

A. Selon le contexte. The boldfaced word in each of the following sentences can have a different meaning, depending on the context. Can you guess the different meanings?

> Bravo! **Encore! Encore!**
> Ça, c'est **encore** plus compliqué.
> Je suis au premier étage, alors je monte **encore** un étage pour aller au deuxième?

B. Vous savez déjà... You already know the boldfaced words in sentence **a.** Guess the meaning of the boldfaced words in sentence **b,** using the context.

1. **a. Ouvrez** votre livre, **lisez** le paragraphe et **fermez** le livre.
   b. Robert **ouvre** la lettre de Thomas, **lit** les instructions et **referme** la lettre.
2. **a. Prenez** une feuille de papier.
   b. Elle **prend** la lettre.
3. **a. Donnez**-moi un café, s'il vous plaît.
   b. Thomas **donne** l'adresse de l'appartement à Robert.

Lecture: Un nouvel appartement

CD 2-4

Robert, un jeune Américain de Louisiane, arrive devant l'immeuble où habitent Thomas et son colocataire Claude.

Robert ouvre la lettre de Thomas, consulte les instructions et vérifie l'adresse. Il lit: «*Mon appartement se trouve 38, rue Dauphine. C'est un grand immeuble avec une porte bleue. J'habite au deuxième étage.*» «Oui, c'est bien là», pense-t-il. Il descend de la voiture, entre dans l'immeuble et monte l'escalier.

Il sonne à la porte de l'appartement. Quelques instants après, une jolie jeune femme lui ouvre la porte.

—Euh... Bonjour, mademoiselle, je suis Robert. C'est bien ici que Claude et Thomas habitent?

—Claude, c'est moi. Mais...

Robert, très surpris, l'interrompt et s'exclame:

—Claude, c'est vous? Euh... Mais vous êtes une femme!

—Eh oui, monsieur, je suis bien une femme! répond la jeune femme.

—Euh... je veux dire que... C'est que, vous comprenez, en anglais, Claude, c'est un prénom masculin, dit Robert.

—En français, monsieur, le prénom Claude est utilisé aussi bien pour une femme que pour un homme, répond la jeune femme.

—Ah, je comprends! Excusez-moi, mademoiselle. Je suis confus. Alors, vous êtes Claude. Moi, je suis Robert, Robert Martin. Est-ce que Thomas est ici?

—Thomas? dit-elle d'un air surpris.

—Eh oui, Thomas, mon ami. Il habite ici avec vous, n'est-ce pas?

—Mais certainement pas, monsieur! dit-elle d'un ton énervé.

Quand elle essaie de fermer la porte, Robert s'exclame:

—Un instant, s'il vous plaît, mademoiselle. Regardez! Voici l'adresse que mon ami m'a donnée.

Elle prend la lettre, lit les instructions et commence à comprendre.

—Oui, monsieur, c'est bien ici le 38, rue Dauphine, mais vous êtes au premier étage et votre ami habite au deuxième étage.

—Au premier étage? Ah! Oui, je comprends maintenant. *First floor,* c'est le rez de-chaussée et *second floor,* c'est le premier étage. Alors, je monte encore un étage pour trouver l'appartement de mon ami?

—Oui, monsieur, c'est bien ça. Au revoir, et bienvenue au Québec!

—Au revoir, mademoiselle, et merci.

A. Vrai ou faux?

1. Robert arrive au 38, rue Dauphine, l'adresse de son ami Thomas.
2. Il monte directement au deuxième étage.
3. Il sonne et Claude, la jeune femme qui habite avec Thomas, ouvre la porte.
4. Robert est surpris de voir une femme.
5. Claude est un prénom masculin et aussi un prénom féminin en français.
6. En France et au Québec, le *first floor,* c'est le rez-de-chaussée et le *second floor,* c'est le premier étage.

B. Voilà pourquoi. Complétez le paragraphe pour expliquer la confusion de Robert.

homme	premier	premier	deuxième	deuxième	Thomas	Thomas

Robert entre dans l'immeuble pour trouver l'appartement de (1) _____. Thomas habite au (2) _____ étage avec Claude, un ami. Robert monte au (3) _____ étage et sonne. Une jeune femme ouvre la porte. C'est Claude, mais elle n'habite pas avec Thomas. Robert ne comprend pas; il pense que la jeune femme habite avec (4) _____. Voilà le problème: Robert est au (5) _____ étage et Thomas et Claude habitent au (6) _____ étage. C'est un autre Claude, un jeune (7) _____, pas une jeune femme, qui habite avec Thomas.

Talking about your possessions

Vocabulaire supplémentaire

un assistant personnel *a personal organizer*
une cassette
une cuisinière *a stove*
un (four à) micro-ondes *a microwave (oven)*
un futon
un lave-vaisselle *a dishwasher*
un lave-linge *a washer*
un lecteur MP3 *an MP3 player*
un magnétoscope *a VCR*
une moto *a motorcycle*
une radio cassette (K7) *a boombox*
un réfrigérateur (un frigo)
un sèche-linge *a dryer*
une table basse *a coffee table*

Les effets personnels

Avez-vous beaucoup de **choses**? Moi, **j'ai...**

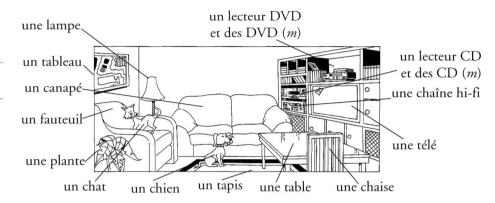

un lecteur DVD et des DVD *(m)*
un lecteur CD et des CD *(m)*
une chaîne hi-fi
une télé
une lampe
un tableau
un canapé
un fauteuil
une plante
un chat   un chien   un tapis   une table   une chaise

beaucoup de vêtements *(m)*   une voiture   un vélo   un portable (un ordinateur)   un portable   un iPod

Chez Thomas **tout est en ordre** et **bien rangé.** Qu'est-ce qu'il y a... ?

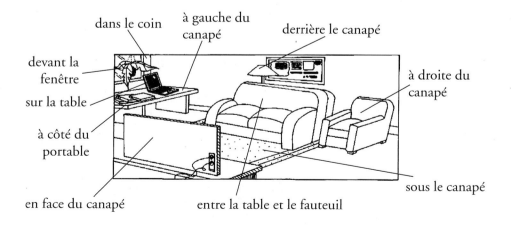

dans le coin   à gauche du canapé   derrière le canapé
devant la fenêtre
à droite du canapé
sur la table
à côté du portable
en face du canapé   entre la table et le fauteuil   sous le canapé

Avez-vous (avoir *to have***)**   **une chose** *a thing*   **j'ai (avoir** *to have*)   **tout est en ordre** *everything is in order (in its place)*
bien rangé(e) *orderly, put away, in its place*

Avant d'arriver au Québec, Robert **cherche** un appartement. Il téléphone à Thomas.

THOMAS: Tu cherches un appartement ici à Québec? Écoute, tu sais, moi, je **partage** un appartement avec mon ami Claude. **Nous avons** trois chambres; tu voudrais habiter avec nous?

ROBERT: **Peut-être.** Comment est **ton** appartement?

THOMAS: Il est assez grand et confortable, mais pas trop cher. Tu aimes les animaux?

ROBERT: Oui, pourquoi? **Tu as** des animaux?

THOMAS: Claude **a** un chien et un chat. Ils sont quelquefois **embêtants** et ils aiment dormir **partout.**

ROBERT: Pas de problème. J'aime bien les animaux. Vous **fumez**?

THOMAS: Non, je ne fume pas et Claude **non plus.**

ROBERT: Bon, moi non plus. Alors ça va.

A. Tu as... ? Demandez à votre partenaire s'il/si elle a ces choses.

EXEMPLE — **Tu as une voiture?**
— **Oui, j'ai une voiture. / Non, je n'ai pas de voiture.**

1.  **2.** **3.** **4.**

5.  **6.** **7.**  **8.**

B. Qu'est-ce que c'est? Regardez l'illustration du salon de Thomas en bas de la page précédente. Qu'est-ce qu'il y a dans chaque endroit *(place)*?

EXEMPLE sur la table **Les livres sont sur la table.**

1. devant la fenêtre
2. en face du canapé
3. derrière le canapé
4. à droite des livres
5. à côté du portable

6. dans le coin
7. à gauche du portable
8. à droite du canapé
9. entre le fauteuil et la table
10. sous le canapé

C. Conversation. Avec un(e) partenaire, relisez à haute voix la conversation entre Robert et Thomas en haut de la page. Ensuite, imaginez que votre partenaire va habiter *(is going to live)* chez vous et changez la conversation pour décrire votre propre situation.

You can find a list of the new words from the vocabulary and grammar sections of this **Compétence** on page 138 and a recording of this list on track 2-6 of your *Text Audio CD*.

---

chercher *to look for*   **partager** *to share*   **Nous avons (avoir** *to have)*   **Peut-être** *Maybe, Perhaps*   **ton/ta/tes** *your (singular familiar)*   **Tu as (avoir** *to have)*   **a (avoir** *to have)*   **embêtant(e)** *annoying*   **partout** *everywhere*   **fumer** *to smoke*   **non plus** *neither*

Pour vérifier

1. What does **avoir** mean? What are its forms? Why might one confuse the **tu** and **ils/elles** forms of **avoir** (to have) with those of **être** (to be)?

2. What does the indefinite article (**un, une, des**) change to after expressions of quantity such as **combien** or **beaucoup**? When else does this change occur?

3. Which of these nouns would have a plural ending with **-x** instead of **-s: un hôpital, un animal, un tableau, un bureau, une table, un canapé**?

Saying what you have

Le verbe **avoir**

To say what someone has, use the verb **avoir.** Its conjugation is irregular.

AVOIR *(to have)*	
j' **ai**	nous^z **avons**
tu **as**	vous^z **avez**
il/elle **a**	ils/elles^z **ont**

Use **de (d')** rather than **des** after **combien** *(how much, how many),* as you do after quantity expressions like **beaucoup** and **assez.** Also remember to use **de (d')** instead of **un, une,** or **des** in most negative sentences, unless the negated verb is a form of the verb **être.**

AFFIRMATIVE	NEGATIVE	AFTER A QUANTITY EXPRESSION
J'ai **des** chats.	Je n'ai pas **de** chats.	Combien **de** chats as-tu?
BUT:		
C'est **un** chat.	Ce ne sont pas **des** chats.	C'est beaucoup **de** chats.

Although the plural of most nouns and adjectives is formed by adding **-s,** words ending in **-eau, -au,** or **-eu** usually form their plural with **-x.** Words ending in **-al** often change this ending to **-aux** in the plural. Abbreviations like **DVD** and **CD** do not add **-s** in the plural.

un tableau	un bureau	un animal	un CD	un DVD
des tableau**x**	des bureau**x**	des anim**aux**	des CD	des DVD

Prononciation

Avoir et Être

Be careful to pronounce the forms of the verbs **avoir** and **être** distinctly. Open your mouth wide to pronounce the **a** in **tu as** and **il/elle a.** Contrast this with the vowel sound in **es** and **est.** Pronounce **ils sont** with an **s** sound, and the liaison in **ils ont** with a **z** sound.

être: Tu es professeur.	avoir: Tu as beaucoup de cours.
Elle est professeur.	Elle a beaucoup de cours.
Ils sont professeurs.	Ils _z ont beaucoup de cours.

A. Avoir ou être? Posez ces questions à un(e) camarade de classe. Faites attention à la prononciation des verbes **avoir** et **être.**

> EXEMPLE   a. — **Tu es extraverti(e)?**
> — **Oui, je suis extravertie. / Non, je ne suis pas extraverti(e).**
> b. — **Tu as beaucoup d'amis?**
> — **Oui, j'ai beaucoup d'amis. / Non, je n'ai pas beaucoup d'amis.**

1. **a.** Tu es d'ici?   **b.** Tu as beaucoup de choses chez toi?
2. **a.** Ton meilleur ami est sympa?   **b.** Il a beaucoup d'amis?
3. **a.** Tes parents, ils sont sportifs?   **b.** Ils ont un vélo?
4. **a.** Ils sont d'ici?   **b.** Ils ont une grande maison?

B. Qu'est-ce qu'ils ont? Complétez ces phrases selon le modèle.

> **EXEMPLE**   Moi, je (j')... (un chat, un chien).
> **Moi, j'ai un chat. Je n'ai pas de chien.**

1. Chez moi, je (j')... (une chaîne hi-fi, des CD de musique française, un portable, des plantes, un lecteur DVD, beaucoup de DVD, un iPod).
2. Mon meilleur ami (Ma meilleure amie)... (un chien, un chat, beaucoup de vêtements, une voiture, un vélo, un portable, des plantes).
3. Dans le cours de français, nous... (beaucoup de devoirs, beaucoup d'examens, cours le lundi, cours le mardi, un examen aujourd'hui).
4. Généralement, les étudiants à l'université... (un vélo, une voiture, beaucoup de temps libre, 25 heures de cours par semaine)

C. Combien? Demandez à un(e) camarade de classe combien de ces choses il/elle a.

> **EXEMPLE**   **— Combien de chiens est-ce que tu as?**
> **— J'ai un (deux, trois...) chien(s). / J'ai beaucoup de chiens. /**
> **Je n'ai pas de chiens.**

EXEMPLE

1.   **2.**

3.   **4.**   **5.**

D. Oui ou non? Vous cherchez un nouveau logement et vous parlez à d'autres étudiants qui voudraient partager leur *(their)* appartement / maison. Complétez leurs phrases avec la forme correcte du verbe **avoir**. Ensuite, dites si vous voudriez habiter avec ces personnes. Répondez **oui, non** ou **peut-être.**

1. J'_____ un très bel appartement et le loyer n'est pas trop cher.
2. Tu aimes les animaux? J'_____ trois colocataires et ils _____ neuf chats et trois petits chiens.
3. Nous _____ une grande maison près de l'université. Les chambres _____ beaucoup de fenêtres et une belle vue *(view)*.
4. Mon colocataire _____ beaucoup d'amis qui fument dans l'appartement.
5. Tu _____ une voiture? Mon immeuble n'_____ pas de parking mais il est près de tout. Moi, j'_____ un vélo.
6. J'_____ un appartement. Il est au cinquième étage mais nous _____ deux nouveaux ascenseurs.
7. L'immeuble n'_____ pas assez d'eau chaude, mais le loyer est seulement *(only)* de deux cents dollars par mois et j'_____ un très joli appartement.

Pour vérifier

1. How do you say *on? under? facing? next to?*
2. What does the preposition **de** mean? With which two forms of the definite article does it combine to form **du** and **des?**

Saying where something is

Quelques prépositions

You can use the following prepositions to tell where something or someone is.

sur *on*	**près (de)** *near*
sous *under*	**loin (de)** *far (from)*
entre *between*	**à côté (de)** *next to, beside*
dans *in*	**à droite (de)** *to the right (of)*
devant *in front of*	**à gauche (de)** *to the left (of)*
derrière *behind*	**en face (de)** *across (from), facing*
	dans le coin (de) *in the corner (of)*

When used by itself, the preposition **de** means *of, from,* or *about.* It is also used with some of the prepositions above. When **de** is followed by a definite article and a noun, it combines with the masculine singular **le** and the plural **les** to form the contractions **du** and **des.** It does not change when followed by **la** or **l'.**

CONTRACTIONS WITH *DE*			
de + le	→	du	J'habite près **du** centre-ville.
de + la	→	de la	La salle de classe est près **de la** bibliothèque.
de + l'	→	de l'	Mon appartement est près **de l'**université.
de + les	→	des	Il n'y a pas de parking près **des** résidences.

CD 2-8

Prononciation

De, du, des

Be careful to pronounce **de, du,** and **des** distinctly.

- As you know, the **e** in words like **de, le,** and **ne** is pronounced with the lips slightly puckered. The tongue is held firm in the lower part of the mouth.
- The **u** in **du,** as in **tu,** is pronounced with the tongue arched firmly near the roof of the mouth, as when pronouncing the French vowel **i** in **il,** but with the lips puckered.
- The vowel in **des** is a sharp sound like the **é** in **café,** pronounced with the corners of the lips spread.

A. Dans la salle de classe. Choisissez les mots en italique qui décrivent le mieux votre cours de français.

1. Le professeur *est / n'est pas* dans la salle de classe maintenant.
2. D'habitude, le professeur est *devant / derrière* les étudiants.
3. Le professeur *est / n'est pas* en face de moi maintenant.
4. Moi, je suis *près / loin* de la porte.
5. La porte est *à gauche de / à droite de / devant / derrière* nous.
6. *Je suis / Je ne suis pas* entre le professeur et la porte.
7. *Je suis / Je ne suis pas* dans le coin de la salle de classe.
8. Le tableau est *devant les étudiants / derrière les étudiants / à côté des étudiants.*

B. C'est où? Une amie de Thomas décrit *(is describing)* le salon chez elle. Complétez ses phrases avec la forme convenable de la préposition **de (de, du, de la, de l', des)**. Ensuite *(Then),* regardez l'illustration et dites si les phrases sont vraies ou fausses. Corrigez les phrases fausses.

1. Sur la table, les livres sont à gauche _____ ordinateur.
2. L'ordinateur est à côté _____ mes livres.
3. La télé est en face _____ fauteuil.
4. L'escalier est à gauche _____ table.
5. La télé est à côté _____ plantes.
6. La lampe est à côté _____ fauteuil.
7. Le chien est à droite _____ télé.
8. La porte est en face _____ escalier.

C. Descriptions. Faites des phrases pour décrire le salon dans *B. C'est où?*

EXEMPLE   les livres / la table
      Les livres sont sur la table.

1. le chat / la table
2. la télé / le fauteuil
3. les plantes / la télé
4. le chien / le fauteuil et la télé
5. le chien / le fauteuil
6. la table / le salon
7. la porte / le fauteuil
8. les livres / l'ordinateur
9. l'ordinateur / la table
10. l'escalier / les tableaux

Maintenant, posez ces questions à un(e) camarade de classe.

1. Qu'est-ce qu'il y a sur la table? sous la table? à gauche des livres? à droite de la table?
2. Qu'est-ce qu'il y a devant le fauteuil? à côté du fauteuil? en face de la télé? derrière la télé?
3. Où est la lampe par rapport *(in relationship)* au fauteuil?
4. Où est la télé par rapport aux plantes? par rapport au fauteuil?
5. Où est le chien par rapport à la télé et au fauteuil?

D. À vendre. Avec un(e) partenaire, préparez au moins huit phrases décrivant cette maison.

EXEMPLE   **Quand vous entrez *(enter)* dans la maison, les toilettes sont à gauche de la porte et le bureau est à droite. Derrière les toilettes il y a...**

au rez-de-chaussée

au premier étage

Describing your room

Note culturelle

Thomas montre l'appartement à Robert parce que Robert va habiter avec lui *(him)*. Si *(If)* vous êtes invité(e) chez un(e) Québécois(e) ou un(e) Français(e), ne vous attendez pas à *(don't expect to)* faire le tour de sa maison ou de son appartement. En général, dans les cultures francophones, on *(one)* reste dans le salon et la salle à manger. Est-ce qu'on montre souvent sa maison aux invités dans votre région? Pourquoi ou pourquoi pas?

Les meubles et les couleurs

Thomas **montre** les chambres à Robert.

un placard • une affiche • des rideaux *(m)* • une commode • un bureau • un lit • un tapis • une étagère

Voilà **ma** chambre. **Les murs** sont beiges et le tapis et les rideaux sont bleus. **La couverture** est bleue, rouge et verte.
Ma chambre est toujours **propre** et en ordre. Tout est **à sa place.**

Note de vocabulaire

Laisser means *to leave* in the sense of leaving something somewhere, but not in the sense of leaving a place.

Voilà la chambre de Claude. **Sa** chambre est souvent un peu **sale** et en désordre. Il **laisse** tout **par terre.**

Et vous? Comment est votre chambre, en ordre ou en désordre? De quelle couleur *(f)* est votre tapis? De quelle couleur sont vos murs? Voici des adjectifs pour indiquer la couleur de quelque chose.

Note de grammaire

As adjectives, the words for colors follow the noun they describe and must agree with it in gender and number: **des chaises bleues. Orange** and **marron** are exceptions. They are invariable and never change form. All colors are invariable when followed by adjectives such as **clair** *(light)*, **foncé** *(dark)*, or **vif** *(bright)*: **Ma voiture est bleu clair.**

Vocabulaire supplémentaire

bleu clair	*light blue*
bleu foncé	*dark blue*
bleu vif	*bright blue*
de toutes les couleurs	*with all colors*
multicolore	*multicolored*
à fleurs	*floral*
écossais(e)	*plaid*
imprimé(e)	*print*
rayé(e)	*striped*
uni(e)	*solid-colored*

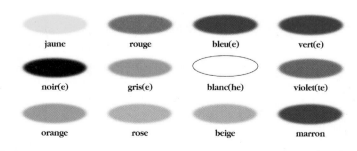

jaune • rouge • bleu(e) • vert(e)
noir(e) • gris(e) • blanc(he) • violet(te)
orange • rose • beige • marron

Les meubles *Furniture, Furnishings*   **montrer** *to show*   **mon/ma/mes** *my*   **un mur** *a wall*   **une couverture** *a blanket, a cover*
propre *clean*   **à sa place** *in its place*   **son/sa/ses** *his/her/its*   **sale** *dirty*   **laisser** *to leave*   **par terre** *on the floor, on the ground*

CD 2-9

Thomas montre les chambres à Robert.

THOMAS: Voici la chambre de Claude à côté de la cuisine. Sa chambre est toujours en désordre. Il laisse ses vêtements partout.

ROBERT: C'est ta chambre en face de la chambre de Claude?

THOMAS: Oui, **comme tu vois,** je préfère avoir tout bien rangé et **chaque chose** à sa place.

ROBERT: Et ça, c'est ma chambre **au bout du couloir**?

THOMAS: Oui, **viens voir...** Tu as un lit, un bureau et une grande fenêtre avec **une** belle **vue.** J'**espère** que **ça te plaît.**

ROBERT: Oui, **ça me plaît** beaucoup!

THOMAS: Les murs sont blancs. Tu préfères une autre couleur?

ROBERT: Non, **justement,** le blanc, c'est ma couleur **préférée.**

THOMAS: Moi, je préfère le vert.

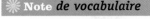

Note *de vocabulaire*

The formal/plural version of **ça te plaît** is **ça vous plaît.**

A. Chez vous? Décrivez votre chambre en choisissant l'adverbe qui convient.

(presque) toujours   **souvent**   **quelquefois**
      rarement   **ne... jamais**

EXEMPLE   Ma chambre est en ordre.
**Ma chambre est presque toujours en ordre. /
Ma chambre n'est jamais en ordre.**

1. Ma chambre est propre.
2. Ma chambre est en désordre.
3. Mes livres sont sur l'étagère.
4. Ma chambre est sale.
5. Mes vêtements sont par terre.
6. Mes livres sont sur le lit.
7. Je laisse mes vêtements partout.
8. Mes vêtements sont dans le placard ou dans la commode.

B. Les couleurs. Complétez les phases suivantes avec le nom d'une couleur.

1. Je préfère les vêtements...
2. J'ai beaucoup de vêtements...
3. Je préfère avoir des murs...
4. Les murs de ma chambre sont...
5. La couverture de mon lit est...
6. Je préfère les voitures...
7. Ma voiture est...
8. Je préfère les meubles...
9. Chez moi, le canapé est...
10. Ma couleur préférée, c'est le...

C. Conversation. Avec un(e) partenaire, relisez la conversation entre Robert et Thomas en haut de la page. Ensuite, imaginez que votre partenaire va habiter *(is going to live)* chez vous et changez la conversation pour décrire votre propre maison / appartement.

---

comme tu vois *as you see*   **chaque chose** *each thing*   **au bout de** *at the end of*   **le couloir** *the hallway, the corridor*   **viens voir** *come see*   **une vue** *a view*   **espérer** *(conjugated like* **préférer***) to hope*   **ça te plaît** *you like it*   **ça me plaît** *I like it*   **justement** *as a matter of fact, precisely, exactly*   **préféré(e)** *favorite*

You can find a list of the new words from CD 2-10 the vocabulary and grammar sections of this **Compétence** on page 139 and a recording of this list on track 2-10 of your *Text Audio CD.*

Pour vérifier

1. How do you say *John's friend* and *Mary's car* in French?

2. With which two forms of the definite article does **de** combine to form the contractions **du** and **des**?

3. How do you say *my*? How do you say *your* (singular familiar)? What are the forms of each word?

4. When do you use **mon, ton,** and **son,** instead of **ma, ta,** and **sa** before a feminine noun?

5. Does French have different words for *his, her,* and *its*? How do you say *his house* and *her house* in French? How do you say *his dog* and *her dog*?

To download a podcast on Possessives, go to **academic.cengage.com/french.**

Identifying your belongings

La possession et les adjectifs possessifs **mon, ton** *et* **son**

In French, use a phrase with **de,** rather than *'s* to indicate possession or relationship.

There is Thomas's room.	Voilà la chambre **de** Thomas.
That's Claude's dog.	C'est le chien **de** Claude.

Remember that **de** contracts with the articles **le** and **les** to form **du** and **des.** It does not change when followed by **la** or **l'.**

le livre **du** professeur	les livres **des** étudiants
la porte **de l'**appartement	la porte **de la** cuisine

The possessive adjectives **mon/ma/mes** *(my),* **ton/ta/tes** *(your* [singular familiar]*),* and **son/sa/ses** *(his, her, its)* agree in gender and number with the noun they precede. However, use the masculine form before feminine singular nouns that begin with a vowel sound.

	MASCULINE SINGULAR	FEMININE SINGULAR *(plus consonant sound)*	FEMININE SINGULAR *(plus vowel sound)*	PLURAL
my	**mon** lit	**ma** commode	**mon** affiche	**mes** rideaux
your	**ton** lit	**ta** commode	**ton** affiche	**tes** rideaux
his/her/its	**son** lit	**sa** commode	**son** affiche	**ses** rideaux

—C'est **la couverture de Thomas**?
—Non, ce n'est pas **sa** couverture. C'est **ma** couverture. Et ce sont **mes** rideaux aussi.

The use of the forms **son/sa/ses** *(his, her, its)* depends on the gender and number of the object possessed, not the person who owns it. **Son/sa/ses** can all mean *his, her,* or *its.*

C'est **son** fauteuil.

C'est **son** fauteuil.

Et c'est **son** fauteuil aussi.

A. Compliments. Une amie vous montre *(is showing you)* sa maison. Faites un compliment avec la phrase la plus logique.

> **EXEMPLE** maison (jolie, laide)
> **Ta maison est jolie.**

1. bureau (en désordre, en ordre)
2. tapis (beau, laid)
3. chambre (désagréable, agréable)
4. maison (grande, petite)
5. affiches (intéressantes, ennuyeuses)
6. placards (trop petits, immenses)
7. étagère (en désordre, bien rangée)
8. chien (beau, laid)

B. De quelle couleur? Demandez à votre partenaire de quelle couleur sont ces choses. Utilisez **ton, ta** ou **tes.**

EXEMPLE   voiture
—**De quelle couleur est ta voiture?**
—**Ma voiture est grise. / Je n'ai pas de voiture.**

chambre   canapé   couverture   tapis   rideaux   vêtements préférés   portable

Maintenant, décrivez les affaires *(belongings)* de votre partenaire à la classe.

EXEMPLE   **Sa voiture est grise. / Il/Elle n'a pas de voiture.**

C. C'est à moi! Un locataire change d'appartement et il voudrait tout prendre avec lui *(him)* mais l'autre locataire n'est pas d'accord. Jouez les rôles avec un(e) partenaire.

EXEMPLE   la plante
—**Bon, je prends *(I'm taking)* ma plante.**
—**Ah non, ce n'est pas ta plante. C'est ma plante!**

1. le bureau
2. les rideaux
3. le tapis
4. l'affiche
5. la commode
6. le fauteuil
7. l'étagère
8. le lecteur CD
9. les animaux

D. La chambre de qui? Complétez chaque phrase avec **son, sa** ou **ses** et dites si la phrase décrit la chambre de Robert ou la chambre de Claude.

EXEMPLE   <u>Sa</u> chambre est en ordre.
La chambre de Robert est en ordre.

la chambre de Robert

1. _____ tapis est jaune.
2. _____ rideaux sont gris.
3. _____ vélo est rouge.
4. _____ couverture est verte.
5. _____ murs sont blancs.
6. Il n'y a pas d'affiches dans _____ chambre.
7. Beaucoup de _____ affaires *(belongings)* sont par terre.
8. Il y a un livre rouge sous _____ bureau.
9. _____ chambre est propre.
10. _____ chambre est un peu sale.

la chambre de Claude

E. Comparaisons. Regardez bien les illustrations de l'activité **D. La chambre de qui?** Fermez votre livre et travaillez en groupe pour comparer de mémoire la chambre de Robert et la chambre de Claude. Le groupe qui trouve le plus grand nombre de comparaisons correctes gagne.

EXEMPLE   **Les murs de Robert sont blancs mais les murs de Claude sont gris. Le bureau de Robert est devant sa fenêtre et...**

Indicating to whom something belongs

*Les adjectifs possessifs **notre**, **votre** et **leur***

The possessive adjectives for *our, your* (formal or plural), and *their* have only two forms, singular and plural.

	MASCULINE SINGULAR	FEMININE SINGULAR *(plus consonant sound)*	FEMININE SINGULAR *(plus vowel sound)*	PLURAL
my	**mon** lit	**ma** chambre	**mon** amie	**mes** livres
your (sing. fam.)	**ton** lit	**ta** chambre	**ton** amie	**tes** livres
his, her, its	**son** lit	**sa** chambre	**son** amie	**ses** livres
our	**notre** lit	**notre** chambre	**notre** amie	**nos** livres
your (form./pl.)	**votre** lit	**votre** chambre	**votre** amie	**vos** livres
their	**leur** lit	**leur** chambre	**leur** amie	**leurs** livres

CD 2-11

Prononciation

*La voyelle **o** de **notre** / **votre** et de **nos** / **vos***

Compare the **o** sounds in **notre** / **votre** and **nos** / **vos.** The lips are puckered to make both of these sounds and the tongue is held firm, but the **o** in **nos** / **vos** is pronounced with the back of the tongue arched higher in the mouth than for the **o** in **notre** and **votre.** The letter **o** is pronounced with the sound of **nos** when it is the last sound in a syllable, when it is followed by an **s,** or when it is written **ô.** Otherwise, it is pronounced with the more open sound of **notre.**

notre chien / nos chiens   votre chat / vos chats

A. Chez nous. Complétez les questions suivantes avec **votre** ou **vos.** Imaginez que deux amis voudraient persuader un troisième ami de partager leur appartement. Comment répondent-ils aux questions? Utilisez **notre** ou **nos** dans les réponses.

EXEMPLE   —**Votre** quartier est joli?
            —**Oui, notre quartier est très joli.**

1. _____ appartement est très cher?
2. _____ chiens sont méchants?
3. _____ cuisine est grande?
4. _____ parents passent beaucoup de temps à l'appartement?
5. _____ appartement a beaucoup de fenêtres?

B. Tu ou vous? Robert passe le week-end chez les parents de ses amis Patrick et Antoine Dupont et il veut savoir à qui chaque chose appartient *(wants to know to whom everything belongs).* Complétez ce qu'il dit avec **ton/ta/tes** ou **votre/vos**.

> **EXEMPLES** Patrick, c'est ___ vélo?   Mme Dupont, c'est ___ voiture?
> **Patrick, c'est ton vélo?**   **Mme Dupont, c'est votre voiture?**

1. Patrick et Antoine, c'est _____ maison? Ce sont _____ parents?
2. M. Dupont, c'est _____ garage? Ce sont _____ voitures?
3. M. et Mme Dupont, j'aime bien _____ quartier. Ce sont _____ voisins *(neighbors)*?
4. Patrick, c'est _____ chambre? Tu laisses souvent _____ vêtements par terre ou ils sont toujours dans _____ placard ou dans _____ commode?
5. M. et Mme Dupont, c'est _____ bureau? J'aime bien _____ étagère. Il y a de la place pour tous _____ livres.
6. Patrick et Antoine, c'est _____ salle de jeux. Où sont _____ jeux vidéo? Ah, voila... ça, Antoine, c'est _____ jeu préféré, non?

C. L'université Laval. Comparez votre université avec l'université Laval en complétant les phases avec **notre/nos** ou **leur/leurs.**

> **EXEMPLE** Fondée en 1852, l'université Laval est la première université francophone en Amérique.
> **Leur** université est plus vieille que **notre** université. / **Notre** université est plus vieille que **leur** université.

1. Il y a approximativement 38 000 étudiants à l'université Laval. _____ université est plus grande que _____ université.
2. Les frais de scolarité *(tuition)* sont de 909$ canadiens (= 777$ américains) par an *(per year).* _____ université est plus chère que _____ université.
3. Le semestre d'automne commence le 3 septembre à l'université Laval. _____ cours commencent avant _____ cours.
4. Il y a 10 000 places pour les voitures dans les parkings de l'université Laval. _____ parkings sont plus grands que _____ parkings.
5. L'université Laval est située à Québec, une ville de 718 000 habitants. _____ ville est plus grande que _____ ville.

D. Préférences. Aimez-vous ces choses? Utilisez **leur/leurs** ou **son/sa/ses** dans vos réponses.

> **EXEMPLES** les vieux films avec Fred Astaire et Ginger Rogers
> **J'aime bien leurs films.**
>
> les vieux films d'Alfred Hitchcock
> **Je n'aime pas beaucoup ses films.**

L'université Laval

1. les films de Steven Spielberg
2. les vieux films avec les «Three Stooges»
3. la musique des Beatles
4. la musique de Jennifer Lopez
5. les CD des Dixie Chicks
6. les CD de Sting

Giving your address and phone number

Des renseignements

Pour **s'inscrire** à l'université, Robert **doit** donner les **renseignements suivants.**

Quel est votre nom de famille?   Martin.
Quel est votre prénom?   Robert.
Quelle est votre adresse?   C'est le 215, Ursline St.
Quelle est votre (adresse) mail?   RobMart@airmail.net
Quel est votre numéro de téléphone?   C'est le (337) 988–1284.
Dans quel pays habitez-vous?   Les États-Unis.
Quel état? (Quelle province?)   La Louisiane.
Quelle ville?   Lafayette.
Quelle est votre nationalité?   Américaine.

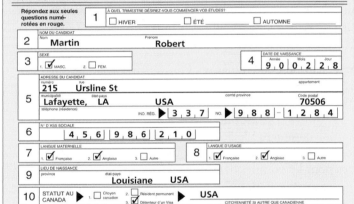

 Robert parle de son appartement et son ami Alain lui **pose des questions.**

CD 2-12

ALAIN: Quelle est ton adresse?
ROBERT: C'est le 38, **rue** Dauphine.
ALAIN: Et c'est quel appartement?
ROBERT: C'est l'appartement numéro 231.
ALAIN: Et le code postal?
ROBERT: G1K 7X2.
ALAIN: Quel est ton numéro de téléphone?
ROBERT: C'est le 692-2691.
ALAIN: Et comment est le quartier?
ROBERT: Il est agréable et près de tout.
ALAIN: L'appartement n'est pas trop cher? C'est combien, le loyer?
ROBERT: Je partage mon appartement avec deux amis, Thomas et Claude. C'est 825 dollars par mois, partagés entre nous trois. Alors pour moi, ça fait 275 dollars.

s'inscrire *to register*   **doit (devoir** *must, to have to)*   **les renseignements** *(m) information*   **suivant(e)** *following*
poser une question *to ask a question*   **une rue** *a street*

A. Et Thomas? Quels renseignements est-ce que Thomas donne?

EXEMPLE Bertrand
C'est son nom de famille.

1. Thomas
2. Québec
3. le Québec
4. le Canada
5. le 38, rue Dauphine
6. G1K 7X2
7. le 692–2691
8. Thomas1@homemail.com
9. 825$ par mois

❋ Note *de vocabulaire*

In French, the province is **le Québec** and the city, **Québec.** When people say **J'habite au Québec,** they are talking about the province. When they say **J'habite à Québec,** they are talking about the city.

B. Et vous? Répondez aux questions suivantes.

1. Quel est votre nom de famille? Quel est votre prénom?
2. Quelle est votre adresse? Vous habitez dans quelle ville? Quel est votre code postal?
3. Quel est votre numéro de téléphone? Quelle est votre (adresse) mail?
4. Quelle est votre nationalité?

C. Un abonnement. Vous vendez des abonnements *(are selling subscriptions)* pour la revue *Brune.* Demandez les renseignements nécessaires pour compléter le formulaire d'abonnement à plusieurs camarades de classe.

EXEMPLE — **Quel est ton nom de famille?**
— **Mon nom de famille? C'est Sodji.**

You can find a list of the new words from
CD 2-13 the vocabulary and grammar sections of this ***Compétence*** on page 139 and a recording of this list on track 2-13 of your *Text Audio CD.*

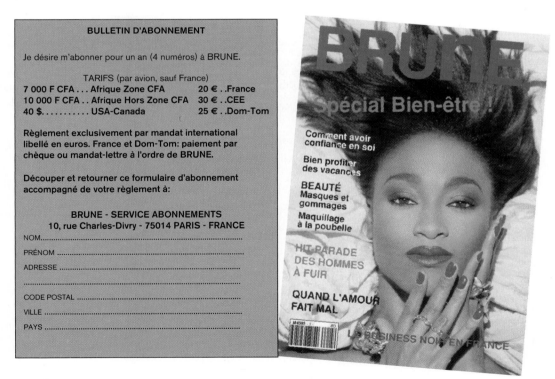

BULLETIN D'ABONNEMENT

Je désire m'abonner pour un an (4 numéros) à BRUNE.

TARIFS (par avion, sauf France)
7 000 F CFA . . . Afrique Zone CFA   20 € . .France
10 000 F CFA . . Afrique Hors Zone CFA   30 € . .CEE
40 $. . . . . USA-Canada   25 € . .Dom-Tom

Règlement exclusivement par mandat international libellé en euros. France et Dom-Tom: paiement par chèque ou mandat-lettre à l'ordre de BRUNE.

Découper et retourner ce formulaire d'abonnement accompagné de votre règlement à:

BRUNE - SERVICE ABONNEMENTS
10, rue Charles-Divry - 75014 PARIS - FRANCE

NOM...

PRÉNOM ....

ADRESSE ....
....

CODE POSTAL ....

VILLE ....

PAYS ....

D. Conversation. Avec un(e) partenaire, relisez à haute voix la conversation entre Robert et son ami à la page précédente. Ensuite, changez la conversation pour décrire votre propre situation.

Pour vérifier

1. When do you use **quel** to say *what*? When do you use **qu'est-ce que** or **que**? What are the four forms of **quel**?

2. How do you say *this*, *that*, *these*, and *those*? When do you use the alternate masculine form **cet**?

✳ Note *de vocabulaire*

Quel followed by a noun is also used as an exclamation. It is most often the equivalent of *What . . . !* or *What a . . . !* in English.

Quelle belle maison!	*What a pretty house!*
Quels chiens embêtants!	*What annoying dogs!*
Quelle chance!	*What luck!*

✳ Note *de vocabulaire*

If you need to distinguish *this* from *that*, you can add the suffixes **-ci** and **-là** to the noun.

ce livre-ci *this book*
ces maisons-là *those houses*

Telling which one

Les adjectifs **quel** *et* **ce**

To say *which* or *what* before a noun, use **quel.** The form you use depends on the gender and number of the noun.

	MASCULINE	FEMININE
SINGULAR	quel	quelle
PLURAL	quels	quelles

Vous habitez dans **quel pays**?   Vous êtes de **quelle ville**?

Quels pays voudriez-vous visiter?   **Quelles villes** voudriez-vous voir?

Quel may be separated from the noun by **est** or **sont,** but it still agrees with the noun.

Quel est votre **nom de famille**?   **Quelle** est votre **adresse**?

Remember to use **qu'est-ce que** or **que** to say *what* when it is the object of the verb. They are followed by a subject and a verb.

Qu'est-ce que Robert aime faire?   **Que** voudrais-tu faire ce soir?

To point out which item or person you are talking about, use the adjective **ce (cet)/cette/ces** to say both *this/these* and *that/those.* The masculine **ce** becomes **cet** before masculine singular nouns beginning with a vowel sound. Use **ces** with all plural nouns.

Tu aimes **cette** voiture?
Do you like this car?

	SINGULAR	PLURAL
MASCULINE (plus consonant sound)	ce canapé	ces canapés
MASCULINE (plus vowel sound)	cet appartement	ces appartements
FEMININE	cette étagère	ces étagères

CD 2-14

Prononciation

La voyelle **e** *de* **ce/cet/cette/ces**

You already know that a final **e** is usually not pronounced in French, except in short words like **je.** As you notice in **ce/cet/cette/ces,** unaccented **e** has three different pronunciations, depending on what follows it.

In short words like **ce** and **que,** or when **e** is followed by a single consonant within a word, pronounce it as in:

je   ne   le   regarde   vendredi

When, as in **ces, e** is followed by an unpronounced consonant at the end of a word, pronounce it as in:

les   mes   parlez   manger   premier

In words like **cette** and **cet,** where **e** is followed by two consonants within a word, or a single pronounced consonant at the end of a word, pronounce it as in:

quel   cher   belle   elle   cherche

A. Entretien. Complétez les questions suivantes avec la forme convenable de **quel** ou avec **qu'est-ce que.** Ensuite, posez les questions à votre partenaire.

1. _____ il y a dans ta chambre?
2. Dans _____ pièce est-ce que tu passes le plus de temps?
3. _____ tu voudrais acheter *(to buy)* pour ton salon ou pour ta chambre?
4. Dans _____ rue est-ce que tu habites?
5. Ta chambre est à _____ étage?
6. De _____ couleur sont les murs de ta chambre?
7. _____ tu voudrais changer chez toi?

B. Goûts. Demandez à un(e) camarade de classe s'il / si elle aime ces choses.

> **EXEMPLE** maison
> — **Tu aimes cette maison?**
> — **Oui, j'aime bien cette maison. / Non, je n'aime pas cette maison.**

EXEMPLE maison

1. canapé

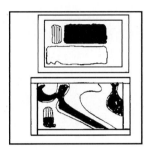

2. tableaux

3. escalier

4. appartements

5. étagère

6. maisons

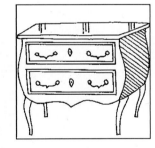

7. commode

C. Préférences. Demandez à votre partenaire quelles sont ses préférences. Après, donnez votre réaction à sa réponse en utilisant **ce, cet, cette** ou **ces.** *(If you aren't familiar with what he/she names, say* **Je ne connais pas...** *)*

> **EXEMPLE** son restaurant préféré
> — **Quel est ton restaurant préféré?**
> — **J'aime beaucoup Pizza Nizza.**
> — **Moi aussi, j'aime beaucoup ce restaurant. / Moi, je n'aime pas ce restaurant. / Je ne connais pas ce restaurant.**

1. sa librairie préférée
2. son livre préféré
3. son acteur préféré
4. son actrice préférée
5. ses films préférés
6. ses voitures préférées

Reprise

Saying where you live and what you have

In **Chapitre 3,** you learned to talk about your belongings and where you live. Now you have a chance to review what you learned.

A. Quelques questions. D'abord, complétez les questions avec **de, d', du, de la, de l'** ou **des.** Ensuite, posez les questions à votre partenaire.

1. Est-ce que tu habites près ou loin _____ centre-ville?
2. Tu habites près _____ université?
3. Y a-t-il un arrêt d'autobus près _____ chez toi?
4. Qu'est-ce qu'il y a en face _____ chez toi?
5. Est-ce que ta chambre est près _____ cuisine?
6. Dans ta chambre, qu'est-ce qu'il y a en face _____ lit?
7. Dans le salon, qu'est-ce qu'il y a en face _____ télé?

B. Une maison. Dites où les choses suivantes sont l'une par rapport à l'autre *(in relationship to each other)*. Suivez l'exemple.

> **EXEMPLE**   le salon / les toilettes
> **Le salon est à gauche des toilettes.**

1. le salon / la cuisine et les toilettes
2. la salle de bains / la chambre
3. le canapé / le salon
4. la lampe / le fauteuil
5. le fauteuil / l'escalier
6. la salle à manger / la cuisine
7. la table / la salle à manger
8. la table / le tapis

Maintenant, travaillez avec un(e) partenaire pour continuer la description de la maison.

> **EXEMPLE**   C'est une grande maison. Au rez-de-chaussée, il y a... Dans le salon...

C. Qu'est-ce que vous avez? Complétez les phrases suivantes avec le verbe **avoir** dans le premier blanc et un adjectif possessif dans le deuxième.

EXEMPLE   J'**ai** un portable. **Mon** numéro de téléphone, c'est le 825–5479.

1. J'_____ un appartement au centre-ville. _____ adresse, c'est le 202, rue Voltaire.
2. Nous _____ beaucoup de restaurants dans _____ quartier.
3. Mes parents _____ une maison en banlieue. _____ jardin *(yard)* est très joli.
4. Mon meilleur ami (Ma meilleure amie) _____ un grand appartement très élégant. _____ loyer est de plus de mille dollars par mois.
5. J'_____ un appartement dans un quartier très agréable. _____ rue est très jolie.
6. Mon meilleur ami (Ma meilleure amie) _____ une belle voiture. _____ voiture est bleue.
7. À l'université, nous n'_____ pas beaucoup de parkings pour _____ voitures.

Maintenant, changez les phrases pour décrire votre situation ou celle de *(that of)* vos amis.

D. C'est combien?   Vous cherchez du mobilier *(furnishings)* dans les petites annonces *(classified ads)* au Québec. Donnez le prix de chaque objet comme dans l'exemple. Utilisez **ce, cet, cette** ou **ces**.

EXEMPLE

> MOBILIER CUISINE:
> table, 6 chaises 450$.
> Tél: 678-2665.

Cette table et ces chaises coûtent *(cost)* quatre cent cinquante dollars.

1. TABLE SALLE À MANGER, laquée noire, 6 chaises laquées noires. Très propres. 1 150$. Tél: 760-7883.

2. MOBILIER salon fleuri (fauteuil, canapé) 550$. Tél: 842-5835.

3. TÉLÉ 48", Sony, état neuf 700$. Tél: 881-9896.

4. LIT D'EAU "king" complet: base, lit en pin, matelas anti-vagues, éléments chauffants. Le tout en très bon état, 150$. Tél: 653-5216.

5. TABLE D'ORDINATEUR: blanche, 3 tiroirs, en bon état, 115$. Tél: 832-7175.

6. FAUTEUIL en cuir noir. Excellente condition. 495$. Tél: 542-7060.

Rue résidentielle au Québec

Lecture et Composition

Lecture

⚘ Pour mieux lire: *Previewing content*

Looking at the title of an article and thinking about what you know or think about the topic can help you anticipate its content and read it more easily. You are going to read an article by an interior decorator in Quebec about how colors can change your moods. Before you begin to read, look at the title of the article that follows. What is it about? What feelings do you associate with the following colors?

le rouge   le jaune   le rose   le noir   le bleu   le blanc

Associations. Quelle couleur associez-vous le plus aux choses suivantes?

1. la passion
2. la dépression
3. la concentration
4. l'énergie
5. la relaxation
6. la pureté
7. l'appétit
8. l'irritation

Les couleurs et leurs effets sur la nature humaine

Les couleurs changent nos **humeurs** et par conséquent reflètent notre personnalité. **Pour mieux vous faire connaître** les effets qu'ont les couleurs sur la nature humaine, nous avons préparé un guide qui va vous aider à choisir les couleurs pour votre maison ou appartement.

Les couleurs chaudes: le rouge et le jaune.
Le rouge stimule le métabolisme, le rythme cardiaque et la température **corporelle.** Le rouge est **perçu comme** une couleur agressive, **forte,** vitale et passionnante. **Puisque** c'est une couleur qui stimule l'appétit, le rouge est souvent utilisé pour les salles à manger et les restaurants.

Le jaune stimule la mémoire, le mouvement, la coordination et le système digestif. Le jaune et le rouge sont considérés comme «énergiques». Mais **faites attention,** le jaune dans une chambre de bébé **peut rendre** l'enfant irritable.

Les couleurs froides: le bleu et le vert.
Le bleu encourage la concentration. Le rythme cardiaque et la respiration **ralentissent.** La température du **corps baisse.** Cette couleur est très recommandée dans un bureau.

Le vert augmente la relaxation. Le corps et **l'esprit se détendent** dans une atmosphère verte. Le vert diminue l'anxiété, **la peur** et **les cauchemars.** Le vert encourage le sentiment de bien-être. Il est **donc parfait** pour une chambre à coucher.

Les couleurs neutres: le blanc, le gris et le noir.
Le blanc stimule les fonctions vitales, par conséquent **le sommeil** n'est pas aussi **bénéfique** dans une chambre blanche. Le blanc est aussi associé à la pureté et à l'honnêteté.

Le gris incite à la dépression et à l'indifférence. Il est préférable de l'utiliser comme accent plutôt que couleur dominante dans votre décor.

Le noir est une couleur distincte, audacieuse et classique. Le noir est un fond idéal **pour faire ressortir** les autres couleurs, mais il peut être **étouffant** en trop grande quantité.

---

humeurs *moods*   **Pour mieux vous faire connaître** *To inform you better about*   **corporelle** *body*   **perçu comme** *perceived as*   **forte** *strong*   **Puisque** *Since*   **faites attention** *be careful*   **peut rendre** *can make*   **froides** *cold*   **ralentissent** *slow down*   **corps** *body*   **baisse** *lowers*   **l'esprit** *the mind*   **se détendent** *relax*   **la peur** *fear*   **les cauchemars** *nightmares*   **donc** *therefore*   **parfait** *perfect*   **le sommeil** *sleep*   **bénéfique** *beneficial*   **pour faire ressortir** *to make stand out*   **étouffant** *stifling*

Compréhension

Quelles couleurs? Complétez les phrases suivantes avec les couleurs appropriées d'après la lecture *Les couleurs et leurs effets sur la nature humaine*.

1. Si vous désirez manger moins, évitez *(avoid)* le _____ pour décorer votre salle à manger.

2. Pour mieux vous concentrer, étudiez dans une pièce _____ .

3. Si votre bébé pleure *(cries)* beaucoup, utilisez le _____ dans sa chambre et évitez le _____ .

4. Si vous désirez mieux dormir, les murs _____ ne sont pas recommandés dans votre chambre.

5. Si vous souffrez de dépression, évitez le _____ dans votre décor.

6. Si vous avez souvent froid *(feel cold)* chez vous, utilisez le _____ et évitez le _____ .

Composition

❀ Pour mieux écrire: *Brainstorming*

Brainstorming on a topic before you begin writing about it can simplify your task. To brainstorm, first think about what general sections you will want to include in your writing, then jot down as many notes for each section as you can. Finally, use these sections to organize your writing.

Organisez-vous. Imagine that you are responding to a roommate ad in Quebec. What would you want to know about the apartment and its occupant? Jot down as many words and phrases in French as you can under each heading in this chart, using a separate piece of paper.

location	rooms and furnishings	roommate's personality

Une lettre

You are moving to Quebec and respond to an ad for a roommate in the newspaper. Write a letter in which you introduce yourself and tell the sort of place you are looking for. Then, write three paragraphs asking about the apartment's location, the rooms and furnishings, and what the roommate is like. Begin the letter with **Cher monsieur / Chère madame / Chère mademoiselle.** End the letter with **En attendant votre réponse,** and sign your name.

SYSTÈME-D

If you have access to SYSTÈME-D software, you will find the following phrases, vocabulary, grammar, and dictionary aids there.

Phrases: Writing a letter; Introducing; Describing people; Asking for information

Vocabulary: House; Rooms; Furniture; Kitchen; Living room; Bedroom; Personality; Numbers; Direction and distance; Money

Grammar: Possessive adjectives; Demonstrative adjectives; Interrogative adjective

Dictionary: The verb **avoir**

Le Québec d'aujourd'hui

Grâce à son histoire, à sa langue et à **ses coutumes,** le Québec est, **à bien des égards,** une société distincte à l'intérieur du Canada. Dans cette province, **la seule** où le français est **l'unique** langue officielle, 83% de la population parle français à la maison, 10% parle anglais et 6% parle d'autres langues.

Pour comprendre la culture québécoise, **il faut connaître** un peu son histoire.

Au 16ᵉ siècle, les Français et les Anglais **ont commencé** à coloniser le Canada. Les Français **se sont établis** au Québec et dans **la partie est du** Canada. La majorité des francophones québécois d'aujourd'hui sont les descendants de ces premiers **colons** français. Les Britanniques se sont établis dans d'autres parties du Canada. **Certains** anglophones québécois d'aujourd'hui sont les descendants de ces premiers colons. Beaucoup d'autres sont des **immigrés** ou les descendants d'immigrés britanniques ou d'immigrés d'autres pays.

Jacques Cartier, explorateur français

Au cours du 17ᵉ et du 18ᵉ siècles, les Français et les Anglais **se sont battus** pour le contrôle du Canada. En 1763, la France a cédé ses territoires canadiens aux Anglais et pendant 200 **ans,** les Québécois **ont vécu** sous la domination de la minorité anglophone.

Grâce à *Thanks to*   **ses coutumes** *its customs*   **à bien des égards** *in many regards*   **la seule** *the only one*   **l'unique** *the only*   **il faut connaître** *it is necessary to know*
Au 16ᵉ siècle *In the 16ᵗʰ century*   **ont commencé** *began*   **se sont établis** *established themselves*   **la partie est du** *the eastern part of*   **colons** *colonists*   **Certains** *Some*
immigrés *immigrants*   **Au cours du 17ᵉ et du 18ᵉ siècles** *In the course of the 17ᵗʰ and 18ᵗʰ centuries*   **se sont battus** *battled*   **ans** *years*   **ont vécu** *lived*

Pendant les années 60, un mouvement pour la préservation de la francophonie a commencé et plusieurs mesures **ont été mises en place** pour la protection de l'identité québécoise.

Plus de 700 000 immigrés **venant** d'Europe, d'Asie, d'Afrique et des Amériques habitent au Québec et plus de 35 000 **viennent s'y établir chaque année.** Cette immigration **a eu** une forte influence sur l'identité québécoise.

Fier de ses racines et de ses traditions, le Québec d'aujourd'hui est une société francophone qui **s'inspire de** la culture franco-européenne **aussi bien que de** la culture anglo-américaine. Mais c'est aussi une société multi-ethnique qui **s'ouvre aux contributions que lui apportent ses peuples indigènes** (les Inuits et les Amérindiens) et ses immigrés venant de partout dans **le monde.**

Source: www.gouv.qc.ca

Comprehénsion

 Visit **academic.cengage.com/french** for YouTube video cultural correlations, cultural information and activities.

1. Au Québec, 83% de la population parle _____, 10% parle _____ et 6% parle d'_____. Quelle est la situation linguistique dans votre région?

2. Au cours du 17ᵉ et du 18ᵉ siècles, les _____ et les _____ se sont battus pour le contrôle du Canada. En 1763, les _____ ont gagné la guerre *(won the war)*. Comment est-ce que l'histoire de votre région a influencé sa situation linguistique?

3. Le Québec d'aujourd'hui est une société francophone qui s'inspire de la culture _____ aussi bien que de la culture _____. Mais c'est aussi une société multi-ethnique qui s'ouvre aux contributions que lui apportent ses peuples _____ et ses _____ venant de toutes les parties du monde. Quelles cultures ont influencé votre société?

Pendant les années 60 *During the sixties* **ont été mises en place** *were put in place* **venant** *coming from* **viennent s'y établir chaque année** *come settle there each year* **a eu** *has had* **Fier de ses racines** *Proud of its roots* **s'inspire de** *is inspired by* **aussi bien que de** *as well as by* **s'ouvre aux contributions que lui apportent ses peuples indigènes** *is open to the contributions brought to it by its indigenous peoples* **le monde** *the world*

Résumé de grammaire

cent = *one hundred*
mille = *one thousand*
un million = *one million*
un million d'habitants

300	trois cents
301	trois cent un
3 000	trois mille
3 100 000	trois millions cent mille

Ma rue, c'est la première (deuxième, troisième, quatrième, cinquième, sixième, septième, huitième, neuvième, dixième, onzième...) rue à droite.

—J'**ai** un appartement. Et toi? Tu **as** une maison?
—Ma famille **a** une petite maison. J'habite chez mes parents.

—Tu as **des** chats, non?
—Non, ce ne sont pas **des** chats. J'ai **des** chiens.
—Combien **de** chiens as-tu?
—Quatre.
—Tu n'as pas **de** problèmes avec tes colocataires?
—Non, je n'ai pas **de** colocataire.

un tableau → des tableaux
un bureau → des bureaux
un animal → des animaux

Je rentre **de** l'université à cinq heures.

Ma résidence est **près d'**ici, **derrière** la bibliothèque et **à côté de** la librairie.

Numbers above 100

- Use **un** in **un million,** but not before the words **cent** and **mille.** The word **million(s)** is followed by **de (d')** when followed directly by a noun.
- **Million** takes an **s** when plural. **Cent** generally only takes an **s** when plural if not followed by another number. Never add an **s** to **mille.**
- There is no hyphen between the words **cent, mille,** or **million** and another number.
- Use commas to denote decimals, and spaces or periods to set off numbers in the thousands, millions, etc.

Ordinal numbers

Use **premier (première)** to say *first.* To form the other ordinal numbers *(second, third, fourth . . .),* add the suffix **-ième** to the cardinal numbers **(deux, trois, quatre...).** Drop the final **-e** of cardinal numbers before adding **-ième.** Note the spelling changes in **cinquième** *(fifth)* and **neuvième** *(ninth).*

Avoir

The verb **avoir** *(to have)* is irregular.

j'	**ai**	nous	**avons**
tu	**as**	vous	**avez**
il/elle	**a**	ils/elles	**ont**

Un, une, des → de (d')

Use **de (d')** rather than **un, une,** or **des** after . . .

- most negated verbs, except **être.**
- quantity expressions like **combien, beaucoup,** and **assez.**

Plurals ending with -x

In the plural, most words ending in **-eau, -au,** or **-eu** have **-x** rather than **-s,** and the ending **-al** becomes **-aux.**

Prepositions

When used alone, the preposition **de** means *of, from,* or *about.* **De** is also used in some of the following prepositions.

sur	*on*	**près (de)**	*near*
sous	*under*	**loin (de)**	*far (from)*
entre	*between*	**à côté (de)**	*next to, beside*
dans	*in*	**à droite / gauche (de)**	*to the right / left (of)*
devant	*in front of*	**en face (de)**	*across (from), facing*
derrière	*behind*	**dans le coin (de)**	*in the corner (of)*

De contracts with the articles **le** and **les,** but not with **la** or **l'.**

CONTRACTION:			NO CONTRACTION:		
de + le	→	du	de + la	→	de la
de + les	→	des	de + l'	→	de l'

Je n'aime pas habiter à la résidence parce qu'elle est loin **du** parking et ma chambre est en face **des** ascenseurs, à côté **de l'**escalier et loin **de la** salle de bains!

Possession

De is used instead of *'s* to indicate possession. Remember the contractions **de + le → du** and **de + les → des.**

le bureau du professeur	*the professor's office*
la voiture de mon frère	*my brother's car*

The possessive adjectives also indicate possession.

	MASCULINE SINGULAR	FEMININE SINGULAR *(+ consonant sound)*	FEMININE SINGULAR *(+ vowel sound)*	PLURAL
my	**mon** vélo	**ma** voiture	**mon** adresse	**mes** meubles
your (sing. fam.)	**ton** vélo	**ta** voiture	**ton** adresse	**tes** meubles
his/her/its	**son** vélo	**sa** voiture	**son** adresse	**ses** meubles
our	**notre** vélo	**notre** voiture	**notre** adresse	**nos** meubles
your (form./pl.)	**votre** vélo	**votre** voiture	**votre** adresse	**vos** meubles
their	**leur** vélo	**leur** voiture	**leur** adresse	**leurs** meubles

Use the forms **mon, ton,** and **son** rather than **ma, ta,** and **sa** before feminine nouns beginning with vowel sounds.

The use of the forms **son/sa/ses** *(his, her, its)* depends on the gender and number of the object possessed, not the person who owns it. **Son/sa/ses** can all mean *his, her,* or *its.*

— C'est ta voiture?
— Non, c'est la voiture **de** mon amie.

— C'est la porte **de la** salle de bains?
— Non, c'est la porte **du** placard.

— Tu habites encore chez **tes** parents?
— Non, j'habite chez **mon** frère.
— Où est **sa** maison?
— Pas loin de chez **nos** parents.
— Dans quelle rue est la maison de **vos** parents?
— **Leur** maison est dans la rue Martin.

Mon amie s'appelle Monique.

son quartier = *his/her/its neighborhood*
sa porte = *his/her/its door*
ses murs = *his/her/its walls*

Quel/quelle/quels/quelles and *ce (cet)/cette/ces*

Use **quel/quelle/quels/quelles** to say *which* or *what* directly before a noun or the verbs **est** and **sont.** It agrees with the gender and number of the noun it modifies.

	MASCULINE	FEMININE
SINGULAR	quel état	quelle ville
PLURAL	quels états	quelles villes

Use the demonstrative adjective **ce (cet)/cette/ces** to say both *this/these* and *that/those.* The masculine **ce** becomes **cet** before masculine singular nouns beginning with a vowel sound.

	SINGULAR	PLURAL
MASCULINE (+ consonant sound)	ce chien	ces chiens
MASCULINE (+ vowel sound)	cet animal	ces animaux
FEMININE	cette étagère	ces étagères

— Dans **quelle** ville habites-tu?
— J'habite à Sherbrooke.
— **Quelle** est ton adresse?
— C'est le 1202, rue Galt.
— **Quel** est ton numéro de téléphone?
— C'est le (819) 569–1208.

— Tu habites dans **cette** rue?
— Oui, j'aime beaucoup **ce** quartier. Mon appartement est dans **cet** immeuble.
— Mon appartement est derrière **ces** arbres.

CD2

Vocabulaire

Talking about where you live

NOMS MASCULINS

un appartement	an apartment
un arrêt d'autobus	a bus stop
un ascenseur	an elevator
le centre-ville	downtown
un dollar	a dollar
un escalier	stairs, a staircase
un étage	a floor
un immeuble	an apartment building
le logement	lodging, housing
le loyer	the rent
le rez-de-chaussée	the ground floor
un salon	a living room
le sous-sol	the basement

NOMS FÉMININS

la banlieue	the suburbs
la campagne	the country(side)
une chambre	a bedroom
une cuisine	a kitchen
une fenêtre	a window
une maison	a house
une pièce	a room
une porte	a door
une salle à manger	a dining room
une salle de bains	a bathroom
des toilettes	a restroom, a toilet
une ville	a city

ADJECTIFS

cher (chère)	expensive
commode	convenient
confortable	comfortable

DIVERS

à la campagne	in the country
à la résidence universitaire	in the university dorm
À quel étage?	On what floor?
au sous-sol	in the basement
au rez-de-chaussée	on the ground floor
au premier (deuxième...) étage	on the second (third . . .) floor
au centre-ville	downtown
cent	a/one hundred
en banlieue	in the suburbs
en ville	in town
Je n'ai pas de...	I don't have . . .
loin (de)	far (from)
mille	a/one thousand
un million (de)	a/one million
par mois	per month
(tout) près (de)	(very) near
trop	too (much)
va	is going, goes

Pour les nombres ordinaux, voir la page 110.

Talking about your possessions

NOMS MASCULINS

un animal (*pl* des animaux)	an animal
un canapé	a couch
un CD	a CD
un chat	a cat
un chien	a dog
un DVD	a DVD
des effets personnels	personal belongings
un fauteuil	an armchair
un iPod	an iPod
un lecteur CD/DVD	a CD/DVD player
un ordinateur	a computer
un portable	a laptop, a cell phone
un tableau	a painting
un tapis	a rug
un vélo	a bicycle
des vêtements	clothes

NOMS FÉMININS

une chaîne hi-fi	a stereo
une chaise	a chair
une chose	a thing
une lampe	a lamp
une plante	a plant
une table	a table
une télé	a TV
une voiture	a car

PRÉPOSITIONS

à côté (de)	next to, beside
à droite (de)	to the right (of)
à gauche (de)	to the left (of)
dans	in
dans le coin (de)	in the corner (of)
de	of, from, about
derrière	behind
devant	in front of
en face (de)	across from, facing
entre	between
sous	under
sur	on

VERBES

arriver	to arrive
avoir	to have
chercher	to look for
fumer	to smoke
partager	to share
téléphoner (à)	to phone

DIVERS

combien (de)	how many, how much
embêtant(e)	annoying
en ordre	in order, orderly
non plus	neither
partout	everywhere
Pas de problème.	No problem.
peut-être	maybe, perhaps
bien rangé(e)	orderly, put away, in its place
ton/ta/tes	your (sing. fam.)
tout	everything, all

Describing your room

NOMS MASCULINS

un adjectif	an adjective
un bureau (*pl* des bureaux)	a desk
un couloir	a hall, a corridor
un lit	a bed
des meubles	furniture, furnishings
un mur	a wall
un placard	a closet
un rideau (*pl* des rideaux)	a curtain

NOMS FÉMININS

une affiche	a poster
une commode	a dresser, a chest of drawers
une couleur	a color
une couverture	a cover, a blanket
une étagère	a bookcase, a shelf
une vue	a view

ADJECTIFS POSSESSIFS

mon/ma/mes	my
ton/ta/tes	your
son/sa/ses	his, her, its
notre/nos	our
votre/vos	your
leur/leurs	their

EXPRESSIONS VERBALES

Ça te plaît. / Ça me plaît.	You like it. / I like it.
comme tu vois	as you see
espérer	to hope
indiquer	to indicate
laisser	to leave
montrer	to show
Viens voir!	Come see!

LES COULEURS

De quelle couleur est... ?	What color is . . . ?
De quelle couleur sont... ?	What color are . . . ?
beige	beige
blanc(he)	white
bleu(e)	blue
gris(e)	gray
jaune	yellow
marron	brown
noir(e)	black
orange	orange
rose	pink
rouge	red
vert(e)	green
violet(te)	purple

DIVERS

à sa place	in its place
au bout (de)	at the end (of)
chaque	each
en désordre	in disorder, disorderly
justement	as a matter of fact, precisely, exactly
par terre	on the floor, on the ground
préféré(e)	favorite
propre	clean
sale	dirty

Giving your address and phone number

NOMS MASCULINS

un code postal	a zip code
un état	a state
les États-Unis	the United States
un nom (de famille)	a (sur/last)name, a noun
un numéro de téléphone	a telephone number
un pays	a country
un prénom	a first name
des renseignements	information

NOMS FÉMININS

une adresse (mail)	an (e-mail) address
la Louisiane	Louisiana
une nationalité	a nationality
une province	a province
une rue	a street

DIVERS

ce (cet)/cette	this, that
ces	these, those
il/elle doit...	he/she must . . .
partagé(e)	shared, divided
poser une question	to ask a question
quel/quelle/quels/quelles	which, what
s'inscrire	to register
suivant(e)	following

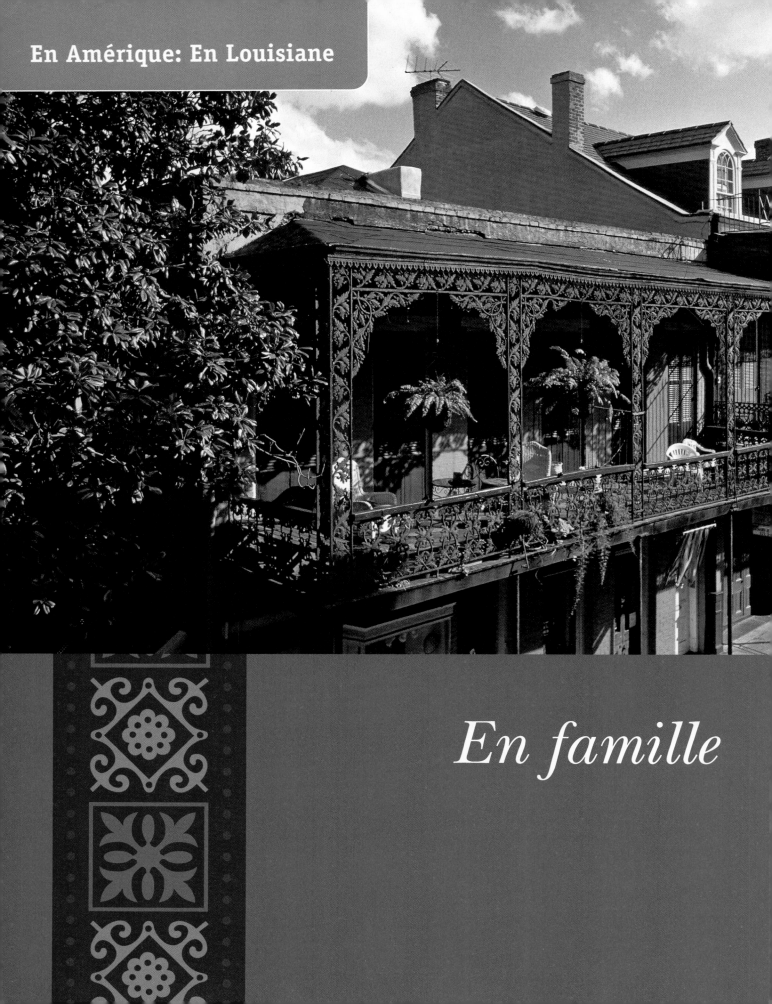

En famille

Chapitre 4

iLrn iLrn Heinle Learning Center

academic.cengage.com/french/horizons

Système-D

Audio   iRadio

Expand your knowledge of aspects of Creole and Cajun culture by searching the Web for **1.** a brief history of **le Vieux Carré** in New Orleans and a brief history of the Acadiana region, as well as points of interest in each place **2.** the ingredients of the Cajun dishes mentioned on p. 143 and other aspects of Cajun cuisine **3.** a brief history of zydeco music and its major artists.

Quand vous pensez à la Louisiane francophone, pensez-vous à la tradition créole et à La Nouvelle-Orléans avec son **Vieux Carré** et son célèbre Mardi gras? Ou pensez-vous **plutôt** à la culture cadienne et à sa fameuse musique et à sa délicieuse cuisine?

Les origines des francophones en Louisiane sont **nombreuses** et variées. Les plus grands groupes culturels sont **les Cadiens** et les Créoles. Les Cadiens d'aujourd'hui sont les descendants des **Acadiens expulsés du** Canada par les Anglais **au 18ᵉ siècle.** Les Créoles sont les descendants des résidents de Louisiane avant son annexion par les États-Unis en 1803. Les Créoles sont principalement d'origines française, africaine et espagnole.

La Nouvelle-Orléans est célèbre pour son Vieux Carré.

La Nouvelle-Orléans est **au cœur de** la région créole. La région cadienne, l'Acadiana, **comprend 22 paroisses** dans **la partie sud** de la Louisiane. Lafayette est au cœur de cette région.

La Nouvelle-Orléans

Lafayette

Le Village Acadien près de Lafayette **met en scène la vie quotidienne** des Acadiens dans **le passé.**

Le Mardi gras à La Nouvelle-Orléans est **connu dans le monde entier.**

le Vieux Carré *the French Quarter*   **plutôt** *instead, rather*   **nombreuses** *numerous*   **les Cadiens,** *the Cajuns*   **les Acadiens** *the Acadians (the first French colonists in Nova Scotia, New Brunswick and on Prince Edward Island)*   **expulsés du** *thrown out of*   **au 18ᵉ siècle** *in the 18ᵗʰ century*   **au cœur de** *in the heart of*   **comprend 22 paroisses** *includes 22 parishes (equivalent to counties)*   **la partie sud** *the southern part*   **connu dans le monde entier** *known throughout the world*   **met en scène la vie quotidienne** *depicts daily life*   **le passé** *the past*

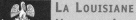

La Louisiane

Nombre d'habitants: 4 287 768 (les Louisianais) (Un peu moins de 200 000 parlent français, cadien *(cajun)* ou créole à la maison.)

Capitale: Baton Rouge Visit it live on Google Earth!

Connaissez-vous la cuisine cadienne? la cuisine créole? Aimez-vous le boudin, l'andouille, le jambalaya, **les écrevisses**?

Aimez-vous la musique cadienne? le zydeco? le swamp-pop? **Laissez les bons temps rouler!**

❀ Qu'en savez-vous?

Voici quelques définitions de mots associés à la Louisiane. Quel mot de la liste va avec chaque définition? Devinez *(Guess)* si vous n'êtes pas sûr(e) de la réponse.

les Créoles	**les Cadiens**	**le Vieux Carré**	**l'Acadiana**
l'andouille	**le jambalaya**	**le zydeco**	**un fais do-do**

1. un genre musical en Louisiane influencé par le blues et le plus souvent joué à l'accordéon
2. un plat de riz *(rice dish)* avec des tomates, de la viande *(meat)* et du bouillon
3. une soirée de danse
4. une saucisse épicée *(spiced sausage)* préparée avec du porc
5. le quartier français à La Nouvelle-Orléans
6. les 22 paroisses de la région cadienne
7. les descendants des francophones venus en Louisiane de l'Acadie au Canada, la région qui comprend aujourd'hui la Nouvelle-Écosse, le Nouveau-Brunswick et l'Île-du-Prince-Édouard
8. les descendants des habitants de Louisiane avant son annexion par les États-Unis; principalement d'origines française, africaine et espagnole

---

Connaissez-vous... ? *Do you know . . . ?* **les écrevisses** *crawfish* **Laissez les bons temps rouler!** *Let the good times roll!* (regional)

Describing your family

Note *culturelle*

En 1916, l'état de Louisiane exige que la scolarité soit faite *(requires that education be done)* en anglais et l'anglais commence à être la langue prédominante chez les jeunes. Plus de 90% de la population en Acadiana née *(born)* avant cette époque est bilingue français-anglais, mais moins de 10% de leurs petits-enfants *(grandchildren)* parlent français. Certains Américains voudraient établir *(to establish)* l'anglais comme la seule langue officielle aux États-Unis. Que pensez-vous de cette idée?

Ma famille

Robert et ses amis **ont l'intention de** passer une semaine de **vacances** *(f)* chez **le père** de Robert à Lafayette. Robert parle de sa famille.

Voici ma famille. Mes parents sont divorcés maintenant. Ils ont quatre **enfants,** trois **garçons** et **une fille.**

mon grand-père (Il est **décédé** maintenant) — (mes grands-parents) — ma grand-mère

(mes parents)

mon père — ma mère — mon oncle — ma tante

moi — mes frères — ma sœur — mon cousin — ma cousine

le **fils** et la fille de ma sœur (mon neveu et ma nièce)

Vocabulaire supplémentaire

adopté(e) *adopted*
des beaux-parents *(m) stepparents, in-laws*
un beau-frère *a brother-in-law*
une belle-sœur *a sister-in-law*
l'aîné (l'aînée) *the oldest child*
le cadet (la cadette) *the middle child, the younger child (of two)*
le benjamin (la benjamine) *the youngest child (of more than two)*
un demi-frère (une demi-sœur) *a stepbrother, a half-brother (a stepsister, a half-sister)*
un ex-mari (une ex-femme) *an ex-husband (an ex-wife)*
un fils unique (une fille unique) *an only child*
des petits-enfants (un petit-fils, une petite-fille) *grandchildren (a grandson, a granddaughter)*
porter des lentilles *(f) to wear contact lenses*

Note *de vocabulaire*

Use **avoir l'air** *(+ adjective)* to say someone *looks young, happy, intelligent* . . . Do not use it to say someone *looks like* another person. Use the verb **ressembler à** instead: **Je ressemble à ma mère.**

Mon père s'appelle Luke.
Il **a environ 50 ans** *(m).*
Il **a l'air** *(m)* **encore** jeune.
Il est **de taille moyenne.**
Il **a les cheveux courts** et gris.

Il **a les yeux** *(m)* marron.
Il a **une barbe** grise et une moustache.
Il **porte des lunettes** *(f).*

Et vous? Comment êtes-vous?

J'ai les yeux **noirs** / marron / **noisette** / verts / bleus / gris.
J'ai les cheveux courts / **mi-longs** / longs et noirs / **bruns** / **châtains** / auburn / blonds / gris / blancs / **roux.**

---

avoir l'intention de *to intend to* **les vacances** *(f) vacation* **le père** *the father* **des enfants** *children* **un garçon** *a boy* **une fille** *a daughter, a girl* **décédé(e)** *deceased* **un fils** *a son* **avoir ... ans** *to be ...years old* **environ** *about* **avoir l'air...** *to look, to seem ...* **encore** *still* **de taille moyenne** *of medium height* **avoir les cheveux...** *to have ...hair* **court(e)** *short* **avoir les yeux...** *to have ...eyes* **une barbe** *a beard* **porter** *to wear* **des lunettes** *(f) glasses* **noirs** *(with eyes) very dark brown* **noisette** *(inv) hazel* **mi-longs** *(with hair) shoulder-length* **bruns** *(with hair) medium to dark brown* **châtains** *(with hair) light to medium brown* **roux** *(with hair) red*

Robert parle de sa famille avec Thomas.

THOMAS: Vous êtes combien dans ta famille?

ROBERT: Nous sommes sept: mon père, **ma belle-mère,** ma mère, mes deux frères, ma sœur et moi. Ma sœur est mariée et elle habite à La Nouvelle-Orléans.

THOMAS: Elle est plus jeune ou **plus âgée que** toi? Quel âge a-t-elle?

ROBERT: Elle a 28 ans.

THOMAS: Comment s'appelle-t-elle?

ROBERT: Elle s'appelle Sarah.

A. La famille. Donnez l'équivalent féminin.

EXEMPLE le frère **la sœur**

1. le père
2. l'oncle
3. le garçon
4. le neveu
5. le beau-père
6. le cousin
7. le fils
8. le grand-père

B. Généalogie. Complétez les phrases.

EXEMPLE Les parents de mon père, **ce sont mes grands-parents.**

1. Le mari de ma tante, c'est _____.
2. Le fils de ma sœur, c'est _____. Sa fille, c'est _____.
3. La fille de mon oncle, c'est _____ et son fils, c'est _____.
4. La femme de mon oncle, c'est _____.

C. Mon meilleur ami. Faites des phrases pour décrire votre meilleur ami.

EXEMPLE Il s'appelle *Philippe / Chuong / ???.*
Il s'appelle Emmitt.

1. Il s'appelle *Philippe / Chuong / ???.*
2. Il est *grand / petit / de taille moyenne.*
3. Il a *18 / 25 / 38 / 45 / ???* ans.
4. Il a les cheveux *longs / mi-longs / courts* et *blonds / noirs / ???.*
5. Il a les yeux *marron / gris / ???.*
6. Il a l'air *intellectuel / sportif / jeune / bête / ???.*

D. Entretien. Interviewez votre partenaire.

1. Vous êtes combien dans ta famille? Tu as des frères ou des sœurs? Ils sont plus âgés que toi ou moins âgés que toi? Avec quel membre de la famille préfères-tu passer du temps? Comment s'appelle-t-il/elle? Quel âge a-t-il/elle? Comment est-il/elle?
2. Tu as des enfants? (Si oui:) Comment s'appellent-ils? Quel âge ont-ils? (Sinon:) Voudrais-tu avoir des enfants un jour *(one day)*? Préfères-tu avoir une fille ou un garçon?

E. Conversation. Avec un(e) partenaire, relisez à haute voix la conversation entre Robert et Thomas en haut de la page. Ensuite, changez la conversation pour décrire un membre de votre famille.

You can find a list of the new words from the vocabulary and grammar sections of this *Compétence* on page 174 and a recording of this list on track 2-16 of your *Text Audio CD.*

---

une belle-mère (un beau-père) *a stepmother, a mother-in-law (a stepfather, a father-in-law)*   **plus âgé(e) que** *older than*

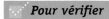

Pour vérifier

How do you say *I'm hungry? I'm thirsty? I'm hot? I'm cold? I'm sleepy? I'm afraid? I'm right? I'm never wrong? I need to stay home? I feel like staying home? I intend to stay home?*

Describing feelings and appearance

*Les expressions avec **avoir***

Use these expressions with **avoir** to describe people or say how they feel.

avoir (environ)... ans	to be (around) . . . years old	avoir faim	to be hungry
avoir l'air...	to look . . . , to seem . . .	avoir soif	to be thirsty
avoir une barbe /	to have a beard /	avoir froid	to be cold
une moustache /	a mustache /	avoir chaud	to be hot
des lunettes	glasses	avoir raison	to be right
avoir les yeux noirs /	to have dark brown /	avoir tort	to be wrong
verts...	green . . . eyes	avoir peur (de)	to be afraid (of)
avoir les cheveux	to have long /	avoir sommeil	to be happy
longs / roux ...	red . . . hair		

— Mon fils a peur des chiens.   — *My son is afraid of dogs.*
— Quel âge a-t-il? Il a l'air très jeune.   — *How old is he? He looks very young.*
— Tu as raison. Il a quatre ans.   — *You're right. He's four.*

The French equivalents of the English verbs *to need, to feel like,* and *to intend* are also expressions with **avoir. Avoir l'intention de** is followed by an infinitive. **Avoir besoin de** and **avoir envie de** can be followed by an infinitive or by a noun.

avoir l'intention de (d')	to intend
avoir besoin de (d')	to need
avoir envie de (d')	to feel like

J'ai besoin de la voiture. J'ai besoin d'aller en cours. J'ai l'intention de rentrer dans deux heures.
I need the car. I need to go to class. I intend to return in two hours.

Tu as envie de manger? Tu as envie d'un sandwich?
You feel like eating? You feel like a sandwich?

✳ **Notes** *de vocabulaire*

1. Use the definite article **les** when talking about someone's hair and eyes. **Les cheveux** and **les yeux** are both masculine plural, so follow them with an adjective in the masculine plural form. **Ma sœur a les cheveux bruns et les yeux verts. Auburn, marron,** and **noisette,** however, are invariable.
2. Brown eyes can be **noirs** *(dark brown)* or **marron** *(light to medium brown).* Brown hair can be **bruns** *(dark or medium brown)* or **châtains** *(light to medium brown).* The words **brun, roux, auburn,** and **châtain** are mainly used to describe someone's hair.
3. You can say that someone is *blond* or *a blond, brunette* or *a brunette,* or *red-headed* or *a red-head,* using **blond(e), brun(e),** or **roux (rousse). Elle est rousse mais son frère est blond.** *She's a red-head, but her brother's a blond.*
4. To say you are *very hot / cold / hungry* . . . use **très. J'ai très chaud.**

Vocabulaire supplémentaire
avoir un tatoo / un piercing
avoir un bouc *to have a goatee*
avoir des favoris *(m) to have sideburns*
être chauve *to be bald*
avoir la tête rasée *to have a shaved head*

A. Comment est-il? Répondez aux questions pour faire une description du meilleur ami de Robert.

Antoine, 20 ans

1. Comment s'appelle-t-il?
2. Quel âge a-t-il?
3. Il a les cheveux de quelle couleur? Il a les cheveux longs ou courts? Il a les yeux de quelle couleur?
4. Il a une barbe ou une moustache? Il porte des lunettes? Il a l'air content *(happy)*?

B. Descriptions. Changez la description d'Antoine de l'exercice **A. Comment est-il?** pour parler de votre meilleur(e) ami(e).

EXEMPLE   **Mon meilleur ami (Ma meilleure amie) s'appelle Pat. Il/Elle a 25 ans. Il/Elle a les cheveux...**

C. Les activités de Robert. Quelles sont les activités que Robert a probablement envie de faire? Quelles sont les activités qu'il a probablement besoin de faire?

EXEMPLES   faire les devoirs   **Il a besoin de faire les devoirs.**
regarder la télé   **Il a envie de regarder la télé.**

1. aller au cinéma
2. aller prendre un verre
3. aller travailler
4. préparer les cours
5. sortir avec des amis
6. aller en cours

D. Et toi? Demandez à votre partenaire s'il/si elle a l'intention de faire les activités mentionnées dans l'exercice précédent demain.

EXEMPLE   faire les devoirs
— **As-tu l'intention de faire les devoirs demain?**
— **Non, je n'ai pas l'intention de faire les devoirs demain.**

E. Moi, j'ai... Utilisez une expression avec **avoir** de la liste à la page précédente selon le contexte.

EXEMPLE   Je voudrais aller prendre un verre.   **J'ai soif.**

1. Brrrr... Fermez la fenêtre.
2. Ah! C'est un serpent!
3. Voilà. Ma réponse est correcte.
4. J'ai envie de manger quelque chose.
5. Je voudrais un coca.
6. J'ai besoin de dormir.

F. Qu'est-ce qu'ils ont? Aujourd'hui la nièce de Robert fête ses cinq ans *(is celebrating her fifth birthday)*. Que dit sa mère? Utilisez une expression avec **avoir**.

1. Ma fille...
   aujourd'hui.

2. Ses amis...

3. Mon frère...

4. Mes cousins...

5. Mon mari et
   moi, nous...

6. Moi, j'...

7. Le chien de
   mon fils...

8. Tu... de faire
   ça au chien!

G. Entretien. Interviewez votre partenaire.

1. Tu as l'intention de voir ta famille ce week-end? Qu'est-ce que tu as envie de faire ce week-end? Qu'est-ce que tu as besoin de faire? Où as-tu l'intention de dîner samedi soir? Qu'est-ce que tu as l'intention de faire dimanche soir?
2. Comment s'appelle ton meilleur ami? Quel âge a-t-il? Il a les yeux et les cheveux de quelle couleur? Est-il grand, petit ou de taille moyenne? Porte-t-il des lunettes? A-t-il l'air plutôt sportif ou plutôt intellectuel?
3. Où aimes-tu dîner quand tu as très faim? Tu as faim maintenant? Tu as soif? Est-ce que tu as l'intention de manger quelque chose après le cours? As-tu sommeil maintenant? As-tu l'intention de dormir après le cours?

Stratégies et Compréhension auditive

⚛ Pour mieux comprendre: *Asking for clarification*

When you do not understand something, it is useful to be able to ask for clarification. You already know three ways to do this: by asking for something to be repeated, by asking what a word means, or by asking how a word is spelled.

> Comment? Répétez, s'il vous plaît.
> Je ne comprends pas. Qu'est-ce que ça veut dire **belle-sœur**?
> Ça s'écrit comment?

A. Je ne comprends pas. Listen to three conversations. In each, which method is used to ask for clarification: **a**, **b**, or **c**?

CD 2-17

a. asking for something to be repeated (**Comment? Répétez, s'il vous plaît.**)
b. asking the meaning of a word (**Qu'est-ce que ça veut dire… ?**)
c. asking the spelling of a word (**Ça s'écrit comment?**)

B. Comment? Listen to these three other scenes, in which one of the speakers is having difficulty understanding. In each case, what could he or she say to ask for clarification?

CD 2-18

Compréhension auditive: La famille de Robert

CD 2-19 Robert is describing his family to a friend who is studying French. Use what you know and your ability to guess logically to help you understand what he says. The first time, listen only for the number of times his friend asks for clarification.

A. La famille de Robert. Écoutez encore une fois *(again)* la description de la famille de Robert et complétez l'arbre généalogique *(family tree)* avec les prénoms des membres de sa famille.

Robert

B. C'est qui? Écoutez encore une fois la description de la famille de Robert et répondez aux questions.

1. Qui habite à Lafayette?
2. Qui habite à Atlanta?
3. Qui habite à La Nouvelle-Orléans?
4. Qui est marié?
5. Qui est divorcé?
6. Comment dit-on **pédiatre** en anglais?
7. Dans la famille de Robert, qui est pédiatre?
8. Quelle est la profession du père de Robert?

Saying where you go in your free time

Vocabulaire supplémentaire

à la synagogue
à la mosquée
au temple to church (Protestant), to temple
au lac to the lake
au bar
à une fête to a party
chez un ami to a friend's house

Note de grammaire

1. Use **pour** before infinitives to say *in order to*. Note that in English, *in order to* may be shortened to just *to*: *One goes to the bookstore (in order) to buy books.* **On va à la librairie pour acheter des livres.**

2. With the verb **retrouver** you must state whom you are meeting: **Je retrouve mes amis au café.** To say *We meet (each other) at the café*, use **On se retrouve au café.**

3. Notice the accent spelling change in the conjugation of **acheter** (to buy).

j' achète	**nous achetons**
tu achètes	**vous achetez**
il/elle achète	**ils/elles achètent**

4. The name of a place generally follows the type of place. For example, for *Tinseltown Cinema*, you say **le cinéma Tinseltown**.

Le temps libre

Chez vous, où est-ce qu'**on va** pour passer **son temps libre**?

On aime beaucoup les activités culturelles et **de temps en temps** on va...

 au musée pour voir **une exposition**

 au théâtre pour voir **une pièce**

 à un concert ou à un festival de musique

On aime aussi **les activités de plein air** et on va souvent...

 au parc pour faire du jogging

 à la piscine pour nager

 à la plage pour **prendre un bain de soleil**

Pour **retrouver des amis**, on va...

 à un match de basket

 en boîte

 à l'église

Pour faire du shopping, on va...

Et pour **acheter** des livres, on va...

 au centre commercial

 dans les petits magasins

 à la librairie

on va one goes **son temps libre** one's free time **de temps en temps** from time to time **une exposition** an exhibit **une pièce** a play **les activités de plein air** outdoor activities **prendre un bain de soleil** to sunbathe **retrouver des amis** to meet friends **acheter** to buy

Robert et Claude parlent de leurs projets *(m)* pour ce soir.

CLAUDE: **On sort** ce soir?

ROBERT: D'accord. **On va** au cinéma?

CLAUDE: Ah, non, je préfère **connaître** un peu la région. **On dit que** la cuisine **cadienne** est **extra**! **Allons plutôt** au restaurant.

ROBERT: D'accord. Allons dîner au restaurant Préjean. C'est un très bon restaurant où **on sert** les spécialités de la région et il y a un orchestre cadien. **Ça te dit?**

CLAUDE: Oui, bonne idée. Allons au restaurant et après allons écouter de la musique zydeco.

ROBERT: Pas de problème. **On peut** toujours **trouver** des concerts ici!

A. Où va-t-on pour... Demandez à un(e) camarade de classe où on va pour faire les choses suivantes.

EXEMPLE lire
— **Où est-ce qu'on va pour lire?**
— **On va à la bibliothèque.**

1. dîner	**6.** nager
2. voir une pièce	**7.** voir une exposition
3. retrouver des amis	**8.** prendre un bain de soleil
4. prendre un verre	**9.** acheter des livres
5. faire du shopping	

> au restaurant
> au musée
> à la piscine
> au café
> au centre commercial
> à l'église
> au parc
> au théâtre
> à la plage
> à la librairie
> à la bibliothèque

B. Entretien. Interviewez votre partenaire.

1. Où aimes-tu retrouver tes amis? Où aimez-vous aller ensemble? Aimez-vous les activités de plein air? Préférez-vous aller à la plage, à la piscine ou au parc?

2. Dans quel restaurant aimes-tu manger? Ce restaurant est près de l'université? Il est cher?

3. Dans quel magasin aimes-tu acheter des vêtements? Ce magasin est au centre commercial? C'est un magasin cher? Aimes-tu faire du shopping? Aimes-tu mieux acheter des vêtements, des livres, des DVD ou des CD?

4. Aimes-tu les activités culturelles? Est-ce qu'il y a beaucoup de théâtres dans le quartier universitaire? beaucoup de musées? beaucoup de concerts? Préfères-tu aller à un concert ou au théâtre? Préfères-tu aller voir une pièce ou aller voir un film?

C. Conversation. Avec un(e) partenaire, relisez à haute voix la conversation entre Robert et Claude en haut de la page. Ensuite, imaginez que vous êtes chez un(e) ami(e) qui habite dans une autre ville et que vous allez sortir ensemble. Choisissez une sorte de cuisine (mexicaine, italienne, française, japonaise, chinoise...) et un genre de musique (du rock, du jazz, du hip-hop, de la country, de la pop, de la musique classique...) populaire dans votre région.

On sort... ? *How about going out . . . ?* **On va... ?** *How about going . . . ?* **connaître** *to know, to get to know* **On dit que** *They say that* **cadien(ne)** *Cajun* **extra(ordinaire)** *great* **Allons...** *Let's go . . .* **plutôt** *instead, rather* **on sert (servir** *to serve)* **Ça te dit?** *How does that sound to you?* **On peut** *One can* **(pouvoir** *can, may, to be able)* **trouver** *to find*

You can find a list of the new words from CD 2-21 the vocabulary and grammar sections of this **Compétence** on page 174 and a recording of this list on track 2-21 of your *Text Audio CD*.

Pour vérifier

1. What are the forms of **aller**?
2. With which forms of the definite article does **à** contract? What are the contracted forms? With which forms does it not contract? How do you say *to the café*? *to the library*? *to the university*? *to the students*?
3. What does the word **y** mean?
4. Where do you place **y** in a sentence where there is a verb followed by an infinitive? Where do you place it otherwise?
5. What happens to words like **je** and **ne** before **y**?

Saying where you are going

*Le verbe **aller**, la préposition **à** et le pronom **y***

To talk about going places, use the irregular verb **aller** *(to go)*.

ALLER *(to go)*	
je **vais**	nous ‿ **allons**
tu **vas**	vous ‿ **allez**
il/elle **va**	ils/elles **vont**

Use the preposition **à** *(to, at, in)* to say where you are going. When **à** falls before **le** or **les,** the two words contract to **au** and **aux.**

CONTRACTIONS WITH À	
à + le → au	Je vais **au** cinéma.
à + la → à la	Je vais **à la** librairie.
à + l' → à l'	Claude va **à l'**université.
à + les → aux	Robert va **aux** festivals de musique de la région.

The pronoun **y** *(there)* is used to avoid repeating the name of the place where one is going. Treat **y** as a vowel sound and use elision and liaison before it.

Je vais **au parc.** J'**y** vais avec mes cousins. Nous ‿ **y** allons à trois heures.

Y is generally placed *immediately* before the verb. It goes before the infinitive if there is one. If not, it goes before the conjugated verb.

— Il voudrait aller **au cinéma**?   — Ils vont **au musée**?
— Oui, il voudrait **y** aller.   — Oui, ils **y** vont.

In the negative, **y** remains *immediately* before the conjugated verb or the infinitive.

— Tu **y** vas?   — Tu voudrais **y** aller?
— Non, je n'**y** vais pas.   — Non, je ne voudrais pas **y** aller.

Whenever you use **aller** to talk about going somewhere and don't name the place you are going, use **y** even when the word *there* would not be stated in English.

On y va?   *Shall we go (there)?*   J'y vais. *I'm going (there).*

CD 2-22

Prononciation

*Les lettres **a, au** et **ai***

- Pronounce **a** or **à** with the mouth wide open as in the word *father,* but with the tongue slightly higher and closer to the front of the mouth.
  Ton ami va à Paris.   Tu vas à Paris avec ta camarade?

- Pronounce **au** like the **o** in **nos.**
  Laure va au restaurant?   Les autres y vont aussi?

- Pronounce the **ai** of **je vais** like the **ais** of **français.** Be sure to distinguish this sound from the **a** of **tu vas** or **il va.**
  Je vais au café.   Tu n'y vas jamais?

A. Vous y allez souvent? Ces personnes vont-elles souvent, quelquefois, rarement ou jamais aux endroits indiqués?

> **EXEMPLE** Moi, je... (le musée)
> **Moi, je vais rarement au musée. / Je ne vais jamais au musée.**

1. Moi, je... (l'université, la plage, le théâtre, le cinéma, l'opéra)
2. Mes parents... (le cinéma, Paris, le parc, le centre commercial)
3. Mon meilleur ami (Ma meilleure amie)... (l'église, la piscine, les matchs de basket de notre équipe *(team)*, le musée)
4. Mes amis et moi, nous... (les matchs de football américain de notre équipe, la bibliothèque, les festivals de musique de la région)

B. On sort. Robert parle de ses amis et de sa famille. Où vont-ils?

> **EXEMPLE** Moi, je **vais à la piscine.**

1. Thomas et moi...

2. Mon oncle et ma tante...

3. Thomas...

4. Claude et son frère...

5. Mon père...

6. Le chien de ma sœur...

C. Et toi? Demandez à votre partenaire s'il/si elle va quelquefois aux endroits *(places)* illustrés dans *B. On sort.* Votre partenaire va répondre avec le pronom **y.**

> **EXEMPLE** — **Est-ce que tu vas à la piscine quelquefois?**
> — **Oui, j'y vais souvent (de temps en temps, rarement...).**

Maintenant, demandez à votre partenaire s'il/si elle aime aller aux endroits *(places)* illustrés dans *B. On sort.* Votre partenaire va répondre avec le pronom **y.**

> **EXEMPLE** — **Est-ce que tu aimes aller à la piscine?**
> — **Oui, j'aime beaucoup (assez...) y aller.**
> **Non, je n'aime pas y aller.**

D. Entretien. Interviewez votre partenaire.

1. Où aimes-tu passer ton temps libre? Tu vas souvent au théâtre? au musée? Tu préfères aller voir un concert ou aller voir une exposition?
2. Avec quel membre de ta famille préfères-tu passer ton temps libre? Où aimez-vous aller ensemble? Vous y allez souvent ensemble?
3. Tu aimes les activités de plein air? Tu vas souvent au parc? Tu préfères aller à la piscine ou à la plage? Tu y vas souvent? Tu y vas pour nager ou plutôt pour prendre un bain de soleil?

Pour vérifier

1. What are the three possible uses of the pronoun **on**? What form of the verb do you use with **on**?

2. How do you form the imperative? What is it used for?

3. With which verbs do you drop the final **-s** in the **tu** form of the imperative?

4. Which two verbs have irregular command forms? What are the forms? How would you say to a friend: *Be on time! Be good! Let's be calm! Have confidence! Let's have patience!*

 To download a podcast on the Imperative and Subject Pronouns, go to **academic.cengage.com/french.**

Suggesting activities and telling people what to do

Le pronom sujet on et l'impératif

Use **on** as the subject of a sentence when you are referring to people in general *(one, people, they)*. Consider the difference between these sentences.

À Paris, **on** parle français.	*In Paris, they speak French.* (general group)
Tes amis? **Ils** parlent français?	*Your friends? Do they speak French?* (specific people)

The pronoun **on** is also often used instead of **nous** to say *we*. **On** takes the same form of the verb as **il** and **elle,** regardless of its translation in English.

Claude et moi, **on** aime sortir.   *Claude and I, we like to go out.*

You can propose doing something with someone *(How about . . . ? Shall we . . . ?)* by asking a question with **on.**

On va au cinéma?	*How about going to the movies?*
Qu'est-ce qu'**on** fait ce soir?	*What shall we do this evening?*

The imperative (command form) can also be used to make suggestions, as well as to tell someone else to do something. Use the imperative as follows.

• To make suggestions with *Let's . . .,* use the **nous** form of the verb, without the pronoun **nous.**

Allons au cinéma!	*Let's go to the movies!*
Ne **restons** pas à la maison!	*Let's not stay home!*

• To give instructions, or to tell someone to do something, use either the **tu** form of the verb or the **vous** form of the verb, as appropriate, without the pronoun. In **tu** form commands, drop the final **-s** of **-er** verbs and of **aller.** However, as you learn other verbs that do not end in **-er,** do not drop the **-s** in the commands.

Va à la bibliothèque! / **Allez** à la bibliothèque!	*Go to the library!*
Ne **mange** pas ça! / Ne **mangez** pas ça!	*Don't eat that!*

The verbs **être** and **avoir** have irregular command forms.

ÊTRE *(be . . .)*		AVOIR *(have . . .)*	
Sois sage!	*Be good!*	**Aie** confiance!	*Have confidence!*
Soyons calmes!	*Let's be calm!*	**Ayons** de la patience!	*Let's have patience!*
Soyez à l'heure!	*Be on time!*	**Ayez** confiance!	*Have confidence!*

A. Où? Est-ce qu'on fait plus souvent ces choses **en Louisiane** ou **au Québec**?

EXEMPLE   écouter de la musique zydeco
          On écoute plus souvent de la musique zydeco en Louisiane.

1. aller à des festivals de neige *(snow)*
2. fêter *(to celebrate)* Mardi gras
3. fêter le 4 juillet *(July)*
4. écouter de la musique québécoise
5. manger des po-boys
6. aller à des festivals de danse cadienne

B. Tes amis et toi? Posez ces questions à votre partenaire. Il/Elle va répondre en utilisant le pronom **on.**

> **EXEMPLE** — Tes amis et toi, vous préférez aller à quel restaurant?
> — **On préfère aller au restaurant Vermilionville.**

1. Tes amis et toi, quand aimez-vous sortir ensemble?
2. Où aimez-vous aller ensemble?
3. Dans quel restaurant mangez-vous le plus souvent?
4. Parlez-vous beaucoup au téléphone?
5. Vous allez souvent au parc ensemble?
6. Vous jouez au basket ou au tennis ensemble?

C. On... ? Un(e) ami(e) vous invite *(invites you)* à faire ces choses. Répondez à ses suggestions selon vos goûts *(according to your tastes).*

> **EXEMPLE** — **On joue à des jeux vidéo?**
> — **D'accord. Jouons à des jeux vidéo.**
> **Non, ne jouons pas à des jeux vidéo.**

1.  2.  3.  4.

D. Pour réussir. Donnez des conseils à un groupe de nouveaux étudiants. Utilisez l'impératif.

> **EXEMPLE** préparer les examens avec d'autres étudiants
> **Préparez les examens avec d'autres étudiants.**
> **Ne préparez pas les examens avec d'autres étudiants.**

1. aller à tous les cours
2. être à l'heure
3. avoir confiance
4. regarder les examens des autres
5. aller en boîte tous les soirs
6. avoir peur de parler au prof

E. Des parents difficiles. Un jeune homme paresseux de trente ans habite encore chez ses parents. Ils lui disent ce qu'il doit faire *(must do)* avec l'un des verbes de chaque paire et ce qu'il ne doit pas faire avec l'autre. Qu'est-ce qu'ils lui disent? Utilisez l'impératif et soyez logique!

> **EXEMPLE** arrêter *(to stop)* de fumer / fumer dans la maison
> **Arrête de fumer. Ne fume pas dans la maison.**

1. être plus propre / laisser tes vêtements partout
2. être timide / demander plus d'argent au travail
3. rester au lit tout le temps / être plus dynamique
4. jouer à des jeux vidéo toute la journée / avoir un peu d'ambition
5. aller prendre un verre avec tes amis après le travail / rentrer à la maison
6. manger toujours la même chose / avoir un peu d'imagination

Saying what you are going to do

Le week-end prochain

Robert va passer le week-end prochain à La Nouvelle-Orléans. Et vous? Qu'est-ce que vous allez faire?

Je vais... / Je ne vais pas...

quitter la maison **tôt**

partir pour le week-end

visiter une autre ville

faire un tour de la ville

aller **boire** quelque chose au café

rentrer **tard**

CD 2-23

Robert et Thomas **font des projets** pour le week-end prochain.

THOMAS: Qu'est-ce qu'on fait ce week-end?
ROBERT: J'ai beaucoup de projets pour ce week-end. Jeudi matin, on va partir très tôt pour La Nouvelle-Orléans. **D'abord,** on va visiter la ville. **Ensuite,** on va **aller voir** ma sœur. On va **passer la soirée** chez elle. Vendredi on va faire un tour du **Vieux Carré.** On va rentrer à Lafayette assez tard.
THOMAS: Et samedi?
ROBERT: À midi, on va déjeuner au restaurant Prudhomme. C'est un restau-rant célèbre pour sa cuisine régionale. **Et puis,** le soir, on va aller à Eunice, une petite ville pas loin de Lafayette. Il y a une soirée de musique et de folklore cadiens tous les samedis.
THOMAS: **Génial!**

Le week-end prochain *Next weekend* **quitter** *to leave* **tôt** *early* **partir** *to leave* **boire** *to drink* **tard** *late* **faire des projets** *to make plans* **D'abord** *First* **Ensuite** *Then, Afterwards* **aller voir** *to go see, to visit (a person)* **passer la soirée** *to spend the evening* **le Vieux Carré** *the French Quarter* **Et puis** *And then* **Génial!** *Great!*

A. Le week-end prochain. Est-ce que vous allez faire les choses suivantes samedi prochain?

EXEMPLE   rester à la maison
Je vais rester à la maison. / Je ne vais pas rester à la maison.

1. quitter la maison tôt
2. partir pour la journée
3. faire un tour de la ville
4. visiter une autre ville
5. aller voir des amis
6. retrouver des amis en ville
7. aller boire quelque chose
8. dîner au restaurant
9. rentrer tard
10. inviter des amis à la maison
11. regarder un DVD
12. passer la soirée à la maison

B. Entretien. Interviewez votre partenaire.

1. D'habitude, à quelle heure est-ce que tu quittes la maison le lundi? le mardi? À quelle heure est-ce que tu rentres?
2. Quelle ville est-ce que tu aimes visiter? Qu'est-ce que tu aimes faire dans cette ville?
3. Est-ce que tu voudrais partir pour le week-end? (Où est-ce que tu voudrais aller?)
4. Vas-tu souvent au café? Qu'est-ce que tu aimes boire quand tu as très soif? Et quand tu as froid? Et quand tu as chaud?
5. En général, quels jours est-ce que tu passes la journée à la maison? Et la soirée? Est-ce que tu passes toute la journée chez toi de temps en temps?

C. Conversation. Avec un(e) partenaire, relisez à haute voix la conversation entre Robert et Thomas en bas de la page précédente. Ensuite, imaginez qu'un(e) ami(e) passe le week-end chez vous et que vous allez visiter une autre ville ensemble. Décidez quelle ville vous allez visiter et parlez de vos projets.

À La Nouvelle-Orléans

CD 2-24   You can find a list of the new words from the vocabulary and grammar sections of this ***Compétence*** on page 175 and a recording of this list on track 2-24 of your *Text Audio CD*.

Pour vérifier

1. How do you say what you are going to do?
   How do you say what you are not going to do?
   How would you say *I'm going to stay home?*
   *I'm not going to work today? I'm going to go
   to the mall?*

2. Where do you place the pronoun **y** in the
   immediate future?

3. What is the immediate future form of **il y a**?
   How do you negate it?

Saying what you are going to do

Le futur immédiat

To say what you *are going to do,* use a form of **aller** followed by an infinitive.

je vais étudier	nous allons rentrer
tu vas travailler	vous allez sortir
il/elle/on va lire	ils/elles vont nager

— Qu'est-ce que tu **vas faire** demain?   — *What are you going to do tomorrow?*

— Je **vais travailler.**   — *I'm going to work.*

In the negative, put the **ne... pas** around the conjugated form of **aller.** Place the pronoun **y,** when needed, *immediately* before the infinitive.

Ma sœur va rester à la maison mais moi, je **ne vais pas y rester.**

Il y a becomes **il va y avoir** when saying *there is/are going to be.*

Il va y avoir un concert demain. **Il ne va pas y avoir** de problèmes.

Use these expressions to tell when you are going to do something.

maintenant *now*	**plus tard** *later*
aujourd'hui *today*	**demain** *tomorrow*
ce matin *this morning*	**demain matin** *tomorrow morning*
cet après-midi *this afternoon*	**demain après-midi** *tomorrow afternoon*
ce soir *tonight*	**demain soir** *tomorrow evening*
lundi *Monday*	**lundi prochain** *next Monday*
ce week-end *this weekend*	**le week-end prochain** *next weekend*
cette semaine *this week*	**la semaine prochaine** *next week*
ce mois-ci *this month*	**le mois prochain** *next month*
cette année *this year*	**l'année prochaine** *next year*

A. Et ensuite? Qu'est-ce que ces gens vont faire *d'abord* et qu'est-ce qu'ils vont faire *ensuite*?

> **EXEMPLE**   moi, je: manger / préparer le dîner
> **D'abord, je vais préparer le dîner et ensuite, je vais manger.**

1. nous: travailler tout l'après-midi / aller prendre un verre
2. moi, je: dormir / rentrer à la maison
3. mon frère: retrouver sa petite amie en ville / dîner au restaurant avec elle
4. vous: dîner au restaurant / sortir danser
5. mes amis: préparer le dîner / aller au supermarché *(supermarket)*

B. Dans ma famille. Qui de votre famille va probablement faire les choses suivantes le week-end prochain? Employez **personne ne va...** pour dire *nobody is going to . . .*

> **EXEMPLE**   travailler
> **Moi, je vais travailler le week-end prochain.**
> **Ma mère et moi allons travailler le week-end prochain.**
> **On va tous travailler le week-end prochain.**
> **Personne ne va travailler le week-end prochain.**

1. jouer à des jeux vidéo
2. sortir en boîte
3. rester à la maison
4. faire du shopping
5. aller nager

6. retrouver des amis en ville
7. voir une exposition au musée
8. aller à un concert
9. voir un film
10. travailler dans le jardin

C. Projets.
Demandez à un(e) camarade de classe ce qu'il/elle va faire aux moments indiqués.

EXEMPLE ce soir
— **David, qu'est-ce que tu vas faire ce soir?**
— **Je vais travailler ce soir.**

1. plus tard, après les cours
2. demain matin
3. demain soir
4. le week-end prochain
5. la semaine prochaine
6. l'année prochaine

rentrer à la maison	???	préparer les cours	travailler
sortir	manger	aller au cinéma	être en cours	aller...
partir pour le week-end	dormir	aller voir des amis	

D. Leurs projets.
De retour au *(Back in)* Québec, Thomas parle à Robert de leurs projets pour le lendemain *(the next day)*. Qu'est-ce que Thomas dit?

EXEMPLE Tu... avec Claude?
Tu vas jouer à des jeux vidéo avec Claude?

1. Moi, je... jusqu'à midi.
2. Claude...
3. Toi et moi, nous... ?
4. Ta petite amie et toi, vous... ?

5. Nos amis...
6. Nos autres amis...
7. Mes amis et moi, on...
8. Claude et sa cousine...

F. Entretien.
Interviewez votre partenaire.

1. À quelle heure est-ce que tu vas rentrer chez toi aujourd'hui? Est-ce que tu vas y passer toute la soirée? Est-ce que vas être chez toi demain matin? Tu habites dans un appartement, dans une maison ou dans une résidence à l'université? Tu y habites seul(e)? Tu aimes y habiter? Tu vas y habiter l'année prochaine?
2. Dans quel restaurant est-ce que tu manges le plus souvent? Tu vas y manger ce week-end? Avec qui est-ce que tu y manges généralement?

Pour vérifier

1. Do you generally use cardinal or ordinal numbers to give dates in French? What is the exception?
2. In what two ways can the year 1789 be expressed in French? How do you say the year 2010?
3. What are these dates in French: 15/3/1951 and 11/1/2012?

Vocabulaire supplémentaire
Les fêtes

un anniversaire de mariage *a wedding anniversary*
la fête des Mères / Pères
la fête nationale *Independence Day*
Hanoukka *(f)*
le jour d'Action de Grâce *Thanksgiving*
le (réveillon du) jour de l'an *New Year's (Eve)*
Noël *(m) Christmas*
Pâques *(f) Easter*
la pâque juive *Passover*
le ramadan
la Saint-Valentin
Yom Kippour
Bon anniversaire! *Happy Birthday!*
Bonne année! *Happy New Year!*
Joyeux Noël! *Merry Christmas!*

Saying when you are going to do something

Les dates

You often need to give dates to say when you are going to do something.

Je vais partir en vacances le 30 décembre.

In French, dates are expressed using **le** and cardinal numbers (**deux, trois...**), rather than ordinal numbers (**deuxième, troisième...**), except to say *the first* of the month. For *the first,* use **le premier (1ᵉʳ).** To ask the date, say **Quelle est la date?**

— Quelle est la date de votre fête *(holiday)* préférée?
— C'est le premier... le deux... le trois... le quatre...

janvier	avril	juillet	octobre
février	mai	août	novembre
mars	juin	septembre	décembre

There are two ways of expressing the years 1100–1999 in French. Years starting at 2000 are only expressed using the word **mille.**

1991: mille neuf cent quatre-vingt-onze / dix-neuf cent quatre-vingt-onze
2009: deux mille neuf

Note that the day goes before the month in French.

14/8/1957 = le quatorze août 1957

Use **en** to say *in* what month or year.

— Ton anniversaire *(birthday)*, c'est **en** quel mois?
— C'est **en** novembre.

— **En** quelle année vas-tu finir tes études?
— **En** 2012.

A. C'est en quel mois? Quel mois associez-vous avec... ?

1. le début *(beginning)* de l'année? la fin *(end)* de l'année?
2. le début de l'année scolaire? le début de ce semestre / trimestre?
3. la fin de ce semestre / trimestre?
4. la fête nationale américaine? canadienne? française?
5. la fête des Mères? la fête des Pères?
6. le jour d'Action de Grâce *(Thanksgiving)*?

B. Encore des dates. Quelle est la date... ?

1. aujourd'hui
2. demain
3. du prochain cours de français
4. de la fête nationale américaine / canadienne
5. de Noël
6. de *Halloween*
7. du jour de l'an *(New Year's Day)*
8. de la fête nationale française

C. Votre anniversaire. Vos camarades de classe devineront *(will guess)* la date de votre anniversaire. Répondez **avant** ou **après** jusqu'à ce qu'ils devinent juste *(right)*.

EXEMPLE — **Ton anniversaire, c'est en mars?**
— **Après.**
— **C'est en mai?**
— **Oui.**
— **C'est le quinze mai?**
— **Avant...**

D. Dates importantes. Lisez à haute voix ces dates importantes.

EXEMPLE 4/7/1776 (le début de la Révolution américaine)
le quatre juillet mille sept cent soixante-seize
(le quatre juillet dix-sept cent soixante-seize)

1. 1/11/1718 (Bienville fonde La Nouvelle-Orléans.)
2. 14/7/1789 (le début de la Révolution française)
3. 30/4/1812 (La Louisiane devient *[becomes]* un état des États-Unis.)
4. 11/11/1918 (le jour de l'Armistice)
5. 6/6/1944 (le jour du débarquement en Normandie)

E. À quelle date? Dites à quelle date chacun va faire les choses indiquées.

EXEMPLE Robert / rentrer chez son père...
Robert va rentrer chez son père le 25 décembre.

1. Beaucoup d'Améri-cains / faire un pique-nique...

2. Les Français / célébrer leur fête nationale...

3. Beaucoup de couples / dîner au restaurant...

4. On / sortir avec des amis...

5. Thomas / passer la journée avec sa famille...

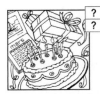

6. Moi, je / fêter *(to celebrate)* mon anniversaire...

F. Entretien. Interviewez votre partenaire.

1. Quelle est la date aujourd'hui? Quelle est la date de ton anniversaire? Qu'est-ce que tu vas probablement faire ce jour-là? Quelle est la date de ta fête préférée? Qu'est-ce que tu aimes faire ce jour-là?
2. Quelle est la date du dernier *(last)* jour du cours de français? Qu'est-ce que tu vas faire après ton dernier cours ce semestre / trimestre? Vas-tu partir en vacances après la fin *(end)* du semestre / trimestre? Que vas-tu faire? Est-ce que tu vas continuer à étudier ici l'année prochaine?

Planning how to get there

❋ Notes *de vocabulaire*

1. **Un bus** runs within cities and **un car** runs between cities. *A tour bus* is also called **un car.** *A school bus* is **un car scolaire.**
2. Although traditionally it is considered correct to say **à vélo / à moto / à vélomoteur,** many people say **en vélo / en moto / en vélomoteur.**

Vocabulaire supplémentaire

à moto(cyclette) *(f) by motorcycle*
à vélomoteur *(m) by moped*

Les moyens de transport

Robert et ses amis vont aller à La Nouvelle-Orléans en voiture. Et vous? Comment préférez-vous voyager?

Pour visiter une autre ville je préfère y aller...

en avion *(m)*   en train *(m)*   en bateau *(m)*   en car / en autocar *(m)*

Il y a d'autres possibilités pour aller en ville. Comment **venez-vous** en cours?

Je viens en cours...

à pied *(m)*   à vélo *(m)*   en taxi *(m)*

en voiture *(f)*   en métro *(m)*   en bus / en autobus *(m)*

CD 2-25

Robert parle à Thomas du voyage à La Nouvelle-Orléans.

ROBERT: Écoute, demain matin on va partir à La Nouvelle-Orléans. Tout est **prêt**?
THOMAS: Oui. On y va en car?
ROBERT: Non, on va **louer** une voiture, c'est plus commode.
THOMAS: C'est loin? **Ça prend combien de temps** pour y aller?
ROBERT: Ça prend environ deux heures et demie en voiture, **pas plus.**
THOMAS: Et **on revient** quand?
ROBERT: On revient vendredi soir.

---

les moyens *(m)* **de transport** *means of transportation*   **vous venez (venir** *to come)*   **Je viens (venir** *to come)*   **prêt(e)** *ready*
louer *to rent*   **Ça prend combien de temps...** *How long does it take . . .*   **pas plus** *no more*   **on revient (revenir** *to come back)*

A. Moyens de transport. Complétez les phrases pour parler de vous.

1. Pour faire un long voyage, je préfère voyager...
2. Je n'aime pas beaucoup voyager...
3. Je préfère aller en ville...
4. Je n'aime pas beaucoup aller en ville...
5. D'habitude, je viens en cours...
6. Après les cours, je rentre chez moi...
7. Pour aller voir mes parents, j'y vais...

B. On y va comment? Dites où chacun va et comment.

EXEMPLE   **Ils vont à La Nouvelle-Orléans en voiture.**

Ils...

1. Je...

2. Ils...

3. Vous...

4. Nous...

5. Elle...

C. Entretien. Interviewez votre partenaire.

1. Tu préfères prendre l'avion, le train ou l'autocar pour faire un long voyage?
2. Quelle autre ville est-ce que tu visites souvent? Comment est-ce que tu y vas? (en voiture? en train? en avion?) Ça prend combien de temps pour y aller?
3. Tu voyages souvent en avion? Tu as peur de prendre l'avion? Pour aller à l'aéroport de chez toi, ça prend combien de temps? Qu'est-ce que tu aimes faire pendant *(during)* les longs voyages en avion? (dormir? lire? parler?...)
4. Quels jours est-ce que tu viens en cours? Comment viens-tu en cours d'habitude?

D. Conversation. Avec un(e) partenaire, relisez à haute voix la conversation entre Robert et Thomas en bas de la page précédente. Ensuite, changez la conversation pour parler d'un voyage que vous allez faire ensemble pour visiter une autre ville. Parlez de comment vous allez voyager et de combien de temps ça va prendre pour y aller.

CD 2-26   You can find a list of the new words from the vocabulary and grammar sections of this *Compétence* on page 175 and a recording of this list on track 2-26 of your *Text Audio CD.*

Pour vérifier

1. What are the forms of **venir**? of **prendre**? What two verbs are conjugated like **venir**? like **prendre**? What verb do you use to say you are having something to eat or drink? When is **apprendre** followed by **à**?

2. In what forms of the verbs **venir** and **prendre** are the vowels nasal? **Je viens / tu viens / il vient** rhyme with what word? **Je prends / tu prends / il prend** rhyme with what word? How do you pronounce the **ils/elles viennent** form? the **ils/elles prennent** form?

☀ Notes de vocabulaire

1. Use **en** with **aller, venir,** or **voyager** to say you are traveling *by* a means of transportation. **Je viens *en* bus, *en* taxi, *en* train...**

2. Use **prendre** to say what means of transportation you are *taking*. In this case, you can generally use the same article with the noun that you would in English: *I take* **the** *bus,* **a** *cab,* **the** *train . . .* **Je prends *le* bus, *un* taxi, *le* train...**

Deciding how to get there and come back

*Les verbes **prendre** et **venir** et les moyens de transport*

The conjugations of **prendre** *(to take)* and **venir** *(to come)* are irregular.

PRENDRE *(to take)*		VENIR *(to come)*	
je **prends**	nous **prenons**	je **viens**	nous **venons**
tu **prends**	vous **prenez**	tu **viens**	vous **venez**
il/elle/on **prend**	ils/elles **prennent**	il/elle/on **vient**	ils/elles **viennent**

You can use **prendre** to say that you are *taking* a means of transportation.

  Je **prends** mon vélo.   Je **prends** l'avion.

You can also use **prendre** as *to have* when talking about having something to eat or drink.

  Je vais **prendre** un sandwich et une eau minérale.

Comprendre *(to understand)* and **apprendre** *(to learn)* are conjugated like **prendre.** When **apprendre** is followed by an infinitive, the infinitive is preceded by **à.**

  Tu **comprends** le français, non? Moi, **j'apprends à** parler français.
  Ma sœur **apprend** le français aussi.

You can also use **aller, venir,** or **voyager** and the preposition **en** (or **à** with **vélo**) to say that you are *going, coming,* or *traveling by* a particular means of transportation. To say *on foot,* use **à pied.**

  Je **viens** en cours à pied.   J'y **vais** à vélo.   Je **voyage** en avion.

Revenir *(to come back)* and **devenir** *(to become)* are conjugated like **venir.**

  Elle **revient** tard.   *She comes back late.*
  Il **devient** impatient.   *He is becoming impatient.*

CD 2-27

Prononciation

*Les verbes **prendre** et **venir***

In the **je, tu,** and **il/elle/on** forms of the verb **venir,** the vowel combination **ie** has the nasal sound [jɛ̃]. The consonants after **ie** are all silent. All three forms rhyme with the word **bien.** In the **ils/elles viennent** form, however, the **ie** is not nasal and the **nn** is pronounced.

  je viens   tu viens   il vient   ils viennent   elles viennent

Similarly, the **e** in the **je, tu,** and **il/elle/on** forms of the verb **prendre** is nasal and the consonants after the vowel are silent. All three forms rhyme with the word **quand.** In the **ils/elles prennent** form, however, the **e** is not nasal. It is pronounced like the **è** in **mère** and the **nn** is pronounced.

  je prends   tu prends   il prend   ils prennent   elles prennent

The **e** in the **nous** and **vous** forms of both verbs is pronounced like the **e** in **je.**

  nous venons   vous venez   nous prenons   vous prenez

A. Qu'est-ce qu'on fait? Conjuguez les verbes entre parenthèses et posez les questions à votre partenaire.

1. Quels jours est-ce que tu *(venir)* en cours? Est-ce que tu *(venir)* toujours en cours? Est-ce que tu *(prendre)* le bus pour venir en cours?
2. Est-ce que les autres étudiants du cours de français *(venir)* toujours en cours? Est-ce qu'ils *(comprendre)* bien le français?
3. Est-ce que le cours de français *(devenir)* plus difficile? Est-ce que tu *(prendre)* beaucoup de notes en cours?
4. Est-ce que le professeur de français *(venir)* toujours en cours à l'heure?
5. Est-ce que le prof *(devenir)* impatient(e) quand les étudiants ne préparent pas bien le cours? Est-ce que tu *(apprendre)* bien le vocabulaire?
6. Est-ce que tu *(avoir)* l'intention de revenir à cette université l'année prochaine? Est-ce que tu *(avoir)* l'intention de devenir prof après tes études?

B. Que font-ils? Décrivez votre cours de français. Combien de phrases logiques pouvez-vous faire en employant *(can you make using)* un élément de chaque colonne?

> **EXEMPLE**   **Moi, je ne viens pas en cours en autobus.**

		des notes / un café
		toujours le professeur
		beaucoup de verbes / de vocabulaire
Moi, je...	prendre	beaucoup / peu de français
Le professeur...	apprendre	à l'université le soir / le week-end
Nous... (ne/n')	comprendre (pas)	paresseux (paresseuse)(s) / timide(s) / impatient(e)(s)
Beaucoup d'étudiants...	venir	l'autobus pour venir en cours
	revenir	en cours à pied / en voiture /
	devenir	en autobus / à vélo

C. La santé. Votre ami voudrait améliorer sa santé *(to improve his health)*. Donnez-lui des conseils. Utilisez l'impératif.

> **EXEMPLE**   Je prends un coca ou un jus d'orange?
> **Prends un jus d'orange!**

1. Je prends une bière ou une eau minérale?
2. Je prends un café ou un jus de fruit?
3. Je viens en cours en voiture ou à vélo?
4. Je prends une salade ou des frites?
5. Je vais au parc ou je reste à la maison?
6. Je vais au parc en voiture ou à pied?
7. Je prends un bain de soleil ou je nage?

Faire du vélo, c'est bon pour la santé.

D. Une sortie. Avec un(e) partenaire, préparez une conversation basée sur cette situation pour présenter à la classe.

Vous demandez à un(e) ami(e) s'il/si elle a envie de faire quelque chose avec vous. Parlez de quand vous allez y aller et de quel moyen de transport vous allez prendre.

Reprise

Talking about your family and free time

Didier Landry   Anne Landry

Christine   Éric

Philippe et Marie Broussard

In *Chapitre 4,* you learned to describe your family, say where you go and how you get there, invite or tell someone to do something, and talk about your plans for the near future. Now you have a chance to practice what you learned.

A. Descriptions. Vous allez passer un mois chez cette famille francophone à Lafayette. La mère décrit chaque personne de la famille. Complétez ses descriptions d'une façon logique.

Mes parents habitent chez nous. Mon __1__ a soixante-quinze ans. Il a une __2__ mais il n'a pas de barbe. Il a besoin de __3__ pour lire. Ma __4__ a soixante-douze __5__. Ils ont tous les deux *(both)* les __6__ gris. Mon __7__ et moi, nous __8__ quarante-sept __9__. Nous __10__ deux enfants, un __11__ et une __12__. Notre fils a les cheveux __13__ comme nous, mais notre __14__ a les cheveux __15__.

B. Chez les Landry. Les Landry sont à la maison. Complétez les phrases suivantes pour décrire la situation des membres de la famille. Utilisez une expression avec **avoir.**

> **EXEMPLE**   Les Broussard vont boire quelque chose parce qu'ils **ont soif.**

1. Madame Broussard voudrait manger quelque chose aussi parce qu'elle _____.
2. Éric voudrait mettre un pull *(to put on a sweater)* parce qu'il _____.
3. Christine voudrait enlever *(to take off)* son pull parce qu'elle _____.
4. Monsieur Broussard voudrait faire la sieste *(to take a nap)* parce qu'il _____.
5. Anne _____ d'étudier parce qu'elle a un examen demain.

C. Qu'est-ce qu'on fait? Vous voulez profiter au maximum de *(to make the most of)* votre visite à Lafayette. Répondez aux suggestions de la famille chez qui vous habitez. Utilisez l'impératif.

> **EXEMPLE**   Alors, on parle anglais ou français?
> **Parlons français!**

1. On reste à la maison aujourd'hui ou on va en ville?
2. On prend un coca au McDonald ou on prend un café dans un petit café du quartier?
3. On mange un hamburger ou on mange dans un restaurant créole?
4. On visite le musée ou on rentre à la maison?
5. On va voir un film américain ou on va voir un film français?
6. On écoute un CD de Beyoncé ou on écoute un CD de musique cadienne?
7. On loue un DVD en français ou en anglais?

Maintenant, dites à une amie de faire ces mêmes choses.

> **EXEMPLE**   **Ne parle pas anglais. Parle français.**

D. À La Nouvelle-Orléans. Une amie des Landry va visiter La Nouvelle-Orléans. Dites-lui *(Tell her)* de faire ou de ne pas faire ces choses. Utilisez l'impératif.

EXEMPLE   venir en juillet
Ne viens pas en juillet!

1. venir pour Mardi gras
2. visiter le Vieux Carré
3. manger de la cuisine créole
4. prendre un café au Café du Monde
5. rester à l'hôtel le soir
6. visiter la rue Bourbon

E. Comment vont-ils en ville? Anne Landry parle des projets de sa famille pour aujourd'hui. Complétez ces phrases avec la forme convenable du verbe **prendre.**

EXEMPLE   Papa **prend** le bus pour aller acheter des livres.

1. Didier _____ sa voiture pour aller voir un film.
2. Les enfants _____ le bus pour aller nager.
3. Moi, je _____ ma voiture pour aller faire du shopping.
4. Mes parents _____ un taxi pour aller voir une exposition.
5. Mon mari et moi _____ la voiture pour aller dîner ensemble.

Maintenant, dites où chacun va et comment il y va.

la librairie / le musée / le centre commercial / le restaurant / le cinéma / la piscine

EXEMPLE   **Papa va à la librairie. Il y va en bus.**

F. Des visites. Presque tous les membres de sa famille viennent voir Didier à Lafayette cette année. Didier parle avec sa mère au téléphone pour savoir quand chacun vient. Qu'est-ce qu'ils disent?

EXEMPLE   8/8 (mes cousins)
— **Quand est-ce que mes cousins viennent?**
— **Le huit août.**

1. 1/1 (ma sœur)
2. 15/6 (tu)
3. 17/9 (mon oncle)
4. 15/3 (mes frères)

Maintenant, Didier parle de ce que tous les membres de sa famille vont faire aux dates indiquées. Complétez ses phrases logiquement au futur immédiat.

EXEMPLE   12/25 (mes enfants)
Le vingt-cinq décembre, mes enfants vont passer du temps en famille.

1. (14/2) ma femme et moi
2. (4/7) mes enfants
3. (31/12) ma tante
4. (1/1) moi, je

Maintenant, demandez à votre partenaire ce qu'il/elle va probablement faire aux dates indiquées.

EXEMPLE   — **Qu'est-ce que tu vas probablement faire le vingt-cinq décembre?**
— **Je vais passer du temps en famille.**
Je ne vais rien faire de spécial.

---

passer du temps en famille /
 avec des amis / seul(e)...

sortir avec des amis

inviter des amis à la maison

faire une fête *(to have a party)*

dîner au restaurant

dormir toute la journée

aller voir un défilé *(parade)*

aller danser

rester à la maison

???

Lecture et Composition

Lecture

⚙ Pour mieux lire: *Using word families*

Music is an integral part of life on the bayou. You are going to read the lyrics to the song ***Cœur des Cajuns** (Heart of the Cajuns)* by Bruce Daigrepont, in which he sees Cajun music as the expression of both the **joie de vivre** *(joy of living)* and the **chagrin de cœur** *(heartache)* of the Cajun people. Learning to recognize related words that have the same root will help expand your vocabulary and facilitate your reading. Before reading the lyrics, do this activity to make your reading easier.

Familles de mots. Servez-vous des mots donnés pour déterminer le sens des mots en caractères gras.

danser: *to dance* → **une danse:** *a* _____
chanter: *to sing* → **une chanson:** *a* _____
prier: *to pray* → **une prière:** *a* _____
valser: *to waltz* → **une valse:** *a* _____
vivre: *to live* → **une vie:** *a* _____

Cœur des Cajuns

La joie de vivre, c'est dans l'accordéon,
La joie de vivre, c'est dans les belles chansons.
La musique c'est une tradition
Et c'est dans les cœurs de tous les Cajuns.

Chagrin de cœur, c'est dans l'accordéon,
Chagrin de cœur, c'est dans les belles chansons.
La musique c'est une tradition
Et c'est dans les cœurs de tous les Cajuns.

Dansez ensemble les vieux et les jeunes.
Priez ensemble les vieux et les jeunes.
La tradition c'est **pour tout quelques-uns**
Et c'est dans les cœurs de tous les Cajuns.

Un **'tit** bébé dans **les bras** de sa maman,
Aprévalser dans les bras de sa maman.
Il va apprendre la tradition
Et c'est dans les cœurs de tous les Cajuns.

La joie de vivre, c'est dans l'accordéon,
La joie de vivre, c'est dans les belles chansons.
La musique c'est une tradition
Et c'est dans les cœurs de tous les Cajuns.

Chagrin de cœur, c'est dans l'accordéon,
Chagrin de cœur, c'est dans les belles chansons.
La musique c'est une tradition
Et c'est dans les cœurs de tous les Cajuns.

by Bruce Daigrepont
(Bayou Pon Pon, ASCAP-Happy Valley Music, BMI) from *Cœur des Cajuns* on Rounder Records (#6026)

---

pour tout quelques-uns *for everyone* (regional) **'tit** = *petit* **les bras** *the arms*
Aprévalser *Waltzing* (regional)

Compréhension

Cœur des Cajuns. Lisez *Cœur des Cajuns* et complétez ces phrases.

1. La musique est une expression de la joie de vivre et aussi du _____.

2. La musique est une tradition qui se trouve *(is found)* dans les _____ de tous les Cajuns.

3. _____ est un instrument de musique populaire.

4. Les vieux et les jeunes vont danser, valser et _____ ensemble.

Composition

> ⚛ **Pour mieux écrire:** *Visualizing your topic*

Sometimes it is easier to write a description of people or things if you visualize or look at images of them. An image such as a family tree provides a logical order to a description.

Organisez-vous. Vous allez écrire une description de votre famille. D'abord, regardez des photos de votre famille. Ensuite, dessinez *(draw)* un arbre généalogique de votre famille. Si vous êtes marié(e) ou divorcé(e), dessinez votre (ex-)mari / (ex-)femme et vos enfants. Sinon *(Otherwise),* dessinez vos parents et vos frères et sœurs. À côté de chaque membre de votre famille sur l'arbre généalogique, écrivez tous le mots que vous associez à cette personne: son âge, sa profession, son apparence physique, son caractère et ses activités. Si nécessaire, cherchez des mots dans un dictionnaire.

If you have access to SYSTÈME-D software, you will find the following phrases, vocabulary, grammar, and dictionary aids there.

Phrases: Describing people; Asking for information
Vocabulary: Family members; Personality; Hair colors; Animals
Grammar: Adjective position; Contractions with **à**; Possessive adjectives
Dictionary: The verb **aller**

Ma famille

Écrivez une description détaillée de votre famille. Basez votre description sur l'arbre généalogique de la section précédente.

Comparaisons culturelles

La francophonie en Louisiane et ses origines

La majorité des Créoles en Louisiane aujourd'hui sont d'origine française, d'origine africaine, d'origine européenne ou d'origine mixte.

En 1682, la France prend possession de la Louisiane et en 1718, La Nouvelle-Orléans est **fondée.** Certains Créoles d'aujourd'hui sont les descendants des premiers **colons** français et européens. Ces colons **faisaient souvent partie de** l'aristocratie ou de **la haute bourgeoisie.**

D'autres Créoles sont les descendants d'immigrés français **venus** en Louisiane pour **échapper** aux campagnes militaires de Napoléon.

Encore d'autres Créoles sont les descendants d'**esclaves** échappés des îles caraïbes ou d'immigrés de ces îles.

Par contre, la majorité des Cadiens sont les descendants des Acadiens, **expulsés du** Canada **par** les Anglais **au 18ᵉ siècle.** (Le mot *cajun* **est dérivé du mot** *acadien.*)

En 1604, les Français fondent l'Acadie, aujourd'hui la Nouvelle-Écosse, le Nouveau-Brunswick et l'Île-du-Prince-Édouard. En 1713, les Anglais prennent possession de l'Acadie. En 1755, ils commencent à expulser les Français. Cette expulsion des Acadiens du Canada est **connue comme** le Grand Dérangement. En 2004, la gouverneure générale du Canada, Adrienne Clarkson, reconnaît le génocide des Acadiens au 18ᵉ siècle et **établit** le 28 juillet comme *Une Journée de Commémoration du Grand Dérangement.*

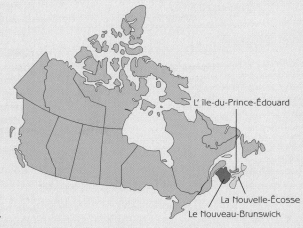

L'île-du-Prince-Édouard

La Nouvelle-Écosse
Le Nouveau-Brunswick

fondée *founded*   **des colons** *colonists*   **faisaient souvent partie de** *were often part of*   **la haute bourgeoisie** *the upper middle class*   **venus** *who came*   **échapper** *to escape*   **Encore d'autres** *Still other*   **esclaves** *slaves*   **Par contre** *On the other hand*   **expulsés du** *thrown out of*   **par** *by*   **au 18ᵉ siècle** *in the 18ᵗʰ century*   **est dérivé du mot** *is derived from the word*   **connue comme** *known as*   **établit** *establishes*

En raison de l'inaccessibilité de la région, les francophones en Louisiane restent **isolés pendant** plus de 200 ans et la culture et la langue des francophones restent dominantes dans **le sud** de la Louisiane.

Vers la fin du 19ᵉ siècle, pourtant, des vagues d'anglophones commencent à arriver dans la région. En 1916, l'état de Louisiane **exige que la scolarité soit faite** en anglais et l'anglais devient la langue prédominante chez les jeunes. L'usage du français en Louisiane **diminue.**

Après un certain temps, un mouvement pour le développement et la protection de la langue et de la culture françaises **surgit.** En 1968, l'état établit CODOFIL, le Conseil pour le Développement du Français en Louisiane. L'assemblée législative **crée** la région d'Acadiana. Un amendement est **ajouté** à la Constitution de l'état pour encourager la préservation de la culture française en Louisiane et les écoles commencent à établir des programmes d'immersion en français.

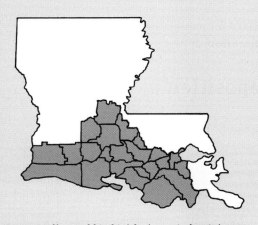

En 1971, l'assemblée législative crée la région d'Acadiana, **comprenant 22 paroisses** francophones.

En 2005, après la dévastation de l'ouragan Katrina, les millions de dollars d'aide venus des pays francophones sont **témoignage des liens** culturels de cette région avec la Francophonie.

Compréhension

1. Quels sont les deux plus grands groupes culturels parmi *(among)* les francophones en Louisiane? Quelles sont les origines de chaque groupe?

2. Qu'est-ce que c'est que le Grand Dérangement?

3. Quelle est la différence entre les deux régions d'Acadie et d'Acadiana?

4. Quel est le but *(purpose)* de l'organisation CODOFIL? Que pensez-vous de cette idée de créer une agence pour la défense de la langue et de la culture d'une minorité?

5. Dans certaines écoles primaires *(elementary schools)* en Louisiane, il y a des programmes d'immersion en français. À votre avis *(In your opinion)*, à quel âge est-ce qu'on devrait *(should)* commencer à étudier une autre langue? Est-il plus important d'étudier une autre langue si on est d'une famille d'une autre tradition linguistique?

Visit **academic.cengage.com/french** for YouTube video cultural correlations, cultural information and activities.

En raison de *Because of* **isolés pendant** *isolated for* **le sud** *the south* **Vers la fin du 19ᵉ siècle** *Towards the end of the 19ᵗʰ century* **pourtant** *however* **des vagues** *waves* **exige que la scolarité soit faite** *requires that education be done* **diminue** *diminishes* **surgit** *surges, arises* **crée** *creates* **ajouté** *added* **comprenant 22 paroisses** *including 22 parishes (equivalent to counties)* **témoignage des liens** *testimony of the ties*

Résumé de grammaire

Expressions with *avoir*

The following expressions use **avoir** to describe someone or say how someone feels.

Note the use of the definite article with **avoir les yeux / les cheveux.**

Ma tante s'appelle Sylvie. Elle **a 34 ans.** Elle **a les cheveux longs et châtains** et **les yeux noirs.** Elle **a des lunettes.** Elle **a l'air** intellectuel.

avoir... ans	avoir l'air
avoir faim	avoir soif
avoir froid	avoir chaud
avoir raison	avoir tort
avoir peur (de)	avoir sommeil
avoir les yeux...	
avoir les cheveux...	
avoir une barbe / une moustache / des lunettes	

— J'ai faim. Je vais aller au restaurant. Qu'est-ce que tu **as l'intention de** faire?

— Je ne sais pas. J'**ai besoin de** travailler, mais j'**ai envie de** sortir.

Use **avoir besoin de** (+ noun or infinitive) for *to need,* **avoir envie de** (+ noun or infinitive) for *to feel like,* and **avoir l'intention de** (+ infinitive) for *to intend to.*

The verb *aller,* the preposition *à,* and the pronoun *y*

The verb **aller** *(to go)* is irregular.

— Où **vas**-tu?

— Je **vais** au cinéma. Mes parents y **vont** aussi, mais ma sœur n'y **va** pas. Et toi?

— Philippe et moi **allons** au café.

ALLER *(to go)*	
je **vais**	nous *z* **allons**
tu **vas**	vous *z* **allez**
il/elle **va**	ils/elles **vont**

J'aime aller **au** centre commercial, mais j'aime mieux aller **à la** librairie.

Aimes-tu aller **aux** festivals de musique de la région?

— Je vais à l'université. Tu voudrais **y** aller avec moi?

— Non, je n'**y** vais pas aujourd'hui.

Use the preposition **à** *(to, at, in)* to say where you are going. When **à** falls before **le** or **les,** the two words contract to **au** and **aux.**

Use the pronoun **y** to mean *there,* even when *there* is only implied in English. Place it *immediately* before the infinitive if there is one. Otherwise, place it *immediately* before the conjugated verb. Treat **y** as a vowel for purposes of elision and liaison.

The subject pronoun *on* and command forms *(l'impératif)*

On parle français en Louisiane.

Use **on** as the subject of a sentence to refer to people in general *(one, people, they),* or instead of **nous** to say *we.* **On** takes the same verb form as **il/elle,** no matter what the translation in English.

— **On sort** ce soir?

— D'accord. **Allons** au cinéma.

— Non, **n'allons pas** au cinéma. **Dînons** plutôt au restaurant.

You can invite someone to do something with you by asking a question with **on** *(Shall we . . . ? / How about . . . ?).* To say *Let's . . . ,* use the **nous** form of the appropriate verb without the pronoun **nous.**

To tell someone to do something, use the **tu** or **vous** form of the verb, as appropriate, without the pronoun **tu** or **vous.** In **tu** form commands, drop the final **-s** of **-er** verbs and **aller.**

Avoir and **être** have irregular command forms.

ÊTRE *(be . . .)*	AVOIR *(have . . .)*
sois	aie
soyons	ayons
soyez	ayez

Va au restaurant Préjean et **mange** les spécialités de la maison.
Mangez bien. **Ne mangez pas** de dessert.

Sois à l'heure pour tes cours.
N'**aie** pas peur — **aie** confiance!
Soyons calmes!
Ayez de la patience!

The immediate future *(Le futur immédiat)*

To talk about what someone *is going to do,* use a conjugated form of the verb **aller** followed by an infinitive. To say what someone is *not* going to do, place **ne... pas** around the conjugated form of **aller. Il y a** becomes **il va y avoir** in the immediate future.

— Qu'est-ce que tu **vas faire** ce soir? Tu **vas sortir?**
— Non, je **ne vais pas sortir. Je vais rester** à la maison. **Il va y avoir** un festival de films à la télé.

Dates

To tell the date, use **le** and the cardinal numbers (**deux, trois, quatre...**), except for *the first* (**le premier**). The day goes before the month: 30/9/2007.

You can express the years 1100–1999 in two ways. Years from 2000 on are only expressed using the word **mille.**

Use **en** to say in what year or month.

— Quelle est la date aujourd'hui? C'est **le trente septembre?**
— Non, c'est **le premier octobre.**

1910 **mille neuf cent dix / dix-neuf cent dix**
2010 **deux mille dix**

Mon anniversaire, c'est **en** mars.
Je vais finir mes études **en** 2012.

The verbs *prendre* and *venir* and means of transportation

Prendre *(to take)* and **venir** *(to come)* are irregular.

PRENDRE *(to take)*		VENIR *(to come)*	
je **prends**	nous **prenons**	je **viens**	nous **venons**
tu **prends**	vous **prenez**	tu **viens**	vous **venez**
il/elle/on **prend**	ils/elles **prennent**	il/elle/on **vient**	ils/elles **viennent**

— **Venez**-vous à l'université en voiture?
— Non, je ne **viens** pas en cours en voiture. Je **prends** mon vélo. **Prenez**-vous votre voiture?

Le matin, il **prend** un café et un croissant.

Prendre means *to take.* You can also use it as *to have* when talking about having something to eat or drink. **Comprendre** *(to understand)* and **apprendre** *(to learn)* are conjugated like **prendre.**

Tu **comprends?**

Nous **apprenons** beaucoup dans ce cours.

Revenir *(to come back)* and **devenir** *(to become)* are conjugated like **venir.**

Les fils **reviennent** tard et le père **devient** impatient.

Use the preposition **en** (or **à** with **vélo**) to say *by* what means you are traveling with verbs like **aller, venir,** and **voyager.** When using **prendre** to say what means of transportation you are taking, you can often use the same article with the noun that you would in English.

D'habitude, ils **voyagent en avion** mais aujourd'hui ils **prennent le train.**

CD 2

Describing your family

LA FAMILLE

un beau-père / une belle-mère	a stepfather, a father-in-law / a stepmother, a mother-in-law
un(e) cousin(e)	a cousin
un(e) enfant	a child
un fils / une fille	a son / a daughter
un frère / une sœur	a brother / a sister
un garçon / une fille	a boy / a girl
des grands-parents / un grand-père / une grand-mère	grandparents / a grandfather / a grandmother
un neveu (*pl* des neveux) / une nièce	a nephew / a niece
un oncle / une tante	an uncle / an aunt
des parents / un père / une mère	parents / a father / a mother

NOMS FÉMININS

une barbe	a beard
des lunettes	glasses
une moustache	a mustache
des vacances	vacation

ADJECTIFS

âgé(e)	old
auburn (inv)	auburn
blond(e)	blond(e)
brun(e)	medium / dark brown (with hair)
châtain	light / medium brown (with hair)
court(e)	short
décédé(e)	deceased
long(ue)	long
mi-longs	shoulder-length (with hair)
noir(e)	black, very dark brown (with hair)
noisette (inv)	hazel (with eyes)
roux (rousse)	red (with hair)

EXPRESSIONS VERBALES

avoir besoin de	to need
avoir chaud / froid	to be hot / cold
avoir envie de	to feel like, to want
avoir faim / soif	to be hungry / thirsty
avoir l'air...	to look . . . , to seem . . .
avoir les cheveux / les yeux...	to have . . . hair / eyes
avoir l'intention de	to intend to
avoir peur (de)	to be afraid (of)
avoir raison / tort	to be right / wrong
avoir sommeil	to be sleepy
Comment s'appelle-t-il/elle?	What is his/her name?
Il/Elle s'appelle...	His/Her name is . . .
porter	to wear, to carry
Quel âge a... ?	How old is . . . ?
avoir (environ)... ans	to be (about) . . . years old
Vous êtes combien dans votre (ta) famille?	How many people are there in your family?
Nous sommes...	There are . . . of us.

DIVERS

de taille moyenne	of medium height
encore	still
environ	about
La Nouvelle-Orléans	New Orleans

Saying where you go in your free time

NOMS MASCULINS

un centre commercial	a shopping mall
un concert	a concert
un festival	a festival
un magasin	a store
un musée	a museum
un orchestre	an orchestra, a band
un parc	a park
des projets	plans
le temps libre	free time
un théâtre	a theater

NOMS FÉMININS

une activité (de plein air)	an (outdoor) activity
la cuisine	cooking, cuisine
une église	a church
une exposition	an exhibit
une librairie	a bookstore
la musique zydeco	zydeco music
une pièce	a play
une piscine	a swimming pool
une plage	a beach
une région	a region
une spécialité	a specialty

EXPRESSIONS VERBALES

acheter	to buy
aie, ayons, ayez	have, let's have, have
aller (à)	to go (to)
avoir confiance	to have confidence
avoir de la patience	to have patience
connaître	to know, to get to know, to be acquainted / familiar with
prendre un bain de soleil	to sunbathe
retrouver	to meet
servir	to serve
sois, soyons, soyez	be, let's be, be
trouver	to find

DIVERS

à l'heure	on time
bonne idée	good idea
cadien(ne)	Cajun
calme	calm
Ça te dit?	How does that sound?
culturel(le)	cultural
de temps en temps	from time to time
extra(ordinaire)	great
on	one, people, they, we
On... ?	Shall we . . . ?, How about . . . ?
on dit que	they say that
on peut	one can
plutôt	rather, instead
pour	in order to
sage	good, well-behaved
y	there

Saying what you are going to do

NOMS MASCULINS

un anniversaire	*a birthday*
le folklore	*folklore*

NOMS FÉMININS

une fête	*a holiday, a party*
la soirée	*the evening*

EXPRESSIONS VERBALES

aller voir	*to go see, to visit (a person)*
boire	*to drink*
faire des projets	*to make plans*
faire un tour	*to take a tour, to go for a ride*
il va y avoir	*there is / are going to be*
partir (en vacances, pour le week-end)	*to go away, to leave (on vacation, for the weekend)*
quitter	*to leave*
visiter	*to visit (a place)*

LES DATES

En quelle année?	*In what year?*
En quel mois?	*In what month?*
Quelle est la date?	*What is the date?*
C'est le premier (deux, trois...)	*It's the first (second, third . . .) of*
janvier / février / mars / avril / mai / juin / juillet / août / septembre / octobre / novembre / décembre	*January / February / March / April / May / June / July / August / September / October / November / December*

EXPRESSIONS ADVERBIALES

ce matin	*this morning*
ce mois-ci	*this month*
ce soir	*tonight, this evening*
ce week-end	*this weekend*
cet après-midi	*this afternoon*
cette année	*this year*
cette semaine	*this week*
d'abord	*first*
demain matin / après-midi / soir	*tomorrow morning / afternoon / evening*
ensuite	*then, afterwards*
l'année prochaine	*next year*
la semaine prochaine	*next week*
le mois prochain	*next month*
le week-end prochain	*next weekend*
lundi (mardi) prochain	*next Monday (Tuesday)*
plus tard	*later*
(et) puis	*(and) then*
tard	*late*
tôt	*early*

DIVERS

célèbre	*famous*
génial(e) (*m.pl.* géniaux)	*great*
régional(e) (*m.pl.* régionaux)	*regional*
le Vieux Carré	*the French Quarter*

Planning how to get there

NOMS MASCULINS

un (auto)bus	*a bus*
un (auto)car	*a bus*
un avion	*a plane*
un bateau	*a boat*
le métro	*the subway*
un moyen de transport	*a means of transportation*
un taxi	*a cab, a taxi*
un train	*a train*
un voyage	*a trip*

NOM FÉMININ

une possibilité	*a possibility*

EXPRESSIONS VERBALES

aller à pied	*to go on foot*
à vélo	*by bike*
en (auto)car	*by bus*
en (auto)bus	*by bus*
en avion	*by plane*
en bateau	*by boat*
en métro	*by subway*
en taxi	*by taxi*
en train	*by train*
en voiture	*by car*
apprendre	*to learn*
comprendre	*to understand*
devenir	*to become*
louer	*to rent*
prendre	*to take*
revenir	*to come back*
venir	*to come*

DIVERS

Ça prend combien de temps?	*How long does it take?*
Ça prend...	*It takes . . .*
impatient(e)	*impatient*
pas plus	*no more*
prêt(e)	*ready*

Bruce Daigrepont présente des concerts de musique cadienne partout dans le monde.

Nonc Willie

BRUCE DAIGREPONT

Bruce Daigrepont, true to his Cajun heritage, focuses his music around the traditional Cajun instruments, the accordion and fiddle, backed by drums, bass, rubboard, and triangle. His sets are comprised of Cajun waltzes and two-steps, fiddle reels, deep blues, swamp pop, zydeco, and R&B.

A. Chez Nonc Willie. Dans la chanson *(song)* **Nonc Willie** *(Uncle Willie)*, le chanteur invite des amis à aller chez Nonc Willie pour s'amuser *(to have fun)*. Voilà les choses à faire chez Nonc Willie. Devinez le sens des mots que vous ne connaissez pas. *(Guess the meaning of the words you don't know.)*

gagner de l'argent	s'amuser	boire de la bière
jouer à des jeux de cartes	acheter des bonbons	

B. Dans le passé. Le chanteur dit «je me souviens» *(I remember)* pour parler de quand il était *(was)* petit. Dans les phrases suivantes, tous les verbes sont au passé. Utilisez le contexte pour deviner leur sens.

Nonc Willie *était* le frère de mon grand-père. Il n'*avait* pas beaucoup d'argent, mais il *s'amusait* bien. Tous ses amis *se rassemblaient* le samedi soir pour jouer aux cartes ensemble. Le gagneur *donnait* un peu d'argent aux enfants qui *observaient* le jeu.

 You can access these songs at the iTunes playlist on **academic.cengage.com/french/horizons.**

Fille de ville

MARIE-ÉLAINE THIBERT

Marie-Élaine Thibert has always had a passion for music. To fulfill her dream, she had to work hard and also overcome her shyness. That dream, to sing on stage no matter how long it took her to get there, became a reality for her when she was selected to sing on *Star Académie* (the equivalent of *American Idol*) and quickly became a star.

Fille de ville. Dans cette chanson, Marie-Élaine Thibert indique qu'elle n'a rien contre *(has nothing against)* la campagne. Pourtant, née *(born)* dans la grande ville de Montréal, elle se proclame *(proclaims herself)* clairement une «fille de ville». Regardez la liste de mots et d'expressions qui suit. Avec quel endroit *(place)* associez-vous chacun, **la campagne** ou **la ville**?

Depuis toujours fan de *(a fan of)* Céline Dion, Marie-Élaine Thibert a chanté avec elle à Las Vegas.

les champs *(fields)*

les lumières *(lights)*

le bruit *(noise)*

les bois *(woods)*

gronder *(to rumble)*

les lacs et les rivières

le béton *(concrete)* et le traffic

l'espace *(space)*

les montagnes

l'énergie

les plaines

les odeurs

les millions de choses à faire

les oiseaux *(birds)* et les fleurs

Les projets

Chapitre 5

iLrn Heinle Learning Center

academic.cengage.com/french/horizons

Système-D

Audio   iRadio

What part of France would you like to visit? Would you like to do a special kind of trip like a bicycle tour or a cooking or wine-tasting tour? Do an online search for various trips to France. Find a trip you would like to take and describe where you are going to go and what you are going to do.

LA FRANCE

Voudriez-vous visiter la France? **Aimeriez-vous** visiter Paris ou les autres régions de la France? La France vous offre une grande variété. Il y a...

de grandes villes

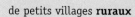

des plaines

de petits villages **ruraux**

Aimeriez-vous... Would you like . . .   **ruraux** rural

Visit it live on Google Earth!

des rochers escarpés

des plages de sable

des fleuves

des montagnes

❀ Qu'en savez-vous?

Est-ce que vous connaissez *(know)* un peu la France?
Regardez la carte *(map)* de la France au commencement du *(at the beginning of the)* livre. Ensuite, répondez à ces questions. Si vous ne savez pas, devinez! *(If you don't know, guess!)*

1. La France a à peu près la même superficie *(about the same area)* que...

   a. l'Alaska   b. le Texas   c. la Louisiane

2. Regardez la carte de la France. À cause de *(Because of)* sa forme, on appelle la France...

   a. le Pentagone   b. l'Octogone   c. l'Hexagone

3. Nommez les huit pays et les quatre masses d'eau qui bordent la France.

4. Nommez cinq chaînes et massifs montagneux *(mountain ranges)* en France. Lequel *(Which one)* ne forme pas de frontière entre la France et un autre pays?

5. Nommez sept fleuves en France. Lequel traverse *(crosses)* Paris?

6. Paris est la capitale de la France. Nommez deux autres villes importantes.

7. La France est un centre important de commerce, d'industrie et de technologie. Est-ce que l'agriculture joue aussi un rôle important?

des fleuves *rivers*

Saying what you did

Le week-end dernier

Alice Pérez, **femme d'affaires** américaine **travaillant** à Paris, parle de ses activités de **samedi dernier.** Et vous?

Où est-ce que vous êtes allé(e)? Qu'est-ce que vous avez fait?

Samedi matin...

je ne suis pas sortie, je suis restée chez moi.

J'ai dormi jusqu'à 10 heures.

J'ai **pris** mon **petit déjeuner.**

Samedi après-midi...

je suis allée en ville.

Je n'ai pas travaillé.

J'ai déjeuné avec une amie et j'ai bien mangé.

Samedi soir...

je suis sortie.

J'ai vu un film étranger.

J'ai retrouvé un ami au café.

je suis rentrée chez moi.

J'ai lu le journal.

Je **n'**ai **rien** fait.

Le week-end dernier *Last weekend*   **une femme d'affaires (un homme d'affaires)** *a business woman (a business man)*
travaillant *working*   **samedi dernier** *last Saturday*   **Où est-ce que vous êtes allé(e)?** *Where did you go?*   **Qu'est-ce que vous avez fait?** *What did you do?*   **prendre son petit déjeuner** *to have one's breakfast*   **ne... rien** *nothing*

C'est lundi et Cathy, la fille d'Alice, parle avec un ami des activités du week-end dernier.

CATHY: Tu as passé un bon week-end?

EDGAR: Oui, génial. Samedi matin, j'ai préparé les cours et samedi après-midi, j'ai joué au foot avec des amis.

CATHY: Qu'est-ce que tu as fait samedi soir?

EDGAR: Je suis sorti. Je suis allé en boîte et j'ai beaucoup dansé.

CATHY: Et **hier**?

EDGAR: Hier matin, **j'ai fait une promenade** sur les Champs-Élysées où j'ai fait du shopping. **Hier soir,** je suis resté à la maison et j'ai regardé la télé.

A. Activités logiques. Formez des phrases logiques. Complétez les phrases de la première colonne avec un choix logique de la deuxième colonne.

1. Je suis resté(e) au lit et...
2. J'ai retrouvé des amis au café où...
3. J'ai dîné au restaurant où...
4. Je suis allé(e) au cinéma où...
5. Je suis allé(e) en boîte où...
6. J'ai joué au tennis avec une amie mais...
7. Je suis allé(e) au parc où...

j'ai pris un verre.
j'ai dormi.
j'ai beaucoup dansé.
je n'ai pas gagné.
j'ai vu un film étranger.
j'ai très bien mangé.
j'ai fait une promenade.

B. Et vous? Complétez les phrases pour indiquer comment vous avez passé la journée d'hier.

1. J'ai dormi jusqu'à *8 heures / 10 heures / ???*.
2. J'ai pris le petit déjeuner *chez moi / au café / chez une amie / ???. (Je n'ai pas pris de petit déjeuner.)*
3. J'ai lu *le journal / un livre / ???. (Je n'ai rien lu.)*
4. *Je suis allé(e) / Je ne suis pas allé(e)* en cours.
5. J'ai déjeuné *chez moi / chez des amis / au restaurant / ???. (Je n'ai pas déjeuné.)*
6. *J'ai travaillé. / Je n'ai pas travaillé.*
7. J'ai dîné *chez moi / chez mes parents / dans un fast-food / ???. (Je n'ai pas dîné.)*
8. J'ai *beaucoup / peu* mangé. *(Je n'ai pas mangé.)*
9. Le soir, *je suis resté(e) chez moi / je suis sorti(e) / ???.*

Le week-end dernier, j'ai fait une promenade au jardin des Tuileries.

C. Conversation. Avec un(e) partenaire, relisez à haute voix la conversation entre Cathy et Edgar en haut de la page. Ensuite, imaginez que c'est lundi matin et changez la conversation pour parler de votre week-end passé.

Note: You may not know how to say everything you did. Pick two or three things that you know how to say or ask your instructor for help.

You can find a list of the new words from the vocabulary and grammar sections of this **Compétence** on page 214 and a recording of this list on track 2-29 of your *Text Audio CD.*

---

hier *yesterday*   **faire une promenade** *to take a walk*   **hier soir** *last night, yesterday evening*

1. The **passé composé** always has two parts. What are they called?

2. What verb is usually used as the auxiliary verb? Do you conjugate it?

3. How do you form the past participle of all **-er** and most **-ir** verbs? Which verbs that you know have irregular past participles? What are their past participles?

4. How do you negate verbs in the **passé composé**? How do you say *I did nothing / I didn't do anything*?

5. In the **passé composé**, where do you place adverbs like **souvent** or **bien**?

6. What are the three possible English translations of **j'ai mangé**?

To download a podcast on the Compound Past Tense, go to **academic.cengage.com/french.**

✳ Note *de grammaire*

Some verbs expressing *going, coming,* and *staying,* such as **aller, sortir, rentrer,** and **rester,** have **être,** not **avoir,** as their auxiliary verb. You will learn about them in the next **Compétence.** For now, remember to use **je suis allé(e), je suis sorti(e), je suis resté(e),** and **je suis rentré(e)** if you want to say *I went, I went out, I stayed,* and *I returned.* (If you are a female, add an extra **-e** to the past participle of these verbs, just as you do with adjectives. Do not add this feminine **-e** to the verbs you are learning to conjugate with the auxiliary **avoir** in this **Compétence.**)

Saying what you did

*Le passé composé avec **avoir***

To say what happened in the past, put the verb in the **passé composé.** It is composed of two parts, the auxiliary verb and the past participle. The auxiliary verb, usually **avoir,** is conjugated. The past participle of all **-er** verbs ends in **-é,** that of many **-ir** verbs ends in **-i.**

PARLER		DORMIR	
j'**ai parlé**	nous **avons parlé**	j'**ai dormi**	nous **avons dormi**
tu **as parlé**	vous **avez parlé**	tu **as dormi**	vous **avez dormi**
il/elle/on **a parlé**	ils/elles **ont parlé**	il/elle/on **a dormi**	ils/elles **ont dormi**

Many irregular verbs have irregular past participles that must be memorized.

avoir	j'ai **eu,** tu as **eu**...	**être**	j'ai **été,** tu as **été**...
il y a	il y a **eu**	**faire**	j'ai **fait,** tu as f**ait**...
boire	j'ai **bu,** tu as **bu**...	**écrire**	j'ai **écrit,** tu as **écrit**...
lire	j'ai **lu,** tu as **lu**...	**prendre**	j'ai **pris,** tu as **pris**...
voir	j'ai **vu,** tu as **vu**...	(**apprendre**	j'ai **appris**...
		comprendre	j'ai **compris**...)

Adverbs indicating how often (**toujours, souvent...**) and how well (**bien, mal...**) are usually placed between the auxiliary verb and the past participle. Place **ne... pas, ne... jamais,** and **ne... rien** around the auxiliary verb.

Nous avons **souvent** mangé ici. Nous avons **bien** mangé.

Je **n'**ai **pas** travaillé hier. Je **n'**ai **rien** fait.

The **passé composé** can be translated in a variety of ways in English.

I took the bus.
I have taken the bus. } J'ai pris l'autobus.
I did take the bus.

A. La journée de Cathy. Voilà les activités de Cathy le week-end dernier. Est-ce qu'elle a fait les choses suivantes?

> **EXEMPLE** Samedi matin, Cathy (quitter la maison très tôt)
> **Samedi matin, Cathy n'a pas quitté la maison très tôt.**

Samedi matin, Cathy (dormir, travailler, faire du jogging)

Samedi après-midi, elle (visiter un musée, faire du ski nautique *[to waterski]*, lire un livre)

Samedi soir, Cathy et ses amis (passer la soirée au café, boire un café, beaucoup parler)

B. Qu'avez-vous fait? Dites si ces personnes ont fait les choses suivantes la dernière fois que vous êtes allés *(went)* en cours.

>   **EXEMPLE**   Moi, je (j') / dormir jusqu'à 10 heures
>   **Moi, j'ai dormi jusqu'à dix heures.**
>   **Moi, je n'ai pas dormi jusqu'à dix heures.**

AVANT LE COURS

Moi, je (j')...

1. être dans un autre cours
2. passer la matinée chez moi
3. lire le journal
4. retrouver des amis au café
5. faire mes devoirs

Mon (Ma) meilleur(e) ami(e)...

6. boire un café avec moi
7. manger avec moi
8. passer la matinée avec moi
9. faire une promenade avec moi
10. faire les devoirs avec moi

EN COURS

Les étudiants...

11. dormir en cours
12. bien écouter la leçon
13. beaucoup apprendre
14. boire un café en cours
15. comprendre la leçon

Nous...

16. avoir un examen
17. écrire beaucoup d'exercices
18. voir un film français
19. travailler ensemble
20. commencer un nouveau chapitre

C. Et toi? Posez des questions à votre partenaire sur ce qu'il/elle a fait hier. Basez vos questions sur les phrases données.

>   **EXEMPLE**   À quelle heure / quitter la maison
>   **— À quelle heure est-ce que tu as quitté la maison hier?**
>   **— J'ai quitté la maison vers 9 heures.**
>   **Je n'ai pas quitté la maison hier.**

1. jusqu'à quelle heure / dormir
2. quand / quitter la maison
3. où / prendre ton petit déjeuner
4. avec qui / déjeuner
5. que / étudier
6. que / faire hier soir

Après, décrivez la journée de votre partenaire à la classe.

>   **EXEMPLE**   **Rachel a dormi jusqu'à sept heures. Elle a quitté la maison...**

D. Devinez! Dites à votre partenaire combien des choses suivantes vous avez faites récemment *(recently)* avec des ami(e)s. Votre partenaire va deviner lesquelles *(guess which ones)*.

| boire un café   louer un DVD   voir un film au cinéma   visiter une autre ville |
| faire une promenade   prendre un verre   déjeuner   dîner |
| prendre le petit déjeuner   faire du jogging |

>   **EXEMPLE**   **— Mes amis et moi, on a fait cinq choses de la liste récemment.**
>   **— Vous avez bu un café ensemble?**
>   **— Oui, on a bu un café. / Non, on n'a pas bu de café.**
>   **— Vous avez loué un DVD?...**

Stratégies et Lecture

❀ Pour mieux lire: *Using the sequence of events to make logical guesses*

You can often guess the meaning of unfamiliar verbs in a narrative by imagining what the logical order of actions would be. For example, when taking the bus, you wait for the bus first, get on the bus, then get off at your destination. Learn to read a whole sentence or paragraph, rather than one word at a time.

Notice that the prefix **re-** means that an action in a sequence is done again, as in English (*do* and *redo, read* and *reread*).

You will also notice that prepositions can indicate relationships between actions. **Pour** means *in order to* when it is followed by a verb. **Sans,** meaning *without,* can also be followed by an infinitive.

A. Devinez! Use the sequence of events in this passage to guess the meaning of the boldfaced words.

Cathy a pris une enveloppe. Elle **a ouvert** l'enveloppe et elle en **a sorti** une feuille de papier. Elle **a lu** les instructions sur la feuille mais elle n'a pas compris. Alors, elle **a relu** les instructions et elle **a remis** la feuille de papier dans l'enveloppe.

Cathy **a attendu** l'autobus devant son appartement. Quand il est arrivé, elle **est montée** dedans, et elle **est descendue** quand elle est arrivée à sa destination. Elle **est entrée** dans un café et a commandé un coca. Elle a bu son coca, elle **a payé l'addition** et elle **est repartie.**

Elle est entrée dans une station de métro et elle a acheté un ticket **au guichet,** mais elle n'a pas pris le métro. Elle **a mis** le ticket dans son enveloppe et elle a quitté la station.

Cathy est arrivée devant un magasin de vélo où elle a admiré un vélo rouge dans **la vitrine.** Elle est entrée dans le magasin et a demandé **le prix** du vélo.

B. Dans l'ordre logique. Mettez les activités suivantes de Cathy dans l'ordre logique. La première et la dernière *(last)* sont indiquées.

_____ Elle est allée vers la porte.
_____ Elle a lu les instructions sur la feuille de papier.
__1__ Cathy a vu une enveloppe sur la table.
_____ Elle a sorti une feuille de papier de l'enveloppe.
_____ Elle a pris l'enveloppe.
_____ Elle a ouvert l'enveloppe.
__8__ Elle a ouvert la porte et elle est sortie.
_____ Elle a remis la feuille dans l'enveloppe.

C. Quel verbe? Complétez ces phrases logiquement. N'oubliez pas *(Don't forget)* que **pour** veut dire *in order to* et **sans** veut dire *without.*

1. Cathy a quitté l'appartement sans... (boire son café, ouvrir la porte).
2. Elle a pris l'autobus pour... (rester à la maison, aller en ville).
3. Elle a retrouvé des amis pour... (passer le week-end seule, aller au cinéma).
4. Elle est allée au guichet pour... (acheter des tickets, boire une bière).
5. Après, elle est allée au café avec des amis pour... (boire quelque chose, danser).
6. Elle est rentrée à la maison sans... (quitter le café, prendre l'autobus).

Lecture: Qu'est-ce qu'elle a fait?

Seule dans son appartement, Cathy Pérez avait l'air un peu agitée. Elle a pris une enveloppe qui était sur la table et en a sorti une feuille de papier. Elle a lu les instructions et a remis la feuille dans l'enveloppe. Elle a pris l'enveloppe et a quitté son appartement.

Cathy est entrée dans un café où elle a commandé un coca et ensuite, elle a demandé l'addition. Quand l'addition est arrivée, elle a payé le garçon. Elle a ouvert l'enveloppe, a relu les instructions, a mis l'addition dans l'enveloppe et a quitté le café sans boire son coca. C'est bien bizarre! Pourquoi avait-elle l'air si agitée?

Ensuite, Cathy est allée à la station de métro. Elle est entrée dans la station et sans regarder le plan, est allée au guichet et a demandé un ticket. Quand on lui a donné son ticket, elle l'a mis dans l'enveloppe, a remonté l'escalier et a quitté la station de métro. Pourquoi a-t-elle acheté un ticket sans prendre le métro? Tout cela est fort bizarre!

Cathy a continué sa route jusqu'à un magasin de vélo. Elle a regardé un vélo rouge qui était dans la vitrine. Elle est entrée dans le magasin et elle a demandé le prix du vélo. Elle a écrit le prix du vélo sur une feuille de papier et elle a mis la feuille de papier dans l'enveloppe. Ensuite, elle est sortie du magasin.

Cathy est allée au coin de la rue pour attendre l'autobus. Quand l'autobus est arrivé, elle l'a pris et puis elle est descendue à l'université. Elle avait l'air un peu plus calme. Pourquoi a-t-elle fait tout ça? Pourquoi a-t-elle mis ces choses dans l'enveloppe? Pourquoi est-elle plus calme maintenant?

A. Comprenez-vous? Dites si Cathy a fait ces choses ou non.

1. Cathy a sorti une feuille de papier d'une enveloppe et a lu des instructions.
2. Elle a quitté son appartement et elle est allée directement à l'université.
3. Au café, elle a retrouvé une amie et elles ont commandé un café au lait.
4. Au café, elle a commandé un coca mais elle est partie sans boire le coca.
5. Elle a acheté un ticket de métro mais elle n'a pas pris le métro.

B. Maintenant... c'est à vous! Est-ce que vous trouvez les actions de Cathy plutôt bizarres? Pourquoi est-ce qu'elle a fait tout ça? Imaginez une explication.

Est-ce qu'elle... est agent de police ou détective privé? souffre d'amnésie? travaille pour la CIA? est espionne comme James Bond? collectionne des souvenirs de Paris? fait un exercice pour son cours de français?

Réponse:
Il y a une explication simple et logique! Cathy suit (*is taking*) un cours de français pour étrangers à Paris. Ses devoirs, dans l'enveloppe, consistent à prouver au professeur qu'elle est capable de commander quelque chose à boire au café, de demander un vélo et d'acheter un ticket de métro. Elle doit rapporter (*needs to bring back*) l'addition, le prix du vélo et le ticket de métro à son professeur.

Telling where you went

❋ **Note** *culturelle*

D'après une enquête *(survey)* récente, 48% des Français sont partis en week-end au moins une fois l'année précédente, 26% l'ont fait *(have done so)* au moins quatre fois et 13% au moins dix fois. 84% sont allés voir leur famille ou des amis et 40% sont allés à la campagne. Combien de fois êtes-vous parti(e) en week-end l'année dernière? Où êtes-vous allé(e)?

❋ **Note** *de vocabulaire*

1. It is common to say either **je suis descendu(e)** or **je suis resté(e)** with **à l'hôtel** or **dans un camping.** It is more common to use **rester** for *to stay* with **chez...** Also use **rester** to say how long you stayed.
2. Use **des parents** to say *relatives* and **mes parents** to say *my parents.*

Je suis parti(e) en voyage

La dernière fois que vous êtes parti(e) en voyage, où est-ce que vous êtes allé(e)? Qu'est-ce que vous avez fait?

Je suis allé(e)	à Denver. à New York. ???	**J'y suis allé(e)**	en avion. en train. en autocar. en voiture **(de location).**
Je suis parti(e)	en mars. le matin. vers trois heures. ???	Je suis arrivé(e)	le même jour. trois heures plus tard. **le lendemain.** ???
Je suis descendu(e)	à l'hôtel. dans un camping.	Je suis resté(e)	**une nuit.** le week-end. trois jours.
Je suis resté(e)	chez des amis. chez **des parents.**		
Je suis allé(e)	à la plage. à un concert. dans un club.	Je suis rentré(e)	trois jours après. la semaine suivante. deux semaines plus tard.

CD 2-31

Alice est partie en week-end. Le mardi suivant, elle parle avec son amie Claire du voyage qu'elle a fait le week-end passé.

CLAIRE: Qu'est-ce que tu as fait le week-end dernier?
ALICE: J'ai pris le train pour aller à Deauville.
CLAIRE: Quand est-ce que tu es partie?
ALICE: Je suis partie samedi matin et je suis rentrée hier soir.
CLAIRE: Tu as trouvé un bon hôtel?
ALICE: Je suis descendue dans un petit hôtel confortable, pas trop loin de la plage.
CLAIRE: **Quelle chance!** Moi aussi, j'ai envie de visiter Deauville.

A. En week-end Décrivez la dernière fois que vous êtes parti(e) en voyage.

1. Je suis allé(e) à (Chicago, Houston, ???).
2. J'y suis allé(e) (en avion, en train, ???).
3. Je suis parti(e) (le soir, vers cinq heures, ???).
4. Je suis arrivé(e) (une heure, trois jours, ???) plus tard.
5. Je suis descendu(e) (à l'hôtel, dans un camping, ???).
6. Je suis resté(e) (deux jours, une semaine, ???).
7. Je suis allé(e) (en ville, en boîte, ???).
8. Je suis rentré(e) (le lendemain, trois jours après, ???).

La dernière fois *The last time*   **J'y suis allé(e)** *I went there*   **de location** *rental*   **le lendemain** *the next day, the following day*
Je suis descendu(e) (descendre [de / dans / à]) *I stayed (to descend, to come down, to get off / out [of], to stay [at])*   **une nuit** *one night*   **des parents** *relatives*   **Quelle chance!** *What luck!*

B. Un tour de Paris. Alice et sa famille adorent visiter Paris et la région parisienne. Regardez les photos et complétez les phrases avec une expression de la colonne de droite.

1. Son mari, Vincent, est allé à la Sainte-Chapelle pour...
2. Ses enfants sont allés à Versailles pour...
3. Ils sont allés à Notre-Dame pour...
4. Ils sont allés au musée d'Orsay pour...
5. Ils sont allés au café sur les Champs-Élysées pour...
6. Alice est allée au jardin du Luxembourg pour...

voir une nouvelle exposition.
faire une promenade.
prendre un café.
voir son architecture gothique.
admirer les vitraux *(stained-glass windows)*.
visiter le château de Versailles.

Les Champs-Élysées

La Sainte-Chapelle

Le château de Versailles

Le musée d'Orsay

Notre-Dame

Le jardin du Luxembourg

C. Conversation. Avec un(e) partenaire, relisez à haute voix la conversation entre Alice et Claire à la page précédente. Ensuite, changez la conversation pour parler de la dernière fois que vous êtes parti(e) en week-end. Après, changez de rôles et parlez du dernier voyage de votre partenaire.

CD 2-32 You can find a list of the new words from the vocabulary and grammar sections of this **Compétence** on page 214 and a recording of this list on track 2-32 of your *Text Audio CD.*

Pour vérifier

1. Which verbs have **être** as the auxiliary in the **passé composé**? What do you have to remember to do with the past participle of these verbs that you don't do with verbs that have **avoir** as their auxiliary?

2. How do you say *to enter*? What preposition do you use with it? How do you say *to go out*? *to go out of*?

3. What preposition do you use with **partir** to say *to leave from*? What is the difference between **partir** and **quitter**?

4. How do you say *to go/come down, to descend*? *to get out of/down from/off of*? *to stay at*? How do you say *to go up*? *to get on/in*?

5. You are staying at a hotel in Paris and you go out to see **la tour Eiffel**. Would you use **rentrer** or **retourner** to say *to go back* to the hotel? *to go back* to see **la tour Eiffel** again?

❋ Note *de grammaire*

1. When **on** means *we*, its past participle may either be left in the masculine singular form (**On est sorti.**) or it may agree (**On est sorti[e]s**). Either form is considered correct.

2. **Passer** takes **avoir** in the **passé composé** when it means *to spend time*. It takes **être** when it means *to pass by*. **J'ai passé** une semaine à Austin. Je **suis passé(e)** chez mes parents.

To download a podcast on the Compound Past Tense, go to **academic.cengage.com/french.**

Telling where you went

Le passé composé avec **être**

Some verbs have **être** as their auxiliary verb in the **passé composé**. The past participle of these verbs must agree with the subject in number and gender. Remember that you do not make this agreement when **avoir** is the auxiliary: **Elle est parti(e)** hier. Elle a *pris* le train.

ALLER → ALLÉ		SORTIR → SORTI	
je **suis allé(e)**	nous **sommes allé(e)s**	je **suis sorti(e)**	nous **sommes sorti(e)s**
tu **es allé(e)**	vous **êtes allé(e)(s)**	tu **es sorti(e)**	vous **êtes sorti(e)(s)**
il **est allé**	ils **sont allés**	il **est sorti**	ils **sont sortis**
elle **est allée**	elles **sont allées**	elle **est sortie**	elles **sont sorties**
on **est allé(e)(s)**		on **est sorti(e)(s)**	

Notice that many of the verbs that have **être** as the auxiliary are verbs of *arriving* and *leaving*.

aller	je suis allé(e)	*I went*
venir/devenir/revenir	je suis venu(e)/devenu(e)/ revenu(e)	*I came/became/came back*
arriver	je suis arrivé(e)	*I arrived*
rester	je suis resté(e)	*I stayed, I remained*
entrer (dans)	je suis entré(e) (dans)	*I entered, I went in*
sortir (de)	je suis sorti(e) (de)	*I went/came out (of)*
partir (de)	je suis parti(e) (de)	*I left*
rentrer	je suis rentré(e)	*I came home, I returned*
retourner	je suis retourné(e)	*I returned, I went back*
monter (dans)	je suis monté(e) (dans)	*I went up, I got on/in*
descendre (de / dans / à)	je suis descendu(e) (de / dans / à)	*I came down, I got out/ off (of), I stayed (at)*
tomber	je suis tombé(e)	*I fell (down)*
naître	je suis né(e)	*I was born*
mourir	il/elle est mort(e)	*he/she died*

Rentrer means *to return / go back home* (or to the place you are staying). Use **retourner** for *to return* in most other cases. **Partir** and **quitter** both mean *to leave*. **Partir** uses **être** as its auxiliary, but **quitter** does not. It takes **avoir** as its auxiliary verb and *must* have a direct object: **Elle *est partie* tôt. Elle *a quitté* la maison à six heures.**

Place **y** *immediately* before the auxiliary verb in the **passé composé**.

J'**y** suis allé(e).   Je n'**y** suis pas allé(e).

Prononciation

CD 2-33

Les verbes auxiliaires **avoir** *et* **être**

As you practice when to use **avoir** and when to use **être** to form the **passé composé**, be careful to pronounce the forms of these auxiliary verbs distinctly.

tu as parlé / tu es parti(e)   il a parlé / il est parti

ils ᶻont parlé / ils sont partis

A. Qu'est-ce que vous avez fait? Parlez de la dernière fois que vous avez mangé au restaurant avec un(e) ami(e) ou avec des amis.

> **EXEMPLE** je / sortir (avec qui?)
> **Je suis sorti(e) avec Thomas et Karima.**

1. je / sortir (avec qui?)
2. je / partir de la maison (à quelle heure?)
3. nous / aller (à quel restaurant?)
4. nous / arriver au restaurant (vers quelle heure?)
5. nous / rester au restaurant (combien de temps)
6. après ça, nous / aller (où?)
7. je / rentrer (vers quelle heure?)
8. le lendemain, je / rester au lit (jusqu'à quelle heure?)

B. Tu es parti(e) en week-end? Pensez à la dernière fois que vous êtes parti(e) en week-end. Votre partenaire va vous poser des questions au sujet de ce week-end.

> **EXEMPLE** où / aller
> —**Où est-ce que tu es allé(e)?**
> —**Je suis allé(e) à Deauville.**

1. quand / partir
2. avec qui / voyager
3. comment / y aller
4. quand / arriver
5. où / descendre
6. combien de temps / rester
7. que / faire
8. quand / rentrer

Maintenant créez cinq questions pour poser à votre professeur au sujet de son dernier voyage.

> **EXEMPLE** **Comment est-ce que vous avez voyagé?**

C. Un voyage. Alice a visité Deauville avec son mari Vincent et leurs enfants. Regardez les illustrations et dites s'ils ont fait les choses indiquées. *Attention!* Certains verbes utilisent **avoir** comme auxiliaire, mais d'autres utilisent **être**.

> **EXEMPLE** samedi matin
> Alice: rester à la maison
> **Alice n'est pas restée à la maison.**

samedi matin: Alice: partir en week-end seule, Alice et sa famille: aller à Nice, ils: visiter Deauville, ils: prendre la voiture, ils: y aller en train, ils: partir vers neuf heures

samedi après-midi: les Pérez: rester chez des amis, ils: descendre à l'hôtel, ils: y arriver en taxi, ils: y arriver vers midi et quart, Alice: payer le chauffeur de taxi, Vincent: prendre tous les bagages

dimanche matin: les Pérez: rester à l'hôtel, ils: sortir avant neuf heures, ils: aller à la plage, ils: louer un bateau *(boat)*, Cathy: faire du ski nautique *(to waterski)*

dimanche soir: les Pérez: rentrer à la maison, ils: laisser tous leurs bagages à l'hôtel, ils: revenir en taxi, ils: arriver à la maison avant minuit, Vincent: payer le chauffeur de taxi

Les expressions qui désignent le passé et reprise du passé composé

The following expressions are useful when talking about the past.

hier (matin, après-midi)	*yesterday (morning, afternoon)*
hier soir	*last night, yesterday evening*
lundi (mardi...) dernier	*last Monday (Tuesday . . .)*
le week-end dernier	*last weekend*
la semaine dernière	*last week*
le mois dernier	*last month*
l'année dernière	*last year*
la dernière fois	*the last time*
récemment	*recently*
Pendant combien de temps?	*For how long?*
pendant deux heures (longtemps)	*for two hours (a long time)*
Il y a combien de temps?	*How long ago?*
il y a quelques secondes (cinq minutes, trois jours, cinq ans)	*a few seconds (five minutes, three days, five years) ago*
déjà	*already, ever*
ne... pas encore	*not yet*

Most of these time expressions go at the beginning or end of a clause or sentence. However, **déjà** is placed between the auxiliary verb and the past participle. **Ne... pas encore** goes around the auxiliary verb.

—Tu as **déjà** vu ce film?   —*Have you **already** seen this movie?*

—Non, je **n'ai pas encore** vu ce film.   —*No, I haven't seen this movie **yet**.*

—Moi, j'ai vu ce film **hier soir**.   —*I saw this movie **last night**.*

A. Et vous? Indiquez la dernière fois que vous avez fait les choses suivantes.

EXEMPLE   descendre dans un camping
      Je suis descendu(e) dans un camping l'année dernière / en juin / il y a longtemps.
      Je ne suis pas descendu(e) dans un camping récemment.
      Je ne suis jamais descendu(e) dans un camping.

1. aller au cinéma	**6.** rentrer tard
2. lire un bon livre	**7.** descendre à l'hôtel
3. sortir avec des amis	**8.** être chez mes parents
4. visiter une autre ville	**9.** dormir toute la matinée
5. passer la journée chez moi	**10.** avoir un accident de voiture

B. Et toi? Posez des questions à vos camarades de classe pour trouver quelqu'un qui a fait chacune des choses suivantes récemment. Après, dites à la classe qui a fait chaque chose et quand il/elle l'a faite.

EXEMPLES   voir un bon film
      — Sam, tu as vu un bon film récemment?
      — Non, je n'ai pas vu de bon film récemment.

      — Lisa, tu as vu un bon film récemment?
      — Oui, j'ai vu un bon film hier soir.

Après, à la classe: **Lisa a vu un bon film hier soir.**

1. voir un bon film
2. aller au café avec des amis
3. faire de l'exercice
4. sortir avec des amis
5. partir en week-end
6. arriver en cours en retard *(late)*
7. être malade *(sick)*
8. rentrer à la maison après minuit

C. Quand? Voilà le calendrier de Cathy. Quand est-ce qu'elle a fait les choses indiquées? Aujourd'hui, c'est le 14 novembre.

il y a un mois
il y a six semaines
le mois dernier
hier
le week-end dernier
mardi dernier
la semaine dernière
il y a une semaine
il y a deux jours

EXEMPLE   beaucoup travailler
Cathy a beaucoup travaillé le mois dernier.

1. dîner chez une amie
2. aller au Louvre
3. préparer un examen
4. rentrer de Deauville
5. faire du shopping
6. passer *(to take)* un examen
7. passer le week-end à Deauville

D. Déjà? Demandez à un(e) camarade de classe s'il/si elle a déjà fait les choses indiquées. N'oubliez pas *(Don't forget)* d'utiliser **ne... pas encore** au négatif.

EXEMPLE   manger des escargots
— Tu as déjà mangé des escargots?
— Oui, j'ai déjà mangé des escargots.
Non, je n'ai pas encore mangé d'escargots.

1. visiter un pays francophone
2. aller à Paris
3. monter à la tour Eiffel
4. boire du champagne français
5. visiter l'Asie *(Asia)*

E. Entretien. Interviewez votre partenaire.

1. Tu es resté(e) chez toi samedi matin? Tu es resté(e) au lit jusqu'à quelle heure? Tu as pris un café? Où est-ce que tu as pris ton petit déjeuner?
2. Est-ce que tu es allé(e) au cinéma le week-end dernier? Quel film est-ce que tu as vu récemment? Est-ce que tu as aimé ce film?
3. Tu es sorti(e) avec des amis samedi soir ou tu as passé la soirée à la maison? La dernière fois que tu es sorti(e) avec des ami(e)s, où est-ce que vous êtes allé(e)s? Qu'est-ce que vous avez fait ensemble? Est-ce que tu es rentré(e) tard?

Discussing the weather and your activities

Vocabulaire supplémentaire

Il fait bon. *The weather's nice.*
Il fait humide. *It's humid.*
Il fait sec. *It's dry.*
Il y a des nuages. *It's cloudy.*
Il y a du brouillard. *It's foggy.*
Il y a du verglas. *It's icy.*
Il y a un orage. *There's a storm.*
Il y a des éclairs. *There's lightning.*
Il y a du tonnerre. *There's thunder.*
Le ciel est couvert. *The sky is overcast.*

Le temps et les projets

Quelquefois les projets **dépendent du temps qu'il fait.**

Et chez vous? **Quel temps fait-il** aujourd'hui?

Il fait froid. Il fait frais. Il fait chaud. Il fait beau. Il fait mauvais.

Il fait du soleil. Il fait du vent. Il pleut. Il neige.

Quelle **saison** préférez-vous? Qu'est-ce que vous faites **pendant** cette saison?

Je préfère **l'été** *(m)*. En été...

je vais à la plage.
je fais du bateau et du ski nautique.

Je préfère l'automne *(m)*. En automne...

je fais du camping.
je **fais du VTT.**

Je préfère **l'hiver** *(m)*. En hiver...

je vais à la montagne.
je fais du ski.

Je préfère **le printemps.** Au printemps...

je vais au parc.
je fais des promenades.

CD 2-34

C'est vendredi après-midi et Alice et Cathy parlent de leurs projets pour le week-end.

ALICE: **S'il** fait beau demain, je vais faire une promenade au jardin du Luxembourg. J'ai besoin de faire de l'exercice. Et toi, qu'est-ce que tu as l'intention de faire?

CATHY: S'il fait beau, j'ai envie de faire du jogging.

ALICE: Et s'il fait mauvais?

CATHY: S'il fait mauvais, je ne vais rien faire de spécial.

Le temps *Weather* **dépendre de** *to depend on* **le temps qu'il fait** *what the weather is like* **Quel temps fait-il?** *What is the weather like?* **la saison** *the season* **pendant** *during, for* **l'été** *(m) summer* **faire du VTT (vélo tout terrain)** *to go all-terrain biking* **l'hiver** *(m) winter* **le printemps** *spring* **S'il** *If it* **(si** *if)*

A. Et chez vous? Chez vous, en quelle saison fait-il le temps indiqué?

> **EXEMPLE**   Il neige.
> **Ici, il neige souvent (rarement, quelquefois) en hiver.**
> **Ici, il ne neige jamais.**

1. Il fait frais.
2. Il fait du vent.
3. Il fait mauvais.
4. Il fait très beau.
5. Il fait froid.
6. Il fait chaud.
7. Il fait du soleil.
8. Il pleut.
9. Il neige.

B. Et vous? Complétez les phrases.

1. Quand il fait beau, j'aime...
2. S'il fait beau ce week-end, j'ai l'intention de...
3. Quand il pleut, je préfère...
4. Quand il fait chaud, j'aime...
5. Quand il neige, j'aime...
6. Au printemps, j'aime...
7. Je ne fais rien quand...
8. À la montagne, j'aime...
9. À la plage, j'aime...
10. Aujourd'hui, il fait... et j'ai envie de...

C. Quel temps fait-il? Demandez à un(e) camarade de classe quel temps il fait aux moments indiqués. Il/Elle doit répondre en utilisant au moins *deux* expressions pour décrire le temps.

> **EXEMPLE**   en automne
> **— Quel temps fait-il en automne?**
> **— Il fait beau et il fait frais.**

1. en hiver
2. en été
3. en automne
4. au printemps
5. aujourd'hui

D. Entretien. Posez ces questions à votre partenaire.

1. Aimes-tu l'été? Aimes-tu aller à la plage? Aimes-tu nager? Préfères-tu faire du bateau ou faire du ski nautique?
2. Aimes-tu l'hiver? Aimes-tu aller à la montagne? Préfères-tu faire des promenades ou faire du ski?
3. Qu'est-ce que tu aimes faire quand il fait chaud? Et quand il fait froid? Et quand il neige?
4. Quelle saison préfères-tu? Quel temps fait-il d'habitude? Qu'est-ce que tu aimes faire pendant cette saison?
5. Quel temps fait-il aujourd'hui? Qu'est-ce que tu as envie de faire? Qu'est-ce que tu vas faire après les cours?

E. Conversation. Avec un(e) partenaire, relisez la conversation entre Alice et Cathy en bas de la page précédente. Ensuite, changez la conversation pour parler de vos projets pour le week-end.

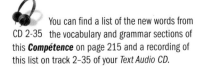

You can find a list of the new words from the vocabulary and grammar sections of this **Compétence** on page 215 and a recording of this list on track 2-35 of your *Text Audio CD.*

CD 2-35

Pour vérifier

1. How do you say *to make* or *to do* in French? What is the present tense of **faire**? How is the **vous** form of this verb different from the usual **vous** form of a verb?

2. How do you say that you are doing *nothing*?

3. How do you say *What is the weather like? The weather is nice? It is raining? It is snowing?* How do you say *What is the weather going to be like? It is going to be nice? It is going to rain? It is going to snow?* How do you say *What was the weather like? It was nice? It rained? It snowed?*

4. How do you say *I like snow? I like rain?*

✳ Note *de prononciation*

The **ai** in **fais, fait,** and **faites** rhymes with the **ai** in **français** and **française,** but the **ai** of **faisons** rhymes with the **e** in **je.**

Talking about the weather and what you do

*Le verbe **faire**, l'expression **ne... rien** et les expressions pour décrire le temps*

To say *to make* or *to do,* use the irregular verb **faire.**

FAIRE (to make, to do)	
je **fais**	nous **faisons**
tu **fais**	vous **faites**
il/elle/on **fait**	ils/elles **font**
PASSÉ COMPOSÉ: **j'ai fait**	

— Qu'est-ce que tu fais ce soir?　　— Qu'est-ce que Papa fait dans la cuisine?
— Je reste à la maison. Je fais　　— Il fait des sandwichs.
　mes devoirs.

To say that you do *nothing* or you do *not* do *anything,* use **ne... rien.** This expression can be the subject or object of the verb, or the object of a preposition.

Rien n'est prêt.　　　Je **n'**achète **rien.**　　　Je **n'ai** besoin de **rien.**

When negating an infinitive, place both parts of the negative expression before it.

Je préfère **ne pas** sortir ce soir.　　Je voudrais **ne rien** faire demain soir.

The verb **faire** is used in many, but not all, weather expressions. You will also need the infinitives and past participles **pleuvoir** *(to rain)* → **plu** and **neiger** *(to snow)* → **neigé.** Use **la pluie** to say *(the) rain* and **la neige** to say *(the) snow.*

aujourd'hui	demain	hier
Quel temps fait-il?	Quel temps va-t-il faire?	Quel temps a-t-il fait?
Il fait beau / du vent...	Il va faire beau / du vent...	Il a fait beau / du vent...
Il pleut.	Il va pleuvoir.	Il a plu.
Il neige.	Il va neiger.	Il a neigé.

A. Que faites-vous? Dites ou demandez si ces personnes font les choses indiquées.

1. Moi, je... (faire beaucoup de choses seul[e], faire souvent des bêtises *[stupid things]*, faire beaucoup de choses avec ma famille)
2. Mon meilleur ami (Ma meilleure amie)... (faire beaucoup de choses pour moi, faire beaucoup de choses le week-end, faire souvent de l'exercice)
3. En cours, nous... (faire beaucoup d'exercices oraux, faire beaucoup d'exercices ensemble, faire les devoirs dans le cahier)
4. Mes parents... (faire beaucoup de choses le week-end, faire beaucoup de choses avec moi, faire beaucoup de choses pour moi)
5. *[au professeur]* Est-ce que vous... ? (faire quelque chose d'intéressant après le cours de français, faire quelque chose avec vos amis ce week-end, faire souvent du sport)

B. Quel temps fait-il? Quel temps fait-il aujourd'hui dans ces régions? Quel temps va-t-il faire demain?

Dans les Alpes

En Normandie

En Guadeloupe

C. Qu'est-ce qu'ils ont fait? Alice parle des activités récentes de sa famille et du temps qu'il a fait ce jour-là. Complétez ses phrases.

> **EXEMPLE**   Hier, j'**ai lu un livre**. Il **a plu** toute la journée.

EXEMPLE Hier, j'...
Il... toute la journée.

1. À Deauville,
nous... Il...

2. Vendredi dernier,
mon mari Vin-
cent et moi... Il...

3. À Chamonix, les
enfants... Il...

4. Hier, Vincent...
Il...

5. Ce matin, Vincent
et notre fils... Il...

D. Entretien. Interviewez votre partenaire.

1. Qu'est-ce que tu aimes faire le vendredi soir? le samedi soir? Qu'est-ce que tu fais d'habitude le dimanche matin? Quand est-ce que tu ne fais rien?
2. Quel temps va-t-il faire ce week-end? Qu'est-ce que tu as envie de faire s'il fait beau? Qu'est-ce que tu as l'intention de faire s'il fait mauvais? Qu'est-ce que tu vas faire samedi soir? Est-ce que tu préfères ne rien faire quelquefois?
3. Ton meilleur ami (Ta meilleure amie) et toi, quand est-ce que vous aimez sortir ensemble? Qu'est-ce que vous faites souvent ensemble?

> ✳ **Note** *de grammaire*
>
> Questions asked with **faire** are often answered with a different verb.
> **—Qu'est-ce que tu fais le samedi matin?**
> **—Je regarde la télé.**

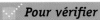

Pour vérifier

1. How do you say *to go camping*? *to take a trip*? *to do housework*? *to do laundry*?

2. In the expressions with **faire,** which articles change to **de (d')** in a negative sentence? Which do not?

Vocabulaire supplémentaire

aller à la chasse *to go hunting*
aller à la pêche *to go fishing*
faire de l'alpinisme *to go mountain climbing*
faire de la marche à pied *to go walking*
faire de la musculation *to do weight training*
faire de la varappe / de l'escalade *to go rock climbing*
faire du cheval *to go horseback riding*
faire du patin (à glace) *to go (ice-)skating*
faire du roller *to go rollerblading*
faire du snowboarding *to go snowboarding*
faire la fête *to party*
faire sa toilette *to get cleaned up, to get ready*
faire une randonnée (des randonnées) *to go for a hike (hiking)*

Talking about activities

Les expressions avec *faire*

The verb **faire** can have a variety of meanings in idiomatic expressions.

LE SPORT ET LES DISTRACTIONS	LE MÉNAGE ET LES COURSES
faire de l'exercice	faire des courses *(to run errands)*
faire du bateau	faire du jardinage *(to garden)*
faire du camping	faire la cuisine *(to cook)*
faire du jogging	faire la lessive *(to do laundry)*
faire du shopping	faire la vaisselle *(to do the dishes)*
faire du ski (nautique)	faire le ménage *(to do housework)*
faire du sport (du tennis, du hockey...)	
faire du vélo	
faire du VTT	
faire une promenade	
faire un voyage *(to take a trip)*	

The **un, une, des, du, de la,** and **de l'** in the expressions with **faire** become **de (d')** when the verb is negated. The definite article (**le, la, l', les**) does not change.

Je fais **du** jogging en été.   Nous faisons **la** cuisine le soir.

Je ne fais pas **de** jogging en hiver.   Nous ne faisons pas **la** cuisine le matin.

A. Un besoin ou une envie? Commencez ces phrases logiquement avec **J'ai envie de...** ou **J'ai besoin de...**

> EXEMPLES   faire des devoirs   **J'ai besoin de faire des devoirs.**
> faire du ski   **J'ai envie de faire du ski.**

1. faire des courses
2. faire du bateau
3. faire la lessive
4. faire du vélo
5. faire le ménage
6. faire la cuisine
7. faire la vaisselle
8. rester à la maison et ne rien faire

Avez-vous envie de faire du camping?

B. Préférences. Sur une feuille de papier, écrivez les activités suivantes dans l'ordre de vos préférences. Votre partenaire va vous poser des questions pour déterminer l'ordre des activités sur votre feuille de papier.

> faire du jogging / faire du camping / faire du jardinage /
> faire la cuisine / faire du vélo / ne rien faire

> EXEMPLE   **— Préfères-tu faire du jogging ou ne rien faire?**
> **— Je préfère ne rien faire.**
> **— Préfères-tu ne rien faire ou faire la cuisine?...**

C. Que font-ils?
Éric, le fils d'Alice, parle avec sa mère des projets de la famille pour aujourd'hui. Complétez ses phrases avec une expression avec **faire.**

1. Maman, est-ce que tu... ce matin?

2. Michel et toi, vous... cet après-midi.

3. Papa...

4. Papa et toi, vous...

5. Cathy et moi, nous...

6. Moi, je...

D. Quel temps?
Quel temps fait-il quand vous faites ces choses?

1. Je fais du ski quand...
2. Je fais du jardinage quand...
3. J'aime aller à la piscine quand...
4. J'aime ne rien faire quand...
5. Je n'aime pas rester à la maison quand...
6. Je n'aime pas faire de sport quand...

E. Conseils.
Donnez des conseils à un ami. Utilisez l'impératif.

faire le ménage   louer un DVD   faire du shopping
faire la vaisselle   rester à la maison   faire du vélo   faire une promenade
faire la cuisine   faire la lessive   faire tes devoirs   ne rien faire

EXEMPLE —La vaisselle est sale.
—Eh bien, fais la vaisselle!

1. J'ai faim.
2. Tous mes vêtements sont sales.
3. J'ai envie de faire de l'exercice.
4. J'ai besoin d'acheter de nouveaux vêtements.
5. Mon appartement est très sale.
6. Je n'ai pas envie de sortir ce soir.
7. J'ai beaucoup de devoirs à faire ce soir!
8. Je voudrais voir un film mais je n'ai pas envie d'aller au cinéma.

Deciding what to wear and buying clothes

Vocabulaire supplémentaire

D'AUTRES VÊTEMENTS

un blouson *a windbreaker, a jacket*
une casquette *a cap*
une ceinture *a belt*
un chapeau *a hat*
des chaussettes *(f) socks*
une écharpe *a winter scarf*
un foulard *a dress scarf*
des gants *(m) gloves*
un gilet *a vest, a cardigan*
des hauts talons *(m) high heels*
un sweat *a sweatshirt*
un tailleur *a woman's suit*
une veste *a sports coat*

DES BIJOUX (M) JEWELRY

une bague *a ring*
des boucles d'oreille *(f) earrings*
un bracelet
un collier *a necklace*

DES SOUS-VÊTEMENTS (M) / DE LA LINGERIE
UNDERWEAR / LINGERIE

une chemise de nuit *a nightgown*
un collant *pantyhose*
une combinaison *a slip*
une culotte *panties*
un pyjama *pajamas*
un slip *briefs*
un soutien-gorge *a bra*

✳ Note *de vocabulaire*

Porter means *to carry* or *to wear* and **mettre** *to put, to put on,* or *to wear.* They can both be used to say what one *wears* in general, although **mettre** is more commonly used in this case and in the **passé composé. Il porte/met souvent un jean. Il a mis un jean hier.** Use **porter** to say what someone is wearing at a particular moment. **Aujourd'hui il porte un pantalon blanc.**

The forms of **mettre** are:

je	**mets**	nous	**mettons**
tu	**mets**	vous	**mettez**
il/elle/on	**met**	ils/elles	**mettent**

PASSÉ COMPOSÉ: **j'ai mis**

Les vêtements

Qu'est-ce que vous **mettez** pour aller en cours? pour sortir le soir? Qu'est-ce que vous **avez mis** ce matin? hier soir?

Je mets souvent...   Je mets **parfois**...   Ce matin, j'ai mis...

un jean

un short

un pantalon

une jupe

un pull

un polo ou
un tee-shirt

une chemise et
une cravate

un chemisier

un survêtement

une robe

un costume

des chaussures *(f)*, des
bottes *(f)*, des sandales *(f)*
ou des baskets *(f)*

un anorak

un imperméable

un manteau

un maillot de bain ou
un bikini

Portez-vous quelquefois... ?

un parapluie

un sac ou un portefeuille

une montre

des lunettes *(f)*
de soleil

---

mettez (mettre *to put, to put on)*   **avez mis (mettre** *past participle:* **mis)**   **parfois** *sometimes*

Alice Pérez cherche un nouveau maillot de bain. Elle entre dans un magasin.

CD 2-36

LA VENDEUSE:	Bonjour, madame. **Je peux vous aider?**
ALICE:	Je cherche un maillot de bain.
LA VENDEUSE:	**Quelle taille faites-vous?**
ALICE:	**Je fais du** 42.
LA VENDEUSE:	Nous avons **ces maillots-ci.** Ils sont très jolis et ils sont **en solde.**
ALICE:	J'aime bien ce maillot noir. **Je peux l'essayer?**
LA VENDEUSE:	**Bien sûr,** madame. **La cabine d'essayage** est **par ici.**

Alice sort de la cabine d'essayage.

LA VENDEUSE:	Alors, **qu'en pensez-vous?**
ALICE:	**Il me plaît** beaucoup. Il **coûte** combien?
LA VENDEUSE:	**Voyons,** c'est 65 euros.
ALICE:	C'est bien. Alors, je **le** prends.

Note *culturelle*

Notez que les tailles en France ne sont pas les mêmes qu'aux USA.

Robes et chemisiers		Chemises hommes	
USA	FRANCE	USA	FRANCE
8	38	15	38
10	40	15 ½	39
12	42	16	40
14	44	16 ½	41
16	46	17	42

A. Et vous? Regardez les illustrations à la page précédente. Dites si vous mettez souvent chaque chose.

> **EXEMPLE** **Je mets souvent un jean. / Parfois je mets un jean. / Je ne mets jamais de jean.**

B. Quel temps fait-il? Pour chaque saison, décrivez le temps qu'il fait chez vous. Parlez aussi des vêtements que vous portez typiquement en cette saison.

> **EXEMPLE** **Ici, en automne, il fait frais et il fait du vent. Je mets souvent un jean et un pull.**

C. Préférences. Complétez les phrases suivantes pour exprimer vos préférences.

1. Je préfère acheter mes vêtements *en solde / dans les meilleurs magasins / dans les magasins du quartier / dans un magasin de vêtements d'occasion* (second hand) */ ???.*
2. Si quelque chose me plaît, je préfère l'essayer *dans le magasin / à la maison.*
3. Pour sortir le soir, je mets souvent *un jean / un pantalon / ???.*
4. Quand je voyage en voiture, je mets souvent *un jean / ???.*
5. Pour aller à la plage, je mets *un short / ???.*
6. Pour aller en cours, je mets *un pantalon / ???.*
7. Quand je suis chez moi, je mets souvent *un jean / ???.*
8. Je ne mets presque jamais *de short / ???.*

D. Conversation. Avec un(e) partenaire, relisez la conversation entre Alice et la vendeuse en haut de la page. Ensuite, changez la conversation pour acheter un jean, un anorak ou un manteau. Après, changez de rôles et jouez le rôle du vendeur / de la vendeuse pour votre partenaire.

CD 2-37 You can find a list of the new words from the vocabulary and grammar sections of this **Compétence** on page 215 and a recording of this list on track 2-37 of your *Text Audio CD.*

---

une vendeuse (un vendeur) *a salesclerk* **Je peux vous aider?** *Can I help you?* **Quelle taille faites-vous?** *What size do you wear?* **Je fais du...** *I wear size . . .* **ces... -ci** *these . . . over here* **en solde** *on sale* **Je peux l'essayer?** (essayer) *Can I try it on? (to try, to try on)* **Bien sûr** *Of course* **La cabine d'essayage** *The fitting room* **par ici** *this way* **qu'en pensez-vous?** *what do you think about it?* **Il me plaît. (plaire)** *I like it. / It pleases me. (to please)* **coûter** *to cost* **Voyons** *Let's see* **le (l')** *it, him* **(la, l'** *it, her)*

Pour vérifier

1. How do you say the direct object pronouns *him, her, it,* and *them* in French?

2. Where do you place the direct object pronouns and **y** when there is an infinitive? in the **passé composé**? Where do you place them otherwise? Where do you place them in a negative sentence?

Avoiding repetition

Les pronoms *le, la, l'* et *les*

Use the direct object pronouns **le, la, l',** and **les** to replace a person, animal, or thing that is the direct object of the verb. Use **le** *(him, it)* to replace masculine singular nouns and **la** *(her, it)* to replace feminine singular nouns. **Les** *(Them)* replaces all plural nouns. **Le** and **la** become **l'** when the following word begins with a vowel or silent **h.**

—Tu prends ce maillot?

—Oui, je **le** prends.

—Tu achètes cette chemise?

—Oui, je **l'**achète.

—Tu prends cette robe aussi?

—Oui, je **la** prends.

—Tu achètes ces bottes?

—Oui, je **les** achète.

	BEFORE A CONSONANT SOUND	BEFORE A VOWEL OR SILENT H
him, it (masculine)	le	l'
her, it (feminine)	la	l'
them	les	les

Like **y,** these pronouns are generally placed *immediately* before the verb. They go before the infinitive if there is one. Otherwise, place them before the conjugated verb. In the negative, the pronoun remains *immediately* before the conjugated verb or the infinitive.

— Tu aimes **cette chemise**?

— Oui, je **l'**aime bien.

   Non, je ne **l'**aime pas.

— Tu vas acheter **cette chemise**?

— Oui, je vais **l'**acheter.

   Non, je ne vais pas **l'**acheter.

In the **passé composé,** direct object pronouns and **y** are placed *immediately* before the auxiliary (conjugated) verb.

Je **l'**ai fait.

Je ne **l'**ai pas fait.

J'**y** suis allé(e).

Je n'**y** suis pas allé(e).

You know that in the **passé composé,** the past participle generally agrees in gender and number with the subject when the auxiliary verb is **être,** but not when it is **avoir.**

Hier, Cathy est all**ée** au centre commercial. Elle a achet**é** ces bottes.

However, the past participle used with **avoir** will agree with the *direct object* of the verb, but only if it *precedes* the verb, as with a direct object pronoun.

—Où est-ce que Vincent a achet**é ses bottes**?

—Il **les** a achet**ées** au centre commercial.

A. Au magasin de vêtements. Alice et Vincent sont au magasin de vêtements. Complétez ce que chacun dit avec le pronom convenable **(le, la, l', les).**

1. J'aime ce maillot de bain. Je peux _____ essayer?

2. J'aime ces bottes. Je _____ prends.

3. Je n'aime pas ce bikini. Je ne _____ prends pas.

4. Comment trouves-tu cette robe? Voudrais-tu _____ essayer?

5. Je n'aime pas cet anorak. Je ne vais pas _____ prendre.

6. Regarde cette belle cravate! Je _____ trouve super!

B. À Paris. Dites si vous reconnaissez *(recognize)* ces sites parisiens. Utilisez
Je reconnais... *(I recognize ...)* et le pronom convenable **(le, la, l', les)**.

> **EXEMPLE**   Cette avenue?
> **Oui, je la reconnais. C'est les Champs-Élysées.**
> **Non, je ne la reconnais pas.**

EXEMPLE   Cette avenue?   **1.** Cette cathédrale?   **2.** Ce musée?

3. Cette tour?   **4.** Cette place?   **5.** Ce fleuve *(river)*?

C. Intentions. Un(e) ami(e) voudrait savoir ce que vous allez faire avec les
choses suivantes. Répondez en utilisant un pronom complément d'objet direct
(le, la, l', les) et un verbe logique. Jouez les deux rôles avec un(e) partenaire.

> **EXEMPLE**   ces frites
> —**Qu'est-ce que tu vas faire avec ces frites?**
> —**Je vais les manger!**

1. ces vêtements   **4.** ce jus de fruit   **7.** ces bottes
2. ce DVD   **5.** cette chemise   **8.** cette eau minérale
3. ce sandwich   **6.** ce journal   **9.** ce CD

D. Et vous? Avez-vous fait ces choses le week-end dernier? Répondez en
employant le pronom convenable: **y, le, la, l'** ou **les**.

> **EXEMPLE**   Vous avez regardé *la télé* le week-end dernier?
> **Oui, je l'ai regardée.**
> **Non, je ne l'ai pas regardée.**

1. Vous avez passé tout le week-end *chez vous*?
2. Vous avez fait *le ménage*?
3. Vous avez fait *la lessive*?
4. Vous avez lu *le livre de français*?
5. Vous avez fait *les devoirs*?
6. Vous avez dîné *au restaurant*?
7. Vous êtes rentré(e) *chez vous* après 10 heures?

E. Le week-end des Pérez. Regardez les explications de ce que les Pérez ont fait le week-end dernier et complétez les réponses aux questions qui suivent. Utilisez **y, le, la, l'** ou **les.**

EXEMPLE Qui est allé *au Quartier latin?*
Éric et Michèle **y sont allés.**

Vendredi après-midi, Éric et sa petite amie Michèle sont allés au Quartier latin où ils ont mangé dans un restaurant italien. Michèle a mangé des ravioli et Éric a commandé des spaghetti carbonara. Après le repas, ils sont allés dans une librairie où Michèle a acheté le nouveau livre de Jean-Christophe Rufin. Après ça, ils ont retrouvé des amis dans un café du quartier et ils ont pris un café ensemble à la terrasse. Plus tard, Éric et Michèle sont allés au cinéma du Panthéon pour voir le nouveau film avec Natalie Baye.

1. Quel jour est-ce qu'ils sont allés *au Quartier latin?*
Ils _____ vendredi après-midi.

2. Qui a commandé *les spaghetti carbonara?*
Éric _____.

3. Qui a acheté *le nouveau livre de Jean-Christophe Rufin?*
Michèle _____.

4. Où est-ce qu'ils ont retrouvé *leurs amis?*
Ils _____ dans un café du quartier.

5. Avec qui est-ce qu'ils ont pris *leur café?*
Ils _____ avec des amis.

6. Où est-ce qu'Éric et Michèle ont vu *le film avec Natalie Baye?*
Ils _____ au cinéma du Panthéon.

7. Quel jour est-ce qu'Alice est allée *au musée d'Orsay?*
Elle _____ samedi matin.

8. Où est-ce qu'elle a vu *la nouvelle exposition de Cézanne?*
Elle _____ au musée d'Orsay.

9. Elle a visité *les autres expositions au musée?*
Non, elle _____.

10. Elle est allée *au cinéma* après le musée?
Non, elle _____.

11. Où est-ce qu'elle a retrouvé *Vincent?*
Elle _____ dans un restaurant du quartier.

Samedi matin, Alice est allée au musée d'Orsay où elle a vu la nouvelle exposition de Cézanne. Elle n'a pas eu le temps de visiter les autres expositions parce qu'elle est allée faire une course dans un magasin de vêtements. Vers une heure et demie, elle a retrouvé Vincent dans un restaurant du quartier.

12. Pourquoi est-ce que Cathy est allée *au Printemps*?
Elle _____ pour faire du shopping.

13. Où est-ce qu'elle a acheté *ses chaussures rouges*?
Elle _____ au Printemps.

14. Où est-ce qu'elle a acheté *sa robe bleue*?
Elle _____ au Printemps aussi.

15. Qui n'a pas aimé *les nouvelles chaussures de Cathy*?
Sa mère _____.

F. Préférences. Un(e) ami(e) vous pose des questions. Répondez à ses questions en remplaçant les mots en italique par le pronom convenable.

Samedi matin, Cathy est allée faire du shopping au Printemps. Elle a acheté des chaussures rouges et une robe d'été bleue. Ensuite, elle est allée retrouver ses parents au restaurant. Quand elle a montré ses chaussures et sa robe à ses parents, sa mère n'a pas aimé ses nouvelles chaussures rouges!

> **EXEMPLE** — Je prépare mes leçons tous les jours. Et toi?
> — **Moi aussi, je les prépare tous les jours. Moi non, je ne les prépare pas tous les jours.**

1. Je regarde souvent *la télé* le week-end. Et toi?
2. J'ai envie de regarder *la télé* ce soir. Et toi?
3. J'invite souvent *mes parents* à la maison. Et toi?
4. Ce week-end, j'ai l'intention de voir *mes parents*. Et toi?
5. Je trouve *mes cours* plutôt difficiles. Et toi?
6. Ce soir, je vais préparer *le prochain examen de français*. Et toi?
7. Samedi soir, je vais faire *mes devoirs*. Et toi?
8. Samedi dernier, je suis allé(e) *au cinéma*. Et toi?
9. Dimanche dernier, j'ai fait *mes devoirs*. Et toi?
10. Hier soir, j'ai regardé *la télé*. Et toi?

G. Entretien. Interviewez votre partenaire. Utilisez un pronom complément d'objet direct pour remplacer les mots en italique dans vos réponses.

1. Vas-tu voir *tes parents* ce week-end? Invites-tu souvent *tes amis* chez toi? Où est-ce que tu préfères retrouver *tes amis*? La dernière fois que tu es sorti(e) avec des amis, où est-ce que tu as retrouvé *tes amis*?
2. Chez toi, dans quelle pièce est-ce que tu préfères regarder *la télé*? écouter *la chaîne hi-fi*? faire *tes devoirs*? passer *ton temps libre*? Où est-ce que tu as passé *la soirée* hier soir?
3. Est-ce que tu achètes *tes vêtements* au centre commercial? Dans quel magasin est-ce que tu achètes *tes vêtements* le plus souvent? Où est-ce que tu as acheté *les vêtements que tu portes maintenant*?

Reprise

Talking about activities and making plans

Dans le *Chapitre 5*, vous avez parlé d'où vous êtes allé(e) et de ce que vous avez fait récemment. Vous avez appris à parler du temps, de vos sorties, de vos activités préférées et des vêtements. Maintenant vous allez réviser ce que vous avez appris.

A. Récemment. Dites quand ces personnes ont fait les choses indiquées récemment.

> **EXEMPLE** je / passer toute la journée à la maison
> **J'ai passé toute la journée à la maison il y a trois jours.**
> **Je n'ai pas passé toute la journée à la maison récemment.**
> **Je n'ai jamais passé toute la journée à la maison.**

1. je / rester au lit jusqu'à midi
2. je / travailler
3. je / rentrer tard
4. je / aller au cinéma
5. je / sortir avec des amis
6. mes amis et moi / sortir ensemble
7. nous / manger ensemble
8. nous / rentrer tard
9. mon meilleur ami (ma meilleure amie) / téléphoner
10. il (elle) / dîner avec moi
11. mes parents / venir chez moi
12. mes parents / sortir avec moi

B. Entretien. Interviewez votre partenaire.

1. Est-ce que tu es sorti(e) avec des amis récemment? Quand est-ce que tu es sorti(e) avec des amis? Quels vêtements est-ce que tu as mis? Où est-ce que vous êtes allés ensemble? Qu'est-ce que vous avez fait? Est-ce que vous êtes rentrés tard?
2. D'habitude, est-ce que tu quittes la maison tôt ou tard le matin pendant la semaine? Est-ce que tu as quitté la maison tôt ce matin? À quelle heure est-ce que tu es arrivé(e) à ton premier cours? Jusqu'à quelle heure vas-tu rester ici? Est-ce que tu vas rentrer chez toi tôt ou tard aujourd'hui? À quelle heure est-ce que tu es rentré(e) hier?
3. Est-ce que tu es parti(e) en week-end récemment? La dernière fois que tu es parti(e) en week-end, où est-ce que tu es allé(e)? Quand est-ce que tu es parti(e)? Est-ce que tu as pris ta voiture? Où est-ce que tu es descendu(e)? Combien de temps est-ce que tu es resté(e)? Qu'est-ce que tu as fait? Quand est-ce que tu es rentré(e)?

C. C'est lundi. Avec un(e) camarade de classe, préparez une scène à présenter à la classe basée sur une de ces deux situations.

- C'est lundi matin et vous parlez de ce que *(what)* vous avez fait le week-end dernier. Pour chaque activité que votre camarade mentionne, demandez plus de renseignements.
- Un(e) camarade de classe a été absent(e) pendant le dernier cours. Maintenant, il/elle vous pose des questions pour savoir *(to know)* ce que vous avez fait en cours.

D. Vos activités. Comment passez-vous votre temps? Répondez aux questions en remplaçant les mots en italique par le pronom convenable: **le, la, l'** ou **les**.

1. Est-ce que vous retrouvez souvent *vos camarades de classe* après les cours? Est-ce que vous faites souvent *les devoirs* ensemble? Est-ce que vous avez retrouvé *vos camarades de classe* hier soir? Est-ce que vous avez fait *les devoirs* ensemble? Est-ce que vous allez préparer *le prochain examen de français* ensemble?

2. Est-ce que vous prenez *votre petit déjeuner* à la maison d'habitude? Est-ce que vous avez pris *le petit déjeuner* chez vous hier? Préférez-vous prendre *le petit déjeuner* chez vous, au restaurant, au café ou dans un fast-food?

3. Est-ce que vous invitez souvent *vos amis* chez vous? Est-ce que vous aimez regarder *la télé* ensemble? Est-ce que vous avez regardé *la télé* ensemble hier soir? Est-ce que vous allez regarder *la télé* ensemble ce soir?

E. Quel temps fait-il? Donnez deux expressions pour décrire le temps sur chaque illustration. Ensuite, dites quels vêtements on met et ce qu'on porte dans ces circonstances.

EXEMPLE

Il pleut et il fait mauvais. On met un imperméable et des bottes ou on porte un parapluie quand il fait mauvais.

1.

2.

3.

F. Souvent? Est-ce que ces gens font souvent les choses indiquées?

EXEMPLE

Mes amis **font souvent du bateau.**
Mes amis **ne font pas souvent de bateau.**

1. Le week-end, mes parents...

2. Mon oncle...

3. Mes amies et moi...

4. Ma mère...

5. Moi, je...

6. Mon père...

Lecture et Composition

Lecture

⚙ Pour mieux lire: *Guessing meaning from context*

You can guess the meaning of words you don't know using the context in which they occur. This exercise will help you to read the article on the typical French day that follows.

En contexte. Utilisez le contexte pour deviner le sens des mots en italique.

1. Les Français modernes sont toujours *pressés*. On n'a jamais assez de temps.
2. Beaucoup de gens ne *consacrent* pas assez de temps à *s'occuper d'eux-mêmes*. Ils ne dorment pas assez et ils mangent mal et trop rapidement.
3. Le *sommeil* prend le plus de temps sur une journée. Les hommes actifs dorment en moyenne huit heures et trente minutes par jour.
4. On prend moins de *repas* ensemble et on mange plus souvent dans des fast-foods.
5. Les femmes *s'occupent* plus des enfants que les hommes, qui consacrent peu de temps aux *soins aux enfants*.

	Hommes		Femmes	
	Actifs	**Inactifs**	**Actives**	**Inactives**
***Temps physiologique*, dont**	***11h22***	***12h39***	***11h35***	***12h37***
- Sommeil	8h30	9h34	8h37	9h32
- Toilette	42	46	49	53
- Repas	2h16	2h18	2h09	2h12
***Temps professionnel et de formation*, dont**	***6h22***	***1h32***	***5h01***	***59***
- Travail professionnel	5h42	13	4h28	5
- Transport domicile-travail	37	9	30	5
- Études	1	1h07	0	47
***Temps domestique*, dont**	***1h59***	***2h55***	***3h48***	***4h47***
- Ménage, cuisine, lessive, courses	1h04	1h35	3h06	3h58
- Soins aux enfants et adultes	11	6	27	26
- Bricolage	30	36	4	5
- Jardinage, soins aux animaux	14	38	11	18
***Temps de loisirs*, dont**	***2h57***	***5h06***	***2h19***	***3h57***
- Télévision	1h47	2h44	1h24	2h28
- Lecture	16	36	17	30
- Promenade	15	32	14	22
- Jeux	12	30	6	15
- Sport	10	15	5	5
***Temps de sociabilité (hors repas)*, dont**	***47***	***1h10***	***43***	***1h04***
- Conversations, téléphone, **courrier**	13	20	16	22
- Visites, réceptions	26	36	22	33
Transport (hors domicile-travail)	***33***	***38***	***34***	***35***

L'emploi du temps des Français

L'homme et la femme modernes sont des individus pressés. 80% des Français estiment qu'ils ne consacrent pas assez de temps sur une journée à leurs amis, 74% à leur famille, 69% à s'occuper d'eux-mêmes, 38% à leur vie professionnelle. Le tableau à gauche présente les résultats d'une enquête récente sur l'emploi du temps des Français (en heures et en minutes).

---

l'emploi du temps *schedule* **actifs** *working* **dont** *out of which* **toilette** *getting ready, getting cleaned up* **lecture** *reading* **hors** *outside of* **courrier** *mail*

Compréhension

1. À qui et à quoi *(what)* est-ce que les Français voudraient consacrer plus de temps?
2. Est-ce que les Français passent plus de temps à dormir ou à travailler? à étudier ou à faire le ménage? à faire du jardinage ou à lire? à faire des promenades ou à faire du sport? Pendant combien de temps est-ce que les Français ont fait chacune *(each one)* de ces activités hier s'ils ont travaillé? s'ils n'ont pas travaillé? Et les Françaises?
3. Quelles sont les différences les plus importantes entre les emplois du temps des hommes et ceux *(those)* des femmes? entre les personnes actives et inactives?
4. Selon vous *(According to you)*, en quoi est-ce que l'emploi du temps d'un étudiant diffère de l'emploi du temps des gens actifs ou inactifs?
5. En quoi est-ce que l'emploi du temps des gens de votre région diffère de celui des *(that of the)* Français?

Composition

If you have access to SYSTÈME-D software, you will find the following phrases, vocabulary, grammar, and dictionary aids there.
Phrases: Telling time; Linking ideas; Sequencing events
Vocabulary: Leisure; Sports; City
Grammar: Compound past tense; Locative pronoun **y**
Dictionary: The verb **faire**

❀ Pour mieux écrire: *Using standard organizing techniques*

To write a good composition, you first need to organize your ideas. You can sometimes base your organization on a document you already have or can easily create. For example, you can organize a description of your family around photos or a family tree. To describe a book you have read, you can use the table of contents to organize your thoughts. To talk about a trip you have taken, you can use your itinerary.

Organisez-vous. Vous allez décrire une semaine imaginaire à Paris. D'abord, sur une feuille de papier, créez votre itinéraire imaginaire.

1.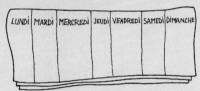

LUNDI | MARDI | MERCREDI | JEUDI | VENDREDI | SAMEDI | DIMANCHE

2. Sous chaque jour, écrivez des phrases pour décrire *(describe)* une progression logique de votre séjour *(your stay)*. Dites:

   - avec qui et comment vous avez voyagé
   - quand vous êtes parti(e) pour Paris
   - à quelle heure vous êtes arrivé(e) à Paris
   - dans quelle sorte d'hôtel vous êtes descendu(e)
   - ce que *(what)* vous avez fait chaque jour, quels sites vous avez visités et où vous avez mangé
   - ce que vous avez aimé le plus
   - quand vous avez quitté Paris
   - si vous avez l'intention d'y retourner un jour

Un voyage à Paris

En vous basant *(Based)* sur votre itinéraire, écrivez une description de votre voyage imaginaire.

EXEMPLE   **L'été dernier, je suis allé(e) à Paris avec...**

Le centre Georges Pompidou

Comparaisons culturelles

Les loisirs des Français

Si on **met à part les repas,** qui représentent un temps libre «obligatoire», la télévision occupe de loin la plus grande partie du temps de loisir des Français. Ils sont exposés aux médias en moyenne environ 6h30 par jour, dont 3h38 pour la télévision et 1h57 pour la radio. Mais le temps qu'ils consacrent **à chacun à titre exclusif** est très inférieur; **on peut** écouter par exemple la radio ou regarder la télévision tout en faisant la cuisine ou le ménage, **voire** en travaillant. Les Français regardent la télévision à titre principal en moyenne 2h07 par jour. Ils **n'**écoutent la radio **que** 4 minutes, ce qui signifie qu'ils l'écoutent presque toujours à titre secondaire, en même temps qu'ils pratiquent une autre activité, considérée comme principale.

Temps consacré à des activités de loisirs

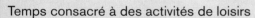

ACTIVITÉS DE LOISIRS:	MINUTES PAR JOUR
Télévision	127
Lecture	25
Promenade et tourisme	20
Conversations, téléphone, **courrier** et autres (non professionnel)	17
Visites à des parents et connaissances	16
Jeux (enfants, adultes)	16
Pratique sportive	16
Autres sorties	9
Ne rien faire, **réfléchir**	7
Participation associative et activités civiques	6
Spectacles	5
Radio, disques, cassettes	4
Participation religieuse	2
Pêche et chasse	2
TOTAL: 4 h 23	263

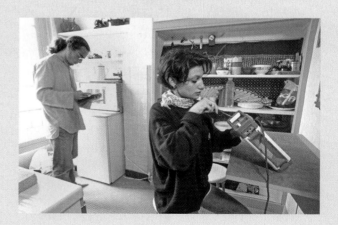

---

met à part les repas *sets aside meals*   **à chacun à titre exclusif** *to each one exclusively*   **on peut** *one can*   **voire** *even*
ne... que *only*   **lecture** *reading*   **courrier** *mail*   **réfléchir** *to think, to reflect*   **pêche et chasse** *fishing and hunting*

Actives ou non, les femmes disposent **en moyenne** de moins de temps libre que les hommes: 4h12 par jour contre 4h52 (activités de loisir et de sociabilité). Dans le domaine des médias, les femmes inactives constituent **la cible privilégiée** des radios, mais elles regardent moins la télévision et sont moins souvent **lectrices des quotidiens nationaux** que les hommes. Elles lisent **en revanche davantage de** livres et de magazines et constituent la clientèle majoritaire du théâtre.

Temps quotidien consacré aux loisirs (en heures et en minutes)

| | Actifs | | Femmes | 60 ans et plus | |
	Hommes	Femmes	au foyer*	Hommes	Femmes
Sociabilité	47	43	57	58	1 h 00
Télévision	1 h 45	1 h 22	2 h 08	3 h 01	2 h 51
Lecture	16	17	19	51	41
Promenade	18	14	18	44	25
Sport	10	5	6	10	2
Semi-loisirs**	45	20	38	1 h 51	48

*Moins de 60 ans.

Les semi-loisirs (jardinage, bricolage, **entretien des voitures, **soins aux** animaux, **travaux d'aiguille, confection de conserves**, gâteaux, confitures) ont été considérés comme faisant partie du temps libre et non du temps domestique.

Compréhension

1. Est-ce qu'il y a une grande différence entre les loisirs préférés des hommes et des femmes en France? entre les personnes actives et les retraités *(retired people)*? Quelles différences y a-t-il dans votre région?

2. Comparez les passe-temps préférés des Français avec les passe-temps préférés dans votre région. Sont-ils les mêmes? Quelles sont les différences? Pourquoi est-ce qu'il y a des différences, à votre avis? Est-ce qu'il y a peut-être des différences de valeurs *(values)*, d'intérêts, de géographie ou de climat qui influencent les préférences des gens?

 Visit **academic.cengage.com/french** for YouTube video cultural correlations, cultural information and activities.

Actives *Working* **en moyenne** *on average* **la cible privilégiée** *the favored target* **lectrices des quotidiens nationaux** *readers of national daily newspapers* **en revanche** *on the other hand* **davantage de** *more* **femmes au foyer** *homemakers* **entretien** *maintenance* **soins aux** *care for* **travaux d'aiguille** *needlework* **confection de conserves, gâteaux, confitures** *making preserves, cakes, jelly*

Passé composé

To say what happened in the past, put the verb in the **passé composé.** It may be translated in a variety of ways. The **passé composé** is composed of an auxiliary verb and a past participle. For most verbs the auxiliary verb is **avoir,** but for a few verbs it is **être.** All **-er** verbs have past participles with **-é** (**parler: j'ai parlé**) and most **-ir** verbs with **-i** (**dormir: j'ai dormi**).

J'ai mangé. = *I ate. / I have eaten. / I did eat.*

Ils n'ont pas beaucoup dormi. = *They didn't sleep much. / They haven't slept much.*

—Qu'est-ce que tu **as fait** hier soir?
—J'**ai vu** un film avec des amis et après on **a pris** un verre au café.

PARLER → PARLÉ	
j' **ai parlé**	nous **avons parlé**
tu **as parlé**	vous **avez parlé**
il/elle/on **a parlé**	ils/elles **ont parlé**

These verbs conjugated with **avoir** have irregular past participles.

avoir:	j'ai eu	mettre:	j'ai mis	être:	j'ai été
il y a:	il y a eu	prendre:	j'ai pris	faire:	j'ai fait
boire:	j'ai bu	apprendre:	j'ai appris	écrire:	j'ai écrit
lire:	j'ai lu	comprendre:	j'ai compris		
pleuvoir:	il a plu				
voir:	j'ai vu				

A few verbs have **être** as their auxiliary. With these verbs, the past participle agrees with the subject for gender and plurality.

ALLER → ALLÉ	
je **suis allé(e)**	nous **sommes allé(e)s**
tu **es allé(e)**	vous **êtes allé(e)(s)**
il **est allé**	ils **sont allés**
elle **est allée**	elles **sont allées**
on **est allé(e)(s)**	

Here are some verbs that have **être** as their auxiliary verb.

—Est-ce que ta mère et ta tante **sont allées** à Paris avec toi?
—Oui, elles ont fait le voyage avec moi mais je **suis restée** plus longtemps. Elles **sont rentrées** une semaine avant moi.

aller:	je suis allé(e)	monter:	je suis monté(e)
arriver:	je suis arrivé(e)	descendre:	je suis descendu(e)
rester:	je suis resté(e)	venir:	je suis venu(e)
entrer:	je suis entré(e)	revenir:	je suis revenu(e)
sortir:	je suis sorti(e)	devenir:	je suis devenu(e)
partir:	je suis parti(e)	naître:	je suis né(e)
rentrer:	je suis rentré(e)	mourir:	il/elle est mort(e)
retourner:	je suis retourné(e)	tomber:	je suis tombé(e)

—Tu as **déjà** visité Nice?
—Non, je **n'**ai **pas encore** été à Nice.
—Qu'est-ce que ton mari et toi avez fait l'année dernière pour les vacances?
—On **n'**a **rien** fait.

Place **ne... pas, ne... rien** *(nothing),* or **ne... jamais** around the auxiliary verb. Use **ne... pas encore** to say *not yet* and **déjà** to say *already* or *ever.* **Déjà** and adverbs indicating how often (**toujours, souvent...**) and how well (**bien, mal...**) are usually placed between the auxiliary verb and the past participle.

The following adverbs indicate when something happened in the past. They may be placed at the beginning or end of the sentence.

hier (matin, après-midi, soir)	récemment
le week-end (le mois) dernier	pendant deux heures (longtemps)
la semaine (l'année) dernière	il y a quelques secondes (cinq minutes, cinq ans...)
la dernière fois	

—Tu as été en vacances pendant combien de temps?
—Pendant quinze jours.
—Tu es rentré il y a combien de temps?
—Je suis rentré mardi dernier.

Faire

The verb **faire** *(to do, to make)* is irregular.

FAIRE *(to do)*	
je **fais**	nous **faisons**
tu **fais**	vous **faites**
il/elle/on **fait**	ils/elles **font**
PASSÉ COMPOSÉ: **j'ai fait**	

Faire is also used in many weather expressions, as well as the expressions listed on page 198.

The **un, une, des, du, de la,** and **de l'** in the expressions with **faire** become **de (d')** when the verb is negated. The definite article (**le, la, l', les**) does not change.

Je ne **fais** rien ce week-end.
Qu'est-ce que tu **fais**?
On **fait** quelque chose ensemble?
Faisons quelque chose avec mes amis.
Que **faites**-vous généralement?
Mes amis **font** beaucoup de sport.

— Quel temps fait-il?
— Il fait beau (mauvais, froid, chaud, frais, du soleil, du vent).

Ils font la cuisine et nous faisons la vaisselle.
They cook and we do the dishes.

Je ne fais jamais **d'**exercice.
Mon colocataire ne fait jamais **le** ménage.

Ne... rien

Ne... rien means *nothing* or *not anything*. This expression can be the subject or object of the verb, or the object of a preposition.

When negating an infinitive, place both parts of the negative expression before it.

Rien n'est en solde?
Tu **n'**achètes **rien**?
Je **n'**ai besoin de **rien.**

Je préfère **ne rien** acheter.

Direct object pronouns

The direct object pronouns are **le, la, l',** and **les.** Use **le** *(him, it)* to replace masculine singular nouns and **la** *(her, it)* to replace feminine singular nouns. **Les** *(Them)* replaces all plural nouns. **Le** and **la** become **l'** when the following word begins with a vowel or silent **h.**

	BEFORE A CONSONANT	BEFORE A VOWEL OR SILENT *H*
him, it (masculine)	le	l'
her, it (feminine)	la	l'
them	les	les

— Tu prends ce sac?
— Oui, je **le** prends.
— *Are you taking this purse?*
— *Yes, I'm taking it.*

— Tu aimes cette robe aussi?
— Oui, je **l'**aime bien.
— *Do you like this dress too?*
— *Yes, I like it.*

— Tu achètes tes vêtements ici?
— Oui, je **les** achète souvent ici.
— *Do you buy your clothes here?*
— *Yes, I often buy them here.*

These pronouns are generally placed *immediately* before the verb. They go before the infinitive if there is one. If not, they go before the conjugated verb. In the negative, the pronoun remains *immediately* before the conjugated verb or the infinitive.

In the **passé composé,** direct object pronouns are placed just before the auxiliary verb **avoir** and the past participle agrees with them for gender and plurality by adding **-e, -s,** or **-es.**

Je **les** achète.
Je ne **les** achète pas.
Je vais **les** acheter.
Je ne vais pas **les** acheter.

A-t-il acheté les chaussures?
Oui, il **les** a acheté**es.**
Non, il ne **les** a pas acheté**es.**

Saying what you did

NOMS MASCULINS

un homme d'affaires	a businessman
le journal	the newspaper
le petit déjeuner	breakfast

NOMS FÉMININS

une femme d'affaires	a businesswoman

EXPRESSIONS ADVERBIALES

hier	yesterday
hier soir	last night, yesterday evening
samedi dernier	last Saturday
le week-end dernier	last weekend

DIVERS

dernier (dernière)	last
faire une promenade	to take a walk
ne... rien	nothing, not anything
prendre son petit déjeuner	to have one's breakfast
travaillant	working

Telling where you went

NOMS MASCULINS

un an	a year
un camping	a campground
un club	a club
un hôtel	a hotel
le lendemain	the next day, the following day
des parents	relatives

NOMS FÉMININS

la chance	luck
une heure	an hour
une minute	a minute
une nuit	a night
une seconde	a second (in time)
une voiture de location	a rental car

EXPRESSIONS VERBALES

descendre (de / dans / à)	to descend, to come down, to get off/out (of), to stay (at)
entrer (dans)	to enter
monter (dans)	to go up, to get on/in
mourir (mort[e])	to die (dead)
naître (né[e])	to be born (born)
partir en voyage	to leave on a trip
partir en week-end	to go away for the weekend
retourner	to return, to go back
tomber	to fall

EXPRESSIONS ADVERBIALES

l'année dernière	last year
déjà	already, ever
la dernière fois	the last time
hier (matin, après-midi)	yesterday (morning, afternoon)
hier soir	last night, yesterday evening
Il y a combien de temps?	How long ago?
il y a quelques secondes	a few seconds ago
longtemps	a long time
lundi (mardi...) dernier	last Monday (Tuesday . . .)
le mois dernier	last month
ne... pas encore	not yet
Pendant combien de temps?	For how long?
pendant deux heures	for two hours
récemment	recently
la semaine dernière	last week
le week-end dernier	last weekend

DIVERS

Quelle chance!	What luck!
quelques	some, a few

Discussing the weather and your activities

NOMS MASCULINS

l'automne (en automne)	*autumn (in autumn)*
l'été (en été)	*summer (in summer)*
l'hiver (en hiver)	*winter (in winter)*
un jardin	*a garden*
le printemps (au printemps)	*spring (in spring)*
le temps	*the weather, time*

NOMS FÉMININS

des distractions	*entertainment*
la neige	*snow*
la pluie	*rain*
une saison	*a season*

EXPRESSIONS VERBALES

aller à la montagne	*to go to the mountains*
dépendre (de)	*to depend (on)*
faire de l'exercice	*to exercise*
faire des courses	*to run errands*
faire du bateau	*to go boating*
faire du camping	*to go camping*
faire du jardinage	*to garden*
faire du jogging	*to go jogging*
faire du shopping	*to go shopping*
faire du ski (nautique)	*to (water)ski*
faire du sport (du tennis, du hockey...)	*to play sports (tennis, hockey . . .)*
faire du vélo	*to go bike-riding*
faire du VTT	*to go all-terrain biking*
faire la cuisine	*to cook*
faire la lessive	*to do laundry*
faire la vaisselle	*to do the dishes*
faire le ménage	*to do housework*
faire une promenade	*to take a walk*
faire un voyage	*to take a trip*
neiger	*to snow*
pleuvoir	*to rain*

DIVERS

ne... rien (de spécial)	*nothing, not anything (special)*
pendant	*during, for*
Quel temps fait-il?	*What's the weather like?*
Il fait beau / chaud / frais / froid / mauvais / du soleil / du vent.	*It's nice / hot / cool / cold / bad / sunny / windy.*
Il pleut.	*It is raining., It rains.*
Il neige.	*It is snowing., It snows.*
Quel temps va-t-il faire?	*What's the weather going to be like?*
Il va faire...	*It's going to be . . .*
Il va pleuvoir/neiger.	*It's going to rain / to snow.*
si	*if*

Deciding what to wear and buying clothes

NOMS MASCULINS

un anorak	*a ski jacket*
un bikini	*a bikini*
un chemisier	*a blouse*
un costume	*a suit (for a man)*
un imperméable	*a raincoat*
un jean	*jeans*
un maillot de bain	*a swimsuit*
un manteau	*an overcoat*
un pantalon	*pants*
un parapluie	*an umbrella*
un polo	*a knit shirt*
un portefeuille	*a wallet*
un pull	*a pullover sweater*
un sac	*a purse, a sack*
un short	*shorts*
un survêtement	*a jogging suit*
un tee-shirt	*a T-shirt*
un vendeur	*a salesclerk*

NOMS FÉMININS

des baskets	*tennis shoes*
des bottes	*boots*
une cabine d'essayage	*a fitting room*
des chaussures	*shoes*
une chemise	*a shirt*
une cravate	*a tie*
une jupe	*a skirt*
des lunettes (de soleil)	*(sun)glasses*
une montre	*a watch*
une robe	*a dress*
des sandales	*sandals*
une vendeuse	*a salesclerk*

EXPRESSIONS VERBALES

coûter	*to cost*
essayer	*to try, to try on*
Il/Elle me plaît.	*I like it.*
mettre (je mets, vous mettez)	*to wear, to put, to put on*

DIVERS

Bien sûr!	*Of course!*
ce (cet, cette, ces)...-ci	*this/these . . . over here*
en solde	*on sale*
Je peux vous aider?	*May I help you?*
le (l') / la (l')	*him, it / her, it*
les	*them*
parfois	*sometimes*
par ici	*this way*
Quelle taille faites-vous?	*What size do you wear?*
Je fais du...	*I wear size . . .*
Qu'en pensez-vous?	*What do you think about it?*
voyons	*let's see*

Bienvenue en Europe francophone

On parle français en Suisse.

EN EUROPE, le français est une langue officielle dans quatre pays et une principauté. **Lesquels aimeriez-vous** visiter?

Le duché du Luxembourg est un des plus petits états d'Europe. **À la tête du gouvernement** se trouvent le Grand-Duc et le Premier ministre. Il y a trois langues **courantes** au Luxembourg: le luxembourgeois, le français et l'allemand. Le français est souvent employé dans l'administration, dans **les écoles** secondaires et dans **le monde** des affaires. Le Luxembourg **attire** l'attention internationale par sa place financière dans l'Europe moderne et, par sa forte immigration (37%), le Luxembourg est devenu un microcosme de l'Europe.

Le Luxembourg

Bienvenue Welcome   **Lesquels aimeriez-vous** Which ones would you like   **Le duché** The duchy   **À la tête du gouvernement** At the head of the government   **courantes** common   **les écoles** schools   **le monde** the world   **attire** attracts

La Suisse, ou la Confédération suisse, est une république fédérale composée de 26 cantons **liés** par la Constitution de 1848. **Toutefois,** une grande partie du **pouvoir** politique **demeure au niveau du** canton. La Suisse **garde depuis** 1515 la neutralité dans tous les conflits internationaux. Ce pays a quatre langues officielles: l'allemand, le français, l'italien et le romanche.

Lausanne, en Suisse

Genève, en Suisse

---

liés *linked*   **Toutefois** *However*   **pouvoir** *power*   **demeure au niveau du** *remains at the level of the*   **garde depuis** *has kept since*

La Belgique

La Belgique est une monarchie fondée sur une démocratie parlementaire. **Les Flamands** (58% de la population) parlent **néerlandais.** Les Wallons (32% de la population) parlent français. Pour le reste, 9% sont bilingues et 1% parle allemand. Cette division culturelle et linguistique a longtemps été une source de conflits. Pour dissiper cet antagonisme, un effort de décentralisation a donné plus de pouvoir aux trois régions qui forment ce pays: la Région flamande, la Région wallonne et la Région de Bruxelles (la capitale).

Monaco, **dont** la langue officielle est le français, est **une principauté** depuis plus de 300 ans. **Bien qu'elle soit devenue** un protectorat de la France en 1861, le prince y a gardé le pouvoir absolu jusqu'à l'établissement de la Constitution de 1911. Aujourd'hui une monarchie constitutionnelle, cette principauté est célèbre dans le monde entier pour le tourisme, le luxe, **les courses** de Formule 1 et pour ses casinos. Le français y est la langue officielle et on y parle aussi anglais et italien. Environ 5000 personnes parlent **monégasque.**

Monaco

Monaco

Les Flamands *The Flemish*   **néerlandais** *Dutch*   **dont** *whose, of which*   **une principauté** *a principality*   **Bien qu'elle soit devenue** *Although it became*   **les courses** *races*   **monégasque** *Monegasque (people and language native to Monaco)*

Avant d'être une république, la France a été une monarchie et un empire. Aujourd'hui, la France est un régime parlementaire qui a à sa tête le Président de la République et son Premier ministre. La France est divisée en 96 départements et 4 départements **d'outre-mer:** la Guadeloupe, la Martinique, la Guyane et La Réunion.

Strasbourg, en France

La France a aussi plusieurs territoires. La Polynésie française, Wallis-et-Futuna, Mayotte et Saint-Pierre-et-Miquelon sont des collectivités d'outre-mer. La Nouvelle-Calédonie est aujourd'hui un pays d'outre-mer. La France possède aussi les Terres australes et antarctiques françaises.

La Corse, en France

Un village en France

Aix-en-Provence, en France

d'outre-mer *overseas*

Les sorties

 iLrn Heinle Learning Center

 academic.cengage.com/french/horizons

 Système-D

 Audio   iRadio

PARIS

 Sur ces pages vous voyez quelques-uns des 180 musées et monuments à Paris. Cherchez des tours virtuels de la ville de Paris ou du musée du Louvre sur Internet. Voici quelques autres sites touristiques à rechercher sur Internet: le Centre Pompidou, la Conciergerie, la Défense et la Grande Arche, les Invalides, le musée d'Orsay, l'Opéra, le Panthéon, la place de la Concorde, la place Vendôme, la Sainte-Chapelle, le Trocadéro.

Quand vous pensez à Paris, quels mots **viennent à l'esprit**? Centre de **mode** et de luxe? centre politique et économique? ville historique **pleine de** monuments et de musées?

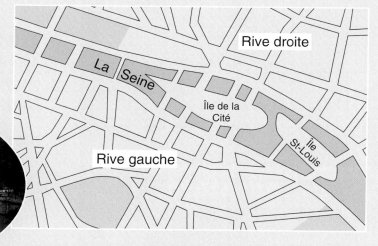

Rive droite

La Seine

Île de la Cité

Île St-Louis

Rive gauche

Paris, la capitale de la France, est une des plus belles villes **du monde.** La Seine sépare la ville en deux parties, **la rive** gauche et la rive droite. Les deux îles situées **au milieu de** la Seine sont l'île de la Cité et l'île St-Louis. C'est sur l'île de la Cité que la ville de Paris est née il y a plus de 2 000 ans.

La célèbre avenue des Champs-Élysées **s'étend** de la place de la Concorde à l'arc de Triomphe.

Le Louvre, l'un des plus grands musées d'art du monde, fait presque un kilomètre de longueur.

---

viennent à l'esprit *come to mind*   **la mode** *fashion*   **pleine de** *full of*   **du monde** *in the world*   **la rive** *the bank* (of a river)
au milieu de *in the middle of*   **s'étend** *extends*

PARIS
NOMBRE D'HABITANTS: 2 153 600 (avec la région
parisienne: plus de 11 100 000) (les Parisiens)
DÉPARTMENT: Paris
PROVINCE: Île-de-France

 Visit it live on Google Earth!

Pour avoir une vue panoramique de la
ville, on peut monter à la tour Eiffel.

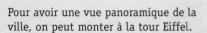

Le Quartier latin est un des quartiers les plus
sympathiques de Paris.

❀ Qu'en savez-vous?

Devinez quel site touristique des photos ici ou à la page 189
correspond à chaque description.

1. La construction de ce chef-d'œuvre d'architecture
   gothique a duré de 1163 à 1345. Après la tour Eiffel,
   c'est le deuxième monument le plus visité de France.
2. Cet ancien palais royal datant de 1190 **a subi** plusieurs addi-
   tions et transformations et il est devenu un musée en 1791.
3. Dans ce quartier, Robert de Sorbon a établi en 1253 ce
   qui est aujourd'hui l'université de Paris, appelée la Sorbonne. Le latin était la langue officielle dans le quartier
   jusqu'en 1793.
4. Longue de presque deux kilomètres et s'étendant de l'arc de
   Triomphe et la place de l'Étoile à l'extrémité **ouest** jusqu'à
   la place de la Concorde et le Louvre à **l'est**, le développement de cette célèbre avenue a commencé en 1640.
5. En 1806, Napoléon a commandé la construction de ce
   monument en honneur de l'armée. **La chute** de Napoléon
   a interrompu **les travaux** sur le monument jusqu'en 1825.
   Terminé en 1836, ce monument est situé sur la place de
   l'Étoile au bout des Champs-Élysées.
6. En 1860, la ville de Paris a annexé ce quartier situé sur
   une colline avec une vue panoramique de la ville. La
   basilique du Sacré-Cœur, construite entre 1875 et 1914,
   est le point **le plus haut** de Paris.
7. L'ingénieur qui a construit ce monument pour l'Exposition
   universelle en 1889 a travaillé aussi sur la statue de la
   Liberté à New York. C'est le site touristique le plus visité
   de France.

Si vous aimez **la vie** de bohème,
visitez le quartier de Montmartre.

---

la vie life   **a subi** has undergone   **ouest** west   **l'est** the east   **La chute** The fall   **les travaux** work   **une colline** a hill   **le plus haut** highest

Inviting someone to go out

Les invitations

Éric Pérez **veut** inviter sa petite amie Michèle à sortir. Et vous, si **vous voulez** inviter **quelqu'un, vous pouvez dire...**

À UN(E) AMI(E)	À UNE AUTRE PERSONNE OU À UN GROUPE DE PERSONNES
Tu veux... ?	Vous voulez... ?
Tu voudrais... ?	Vous voudriez... ?
Je t'invite à...	Je voudrais vous inviter à...

Si **quelqu'un vous invite,** vous pouvez répondre...

POUR DIRE OUI	POUR DIRE NON	POUR SUGGÉRER UNE AUTRE ACTIVITÉ
Oui, je veux bien...	Je regrette mais...	Je préfère...
Quelle bonne idée!	je ne suis pas libre.	J'aime mieux...
Avec plaisir!	**je ne peux** vraiment **pas.**	Allons plutôt à...
	je dois travailler.	

Les Français **utilisent** l'heure officielle pour tous **les horaires** (le train, l'avion, le cinéma, le théâtre, la télé, **les heures d'ouverture**). Pour lire l'heure officielle, on utilise uniquement des chiffres. Aux USA, on **appelle** cette **façon** de lire l'heure *military time.*

L'HEURE OFFICIELLE		L'HEURE FAMILIÈRE
0h05	zéro heure cinq	minuit cinq
1h15	une heure quinze	une heure et quart (du matin)
12h20	douze heures vingt	midi vingt
13h30	treize heures trente	une heure et demie (de l'après-midi)
15h40	quinze heures quarante	quatre heures moins vingt (de l'après-midi)
21h45	vingt et une heures quarante-cinq	dix heures moins le quart (du soir)

il veut (vouloir *to want)* **vous voulez (vouloir** *to want)* **quelqu'un** *someone* **vous pouvez (pouvoir** *can, may, to be able)* **dire** *to say* **Tu veux (vouloir** *to want)* **quelqu'un vous invite** *someone invites you* **je ne peux pas (pouvoir** *can, may, to be able)* **je dois (devoir** *must, to have to)* **utiliser** *to use, to utilize* **un horaire** *a schedule* **les heures d'ouverture** *opening times* **appeler** *to call* **une façon** *a way*

Éric téléphone à sa petite amie Michèle.

MICHÈLE:	Allô?
ÉRIC:	Salut, Michèle. C'est moi, Éric. Ça va?
MICHÈLE:	Oui, très bien. Et toi?
ÉRIC:	Moi, ça va. Écoute, tu es libre ce soir? Tu voudrais sortir?
MICHÈLE:	Oui, je veux bien. Qu'est-ce que tu as envie de faire?
ÉRIC:	**Je pensais** aller voir la nouvelle comédie qu'on **passe** au cinéma Gaumont.
MICHÈLE:	Tu sais, moi, je n'aime pas **tellement** les comédies. Je préfère les films d'**amour**. Allons plutôt voir le nouveau film d'amour au cinéma Rex.
ÉRIC:	Bon, je veux bien. À quelle heure?
MICHÈLE:	Il y a **une séance** à vingt heures quarante-cinq.
ÉRIC:	Alors, je passe chez toi vers huit heures?
MICHÈLE:	D'accord. Alors, au revoir.
ÉRIC:	À tout à l'heure, Michèle.

A. Invitations. Utilisez une variété d'expressions pour inviter un(e) partenaire. Il/Elle va accepter ou refuser chacune de vos invitations ou proposer une autre activité.

INVITEZ UN(E) AMI(E) À...

1. aller danser samedi soir
2. dîner au restaurant ce soir
3. aller voir une exposition demain
4. aller prendre un verre aujourd'hui après les cours

INVITEZ UN GROUPE D'AMIS À...

5. aller voir un film d'amour demain
6. préparer les cours ensemble ce soir
7. faire du vélo au parc ce week-end
8. aller au match de football américain / de basket ce week-end

B. À quelle heure? Regardez la liste des séances du film *Pur week-end* au cinéma Gaumont Champs-Élysées et au cinéma Ugc Ciné Cité Bercy à la page 229. Exprimez l'heure de chaque séance de deux façons.

EXEMPLE   12h

La première séance est à douze heures; c'est-à-dire *(that is to say)* à midi.

C. Conversation. Avec un(e) partenaire, relisez à haute voix la conversation entre Michèle et Éric en haut de la page. Ensuite, changez la conversation pour faire des projets pour aller au cinéma avec un(e) ami(e). Parlez de:

- quel(s) genre(s) de film vous aimez ou n'aimez pas. (Servez-vous des expressions données dans la liste de *Vocabulaire supplémentaire.*)
- quel film vous voudriez voir.
- où et à quelle heure on passe ce film.
- où et comment vous allez vous retrouver *(you are going to meet up).*

Je pensais *I was thinking*   **passer (un film)** *to show (a movie)*   **tellement** *so much*   l'amour *(m) love*   **une séance** *a showing*

Vocabulaire supplémentaire

LES FILMS
un dessin animé *a cartoon*
un drame
un film d'aventures
un film d'épouvante *a horror film*
un film de science-fiction
un film policier

POUR SE RETROUVER
Je passe chez toi / chez vous. *I'll come by your place.*
Passe / Passez chez moi. *Come by my place.*
Rendez-vous à... *Let's meet at . . .*

You can find a list of the new words from the vocabulary and grammar sections of this *Compétence* on page 254 and a recording of this list on track 3-3 of your *Text Audio CD.*

1. What does **vouloir** mean? What are three meanings of **pouvoir**? What are the meanings of **devoir**? What are the conjugations of these three verbs?

2. The **nous** and **vous** forms have the same vowels in the stem as the infinitive. What vowels do the other forms have?

3. What auxiliary verb do you use to form the **passé composé** of these three verbs? What are their past participles?

Issuing and accepting invitations

Les verbes **vouloir**, **pouvoir** *et* **devoir**

The verbs **vouloir** *(to want)* and **pouvoir** *(can, may, to be able)* are useful when inviting someone to do something. They have similar conjugations.

VOULOIR (to want)	
je **veux**	nous **voulons**
tu **veux**	vous **voulez**
il/elle/on **veut**	ils/elles **veulent**
PASSÉ COMPOSÉ: **j'ai voulu**	

POUVOIR (can, may, to be able)	
je **peux**	nous **pouvons**
tu **peux**	vous **pouvez**
il/elle/on **peut**	ils/elles **peuvent**
PASSÉ COMPOSÉ: **j'ai pu**	

Je **veux** sortir mais je ne **peux** pas.   *I **want** to go out, but I **can't**.*

Use **devoir** followed by an infinitive to say what you *must* or *have to* do. **Devoir** also means *to owe*.

DEVOIR (must, to have to, to owe)	
je **dois**	nous **devons**
tu **dois**	vous **devez**
il/elle/on **doit**	ils/elles **doivent**
PASSÉ COMPOSÉ: **j'ai dû**	

Je **dois** travailler demain.   *I **have to** work tomorrow.*
Je **dois** 100 dollars à mon frère.   *I **owe** my brother 100 dollars.*

In the **passé composé, devoir** can mean that someone *had to* do something or *must have* done something. Context will clarify the meaning.

Michèle n'est pas chez elle. Elle **a dû** partir.
*Michèle isn't home. She **had to** leave. / She **must have** left.*

Il n'a pas pu sortir parce qu'il **a dû** travailler.
*He wasn't able to go out because he **had to** work.*

A. Activités. Demandez à votre partenaire ce que chacune de ces personnes veut faire aux moments indiqués. Si votre partenaire n'est pas sûr(e), il/elle doit proposer quelque chose.

EXEMPLE   toi (aujourd'hui après les cours?)
        — **Qu'est-ce que tu veux faire aujourd'hui après les cours?**
        — **Je veux rentrer à la maison.**

1. toi (ce soir? demain soir? ce week-end?)
2. tes amis et toi (vendredi soir? samedi après-midi? dimanche matin?)
3. ton meilleur ami / ta meilleure amie (demain soir? ce week-end? pendant les prochaines vacances *[vacation]*?)
4. les autres étudiants (après les cours aujourd'hui? au prochain cours de français? ce week-end?)

B. En cours. Dites si ces personnes peuvent faire chacune des choses indiquées en cours de français.

EXEMPLE Je... manger **Je ne peux pas manger en cours.**

1. Je...
   parler aux autres étudiants
   boire un café
   dormir
2. Nous...
   toujours parler anglais
   fumer
   poser des questions
3. Le prof...
   quitter la classe maintenant
   toujours comprendre les étudiants
   parler au téléphone
4. Les étudiants...
   dormir
   souvent partir en avance *(early)*
   répondre à leur portable

C. Qu'est-ce qu'on doit faire? Pour chaque paire d'activités proposées, indiquez ce que chacun doit et ne doit pas faire au cours de français.

EXEMPLE Le prof (être patient / être impatient)
Le prof doit être patient. Il ne doit pas être impatient.

1. Le prof (insulter les étudiants / aider les étudiants)
   (donner de bons examens / donner des examens trop difficiles)
   (toujours parler anglais en classe / souvent parler français en classe)
2. Les étudiants (dormir en cours / écouter le prof)
   (faire les devoirs / sortir tous les soirs)
   (bien préparer l'examen / copier les réponses des autres)
3. Moi, je (bien préparer mes cours / toujours sortir avec des amis)
   (dormir en cours / écouter en cours)
   (souvent écouter le CD de français / regarder la télé tout le temps)

D. On veut... Aujourd'hui, les Pérez ne peuvent pas faire ce qu'ils veulent. Jouez le rôle d'Alice et expliquez ce que chacun veut et doit faire.

EXEMPLE **Moi, je veux dormir, mais je dois sortir avec le chien.**

Moi...

1. Éric...

2. Éric et Cathy...

3. Vincent...

4. Nos amis...

5. Michel...

E. Encore des explications. Plus tard, Alice dit que chacun n'a pas pu faire ce qu'il voulait *(wanted)* et elle explique ce qu'ils ont dû faire. Qu'est-ce qu'elle dit? Utilisez le passé composé.

EXEMPLE **Moi, je n'ai pas pu dormir. J'ai dû sortir avec le chien.**

Stratégies et Compréhension auditive

When making plans, we often jot down important information for later reference. If a friend invited you to do something, what sort of information would you want to remember? Look at the following invitation and think about what information is given.

Nous vous attendons

le *Samedi 18 novembre*

à _____ *19* _____ heures.

Notre adresse:

85 boulevard St Michel

Téléphone *02.43.29.69.50*

R.S.V.P.

CD 3-4

A. Prenez des notes. Trois amis invitent Éric à faire quelque chose. Écoutez chaque invitation et prenez des notes en français. Qu'est-ce qu'ils vont faire? Où? Quel jour? À quelle heure?

B. À vous. Éric demande à Michèle de l'accompagner. Utilisez vos notes de l'exercice précédent pour jouer les rôles d'Éric et de Michèle avec un(e) partenaire.

EXEMPLE —**Je vais jouer au tennis avec Marc demain à... Est-ce que tu voudrais jouer avec nous?**
—**Oui, je veux bien!**

Compréhension auditive: On va au cinéma?

CD 3-5 Vincent demande à Alice si elle voudrait aller au cinéma. Lisez les questions de l'exercice suivant. Ensuite, écoutez la conversation et notez les détails importants sur une feuille de papier.

A. Quel film? Répondez aux questions suivantes d'après la conversation entre Alice et son mari.

1. Comment est-ce qu'Alice trouve les films de science-fiction?
2. Quel genre *(type)* de film est-ce qu'ils décident d'aller voir?
3. À quelle séance est-ce qu'ils vont aller?

B. Vos notes. Utilisez vos notes pour recréer *(to recreate)* la conversation entre Alice et Vincent avec un(e) camarade de classe.

C. Tu veux sortir? Invitez un(e) camarade de classe à aller voir un film avec vous. Choisissez une séance et décidez à quelle heure vous allez passer chez votre ami(e).

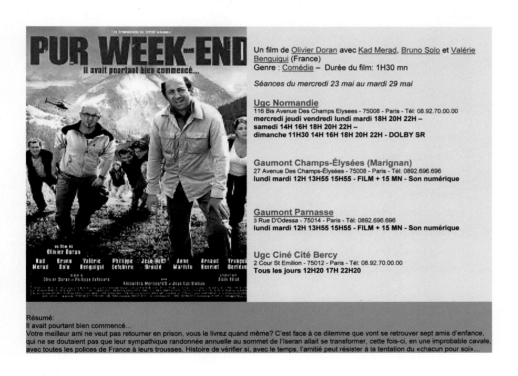

Un film de Olivier Doran avec Kad Merad, Bruno Solo et Valérie Benguigui (France)
Genre : Comédie – Durée du film: 1H30 mn

Séances du mercredi 23 mai au mardi 29 mai

Ugc Normandie
116 Bis Avenue Des Champs Elysees - 75008 - Paris - Tél: 08.92.70.00.00
**mercredi jeudi vendredi lundi mardi 18H 20H 22H –
samedi 14H 16H 18H 20H 22H –
dimanche 11H30 14H 16H 18H 20H 22H - DOLBY SR**

Gaumont Champs-Élysées (Marignan)
27 Avenue Des Champs-Élysées - 75008 - Paris - Tél: 0892.696.696
lundi mardi 12H 13H55 15H55 - FILM + 15 MN - Son numérique

Gaumont Parnasse
3 Rue D'Odessa - 75014 - Paris - Tél: 0892.696.696
lundi mardi 12H 13H55 15H55 - FILM + 15 MN - Son numérique

Ugc Ciné Cité Bercy
2 Cour St Emilion - 75012 - Paris - Tél: 08.92.70.00.00
Tous les jours 12H20 17H 22H20

Résumé:
Il avait pourtant bien commencé...
Votre meilleur ami ne veut pas retourner en prison, vous le livrez quand même? C'est face à ce dilemme que vont se retrouver sept amis d'enfance, qui ne se doutaient pas que leur sympathique randonnée annuelle au sommet de l'Iseran allait se transformer, cette fois-ci, en une improbable cavale, avec toutes les polices de France à leurs trousses. Histoire de vérifier si, avec le temps, l'amitié peut résister à la tentation du «chacun pour soi»...

Talking about how you spend and used to spend your time

Aujourd'hui et dans le passé

Michèle compare sa **vie** quand **elle était** au **lycée** avec sa vie d'aujourd'hui.

Quand j'étais au lycée...

Aujourd'hui...

J'avais 15 ans.	J'ai 21 ans.
J'étais **lycéenne.**	Je suis étudiante à l'université.
J'habitais avec ma famille.	J'habite avec ma famille.
J'avais cours du lundi au vendredi et le samedi matin aussi.	J'ai cours du lundi au vendredi.
Je n'aimais pas beaucoup **l'école** *(f).*	J'aime l'université.
Je rentrais souvent à la maison pour déjeuner.	En général, je déjeune au **restau-u.**
Le week-end, j'étais toujours **fatiguée** et **je dormais** beaucoup.	Le week-end, **je suis** souvent fatiguée et je dors beaucoup.
Le vendredi soir, je passais du temps avec ma famille ou **je sortais** avec **des copains.** On allait au cinéma, au café ou à **une boum.**	Le vendredi soir, **je sors** souvent avec des copains. On va au cinéma, en boîte ou à une fête.
Le samedi, je faisais du sport avec des amis: on jouait au foot, **on faisait du roller...** et on jouait au tennis.	Chaque samedi, je joue au tennis avec des amis et je fais aussi souvent du roller.

---

dans le passé *in the past*   **la vie** *life*   **elle était** *she was*   **le lycée** *high school*   **J'avais 15 ans.** *I was fifteen.*   **un(e) lycéen(ne)** *a high school student*   **J'habitais** *I lived, I used to live*   **J'avais cours** *I had class, I used to have class*   **l'école** *(f) school*   **le restau-u** *the university cafeteria*   **fatigué(e)** *tired*   **je dormais** *I slept, I used to sleep*   **je sortais** *I went out, I used to go out*   **un copain (une copine)** *a friend, a pal*   **une boum** *a party*   **je sors (sortir)** *I go out (to go out)*   **on faisait du roller** *we went in-line skating, we used to go in-line skating*

Michèle demande à Éric **ce qu'**il faisait quand il était au lycée.

MICHÈLE:	Qu'est-ce que tu aimais faire quand tu étais au lycée?
ÉRIC	J'aimais passer le temps avec des copains. Le vendredi soir, on allait aux matchs de football américain ou de basket au lycée.
MICHÈLE:	Et le samedi?
ÉRIC	Le samedi matin, je travaillais. Le samedi après-midi, on faisait du skateboard. Le samedi soir, je sortais avec ma petite amie. On allait au cinéma.
MICHÈLE:	Et qu'est-ce que tu faisais le dimanche?
ÉRIC	Le dimanche, je ne faisais rien de spécial. Je restais à la maison. Je regardais la télé ou je louais une vidéo.

A. Maintenant ou dans le passé?

Est-ce que Michèle parle de sa vie maintenant ou de quand elle avait 15 ans? Commencez chaque phrase avec **Quand j'avais 15 ans...** ou **Maintenant...**

1. J'étais lycéenne.
2. J'ai cours du lundi au vendredi.
3. Je n'aimais pas beaucoup l'école.
4. D'habitude, je déjeunais à la maison.
5. Je sors beaucoup le week-end.
6. J'aime sortir avec des copains.
7. Mes copains et moi, on aimait aller au café.
8. On faisait souvent du sport ensemble.

B. Et vous?

Dites si vous faites ces choses maintenant et si vous faisiez ces choses quand vous aviez 10 ans.

EXEMPLES   Maintenant, j'habite avec ma famille.
Maintenant, j'habite avec ma famille.
Maintenant, je n'habite pas avec ma famille.

Quand j'avais 10 ans, j'habitais avec ma famille.
Quand j'avais 10 ans, j'habitais avec ma famille.
Quand j'avais 10 ans, je n'habitais pas avec ma famille.

1. Maintenant, je suis souvent fatigué(e).
   Quand j'avais 10 ans, j'étais souvent fatigué(e).
2. Maintenant, je dors bien.
   Quand j'avais 10 ans, je dormais bien.
3. Maintenant, je sors souvent le vendredi soir.
   Quand j'avais 10 ans, je sortais souvent le vendredi soir.
4. Maintenant, mes copains et moi, on fait souvent du sport ensemble.
   Quand j'avais 10 ans, on faisait souvent du sport ensemble.
5. Maintenant, je travaille.
   Quand j'avais 10 ans, je travaillais.

C. Conversation.

Avec un(e) partenaire, relisez à haute voix la conversation entre Michèle et Éric en haut de la page. Ensuite, changez la conversation pour parler de ce que vous faisiez *(what you used to do)* quand vous étiez au lycée. Si vous voulez utiliser des verbes que vous n'avez pas encore appris dans cette forme du passé, demandez à votre professeur comment les conjuguer.

You can find a list of the new words from the vocabulary and grammar sections of this *Compétence* on page 254 and a recording of this list on track 3-7 of your *Text Audio CD.*

ce que *what*

Pour vérifier

1. Which form of the present tense do you use to create the stem for all verbs in the imperfect, except for **être**? What is the stem for **être**?

2. You use the **passé composé** to talk about a specific occurrence in the past. When do you use the imperfect?

3. Which imperfect endings are pronounced alike? What single letter distinguishes the **nous** and **vous** forms of the imperfect from the present?

Note *de grammaire*

Note that verbs like **étudier** retain the **i** of the stem before the **imparfait** endings.

| j'étud**i**ais | nous étud**i**ions |
| vous étud**i**iez | ils étud**i**aient |

 To download a podcast on the Imperfect past, go to **academic.cengage.com/french.**

Saying how things used to be

L'imparfait — things you used to Do

You know to use the **passé composé** to talk about an action that took place on a specific occasion in the past. To tell what things used to be like in general, what someone used to do, or what happened over and over in the past, use the **imparfait** *(imperfect)*. The **imparfait** can be translated in a variety of ways in English.

I was working mornings.
I used to work mornings.   Je travaillais le matin.
I worked mornings.

All verbs except **être** form this tense by dropping the **-ons** from the present tense **nous** form and adding the endings you see below. The stem for **être** is **ét-.**

	PARLER (nous parl~~ons~~ → parl-)	**FAIRE** (nous fais~~ons~~ → fais-)	**PRENDRE** (nous pren~~ons~~ → pren-)	**ÊTRE** (ét-)
je (j')	parl**ais**	fais**ais**	pren**ais**	ét**ais**
tu	parl**ais**	fais**ais**	pren**ais**	ét**ais**
il/elle/on	parl**ait**	fais**ait**	pren**ait**	ét**ait**
nous	parl**ions**	fais**ions**	pren**ions**	ét**ions**
vous	parl**iez**	fais**iez**	pren**iez**	ét**iez**
ils/elles	parl**aient**	fais**aient**	pren**aient**	ét**aient**

Spelling changes in the present tense **nous** form of verbs like **manger** and **commencer** occur in the **imparfait** only before endings beginning with an **a.**

MANGER	**COMMENCER**
je mang**e**ais	je commen**ç**ais
tu mang**e**ais	tu commen**ç**ais
il/elle/on mang**e**ait	il/elle/on commen**ç**ait
nous mangions	nous commencions
vous mangiez	vous commenciez
ils/elles mang**e**aient	ils/elles commen**ç**aient

Also learn these expressions in the imperfect.

| c'est → c'était | il y a → il y avait | il pleut → il pleuvait | il neige → il neigeait |

CD 3-8

Prononciation

Les terminaisons de l'imparfait

The **-ais, -ait,** and **-aient** endings of the imperfect are all pronounced alike. The **nous** and **vous** endings of the imperfect, **-ions** and **-iez,** are distinguished from the present only by the vowel **i** in the ending.

Qu'est-ce que vous faisiez?	*What did you use to do?*
Ils travaillaient pour IBM.	*They worked for IBM.*
Nous allions à la plage.	*We used to go to the beach.*

A. La jeunesse. Interviewez un(e) camarade de classe pour savoir ce qu'il/elle faisait quand il/elle était au lycée.

> **EXEMPLE**   fumer / ne pas aimer ça
> > —**Tu fumais quand tu étais au lycée ou tu n'aimais pas ça?**
> > —**Je fumais. / Je n'aimais pas ça.**

1. aller presque toujours en cours / être souvent absent(e)
2. apprendre facilement / avoir des difficultés
3. travailler / ne pas avoir besoin de travailler
4. avoir beaucoup de copains / passer beaucoup de temps seul(e)
5. faire souvent du sport / préférer faire autre chose
6. pouvoir sortir tard / devoir rentrer tôt
7. aller souvent en boîte / ne pas aimer danser
8. aimer dormir tard le week-end / avoir beaucoup d'énergie le matin

Maintenant, avec votre partenaire, préparez six questions pour votre professeur. Demandez ce qu'il/elle faisait quand il/elle était à l'université.

Quand j'avais 10 ans, j'aimais jouer avec mon chien.

B. Chez nous. Que faisaient ces personnes quand vous aviez dix ans? Dites au moins trois choses pour chacune. Utilisez les verbes suggérés ou d'autres verbes si vous préférez.

> **EXEMPLE**   Mon père...
> > **Mon père était très patient. Il travaillait souvent le week-end et il rentrait tard. Il n'était pas souvent à la maison.**

1. Mes parents...	3. Ma mère...	5. Dans ma famille, nous...
2. Mon père...	4. Moi, je...	6. Mes copains et moi...

avoir beaucoup d'amis / un chien	arriver à l'école à... heures
être patient(e)(s) / impatient(e)(s)	rentrer à... heures
travailler le week-end	jouer au golf / aux jeux vidéo
aimer lire / dormir / parler au téléphone	faire souvent du roller / du sport...
être à la maison le week-end	voyager souvent
faire le ménage / du shopping...	aller souvent voir mes cousins...
aimer les maths / les sciences...	aller à la plage / au cinéma...
prendre l'autobus pour aller à l'école	manger dans des fast-foods
	???

C. Entretien. Interviewez votre partenaire.

1. Est-ce que tu habitais ici quand tu étais au lycée? Avec qui habitais-tu? Est-ce que tes grands-parents habitaient près de chez vous? Passais-tu beaucoup de temps avec ta famille? Qu'est-ce que vous faisiez souvent ensemble?
2. Aimais-tu ton lycée? Quels étaient tes cours préférés? Faisais-tu du sport? Est-ce que tes cours étaient faciles ou difficiles? Avais-tu beaucoup de devoirs?
3. Avais-tu beaucoup de copains? Qu'est-ce que tu faisais avec tes copains le week-end? Comment s'appelait ton meilleur ami ou ta meilleure amie? Qu'est-ce que vous aimiez faire ensemble?

Pour vérifier

1. What are the conjugations of **sortir**, **partir**, and **dormir**?
2. When do you use **quitter**?
3. How do you say *to go out* **of**? *to leave* **from**? *to leave* **for**?
4. How do you say *to leave for the weekend*? *to leave on vacation*? *to leave on a trip*?
5. What is the difference in pronunciation between **il sort** and **ils sortent**?

Talking about activities

Les verbes *sortir, partir et dormir*

The verbs **sortir, partir,** and **dormir** have similar patterns of conjugation.

SORTIR (to go out)	PARTIR (to leave)	DORMIR (to sleep)
je **sors**	je **pars**	je **dors**
tu **sors**	tu **pars**	tu **dors**
il/elle/on **sort**	il/elle/on **part**	il/elle/on **dort**
nous **sortons**	nous **partons**	nous **dormons**
vous **sortez**	vous **partez**	vous **dormez**
ils/elles **sortent**	ils/elles **partent**	ils/elles **dorment**
P.C. **je suis sorti(e)**	P.C. **je suis parti(e)**	P.C. **j'ai dormi**
IMP. **je sortais**	IMP. **je partais**	IMP. **je dormais**

You have already seen that **sortir** can mean *to go out,* in the sense of going out with friends. It can also mean *to go/come out of,* in the sense of going out of a place. It is the opposite of **entrer.** Use **de** to say *of.*

> Je suis sorti **de** l'appartement en pyjama pour aller chercher le journal.

Partir means *to leave* in the sense of *to go away.* It is the opposite of **arriver.** Some common expressions with **partir** are: **partir en week-end, partir en vacances, partir en voyage.** To name the place you are leaving, use **partir de.** To say where you are leaving *for,* use **partir pour.**

> Il part en vacances aujourd'hui. Il est parti **de** son bureau à trois heures et il est parti **pour** l'aéroport vers cinq heures.

Quitter means *to leave* a person or a place and is *always* used with a direct object. In the **passé composé,** it is conjugated with **avoir.**

> J'**ai quitté** la maison à midi. J'ai retrouvé mes amis au café. J'**ai quitté** mes amis vers deux heures.

Prononciation

CD 3-9

Les verbes *sortir, partir et dormir*

You can distinguish aurally between the **il/elle** singular and **ils/elles** plural forms of verbs like **sortir, partir,** and **dormir.** Compare these sentences.

ALICE
Elle dort bien.
Elle sort ce soir.
Elle part demain.

ALICE ET SA FILLE
Elles dorment bien.
Elles sortent ce soir.
Elles partent demain.

When a word ends with a pronounced consonant sound in French, it must be released. Note that when you pronounce the boldfaced consonants in the following English phrases, your tongue or lips do not have to move back and release them.

> What par**t**?   What sor**t**?   In the dor**m**.

Compare how the boldfaced consonants in the following plural verb forms are released.

> Ils par**t**ent.   Ils sor**t**ent.   Ils dor**m**ent.

A. Activités. Complétez ces phrases avec la forme correcte du verbe indiqué. Ensuite, dites si elles sont vraies ou fausses pour vous. Corrigez les phrases fausses.

> **EXEMPLE** Je **pars** (partir) rarement en week-end avec mes amis.
> **C'est vrai. Je pars rarement en week-end avec mes amis.**
> **C'est faux. Nous partons souvent en week-end ensemble.**

1. Mon meilleur ami / Ma meilleure amie ne _____ (sortir) presque jamais avec moi le week-end, mais nous _____ (sortir) souvent en semaine.

2. Quand je _____ (sortir) avec mes amis le samedi soir, je suis toujours fatigué(e) le dimanche matin et je _____ (dormir) souvent jusqu'à midi.

3. Mes amis _____ (sortir) souvent pendant la semaine sans moi. Ils _____ (dormir) souvent pendant leurs cours.

4. Je _____ (partir) souvent en vacances avec mes parents. Généralement, nous _____ (partir) en vacances en juillet.

5. Mes parents _____ (partir) souvent en week-end pour faire du camping. Ils _____ (dormir) bien sous une tente, mais moi, je _____ (dormir) mal.

Maintenant dites si ces personnes faisaient ces choses quand vous étiez lycéen(ne).

> **EXEMPLE** **Quand j'étais au lycée, je ne partais jamais en week-end avec mes amis.**

B. Vos habitudes. Formez des phrases pour parler de ce que vous faites les jours du cours de français et quand vous sortez avec des amis. Demandez à votre partenaire s'il/si elle fait les mêmes choses.

> **EXEMPLES** Les jours du cours de français... je / dormir jusqu'à... heures
> **— Les jours du cours de français, je dors jusqu'à 7 heures.**
> **Et toi? Est-ce que tu dors jusqu'à 7 heures aussi?**
> **— Non, je dors jusqu'à 8 heures.**
>
> Quand je sors avec des amis... nous / sortir le plus souvent le... soir
> **— Quand je sors avec des amis, nous sortons le plus souvent le samedi soir. Et vous? Est-ce que vous sortez le plus souvent le samedi soir aussi?**
> **— Oui, nous sortons le plus souvent le samedi soir aussi.**

Les jours du cours de français...

1. je / dormir jusqu'à... heures
2. je / quitter la maison à... heures
3. je / sortir de mon dernier cours à... heures

Quand je sors avec des amis...

4. nous / sortir le plus souvent le... soir
5. nous / quitter la maison à... heures
6. je / dormir jusqu'à... le lendemain *(the next day)*

C. Toujours des questions! Parlez avec votre partenaire de la dernière fois qu'il/elle est sorti(e) avec des amis. Posez les questions indiquées.

> **EXEMPLE** quel jour / sortir ensemble
> **—Quel jour est-ce que vous êtes sortis ensemble?**
> **—On est sortis ensemble samedi dernier.**

1. quand / sortir ensemble
2. où / aller ensemble
3. qu'est-ce que / faire
4. à quelle heure / quitter la maison
5. jusqu'à quelle heure / dormir le lendemain *(the next day)*

Talking about the past

Une sortie

Cathy parle de la dernière fois qu'elle a dîné avec des amis. Et vous? La dernière fois que vous êtes sorti(e) avec des ami(e)s, comment était la soirée? **Qu'est-ce qui s'est passé?**

Il pleuvait quand j'ai quitté l'appartement.

Il était sept heures et demie quand je suis arrivée au restaurant.

On n'avait pas très faim et on n'a pas mangé **tout de suite.**

Le repas était **délicieux** et j'ai beaucoup mangé.

Après le repas, nous étions fatigués et je suis partie.

Quand je suis rentrée chez moi, il était environ dix heures.

Le lendemain, c'était dimanche et je suis restée au lit jusqu'à dix heures.

Qu'est-ce qui s'est passé? *What happened?*   tout de suite *right away*   Le repas *The meal*   délicieux (délicieuse) *delicious*
Le lendemain *The next day*

Cathy et une amie parlent de leurs activités du week-end dernier.

MICHELINE: Je suis allée au restaurant avec des copines ce week-end.
CATHY: Vous êtes allées où?
MICHELINE: Au Bistro Romain.
CATHY: **Ça t'a plu?**
MICHELINE: Beaucoup. C'était délicieux. On a bien mangé et on a beaucoup parlé. C'était vraiment bien!
CATHY: Et qu'est-ce que tu as fait après?
MICHELINE: **Rien du tout.** J'étais fatiguée et je suis rentrée. Et toi, qu'est-ce que tu as fait ce week-end?
CATHY: Moi aussi, je suis sortie avec des copains. On est allés au cinéma.

A. Au restaurant.
La dernière fois que vous êtes allé(e) au restaurant, qu'est-ce qui s'est passé? Changez les mots en italique pour parler de votre sortie.

1. Quand j'ai quitté *la maison*, il était *huit heures* et il *faisait froid.*
2. Quand je suis arrivé(e) au restaurant, il était *neuf heures.*
3. On *avait très faim* et on *a mangé tout de suite.*
4. Le repas était vraiment *médiocre* et j'ai *peu* mangé.
5. Après le repas, nous avions envie de *continuer la soirée* et nous *sommes allés en boîte.*
6. Quand je suis rentré(e), il était *onze heures* et j'*étais fatigué(e).*
7. Le lendemain, c'était *dimanche* et je *suis resté(e) au lit.*

B. La journée d'Alice.
Décrivez la journée d'Alice vendredi dernier.

❋ Note *de grammaire*

You usually answer a question in the same tense in which it is asked.

1. Alice était seule quand elle a quitté l'appartement? Quelle heure était-il? Est-ce qu'il pleuvait? Est-ce qu'il faisait froid? Quels vêtements est-ce qu'elle portait?
2. Alice était seule au café? Elle a mangé quelque chose? A-t-elle bu quelque chose?
3. Quelle heure était-il quand elle est rentrée chez elle?

C. Conversation.
Avec un(e) partenaire, relisez à haute voix la conversation entre Micheline et Cathy en haut de la page. Ensuite, changez la conversation pour parler de la dernière fois que vous avez mangé avec des copains.

You can find a list of the new words from CD 3-11 the vocabulary and grammar sections of this **Compétence** on page 255 and a recording of this list on track 3-11 of your *Text Audio CD.*

Ça t'a plu? *Did you like it?*   **Rien du tout.** *Nothing at all.*

Pour vérifier

1. With a sequence of events that happen one after another, are the verbs in the **passé composé** or the **imparfait**?

2. If one action interrupts another one that is already in progress, which one is in the **passé composé** and which one is in the **imparfait**?

 To download a podcast on the Compound Tense and the Imperfect past, go to **academic.cengage.com/french.**

Telling what was going on when something else happened

L'imparfait et le passé composé

In French, the **passé composé** and **imparfait** convey different meanings. In English, the use of different past tenses also changes a message. Is the message the same in these sentences?

> *When her husband came home, they kissed.*
> *When her husband came home, they were kissing.*

Use the **passé composé** for a sequence of events that happened one after another.

Ce matin, **j'ai quitté** la maison à midi et **je suis arrivé** à l'université à midi vingt.

When saying what was going on when something else occurred, use the **imparfait** for the action in progress and use the **passé composé** to say what happened, interrupting it.

ACTIONS IN PROGRESS	INTERRUPTING ACTIONS
Le professeur parlait...	quand je suis entré(e) dans la salle de classe.
Il pleuvait ce matin...	quand j'ai quitté la maison.

Prononciation

CD 3-12 *Le passé composé et l'imparfait*

Since the use of the **passé composé** or the **imparfait** imparts a different message, it is important that you differentiate what you hear and that you pronounce each tense distinctly. Listen to these pairs of sentences. Where do you hear a difference?

Je travaillais.	Elle mangeait.	Tu parlais.	Il allait.
J'ai travaillé.	Elle a mangé.	Tu as parlé.	Il est allé.

A. Quand ils sont rentrés... Deux couples ont laissé leurs enfants avec une nouvelle baby-sitter le week-end dernier. Qui faisait les choses suivantes quand ils sont rentrés?

> **EXEMPLE** porter les vêtements de sa mère
> **Annick portait les vêtements de sa mère quand ils sont rentrés.**

1. embrasser *(to kiss)* son petit ami
2. parler au téléphone
3. fumer
4. jouer dans l'escalier
5. jouer à des jeux vidéo
6. manger quelque chose sur la table

Répondez aux questions suivantes d'après l'illustration à la page précédente.

1. Quelle heure était-il quand les parents sont rentrés?
2. Qui écrivait *(was writing)* sur le mur?
3. Que faisait le chien?
4. Combien d'enfants est-ce qu'il y avait dans la maison?
5. Qui était avec la baby-sitter?

B. Que faisaient-ils? Expliquez ce qui s'est passé. Suivez l'exemple.

EXEMPLE   Alice (lire un livre) / quand une amie (arriver)
Alice lisait un livre quand une amie est arrivée.

1.

Cathy (préparer ses cours) / quand un ami (téléphoner)

2.

Vincent (jouer au golf) / quand il (commencer à pleuvoir)

3.

Michèle (embrasser *[to kiss]* un copain) / Éric (arriver)

4.

Quand le chien (entrer) / le chat (dormir)

5.

Alice (faire la cuisine) / quand le chat (voir le chien)

6.

Quand Vincent (rentrer) / Alice (nettoyer *[to clean]* la cuisine)

C. Hier. Demandez à votre partenaire ce qui se passait *(what was happening)* quand il/elle a fait ces choses. Utilisez les questions qui suivent.

1. Quand tu es rentré(e) chez toi hier...
2. Quand tu as dîné hier soir...

- Quelle heure était-il? Quel temps faisait-il?
- Est-ce que tu étais seul(e)? Sinon, qui était là? Qu'est-ce qu'il/elle faisait (Qu'est-ce qu'ils/elles faisaient)?
- Est-ce que tu étais fatigué(e) ou malade? Est-ce que tu avais faim?
- Qu'est-ce que tu avais envie de faire? Est-ce que tu avais besoin de faire quelque chose en particulier ou est-ce que tu pouvais faire ce que tu voulais?

Pour vérifier

1. Do you generally use the **passé composé** or the **imparfait** to say what happened at a specific moment, for a specific duration, or a specific number of times? to describe how things were or used to be or to talk about actions in progress?

2. Which would you use to talk about how you were feeling? to describe a change in a mental or physical state?

3. Which tense do you use to say what was going to happen?

Telling what happened and describing the circumstances

Le passé composé et l'imparfait

You know to use the **imparfait** to tell how things used to be or what was going on when something else occurred. The **imparfait** is used to describe continuing actions or states, whereas the **passé composé** is used for actions that happened and were finished.

USE THE *IMPARFAIT* TO SAY:	USE THE *PASSÉ COMPOSÉ* TO SAY:
1. **HOW THINGS USED TO BE OR WHAT USED TO HAPPEN** • continuing actions, states, or situations • repeated or habitual actions of an unspecified duration	1. **WHAT HAPPENED AT A PRECISE MOMENT OR FOR A SPECIFIC DURATION OR NUMBER OF TIMES** • completed actions • actions that occurred for a specific duration or a specific number of times

Notre amie habitait à côté de chez nous.
Our friend lived next to us.
Elle invitait toujours des amis chez elle.
She always invited friends over.

Elle a fait une soirée le mois dernier.
She had a party last month.
Nous sommes allées à cinq de ses soirées.
We went to five of her parties.

| 2. **WHAT THINGS WERE LIKE OR HOW SOMEONE FELT**
 • physical or mental states | 2. **WHAT CHANGED**
 • changes in states |

✳ Note *de grammaire*

You generally use the verb **vouloir** in the **imparfait** to say what someone wanted to do. Use **pouvoir** in the **imparfait** to say what people could do if they might have wanted to, but use it in the **passé composé** to say what they managed to do on an occasion when they tried. Use **devoir** in the **imparfait** to say what one was supposed to do, but in the **passé composé** for what one must have done, or had to do on a specific occasion.

Tout le monde allait bien, mais moi, j'étais fatiguée.
Everyone was doing fine, but I was tired.

Tout à coup, j'ai eu peur.
All of a sudden, I got frightened.

Watch for words like **tout d'un coup** (*all at once*), **tout à coup** (*all of a sudden*), **soudain** (*suddenly*), **une fois** (*once*), and **un jour** (*one day*) indicating changes in states.

Use the verb **aller** in the **imparfait** followed by an infinitive to say what someone was going to do. Use it in the **passé composé** to say what one went to do.

On allait partir.
We were going to leave.

Je suis allée chercher mon sac.
I went to get my purse.

A. Pourquoi? Expliquez pourquoi Cathy a fait ou n'a pas fait ces choses. Quel verbe doit être au passé composé et lequel *(which one)* doit être à l'imparfait?

EXEMPLE Cathy **était** (être) malade, alors elle **n'a pas travaillé** (ne pas travailler).

1. Cathy _____ (ne pas aller) en cours hier parce qu'elle _____ (être) malade.
2. Elle _____ (être) trop fatiguée, alors elle _____ (ne pas faire) les devoirs.
3. Elle _____ (faire) du shopping parce qu'elle _____ (vouloir) acheter une nouvelle robe.
4. Elle _____ (mettre) un pull parce qu'elle _____ (avoir) froid.
5. Elle _____ (avoir) besoin de préparer un examen, alors elle _____ (ne pas sortir) avec ses amis.

B. Ce matin chez les Pérez. Alice Pérez décrit la journée de sa famille. Qu'est-ce qu'elle dit? Mettez les verbes au passé composé ou à l'imparfait comme dans l'exemple.

EXEMPLE **Moi, j'ai fait du jogging ce matin. Je voulais dormir.**

1.  **2.**

Moi...	Éric et Cathy...
faire du jogging ce matin	préparer le déjeuner aujourd'hui
vouloir dormir	vouloir faire du shopping
avoir sommeil	déjeuner avant de sortir
ne pas avoir envie de sortir	aller au centre commercial à une heure
mettre mon survêtement	avoir l'intention d'acheter des vêtements
sortir à sept heures	aller rentrer vers cinq heures
rentrer une heure plus tard	avoir faim
avoir besoin d'un bain *(bath)*	retrouver des amis au restaurant
aller dans la salle de bains	rentrer à neuf heures
prendre un long bain	

C. Entretien. Interviewez votre partenaire au sujet de la dernière fois qu'il/elle est allé(e) au restaurant avec des amis.

La dernière fois que tu es allé(e) au restaurant avec des amis...

1. Quel temps faisait-il? Qu'est-ce que tu as mis pour sortir? un jean? une robe?
2. Quelle heure était-il quand tu es arrivé(e) au restaurant?
3. Avais-tu très faim? As-tu mangé tout de suite?
4. Comment était le repas?
5. Qu'est-ce que tu as fait après le repas?
6. Quelle heure était-il quand tu es rentré(e)? Étais-tu fatigué(e)? Est-ce que tu es allé(e) tout de suite au lit? As-tu bien dormi?
7. Le lendemain, jusqu'à quelle heure es-tu resté(e) au lit?

Narrating in the past

Les contes

Éric et Michèle sont allés voir le film classique ***La Belle et la Bête*** de Jean Cocteau. **Connaissez-vous** ce film? Connaissez-vous **le conte de fée** sur **lequel** il est basé?

Il était une fois un vieux **marchand** qui avait trois filles. Sa plus jeune fille, Belle, était très jolie, **douce** et **gracieuse.**

Un jour, la Bête a emprisonné le marchand. Belle **a promis** à la Bête de venir prendre la place de son père.

La Bête était horrible! Il était grand et laid et il avait l'air **féroce. Au début,** Belle avait très peur de **lui.** Mais elle était toujours gentille et patiente avec lui.

Petit à petit les choses ont changé. Belle et la Bête ont commencé à **se parler.** La Bête a beaucoup changé et Belle a appris à apprécier le monstre. Finalement, Belle **est tombée amoureuse de** lui! Et la Bête a aussi appris à aimer.

À suivre...

CD 3-13

Cathy parle à son frère de ses activités du week-end dernier.

CATHY: Tu es sorti ce week-end?
ÉRIC: Oui, je suis allé au cinéclub avec Michèle.
CATHY: Quel film est-ce que vous avez vu?
ÉRIC: Nous avons vu *La Belle et la Bête* de Cocteau.
CATHY: C'est un classique! Il t'a plu?
ÉRIC: Oui, il m'a beaucoup plu. C'était très intéressant. Les acteurs **ont bien joué.** Les effets spéciaux étaient excellents et il n'y avait pas **trop de** violence.

---

un conte *a story*   ***La Belle et la Bête*** *Beauty and the Beast*   **Connaissez-vous... ?** *Do you know . . . ?*   **un conte de fée** *a fairy tale*   **lequel (laquelle)** *which*   **Il était une fois...** *Once upon a time there was . . .*   **un marchand** *a merchant, a shopkeeper*   **doux (douce)** *sweet, soft, gentle*   **gracieux (gracieuse)** *gracious*   **elle a promis (promettre** *to promise [past participle* **promis])**   **féroce** *ferocious*   **Au début** *At the beginning*   **lui** *him*   **se parler** *to talk to each other*   **tomber amoureux (amoureuse) de** *to fall in love with*   **À suivre** *To be continued*   **bien jouer** *to act well (in movies and theater)*   **Les effets spéciaux** *The special effects*   **trop de** *too much*

A. C'est qui? Décidez lequel des personnages les adjectifs suivants décrivent: **le père de Belle, Belle, la Bête.** N'oubliez pas d'utiliser l'imparfait pour faire une description!

> **EXEMPLE**   douce   **Belle était douce.**

1. jolie
2. grande et laide
3. toujours gentille
4. vieux
5. gracieuse
6. horrible

Maintenant, dites qui a fait les choses suivantes. N'oubliez pas d'utiliser le passé composé pour raconter la séquence du déroulement des faits *(sequence of events)*!

> **EXEMPLE**   promettre de venir prendre la place de son père
> **Belle a promis de venir prendre la place de son père.**

1. emprisonner le marchand
2. prendre la place de son père
3. commencer à parler avec la Bête
4. beaucoup changer
5. apprendre à apprécier la Bête
6. tomber amoureuse de la Bête
7. apprendre à aimer

B. Entretien. Interviewez votre partenaire.

1. Quel film est-ce que tu as vu récemment? Est-ce que tu as vu ce film au cinéma ou à la télé? Est-ce que tu as aimé le film? Est-ce que tu recommandes ce film?

2. Qui a joué dans ce film? Est-ce que les acteurs ont bien joué? Est-ce qu'il y avait beaucoup de violence? Il y avait beaucoup d'effets spéciaux?

3. Qu'est-ce que tu as fait après le film?

C. Une sortie au cinéma. Alice parle à une amie du week-end. Complétez la conversation en mettant les verbes au passé composé ou à l'imparfait.

—Tu ___1___ (passer) un bon week-end?
—Assez bon. Mon amie ___2___ (vouloir) aller voir un film au cinéma, alors je ___3___ (sortir) avec elle et je ___4___ (rentrer) tard.
—C'___5___ (être) samedi?
—Non, on ___6___ (sortir) vendredi.
—Quelle heure ___7___ (être)-il quand tu ___8___ (rentrer)?
—On ___9___ (rester) au cinéma jusqu'à 10h30 et après on ___10___ (avoir) faim, alors on ___11___ (aller) manger quelque chose. Il y ___12___ (avoir) beaucoup de gens au restaurant et on ___13___ (devoir) attendre pour avoir une table. Il ___14___ (être) envion 1h00 quand on ___15___ (partir) du restaurant.
—Quel film est-ce que vous ___16___ (voir)?
—C'___17___ (être) le nouveau film avec Audrey Tautou.
—Qu'est-ce que tu ___18___ (faire) samedi et dimanche?
—Je (J') ___19___ (travailler) samedi. Dimanche, j'___20___ (être) fatiguée et il ___21___ (faire) mauvais, alors je ___22___ (rester) à la maison.

D. Conversation. Avec un(e) partenaire, relisez à haute voix la conversation entre Cathy et Éric en bas de la page précédente. Ensuite, changez la conversation pour parler d'un film que vous avez vu récemment.

You can find a list of the new words from CD 3-14 the vocabulary and grammar sections of this **Compétence** on page 255 and a recording of this list on track 3-14 of your *Text Audio CD*.

If you were describing a play that you saw, would you use the **passé composé** or the **imparfait** to describe the setting and what was happening on stage when the curtain went up? Which tense would you use to explain the actions of the actors that advanced the story?

For a chart summarizing all of the uses of the **passé composé** and the **imparfait**, see the *Résumé de grammaire* on page 253.

 To download a podcast on the Compound past tense and the Imperfect past, go to **academic.cengage.com/french.**

Narrating what happened

Le passé composé et l'imparfait (reprise)

When recounting a story in the past, you use both the **passé composé** and the **imparfait.**

USE THE *IMPARFAIT* TO SAY:	USE THE *PASSÉ COMPOSÉ* TO SAY:
WHAT WAS ALREADY GOING ON	WHAT HAPPENED NEXT / WHAT CHANGED
• descriptions of the scene / setting • background information about the characters • interrupted actions in progress	• sequence of events that advance the storyline • actions interrupting something in progress

If you were telling the old French tale **Cendrillon** *(Cinderella),* you might begin . . .

> Il **était** une fois une belle jeune fille qui **s'appelait** Cendrillon. Son père **était** mort et elle **habitait** avec sa belle-mère et ses deux demi-sœurs. Sa belle-mère **était** cruelle et ses demi-sœurs **étaient** laides, bêtes et très gâtées *(spoiled).* C'**était** Cendrillon qui **faisait** tout le travail mais elle **était** toujours belle et gracieuse. Un jour, le prince **a décidé** de donner un bal au palais et un messager **est allé** chez Cendrillon avec une invitation.

There are only two events that occur advancing the story in the preceding paragraph: the prince decided to give a ball and the messenger went to Cinderella's house. These two verbs are in the **passé composé.** All the rest of the paragraph is background information, setting the scene, so the verbs are in the **imparfait.**

When deciding whether to put a verb in the **passé composé** or the **imparfait,** learn to ask yourself whether you are talking about background information or something that was already in progress **(imparfait),** or the next thing that happened in the story **(passé composé).**

A. La journée d'Alice. Alice parle de sa journée. Décidez si chaque phrase décrit la scène / la situation ou raconte le déroulement des faits *(sequence of events).* Récrivez les phrases dans chaque colonne.

Il est sept heures. Il pleut. Je quitte la maison. Il y a beaucoup de voitures sur la route. J'arrive au bureau en retard. Mon patron *(boss)* n'est pas content. Je travaille beaucoup. Je ne déjeune pas. Je rentre à cinq heures. Je suis fatiguée. Il n'y a rien à manger. Nous allons au restaurant. Nous rentrons. Je prends un bain. Il est 11 heures. Je vais au lit.

EXEMPLE

LA SCÈNE / LA SITUATION	LE DÉROULEMENT DES FAITS
Il est sept heures.	**Je quitte la maison.**

Maintenant, récrivez le paragraphe en mettant les verbes qui présentent le déroulement des faits au passé composé et les verbes qui décrivent la scène ou la situation à l'imparfait.

B. Il était une fois... Récrivez le début de l'histoire de *La Belle et la Bête* au passé en mettant les verbes en caractères gras à l'imparfait ou au passé composé.

EXEMPLE   **Il y avait un marchand très riche...**

Il y (1) **a** un marchand très riche qui (2) **a** trois filles. Ils (3) **habitent** tous ensemble dans une belle maison en ville. Mais un jour, des voleurs *(thieves)* (4) **prennent** toute sa fortune et le marchand et ses filles (5) **doivent** aller habiter dans une petite maison à la campagne.

Ses deux filles aînées (6) **sont** très malheureuses *(unhappy)*. Elles (7) **parlent** constamment des choses qu'elles (8) **veulent.** Belle (9) **est** la plus jeune de ses filles. Elle (10) **est** très jolie et aussi très douce. Elle (11) **accepte** sa nouvelle vie et elle (12) **est** heureuse *(happy)*.

Un jour, le marchand (13) **part** pour la ville voisine *(neighboring)*. Il (14) **neige** et il (15) **fait** très froid et en route, il ne (16) **peut** rien voir dans la forêt. Le marchand (17) **pense** qu'il (18) **va** mourir quand, soudain, il (19) **trouve** un château. La porte du château (20) **est** ouverte et il (21) **décide** d'entrer. Il (22) **remarque** [remarquer *to notice*] une grande table couverte de plats délicieux. Il (23) **mange,** puis il (24) **fait** une sieste *(nap)*.

Après sa sieste, il (25) **sort** dans le jardin où il (26) **trouve** une jolie rose qu'il (27) **veut** rapporter *(to bring back)* à Belle. À ce moment-là, un monstre horrible (28) **arrive** et (29) **commence** à crier *(to shout)* qu'il (30) **veut** que Belle vienne habiter chez lui. Sinon *(Otherwise),* la Bête (31) **va** tuer *(to kill)* le marchand.

C. La Belle et la Bête. Continuez l'histoire de la Belle et la Bête en mettant le verbes entre parenthèses au passé composé ou à l'imparfait.

Quand le marchand _____1_____ (rentrer), il _____2_____ (raconter *[to recount]*) ses aventures à ses filles et Belle _____3_____ (décider) d'aller habiter chez la Bête. Quand elle _____4_____ (arriver) au château, elle _____5_____ (trouver) tout ce dont *(that)* elle _____6_____ (avoir) besoin. Chaque jour, elle _____7_____ (avoir) tout ce qu'elle _____8_____ (vouloir). Mais les cinq premiers jours, elle _____9_____ (ne pas voir) la Bête.

Un jour, elle le (l') _____10_____ (voir) pour la première fois pendant *(while)* qu'elle _____11_____ (faire) une promenade dans le jardin. Elle le (l') _____12_____ (trouver) horrible et elle _____13_____ (crier). Belle _____14_____ (avoir) peur et elle _____15_____ (ne pas pouvoir) regarder la Bête dans les yeux, mais elle _____16_____ (aller) faire une promenade avec lui. La conversation _____17_____ (être) agréable. Quand la Bête _____18_____ (demander) à Belle de faire une promenade deux jours plus tard, elle _____19_____ (accepter).

Après ce jour-là, ils _____20_____ (faire) une promenade chaque après-midi. Ils _____21_____ (parler) de tout. Au début, Belle _____22_____ (avoir) très peur de la Bête mais, finalement, Belle _____23_____ (apprendre) à avoir confiance en lui. Après un certain temps, Belle _____24_____ (commencer) à aimer le monstre et un jour elle l' _____25_____ (embrasser *[to kiss]*). Tout à coup, le visage *(face)* de la Bête _____26_____ (changer) et il _____27_____ (devenir) un beau et jeune prince.

Reprise

Issuing invitations and talking about the past

See the **Résumé de grammaire** section at the end of each chapter for a review of all the grammar presented in the chapter.

Dans le *Chapitre 6*, vous avez appris à faire des invitations et à raconter *(to tell)* ce qui s'est passé dans le passé. Maintenant vous allez réviser ce que vous avez appris.

A. Invitations. Invitez un(e) camarade de classe à faire les choses suivantes. Il/Elle va accepter une de vos invitations, refuser une de vos invitations et suggérer une autre activité pour la troisième. Utilisez une variété d'expressions.

> **EXEMPLE** aller au cinéma demain
> **—Tu voudrais aller au cinéma demain?**
> **—Oui, je voudrais bien.**

1. aller prendre un verre après les cours
2. aller danser samedi soir
3. aller voir une exposition au musée dimanche après-midi

Maintenant, refaites les trois invitations pour inviter toute la classe.

> **EXEMPLE** aller au cinéma demain
> **Vous voudriez aller au cinéma demain?**

B. Non, merci. Un ami téléphone à Éric pour l'inviter à sortir, mais Éric préfère ne rien faire et il refuse. L'ami insiste. Éric est très imaginatif dans ses excuses. Jouez les deux rôles avec un(e) partenaire.

C. On ne peut pas toujours faire ce qu'on veut! Éric explique ce que les Pérez ont envie de faire et ce qu'ils ont besoin de faire. Refaites ses phrases en utilisant **vouloir, pouvoir** et **devoir** comme dans l'exemple.

> **EXEMPLE** Maman a envie de dormir, mais elle a besoin de travailler.
> **Maman veut dormir, mais elle ne peut pas parce qu'elle doit travailler.**

1. Papa a envie de jouer au golf, mais il a besoin de faire des courses.
2. Michel a envie de faire du vélo, mais il a besoin de faire ses devoirs.
3. Michèle et moi, nous avons envie de sortir ce soir, mais nous avons besoin de préparer les cours.
4. Nos amis ont envie de sortir aussi, mais ils ont besoin de travailler.
5. Moi, j'ai envie de faire du vélo, mais j'ai besoin de faire la lessive.

D. En cours. Dites si les personnes suivantes font les choses indiquées.

> **EXEMPLE** Moi, je (dormir en cours)
> **Moi, je ne dors pas en cours.**

1. Moi, je (partir de la maison avant 8 heures pour aller en cours, dormir en cours, sortir avec des camarades de classe le samedi soir)
2. Les meilleurs étudiants (partir de la maison tôt pour arriver en cours à l'heure, sortir tous les soirs, dormir dans le laboratoire de langues, faire toujours les devoirs)

3. Les autres étudiants et moi, nous (dormir en cours, faire attention [to pay attention] en cours, sortir du cours en avance [early], sortir ensemble après les cours)
4. Quand il y a un examen, le professeur (sortir de la salle de classe, dormir pendant l'examen, sortir au café avec nous après le cours)

E. Entretien.
Les questions suivantes sont au présent. Mettez-les au passé composé ou à l'imparfait pour demander à un(e) camarade de classe ce qu'il/elle a fait le dernier jour que vous étiez en cours de français.

EXEMPLE   À quelle heure est-ce que tu quittes la maison?
—À quelle heure est-ce que tu as quitté la maison hier (jeudi...)?
—J'ai quitté la maison à huit heures.

1. Qu'est-ce que tu mets pour sortir? un jean? une robe?
2. Quel temps fait-il quand tu quittes la maison?
3. Est-ce que tu veux rester à la maison?
4. Est-ce que tu prends ta voiture ou l'autobus ou est-ce que tu vas en cours à pied?
5. À quelle heure est-ce que le cours de français commence?
6. Est-ce que tu as faim quand tu sors du cours?
7. Est-ce que tu peux faire ce que tu veux après les cours?
8. Quelle heure est-il quand tu rentres?
9. Qui prépare le dîner? Est-ce que c'est bon?
10. Qu'est-ce que tu veux faire après le dîner?
11. Est-ce que tu as besoin de faire quelque chose?
12. Qu'est-ce que tu fais?

Maintenant, écrivez un paragraphe décrivant votre journée le jour du dernier cours de français.

F. Une aventure!
Regardez l'illustration et racontez *(tell)* ce qui s'est passé chez les Fédor le week-end dernier. Utilisez **le voleur** pour *the thief*, **voler** pour *to steal* et **entrer par la fenêtre** pour *to come in through the window*. Avant de commencer, réfléchissez *(think)* aux questions suivantes.

- What night was it?
- What time was it?
- What was the weather like?
- How many people were in the Fédors' living room?
- Why were they there?

- What was each person doing?
- What was in the bedroom?
- What happened?
- What happened next?

le voleur

Les Dupont   Les Fédor   Simon   Pascale

Lecture et Composition

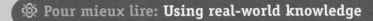

Lecture

✳ Pour mieux lire: Using real-world knowledge

It is often difficult to understand what you read about topics that are unfamiliar to you, even in your own language. On the other hand, the more familiar you are with a topic, the easier it will be to understand what you read in French. When selecting readings to practice French outside of class, select topics of interest about which you know something. Learn to recognize when difficulty reading is due to unfamiliarity with the topic, rather than difficulty with French. You are going to read some opinions about French and American movies. What do you already know about them? What types of American movies are usually the biggest hits? What French movies have you seen?

Titres de films. Lisez la liste des films les plus vus en France de 1945 à 2005 à la page 251. Est-ce que vous pouvez donner leurs titres en anglais?

Le cinéma français et le cinéma américain

Le cinéma est né en France avec **la découverte,** en 1895, de la projection d'images par les frères Lumière. Plus de cent ans après, la France reste **toujours** un des principaux producteurs de films **au monde** et la production cinématographique française continue d'être la plus dynamique en Europe. **Cependant, depuis la Seconde Guerre mondiale,** le cinéma américain a plus de succès que le cinéma français dans le monde et en France. Cette prédominance du cinéma américain provoque beaucoup de discussions et d'explications chez les Français. Voici trois points de vue trouvés sur des forums d'Internet. Êtes-vous d'accord?

«Les cinéastes américains **savent** transporter les spectateurs **loin d'eux-mêmes, en misant sur** des aspirations universelles: l'amour, **le dépassement de soi,** l'héroïsme… alors que les cinéastes français préfèrent explorer **les recoins** — comiques ou dramatiques — de **la vie quotidienne, forcément** moins glamour qu'une love story à NY ou une grande **bataille** dans la Perse antique. Les cinéastes français ont peut-être aussi l'ambition de questionner, d'**éduquer,** de dénoncer… alors que les cinéastes américains préfèrent conforter leur public dans son mode de vie et ses idéaux. La bataille est forcément **inégale**!».

«Je vois le cinéma français un peu comme une transposition à **l'écran** de la vie de tous les jours, c'est **plat** et sans saveur. À quoi bon aller au ciné voir des choses que tu vois dans la vie de tous les jours?»

«C'est sûr qu'**on ne verra jamais** Mathilde Seigner sauver **le monde,** Daniel Auteuil **se battre contre** des extraterrestres, Michel Blanc **fusiller** une armée de **flics** ou Isabelle Carré ayant pour objectif de **faire sauter** l'Élysée. Et c'est bien pour ça que je vote pour les films francais!»

---

la découverte the discovery   **toujours** still   **au monde** in the world   **Cependant, depuis la Seconde Guerre mondiale** However, since the Second World War   **savent** know how to   **loin d'eux-mêmes** far from their own world   **en misant sur** relying on   **le dépassement de soi** surpassing oneself   **les recoins** the nooks and corners   **la vie quotidienne** daily life   **forcément** inevitably   **bataille** battle   **éduquer** to educate   **inégale** unequal   **l'écran** the screen   **plat(e)** flat   **on ne verra jamais** one will never see   **le monde** the world   **se battre contre** fight against   **fusiller** shoot down   **flics** cops   **faire sauter** blow up

Compréhension

Laquelle (Lesquelles) des personnes qui font les commentaires dans la lecture serait (seraient) probablement d'accord *(would probably agree)* avec les phrases suivantes: la première, la deuxième ou la troisième?

1. Je préfère les films français qui transmettent un message social.
2. Les films français sont plus réalistes que les films américains.
3. Généralement, je trouve les films français ennuyeux. Je préfère les films un peu plus fantastiques.
4. Il y a beaucoup de violence dans les films américains. Ça ne me plaît pas!
5. Les cinéastes français veulent souvent que les spectateurs pensent aux problèmes de tous les jours mais les cinéastes américains veulent souvent qu'ils les oublient *(forget)*.

Composition

⚙ Pour mieux écrire: **Using the Internet**

The Internet is a wonderful tool when you are not sure how to word something in French. For example, imagine that you want to say *the worst movie of the year* and you find *worst* in the dictionary as **pire,** but you are not sure whether to place it before or after the word **film.** You are also not sure whether to use **an** or **année** to say *year.* It is easy to find out what people say by going to a French search engine such as http://www.google.fr or http://fr.yahoo.com, searching **"le pire film de l'an"**, **"le pire film de l'année"**, **"le film pire de l'an"** and **"le film pire de l'année"** and comparing how many Web pages you find with each phrase. First search with the phrases in quotes, then without quotes if you do not find them. On most French search engines, you can restrict the search to only Web pages in French or in France. The Web is also a good source to find out information such as how the titles of American movies are translated into French.

Organisez-vous. Vous allez écrire votre avis *(opinion)* sur le meilleur et le pire film de l'année dans un blog. D'abord, faites une liste de cinq films que vous avez vus et cherchez leurs titres en français sur Internet.

Ensuite, utilisez Internet pour determiner quelle expression dans chaque paire qui suit est correcte.

1. "les deux derniers films" / "les derniers deux films"
2. "les acteurs ont joué très bien" / "les acteurs ont très bien joué"
3. "la célèbre actrice" / "l'actrice célèbre"
4. "que j'ai aimé beaucoup" / "que j'ai beaucoup aimé"
5. "l'ami qui j'étais avec" / "l'ami avec qui j'étais"

Forum: Le meilleur et le pire du cinéma cette année

Utilisez le passé composé et l'imparfait pour écrire un paragraphe de six à dix phrases pour un blog sur le meilleur film que vous avez vu récemment. Ensuite, écrivez un autre paragraphe sur le pire film que vous avez vu. Si vous n'avez pas vu de films au cinéma récemment, vous pouvez parler de films moins récents. Expliquez pourquoi vous avez aimé chaque film ou pas.

If you have access to SYSTÈME-D software, you will find the following phrases, vocabulary, grammar, and dictionary aids there.

Phrases: Talking about the movies
Vocabulary: Entertainment
Grammar: Adjective agreement; Adjective position; Comparison

Comparaisons culturelles

Le cinéma: les préférences des Français

Dans **un sondage** où les Français devaient citer les trois films français les plus **inoubliables** du 20ᵉ siècle, ils **ont choisi** surtout des comédies et des satires sociales. Les quatre films les plus cités étaient:

- *La Grande **Vadrouille*** (comédie, 1966) 19%
Pendant la Seconde **Guerre mondiale**, la vie d'**un peintre** et celle d'un chef d'orchestre de Paris sont **dérangées** quand ils sont obligés de devenir résistants pour sauver trois parachutistes britanniques.

- *Les Visiteurs* (comédie, 1993) 12%
Un chevalier du 12ᵉ siècle est transporté de nos jours par **un enchanteur maladroit**.

- *Le Grand Bleu* (drame, 1988) 5%
Deux **plongeurs** rivaux risquent leur vie en descendant **de plus en plus profond** pour obtenir le record du **monde** de plongée.

- *Le Dîner de **cons*** (comédie, 1998) 5%
Pour rigoler, quelques amis font un dîner où chacun doit inviter un con. L'ami qui invite le plus grand con gagne!

Quand on a demandé aux Français de citer les trois acteurs français les plus importants du 20ᵉ siècle, ils ont choisi:

Jean Gabin 38%
Gérard Depardieu 35%
Alain Delon 26%
Jean-Paul Belmondo 25%

Alain Delon

---

un sondage *poll, survey*   **inoubliables** *unforgettable*   **ont choisi** *chose*   **Vadrouille** *Stroll*   **Guerre mondiale** *World War*
un peintre *a painter*   **dérangées** *disturbed*   **Un chevalier** *A knight*   **un enchanteur maladroit** *a clumsy sorcerer*   **plongeurs**
divers   **de plus en plus profond** *deeper and deeper*   **monde** *world*   **cons** *(vulgar) idiots, fools*   **Pour rigoler** *For fun*

Les actrices les plus citées étaient:

Catherine Deneuve 44%

Sophie Marceau 20%

Simone Signoret 19%

Isabelle Adjani 18%

Les acteurs et actrices étrangers les plus mémorables chez les Français étaient:

John Wayne 17%   Marilyn Monroe 20%

Bruce Willis 14%   Sophia Loren 16%

Clint Eastwood 9%   Sharon Stone 12%

Robert de Niro 8%   Jodie Foster 10%

Harrison Ford 8%

Catherine Deneuve

Voici les dix films les plus vus au cinéma en France de 1945 à 2005.

Film	Pays producteur	Nombre d'entrées en millions
Titanic	États-Unis	24,64
La Grande Vadrouille	France, Grande-Bretagne	17,27
Autant en emporte le vent	États-Unis	16,72
Le Livre de la jungle	États-Unis	15,29
Astérix et Obélix: Mission Cléopatre	France	14,37
Les Dix Commandements	États-Unis	14,23
Ben-Hur	États-Unis	13,83
Les Visiteurs	France	13,78
Le Pont de la rivière Kwaï	Grande-Bretagne	13,48
Cendrillon	États-Unis	13,20

D'après les sondages chez les Français, **les cinéastes** français font les meilleures comédies et satires sociales et les Américains sont plus forts pour le grand spectacle et le romantisme.

Compréhension

1. Quel genre de film est-ce que les Français préfèrent? Quels films, acteurs et actrices français connaissez-vous? Que pensez-vous d'eux *(of them)*?

2. Combien de films du tableau ci-dessus *(chart above)* sont américains? français? Certains Français trouvent qu'il y a trop d'influence américaine dans les salles de cinéma en France et que la culture française en est menacée *(is threatened by this)*. Est-ce que ce sentiment est justifié? Quel est le rôle du gouvernement dans la préservation de la culture? Est-ce qu'il doit y avoir une censure? des quotas? des subventions *(subsidies)*?

3. D'après la majorité des Français, quels genres de films est-ce que les cinéastes français font mieux? Et les cinéastes américains? Est-ce que l'industrie cinématographique d'un pays est un reflet de *(a reflection of)* sa culture? Si oui, quelles comparaisons culturelles peut-on faire entre les Français et les Américains?

 Visit **academic.cengage.com/french** for YouTube video cultural correlations, cultural information and activities.

---

les cinéastes *filmmakers*

Résumé de grammaire

The verbs *vouloir, pouvoir,* and *devoir*

Je veux sortir ce soir mais je ne peux pas. Je dois travailler.

Here are the conjugations of **vouloir** *(to want),* **pouvoir** *(can, may, to be able),* and **devoir** *(must, to have to, to owe).*

VOULOIR	POUVOIR	DEVOIR
je **veux**	je **peux**	je **dois**
tu **veux**	tu **peux**	tu **dois**
il/elle/on **veut**	il/elle/on **peut**	il/elle/on **doit**
nous **voulons**	nous **pouvons**	nous **devons**
vous **voulez**	vous **pouvez**	vous **devez**
ils/elles **veulent**	ils/elles **peuvent**	ils/elles **doivent**
P.C. **j'ai voulu**	P.C. **j'ai pu**	P.C. **j'ai dû**
IMP. **je voulais**	IMP. **je pouvais**	IMP. **je devais**

You generally use the verb **vouloir** in the **imparfait** to say what someone wanted to do. Use **pouvoir** in the **imparfait** to say what people could do if they might have wanted to, but use it in the **passé composé** to say what they managed to do on an occasion when they tried. Use **devoir** in the **imparfait** to say what one was supposed to do, but in the **passé composé** for what one must have done, or had to do on a specific occasion.

Nous voulions partir en vacances, mais n'avons pas pu. Nous avons dû travailler.

Elle **a dû** quitter la maison très tôt. Elle **devait** arriver à sept heures. *She must have left / had to leave the house very early. She was supposed to arrive at seven o'clock.*

The verbs *sortir, partir,* and *dormir*

Here are the conjugations of **sortir** *(to go out),* **partir** *(to leave),* and **dormir** *(to sleep).*

Je dors jusqu'à sept heures et je pars pour l'université à huit heures.

SORTIR *(to go out)*	PARTIR *(to leave)*	DORMIR *(to sleep)*
je **sors**	je **pars**	je **dors**
tu **sors**	tu **pars**	tu **dors**
il/elle/on **sort**	il/elle/on **part**	il/elle/on **dort**
nous **sortons**	nous **partons**	nous **dormons**
vous **sortez**	vous **partez**	vous **dormez**
ils/elles **sortent**	ils/elles **partent**	ils/elles **dorment**
P.C. **je suis sorti(e)**	P.C. **je suis parti(e)**	P.C. **j'ai dormi**
IMP. **je sortais**	IMP. **je partais**	IMP. **je dormais**

Ce matin j'ai dormi jusqu'à sept heures et demie et je suis partie pour l'université en retard *(late).*

Avant, je sortais souvent avec des amis mais nous ne sommes pas sortis le week-end dernier.

Sortir means *to go out* both in the sense of going out with friends and going out of a place. Use **partir** to say *to leave* in the sense of *to go away.* **Quitter** means *to leave* a person or a place and *must* be used with a direct object.

Use these prepositions with these verbs:

to go out (of) = **sortir (de)**
to leave (from) = **partir (de)**
to leave (for) = **partir (pour)**

Je **sors** souvent avec ma sœur le samedi. Nous **sortons** de la maison vers neuf heures.

Il **quitte** Paris pour aller travailler à Nice. Il **part** demain.

Je sors **de** la maison à neuf heures.
Je pars **pour** Nice demain.
Je pars **de** chez moi à huit heures.

L'imparfait and le passé composé

All verbs except **être** form the **imparfait** by dropping the **-ons** from the present tense **nous** form and adding these endings. The stem for **être** is **ét-**.

	PARLER (nous parl~~ons~~ → parl-)	FAIRE (nous fais~~ons~~ → fais-)	PRENDRE (nous pren~~ons~~ → pren-)	ÊTRE (ét-)
je (j')	parl**ais**	fais**ais**	pren**ais**	ét**ais**
tu	parl**ais**	fais**ais**	pren**ais**	ét**ais**
il/elle/on	parl**ait**	fais**ait**	pren**ait**	ét**ait**
nous	parl**ions**	fais**ions**	pren**ions**	ét**ions**
vous	parl**iez**	fais**iez**	pren**iez**	ét**iez**
ils/elles	parl**aient**	fais**aient**	pren**aient**	ét**aient**

Quand j'avais 12 ans, j'allais au lycée. Je passais beaucoup de temps avec mes copains. On aimait faire du roller.

Verbs with spelling changes in the present tense **nous** form, like **manger** and **commencer**, retain the spelling changes in the **imparfait** only before endings beginning with an **a.**

Nous mangions bien, mais je mangeais peu.

Note these expressions in the **imparfait:**

il y a	→	il y avait
il pleut	→	il pleuvait
il neige	→	il neigeait

Vous commenciez vos cours à midi, mais moi, je commençais mes cours à 11 heures.

Il y avait du vent, il pleuvait et il faisait froid, mais il ne neigeait pas.

When talking about the past, you will use both the **passé composé** and the **imparfait.** Note their uses:

USE THE *IMPARFAIT* TO SAY:

1. **HOW THINGS USED TO BE OR WHAT USED TO HAPPEN**
   - continuous actions or states
   - repeated or habitual actions of an unspecified duration

2. **WHAT WAS GOING ON**
   - scene or setting
   - interrupted actions in progress

3. **WHAT THINGS WERE LIKE OR HOW SOMEONE FELT**
   - physical or mental states

USE THE *PASSÉ COMPOSÉ* TO SAY:

1. **WHAT HAPPENED AT A PRECISE MOMENT OR FOR A SPECIFIC DURATION**
   - completed actions
   - actions within a specific duration

2. **WHAT HAPPENED NEXT**
   - sequence of events
   - actions interrupting something in progress

3. **WHAT CHANGED**
   - changes in states

Cendrillon **pleurait** *(was crying)* quand sa marraine *(fairy godmother)* **est arrivée.** La marraine **a aidé** Cendrillon et Cendrillon **est allée** au bal du prince. Le prince **est tombé** immédiatement amoureux de Cendrillon. Ils **ont dansé** et ils **ont beaucoup parlé.** À minuit, Cendrillon **est partie** sans dire au prince qui elle **était,** mais elle **a laissé** tomber *(dropped)* une de ses chaussures.

Use the verb **aller** in the **imparfait** followed by an infinitive to say what someone was going to do. Use it in the **passé composé** to say what one went to do.

J'allais faire du shopping.
I was going to go do some shopping.

Je suis allé(e) faire du shopping.
I went to do some shopping.

Vocabulaire

Inviting someone to go out

NOMS MASCULINS

l'amour — *love*
un film d'amour — *a romantic movie, a love story*
un groupe — *a group*
un horaire — *a schedule*

NOMS FÉMININS

une comédie — *a comedy*
une façon — *a way*
l'heure officielle — *official time*
l'heure d'ouverture — *opening time*
une idée — *an idea*
une invitation — *an invitation*
une personne — *a person*
une séance — *a showing*

EXPRESSIONS VERBALES

appeler — *to call*
devoir — *must, to have to, to owe*
dire — *to say, to tell*
passer chez... — *to stop by . . . 's house*
passer un film — *to show a movie*
pouvoir — *can, may, to be able*
regretter — *to regret, to be sorry*
répondre (à) — *to answer, to respond (to)*
suggérer — *to suggest*
téléphoner (à) — *to phone*
utiliser — *to use, to utilize*
vouloir — *to want*

DIVERS

allô — *hello (on the telephone)*
avec plaisir — *gladly, with pleasure*
Je pensais — *I was thinking*
Je t'invite... — *I'm inviting you . . .*
Je voudrais vous inviter... — *I'd like to invite you . . .*
Quelle bonne idée! — *What a good idea!*
quelqu'un — *someone, somebody*
tellement — *so much, so*
uniquement — *uniquely, only*
Vous voudriez... ? — *Would you like . . . ?*

Talking about how you spend and used to spend your time

NOMS MASCULINS

un copain — *a friend, a pal*
un lycée — *a high school*
un lycéen — *a high school student*
un restau-u — *a university cafeteria*

NOMS FÉMININS

une boum — *a party*
une copine — *a friend, a pal*
une école — *a school*
une lycéenne — *a high school student*
les vacances — *vacation*
la vie — *life*

EXPRESSIONS VERBALES

avoir cours — *to have class*
comparer — *to compare*
dormir — *to sleep*
faire du roller — *to go in-line skating*
faire du skateboard — *to skateboard*
partir (de / pour) — *to leave (from / for), to go away (from / to)*
partir en vacances — *to leave on vacation*
partir en voyage — *to leave on a trip*
partir en week-end — *to go away for the weekend*
quitter — *to leave*
sortir (de) — *to go out (of)*

DIVERS

ce que — *what*
dans le passé — *in the past*
fatigué(e) — *tired*
rien de spécial — *nothing special*

Talking about the past

NOMS MASCULINS

un bistro	*a pub, a restaurant*
le lendemain	*the next day*
un repas	*a meal*

NOMS FÉMININS

une fois	*once, one time*
une soirée	*a party*
une sortie	*an outing*

EXPRESSIONS ADVERBIALES

un jour	*one day*
soudain	*suddenly*
tout à coup	*all of a sudden*
tout de suite	*right away*
tout d'un coup	*all at once*

DIVERS

Ça t'a plu?	*Did you like it?*
délicieux (délicieuse)	*delicious*
Qu'est-ce qui s'est passé?	*What happened?*
rien du tout	*nothing at all*
tout le monde	*everybody, everyone*

Narrating in the past

NOMS MASCULINS

un acteur	*an actor*
un bal	*a ball*
un conte	*a story*
un conte de fée	*a fairy tale*
les effets spéciaux	*special effects*
un marchand	*a merchant, a shopkeeper*
un messager	*a messenger*
un monstre	*a monster*
un palais	*a palace*
le travail	*work*

NOMS FÉMININS

une actrice	*an actress*
une bête	*a beast*
une marchande	*a merchant, a shopkeeper*
une messagère	*a messenger*
la violence	*violence*

EXPRESSIONS VERBALES

apprécier	*to appreciate*
à suivre	*to be continued*
changer	*to change*
décider	*to decide*
Connaissez-vous... ?	*Do you know . . . ?*
emprisonner	*to imprison*
jouer	*to act* (in movies and theater)
se parler	*to talk to each other*
prendre la place de	*to take the place of*
promettre	*to promise*
tomber amoureux (amoureuse) de	*to fall in love with*

ADJECTIFS

amoureux (amoureuse) (de)	*in love (with)*
basé(e) (sur)	*based (on)*
classique	*classic*
cruel(le)	*cruel*
doux (douce)	*sweet, soft, gentle*
excellent(e)	*excellent*
féroce	*ferocious*
gâté(e)	*spoiled*
gracieux (gracieuse)	*gracious*
horrible	*horrible*
patient(e)	*patient*

DIVERS

au début (de)	*at the beginning (of)*
finalement	*finally*
Il était une fois...	*Once upon a time there was . . .*
ça m'a plu	*I liked it*
lequel (laquelle)	*which, which one*
lui	*him*
petit à petit	*little by little*
trop de	*too much*

Sélections musicales

Aux Champs-Élysées

SOMA RIBA

Né en banlieue bordelaise, Soma Riba se passionne très jeune pour la musique aussi bien que pour le sport. Il commence sa carrière musicale à 15 ans comme deejay pour des soirées de jeunes, puis il devient plus tard réalisateur artistique de compilations dans lesquelles il révèle sa passion pour le reggae, le zouk et le R&B.

Depuis sa jeunesse à Bordeaux, Soma Riba a une passion pour la musique et aussi pour le sport. C'est dans sa carrière sportive qu'il trouve la source de sa volonté pour réussir *(will to succeed)* comme musicien.

Dans la chanson *Aux Champs-Élysées,* Soma Riba interprète un classique français de Joe Dassin. Né à New York, Dassin a passé une grande partie de sa vie *(life)* en France quand son père est devenu victime de la politique *(policy)* anti-communiste de McCarthy et sa famille a été obligée de quitter les États-Unis. Il a enregistré *(recorded)* des chansons en français, anglais, allemand, espagnol, italien et grec, mais il est surtout connu *(known)* pour les chansons qu'il a composées en français.

Aux Champs-Élysées. Dans la chanson *Aux Champs-Élysées,* le chanteur parle d'une relation amoureuse qui a commencé un jour où il se baladait *(was strolling)* sur les Champs-Élysées. Regardez les expressions qui suivent. Pour chacune, décidez s'il s'agit de *(if it is about)* **quelque chose à faire,** de **quelque chose à voir** ou d'**un sentiment** *(a feeling)*.

You can access these songs at the iTunes playlist on **academic.cengage.com/french/horizons.**

avoir envie de dire n'importe quoi à n'importe qui
   (saying anything to anyone)
se balader *(to stroll)*
avoir le cœur ouvert à l'inconnu *(heart open to the unknown)*
des musiciens, guitare à la main *(in hand)*
chanter et danser avec des fous *(crazy people)*
s'embrasser trouver qu'il suffisait *(it was enough)* de parler
être étourdi(e) *(dazed)*
les oiseaux *(birds)*

Dans mon jeune temps

LYNDA LEMAY

Le thème préféré des chansons de Lynda Lemay est la famille. Dans une interview avec le journal *Le Monde*, elle a dit: «Je parle des générations, des vieux, des enfants, des enfants mal aimés, des enfants anormaux, des enfants désirés. Normalement, la famille, c'est la base, la sécurité, mais certains y ont appris la haine *(hatred)*, la violence; il faut qu'ils se sortent de ces pièges de la vie *(they must get out of these pitfalls in life)*.»

A. Dans mon jeune temps. Dans sa chanson *Dans mon jeune temps*, Lynda Lemay met en contraste ce qu'elle croyait *(what she believed)* quand elle était petite et ses attitudes d'adulte. Pour mieux comprendre cette chanson, regardez ces expressions et déterminez lesquelles représentent probablement les attitudes d'un enfant et lesquelles représentent les attitudes d'un adulte.

Lynda Lemay, chanteuse *(singer)*, guitariste et compositeur de chansons *(songwriter)*, a un très grand succès en France aussi bien qu'au Québec, où elle est née.

  trouver les parents vieux jeu *(old-fashioned)*
  oublier de dire *(to forget to say)* «merci»
  vouloir dire «merci» aux parents, mais trop tard
  croire *(to believe)* que l'amour est gratuit *(free)*
  se rappeler *(to remember)* et parler du passé
  aimer donner des bisous *(kisses on the cheek)*
  s'essuyer *(to wipe off)* les bisous ou fuir *(to flee)* quand on veut l'embrasser
  avoir les yeux rivés sur une bande dessinée *(riveted on a comic book)*
  dire aux enfants de faire attention *(to be careful)*
  trouver qu'on manque *(lacks)* suffisamment de temps dans la vie *(life)*
  penser que la vie est longue
  faire des choses juste pour faire plaisir *(to please)* aux autres

B. Au négatif. Dans la langue parlée, on laisse tomber *(drops)* quelquefois le mot **ne** de l'expression **ne... pas**. Refaites ces phrases en mettant le **ne** qui manque au bon endroit.

  Je voulais pas grandir *(to grow up)*.
  Je disais pas «je t'aime» à mes parents.
  Je voyais pas *(didn't see)* combien coûtait tout ce qu'on me donnait: les toutous *(teddy bears [québécois])*, les jouets *(toys)*, le nouveau papier peint *(new wall paper)*.
  Je comprenais pas pourquoi ma grand-mère radotait *(rambled on)*.
  Je parle de ce que j'ai pas pu faire, les larmes *(tears)* aux yeux.

La Normandie

*La vie
quotidienne*

 iLrn Heinle Learning Center

academic.cengage.com/french/horizons

Système-D

 Audio   iRadio

LA FRANCE ET SA DIVERSITÉ

L'immigration est depuis longtemps la source de beaucoup de débats politiques et sociaux en France. Recherchez des informations sur Internet à ce sujet. Quelles sont les questions qu'on se pose à ce sujet? Est-ce que les attitudes des Français au sujet de l'immigration sont similaires à celles chez vous?

Existe-t-il une identité française? un caractère français? Quand vous pensez à la culture française et au peuple français, comment est-ce que vous les imaginez?

En réalité, la France n'a pas **une seule** identité, ou une seule culture. La France est un pays riche en diversité où chaque région a son **propre** héritage culturel.

Chacune des régions de la France a ses traditions, sa cuisine, sa musique, ses danses et **même parfois** sa langue.

---

une seule *a single*   **propre** *own*   **Chacune** *Each one*   **même parfois** *even at times*

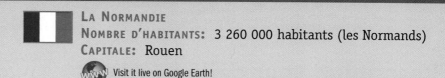

Pourtant, malgré cette diversité, les Français **se sentent** bien français! Une _archi_
histoire qui date de plus de 2 000 ans, **un patrimoine** riche en architecture et en
culture et une tradition **à la fois laïque** et catholique donnent aux Français leur
unité, le sens d'être «français». _Separate La – ique_

Récemment, l'immigration a beaucoup changé le visage de la France. Les nouveaux
immigrés cherchent à **maintenir** leurs langues et leurs traditions.

Ainsi, aujourd'hui la France **fait face à** des questions importantes: Comment
peut-on préserver l'identité de la culture française **tout en respectant** les divers
groupes ethniques qui habitent dans le pays? Est-il possible de combiner l'unité
et la diversité?

✤ Qu'en savez-vous?

Complétez ces phrases.

1. La France n'a pas une seule identité ou une seule culture.
   C'est un pays riche en diversité culturelle, grâce à *(due to)*
   la variété d'héritages culturels de ses ___tradition___ et à
   _____ récente.

2. Dans certaines régions de la France, les gens parlent non
   seulement *(not only)* le français, mais aussi une langue
   régionale. De ces trois langues régionales, devinez
   laquelle *(guess which one)* est parlée dans chacune des
   régions suivantes: niçois, corse, breton.
   En Bretagne, certains parlent _____.
   En Corse, il y a des gens qui parlent _____.
   Dans la région près de Nice, on entend *(hears)* parfois
   parler _____.

3. Malgré cette diversité, les Français se sentent bien
   français. La France a un héritage culturel «français» basé
   surtout sur _____
   _____
   _____

4. À cause de la diversité des cultures qui font aujourd'hui
   partie de la culture française, les Français cherchent à
   trouver une réponse à deux questions importantes:
   _____
   _____

Pourtant, malgré *However, in spite of*   **se sentent** *feel*   **un patrimoine** *a heritage*   **à la fois laïque** *at the same time secular*   **maintenir** *to maintain*   **Ainsi** *Thus*
fait face à *is facing*   **tout en respectant** *while still respecting*

Describing your daily routine

La vie de tous les jours

Quelle est votre **routine quotidienne**?

D'habitude le matin...   Je **fais ma toilette.**

Je me réveille vers six heures.

Je me lève tout de suite.

Je me lave **la figure** et **les mains** *(f)*.

Je prends un bain ou **une douche.**

Je me brosse les cheveux.

Je me brosse les dents.

Je me maquille.

Je m'habille.

Le soir...

Quelquefois **je me repose.**

D'autres fois, je m'amuse avec des amis.

Quand je suis seule, **je m'ennuie.**

Je me déshabille.

Je me couche et **je m'endors** facilement.

---

la routine quotidienne *daily routine*   **faire sa toilette** *to wash up*   **la figure** *the face*   **les mains** *(f) the hands*   **une douche** *a shower*   **je me repose** *(se reposer to rest)*   **D'autres fois** *Other times*   **je m'ennuie** *(s'ennuyer to be bored, to get bored)*   **je m'endors** *(s'endormir to fall asleep)*

Rosalie Toulouse Richard, d'origine française, habite à Atlanta **depuis** son mariage avec un Américain. **Veuve** maintenant, elle retourne en France avec sa **petite-fille** Rose qui ne **connaît** pas du tout la France. **Comme** elles partagent une chambre **pendant** leur **séjour,** elles parlent de leurs routines le matin.

ROSALIE: Tu te lèves vers quelle heure d'habitude?

ROSE: Entre six heures et six heures et demie. Je fais **vite** ma toilette, je m'habille et puis je me maquille. Je suis prête en une demi-heure.

ROSALIE: C'est parfait. Moi, je prends quelquefois une douche le matin mais je préfère prendre mon bain le soir. Je peux très bien **attendre** jusqu'à sept heures pour faire ma toilette.

ROSE: Et moi, je ne quitte jamais la maison avant huit heures et demie. Alors si tu veux, on peut prendre le petit déjeuner ensemble tous les matins.

A. Ma routine. Complétez les phrases avec une expression de la liste.

EXEMPLE   Je me réveille avant six heures.
Je me réveille rarement avant six heures.
Je ne me réveille jamais avant six heures.

❋ **Note** *de grammaire*

Place the **ne** in **ne... jamais** before the word **me** in these sentences, and **jamais** after the verb. Remember that **toujours, souvent,** and **rarement** go right after the verb, but the other adverbial phrases listed go at the end of the sentence.

toujours	tous les jours
souvent	le lundi, le mardi...
quelquefois	le matin, l'après-midi, le soir
de temps en temps	une (deux...) fois par jour (semaine...)
rarement	
ne... jamais	

1. Je me réveille après neuf heures.
2. Je me lève tout de suite.
3. Je prends une douche ou un bain.
4. Je me lave les mains.
5. Je me lave les cheveux.
6. Je me brosse les dents.
7. Je m'habille vite.
8. Je m'ennuie.
9. Je me repose.
10. Je m'amuse bien.
11. Je me couche tard.
12. Je m'endors sur le canapé.

B. Conversation. Avec un(e) partenaire, relisez la conversation entre Rose et sa grand-mère en haut de la page. Ensuite, imaginez que vous allez partager une maison avec votre partenaire et changez la conversation pour parler de votre routine le matin.

You can find a list of the new words from CD 3-16 the vocabulary and grammar sections of this *Compétence* on page 298 and a recording of this list on track 3-16 of your *Text Audio CD.*

---

depuis *since*   **Veuve (Veuf)** *Widow (Widower)*   **une petite-fille (un petit-fils)** *a granddaughter (a grandson)*   **elle connaît** (**connaître** *to know*)   **Comme** *Since, As*   **pendant** *during*   **un séjour** *a stay*   **vite** *quickly, fast*   **attendre** *to wait (for)*

Describing your daily routine

Les verbes réfléchis au présent

 To download a podcast on Reflexive Verbs, go to **academic.cengage.com/french.**

You can say that you are doing something to or for yourself or that you are doing something to or for another person or thing. When someone performs an action on or for himself/herself, a reflexive verb is generally used in French. Compare these sentences.

REFLEXIVE

Je me lave les mains.

NON-REFLEXIVE

Je lave la voiture.

The infinitive of reflexive verbs is preceded by the reflexive pronoun **se.** When you conjugate these verbs, change the reflexive pronoun according to the subject. In the negative, place **ne** directly after the subject and **pas** after the conjugated verb.

SE LAVER (to wash [oneself])		NE PAS SE LAVER	
je me lave	nous nous lavons	je ne me lave pas	nous ne nous lavons pas
tu te laves	vous vous lavez	tu ne te laves pas	vous ne vous lavez pas
il/elle/on se lave	ils/elles se lavent	il/elle/on ne se lave pas	ils/elles ne se lavent pas

Me, te, and **se** change to **m', t',** and **s'** before a vowel sound: **je m'habille, tu t'habilles, elle s'habille, ils s'habillent.**

Here are some reflexive verbs you can use to talk about your daily life:

s'amuser	*to have fun*
s'appeler	*to be named*
se brosser (les cheveux, les dents)	*to brush (one's hair, one's teeth)*
se coucher / se recoucher	*to go to bed / to go back to bed*
s'endormir	*to fall asleep*
s'ennuyer	*to be bored, to get bored*
s'habiller / se déshabiller	*to get dressed / to get undressed*
se laver (les mains, la figure)	*to wash (one's hands, one's face)*
se lever	*to get up*
se maquiller	*to put on make-up*
se raser	*to shave*
se reposer	*to rest*
se réveiller	*to wake up*

The verb **s'endormir** is conjugated like **dormir.**

S'ENDORMIR (to fall asleep)	
je m'endors	nous nous endormons
tu t'endors	vous vous endormez
il/elle/on s'endort	ils/elles s'endorment

Note the spelling change in **s'ennuyer** and other verbs ending in **-yer,** such as **essayer** and **payer.** The **y** changes to **i** in all forms except those of **nous** and **vous.**

S'ENNUYER *(to be bored, to get bored)*	
je m'ennu**i**e	nous nous ennuyons
tu t'ennu**i**es	vous vous ennuyez
il/elle/on s'ennu**i**e	ils/elles s'ennu**i**ent

There is an accent spelling change in the conjugation of **se lever.** Its conjugation is similar to that of **acheter. S'appeler** changes its spelling by doubling the final consonant of the stem in all present tense forms except those of **nous** and **vous.**

SE LEVER *(to get up)*	
je me l**è**ve	nous nous levons
tu te l**è**ves	vous vous levez
il/elle/on se l**è**ve	ils/elles se l**è**vent

S'APPELER *(to be named)*	
je m'appe**ll**e	nous nous appelons
tu t'appe**ll**es	vous vous appelez
il/elle/on s'appe**ll**e	ils/elles s'appe**ll**ent

A. Équivalents. Trouvez le verbe réfléchi correspondant à chaque définition.

1. aller au lit
2. sortir du lit
3. mettre des vêtements
4. faire quelque chose d'amusant
5. faire quelque chose d'ennuyeux
6. ne rien faire
7. commencer à dormir

a. s'endormir
b. s'ennuyer
c. se reposer
d. se lever
e. s'amuser
f. se coucher
g. s'habiller

B. D'abord... Indiquez l'ordre logique des activités données.

EXEMPLE   prendre un bain / se lever
       D'abord, on se lève et puis on prend un bain.

1. se réveiller / se lever
2. se laver la figure / se maquiller
3. s'habiller / prendre un bain ou une douche
4. quitter la maison / s'habiller
5. se reposer / rentrer à la maison après les cours
6. s'amuser / retrouver des amis
7. se déshabiller / se coucher
8. s'endormir / se coucher

C. Un samedi typique. Voilà la routine de Rose le samedi. Qu'est-ce qu'elle fait?

Le samedi matin...

EXEMPLE

... vers neuf heures.
Elle se réveille vers neuf heures.

1. ... tout de suite.

2. ... la figure et les mains.

3. ... les dents.

4. ... les cheveux.

5. ... en jean.

Le samedi soir...

6. ... avec des amis.

7. ... vers deux heures du matin et... facilement.

D. Et vous? Regardez les illustrations de **C. Un samedi typique.** Est-ce que vous faites ces mêmes choses le samedi?

Le samedi matin...

EXEMPLE

... vers neuf heures
Je me réveille vers neuf heures.
Je ne me réveille pas vers neuf heures.

E. Le week-end. Demandez à votre partenaire s'il/si elle fait les choses suivantes le week-end.

EXEMPLE   se réveiller tôt ou tard le samedi matin
    —Est-ce que tu te réveilles tôt ou tard le samedi matin?
    —En général, je me réveille tôt.

1. se lever tôt ou tard le samedi matin
2. prendre un bain ou une douche
3. s'amuser ou s'ennuyer le week-end
4. se coucher tôt ou tard le samedi soir
5. s'endormir facilement

F. Questions. Avec un(e) partenaire, préparez cinq questions à poser au professeur au sujet de sa routine quotidienne. Utilisez des verbes réfléchis.

EXEMPLE   **Est-ce que vous vous couchez tôt ou tard d'habitude?**
    À quelle heure est-ce que vous vous couchez d'habitude?

G. Un week-end entre amis. Demandez à votre partenaire ce qu'il/elle fait avec ses amis quand ils passent un week-end ensemble dans une autre ville.

EXEMPLE   se réveiller tôt ou tard
    —Est-ce que vous vous réveillez tôt ou tard?
    —Nous nous réveillons tard. / On se réveille tard.

1. se réveiller avant ou après dix heures
2. se lever tôt ou tard
3. se reposer plus souvent le matin, l'après-midi ou le soir
4. s'amuser plus souvent le matin, l'après-midi ou le soir
5. s'ennuyer quelquefois
6. se coucher tôt ou tard

H. Vous faites du baby-sitting. Vous faites du baby-sitting pour les deux enfants d'un(e) ami(e). Demandez ces renseignements à votre ami(e). Votre partenaire va jouer le rôle de votre ami(e) et imaginer ses réponses.

Find out . . .

EXEMPLE   *what time they wake up*
    —À quelle heure est-ce qu'ils se réveillent?
    —Ils se réveillent vers huit heures.

1. *if they get up right away*
2. *if they take a bath or a shower in the morning or the evening*
3. *if they rest in the afternoon*
4. *what time they go to bed*
5. *if they fall asleep easily*

Stratégies et Lecture

Recognizing words that belong to the same word family can make reading easier. Can you supply the missing meanings below?

la vie	**vivre**	**se marier**	**le mariage**
life	*to live*	*to marry*	*marriage*
l'arrêt	**s'arrêter**	**espérer**	**l'espoir**
stop	*???*	*to hope*	*???*

Using cognates and word families can help you understand new texts more easily. However, beware of **faux amis,** words that look like cognates but have different meanings. For example, **rester** does not mean *to rest,* but *to stay.* Use cognates, but if a word does not seem right in the context, look it up.

A. Familles de mots. Vous allez voir ces mots dans l'histoire qui suit. Servez-vous du sens des mots donnés pour déterminer le sens des autres mots.

rêver	**un rêve**	**dire**	**dit(e)**
to dream	*a dream*	*to say, to tell*	*said, told*
se souvenir de	**des souvenirs**	**connaître**	**connu(e)**
to remember	*???*	*to know*	*???*
saluer	**une salutation**	**reconnaître**	**reconnu(e)**
to greet	*???*	*to recognize*	*???*
une rose	**un rosier**		
a rose	*???*		

B. Faux amis. Donnez le sens des faux amis en caractères gras selon le contexte.

M. Dupont est dans un fauteuil au jardin quand une jolie jeune fille qui passe **attire** son attention. Il la **salue** et lui dit: «Bonjour, mademoiselle.» Cette fille ressemble à quelqu'un qu'il connaissait dans le passé et il commence à rêver. Il a de beaux **souvenirs** du temps où il était jeune. Il aimait une jeune fille et il **garde** toujours l'espoir de la revoir un jour.

Lecture: Il n'est jamais trop tard!

CD 3-17

Rosalie Toulouse Richard, qui habite à Atlanta depuis son mariage avec un Améri-cain, retourne à Rouen avec sa petite-fille Rose. Son vieil ami, André Dupont, ne sait pas encore que Rosalie est à Rouen.

André Dupont a toujours aimé passer des heures à travailler dans son jardin. Il a une passion pour les roses et depuis des années, il plante des rosiers de toutes les variétés et de toutes les couleurs dans son jardin.

Ses rosiers font l'admiration de tous les gens du quartier et beaucoup d'entre eux passent devant chez lui pour regarder son beau jardin. Aujourd'hui, trois jeunes filles s'arrêtent devant son jardin et lui disent bonjour. Il reconnaît deux d'entre elles, ce sont les petites-filles de son ami Jean Toulouse, mais c'est la troisième qui attire son attention. Il ne l'a jamais vue, et pourtant il a l'impression de la connaître! Elle ressemble à quelqu'un... quelqu'un qu'il a connu il y a très longtemps.

Les souvenirs lui reviennent, comme si c'était hier. C'était il y a longtemps, il avait dix-huit ans et il était amoureux fou d'une jolie jeune fille de son âge. Elle s'appelait Rosalie... ! Il voulait lui dire combien il l'aimait, mais il n'en avait pas le courage. Il était trop timide. Un beau jour, il s'est décidé à tout lui dire. Il a choisi des fleurs de son jardin pour en faire un bouquet, il a pris son vélo et il est allé chez Rosalie. Mais en arrivant, il a trouvé Rosalie en compagnie d'un jeune Américain et elle regardait ce jeune homme d'un regard de femme amoureuse. André, lui, est rentré chez lui sans jamais parler à Rosalie.

Quelques mois après, Rosalie s'est mariée avec le jeune Américain et ils sont partis vivre aux États-Unis. De temps en temps, André avait des nouvelles car le frère de Rosalie et lui étaient de bons amis. Il savait qu'elle habitait à Atlanta, qu'elle avait eu trois enfants, et il y a trois ans, il a appris que son mari était mort. Il gardait toujours l'espoir de la revoir, mais les années passaient et elle ne revenait toujours pas.

—Vos rosiers sont magnifiques, monsieur!
C'est Rosalie qui parle! En un instant, André Dupont revient au présent et ouvre les yeux. C'est la jeune fille qui parle... celle qu'il ne connaît pas.
—Rosalie???
—Moi, monsieur? Non, je m'appelle Rose. Rosalie, c'est ma grand-mère.
—Ta grand-mère?
—Oui. Vous connaissez ma grand-mère?
—Rosalie Toulouse? Oui, je la connais, mais...
—Eh bien, venez la voir, elle est chez son frère Jean! Je suis sûre qu'elle sera contente de revoir un ami d'ici! Allez, venez donc avec nous!

Quoi? C'est trop beau! Est-ce qu'il rêve? Rosalie, ici à Rouen! Comme la vie est à la fois belle et bizarre! Va-t-elle le reconnaître? A-t-il le courage de lui dire qu'il l'aime toujours, après toutes ces années? André Dupont choisit les plus belles roses de son jardin et en fait un magnifique bouquet. Il va enfin pouvoir les offrir à la femme pour qui il a planté tous ces rosiers au cours des années.

Qui parle? Qui parle: André, Rosalie ou Rose?

1. J'adore les fleurs et j'aime faire du jardinage.
2. J'ai eu trois enfants et mon mari est mort il y a trois ans.
3. Je suis passée devant une maison où il y avait des roses splendides.
4. Un monsieur m'a parlé. Il connaît ma grand-mère mais il ne l'a pas vue depuis longtemps.
5. J'ai invité ce monsieur à venir nous voir.
6. Je me suis mariée avec un Américain et je suis allée vivre aux États-Unis.
7. J'étais amoureux de Rosalie mais je n'ai jamais eu le courage de le lui dire.
8. Je garde toujours l'espoir de dire à Rosalie que je l'aime.

Talking about relationships

⚜ **Note** *culturelle*

Depuis un certain temps, on redéfinit la notion traditionnelle du couple et de la famille. Aujourd'hui en France, 33% (pour cent) des adultes habitent seuls et 48% des naissances ont lieu hors *(of births take place outside of)* mariage. Est-ce que la situation est la même dans votre région?

⚜ **Note** *de grammaire*

Se souvenir de is conjugated like **venir.**

je me	souviens
tu te	souviens
il/elle/on se	souvient
nous nous	souvenons
vous vous	souvenez
ils/elles se	souviennent

La vie sentimentale

À l'invitation de Rose, André va chez les Toulouse et André et Rosalie **se rencontrent** pour la première fois depuis des années. Voilà **ce qui se passe.**

André et Rosalie se regardent. — Ils s'embrassent. C'est **le coup de foudre!** — Ils se parlent pendant des heures. — Ils se quittent vers sept heures.

Pendant les semaines qui **suivent,** André et Rosalie passent beaucoup de temps ensemble. Ils **se souviennent de** leur **jeunesse** ensemble. C'est **le grand amour!**

Ils se retrouvent en ville chaque après-midi. — Quelquefois ils se disputent. — Mais **la plupart du temps, ils s'entendent** bien.

Enfin, André et Rosalie **prennent une décision.** Ils vont se marier et vont **s'installer à** Rouen. Ils vont être très **heureux.**

 Un soir, Rosalie parle à sa petite-fille Rose de sa relation avec André.

CD 3-18

ROSE:	Alors, **mamie,** tu as passé une bonne journée?
ROSALIE:	Oui. André et moi, nous sommes allés visiter le Mont-Saint-Michel.
ROSE:	Alors, vous vous entendez bien?
ROSALIE:	Très bien. Nous nous retrouvons tous les jours, nous passons des heures ensemble et nous nous parlons de tout.
ROSE:	**Formidable!** Moi, je **rêve d'une telle** relation.
ROSALIE:	Et ton petit ami et toi, ça va?
ROSE:	Pas très bien. Nous nous disputons souvent et nous ne nous entendons pas très bien.
ROSALIE:	**C'est dommage!**

---

se rencontrer *to meet each other (by chance), to run into each other*   **ce qui** *what*   **se passer** *to happen*   **le coup de foudre** *love at first sight*   **suivent** (**suivre** *to follow*)   **se souvenir de** *to remember*   **la jeunesse** *youth*   **le grand amour** *true love* **la plupart du temps** *most of the time*   **s'entendre** *to get along*   **Enfin** *Finally*   **prendre une décision** *to make a decision* **s'installer (à / dans)** *to settle (in), to move (into)*   **heureux (heureuse)** *happy*   **mamie** *grandma*   **Formidable!** *Great!* **rêver (de)** *to dream (of)*   **un(e) tel(le)** *such a*   **C'est dommage!** *That's too bad!*

A. Test. Faites ce test pour savoir si vous êtes romantique.

Êtes-vous romantique?

I. Indiquez vos opinions sur ces sujets.

1 Pensez-vous que le grand amour...
- **a.** arrive une fois dans la vie?
- **b.** n'existe pas?
- **c.** est sans importance?

2 Pensez-vous qu'un couple peut s'aimer pour toujours?
- **a.** Certainement.
- **b.** Je ne sais pas, on peut essayer.
- **c.** Probablement pas: la vie est trop longue.

3 Au restaurant, **vous voyez** des amoureux qui se regardent dans les yeux pendant tout le dîner. Vous trouvez ça...
- **a.** un peu bête mais charmant.
- **b.** ridicule.
- **c.** adorable.

II. Comment êtes-vous en couple?

1 Vous vous rencontrez **par hasard** et c'est le coup de foudre. Que pensez-vous?
- **a.** C'est juste un désir sexuel.
- **b.** C'est peut-être l'amour.
- **c.** **Attention!**

2 Vous vous disputez. Quelle est la meilleure manière de vous réconcilier?
- **a.** Nous devons nous embrasser.
- **b.** Nous devons essayer de parler calmement du problème.
- **c.** Nous devons nous quitter pendant un certain temps.

3 Vous vous adorez. Vous voulez...
- **a.** essayer de vous voir tous les jours.
- **b.** vous téléphoner tous les jours et vous voir trois ou quatre fois par semaine.
- **c.** vous retrouver le week-end, si vous n'avez pas d'autres projets.

SCORE: **Partie I.** 1. a–2 points 2. a–2 points, b–1 point 3. c–2 points, a–1 point
Partie II. 1. b–2 points, a–1 point 2. a–2 points, b–1 point 3. a–2 points, b–1 point
◆ Si vous avez 10–12 points, vous êtes une personne très (peut-être même un peu trop?) romantique. Attention! **Ne perdez pas votre temps** à attendre un amour parfait. Essayez d'être un peu plus réaliste, quand même.
◆ Si vous avez 6–9 points, vous êtes romantique, mais vous n'exagérez pas. Vous êtes prêt(e) à aimer quand le bon moment arrivera, mais vous ne perdez pas votre temps à chercher l'amour idéal partout.
◆ Si vous avez 0–5 points, vous êtes réaliste, cynique même! Ne voulez-vous pas mettre un peu plus de poésie dans votre vie?

B. En couple. Est-ce qu'on fait ces choses **dans un couple heureux** ou **dans un couple malheureux** *(unhappy)*?

EXEMPLES On se dispute rarement.
On se dispute rarement **dans un couple heureux.**

1. On se dispute tout le temps.
2. On se parle de tout.
3. On ne s'entend pas bien du tout.
4. On s'ennuie ensemble.
5. On s'amuse ensemble.
6. On s'embrasse tout le temps.
7. On ne s'embrasse jamais.

C. Conversation. Avec un(e) partenaire, relisez la conversation entre Rosalie et Rose en bas de la page précédente. Ensuite, changez la conversation pour parler de votre relation avec votre mari, votre femme, votre petit(e) ami(e), votre meilleur(e) ami(e) ou votre camarade de chambre.

CD 3-19   You can find a list of the new words from the vocabulary and grammar sections of this **Compétence** on page 298 and a recording of this list on track 3-19 of your *Text Audio CD.*

---

vous voyez *you see*   **par hasard** *by chance*   **Attention!** *Watch out!*   **Ne perdez pas votre temps** *Don't waste your time*

Pour vérifier

1. When do you use a reciprocal verb?

2. What verbs can be made into reciprocal verbs? How would you say *to look at each other* or *to listen to each other*?

3. When a reflexive or reciprocal verb is used in the infinitive, does the reflexive pronoun change with the subject? How would you say *I am going to get up at 6:00? I am not going to get up at 6:00?*

✳ Note *de grammaire*

Note that although the verbs **se fiancer** and **se marier** are reflexive, **divorcer** is not.

🎧 To download a podcast on Reflexive Verbs, go to **academic.cengage.com/french.**

Saying what people do for each other

Les verbes réciproques au présent et les verbes réfléchis et réciproques au futur immédiat

You have seen that reflexive verbs are used when someone is doing something to or for himself/herself. You use similar verbs to describe reciprocal actions; that is, to indicate that people are doing something to or for each other. Here are some reflexive and reciprocal verbs commonly used to describe relationships:

s'aimer	*to like each other, to love each other*
se détester	*to hate each other*
se disputer	*to argue*
s'embrasser	*to kiss each other, to embrace each other*
s'entendre (bien / mal)	*to get along (well / badly) with each other*
se fiancer	*to get engaged*
se marier	*to get married*
se quitter	*to leave each other*
se réconcilier	*to make up*
se regarder	*to look at each other*
se rencontrer	*to meet* (for the first time), *to run into each other* (by chance)
se retrouver	*to meet* (by design)
se téléphoner	*to telephone each other*

The verb **s'entendre** *(to get along)* is a regular **-re** verb. You will learn how to conjugate other **-re** verbs in the next section on page 276. The forms of **s'entendre** are:

S'ENTENDRE *(to get along)*	
je m'entends	nous nous entendons
tu t'entends	vous vous entendez
il/elle/on s'entend	ils/elles s'entendent

Notice that most verbs indicating actions done to other people can be used reciprocally.

regarder quelqu'un *(to look at someone)*	Je regarde **Jim.**
se regarder *(to look at each other)*	Nous **nous** regardons.

As always, use **aller** to form the immediate future of reflexive and reciprocal verbs. When you use a reflexive or reciprocal verb in the infinitive, the reflexive pronoun varies with the subject. In the negative, put **ne... pas** around the conjugated verb.

SE LEVER *(to get up)*	
je vais me lever	nous allons nous lever
tu vas te lever	vous allez vous lever
il/elle/on va se lever	ils/elles vont se lever

Je ne vais pas **me** lever tôt.   **Nous** aimons **nous** retrouver au café.

Tu préfères **te** coucher tard.   **Vous** allez **vous** marier?

A. Une histoire d'amour. Isabelle, la cousine de Rose, rencontre Luc et ils tombent amoureux. Qu'est-ce qui se passe?

se téléphoner   se regarder   se rencontrer au parc   se marier
s'embrasser   s'installer dans une maison   se quitter   se fiancer
se réconcilier   se parler   se disputer

EXEMPLE   **Ils se téléphonent.**

1.    **2.**    **3.**

4.    **5.**    **6.**

7.   **8.**    **9.**

B. Questions. Rose veut en savoir plus *(to know more)* sur Isabelle et Luc. Avec un(e) partenaire, imaginez ses questions et les réponses qu'Isabelle lui donne.

EXEMPLE   se disputer
         —Est-ce que vous vous disputez souvent?
         —Non, nous ne nous disputons pas souvent.

tous les jours	ne... jamais
souvent	bien
quelquefois	mal
la plupart du temps	beaucoup

1. se téléphoner
2. se retrouver
3. s'embrasser
4. s'entendre
5. s'aimer

C. Isabelle et Luc. Tout va très bien entre Isabelle et Luc. Ils se parlent et ils se retrouvent en ville tous les jours. Est-ce qu'ils vont faire les choses suivantes demain?

> **EXEMPLE**   se disputer
> **Non, ils ne vont pas se disputer.**

1. se téléphoner
2. se retrouver en ville
3. se parler de tout

4. bien s'entendre
5. s'ennuyer ensemble
6. s'embrasser

D. Et demain chez Rose. Dites ce que Rose va faire demain d'après les illustrations.

> **EXEMPLE**    ... vers neuf heures.
> **Elle va se réveiller vers neuf heures.**

1. ... tout de suite.

2. ... la figure et les mains.

3. ... les dents.

4. ... les cheveux.

5. ... en jean.

6. ... vers deux heures du matin.

E. Et toi? Regardez chaque illustration de **D. Et demain chez Rose.** Demandez à un(e) partenaire s'il/si elle va faire la même chose demain.

> **EXEMPLE**    ... vers neuf heures.
> —**Est-ce que tu vas te réveiller vers neuf heures?**
> —**Oui, je vais me réveiller vers neuf heures.**
> **Non, je ne vais pas me réveiller vers neuf heures.**

F. Ce week-end. Dites si ces personnes vont probablement faire ces choses ce week-end.

EXEMPLE   Moi, je... (se lever tôt)
Moi, je vais me lever tôt. / Je ne vais pas me lever tôt.

1. Samedi matin, moi, je...
   se réveiller tard
   se lever tout de suite
   rester au lit quelques minutes
2. Samedi matin, mon meilleur ami / ma meilleure amie...
   se réveiller tôt
   se lever facilement
   prendre son petit déjeuner avec moi
3. Ce week-end, cet(te) ami(e) et moi, nous...
   se retrouver en ville
   s'amuser
   s'ennuyer
   s'entendre bien

G. Partons en week-end. Vous allez faire du camping avec un groupe d'amis ce week-end. Travaillez avec un petit groupe d'étudiants et faites des projets.

EXEMPLE   **On va se réveiller tôt.**

se lever tôt / tard	se laver dans la rivière *(river)*	
faire des randonnées *(to go hiking)*	nager	
se coucher tôt / tard	s'amuser	dormir sous une tente
se brosser les dents avec l'eau de la rivière		

H. Entretien. Interviewez votre partenaire.

1. Est-ce que tu te réveilles facilement ou avec difficulté? Tu te lèves tôt ou tard pendant la semaine en général? Tu te lèves tout de suite? À quelle heure est-ce que tu vas te lever demain?
2. Après les cours, est-ce que tu préfères te reposer ou t'amuser avec des amis? Est-ce que tu vas te reposer ce soir après les cours? Et demain soir?
3. Est-ce que tu te couches tôt ou tard pendant la semaine d'habitude? À quelle heure vas-tu te coucher ce soir? Vas-tu te lever tôt ce week-end? À quelle heure vas-tu te lever? Est-ce que tu préfères te lever tôt ou tard?

Pour vérifier

1. What ending do you add for each subject pronoun after dropping the **-re** from the infinitive of these verbs? What is the conjugation of **perdre**?

2. Which of these **-re** verbs are conjugated with **être** in the **passé composé**?

Talking about activities

Les verbes en -re

Many verbs that end in **-re** follow a regular pattern of conjugation

ATTENDRE (*to wait for*)	
j'attend**s**	nous attend**ons**
tu attend**s**	vous attend**ez**
il/elle/on attend	ils/elles attend**ent**

PASSÉ COMPOSÉ: **j'ai attendu**
IMPARFAIT: **j'attendais**

The following are some common **-re** verbs.

attendre	*to wait (for)*
descendre (de) (à)	*to go down, to get off (of), to stay (at)*
entendre	*to hear*
s'entendre (bien / mal) avec	*to get along (well / badly) with*
perdre	*to lose, to waste*
perdre du temps	*to waste time*
se perdre	*to get lost*
rendre quelque chose à quelqu'un	*to return something to someone, to turn in something to someone*
rendre visite à quelqu'un	*to visit someone*
répondre (à)	*to answer, to respond*
vendre / revendre	*to sell / to sell back, to resell*

❋ Note *de grammaire*

Do not use **pour** after **attendre** to say *for* whom or what you are waiting.

J'attends des amis. *I'm waiting for friends.*

❋ Note *de vocabulaire*

Use **rendre visite à** or **aller voir** to say that you visit a person, and only use **visiter** to say that you visit a place.

In the **passé composé, descendre** and the reflexive verbs are conjugated with **être** as the auxiliary verb. The other verbs in this list are all conjugated with **avoir.**

> J'ai rendu visite à une amie à Paris.   Je suis descendu(e) à l'hôtel Étoile.

A. Votre vie. Est-ce que ces personnes font toujours (souvent, quelquefois, rarement, jamais...) les choses suivantes?

> **EXEMPLE**   Moi, je... (attendre l'autobus pour aller en cours)
> **Moi, je n'attends jamais l'autobus pour aller en cours.**

1. Moi, je...
   rendre visite à mes parents
   attendre le week-end avec impatience
   revendre mes livres à la fin *(end)* du semestre / trimestre

2. Mes amis...
   descendre en ville le week-end
   s'entendre bien
   se rendre visite

3. Mon meilleur ami / Ma meilleure amie...
   perdre patience avec moi
   s'entendre bien avec mes autres amis
   se perdre

4. En cours de français, nous...
   perdre du temps
   répondre bien
   rendre les devoirs au professeur à la fin *(end)* du cours

B. La routine de Rose. En vous servant des phrases données, décrivez la routine de Rose quand elle est à Atlanta. Basez vos réponses sur les illustrations.

EXEMPLE   Rose: attendre l'autobus le matin / aller en cours à pied
Rose attend l'autobus le matin. Elle ne va pas en cours à pied.

1.   **2.**   **3.**   **4.**

1. Rose: perdre patience si l'autobus est en retard *(late)* / attendre patiemment
2. Rose: perdre son temps dans l'autobus / préférer lire
3. Rose: descendre chez un ami / descendre à l'université
4. Rose: répondre mal en cours / répondre bien en cours

5.   **6.**   **7.**   **8.**

5. Les étudiants: travailler bien en cours / perdre leur temps
6. Les étudiants: garder *(to keep)* leurs devoirs / rendre leurs devoirs au professeur
7. Après les cours, Rose: rentrer chez elle / rendre visite à son ami Daniel
8. Rose et son ami: s'entendre mal / s'entendre bien

C. Et toi? Choisissez le verbe logique et complétez les questions. Ensuite, posez les questions à votre partenaire. Utilisez le présent ou le passé composé comme indiqué.

AU PRÉSENT

1. Est-ce que tu _____ souvent visite à tes parents? (rendre, entendre) Ta famille et toi, est-ce que vous _____ bien la plupart du temps? (perdre, s'entendre) Est-ce que tu _____ souvent patience avec tes parents? (perdre, répondre) Est-ce qu'ils _____ souvent patience avec toi? (perdre, répondre)

2. Est-ce que tu _____ tes prochaines vacances avec impatience? (attendre, entendre) Est-ce que tu _____ facilement quand tu es dans une autre ville? (se perdre, vendre) Quand tu voyages avec des amis, est-ce que vous _____ dans un hôtel de luxe? (vendre, descendre)

AU PASSÉ COMPOSÉ

3. Est-ce que tu _____ visite à tes parents récemment? (revendre, rendre) La dernière fois que tu as vu tes parents, est-ce qu'ils _____ patience avec toi? (perdre, vendre)

4. La dernière fois que vous êtes partis en week-end ensemble, est-ce que vous _____ à l'hôtel? (descendre, entendre)

Talking about what you did and used to do

Les activités d'hier

Rose parle de ce qu'elle a fait hier.

Le réveil a sonné et je me suis réveillée.   Je me suis levée.   J'ai pris un bain.

Je me suis brossé les dents.   Je me suis peignée.   Je me suis habillée.

J'ai passé le reste de la journée avec ma cousine et son nouvel ami.

Nous nous sommes promenés.   **Nous nous sommes arrêtés** au restaurant pour manger.

Nous nous sommes bien amusés.   Nous nous sommes quittés vers 10 heures et je me suis couchée vers 11 heures.

Le réveil *The alarm clock*   **sonner** *to ring*   **s'arrêter** *to stop*

Rose parle à sa cousine, Isabelle, qui **raconte** comment elle a rencontré son ami, Luc.

ROSE: Alors, Luc et toi, vous vous êtes rencontrés où?

ISABELLE: J'étais au parc et Luc était à côté de moi. On s'est vus et on s'est parlé un peu. Quelques jours plus tard, il était dans une librairie où j'achetais un livre et **on s'est reconnus.** Il m'a demandé si je voulais aller prendre un verre et j'ai accepté son invitation. On a passé le reste de la journée ensemble.

ROSE: Vous vous êtes bien entendus, **donc**?

ISABELLE: **Parfaitement** bien. On s'est très bien amusés et on s'est retrouvés le lendemain pour aller au cinéma. **Depuis cela,** on s'est téléphoné ou on s'est vus presque tous les jours.

A. Récemment. Quand avez-vous fait ces choses?

ce matin	hier soir	il y a deux semaines
cet après-midi	hier matin	il y a un mois
???	lundi dernier	il y a longtemps

1. Le réveil a sonné et je me suis levé(e) tout de suite...
2. J'ai pris un bain ou une douche...
3. Je me suis brossé les cheveux ou je me suis peigné(e)...
4. Mes amis et moi, nous nous sommes bien amusés ensemble...
5. Nous nous sommes promenés en ville...
6. Je me suis arrêté(e) dans un fast-food pour manger...
7. Je me suis couché(e) après minuit...

B. Ils se sont retrouvés. Décrivez la première fois que Rosalie et André se sont revus après toutes ces années en mettant ces phrases dans l'ordre logique.

1.  2.  3.  4.

_____ Ils se sont embrassés.

__**1**__ André et Rosalie se sont vus.

_____ Ils se sont quittés.

_____ Ils se sont reconnus.

_____ Ils se sont parlé pendant plusieurs heures et ils se sont souvenus du passé.

C. Conversation. Avec un(e) partenaire, relisez la conversation entre Rose et sa cousine en haut de la page. Ensuite, parlez avec votre partenaire de comment vous avez rencontré votre meilleur(e) ami(e) ou votre petit(e) ami(e).

You can find a list of the new words from the vocabulary and grammar sections of this *Compétence* on page 299 and a recording of this list on track 3-21 of your *Text Audio CD*.

---

raconter *to tell*   **on s'est reconnus** (**passé composé** of **se reconnaître** *to recognize each other*)   **donc** *then, thus, so*
Parfaitement *Perfectly*   **Depuis cela** *Since then* (**cela** *that*)

1. Do you use **être** or **avoir** as the auxiliary verb with reflexive and reciprocal verbs in the **passé composé**?

2. Where are reflexive pronouns placed with respect to the auxiliary verb? How do you conjugate **s'amuser** in the **passé composé**?

3. Where do you place **ne... pas** in the negative? How do you say *I didn't wake up early*?

4. When does the past participle agree with the reflexive pronoun and subject? When does it not agree? What are three verbs that you know that do not have agreement?

Notes *de grammaire*

1. When **on** means *we*, its verb may either be left in the masculine singular form **(on s'est levé)** or it may agree **(on s'est levé[e][s])**. Either form is considered correct.

2. Remember that the past participles of regular **-er** verbs end in **-é**, those of regular **-ir** verbs end in **-i**, those of regular **-re** verbs end in **-u: je me suis ennuyé(e), je me suis endormi(e), nous nous sommes entendu(e)s.** Se souvenir (de) is conjugated like **venir: Je me suis souvenu(e).**

Saying what people did

Les verbes réfléchis et réciproques au passé composé

All reflexive and reciprocal verbs have **être** as the auxiliary verb in the **passé composé.** Always place the reflexive pronoun directly before the auxiliary verb.

SE LEVER	
je me suis levé(e)	nous nous sommes levé(e)s
tu t'es levé(e)	vous vous êtes levé(e)(s)
il s'est levé	ils se sont levés
elle s'est levée	elles se sont levées
on s'est levé(e)(s)	

To negate a reflexive verb, place **ne** directly after the subject and **pas** or **jamais** directly after the conjugated form of **être.**

> Je me suis réveillé(e) tôt mais je **ne** me suis **pas** levé(e) tout de suite.

In the **passé composé,** the past participle agrees in gender and number with the reflexive pronoun (and the subject) when it is the direct object of the verb.

> Rosalie **s'**est lev**ée** tôt.   André et Rosalie **se** sont mari**és.**

In this chapter, make the past participle agree except in these cases:

- There is no agreement when a reflexive verb is followed by a noun that is the direct object of the verb. Past participles of verbs like **se laver, se maquiller,** or **se brosser** do not agree with the subject when they are followed by the name of a part of the body.

  Rose et Rosalie se sont lav**ées.**   BUT   Rose et Rosalie se sont lavé **les mains.**
  Rose s'est maquillé**e.**   Rose s'est maquillé **les yeux.**

- With the verbs **se parler, se téléphoner,** and **s'écrire,** there is no agreement because the reflexive pronoun is an *indirect* object, not a *direct* object.

  Ils se sont parlé.   Nous nous sommes téléphoné.   Ils se sont écrit.

A. Hier chez Henri et Patricia. Patricia, la cousine de Rose, parle de ce qu'elle a fait hier. Qu'est-ce qu'elle dit?

EXEMPLE   **Je me suis réveillée à six heures.**

EXEMPLE   Je...   **1.** Je...   **2.** Je...

3. Je... **4.** Je... **5.** Henri et moi, nous...

B. Hier. Regardez les illustrations de *A. Hier chez Henri et Patricia* et expliquez ce que Patricia a fait.

EXEMPLE  **Patricia s'est réveillée à six heures.**

C. Et toi? Demandez à votre partenaire s'il/si elle a fait les choses suivantes hier.

EXEMPLE se lever tôt
—**Est-ce que tu t'es levé(e) tôt hier?**
—**Oui, je me suis levé(e) tôt hier.**
  Non, je ne me suis pas levé(e) tôt hier.

1. se réveiller tôt
2. se lever tout de suite
3. prendre un café au lit
4. prendre un bain ou une douche
5. se laver les cheveux
6. passer la soirée à la maison
7. s'ennuyer
8. s'amuser
9. se coucher tard
10. s'endormir facilement

D. Je veux tout savoir. Utilisez les verbes suivants pour poser des questions à votre partenaire sur ses interactions avec son meilleur ami (sa meilleure amie) cette semaine.

EXEMPLE se téléphoner
—**Est-ce que vous vous êtes téléphoné cette semaine?**
—**Oui, on s'est téléphoné hier.**
  Non, on ne s'est pas téléphoné cette semaine.

se retrouver en ville	se disputer
se promener au parc	s'ennuyer
se voir beaucoup	s'amuser

E. Entretien. Posez ces questions à votre partenaire.

1. À quelle heure est-ce que tu t'es couché(e) hier soir? Est-ce que tu as bien dormi? Jusqu'à quelle heure est-ce que tu as dormi ce matin? Est-ce que tu t'es levé(e) facilement?

2. À quelle heure est-ce que tu dois te réveiller les jours du cours de français? À quelle heure est-ce que tu t'es levé(e) ce matin?

3. Avec qui est-ce que tu es sorti(e) récemment? Où est-ce que vous vous êtes retrouvé(e)s? Qu'est-ce que vous avez fait? Est-ce que vous vous êtes bien amusé(e)s?

1. How do you form the **imparfait** of all verbs except **être**? What is the **imparfait** of **je m'amuse**? of **je ne m'amuse pas**?

2. Do you use the **imparfait** or the **passé composé** to say what happened on a specific occasion? to say how things used to be?

Saying what people did and used to do

Les verbes réfléchis et réciproques à l'imparfait et reprise de l'usage du passé composé et de l'imparfait

Just as with all other verbs (except **être**), the **imparfait** of reflexive verbs is formed by dropping the **-ons** from the present tense **nous** form and adding the endings **-ais, -ais, -ait, -ions, -iez, -aient.**

SE LEVER	NE PAS SE LEVER
je me levais	je ne me levais pas
tu te levais	tu ne te levais pas
il/elle/on se levait	il/elle/on ne se levait pas
nous nous levions	nous ne nous levions pas
vous vous leviez	vous ne vous leviez pas
ils/elles se levaient	ils/elles ne se levaient pas

When talking about your life in the past, remember to use the **imparfait** to tell *what things were like in general* or *what was going on when something else happened* and the **passé composé** to tell *what happened on specific occasions* or to recount *a sequence of events.* Before doing the exercises in this section, review the specific uses of the **passé composé** and the **imparfait** on page 253.

Ce matin, **je me suis levé(e)** à six heures.

Quand j'étais au lycée, **je me levais** à sept heures.

A. À seize ans. Parlez de votre routine quotidienne à l'âge de 16 ans.

> **EXEMPLE** se réveiller souvent tôt
> **À l'âge de seize ans, je me réveillais souvent tôt.**
> **Je ne me réveillais pas souvent tôt.**

1. se réveiller souvent avant six heures
2. se lever facilement
3. prendre un bain / une douche le matin
4. se laver les cheveux tous les jours
5. prendre toujours le petit déjeuner
6. aller toujours en cours
7. s'ennuyer souvent en cours

B. Et hier? Utilisez les verbes de l'exercice précédent pour parler de ce que vous avez fait hier.

> **EXEMPLE** se réveiller tôt
> **Hier, je me suis réveillé(e) tôt.**
> **Je ne me suis pas réveillé(e) tôt.**

C. Et alors? Rosalie parle de ce qui s'est passé hier. Complétez ses phrases logiquement en mettant les verbes donnés au passé composé ou à l'imparfait.

   EXEMPLE   Hier matin, je (j') _____ (être) fatiguée et alors,
                  je _____ (rester) au lit.
                  Hier matin, **j'étais** fatiguée et alors, je **suis restée** au lit.

1. Je (J') _____ (vouloir) préparer le petit déjeuner et alors, je _____ (se laver) les mains.
2. Vers midi, André et moi, nous _____ (avoir) faim et alors, nous _____ (se préparer) des sandwichs.
3. Nous _____ (boire) deux bouteilles d'eau minérale aussi parce que nous _____ (avoir) très soif.
4. Après, André _____ (se coucher) parce qu'il _____ (être) fatigué.
5. Il _____ (se lever) vers trois heures parce qu'il n'_____ (être) plus *(no longer)* fatigué.
6. Il _____ (faire) très beau. Alors, nous _____ (se promener).
7. Quand nous _____ (rentrer), Rose et ses copains _____ (être) à la maison.
8. Nous _____ (se quitter) assez tôt parce que nous _____ (vouloir) nous reposer.

D. Le mariage d'André et de Rosalie. André et Rosalie se sont enfin mariés. Décrivez le jour de leur mariage en mettant les verbes donnés au passé composé ou à l'imparfait.

Le jour de son mariage, Rosalie __1__ (se lever) tôt. André __2__ (arriver) vers neuf heures mais tout de suite après, il __3__ (se souvenir) d'une course qu'il __4__ (devoir) faire et il __5__ (repartir).

Il __6__ (être) trois heures quand André __7__ (revenir). La cérémonie __8__ (commencer) à quatre heures. Tous les invités *(guests)* __9__ (être) dans le jardin. Il __10__ (faire) beau et Rosalie et André __11__ (être) contents. Rosalie __12__ (porter) une jolie robe beige et André __13__ (porter) un costume noir. Rosalie __14__ (être) très jolie! Après la cérémonie, les amis __15__ (rester) et ils __16__ (manger) du gâteau *(cake)*. Ils __17__ (s'amuser) bien quand tout d'un coup il __18__ (commencer) à pleuvoir et alors, ils __19__ (rentrer) dans la maison.

André __20__ (partir) et il __21__ (revenir) avec assez de chaises pour tout le monde. Vers huit heures les invités __22__ (partir). André et Rosalie __23__ (se regarder) et ils __24__ (commencer) à sourire *(to smile)*. Ils __25__ (être) fatigués mais très, très heureux.

E. Entretien. Interviewez votre partenaire.

1. Est-ce que tu t'entendais bien avec tes parents quand tu avais quinze ans? Qu'est-ce que vous faisiez en famille? Est-ce que vous vous disputiez quelquefois? Est-ce que vous vous êtes disputés récemment?
2. À quelle heure est-ce que tu t'es réveillé(e) ce matin? Est-ce que tu t'es levé(e) tout de suite? Qu'est-ce que tu as fait ensuite? À quelle heure est-ce que tu te levais quand tu étais au lycée? Est-ce que tu te levais facilement?
3. Avec qui est-ce que tu es sorti(e) récemment? Où est-ce que vous êtes allé(e)s ensemble? Qu'est-ce que vous avez fait? Est-ce que vous vous êtes bien amusé(e)s? Avec qui aimais-tu sortir quand tu étais au lycée? Qu'est-ce que vous aimiez faire pour vous amuser?

Describing traits and characteristics

Le caractère

Rencontres en ligne: Test de compatibilité

Rangez chaque groupe de réponses de 1 (la réponse qui **exprime** le mieux vos sentiments) à 4 (la réponse qui exprime le moins bien vos sentiments).

Je préfère partager la vie avec quelqu'un qui **s'intéresse...**

1 2 3 4   aux arts
1 2 3 4   au sport
1 2 3 4   à la politique
1 2 3 4   à la nature

Je préfère quelqu'un qui cultive...

1 2 3 4   sa spiritualité
1 2 3 4   son **corps**
1 2 3 4   son **esprit**
1 2 3 4   sa vie professionnelle

Un trait que je cherche chez un(e) partenaire, c'est...

1 2 3 4   un bon sens de l'humour
1 2 3 4   la passion
1 2 3 4   la beauté
1 2 3 4   **la compréhension**

Un trait que je ne **supporte** pas chez une autre personne, c'est...

1 2 3 4   l'indécision *(f)*
1 2 3 4   l'inflexibilité *(f)*
1 2 3 4   **l'insensibilité** *(f)*
1 2 3 4   la vanité

Ce que je supporte le moins dans une relation, c'est...

1 2 3 4   la jalousie
1 2 3 4   l'indifférence *(f)*
1 2 3 4   l'infidélité *(f)*
1 2 3 4   la violence

Chez un(e) partenaire, ce qui a le moins d'importance pour moi, c'est...

1 2 3 4   son argent
1 2 3 4   sa profession
1 2 3 4   sa religion
1 2 3 4   son **aspect physique**

ranger *to arrange, to order*   **exprimer** *to express*   **s'intéresser à** *to be interested in*   **le corps** *the body*   **l'esprit** *(m) the mind, the spirit*   **la compréhension** *understanding*   **supporter** *to bear, to tolerate, to put up with*   **l'insensibilité** *insensitivity*   **Ce que** *What*   **l'aspect physique** *(m) physical appearance*

Rose parle à sa cousine, Isabelle, de son petit ami, Luc.

CD 3-22 ROSE: Alors, tu as trouvé **le bonheur** avec ton nouvel ami, Luc? Il est comment?

ISABELLE: Il a un bon sens de l'humour et il est sympa. Son seul trait que je n'aime pas, c'est qu'il est un peu **jaloux** si je ne passe pas tout mon temps avec lui.

ROSE: Vous vous intéressez aux mêmes choses?

ISABELLE: Oui et non. On aime plus ou moins la même musique et les mêmes films et il s'intéresse à la politique comme moi, mais il est très **conservateur** et moi, tu sais, je suis plutôt libérale.

A. Et vous? Changez les mots en italique pour décrire votre propre situation ou pour exprimer votre opinion.

1. J'ai beaucoup d'amis qui s'intéressent *au sport.*
2. Je ne m'intéresse pas du tout *à la politique.*
3. Je ne supporte pas quelqu'un qui *parle tout le temps des autres.*
4. La plupart de mes amis sont *libéraux.*
5. Dans une relation, je supporte *l'infidélité* moins bien que *la jalousie.*
6. Pour moi, *la beauté* est plus importante que *le sens de l'humour.*
7. Je pense que *la religion* d'une personne est plus importante que *sa profession.*

B. Entretien. Interviewez votre partenaire.

1. Est-ce que tu t'intéresses au sport? aux arts? au cinéma? à la politique? à la philosophie? Est-ce que tu t'ennuies si quelqu'un parle de ces choses?
2. Est-ce que tu passes plus de temps à cultiver ton corps, ton esprit, ta spiritualité ou ta vie professionnelle? Qu'est-ce que tu fais pour le (la) cultiver?
3. Où est-ce que tu as rencontré ton meilleur ami (ta meilleure amie)? Est-ce qu'il/elle a un bon sens de l'humour? Quels sont ses meilleurs traits? A-t-il/elle des traits que tu n'aimes pas? Est-ce qu'il/elle fait des choses quelquefois que tu ne supportes pas? Est-ce que vous vous disputez de temps en temps?

C. Test de compatibilité. Travaillez avec un(e) partenaire pour préparer deux questions supplémentaires pour le test de compatibilité.

EXEMPLE **Quelle activité aimez-vous le moins faire avec une autre personne?**

1 2 3 4 **faire la cuisine**
1 2 3 4 **faire de l'exercice**
1 2 3 4 **faire du shopping**
1 2 3 4 **voyager**

D. Conversation. Avec un(e) partenaire, relisez la conversation entre Rose et Isabelle en haut de la page. Ensuite, changez la conversation pour parler d'un(e) ami(e), de votre petit(e) ami(e) ou de votre mari ou femme. Commencez la conversation en disant: **Alors, tu passes beaucoup de temps avec...** (au lieu de dire *[instead of saying]:* **Alors, tu as trouvé le bonheur avec...**).

CD 3-23 You can find a list of the new words from the vocabulary and grammar sections of this ***Compétence*** on page 299 and a recording of this list on track 3-23 of your *Text Audio CD*.

---

le bonheur *happiness* **jaloux (jalouse)** *jealous* **conservateur (conservatrice)** *conservative*

Pour vérifier

1. Which relative pronoun functions as the subject of a verb? Which one functions as the direct object of a verb? Which one replaces the preposition **de** and its object? Does **qui** or **que** change to **qu'** before a vowel sound?

2. Can **qui, que,** and **dont** all be used for both people and things?

3. Where are relative clauses placed with respect to the noun they describe?

✳ Note de grammaire

Remember that past participles agree with preceding direct objects and therefore agree with the noun that **que** represents: **Je sors avec une femme que j'ai rencontrée pendant mes vacances.**

Specifying which one

Les pronoms relatifs **qui, que** et **dont**

A relative clause gives more information about a person or object you are talking about in a sentence. A relative clause begins with a relative pronoun, a word like *who, that,* or *which* that refers back to the noun being described.

Je sors avec une femme
{ **qui** est beaucoup plus âgée que moi.
{ **que** j'ai rencontrée pendant mes vacances.
{ **dont** je suis amoureux.

I'm going out with a woman
{ ***who*** *is a lot older than I am.*
{ ***that*** *I met during my vacation.*
{ ***with whom*** *I'm in love.*

The relative pronouns **qui, que,** and **dont** are all used for both people and things. The choice depends on how the pronoun functions in the relative clause.

- Use **qui** for both people or things when they are the *subject* of the relative clause. Since **qui** is the subject, it is followed by a verb and it can mean *that, which,* or *who.*

Note how relative pronouns are used to combine two sentences talking about the same thing. The relative clause is placed immediately after the noun it describes.

Comment s'appelle ton ami? **Ton ami** vient de New York.
Comment s'appelle ton ami **qui** vient de New York?

- Use **que (qu')** for people or things when they are the *direct object* in the relative clause. **Que (qu')** can mean *that, which,* or *whom,* or it may be omitted in English. Note that the pronoun **que** makes elision **(qu')** before a vowel sound, but **qui** does not.

Comment s'appelle ton ami? Tu as invité **cet ami** hier.
Comment s'appelle ton ami **que** tu as invité hier?

- Use **dont** to replace the preposition ***de*** + *a person or thing* in relative clauses with verbs such as the following. It can mean *whom, of (about, with) whom, whose, that,* or *of (about, with) which.*

avoir besoin de
avoir envie de
avoir peur de
être amoureux (amoureuse) de
être jaloux (jalouse) de

se souvenir de
parler de
rêver de
tomber amoureux (amoureuse) de
faire la connaissance de (*to make the acquaintance of, to meet* [for the first time])

Comment s'appelle ton ami? Ta sœur parlait **de cet ami** hier.
Comment s'appelle ton ami **dont** ta sœur parlait hier?

A. Préférences. Complétez ces phrases comme dans les exemples. Pour chaque section, utilisez le pronom relatif indiqué.

Utilisez le pronom relatif **qui.** N'oubliez pas de conjuguer le verbe.

> **EXEMPLE**   Je préfère les personnes... (avoir un bon sens de l'humour, avoir beaucoup d'argent)
> **Je préfère les personnes qui ont un bon sens de l'humour.**

1. Je préfère un(e) colocataire (sortir tout le temps, rester souvent à la maison)
2. Je préfère les films (avoir beaucoup d'action, avoir peu de violence)
3. Je préfère un(e) partenaire (cultiver son corps, cultiver son esprit)

Utilisez le pronom relatif **que (qu').**

> **EXEMPLE**   Je préfère les personnes... (je rencontre en cours, je rencontre en boîte)
> **Je préfère les personnes que je rencontre en boîte.**

1. Je préfère les personnes (on rencontre au club de gym, on rencontre à la bibliothèque)
2. Je préfère les activités (je fais seul[e], je fais en groupe)
3. Je préfère la musique (on fait maintenant, on faisait il y a vingt ans)

Utilisez le pronom relatif **dont.**

> **EXEMPLE**   L'argent est une chose (j'ai très envie, je n'ai pas très envie)
> **L'argent est une chose dont je n'ai pas très envie.**

1. L'amour est quelque chose (j'ai très besoin dans ma vie, je n'ai pas vraiment besoin pour le moment)
2. La ville où je suis né(e) est un endroit (je me souviens bien, je ne me souviens pas bien)
3. Ma vie amoureuse, c'est une chose (j'aime bien parler, je n'aime pas beaucoup parler)

B. Identification. C'est André qui parle de sa vie avec Rosalie. Complétez les phrases avec **qui, que** ou **dont.** Ensuite, dites de qui ou de quoi il parle.

> **EXEMPLE**   C'est quelqu'un **dont** je suis tombé amoureux il y a longtemps.
> C'est quelqu'un **que** j'ai revu récemment chez des amis.
> C'est **Rosalie.**

1. C'est quelqu'un _____ j'ai fait la connaissance récemment.
   C'est quelqu'un _____ voyage avec Rosalie.
   C'est quelqu'un _____ j'aimerais connaître mieux.
   C'est _____.

2. C'est un site touristique spectaculaire _____ se trouve *(is located)* sur une île en Normandie.
   C'est un endroit *(place)* _____ Rosalie se souvenait bien.
   C'est un endroit _____ j'ai visité avec Rosalie récemment.
   C'est _____.

3. C'est quelqu'un _____ est venu en France il y a longtemps.
   C'est quelqu'un _____ Rosalie a trouvé très beau.
   C'est quelqu'un _____ j'étais jaloux.
   C'est _____.

Talking about daily life and relationships

Dans le *Chapitre 7,* vous avez appris à parler de votre routine quotidienne et des relations personnelles. Maintenant vous allez réviser ce que vous avez appris.

A. En cours de français. D'abord, dites si ces personnes font les choses indiquées en cours de français. Ensuite, dites si ces mêmes personnes ont fait ces choses la dernière fois que vous étiez en cours.

1. les étudiants / répondre bien aux questions du professeur
2. le professeur / perdre patience avec les étudiants
3. les étudiants / s'entendre bien
4. nous / perdre du temps en cours
5. je / rendre visite au professeur dans son bureau avant le cours
6. je / rendre les devoirs au professeur

B. En cours. Qu'est-ce qui se passe les jours du cours de français? Formez des questions et posez-les à votre partenaire.

> **EXEMPLE** tu / s'amuser en cours
> — **Est-ce que tu t'amuses en cours?**
> — **Oui, je m'amuse en cours.**
>   **Non, je ne m'amuse pas en cours.**

Les jours du cours de français...

1. tu / se lever tôt
2. tu / s'ennuyer en cours
3. tu / s'endormir en cours
4. les autres étudiants et toi, vous / s'amuser bien en cours
5. vous / se disputer
6. vous / se retrouver après les cours
7. les autres étudiants / s'intéresser au cours
8. ils / s'entendre bien
9. le prof / s'amuser en cours
10. le prof / s'endormir en cours

C. Et au dernier cours? Demandez à votre partenaire si chacun a fait les choses indiquées dans *B. En cours* le jour du dernier cours de français.

Le jour du dernier cours de français...

> **EXEMPLE** tu / s'amuser en cours
> — **Est-ce que tu t'es amusé(e) en cours?**
> — **Oui, je me suis amusé(e) en cours.**
>   **Non, je ne me suis pas amusé(e) en cours.**

D. Samedi prochain. Dites si chacun va faire les choses indiquées samedi prochain.

> **EXEMPLE** je / se réveiller avant six heures
> **Je vais me réveiller avant six heures.**
> **Je ne vais pas me réveiller avant six heures.**

1. je / se lever tôt
2. je / se laver les cheveux
3. mes amis et moi, nous / sortir ensemble
4. nous / s'amuser
5. je / se coucher tôt

E. Entretien. D'abord, complétez les questions avec le pronom relatif convenable. Ensuite, interviewez votre partenaire.

1. As-tu plus d'amis _____ tu as rencontrés à l'université ou au lycée? Quand tu sors avec tes amis, quels sont les sujets de conversation _____ vous parlez le plus souvent? Est-ce que tu t'intéresses à des choses _____ tes amis trouvent ennuyeuses ou est-ce que vous vous intéressez aux mêmes choses? As-tu des amis _____ se disputent souvent?

2. Est-ce que tu as beaucoup d'amis _____ sont mariés? Es-tu marié(e)? (Est-ce que tu t'es marié[e] avec la première personne _____ tu es tombé[e] amoureux [amoureuse]?) Est-ce que le mariage est quelque chose _____ tu trouves important ou _____ n'est pas important pour toi?

3. Qu'est-ce qu'on doit faire pour avoir une relation _____ dure *(lasts)*? Y a-t-il des choses _____ tu as peur dans une relation? Est-ce que tu préfères être avec quelqu'un _____ est jaloux ou indifférent?

F. L'histoire de Rosalie. Racontez l'histoire de Rosalie en mettant les verbes donnés à l'imparfait ou au passé composé.

Une jeune fille qui ___1___ (s'appeler) Rosalie ___2___ (habiter) à la campagne près de Rouen. Quand elle ___3___ (avoir) 18 ans, Rosalie ___4___ (finir) ses études et elle ___5___ (devenir) professeur de musique.

Un jour, un jeune Américain ___6___ (venir) en France. Un après-midi, cet homme et Rosalie ___7___ (se rencontrer). Ils ___8___ (se voir) et ils ___9___ (se parler). Ils ___10___ (passer) des heures ensemble et à partir de ce jour-là *(from that day on)*, Rosalie et l'homme ___11___ (se retrouver) presque tous les jours. Le jeune Américain ___12___ (venir) chez Rosalie ou alors ils ___13___ (se retrouver) en ville. Finalement, ils ___14___ (se marier) et ils ___15___ (aller) s'installer à Atlanta. Ils ___16___ (être) très heureux ensemble.

Après la mort de son mari, Rosalie ___17___ (revenir) en France avec sa petite-fille, Rose. Un jour, Rose ___18___ (se promener) avec ses cousines quand elle ___19___ (commencer) à parler avec un monsieur. Ce monsieur, André Dupont, ___20___ (être) l'ancien ami de Rosalie. Il ___21___ (se souvenir) très bien de Rosalie parce qu'il ___22___ (être) amoureux d'elle quand il ___23___ (avoir) 18 ans.

Rosalie ___24___ (être) chez son frère Jean quand elle ___25___ (revoir) André. Ils ___26___ (se voir) et ils ___27___ (tomber) amoureux.

Lecture et Composition

Lecture

 Pour mieux lire: *Recognizing conversational style*

You are going to read a story by Eugène Ionesco (1912–1994) in which a father finds himself alone one morning with his two- or three-year-old daughter.

Sometimes a writer uses language that is not completely "correct" to portray how someone speaks. To appreciate this style and how it tells something about the character who is speaking, you can compare this conversational language with the more "correct" version of the language. In Ionesco's story, the author modifies his language to represent the way a little girl would speak or how someone might speak to a young child.

Du vocabulaire enfantin. Regardez ces phrases. Comment dit-on la même chose d'une façon plus correcte?

1. Tu laves ta figure.
2. Je rase ma barbe.
3. Tu laves ton «dérèr» *(backside)*.

Conte pour enfants de moins de trois ans (extrait)

...papa se lève... Il va dans la salle de bains. Il ferme la porte de la salle de bains. Josette est à la porte de la salle de bains. Elle **frappe** avec ses petits **poings,** elle **pleure.**

Josette dit
Ouvre-moi la porte.

Papa répond
*Je ne peux pas. Je suis **tout nu,** je me lave, après je me rase.*

Josette dit
Et tu fais pipi-caca.

—*Je me lave,* dit papa.

Josette dit
*Tu laves ta figure, tu laves tes **épaules,** tu laves tes **bras,** tu laves ton **dos,** tu laves ton «dérèr», tu laves tes pieds.*

—*Je rase ma barbe,* dit papa.

—*Tu rases ta barbe avec **du savon,** dit Josette. Je veux entrer. Je veux voir.*

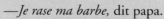

extrait *excerpt*   **frappe** *knocks*   **poings** *fists*   **pleure** *cries*   **tout nu** *completely naked*   **épaules** *shoulders*
bras *arms*   **dos** *back*   **du savon** *soap*

Papa dit

*Tu ne peux pas me voir, parce que je **ne** suis **plus** dans la salle de bains.*

Josette dit (derrière la porte)

Alors, où tu es?

Papa répond

Je ne sais pas, va voir. Je suis peut-être dans la salle à manger, va me chercher.

Josette **court** dans la salle à manger, et papa commence sa toilette. Josette court avec ses petites **jambes,** elle va dans la salle à manger. Papa est tranquille, mais pas pour longtemps. Josette arrive **de nouveau** devant la porte de la salle de bains, elle **crie à travers** la porte:

Josettte

Je t'ai cherché. Tu n'es pas dans la salle à manger.

Papa dit

Tu n'as pas bien cherché. Regarde sous la table.

Josette retourne dans la salle à manger. Elle revient.

Elle dit

Tu n'es pas sous la table.

Papa dit

Alors va voir dans le salon. Regarde bien si je suis sur le fauteuil, sur le canapé, derrière les livres, à la fenêtre.

Josette s'en va. Papa est tranquille, mais pas pour longtemps.

Josette revient.

Elle dit

Non, tu n'es pas dans le fauteuil, tu n'es pas à la fenêtre, tu n'es pas sur le canapé, tu n'es pas derrière les livres, tu n'es pas dans la télévision, tu n'es pas dans le salon.

Papa dit

Alors, va voir si je suis dans la cuisine.

Josette dit

Je vais te chercher dans la cuisine.

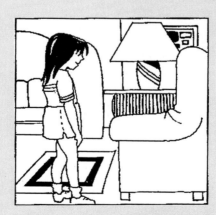

---

ne... plus *no longer*   **court** *runs*   **jambes** *legs*   **de nouveau** *again*   **crie à travers** *yells through*

Josette court à la cuisine. Papa est tranquille, mais pas pour longtemps. Josette revient.

Elle dit
Tu n'es pas dans la cuisine.

Papa dit
*Regarde bien, sous la table de la cuisine, regarde bien si je suis dans le buffet, regarde bien si je suis dans **les casseroles**, regarde bien si je suis dans **le four** avec le poulet.*

Josette va et vient. Papa n'est pas dans le four, papa n'est pas dans les casseroles, papa n'est pas dans le buffet, papa n'est pas sous **le paillasson,** papa n'est pas dans **la poche** de son pantalon, dans la poche du pantalon il y a **seulement le mouchoir.**

Josette revient devant la porte de la salle de bains.

Josette dit
J'ai cherché partout. Je ne t'ai pas trouvé. Où tu es?

Papa dit
Je suis là.

Et papa, qui a eu le temps de faire sa toilette, qui s'est rasé, qui s'est habillé, ouvre la porte.

Il dit
Je suis là.

Il prend Josette dans ses bras, et voilà aussi la porte de la maison qui s'ouvre, **au fond** du couloir, et c'est maman qui arrive...

Eugène Eunesco; *Conte no. 4* © Éditions Gallimard

Compréhension

1. Pourquoi est-ce que le père ne peut pas faire sa toilette tranquillement?

2. Qu'est-ce qu'il fait pour pouvoir faire sa toilette?

3. Où est-ce que la petite fille cherche son papa?

4. Pensez-vous que le père aime sa fille? Pourquoi (pas)?

5. Quels aspects du style d'Ionesco vous fait rire *(make you laugh)*? Quels écrivains comiques qui écrivent en anglais aimez-vous? Est-ce qu'il y a des similarités entre leur style et celui *(that)* d'Ionesco?

---

les casseroles *the pans*   **le four** *the oven*   **le paillasson** *the doormat*   **la poche** *the pocket*   **seulement le mouchoir** *only the handkerchief*   **au fond** *at the end*

Composition

If you have access to SYSTÈME-D software, you will find the following phrases, vocabulary, grammar, and dictionary aids there.

Phrases: Telling time; Linking ideas; Sequencing events; Talking about daily routines
Vocabulary: Toilette
Grammar: Reflexive construction; Reflexive pronouns

⚙ Pour mieux écrire: *Organizing a paragraph*

You know how to use words like **et, ou, mais**, and **parce que** to link ideas together to form sentences. You can also use words like **d'abord, ensuite, alors,** and **et puis** to link your sentences into a well-ordered paragraph. You can also link ideas with the word **pour** to say *in order to*. In this case, **pour** is followed by an infinitive.

Je quitte la maison avant sept heures pour arriver à huit heures.

I leave the house before seven (in order) to arrive before eight.

To say that you do something *before* you do something else, use **avant de.** It is followed by an infinitive.

Je m'habille avant de prendre mon petit déjeuner.

I get dressed before I have (before having) breakfast.

Avant de m'habiller, je prends une douche.

Before I get dressed (before dressing), I take a shower.

Organisez-vous. Vous allez décrire votre routine matinale. Avant de commencer, traduisez les phrases qui suivent.

1. *I'm tired in the morning, so I don't wake up easily.*
2. *First, I eat breakfast. Next, I take a shower. Then, I get dressed. And then, I leave.*
3. *I eat quickly in order to be on time.*
4. *Before I eat, I get dressed. Then, I brush my teeth.*
5. *I take a bath before I put on make-up / shave.*

Le matin chez moi

Décrivez votre routine du matin. Utilisez des mots comme **d'abord, ensuite** et **avant de** pour indiquer l'ordre de vos actions.

EXEMPLE　Le matin, je me lève vers six heures. D'abord...

Comparaisons culturelles

L'amour et le couple

Voici les résultats de **sondages** sur les opinions des Français sur le couple et les relations entre les hommes et les femmes. Quelles sont vos opinions?

Les Français et les Françaises parlent de l'amour.

➧ Êtes-vous amoureux en ce moment?

Oui	Non	Sans réponse
70%	29%	1%

➧ Pour vous, l'amour, est-ce quelque chose de très important, assez important, peu important ou pas important du tout?

Très	Assez	Peu	Pas du tout	Sans opinion
68%	27%	3%	1%	1%

➧ Pour être heureux en amour, estimez-vous que la sexualité est très importante, assez importante, peu importante ou pas importante du tout?

Très	Assez	Peu	Pas du tout	Sans opinion
35%	55%	7%	1%	2%

➧ Parlez-vous de votre vie amoureuse avec vos amis?

Souvent	Rarement	Jamais	Sans réponse
21%	38%	40%	1%

Les femmes parlent de la vie en couple et des hommes.

Pour vous, un couple, c'est **avant tout...**

Vieillir ensemble	53%*
Partager ses idées, ses **valeurs**	49%
Avoir des enfants	32%
Vivre un grand amour	23%
Se soutenir matériellement	14%

Avoir un homme dans votre vie, aujourd'hui, **diriez-vous** que...

C'est indispensable à votre bonheur	59%
Vous pourriez vous en passer	36%
Sans opinion	5%

Avoir des enfants, diriez-vous que...

C'est indispensable à votre bonheur	88%
Vous pourriez vous en passer	9%
Sans opinion	3%

*La totalité des % est supérieure à 100, les personnes interrogées **ayant pu** donner trois réponses.

sondages polls   **avant tout** above all   **Vieillir** To grow old   **valeurs** values   **Vivre** To live   **Se soutenir** To support each other   **diriez-vous** would you say   **Vous pourriez vous en passer** You could do without it   **ayant pu** having been able

Les hommes parlent des femmes.

Quelles sont les principales qualités que vous recherchez chez une femme?

La tendresse	48%
L'intelligence	45%
La fidélité	45%
L'humour	39%
La beauté	24%
Qu'elle tienne bien sa maison	22%
La sensualité	21%
L'indépendance	14%

Qu'est-ce qui pourrait vous faire peur chez une femme?

Le fait qu'elle ait eu beaucoup d'hommes dans sa vie	25%
Sa très grande beauté	21%
Son milieu social	17%
Son audace, le fait qu'elle prenne l'initiative	14%
Son indépendance	13%
Son désir d'avoir un enfant	10%
Son désir de se marier	10%
Son intelligence et sa culture supérieure à la vôtre	10%
Son appétit sexuel	6%
Le fait qu'elle ait une situation professionnelle supérieure à la vôtre	4%

Compréhension

A. Vrai ou faux? D'abord, complétez les phrases suivantes avec le pronom relatif convenable: **qui, que** ou **dont.** Ensuite, dites si les phrases sont vraies ou fausses.

1. La vie amoureuse est quelque chose _____ la majorité des Français parlent souvent avec leurs amis.

2. Une bonne relation sexuelle est quelque chose _____ la majorité des Français trouvent très important pour être heureux en amour.

3. Pour beaucoup de Françaises, un couple, c'est surtout deux personnes _____ restent ensemble jusqu'à la fin *(end)* de la vie.

4. Il y a plus de femmes _____ veulent absolument avoir des enfants dans leur vie que de femmes _____ veulent absolument avoir un homme.

5. Le trait _____ les Français recherchent le plus chez les femmes, c'est la sensualité.

6. La chose _____ les Français ont le plus peur chez les femmes, c'est le désir de se marier.

7. Il y a beaucoup plus d'hommes _____ préfèrent les femmes indépendantes que d'hommes _____ ont peur des femmes indépendantes.

B. Comparaisons. Discutez les questions suivantes.

1. Qu'est-ce que vous trouvez de surprenant *(surprising)* dans les réponses aux sondages des Français? Qu'est-ce qui ne vous surprend pas? Pourquoi?

2. Posez les questions du sondage aux étudiants de votre classe. Quelles différences y a-t-il dans les réponses? Pouvez-vous expliquer ces différences?

3. Dans un sondage sur ce sujet fait dans votre pays, quelles autres questions est-ce qu'on poserait *(would one ask)*? Voyez-vous des attitudes différentes sur ce sujet?

 Visit **academic.cengage.com/french** for YouTube video cultural correlations, cultural information and activities.

La tendresse *Tenderness*   **Qu'elle tienne bien sa maison** *That she keeps house well*   **Qu'est-ce qui pourrait vous faire peur** *What could frighten you*   **Le fait qu'elle ait eu** *The fact that she has had*   **Son audace** *Her boldness*

Résumé de grammaire

Reflexive verbs

Je **me** réveille à six heures et puis, je réveille mes enfants à sept heures.
I wake up **(myself)** *at six o'clock, and then I wake up my children at seven.*

Reflexive verbs are used to say that people do something to or for themselves. In French, the reflexive pronoun corresponding to the subject is placed before the verb.

SE COUCHER *(to go to bed)*	
je **me** couche	nous **nous** couchons
tu **te** couches	vous **vous** couchez
il/elle/on **se** couche	ils/elles **se** couchent

Mon fils de trois ans **s'**habille tout seul.
My three-year-old son dresses all by himself.

The reflexive pronouns **me, te,** and **se** become **m', t',** and **s'** before vowel sounds. Also note the spelling changes with **s'ennuyer, s'appeler** and **se lever.** All verbs ending with **-yer,** such as **essayer** and **payer,** follow the same pattern as **s'ennuyer. Se promener** is conjugated like **se lever.**

—Tu **ne** t'ennu**i**es **pas** dans ce cours?
—Non, je m'intéresse beaucoup au français.

—Comment vous appelez-vous?
—Je m'appe**ll**e Catherine Faure.

—À quelle heure est-ce que vous vous l**e**vez?
—Je me l**è**ve très tôt.

S'ENNUYER *(to be / get bored)*	S'APPELER *(to be named)*	SE LEVER *(to get up)*
je m'ennu**i**e	je m'appe**ll**e	je me l**è**ve
tu t'ennu**i**es	tu t'appe**ll**es	tu te l**è**ves
il/elle/on s'ennu**i**e	il/elle/on s'appe**ll**e	il/elle/on se l**è**ve
nous nous ennuyons	nous nous appelons	nous nous levons
vous vous ennuyez	vous vous appelez	vous vous levez
ils/elles s'ennu**i**ent	ils/elles s'appe**ll**ent	ils/elles se l**è**vent

With negated reflexive verbs, place **ne** directly after the subject and **pas** directly after the conjugated verb.

Mon père **s'**achète une nouvelle voiture chaque année.
My father buys **himself** *a new car each year.*

Verbs that are reflexive in English, such as *to amuse* **oneself** or *to buy* **oneself** *something* will generally also be reflexive in French. Many other verbs are reflexive in French that are not in English. Consult the end-of-chapter vocabulary list to find all the reflexive verbs learned in this chapter.

Je me brosse **les** dents trois fois par jour.
I brush **my** *teeth three times a day.*

Verbs indicating that people are doing something to their own body are generally reflexive in French. After such verbs, in French, you use the definite article **(le, la, l', les)** with a following body part, rather than the possessive adjective *(my, your, his . . .)*.

Reciprocal verbs

Vous **vous** retrouvez après les cours?
Do you meet **each other** *after class?*

Reciprocal verbs indicate that two or more people do something to or for one another. Reciprocal verbs look like reflexive verbs. Most verbs naming something one person might do to another can be made reciprocal by adding a reciprocal pronoun.

Mes voisins ne **se** parlent pas.
My neighbors don't talk **to one another.**

aimer	*to love*	s'aimer	*to love each other*
détester	*to hate*	se détester	*to hate each other*
regarder	*to look at*	se regarder	*to look at each other*

— **Vous** voulez **vous** marier?
— Oui, et **nous** allons **nous** installer dans un petit appartement.

When reflexive / reciprocal verbs are used in the infinitive, the reflexive / reciprocal pronoun changes to match the subject of the conjugated verb.

Past tenses of reflexive and reciprocal verbs

All reflexive / reciprocal verbs are conjugated with **être** in the **passé composé.** The past participle agrees in gender and number with the reflexive / reciprocal pronoun (and the subject) when it is the direct object of the verb.

S'AMUSER	
je me suis amusé(e)	nous nous sommes amusé(e)s
tu t'es amusé(e)	vous vous êtes amusé(e)(s)
il s'est amusé	ils se sont amusés
elle s'est amusée	elles se sont amusées
on s'est amusé(e)(s)	

—Tous tes amis se sont retrouvé**s** chez toi?
—Oui, et on s'est bien amusé**s** jusqu'à très tard. Mon amie Rose s'est endorm**ie** sur le canapé.

With negated verbs, place **ne** directly after the subject and **pas** after the conjugated form of **être.**

Past participles do not agree with reflexive / reciprocal pronouns that are indirect objects. For this reason, there is no agreement with **se parler, se téléphoner, s'écrire,** or when a reflexive verb is followed directly by a noun that is the direct object of the verb, such as a part of the body.

As with all verbs except **être,** form the imperfect of reflexive verbs by dropping the **-ons** from the **nous** form of the verb and adding the imperfect endings: **-ais, -ais, -ait, -ions, -iez, -aient.**

—Vous ne vous êtes pas vu**s** hier?
—Non, mais nous nous sommes téléphoné trois fois.

Ma petite sœur s'est maquill**ée.**
Ma petite sœur s'est maquillé **les yeux.**

—Tu te levais plus tôt l'année dernière?
—Oui, je me levais à six heures.

Regular -re verbs

The following verbs are conjugated like **répondre: descendre, entendre, s'entendre (bien / mal) (avec), perdre, se perdre, rendre visite à quelqu'un, rendre quelque chose à quelqu'un, vendre, revendre.** They all take **avoir** in the **passé composé** except **descendre** and the reflexive verbs.

RÉPONDRE (to answer)	
je répond**s**	nous répond**ons**
tu répond**s**	vous répond**ez**
il/elle/on répond	ils/elles répond**ent**
PASSÉ COMPOSÉ: **j'ai répondu**	
IMPARFAIT: **je répondais**	

—Tu ne rends jamais visite à ton ex-petite amie?
—Non, on a perdu contact. On ne s'entend pas très bien. Si je téléphone chez elle, elle ne répond pas au téléphone.

Relative pronouns

A relative clause is a phrase that describes a noun. The word that begins the phrase, referring back to the noun described is a relative pronoun. The relative pronouns **qui, que,** and **dont** are all used for both people and things. The choice of relative pronoun depends on the pronoun's function in the relative clause. **Qui** replaces the subject of the relative clause, **que (qu')** replaces the direct object, and **dont** replaces the preposition **de** and its object.

Place relative clauses directly after the noun they describe. When **que** is the object of a verb in the **passé composé,** the past participle agrees in number and gender with the noun it represents.

La femme **qui** habite à côté est française. (= La femme est française. **Cette femme** habite à côté.)
La femme **que** j'ai invité**e** est française. (= La femme est française. J'ai invité **cette femme.**)
La femme **dont** je parle souvent est française. (= La femme est française. Je parle souvent **de cette femme.**)

CD3

Vocabulaire

Describing your daily routine

NOMS MASCULINS

un bain	a bath
le mariage	marriage
un petit-fils	a grandson
un séjour	a stay
un veuf	a widower

NOMS FÉMININS

une demi-heure	a half hour
les dents	teeth
une douche	a shower
la figure	the face
la main	the hand
une petite-fille	a granddaughter
une routine	a routine
une veuve	a widow

EXPRESSIONS VERBALES

s'amuser	to have fun
s'appeler	to be named
attendre	to wait (for)
se brosser (les cheveux / les dents)	to brush (one's hair / one's teeth)
connaître	to be familiar with, to be acquainted with, to know
se coucher / se recoucher	to go to bed / to go back to bed
s'endormir	to fall asleep
s'ennuyer	to be bored, to get bored
faire sa toilette	to wash up
s'habiller / se déshabiller	to get dressed / to get undressed
se laver (la figure / les mains)	to wash (one's face / one's hands)
se lever	to get up
se maquiller	to put on makeup
prendre un bain / une douche	to take a bath / a shower
se raser	to shave
se reposer	to rest
se réveiller	to wake up

DIVERS

comme	since, as
d'autres fois	other times
depuis	since, for
d'origine...	of . . . origin
facilement	easily
parfait(e)	perfect
pendant	during
quotidien(ne)	daily
vite	quick(ly), fast

Talking about relationships

NOMS MASCULINS

le coup de foudre	love at first sight
le grand amour	true love

NOMS FÉMININS

la jeunesse	youth
une relation	a relationship

EXPRESSIONS VERBALES

s'aimer	to like each other, to love each other
attendre	to wait (for)
descendre	to go down, to get off, to stay (at a hotel)
se détester	to hate each other
se disputer	to argue
s'embrasser	to kiss each other, to embrace each other
entendre	to hear
s'entendre (bien / mal) (avec)	to get along (well / badly) (with)
se fiancer	to get engaged
s'installer (dans / à)	to move (into), to settle (in)
se marier (avec)	to get married (to)
se parler	to talk to each other
se passer	to happen
perdre	to lose
perdre du temps	to waste time
se perdre	to get lost
prendre une décision	to make a decision
se quitter	to leave each other
se réconcilier	to make up with each other
se regarder	to look at each other
se rencontrer	to meet each other (by chance, for the first time), to run into each other
rendre quelque chose à quelqu'un	to return something to someone
rendre visite à quelqu'un	to visit someone
répondre (à)	to answer
se retrouver	to meet each other (by design)
revendre	to sell back
rêver (de)	to dream (of, about)
se souvenir de	to remember
suivre	to follow
se téléphoner	to phone each other
vendre	to sell

DIVERS

ce qui	what
C'est dommage!	That's too bad!
enfin	finally
formidable	great
heureux (heureuse)	happy
la plupart du temps	most of the time
mamie	grandma
sentimental(e) (mpl sentimentaux)	sentimental, emotional
un(e) tel(le)	such a

Talking about what you did and used to do

NOMS MASCULINS

le reste (de)	the rest (of)
un réveil	an alarm clock

EXPRESSIONS VERBALES

accepter	to accept
s'arrêter	to stop
se peigner	to comb one's hair
se promener	to go walking
raconter	to tell
se reconnaître	to recognize each other
sonner	to ring
se voir	to see each other

DIVERS

cela	that
depuis cela	since then
donc	then, so, thus, therefore
parfaitement	perfectly

Describing traits and characteristics

NOMS MASCULINS

l'aspect physique	physical appearance
le bonheur	happiness
le corps	the body
l'esprit	the mind, the spirit
un groupe	a group
un partenaire	a partner
un sens de l'humour	a sense of humor
un sentiment	a feeling
un test	a test
un trait	a trait

NOMS FÉMININS

la beauté	beauty
la compatibilité	compatibility
la compréhension	understanding
l'importance	importance
l'indécision	indecision
l'indifférence	indifference
l'infidélité	infidelity
l'inflexibilité	inflexibility
l'insensibilité	insensitivity
la jalousie	jealousy
la nature	nature
une partenaire	a partner
la passion	passion
la politique	politics
la profession	the profession
la religion	the religion
une rencontre	an encounter
la spiritualité	spirituality
la vanité	vanity

VERBES

cultiver	to cultivate
exprimer	to express
faire la connaissance de	to make the acquaintance of, to meet (for the first time)
s'intéresser à	to be interested in
ranger	to arrange, to order
supporter	to bear, to tolerate, to put up with

DIVERS

ce que	what
chez (une personne)	with, in (a person)
conservateur (conservatrice)	conservative
dont	whom, of (about, with) whom, whose, that, of (about, with) which
en ligne	online
jaloux (jalouse)	jealous
le mieux	the best
libéral(e) (*mpl* libéraux)	liberal
professionnel(le)	professional
que	that, which, whom
qui	that, which, who

La bonne cuisine

C o m p é t e n c e

 iLrn Heinle Learning Center

 academic.cengage.com/french/horizons

 Système-D

 Audio   iRadio

Élargissez vos connaissances de l'histoire de la Normandie en recherchant les sujets suivants sur Internet: Guillaume le Conquérant et l'invasion normande de l'Angleterre; la tapisserie de Bayeux; l'emprisonnement et l'exécution de Jeanne d'Arc à Rouen; le Jour J *(D-Day)*, le débarquement des Alliés et la bataille de Normandie.

Avez-vous déjà vu des photos de la Normandie? Comment imaginez-vous cette région? Imaginez-vous...

des bateaux **de pêche?**

des fermes normandes?

des pâturages (avec **des moutons** ou **des vaches**)?

---

de pêche *fishing*   **des fermes normandes** *Norman farms*   **des moutons** *sheep*   **des vaches** *cows*

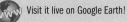

ROUEN

NOMBRE D'HABITANTS: 115 000 habitants (avec ses agglomérations [*metropolitan region*]: 525 000) (les Rouennais)

Visit it live on Google Earth!

d'anciennes villes historiques?

des falaises isolées?

des villes **au bord de la mer telles que** Deauville?

La tapisserie de Bayeux raconte en images la conquête de l'Angleterre par Guillaume le Conquérant, duc de Normandie.

La Normandie, **c'est tout cela! Et même plus!**

�֍ Qu'en savez-vous?

Que savez-vous de *(What do you know about)* l'histoire de la Normandie? Trouvez la date qui correspond à chacun de ces événements historiques.

a. 1066   **b.** le 6 juin 1944

c. 820–911   **d.** 1453

1. le Jour J, jour du débarquement en Normandie des forces alliées (américaines, anglaises, canadiennes et françaises) commandées par le général Eisenhower   B

2. la conquête de la région par les Vikings (Normandie veut dire «*Land of the Northmen*».)   C

3. la fin de la guerre de Cent Ans entre la France et l'Angleterre *(England)* (que la France a gagnée grâce surtout aux batailles [*thanks especially to the battles*] gagnées par Jeanne d'Arc)   D

4. la conquête de l'Angleterre par Guillaume le Conquérant, duc de Normandie   A

---

des falaises *cliffs*   **au bord de la mer** *at the seaside*   **telles que** *such as*   **c'est tout cela! Et même plus!** *it's all that! And even more!*

Ordering at a restaurant

Au restaurant

Aimez-vous la cuisine française? En famille, entre amis ou au restaurant, les Français aiment bien les grands repas traditionnels.

On commence par **une entrée (un hors-d'œuvre):**

de la soupe à l'oignon

du pâté

des œufs *(m)* durs

des crudités *(f)*

de la salade de tomates

des escargots *(m)*

Sur la table, il y a aussi...

du sel et du poivre

du pain

de l'eau minérale

Ensuite, on **sert** le plat principal:

DE LA VIANDE

du rosbif

une côte de porc

un bifteck

DU POISSON

du saumon

du thon

DE LA VOLAILLE

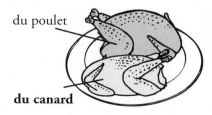
du poulet

du canard

DES FRUITS *(m)* DE MER

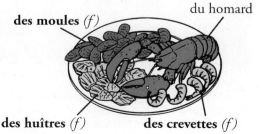
du homard

des moules *(f)*

des huîtres *(f)*

des crevettes *(f)*

---

une entrée *a first course* **un hors-d'œuvre** *an appetizer* **des crudités** (f) *raw vegetables* **sert** (**servir** *to serve*) **de la viande** *meat* **du poisson** *fish* **du thon** *tuna* **de la volaille** *poultry* **du canard** *duck* **des fruits** (m) **de mer** *shellfish* **des moules** (f) *mussels* **des huîtres** (f) *oysters* **des crevettes** (f) *shrimp*

Le plat principal **comprend** aussi **du riz** et des légumes *(m)*:

des pommes de terre *(f)*

des haricots verts

des petits pois

On sert généralement la salade verte après le plat principal. On sert le fromage après ou avec la salade.

une salade

du fromage

On finit le repas avec des fruits—ou un dessert.

de la tarte aux pommes

de la glace à la vanille

du gâteau au chocolat

des fruits *(m)*

un yaourt

Pour finir, on sert le café. Prenez-vous **du sucre,** du lait ou de la crème dans votre café?

du café

Vocabulaire supplémentaire

bleu(e) *very rare*
saignant(e) *rare*
à point *medium rare*
cuit(e) *medium*
bien cuit(e) *well-done*
végétarien(ne) *vegetarian*
végétalien(ne) *vegan*
D'AUTRES PLATS *(dishes):*
  de l'agneau *(m) lamb*
  du bifteck haché *ground meat*
  des coquilles St-Jacques *(f) scallops*
  de la dinde *turkey*
  du rôti de porc *pork roast*
  de la sole *sole*
  de la truite *trout*
  du veau *veal*
POUR METTRE LA TABLE *(to set the table):*
  une assiette *a plate*
  un bol *a bowl*
  un couteau *a knife*
  une cuillère (cuiller) *a spoon*
  une fourchette *a fork*
  une nappe *a tablecloth*
  une serviette *a napkin*
  une tasse *a cup*
  un verre *a glass*
Pour une liste de fruits et de légumes, voir la page 315.

Prononciation

CD 3-24

Le **h** aspiré

In French, **h** is never pronounced and there is usually liaison and elision before it.

J'aime les <u>z</u> huîtres.　　　Il y a beaucoup **d'**huile *(oil)* dans la salade.

Before a few words beginning with **h,** there is no liaison or elision, even though the **h** is silent. These words are said to begin with **h aspiré.** In vocabulary lists, they are indicated by an asterisk (*). The following words have **h aspiré: le homard, les haricots, les hors-d'œuvre.** English words that begin with *h* often have an **h aspiré** when used in French: **les hot-dogs, les hamburgers.**

---

comprend (comprendre *to include*)　**du riz** *rice*　**du sucre** *sugar*

Note *culturelle*

Dans un restaurant français, on peut commander «à la carte», ce qui permet de choisir *(which allows one to choose)* les plats qu'on préfère, ou on peut choisir un menu «à prix fixe». Dans ce cas, on a un choix plus limité mais à un prix plus raisonnable. Regardez la carte à la page 309. Choisissez *(Choose)* une entrée, un plat principal et un dessert et faites le total. Comparez le prix de votre repas à la carte avec le prix des menus à prix fixe (à la page 308). Est-il moins cher de commander un menu à prix fixe ou de commander à la carte? Est-ce qu'il y a des restaurants chez vous qui servent des menus à prix fixe?

André a invité Rosalie au restaurant Maraîchers. Regardez le menu de ce restaurant aux pages 308–309.

CD 3-25

am-euu-riez

LE SERVEUR: Bonsoir, monsieur. Bonsoir, madame. Aimeriez-vous **un apéritif** avant de commander?

ANDRÉ: Rosalie?

ROSALIE: Non, merci, pas ce soir.

ANDRÉ: Pour moi non plus.

LE SERVEUR: Et pour dîner? Est-ce que vous avez décidé?

ANDRÉ: Nous allons prendre le menu à 22 euros.

LE SERVEUR: Très bien, monsieur. Et qu'est-ce que vous désirez **comme** entrée?

ANDRÉ: Pour madame, le saumon fumé, s'il vous plaît. Et pour moi, les huîtres.

LE SERVEUR: Et comme plat principal?

ROSALIE: **La raie** pour moi, s'il vous plaît.

ANDRÉ: Et pour moi, **le pavé de saumon.**

LE SERVEUR: Bien, monsieur. Et comme boisson?

Bootay

ANDRÉ: Une carafe de vin blanc et **une bouteille d'**eau minérale.

LE SERVEUR: Évian ou Perrier?

ROSALIE: L'Évian, s'il vous plaît.

LE SERVEUR: Très bien, madame.

A. Préférences.

Demandez à votre partenaire ce qu'il/qu'elle aime mieux. Pour répondre *neither... nor...,* utilisez **ne... ni... ni...** comme dans l'exemple.

EXEMPLE la viande ou le poisson
— **Est-ce que tu aimes mieux la viande ou le poisson?**
— **J'aime mieux la viande. / J'aime les deux. / Je n'aime ni la viande ni le poisson.**

1. la viande rouge ou la volaille
2. les légumes ou la viande
3. la volaille ou le poisson
4. le poisson ou les fruits de mer
5. les crudités ou la salade verte
6. les pommes de terre ou le riz
7. les haricots verts ou les petits pois
8. les escargots ou les œufs durs
9. le gâteau, la glace ou la tarte
10. les crevettes ou le homard

B. Aujourd'hui on sert...

Voilà ce qu'on sert aujourd'hui. Regardez la liste et indiquez ce qu'il y a par catégorie.

de l'eau minérale   du vin   du canard   du thon
des crevettes   des huîtres
des petits pois   des pommes de terre   du gâteau
de la tarte aux pommes   des côtes de porc   du bifteck
du pâté   des œufs durs   du poulet

EXEMPLE viande
Comme viande, il y a des côtes de porc et...

1. entrée
2. volaille
3. viande
4. poisson
5. dessert
6. légume
7. boisson
8. fruits de mer

---

un serveur (une serveuse) *a server* **un apéritif** *a before-dinner drink* **comme** *for, as a* **la raie** *skate, rayfish* **le pavé de saumon** *salmon steak* **une bouteille de** *a bottle of*

C. Catégories logiques. Quel mot ne va pas logiquement avec les autres? Pourquoi?

EXEMPLE le thé, le jus de fruit, le sel, le lait, l'eau
Le sel, parce que ce n'est pas une boisson.

1. le pain, les petits pois, les pommes de terre, les haricots verts
2. le gâteau au chocolat, le poivre, la tarte aux pommes, la glace
3. la salade de tomates, le pâté, la soupe à l'oignon, le rosbif
4. le déjeuner, le dîner, le petit déjeuner, le sel
5. le homard, le rosbif, les crevettes, les huîtres, les moules
6. les pommes de terre, les petits pois, les haricots verts, le gâteau

D. Chez les Français. Voici les résultats de quelques sondages[1] sur la cuisine et les habitudes des Français. Devinez lequel des chiffres entre parenthèses va dans chaque blanc.

1. (27% [pour cent], 27%, 20%, 14%, 3%)
   _____ des Français préfèrent le café noir, _____ le préfèrent avec du lait, _____ le préfèrent avec du sucre, _____ l'aiment avec de la vanille ou de la noisette *(hazelnut)* et _____ n'aiment pas le café.

2. (45%, 41%, 9%)
   Quand les Français préparent un grand dîner, _____ préfèrent préparer l'entrée, _____ préfèrent préparer le plat principal et _____ le dessert.

3. (29%, 23%, 19%, 15%, 4%)
   _____ des Français mangent la salade verte pendant qu'ils prennent le fromage, _____ la prennent en entrée, _____ avant le fromage, _____ avec le plat principal et _____ à tout moment.

4. (43%, 17%, 13%, 10%, 8%, 8%, 2%)
   Pour terminer un repas, _____ des Français prennent un yaourt ou un fromage blanc *(a creamy soft cheese)*, _____ un fruit, _____ un fromage, _____ une crème dessert, _____ du chocolat, _____ du gâteau ou de la tarte et _____ ne prennent rien.

5. (23%, 18%, 13%, 12%, 12%, 9%, 7%, 6%)
   _____ des Français préfèrent la glace à la vanille, _____ la glace au chocolat, _____ à la fraise, _____ à la menthe, _____ au café, _____ à la pistache, _____ au coco et _____ au rhum et raisin.

Maintenant, dites vos préférences pour chaque question.

E. Un dîner. Voici ce que Rosalie a mangé hier soir. Qu'est-ce qu'elle a mangé? Dans quel ordre? Et vous? Qu'est-ce que vous avez mangé hier soir? Dans quel ordre?

F. Conversation. Avec deux camarades de classe, relisez à haute voix la conversation à la page précédente. Ensuite, imaginez que vous dînez au restaurant Maraîchers avec un(e) ami(e). Commandez un repas complet. Le (La) troisième camarade de classe va jouer le rôle du serveur (de la serveuse).

You can find a list of the new words from the vocabulary and grammar sections of this *Compétence* on page 342 and a recording of this list on track 3-26 of your *Text Audio CD*.
CD 3-26

---

[1]In this chapter, there are several polls about French eating habits and food preferences. They are all from *Le Journal des Femmes* on the website **www.linternaute.com**. There you can find several recipes in French, as well as numerous easy-to-read polls on French eating habits.

37 BISTROT D'ADRIAN 37
RESTAURANT
MARAÎCHERS

Le Bistrot - 15 €.
Service 15% Compris

*Adrian vous propose son petit Menu Bistrot
composé uniquement de produits frais de saison*

Servis Jusqu'à 23 H.

Les Maraîchers - 22 €.
Service 15% Compris

*Les plus beaux produits du Terroir sélectionnés
et cuisinés dans la grande tradition des Maraîchers*

Première Assiette

9 Huîtres "Fines de Claires n°3" Sur lit de glace
Assiette de Coquillages farcis à l'ail
Cocotte de moules marinières
Salade aux Lardons, Oeuf poché
Terrine de canard maison, au poivre vert
Plateau de fruits de mer "l'écailler" + 10 €

Deuxième Assiette

Brochette de poissons, beurre blanc
Moules de pays, frites
Sardines grillées aux herbes
Langue de boeuf, sauce piquante
Poêlée de Rognon de boeuf, flambée au cognac
Bavette poêlée à la fondue d'oignons

Troisième Assiette

Crème Caramel
Fraises au vin ou Fraises au sucre
Feuillantine aux pommes
Glace et sorbet artisanaux
Ile flottante
Coupe normande

**Arrivage Journalier
de Poissons, d'Huîtres et de Fruits de Mer**

Première Assiette

12 Huîtres "Fines de Claires n°3" Sur lit de glace
Saumon fumé par nos soins, Toasts chauds
Poêlon de 12 Escargots de Bourgogne à l'ail
Beignets de Langoustines, Sauce tartare
Salade de cervelle d'agneau poêlée
Plateau de fruits de mer "l'écailler" + 10 €

Deuxième Assiette

Aile de Raie capucine
Daurade entière au lard fumé
Pavé de Saumon Rôti, beurre de moules
Filet de Canard à la Rouennaise
Andouillette à la ficelle "du Père Tafournel"
Faux-filet grillé ou Sauce Poivre

Troisième Assiette

Salade de Saison, ou plateau de fromages

Quatrième Assiette

Tarte tatin chaude, crème fraîche
Bavarois ananas coco
Symphonie aux trois chocolats
Feuillantine aux fraises ou Fraises Melba
Glace et Sorbet artisanaux
Crème Brûlée

depuis 1912

B. BEUNEICHE

La Carte
Service 15% Compris

Nos Huîtres et Fruits de Mer (Arrivage Journalier)

12 Huîtres "Fines de claires" Sur lit deglace n°3 "14€" n°2 "16€"

12 Huîtres "Spéciales St Vaast" Sur lit de glace n°3 "15€" n°2 "17€"

Plateau de fruits de mer "L'Écailler" 18€ "Le marayeur" 30€ "Le Royal" 60€ 1 ou 2 personnes avec 1 Homard frais

Fraîcheur du Marché & Préparations Maison

Soupe de poissons maison, sa rouille et ses croûtons, 6€   Assiette de coquillages farcis 6€

Moules à la crème 7€ – Salade aux Lardons, œuf poché 6€   Terrine de canard maison au poivre 6€

Salade de cervelle d'agneau poêlée 8€   Beignets de Langoustines, Sauce Tartare 10€

Saumon fumé par nos soins Toasts chauds 10€   Poêlon de 12 Escargots de Bourgogne à l'ail 10€

Poissons Frais d'Arrivage

— Brochette de poissons frais, beurre Blanc 7,50€ Moules de pays frites 7,50€

— Sardines grillées aux herbes 7,50€ Pavé de Saumon Rôti, Beurre de Moules 10,50€

— Aile de Raie capucine 10,50€ Daurade entière au lard fumé 10,50€

— Sole Meunière ou Sole Normande 19€

Traditionnels & Spécialités

Langue de Bœuf, sauce piquante 7,50€   Tête de veau Ravigote 7,50€ Bavette poêlée
à la fondue d'oignons 7,50€ Poêlée de Rognon de bœuf Flambée au cognac 7,50€ Faux Filet
Grillé ou Sauce Poivre 10,50€ Filet de canard à la Rouennaise 10,50€ Andouillette à la ficelle 10,50€
Cœur de Filet au Poivre flambé au calvados 15€ Chateaubriand Grillé Beurre Persillé 14,50€

Desserts

Île flottante au caramel 4€   Crème au Caramel 4€   Baiser de vierge 5€   Glace et Sorbet   Plateau de Fromages 5,50€

artisanaux 5€ Fraises au vin ou sucrées 5€ After eight 5€   Coupe normande 5€ Feuillantine aux

Pommes 5,50€ Tarte Tatin crème fraîche 5,50€ Crème Brûlée 5,50€ Bavarois ananas coco 5,50€

Feuillantine aux fraises 6€   Fraises Melba 6€   Symphonie aux trois chocolats 6,50€

Pour vérifier

1. How do you express the idea of *some* in French? What are the forms of the partitive and when do you use each? Can you drop the word for *some* or *any* in French, as you can in English?

2. In what two circumstances do you use **de** instead of the partitive?

Talking about what you eat

Le partitif

To express the idea of *some* or *any*, use the partitive article (**du, de la, de l', des**).

MASCULINE SINGULAR BEGINNING WITH A CONSONANT SOUND	FEMININE SINGULAR BEGINNING WITH A CONSONANT SOUND	SINGULAR NOUNS BEGINNING WITH A VOWEL SOUND	ALL PLURAL NOUNS
du pain	de la glace	de l'eau	des fruits

The words *some* or *any* may be left out in English, but the partitive article must be used in French.

The partitive article becomes **de (d'):**

- after negated verbs (except after the verb **être**).

| Je voudrais **du café.** | *I'd like (some) coffee.* |
| Tu **ne** veux **pas de café**? | *Don't you want (any) coffee?* |

- after expressions of quantity like **beaucoup, combien,** and **trop.**

| J'ai acheté **trop de café.** | *I bought too much coffee.* |

A. Qu'est-ce qu'on sert? Demandez à votre partenaire ce qu'on sert pour chaque plat en France.

> **EXEMPLE** Comme entrée...
> du riz, de la soupe, du gâteau ou de la glace?
> — **Comme entrée, est-ce qu'on sert du riz, de la soupe, du gâteau ou de la glace?**
> — **On sert de la soupe.**

Comme entrée...
1. des œufs durs, des petits pois ou de la tarte?
2. des haricots verts, de la salade de tomates ou du rosbif?

Comme plat principal...
1. du pâté, du saumon ou de la salade verte?
2. du gâteau, des crevettes ou des œufs durs?

Comme légume...
1. des petits pois, des huîtres ou du rosbif?
2. des pommes, de la volaille ou des pommes de terre?

Après le plat principal...
1. de la salade verte, des escargots ou de la soupe?
2. des œufs durs, des fruits de mer ou du fromage?

B. Je prends... Dites si vous prenez souvent les choses suivantes.

> **EXEMPLE** vin
> **Je prends souvent (rarement) du vin.**
> **Je ne prends jamais de vin.**

| 1. pain | 3. eau minérale | 5. crevettes | 7. volaille |
| 2. œufs | 4. viande rouge | 6. poisson | 8. soupe |

C. Comparaisons. Indiquez si les Français prennent souvent ces choses comme entrée, comme plat principal, comme boisson, comme dessert ou comme légume. Ensuite, dites si vous faites souvent la même chose.

EXEMPLE   pâté
Les Français prennent souvent du pâté comme entrée.
Moi aussi, je prends souvent du pâté comme entrée.
Moi, je ne prends jamais de pâté comme entrée.

1. salade de tomates
2. eau minérale
3. petits pois

4. saumon
5. canard
6. tarte

7. gâteau
8. vin
9. pâté

D. Sur la table. Rose est invitée à une fête où il y a beaucoup à manger et à boire. Voici la table de la salle à manger et la table de la cuisine. Faites des comparaisons entre les deux.

EXEMPLE   **Il y a des chips dans la cuisine et dans la salle à manger.**
Il y a de l'eau minérale dans la salle à manger mais il n'y a pas d'eau minérale dans la cuisine.

la salle à manger   la cuisine

E. Entretien. Interviewez votre partenaire.

1. Qu'est-ce que tu manges souvent le soir? Qu'est-ce que tu aimes boire le soir? Qu'est-ce que tu as mangé hier soir?
2. Que préfères-tu manger à midi? (Une salade, un sandwich ou un hamburger?)
3. Est-ce que tu aimes manger dans les fast-foods? Est-ce que tu manges souvent dans un fast-food? Est-ce que tu préfères boire de l'eau ou du coca avec tes repas?

F. Préparatifs. Vous allez inviter des amis chez vous pour un grand repas traditionnel à la française. Avec un(e) partenaire, faites des projets pour ce dîner.

Parlez de:

- quand et où vous allez faire ce dîner et qui vous allez inviter.
- ce que vous allez servir. (Imaginez que tout le monde n'aime pas les mêmes choses et proposez au moins trois possibilités comme entrée, comme plat principal, comme dessert et comme boisson.)

Stratégies et Compréhension auditive

⚛ Pour mieux comprendre: *Planning and predicting*

Since no two cultures are identical, you may sometimes find yourself lacking the cultural knowledge to understand what you hear in French. For example, if the waiter asks «**Évian ou Perrier?**», you will not be able to answer unless you recognize that these are brand names of French mineral waters. In such situations, try to infer what is being asked from the context. Also, when possible, prepare and predict from previous experiences what might be asked or said. For example, before ordering mineral water, glance at the menu to see what kinds are sold.

CD 3-27

A. Pendant le repas. Vous êtes au restaurant. Est-ce qu'on vous dit les choses que vous entendez **avant le repas** ou **à la fin du repas**?

B. Questions. Faites une liste de trois questions qu'un(e) client(e) pose souvent au serveur ou à la serveuse dans un restaurant.

Comprehension auditive: Au restaurant

CD 3-28 Deux touristes sont dans un restaurant français. Écoutez leur conversation. Qu'est-ce qu'ils commandent? Nommez au moins quatre choses.

A. Que demandent-ils? Écoutez encore une fois la conversation au restaurant et écrivez deux questions que les clients posent à la serveuse.

B. Qu'allez-vous choisir? Avec un(e) partenaire, jouez une scène au restaurant entre un serveur (une serveuse) et un(e) client(e). Commandez une entrée, un plat principal, un légume, un dessert et une boisson.

Buying food

Vocabulaire supplémentaire

la confiserie *the candy shop, the confectioner's shop*
la crémerie *the dairy store*
la fromagerie *the cheese shop*
la pâtisserie *the pastry shop*
le marchand de fruits et légumes *the fruit and vegetable market*

Les courses

De plus en plus de Français **font leurs courses** dans les supermarchés et **les grandes surfaces** où on vend de tout. Mais beaucoup préfèrent aller chez les petits **commerçants** du quartier où le service est plus personnalisé.

À la boulangerie, on peut acheter du pain et **des pâtisseries** *(f):*

une baguette   un pain au chocolat   **un pain complet**   une tarte aux **cerises**   une tartelette aux **fraises**

À la boucherie, on achète de la viande:

du poulet   du bœuf   du porc

À la charcuterie, on achète **de la charcuterie** et **des plats préparés:**

du saucisson   du jambon   des saucisses *(f)*   des plats préparés

On achète du poisson et des fruits de mer à la poissonnerie.

Et on va à l'épicerie pour acheter des fruits, des légumes, **des conserves** *(f)* et des produits **surgelés.**

---

faire les courses *to go grocery shopping*   **une grande surface** *a superstore*   **un(e) commerçant(e)** *a shopkeeper*   **une pâtisserie** *a pastry*   **un pain complet** *a loaf of whole-grain bread*   **une cerise** *a cherry*   **une fraise** *a strawberry*   **de la charcuterie** *deli meats, cold cuts*   **un plat préparé** *a ready-to-serve dish*   **des conserves** *(f) canned goods*   **surgelé(e)** *frozen*

Beaucoup de Français **disent** que pour avoir un bon **choix** de légumes et de fruits vraiment **frais, il faut** aller au marché.

Vocabulaire supplémentaire

LÉGUMES
- des **asperges** (f) asparagus
- une **aubergine** an eggplant
- du **brocoli**
- du **céleri**
- des **champignons** (m) mushrooms
- du **chou** cabbage
- du **chou-fleur** cauliflower
- des **choux de Bruxelles** (m) Brussels sprouts
- un **concombre** a cucumber
- une **courgette** a zucchini
- des **épinards** (m) spinach
- du **maïs** corn

FRUITS
- un **abricot** an apricot
- un **ananas** a pineapple
- des **bleuets** (m) blueberries (Canada)
- un **citron vert** a lime
- des **framboises** (f) raspberries
- un **kiwi**
- une **mandarine** a tangerine
- une **mangue** a mango
- un **melon**
- des **myrtilles** (f) blueberries (France)
- une **nectarine**
- un **pamplemousse** a grapefruit
- une **pastèque** a watermelon
- une **prune** a plum
- un **pruneau** a prune
- des **raisins secs** (m) raisins

Au marché, on peut acheter:

des oranges *(f)*

des poires *(f)*

des bananes *(f)*

des pêches *(f)*

du raisin

des laitues *(f)*

des oignons *(m)*

des carottes *(f)*

---

disent (**dire** *to say, to tell*)   **un choix** *a choice*   **frais (fraîche)** *fresh*   **il faut** *it is necessary, one needs, one must*
une laitue *a head of lettuce*

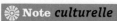
CD 3-29 Rosalie fait ses courses au marché.

ROSALIE:	Bonjour, monsieur.
LE MARCHAND:	Bonjour, madame. **Qu'est-ce qu'il vous faut aujourd'hui?**
ROSALIE:	Euh... voyons... un kilo de pommes de terre, **une livre** de tomates... Vous avez des haricots verts?
LE MARCHAND:	Non, madame, pas aujourd'hui. Mais j'ai des petits pois. Regardez comme ils sont beaux.
ROSALIE:	Non, merci, pas de petits pois aujourd'hui.
LE MARCHAND:	Alors, qu'est-ce que je peux vous proposer d'autre?
ROSALIE:	Donnez-moi aussi 500 grammes de fraises.
LE MARCHAND:	Et voilà, 500 grammes. Et avec ça?
ROSALIE:	C'est tout, merci. Ça fait combien?
LE MARCHAND:	Voilà... Alors, un kilo de pommes de terre —1,20 €, une livre de tomates —1,36 € et 500 grammes de fraises —1,50 €. Ça fait 4,06 €.
ROSALIE:	Voici 5 euros.
LE MARCHAND:	Et voici votre monnaie. Merci, madame, et à bientôt!
ROSALIE:	Merci. Au revoir, monsieur.

A. Devinettes. Qu'est-ce que c'est?

EXEMPLE   C'est un fruit rond, orange et plein de vitamine C.
C'est une orange.

1. C'est le légume préféré de Bugs Bunny.
2. C'est un fruit long et jaune que les chimpanzés adorent.
3. Beaucoup de gens pensent que c'est un légume, mais en réalité, c'est un fruit. Ce fruit est rond et rouge. On le sert souvent en salade.
4. C'est un fruit qui peut être jaune, rouge ou vert. On peut le manger cru *(raw)*, mais on peut aussi faire des gâteaux, des tartes, du jus ou du cidre avec.
5. C'est le légume vert qui est l'ingrédient principal d'une salade.
6. On utilise ce fruit pour faire du vin.
7. Ce sont de petits légumes ronds et verts.
8. Ce sont de petits fruits rouges qu'on utilise souvent pour faire une tarte.

B. C'est... Est-ce que chacun des aliments suivants est **un légume, un plat préparé, une viande, un fruit, de la charcuterie, un fruit de mer** ou **un produit surgelé**?

EXEMPLE   le rosbif
Le rosbif, c'est une viande.

1. le saucisson	4. le pâté	7. le bœuf
2. la glace	5. le porc	8. le homard
3. le raisin	6. la laitue	9. le jambon

C. Dans quel magasin? Dans quel magasin est-ce qu'on vend ces produits?

EXEMPLE   du rosbif
On vend du rosbif à la boucherie.

1. de la viande	5. des tartes	9. des produits surgelés
2. des plats préparés	6. du saucisson	10. des pommes de terre
3. des crevettes	7. du poulet	11. des conserves
4. des oignons	8. des huîtres	12. du pain

Qu'est-ce qu'il vous faut aujourd'hui? *What do you need today?*   **une livre** *half a kilo (≈ a pound)*

D. Qu'est-ce qu'on vend? Nommez au moins quatre choses qu'on vend dans les endroits suivants.

EXEMPLE   à la charcuterie
             À la charcuterie, on vend du jambon...

à la charcuterie	à l'épicerie
à la boucherie	à la boulangerie
au marché	à la poissonnerie

À la charcuterie

E. Les préférences des Français. D'après des sondages *(surveys)*, comment est-ce que les Français ont répondu aux questions suivantes, à votre avis? Devinez l'ordre de préférence des aliments donnés entre parenthèses.

1. Quel fruit attendez-vous avec impatience au marché à l'arrivée de la belle saison?
   (la fraise, la pêche, le raisin, la cerise, le melon)
2. Quel est votre produit préféré à la charcuterie?
   (le jambon cuit *[cooked]*, le jambon cru *[raw ham, prosciutto]*, le pâté, le saucisson)
3. Quels sont vos fruits de mer préférés à la poissonnerie?
   (les huîtres, le crabe, les langoustines *[scampi]*, les crevettes)
4. À la boulangerie, quelle est votre viennoiserie *(sweet bread)* préférée?
   (le pain aux raisins, le pain au chocolat, le chausson aux pommes *[apple turnover]*, le croissant)
5. Quelle est votre viande préférée?
   (le poulet, le porc, le bœuf, le veau *[veal]*, le canard, l'agneau *[lamb]*)

F. Entretien. Interviewez votre partenaire.

1. Aimes-tu faire les courses? Combien de fois par semaine est-ce que tu fais les courses? Où est-ce que tu fais tes courses d'habitude? Est-ce que tu achètes quelquefois des choses chez les petits commerçants?
2. En France, où est-ce qu'on achète du pain? des plats préparés? des fruits et des légumes frais? Qu'est-ce qu'on vend à l'épicerie? à la boulangerie? à la poissonnerie?
3. Aimes-tu les fruits? les légumes? Préfères-tu les fruits ou les légumes? Quels légumes préfères-tu? Quels légumes est-ce que tu n'aimes pas? Quels fruits préfères-tu? Quels fruits est-ce que tu n'aimes pas?

G. Conversation. Avec un(e) partenaire, relisez à haute voix la conversation à la page précédente. Ensuite, imaginez que vous êtes à la boulangerie. Achetez ce que vous voudriez. (Déterminez un prix logique en euros pour chaque chose.)

CD 3-30 You can find a list of the new words from the vocabulary and grammar sections of this ***Compétence*** on page 342 and a recording of this list on track 3-30 of your *Text Audio CD.*

Pour vérifier

What word follows quantity expressions before nouns? Do you use **de** or **des** after a quantity expression followed by a plural noun?

Saying how much

Les expressions de quantité

Use these expressions to specify how much you want at the market or in a restaurant.

un verre de	*a glass of*	une boîte de	*a box of, a can of*
un litre de	*a liter of*	un pot de	*a jar of*
une carafe de	*a carafe of*	un paquet de	*a bag of, a sack of*
une bouteille de	*a bottle of*	une douzaine de	*a dozen*

une tranche de	*a slice of*	300 grammes de	*300 grams of*
un morceau de	*a piece of*	un kilo (et demi) de	*a kilo (and a half) of*
		une livre de	*a half a kilo (1.1 pounds of)*

After quantity expressions like those above, use **de (d')** before a noun instead of **du, de la, de l',** or **des.** This is also true for less specific quantities such as:

combien de	*how much, how many*
(un) peu de	*(a) little*
assez de	*enough*
beaucoup de	*a lot of*
trop de	*too much, too many*
beaucoup trop de	*much too much, much too many*
plus de	*more*
moins de	*less*

J'ai acheté une bouteille **de** vin rouge, un kilo **de** viande et beaucoup **de** légumes!

A. C'est assez? Dans chaque situation, est-ce que la quantité indiquée est suffisante?

EXEMPLE Vous prenez le petit déjeuner seul(e) le matin et il y a un verre de lait dans le réfrigérateur.

Il y a trop de lait. / Il y a assez de lait. / Il y a trop peu de lait.

beaucoup trop	trop	assez	trop peu

1. Vous êtes quatre au restaurant et il y a une demi-bouteille d'eau.
2. Vous allez préparer une salade de tomates pour deux personnes. Vous avez un kilo de tomates.
3. Vous allez faire une omelette pour deux personnes et vous avez un seul œuf.
4. C'est le matin et il y a un verre de lait dans le réfrigérateur chez vous.
5. Vous dînez seul(e) au restaurant et il y a trois carafes d'eau.
6. Vous voulez préparer des carottes pour six personnes et vous avez deux carottes.

B. Mon régime. Quelle quantité de ces aliments mangez-vous?

EXEMPLE   poisson
> **Je mange peu de poisson. / Je ne mange jamais de poisson.**

1. raisin
2. pêches
3. huîtres
4. poulet
5. bananes
6. crevettes
7. produits surgelés
8. viande rouge
9. salade verte

C. Je voudrais... Précisez quelque chose de logique pour chacune des quantités proposées.

Je voudrais...

1. une bouteille de
2. un paquet de
3. une boîte de
4. une livre de
5. deux kilos de
6. un morceau de
7. un litre de
8. dix tranches de

thon	cerises	jambon
vin	tomates	fromage
jus de fruit	rosbif	lait
sel	sucre	riz

D. Donnez-moi... Demandez les quantités indiquées des provisions suivantes.

EXEMPLE **Une bouteille de vin, s'il vous plaît.**

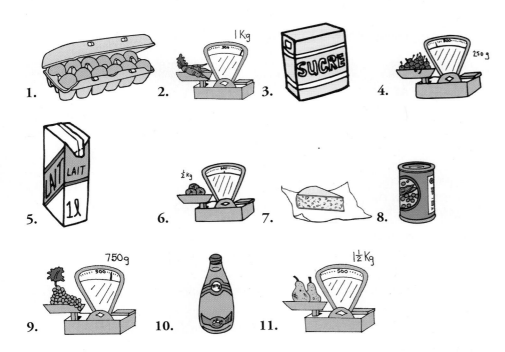

1. 2. 3. 4.

5. 6. 7. 8.

9. 10. 11.

E. Au marché. Imaginez que vous préparez un dîner pour quatre amis. Décidez ce que vous voulez servir et achetez les provisions au marché. Un(e) camarade de classe va jouer le rôle du/de la marchand(e).

Pour vérifier

1. Which article do you use to say *a* in French? Which articles do you use to express the idea of *some* or *any*?

2. Which article do you use to say *the*? to talk about likes, dislikes, and preferences? to make statements about entire categories?

3. Which articles change to **de**? When do they make this change? Which articles never change?

Talking about foods

L'usage des articles

Each article you use with a noun conveys a different meaning. **Un** and **une** mean *a*, whereas **du, de la, de l',** and **des** mean *some* or *any*.

Vous voulez **une** tarte?
*Do you want **a** pie?*
(This refers to a whole pie.)

Vous voulez **de la** tarte?
*Do you want **(some)** pie?*
(This refers to a portion or serving.)

The indefinite article (**un, une, des**) and the partitive (**du, de la, de l'**) change to **de (d')** after expressions of quantity, such as **trop, beaucoup, un kilo, une bouteille...,** and after most negated verbs.

Il ne veut pas **de** dessert parce qu'il a mangé trop **de** chocolats.

Remember to use the definite article (**le, la, l', les**) to say *the,* to express likes, dislikes, and preferences, to make statements about entire categories, or to order from a menu. The definite article does *not* change to **de** after a negative or quantity expression.

Le poisson qu'on achète ici est très bon.	*The fish you buy here is very good.*
Je n'aime pas beaucoup **le** poisson.	*I don't like fish very much.*
Le poisson n'a pas beaucoup de calories.	*Fish doesn't have a lot of calories.*
Je vais prendre **le** saumon fumé.	*I'll have the smoked salmon.*

When using **beaucoup, trop,** or **assez** with **aimer** to say how much you do or don't like something, continue to use the definite article **le, la, l',** or **les.**

J'aime **beaucoup le** thé.   J'aime **assez le** café.   Je n'aime pas **trop le** coca.

	AFFIRMATIVE	NEGATIVE
PARTITIVE ARTICLE *to say* some *or* any	Je voudrais **du** café.	Je ne veux pas **de** café.
INDEFINITE ARTICLE *to say* a; *to indicate a whole or several*	Je voudrais **un** café.	Je ne veux pas **de** café.
DE WITH AN EXPRESSION OF QUANTITY	Je voudrais un kilo **de** café.	Je n'ai pas acheté beaucoup **de** café.
DEFINITE ARTICLE *to say* the; *to express likes; to make general statements about categories*	J'aime beaucoup **le** café.	Je n'aime pas **le** café.

A. Manges-tu bien? Demandez à votre partenaire s'il/si elle mange souvent les choses suivantes.

EXEMPLE   pâté
　　　　　　　—**Manges-tu souvent du pâté?**
　　　　　　　—**Je mange rarement du pâté. / Je ne mange jamais de pâté.**

1. escargots	**4.** viande rouge	**7.** glace
2. tarte	**5.** poulet	**8.** tarte aux pommes
3. légumes	**6.** crudités	**9.** carottes

Maintenant, demandez à votre partenaire s'il/si elle aime ces mêmes choses.

EXEMPLE pâté

—**Aimes-tu le pâté?**

—**J'aime assez le pâté. / Je n'aime pas le pâté.**

B. Vos préférences. Dites si vous achetez souvent les choses suivantes et expliquez pourquoi.

EXEMPLE café

J'achète souvent du café parce que j'aime le café.

Je n'achète jamais de café parce que je n'aime pas le café.

1. fromage	**4.** raisin	**7.** huîtres
2. bananes	**5.** eau minérale	**8.** jus de fruit
3. viande rouge	**6.** jambon	**9.** crevettes

C. Vos goûts. Complétez les phrases suivantes avec le nom d'un aliment (food) ou d'une boisson logique. Utilisez les articles convenables.

1. Moi, j'adore...

2. J'aime bien...

3. Comme viande, je mange souvent...

4. Chez moi, il n'y a jamais...

5. Pour le déjeuner, je prends souvent...

6. La dernière fois que je suis allé(e) au restaurant, j'ai mangé...

D. Ce soir. Rosalie parle du dîner qu'elle va préparer ce soir. Complétez ses phrases avec l'article convenable: **un, une, du, de la, de l', des, le, la, l', les** ou **de**.

Ce soir, je vais servir _____1_____ soupe de légumes, _____2_____ poulet, _____3_____ riz et _____4_____ petits pois. Et comme dessert, je pense préparer _____5_____ tarte aux cerises. Moi, je préfère _____6_____ gâteau, mais André aime beaucoup _____7_____ tarte! Cet après-midi, je dois aller acheter _____8_____ sucre, 500 grammes _____9_____ cerises et beaucoup _____10_____ légumes. Il y a un marché tout près où _____11_____ légumes sont toujours très frais! Je ne mets pas _____12_____ oignons dans la soupe parce qu'André n'aime pas _____13_____ oignons. C'est dommage parce que _____14_____ oignons sont bons pour la santé (health).

E. Entretien. Interviewez votre partenaire.

1. Quels fruits de mer aimes-tu? Quelles viandes? Est-ce que tu manges plus de fruits de mer ou plus de viande?

2. Manges-tu plus souvent des fruits ou des légumes? Quel fruit préfères-tu? Quel légume préfères-tu? Quels fruits et légumes est-ce que tu n'aimes pas? Est-ce que tu achètes plus de légumes surgelés, frais ou en conserve?

3. Tu aimes les desserts? Est-ce que tu préfères le gâteau ou la tarte? la glace au chocolat ou la glace à la vanille? Est-ce que tu manges souvent un dessert quand tu vas au restaurant? Quel dessert prends-tu le plus souvent?

4. À la maison, qu'est-ce que tu manges la plupart du temps? Qu'est-ce que tu ne manges jamais? Pourquoi?

Talking about meals

✳ Note *culturelle*

Seulement 8% des Français ne prennent pas de petit déjeuner. Parmi ceux qui mangent le matin, la plus grande majorité (64%) mangent à la française (pain ou croissant et boisson). 14% prennent seulement une boisson.

En France, les repas se prennent de moins en moins à heures fixes et les familles mangent moins souvent ensemble. Les Français mangent de plus en plus sans se mettre à table: au travail, dans la rue, en voiture ou dans les transports publics, au parc. En effet, à midi, 32% des Français mangent sans se mettre à table. Est-ce que la situation est la même chez vous?

Les repas

En France, le petit déjeuner est généralement un repas **léger.** On prend:

du café au lait   du thé

des tartines (f) ou des croissants (m)

du chocolat   du beurre    de la confiture

De plus en plus de Français, **surtout** les jeunes, prennent aussi des céréales le matin.

Les Américains et les Canadiens prennent souvent un petit déjeuner plus **copieux.** Ils prennent:

des œufs au bacon   des céréales (f)   du pain grillé   des fruits

À midi, certains Français prennent un déjeuner complet. D'autres prennent un repas rapide. Dans les cafés, les fast-foods et les self-services, on peut manger:

    une soupe

    une omelette

    un steak-frites

    une salade

    un hamburger

    une pizza

    un sandwich

Les gens qui prennent un repas rapide à midi mangent souvent un repas plus complet le soir. **Ceux** qui mangent un repas plus copieux à midi mangent **seulement** de la soupe, des légumes, de la charcuterie, une salade, du fromage ou une omelette comme dîner.

---

léger (légère) *light*   **une tartine** *bread with butter and jelly*   **surtout** *especially*   **copieux (copieuse)** *copious, large*
un steak-frites *steak and fries*   **Ceux (Celles)** *Those*   **seulement** *only*

Rose prépare le petit déjeuner avec sa cousine Lucie.

LUCIE: Tu as faim? Je peux te faire des œufs au bacon si tu veux—un vrai petit déjeuner à l'américaine.

ROSE: Merci, c'est gentil, mais je mange très peu le matin. **Pourtant je prendrais volontiers** des céréales et du thé si tu **en** as.

LUCIE: Ah, je regrette... il **n'y a plus** de thé. Mais il y a du café. Tu en veux?

ROSE: Oui, je veux bien. Et toi? Qu'est-ce que tu vas prendre?

LUCIE: Le matin, **je bois** toujours du chocolat chaud et quelquefois je prends des tartines.

ROSE: Oh, regarde! **Il n'y a presque plus** de pain.

LUCIE: Mais **si!** Il y a **encore** une baguette, **là.**

Vocabulaire supplémentaire

des gaufres (f) waffles
des muffins (m) anglais
des pancakes (m)
des petites saucisses breakfast sausages
du sirop d'érable maple syrup
des flocons (m) **d'avoine** oatmeal
une barre de céréales
du pain perdu French toast

A. Vrai ou faux? Corrigez les phrases fausses.

1. En France, on prend plus souvent des œufs le soir ou à midi que le matin.
2. Les Français prennent un repas copieux le matin.
3. Beaucoup de Français prennent seulement du pain et du café le matin.
4. Certains, surtout les jeunes, aiment prendre des céréales.

B. Chez nous. Aux États-Unis et au Canada, à quel(s) repas mange-t-on le plus souvent ces choses: **au petit déjeuner, au déjeuner** ou **au dîner?**

EXEMPLE une omelette
On mange plus souvent une omelette au petit déjeuner.

1. des croissants	4. un hamburger	7. du saumon
2. des céréales	5. de la soupe	8. des œufs au bacon
3. du poisson	6. du pain grillé	9. des légumes

C. Au petit déjeuner. Devinez comment le plus grand nombre de Français ont répondu aux questions suivantes dans des sondages. Après, faites un sondage des étudiants de votre classe.

1. Combien de temps prenez-vous pour le petit déjeuner tous les matins? (5 minutes / de 10 à 15 minutes / de 20 à 30 minutes / Je ne prends pas de petit déjeuner.)
2. Que mangez-vous au petit déjeuner? (des céréales / du pain ou des biscottes *[melba toast]* / des viennoiseries *[sweet breads]* / des biscuits *[cookies, crackers]* / des œufs / rien)
3. Quelle est votre confiture préférée? (cerises / rhubarbe / orange / fraises / abricots / framboises *[raspberry]* / myrtilles *[blueberry]* / mûres *[blackberry]*)
4. Qu'est-ce que vous aimez manger quand vous avez un peu faim entre les repas? (un fruit / des chips / du fromage / des biscuits / du yaourt ou de la compote *[stewed fruit]*)

D. Conversation. Avec un(e) partenaire, relisez à haute voix la conversation entre Lucie et Rose en haut de la page. Ensuite, imaginez que vous passez des vacances avec un(e) ami(e) français(e). Parlez de ce que vous mangez d'habitude le matin.

CD 3-32 You can find a list of the new words from the vocabulary and grammar sections of this *Compétence* on page 343 and a recording of this list on track 3-32 of your *Text Audio CD*.

Pourtant However **je prendrais volontiers** I would gladly have **en** some, any **ne... plus** no more, no longer **je bois (boire** to drink) **Il n'y a presque plus** There is almost no more **si** yes (in response to a question / statement in the negative) **encore** still, again, more **là** there

Pour vérifier

1. In what three instances do you use the pronoun **en**? How is **en** usually translated in English? Can you omit **en** in French as you often can its equivalent in English?

2. How do you say *to drink* in French? What is the conjugation of this verb? How do you say *I drank some coffee this morning? I used to drink a lot of coffee?*

Saying what you eat and drink

*Le pronom **en** et le verbe **boire***

Use the pronoun **en** *(some, any, of it, of them)* to replace a noun preceded by a partitive article, an expression of quantity, **un, une, des,** or a number. Although the equivalent expression may be omitted in English, **en** is always used in French.

—Tu veux un croissant?	—*Do you want a croissant?*
—Oui, j'**en** veux un.	—*Yes, I want one (of them).*

En is placed *immediately* before the verb. It goes before the infinitive if there is one. If not, it goes before the conjugated verb. In the **passé composé,** it is placed before the auxiliary verb.

—Tu prends du gâteau?

—Oui, je vais **en** prendre. / Oui, j'**en** prends. / Non, merci, j'**en** ai déjà pris.

Use **en** to replace:

- a noun preceded by **de, du, de la, de l',** or **des.**

—Tu veux **du café**?	—*Do you want **some coffee**?*
—Non merci, je n'**en** veux pas.	—*No thanks, I don't want **any**.*

- a noun preceded by an expression of quantity. (In this case, repeat the expression of quantity in the sentence containing **en,** unless it's negative.)

—Vous voulez un kilo **de cerises**?	—*Do you want a kilo **of cherries**?*
—Oui, j'**en** veux un kilo.	—*Yes, I want a kilo **(of them)**.*
Non, je n'**en** veux pas.	*No, I don't want **any**.*

- a noun preceded by **un, une,** or a number. (In this case, include **un, une,** or a number in the sentence containing **en,** unless it's negative.)

—Tu as mangé une **tartelette**?	—*You ate a **tart**?*
—Oui, j'**en** ai mangé une.	—*Yes, I ate one **(of them)**.*
Non, je n'**en** ai pas mangé.	*No, I didn't eat **any**.*

Here is the conjugation of **boire** *(to drink)*.

BOIRE *(to drink)*	
je **bois**	nous **buvons**
tu **bois**	vous **buvez**
il/elle/on **boit**	ils/elles **boivent**
PASSÉ COMPOSÉ: j'**ai bu**	
IMPARFAIT: je **buvais**	

Vous avez bu du vin hier soir?   Je buvais du lait quand j'étais petit.

A. À table. Un(e) ami(e) vous propose les choses suivantes au petit déjeuner. Comment répondez-vous? Utilisez le pronom **en** dans vos réponses.

> **EXEMPLE**   du café
> **—Tu veux du café?**
> **—Non merci, je n'en veux pas. / Oui, j'en veux bien.**

1. du café	**3.** des œufs	**5.** des tartines
2. du thé	**4.** de l'eau	**6.** des céréales

B. Des courses. Voilà la liste de Rosalie pour les courses. Combien va-t-elle acheter de chaque chose? Utilisez le pronom **en** dans vos réponses.

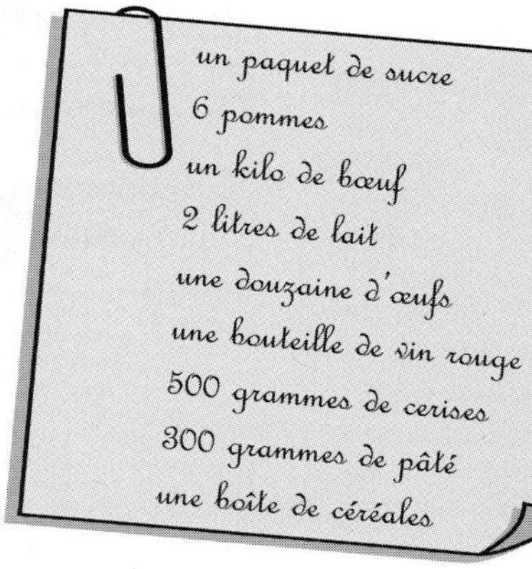

> **EXEMPLE**   du sucre
> **Elle va en acheter un paquet.**

1. des pommes
2. du bœuf
3. du lait
4. des œufs
5. du vin rouge
6. des cerises
7. du pâté
8. des céréales

[handwritten margin note: douzenne]

[shopping list note:]
un paquet de sucre
6 pommes
un kilo de bœuf
2 litres de lait
une douzaine d'œufs
une bouteille de vin rouge
500 grammes de cerises
300 grammes de pâté
une boîte de céréales

C. Et vous? Faites-vous attention à votre santé *(health)*? Répondez à ces questions. Employez le pronom **en.**

> **EXEMPLE**   Vous mangez des œufs?   *(eww)*
> **Oui, j'en mange trop / beaucoup / assez / peu.**
> **Oui, mais je n'en mange pas assez.**
> **Non, je n'en mange pas.**

1. Vous buvez de l'eau?
2. Vous mangez des desserts?
3. Vous faites de l'exercice?
4. Vous mangez des fruits?
5. Vous mangez du poisson?
6. Vous fumez des cigarettes?
7. Vous mangez des légumes?
8. Vous mangez de la viande?

[handwritten margin notes: de-ser spanish; alternatif; Indicatif; une tasse – a cup; du lait de soja; boîter – to limp]

D. Boissons. Complétez les phrases logiquement en utilisant le verbe **boire.**

> **EXEMPLE**   Le matin, je **bois du lait.**

1. Au petit déjeuner, les Français...
2. Au petit déjeuner, les Américains / Canadiens...
3. Le matin, je...
4. Quand j'étais jeune, le matin, je...
5. Ce matin, je (j')...
6. Avec un hamburger, on...
7. Dans cette région, quand il fait chaud, nous...
8. Quand j'ai très soif, je...
9. *[À un(e) camarade de classe]* À une fête, qu'est-ce que tu... ?
10. *[Au professeur]* Est-ce que vous... beaucoup de café?

E. Entretien. Interviewez votre partenaire. Utilisez le pronom **en** dans les réponses.

[handwritten margin note: jeu n'ai deja manger]

1. Manges-tu souvent des légumes? Est-ce que tu en as déjà mangé aujourd'hui? Manges-tu souvent de la viande rouge? En manges-tu tous les jours? Est-ce que tu vas en manger demain?
2. Fais-tu souvent de l'exercice? Combien de fois par semaine est-ce que tu en fais?
3. Est-ce que tu bois du café? En bois-tu trop? Quand est-ce que tu en bois? Et tes amis, est-ce qu'ils en boivent souvent?

1. How do you find the stem of a regular **-ir** verb? What are the endings? What is the conjugation of **grandir**? of **grossir**?

2. What auxiliary do you use in the **passé composé** with the verbs listed here, except with the reflexive verb **se nourrir**? How do you form the past participle? How do you say *I finished*? What is the conjugation of **-ir** verbs in the imperfect?

3. How do you pronounce an initial **s**? a single **s** between vowels? How do you pronounce double **ss**? How can you hear the difference between the singular and plural forms of **-ir** verbs in the present tense?

Talking about choices

Les verbes en -ir

To conjugate regular **-ir** verbs in the present tense, drop the **-ir** and add the following endings. All **-ir** verbs presented here form the **passé composé** with **avoir**, except **se nourrir**.

CHOISIR *(to choose)*	
je chois**is**	nous chois**issons**
tu chois**is**	vous chois**issez**
il/elle/on chois**it**	ils/elles chois**issent**

PASSÉ COMPOSÉ: j'**ai choisi**

IMPARFAIT: je **choisissais**

Note *de vocabulaire*

Notice that some **-ir** verbs are based on a related adjective: (**gros → grossir, grand → grandir**).

 To download a podcast on **-ir** verbs, go to **academic.cengage.com/french**.

Here are some common **-ir** verbs.

choisir (de faire)	*to choose (to do)*
finir (de faire)	*to finish (doing)*
grandir	*to grow (up), to grow taller*
grossir	*to get fatter*
maigrir	*to get thinner, to slim down*
(se) nourrir	*to feed, to nourish, to nurture (oneself)*
obéir (à quelqu'un / à quelque chose)	*to obey (somebody / something)*
réfléchir (à)	*to think (about)*
réussir (à)	*to succeed (at), to pass* [a test]

Prononciation

CD 3-33 *La lettre **s** et les verbes en **-ir***

It can be difficult to remember whether to use one **s** or two when spelling forms of verbs such as **choisir** or **réussir**. Keep in mind that a single **s** between vowels is pronounced like a **z**, and double **ss** is pronounced like an **s**. Initial **s** is always pronounced like **s**.

ils choisissent   nous réussissons   je choisissais   je grossissais

poison / poisson   un désert / un dessert   vous choisissez / vous réussissez

In the present tense, an **s** sound in the ending of **-ir** verbs indicates that you are talking about more than one person.

il grandit / ils grandissent   elle finit / elles finissent   il choisit / ils choisissent

A. Il faut bien choisir. Rosalie parle de ce que chacun choisit de manger. Que dit-elle? Donnez le meilleur choix pour chaque situation.

> **EXEMPLE** Rose veut maigrir. Elle... (de la viande, de la salade)
> Elle **choisit de la salade.**

1. André veut grossir. Il... (de la viande, de la salade)
2. Moi, je veux rester en bonne santé *(healthy)*. Je... (de la glace, des fruits)
3. André et Henri veulent une boisson avec des vitamines. Ils... (du jus de fruit, du café)
4. Rose et moi, nous voulons maigrir. Nous... (des frites, des petits pois)
5. Et toi, Patricia, tu veux être plus forte *(stronger)*? Tu... (du poisson, de la salade)?
6. Et vous, les enfants, vous voulez grandir vite? Vous... (de la viande, du gâteau)?

B. C'est-à-dire... Trouvez une expression équivalente. Utilisez un verbe en **-ir**.

> **EXEMPLE**   Il devient plus mince.
> **Il maigrit.**

1. Tu deviens plus gros.
2. Ils font un choix.
3. Je pense à quelque chose.
4. Les enfants deviennent plus grands.
5. Il a un bon résultat à son examen.
6. Nous terminons quelque chose.

C. Une histoire d'amour. Complétez cette description de la relation de Rosalie et d'André avec la forme correcte des verbes indiqués au présent.

Rosalie est réaliste et elle répète toujours qu'on ne ___1___ (se nourrir) pas d'amour et d'eau fraîche. Cependant *(However),* elle ___2___ (réfléchir) beaucoup à sa vie sentimentale et elle ___3___ (réussir) à trouver le grand amour avec André. Leur amour ___4___ (se nourrir) des plus petites choses, une caresse ou un mot doux *(sweet),* et André ___5___ (choisir) toujours de petits cadeaux *(gifts)* parfaits pour Rosalie. Cet amour ___6___ (grandir) de jour en jour et ils ___7___ (finir) par se marier. Ils ne ___8___ (réfléchir) pas trop aux défauts *(faults)* de l'autre et ils ___9___ (réussir) toujours à avoir un bon sens de l'humour. Ils ___10___ (finir) leur vie ensemble à l'âge de presque cent ans et tous les matins pendant toutes ces années, André ___11___ (choisir) des roses de son jardin pour en faire un bouquet pour Rosalie.

D. En cours de français. Comment est votre cours de français? Dites si les personnes suivantes font les choses indiquées généralement.

> **EXEMPLE**   Le professeur... (choisir des questions très faciles pour l'examen)
> **Généralement, le professeur ne choisit pas de questions très faciles pour l'examen.**

1. Le professeur... (réussir à comprendre les questions des étudiants, finir le cours à l'heure, choisir les mêmes étudiants pour répondre à ses questions)
2. Les étudiants... (finir les devoirs, obéir au prof, réussir à bien parler français)
3. Moi, je... (finir les devoirs, réussir à comprendre la leçon, réfléchir avant de répondre)

Maintenant, dites si ces personnes ont fait ces choses au dernier cours.

> **EXEMPLE**   Le professeur (choisir des questions très faciles pour l'examen)
> **Au dernier cours, le professeur n'a pas choisi de questions très faciles pour l'examen.**

E. Au lycée. Demandez à votre partenaire s'il/si elle faisait généralement les choses suivantes quand il/elle était au lycée.

> **EXEMPLE**   réfléchir avant de répondre
> **—Quand tu étais au lycée, est-ce que tu réfléchissais généralement avant de répondre?**
> **—Oui, je réfléchissais (presque) toujours avant de répondre.**

1. réussir à tous tes cours
2. obéir à tes parents
3. réfléchir à ton avenir *(future)*
4. finir tes devoirs
5. choisir toujours la même chose au déjeuner
6. te nourrir bien

Choosing a healthy lifestyle

La bonne santé

Faites-vous attention à votre santé? **À votre avis,** qu'est-ce qu'il faut faire pour rester en bonne santé?

Pour rester en bonne santé, est-ce qu'**on devrait...**
    manger des plats **sains** et légers?
    manger plus de produits **bios**?
    manger moins de **matières grasses** *(f)*?
    manger plus **lentement**?
    prendre des vitamines?
    éviter l'alcool et le tabac?
    contrôler le stress? (faire du yoga ou de la méditation, parler entre ami[e]s...)

Pour être en forme et pour devenir plus **fort**, est-ce qu'on devrait...
    marcher et **faire des randonnées** *(f)*?
    faire de l'aérobic?
    faire de la muscu(lation)?

 CD 3-34 Patricia demande **des conseils** à Rosalie.

PATRICIA: **Je me sens** toujours fatiguée ces jours-ci. J'ai besoin d'**améliorer** ma santé. Toi, tu as l'air toujours en forme. **Pourrais-tu** me donner des conseils?
ROSALIE: Tu dors assez la nuit?
PATRICIA: Je me couche assez tôt mais je dors très mal. Je me réveille **plusieurs** fois pendant la nuit. Si je pouvais dormir mieux, **je serais** contente.
ROSALIE: Tu devrais boire moins de café pendant la journée. **Tu ferais mieux de** bien manger aussi et de faire de l'exercice régulièrement.
PATRICIA: J'aime bien marcher. Si j'avais plus de temps libre, **j'aimerais** bien faire du sport tous les jours.
ROSALIE: Si tu marchais tous les jours et que tu mangeais mieux, **tu te sentirais sans doute** mieux. Et **n'oublie pas** de boire moins de café et plus d'eau!

---

la santé *health*   **faire attention (à)** *to pay attention (to), to watch out (for)*   **À votre avis** *In your opinion*   **on devrait** *one should*   **sain(e)** *healthy*   **bios (biologiques)** *organic*   **les matières grasses** *(f) fats*   **lentement** *slowly*   **éviter** *to avoid* **fort(e)** *strong*   **marcher** *to walk*   **faire des randonnées** *(f) to go hiking*   **faire de la muscu(lation)** *to do weight training, to do bodybuilding*   **des conseils** *(m) advice*   **Je me sens (se sentir** *to feel)*   **améliorer** *to improve*   **Pourrais-tu** *Could you* **plusieurs** *several*   **je serais** *I would be*   **Tu ferais mieux de** *You would do better to*   **j'aimerais** *I would like*   **tu te sentirais** *you would feel*   **sans doute** *probably*   **n'oublie pas** *don't forget* (**oublier** *to forget*)

A. Des conseils. C'est **un bon conseil** ou **un mauvais conseil** pour la santé?

1. Il faut faire de l'exercice plusieurs fois par semaine.
2. On devrait manger moins de viande rouge et plus de légumes.
3. Il est important de faire de l'aérobic.
4. On devrait éviter les matières grasses.
5. Les plats sains et légers sont bons pour la santé.
6. On peut devenir plus fort si on fait de la muscu.
7. On devrait manger plus vite pour éviter de trop manger.
8. On devrait manger des produits bios.
9. On ferait mieux de rester très stressé, ça donne de l'énergie.
10. Si vous voulez améliorer votre santé, n'oubliez pas de boire assez d'eau.

B. Il faut... Complétez ces phrases. Dites au moins deux choses pour chacune.

1. Pour améliorer sa santé, on devrait...
2. Pour contrôler le stress, on devrait...
3. Pour devenir plus fort, on devrait...
4. Pour se sentir moins fatigué, on devrait...

faire	éviter
obéir	prendre
contrôler	manger

C. Habitudes. Deux amis parlent de ce qu'ils font pour améliorer leur santé. Mettez chaque verbe entre parenthèses à la forme correcte dans le blanc logique.

EXEMPLE Je **maigris** parce que je **choisis** des plats sains et légers.
(choisir, maigrir)

1. Les enfants _____ si on les _____ mal. (grossir, nourrir)
2. Je _____ à ne pas fumer, mais je _____ parce que je mange quand j'ai envie d'une cigarette. (réussir, grossir)
3. Mon meilleur ami _____ parce qu'il _____ toujours des desserts avec beaucoup de sucre. (choisir, grossir)
4. Dans notre famille, nous _____ beaucoup à notre régime (diet): on _____ bien et on _____ rarement le dîner avec un dessert. (réfléchir, finir, se nourrir)
5. Nos enfants _____ toujours et ils _____ tous leurs légumes. (obéir, finir)
6. Tu ne _____ pas à contrôler le stress parce que tu _____ trop à tes problèmes. (réussir, réfléchir)

D. Entretien. Interviewez votre partenaire.

1. Est-ce que tu te sens souvent fatigué(e)? Dors-tu assez? Combien d'heures dors-tu par nuit? Comment est-ce que tu te sens aujourd'hui?
2. Fais-tu attention à ta santé? Que fais-tu pour ta santé?
3. Manges-tu bien? Manges-tu beaucoup de fruits et de légumes? beaucoup de plats sains et légers? beaucoup de produits bios? Est-ce que tu prends des vitamines?
4. Est-ce que tu évites l'alcool ou est-ce que tu en bois? Est-ce que tu fumes?
5. Es-tu stressé(e)? Que fais-tu pour contrôler le stress?
6. Aimes-tu faire de l'exercice? Fais-tu de l'aérobic? de la muscu? des randonnées?

E. Conversation. Avec un(e) partenaire, relisez à haute voix la conversation entre Rosalie et Patricia à la page précédente. Ensuite, imaginez que vous voudriez faire plus attention à votre santé. Demandez des conseils à votre partenaire.

CD 3-35 You can find a list of the new words from the vocabulary and grammar sections of this **Compétence** on page 343 and a recording of this list on track 3-35 of your *Text Audio CD.*

Pour vérifier

1. What other verb tense has the same endings as the conditional? What is the stem for the conditional of most verbs? What are 12 verbs with irregular stems in the conditional? What is the stem of each? Do they use the regular conditional endings? How do you say *there would be*? *it would rain*? *it would be necessary*?

2. How do you express *could* and *should* in French?

3. When do you use the conditional?

 To download a podcast on the Conditional, go to **academic.cengage.com/french.**

✳ Note de *prononciation*

An unaccented **e** is usually not pronounced if you can drop it without bringing three pronounced consonants together (**samedi**). This is called **e caduc** and often occurs in the pronunciation of conditional verb forms (**j'habiterais**).

This occurs in many words in English, as in the words **reference, difference,** and **reverence.**

Saying what you would do

Le conditionnel

To say what one *would, could,* or *should* do, use the conditional form of the verb.

> *would* + verb in English = verb in the conditional in French

*I **would like** to improve my health.*   **Je voudrais** améliorer ma santé.

The conditional of most verbs is formed by adding the same endings as the **imparfait** to the infinitive of the verb. If an infinitive ends in **-e,** the **e** is dropped.

PARLER	FINIR	PERDRE
je parler**ais**	je finir**ais**	je perdr**ais**
tu parler**ais**	tu finir**ais**	tu perdr**ais**
il/elle/on parler**ait**	il/elle/on finir**ait**	il/elle/on perdr**ait**
nous parler**ions**	nous finir**ions**	nous perdr**ions**
vous parler**iez**	vous finir**iez**	vous perdr**iez**
ils/elles parler**aient**	ils/elles finir**aient**	ils/elles perdr**aient**

Most irregular verbs follow this same pattern.

dormir → je dormirais...   prendre → je prendrais...   boire → je boirais...

Verbs like **se lever, payer,** and **appeler** have spelling changes in the conditional stem in *all* the forms (**je me lèverais, je paierais, j'appellerais**). Those like **préférer** do not (**je préférerais**).

The following verbs have irregular stems in the conditional. The endings are regular.

-r-		-vr- / -dr-		-rr-	
aller	ir-	devoir	devr-	voir	verr-
avoir	aur-	vouloir	voudr-	pouvoir	pourr-
être	ser-	venir	viendr-	mourir	mourr-
faire	fer-	devenir	deviendr-		
		revenir	reviendr-		

Si j'avais le temps, **j'irais** plus souvent au club de gym. **Voudriez-vous** venir aussi?
*If I had time, **I would go** to the gym more often. **Would you like** to come too?*

You need to learn these forms too.

il y a	→	il y aurait	*there would be*
il pleut	→	il pleuvrait	*it would rain*
il faut	→	il faudrait	*it would be necessary*

To say *should,* use the conditional of **devoir** plus an infinitive. To say *could,* use the conditional of **pouvoir.**

> *should* + verb in English = **devoir** in the conditional + infinitive
> *could* + verb in English = **pouvoir** in the conditional + infinitive

*I **should** eat better.*   **Je devrais** manger mieux.
***Could you** give me some advice?*   **Pourrais-tu** me donner des conseils?

As you have seen, the conditional is used to say what one *would, could,* or *should* do.

Use the conditional:

- to make polite requests or offers.

Pourrais-tu me passer le sel?	*Could you pass me the salt?*
Voudriez-vous du café?	*Would you like some coffee?*

- to say what someone would do if circumstances were different (to make hypothetical or contrary-to-fact statements).

Si je savais faire la cuisine, je mangerais mieux.
If I knew how to cook, I would eat better.

In statements such as the one above, the **si** clause is in the imperfect and the result clause is in the conditional. Note that either clause can come first.

> **si** + imperfect → conditional

Si nous **avions** plus de temps libre, nous **ferions plus d'exercice.**
*If we **had** more free time, we **would exercise more.***

Nous **ferions plus d'exercice** si nous **avions** plus de temps libre.
*We **would exercise more** if we **had** more free time.*

Prononciation

CD 3-36

La consonne r et le conditionnel

The conditional stem of all verbs in French end in **-r.** To pronounce a French **r,** arch the back of the tongue firmly in the back of the mouth, as if to pronounce a *g,* and pronounce a strong English *h* sound.

je pourrais   tu trouverais   nous serions   il reviendrait   ils devraient

A. Réactions. Quelle serait votre réaction dans les circonstances suivantes?

Je serais... / Je ne serais pas...

heureux (heureuse)	furieux (furieuse)	horrifié(e)
étonné(e) *(astonished)*	surpris(e)	triste *(sad)*
indifférent(e)	fatigué(e)	???

1. Si mon meilleur ami (ma meilleure amie) commençait un cours de muscu...
2. Si je ne pouvais plus manger de viande...
3. Si on découvrait *(discovered)* que le chocolat était très bon pour la santé...
4. Si je devais faire de l'exercice tous les jours...
5. Si mon meilleur ami (ma meilleure amie) devenait végétarien(ne)...
6. S'il était interdit *(forbidden)* de fumer partout...
7. Si le médecin *(doctor)* me disait *(told me)* d'éviter le sucre...

B. Scrupules. Que feriez-vous dans ces circonstances?

1. Si vous voyiez *(saw)* la fiancée de votre frère embrasser un autre garçon, est-ce que vous...
   a. le diriez *(would tell)* à votre frère?
   b. ne feriez rien?
   c. demanderiez 50 dollars à sa fiancée pour garder le silence?

2. Si vous voyiez une copie de l'examen de fin de semestre / trimestre sur le bureau du prof deux jours avant l'examen, est-ce que vous...
   a. la prendriez?
   b. ne feriez rien?
   c. liriez l'examen tout de suite?

3. Si vous trouviez un chien dans la rue, est-ce que vous...
   a. téléphoneriez à la Société protectrice des animaux?
   b. prendriez le chien et chercheriez son maître *(owner)*?
   c. ne feriez rien?

4. Si vous ne veniez pas en cours le jour d'un examen important parce que vous n'étiez pas préparé(e), est-ce que vous...
   a. expliqueriez *(explain)* la situation au professeur?
   b. diriez au professeur que vous étiez malade?
   c. accepteriez d'avoir un zéro à l'examen?

5. Si vous voyiez quelqu'un qui attaquait votre professeur de français, est-ce que vous...
   a. téléphoneriez à la police?
   b. resteriez là pour aider votre professeur?
   c. resteriez là pour aider l'agresseur?

C. Une interview. Barbara Walters vous interviewe. Comment lui répondez-vous?

1. Si vous étiez une autre personne, qui voudriez-vous être?
2. Si vous habitiez dans une autre ville, où voudriez-vous habiter?
3. Si vous étiez un animal, quel animal seriez-vous: un chien, un chat, un poisson, un rat ou un oiseau *(a bird)*?
4. Si vous étiez une saison, quelle saison seriez-vous: l'hiver, l'été... ?
5. Si on écrivait *(wrote)* votre biographie, comment s'appellerait le livre?
6. Si votre vie était un morceau de musique, est-ce que ce serait de la musique populaire, de la musique classique, du rock, du blues... ?
7. Si votre vie était un film, est-ce que ce serait un drame, une comédie, un film d'épouvante *(horror)* ou un film d'aventures?

D. Temps libre. Feriez-vous les choses suivantes si vous aviez plus de temps libre?

> **EXEMPLE** préparer plus souvent des plats sains et légers
> **Oui, je préparerais plus souvent des plats sains et légers.**
> **Non, je ne préparerais pas plus souvent des plats sains et légers.**

1. dormir plus
2. être moins stressé(e)
3. pouvoir me reposer plus
4. apprendre une autre langue
5. aller plus souvent au parc
6. faire plus d'exercice
7. voir plus souvent mes amis
8. rendre plus souvent visite à ma famille

E. Situations. Qu'est-ce que ces gens feraient ou ne feraient pas dans les situations suivantes?

> **EXEMPLE** Si nous n'avions pas cours aujourd'hui, mes amis et moi... (aller au parc)
> **Si nous n'avions pas cours aujourd'hui, nous irions au parc.**
> **Si nous n'avions pas cours aujourd'hui, nous n'irions pas au parc.**

1. Si nous n'avions pas cours aujourd'hui, mes amis et moi... (manger au restaurant, faire de l'aérobic, aller prendre un verre, se reposer)
2. Si Rose voulait améliorer sa santé, elle... (fumer beaucoup, devoir faire plus d'exercice, prendre des vitamines, boire assez d'eau)
3. Si les étudiants voulaient mieux réussir en cours, ils... (faire tous les devoirs, aller à tous les cours, dormir en cours, écouter des CD en français)
4. Si mes parents allaient en vacances en France, ils... (être contents, manger dans des restaurants français, boire du vin français, marcher beaucoup)

F. Décisions. Qu'est-ce que ces gens feraient dans les circonstances données?

> **EXEMPLE** Si je pouvais quitter la classe maintenant, je **rentrerais chez moi.**

1. Si je pouvais faire ce que je voulais en ce moment, je (j')...
2. Si j'avais des vacances la semaine prochaine, je (j')...
3. Si mon meilleur ami (ma meilleure amie) pouvait faire ce qu'il/elle voulait en ce moment, il/si elle...
4. S'il/Si elle gagnait à la loterie, il/elle...
5. Si nous pouvions sortir ensemble ce soir, nous...
6. Si nous avions envie de faire de l'exercice, nous...
7. Si mes parents gagnaient à la loterie, ils...
8. S'ils pouvaient partir en vacances maintenant, ils...
9. Si le professeur nous disait *(told us)* qu'il n'y aurait plus d'examens dans ce cours, nous...

G. Par politesse. Mettez ces phrases au conditionnel pour être plus poli(e) *(polite)*.

> **EXEMPLE** Veux-tu rester en forme?
> **Voudrais-tu rester en forme?**

1. Tu veux faire de l'exercice?
2. Quand as-tu le temps d'aller au club de gym avec moi?
3. Peux-tu passer chez moi vers dix heures?
4. Ton amie veut venir aussi?
5. Qu'est-ce que vous voulez faire après?
6. On peut aller au restaurant végétarien?
7. Est-ce que vous voulez manger leur nouvelle salade?

Talking about food and health

Dans le ***Chapitre 8,*** vous avez appris à commander dans un restaurant, à acheter des provisions au marché, à parler des repas français et à dire ce que vous feriez pour améliorer votre santé. Maintenant vous allez réviser ce que vous avez appris.

A. Chez les petits commerçants. Dites au moins quatre choses qu'on peut acheter dans les endroits suivants.

> **EXEMPLE**   dans un supermarché
> **On peut acheter de l'eau minérale...**

1. dans une boulangerie
2. dans une charcuterie
3. dans une épicerie
4. dans une boucherie
5. au marché
6. dans une poissonnerie

B. Les courses. Rose va préparer un grand dîner ce soir. Voilà la liste de ce qu'elle va acheter. Dites où elle va aller pour acheter chaque chose.

> **EXEMPLE**   *a jar of jelly*
> **Elle va acheter un pot de confiture à l'épicerie.**

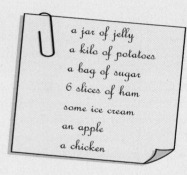

a jar of jelly
a kilo of potatoes
a bag of sugar
6 slices of ham
some ice cream
an apple
a chicken

C. Des gens en bonne santé. Ces personnes font très attention à leur santé. Répondez à chaque question de façon logique pour dire ce qu'elles font ou vont faire. Employez le pronom **en.**

> **EXEMPLE**   Rose mange beaucoup *de desserts sucrés?*
> **Non, elle n'en mange pas beaucoup.**

1. Son meilleur ami mange *de la viande rouge* tous les soirs?
2. Ses petits-enfants mangent *des fruits* le matin?
3. Rosalie boit beaucoup *de vin* tous les jours?
4. Les enfants de Patricia boivent trop *de coca?*
5. Patricia et Henri vont faire *de l'exercice* ce matin?
6. André va boire moins *de café?*
7. Il va prendre *un dessert* ce soir?

D. Qu'est-ce qu'on prend? Indiquez ce qu'on mange et ce qu'on boit dans chacune de ces circonstances. Ensuite, dites ce que vous prenez dans les mêmes circonstances. Nommez autant de *(as many)* choses que possible.

> **EXEMPLE**   En France, au petit déjeuner, on **mange des tartines ou des croissants et on boit du café.** Moi, je **mange des céréales.**

1. En France, au petit déjeuner, on... Moi, je...
2. En France, dans un fast-food, on... Moi, je...
3. En France, pour un repas traditionnel, comme entrée, on... Comme plat principal, on... Comme légume, on... Comme dessert, on... Et comme boisson, on... Moi, comme entrée, je... Comme plat principal, je... Comme légume, je... Comme dessert, je... Et comme boisson, je...
4. En France, pour un dîner léger, on... Moi, je...

E. À table! Complétez avec la forme correcte de l'article convenable.

Ce qu'on mange varie d'une culture à l'autre. Aux États-Unis, par exemple, on prend ___1___ petit déjeuner copieux. On mange souvent ___2___ œufs au bacon et ___3___ pain grillé. On boit ___4___ jus de fruit, ___5___ lait ou ___6___ café. En France, ___7___ petit déjeuner est un repas léger. On boit ___8___ café au lait, ___9___ thé ou ___10___ chocolat et on mange ___11___ tartines.

À midi, on peut manger dans un café où on peut prendre ___12___ omelette, ___13___ salade ou ___14___ sandwich avec ___15___ vin ou ___16___ eau minérale. ___17___ vin français est très bon, mais ___18___ eau minérale est populaire aussi. On peut finir son repas avec une tasse *(cup)* ___19___ café avec un peu ___20___ sucre ou un peu ___21___ lait.

F. Qu'est-ce qu'ils font? Dites si ces personnes font ou ne font pas les choses indiquées. Suivez l'exemple et soyez logique.

EXEMPLE Je ne veux pas grossir. Alors, je (finir) tous mes repas avec un dessert.
Je ne veux pas grossir. Alors, je ne finis pas tous mes repas avec un dessert.

1. Tu fais attention à ta santé. Alors, tu (choisir) des plats sains et tu (boire) beaucoup d'eau.
2. Mes amis (maigrir) parce qu'ils marchent tous les jours.
3. Nous n'aimons pas les boissons alcoolisées. Alors, nous (boire) beaucoup de bière.
4. Comme nous voulons éviter le sucre, nous (finir) tous nos repas avec un dessert.
5. Mes amis veulent rester en bonne forme. Alors, ils (boire) peu de bière.
6. Si on veut rester en forme, on (boire) du jus de fruit et on (choisir) des plats sains.
7. Tes amis et toi, vous voulez rester en forme? Alors, vous (choisir) de bien manger et vous (boire) trop de café.

G. Si... Si ces personnes avaient plus de temps libre, est-ce qu'elles feraient les choses indiquées?

EXEMPLE Moi, je (voyager plus)
Je voyagerais plus. / Je ne voyagerais pas plus.

1. Mon meilleur ami (Ma meilleure amie) (faire de la muscu, travailler plus)
2. Mes parents (faire plus attention à leur santé, partir souvent en voyage)
3. Moi, je (dormir plus, réussir mieux à mes cours)
4. Mes amis (réfléchir plus à leur santé, boire moins de boissons alcoolisées)
5. Mes amis et moi (se reposer, sortir plus souvent, être moins stressés)

Lecture et Composition

Lecture

Déjeuner du matin
Jacques Prévert

Il a mis le café
Dans **la tasse**
Il a mis le lait
Dans la tasse de café
Il a mis le sucre
Dans le café au lait
Avec la petite **cuiller**
Il a tourné
Il a bu le café au lait
Et il a reposé la tasse
Sans me parler
Il a allumé
Une cigarette
Il a fait des ronds
Avec la fumée
Il a mis **les cendres**
Dans le cendrier
Sans me parler
Sans me regarder
Il s'est levé
Il a mis
Son chapeau sur sa tête
Il a mis
Son manteau de pluie
Parce qu'il pleuvait
Et il est parti
Sous la pluie
Sans **une parole**
Sans me regarder
Et moi j'ai pris
Ma tête dans mes mains
Et j'ai pleuré.

"Déjeuner du matin," in *Paroles* © Éditions
Gallimard

---

la tasse *the cup*   **cuiller** *spoon*   **les cendres** *the
ashes*   **une parole** *a word*

✿ Pour mieux lire: *Reading a poem*

In order to fully appreciate a poem, it is important to read it with the right rhythm. Traditionally, French poems have verses with an even number of syllables ranging from six to twelve, with regular pauses approximately in the middle. Modern poets such as Jacques Prévert often break with traditional French versification and use more irregular rhythms to create different feelings or moods. His poem *Déjeuner du matin* can be read in more than one way, creating different impressions. Do the following activity to help you read it.

Sentiments. Jacques Prévert (1900–1977), l'un des poètes les plus célèbres du vingtième siècle *(century),* aimait parler de la vie de tous les jours dans sa poésie. Lisez les phrases suivantes du poème *Déjeuner du matin* en faisant une pause à la fin de chaque vers. Ensuite, relisez les phrases sans pause. Pour vous, quels sentiments sont évoqués par les différentes manières de lire les vers?

l'hésitation	la confusion	la compréhension	l'accord	le désaccord
la décision	l'indécision	l'indifférence	la réflexion	la patience
l'impatience	le calme	l'angoisse	???	

Il a mis
Son chapeau sur sa tête *(head)*

Il a fait des ronds *(rings)*
Avec la fumée *(smoke)*

Et moi, j'ai pris
Ma tête *(head)* dans mes mains
Et j'ai pleuré *(cried)*

Compréhension

Qu'est-ce qui s'est passé? Qu'est-ce qui s'est passé dans le poème?

1. Faites une liste des choses qu'il a faites.
2. Nommez deux choses qu'il n'a pas faites.
3. Quelle a été la réaction de l'autre personne?
4. Qui sont ces personnages? Sont-ils amis? parents? Sont-ils mariés, fiancés, divorcés... ?
5. Pourquoi est-ce qu'ils ne se parlent pas? Qu'est-ce qui s'est passé?

Composition

✿ Pour mieux écrire: *Finding the right word*

You are going to write a review of a restaurant you like or you do not like in your city. When you write, try to use the most precise word possible to get your message across. Note how, in the following English sentence, the word *small* is not clear, and how it can convey different messages, either positive or negative.

> It is a *small* restaurant with only fifteen tables.
> Positive: It is a *cozy (intimate)* restaurant with only fifteen tables.
> Negative: It is a *cramped (crowded)* restaurant with only fifteen tables.

In order to find the right word to express your meaning in French, you may need to use a synonym dictionary. Once you select a French word from an English-French dictionary, double check that you understand its use by looking it up in a French-English dictionary, or search it on the Internet in the context in which you wish to use it.

Organisez-vous. Dans les phrases suivantes, voici quelques mots qu'on pourrait utiliser au lieu des mots en italique pour décrire un restaurant. Trouvez un mot supplémentaire pour chaque liste en cherchant dans un diction-naire des synonymes sur Internet ou à la bibliothèque de votre université.

> Le décor est *joli* (beau, charmant, harmonieux, pittoresque, ???).
> Le décor est *laid* (atroce, hideux, grotesque, vulgaire, ???).
>
> Le menu est *intéressant* (exotique, varié, extraordinaire, sensationnel, phénoménal, ???).
> Le menu est *ennuyeux* (médiocre, ordinaire, limité, commun, insuffisant, banal, ???).
>
> La cuisine est *bonne* (délicieuse, savoureuse, délectable, exquise, succulente, ???).
> La cuisine est *mauvaise* (insipide, déplorable, révoltante, fade, désastreuse, ???).
>
> L'ambiance est *agréable* (sympathique, chaleureuse, intime, charmante, confortable, ???).
> L'ambiance est *désagréable* (déplaisante, inhospitalière, froide, ???).
>
> Le service est *bon* (rapide, animé, enthousiaste, immédiat, plaisant, gracieux, ???).
> Le service est *mauvais* (lent, impoli, hostile, inconsistent, honteux, exaspérant, ???).

Une critique gastronomique

Écrivez une critique gastronomique d'un restaurant de votre ville. Parlez du décor, du menu, de la cuisine, de l'ambiance et du service.

If you have access to SYSTÈME-D software, you will find the following phrases, vocabu-lary, grammar, and dictionary aids there.
Phrases: Appreciating (food), Describing objects, Making a judgment
Vocabulary: Food, Food-seasoning, Meals, Restaurants
Grammar: Indefinite article, Definite article, Partitive

Comparaisons culturelles

À table!

Ce qui est considéré «normal» ou «**poli**» diffère souvent d'une culture à l'autre. Chaque société a ses **propres coutumes** à table, ses plats préférés, et même sa propre **façon** de manger. En France, par exemple, **on garde** toujours les deux mains sur la table. **Après avoir coupé** la viande, on garde sa **fourchette** dans la main gauche. On ne boit jamais de lait avec les repas comme le font certains Américains. De nombreux restaurants et cafés acceptent que leurs clients viennent en compagnie de leur chien, du moment qu'il **se comporte** correctement.

Regardez ces photos. Qu'est-ce que vous **remarquez**?

poli *polite*   **propres coutumes** *own customs*   **façon** *way, manner*   **on garde** *one keeps*   **Après avoir coupé** *After cutting*
fourchette *fork*   **se comporte** *behaves*   **remarquez** *notice*

Lisez ces phrases concernant les coutumes et les bonnes manières. Lesquelles sont vraies dans votre région? Et en France?

	CHEZ NOUS	EN FRANCE
1. Avant de manger, on dit souvent «bon appétit»!	☐	☐
2. On boit quelquefois du lait aux repas.	☐	☐
3. On mange souvent des œufs le matin.	☐	☐
4. On mange plus souvent des œufs le soir ou à midi.	☐	☐
5. On mange assez souvent dans des fast-foods.	☐	☐
6. La présentation est presque aussi importante que le goût *(taste)* d'un plat.	☐	☐
7. Le pain est presque indispensable à tous les repas.	☐	☐
8. Le pain se mange généralement sans beurre, sauf le matin.	☐	☐
9. On fait assez souvent les courses chez les petits commerçants.	☐	☐
10. On mange beaucoup de choses avec les mains.	☐	☐
11. Quand on mange, on garde toujours les deux mains sur la table.	☐	☐
12. On met le pain directement sur la table, pas sur l'assiette *(plate)*.	☐	☐
13. Au restaurant, on peut commander à la carte ou on peut choisir un menu à prix fixe.	☐	☐
14. La carte est toujours affichée *(posted)* à l'extérieur d'un restaurant.	☐	☐

> *Pour la France – Vrai: 1, 4, 5, 6, 7, 8, 9, 11, 12, 13, 14*

Compréhension

1. Quelles différences est-ce qu'il y a entre ce qu'on fait chez vous et ce qu'on fait en France? Quelles similarités?

2. Les opinions des Français ne sont pas toujours reflétées *(reflected)* dans leur vie de tous les jours. Comment pouvez-vous expliquer ce contraste entre ce que les Français pensent et ce qu'ils font?

Visit **academic.cengage.com/french** for YouTube video cultural correlations, cultural information and activities.

Opinions	Actions
Selon *(According to)* les Français:	En France:
Les repas, c'est surtout un moment pour se retrouver en famille ou entre amis.	Les repas se prennent de moins en moins à heures fixes et à la maison et les familles mangent de moins en moins souvent ensemble.
On devrait continuer à préparer des repas traditionnels à la maison quand c'est possible.	De plus en plus, les grands repas traditionnels se limitent aux fêtes.
Les plats déjà préparés, c'est juste pour quand on est pressé *(in a hurry)*.	On passe de moins en moins de temps à préparer les repas en se servant *(using)* de produits tout prêts (salades composées, légumes mélangés *[mixed]*...), de produits surgelés et aussi du four à micro-ondes *(microwave)*.
Le service et la qualité sont meilleurs chez les petits commerçants que dans les grandes surfaces.	On fait de plus en plus souvent les courses dans les grandes surfaces.

Résumé de grammaire

Je vais acheter **de l'**eau, **du** pain, **de la** crème et **des** légumes.
*I'm going to buy **(some)** water, **(some)** bread, **(some)** cream and **(some)** vegetables.*

— Je vais prendre **un** sandwich et **des** frites.
— Je **ne** prends **pas de** frites parce qu'elles ont **trop de** calories.

— Tu **n'**aimes **pas les** frites?
— Mais si, j'aime **beaucoup les** frites, mais **le** riz est meilleur pour **la** santé.
— Mais **les** frites qu'ils servent ici sont délicieuses.

Le matin, je **bois** du thé mais mon mari **boit** du café. À midi, nous **buvons** de l'eau.

Qu'est-ce que tu **as bu** ce matin?
Qu'est-ce qu'tu **buvais** quand tu étais petit?

Les étudiants **réussissent** bien au cours. Tu **réussis** à tes cours?
J'**ai fini** mes devoirs.
Je ne **réfléchissais** pas beaucoup à mon avenir *(future)* quand j'étais jeune.

— Tu veux **de l'**eau?
— Oui, j'**en** veux bien.
   Non merci, je n'**en** veux pas.

— Tu prends un **sandwich**?
— Oui, j'**en** prends **un**.
   Non, j'**en** prends **deux**.
   Non, je n'**en** prends pas.

— Tu as acheté un kilo **de carottes**?
— Oui, j'**en** ai acheté **un kilo**.
   Non, j'**en** ai acheté **une livre**.
   Non, je n'**en** ai pas acheté.

The partitive and review of article use

Use the partitive to convey the idea of *some* or *any*. Use the partitive in French even when *some* or *any* can be omitted in English. Use **de l'** before all singular nouns beginning with a vowel sound, **du** before masculine singular nouns beginning with a consonant, **de la** before feminine singular nouns beginning with a consonant, and **des** before all plural nouns.

Un and **une** mean *a* and **du, de la, de l'**, and **des** express the idea of *some* or *any*. All of these forms change to **de (d')** after most negated verbs and after expressions of quantity. (See page 318 for a list of quantity expressions.)

Use the definite article (**le, la, l', les**) to say *the,* to express likes, dislikes, and preferences, or to make statements about entire categories. The definite article does *not* change to **de** after a negative or quantity expression.

The verb *boire* and regular *-ir* verbs

The verb **boire** *(to drink)* is irregular.

BOIRE *(to drink)*	
je **bois**	nous **buvons**
tu **bois**	vous **buvez**
il/elle/on **boit**	ils/elles **boivent**

PASSÉ COMPOSÉ: **j'ai bu**
IMPARFAIT: **je buvais**

The stem for the present tense of regular **-ir** verbs is obtained by dropping the **-ir.** Add the following endings for the present tense.

RÉUSSIR *(to succeed)*	
je réuss**is**	nous réuss**issons**
tu réuss**is**	vous réuss**issez**
il/elle/on réuss**it**	ils/elles réuss**issent**

PASSÉ COMPOSÉ: **j'ai réussi**
IMPARFAIT : **je réussissais**

See page 326 for a list of common **-ir** verbs. All **-ir** verbs presented in this chapter form the **passé composé** with **avoir,** except the reflexive verb **se nourrir.**

The pronoun *en*

En replaces a noun preceded by a partitive article, an expression of quantity, **un, une,** or a number. When replacing a noun preceded by **un, une,** a number, or an expression of quantity, repeat the **un, une,** number, or expression of quantity in the sentence containing **en,** unless it's negative. In English, **en** is usually translated by *some, any, of it,* or *of them.* Although the equivalent expression may be omitted in English, **en** is always used in French.

En is placed *immediately* before the verb. It goes before the infinitive if there is one. If not, it goes before the conjugated verb. In the **passé composé,** place it before the auxiliary verb.

Je vais **en** prendre.
J'**en** prends.
J'**en** ai pris.

The conditional *(Le conditionnel)*

Use the conditional to say what someone *would, could,* or *should* do. To form the conditional of most verbs, add the same endings as the **imparfait** to the infinitive of the verb. If an infinitive ends in **-e,** drop the **e** before adding the endings.

PARLER		FINIR		PERDRE	
je	parlerais	je	finirais	je	perdrais
tu	parlerais	tu	finirais	tu	perdrais
il/elle/on	parlerait	il/elle/on	finirait	il/elle/on	perdrait
nous	parlerions	nous	finirions	nous	perdrions
vous	parleriez	vous	finiriez	vous	perdriez
ils/elles	parleraient	ils/elles	finiraient	ils/elles	perdraient

Si j'avais plus de temps, **je préparerais** mieux mes cours. **Je finirais** tous mes devoirs et **le prof perdrait** moins souvent patience avec moi.

Most irregular verbs follow this same pattern.

dormir → je dormirais, tu dormirais...
prendre → je prendrais, tu prendrais...
boire → je boirais, tu boirais...

Si tu voulais être en bonne forme, **tu dormirais** plus, **tu prendrais** des vitamines et **tu boirais** assez d'eau.

Verbs like **se lever, payer,** and **appeler** have spelling changes in the conditional stem in *all* the forms **(je me lèverais, je paierais, j'appellerais).** Those like **préférer** do not **(je préférerais).**

Si nous étions en vacances, **nous nous lèverions** plus tard. **Mon ami préférerait** se lever vers neuf heures.

The following verbs have irregular stems in the conditional. The endings are regular.

aller → j'irais, tu irais...
avoir → j'aurais, tu aurais...
être → je serais, tu serais...
faire → je ferais, tu ferais...
devoir → je devrais, tu devrais...
vouloir → je voudrais, tu voudrais...
venir → je viendrais, tu viendrais...
devenir → je deviendrais, tu deviendrais...
revenir → je reviendrais, tu reviendrais...
voir → je verrais, tu verrais...
pouvoir → je pourrais, tu pourrais...
mourir → je mourrais, tu mourrais...

Si j'avais plus de temps libre, **je ferais** beaucoup de choses. **J'irais** plus souvent au parc, **je verrais** plus souvent mes amis et **je serais** content!

Also learn the following:

il y a → il y aurait   il pleut → il pleuvrait   il faut → il faudrait

Si tu visitais la Normandie au printemps, **il y aurait** du vent et **il pleuvrait. Il** te **faudrait** un parapluie!

To say *should,* use the conditional of **devoir** plus an infinitive. To say *could,* use the conditional of **pouvoir** plus an infinitive.

— **Pourrais-tu** me donner des conseils pour rester en bonne santé?
— **Tu devrais** bien manger et faire de l'exercice.

Use the conditional:

- to make polite requests or offers.
- to say what someone would do if circumstances were different.

Voudrais-tu y aller avec moi?
S'il savait faire la cuisine, **il mangerait** mieux.

Ordering at a restaurant

Vocabulaire

NOMS MASCULINS

un apéritif	a before-dinner drink
un dessert	a dessert
un fruit	a fruit
des fruits de mer	shellfish, crustaceans
*des haricots (verts)	(green) beans
*un hors-d'œuvre	an hors d'œuvre, an appetizer
du lait	milk
des légumes	vegetables
un menu à prix fixe	a set-price menu
du pain	bread
un pavé (de)	a thick slice (of)
des petits pois	peas
le plat (principal)	the (main) dish
du poisson (fumé)	(smoked) fish
du poivre	pepper
un repas	a meal
du riz	rice
du sel	salt
un serveur	a server, a waiter
du sucre	sugar

NOMS FÉMININS

une bouteille (de)	a bottle (of)
une carafe (de)	a carafe (of)
la carte	the menu
de la crème	cream
une entrée	a first course
une pomme	an apple
une pomme de terre	a potato
de la raie	rayfish, skate
une salade	a salad
une serveuse	a server, a waitress
de la viande	meat
de la volaille	poultry

DIVERS

Aimeriez-vous... ?	Would you like . . . ?
comme	for, as (a)
comprendre	to include
décider	to decide
du, de la, de l', des	some, any
finir	to finish
fumé(e)	smoked
servir	to serve
traditionnel(le)	traditional
typiquement	typically

Pour les noms des différentes sortes d'entrées, voir la page 304.

Pour les noms des différentes sortes de viandes, de volailles, de poissons et de fruits de mer, voir la page 304.

Pour voir les différentes possibilités pour finir un repas, voir la page 305.

Buying food

NOMS MASCULINS

du bœuf	beef
un choix	a choice
un commerçant	a shopkeeper
un marché	a market
un oignon	an onion
un pain au chocolat	a chocolate-filled croissant
un pain complet	a loaf of whole-grain bread
un plat préparé	a ready-to-serve dish
du porc	pork
un produit	a product
du raisin	grapes
du saucisson	salami
le service personnalisé	personal service
un supermarché	a supermarket

NOMS FÉMININS

une baguette	a loaf of French bread
une banane	a banana
la boucherie	the butcher's shop
la boulangerie	the bakery
une carotte	a carrot
une cerise	a cherry
la charcuterie	the deli
de la charcuterie	deli meats, cold cuts
une commerçante	a shopkeeper
des conserves	canned goods
l'épicerie	the grocery store
une fraise	a strawberry
une grande surface	a superstore
une laitue	lettuce
une orange	an orange
une pâtisserie	a pastry
une pêche	a peach
une poire	a pear
la poissonnerie	the fish market
des saucisses	sausages
une tartelette (aux fraises / aux cerises)	a (strawberry / cherry) tart

DIVERS

C'est tout.	That's all.
de plus en plus	more and more
dire	to say, to tell
faire les courses	to go grocery-shopping
frais (fraîche)	fresh
il faut	it is necessary, one needs, one must
Qu'est-ce que je peux vous proposer d'autre?	What else can I get you?
Qu'est-ce qu'il vous faut?	What do you need?
surgelé(e)	frozen

Pour les expressions de quantité, voir la page 318.

Talking about meals

NOMS MASCULINS

du bacon	bacon
du beurre	butter
du chocolat	chocolate
un croissant	a croissant
le déjeuner	lunch
le dîner	dinner
*un hamburger	a hamburger
du pain grillé	toast
un self-service	a self-service restaurant
un steak-frites	a steak and fries

NOMS FÉMININS

des céréales	cereal
de la confiture	jelly
une omelette	an omelet
une pizza	a pizza
une tartine	bread with butter and jelly

EXPRESSIONS VERBALES

boire	to drink
choisir (de faire)	to choose (to do)
finir (de faire)	to finish (doing)
grandir	to grow, to grow up, to get taller
grossir	to get fatter
maigrir	to get thinner, to slim down
(se) nourrir	to feed, to nourish, to nurture (oneself)
obéir (à)	to obey
réfléchir (à)	to think (about)
réussir (à)	to succeed (at, in), to pass [a test]

DIVERS

à l'américaine	American-style
ceux (celles)	those
complet (complète)	complete
copieux (copieuse)	copious, large
en	some, any, of it, of them
encore	still, again, more
grillé(e)	toasted, grilled
je prendrais	I would have, I would take
là	there
léger (légère)	light
ne... plus	no more, no longer
pourtant	however
rapide	rapid, fast, quick
seulement	only
si	yes (in response to a question or statement in the negative)
surtout	especially
volontiers	gladly
vrai(e)	true

Choosing a healthy lifestyle

NOMS MASCULINS

l'alcool	alcohol
des conseils	advice
des produits bios	organic products
le stress	stress
le tabac	tobacco

NOMS FÉMININS

des matières grasses	fats
la santé	health
des vitamines	vitamins

EXPRESSIONS VERBALES

améliorer	to improve
contrôler	to control
éviter	to avoid
faire attention (à)	to pay attention (to), to watch out (for)
faire de l'aérobic	to do aerobics
faire de la méditation	to meditate
faire de la muscu(lation)	to do weight training, to do bodybuilding
faire des randonnées	to go hiking
faire du yoga	to do yoga
faire mieux (de)	to do better (to)
marcher	to walk
on devrait	one should
oublier	to forget
se sentir	to feel

DIVERS

à votre avis	in your opinion
content(e)	content, happy
en forme	in shape
fort(e)	strong
lentement	slowly
plusieurs	several
régulièrement	regularly
sain(e)	healthy
sans doute	probably

Sélections musicales

C'est quoi, c'est l'habitude

ISABELLE BOULAY

You can access these songs at the iTunes playlist on **academic.cengage.com/french/horizons**.

Très jeune, Isabelle Boulay a commencé à chanter pour les clients du restaurant de ses parents.

Isabelle Boulay est née dans une petite ville à l'est du Québec. À l'âge de 17 ans, ses amis l'ont inscrite *(entered her)* dans un festival de la chanson pour amateurs où elle a connu un grand succès. Arrivée en France en 1992, sa participation, pendant trois ans, dans la comédie musicale *Starmania* avec le célèbre chanteur Michel Fugain l'a faite connaître *(made her know)* en France. Depuis, elle a enregistré *(recorded)* plusieurs albums.

Dans sa chanson *C'est quoi, c'est l'habitude,* de l'album *Tout un jour,* Isabelle Boulay parle des problèmes d'un couple pour lequel l'habitude et la lassitude *(weariness)* rendent la vie monotone et ennuyeuse. Pour mieux comprendre la chanson, faites les exercices suivants avant de l'écouter.

A. On ne s'aime plus. Qu'est-ce qu'on dirait probablement dans une relation où la vie quotidienne est devenue trop monotone et où on s'ennuie? Choisissez la réponse logique dans chaque paire.

1. On s'aime moins. / On s'aime beaucoup.
2. On s'aime encore. / On ne s'aime plus.
3. On se dispute souvent, mais on se réconcilie toujours. / On ne se dit rien.
4. On se raccroche à ce que l'on peut pour croire à notre amour. *(We hold on to what we can to believe in our love.)* / On a trouvé le grand amour ensemble.
5. On s'ennuie ensemble parce qu'on se connaît par cœur *(we know each other by heart).* / On s'amuse toujours ensemble parce qu'on fait quelque chose de nouveau tous les jours.
6. Son silence me ronge et me tue *(is eating at me and killing me).* / Son silence me rassure.
7. On veut être ensemble. / On cherche des plaisirs ailleurs *(elsewhere).*

B. Dis-moi... non, ne me dis pas! Si vous aviez des problèmes dans une relation, est-ce que vous voudriez savoir *(to know)* les choses suivantes? Commencez chaque phrase avec **Dis-moi...** *(Tell me . . .)* ou **Ne me dis pas...** *(Don't tell me . . .).*

1. ... que tu veux être avec moi.
2. ... que tu ne supportes pas le quotidien avec moi.
3. ... que notre amour est perdu.
4. ... que tu préfères être avec quelqu'un d'autre.
5. ... le nom de l'autre personne.

Comme d'habitude

KARIM KACEL

Karim Kacel est né en banlieue parisienne où il a grandi avec des parents immigrés venus d'Algérie.

Enfant, Karim Kacel écoutait toutes sortes de musique: du jazz, du rock, de la musique arabe; mais il aimait surtout la chanson française classique. Cette passion pour les classiques français est évidente dans ses reprises de tubes *(remakes of hits)* du passé, comme la chanson *Comme d'habitude,* chantée à l'origine par le célèbre chanteur Claude François. La chanson *My Way,* de Frank Sinatra, est une reprise en anglais de ce classique français.

De même que *C'est quoi, c'est l'habitude,* à la page précédente, *Comme d'habitude* décrit une rélation où le couple est trop habitué *(used to)* à la vie quotidienne ensemble. Pour mieux comprendre la chanson, faites les exercices suivants avant de l'écouter.

A. Dans une bonne relation? Est-ce que qu'un couple heureux ferait les choses suivantes?

1. se bousculer *(to bump into each other)*
2. se caresser les cheveux
3. se tourner le dos *(to turn their back)*
4. remonter le drap *(to pull up the sheet)* si l'autre a froid
5. faire semblant *(to pretend)* d'être heureux
6. sourire *(to smile)*
7. revenir à une maison vide *(empty)*
8. rire *(to laugh)*
9. se coucher seul(e) dans un lit froid
10. cacher ses larmes *(to hide one's tears)*

B. Le futur. Dans *Comme d'habitude,* il y a quelques verbes au futur. Les formes du futur *(someone will do something)* en français ressemblent aux formes du conditionnel *(someone would do something).* Utilisez les quatre premiers exemples pour traduire les dernières paires de phrases suivantes.

LE CONDITIONNEL

Le jour s'en irait. *The day would pass.*
Tu serais sortie. *You would have gone out.*

Je t'attendrais. *I would wait for you.*

Tu me sourirais. *You would smile at me.*

Je reviendrais.
J'irais me coucher.
Je cacherais mes larmes.
Tu rentrerais.
Tu te déshabillerais.
Tu te coucherais.
On s'embrasserait.

LE FUTUR

Le jour s'en ira. *The day will pass.*
Tu seras sortie. *You will have gone out.*

Je t'attendrai. *I will wait for you.*

Tu me souriras. *You will smile at me.*

Je reviendrai.
J'irai me coucher.
Je cacherai mes larmes.
Tu rentreras.
Tu te déshabilleras.
Tu te coucheras.
On s'embrassera.

En vacances

Chapitre 9

Compétence

 iLrn Heinle Learning Center

 academic.cengage.com/french/horizons

 Système-D

 Audio   iRadio

LA FRANCE D'OUTRE-MER

Connaissez-vous bien la France d'outre-mer? Regardez la liste des départements d'outre-mer et des territoires d'outre-mer de la France. Choisissez une des régions nommées et faites des recherches sur Internet pour trouver des informations à son sujet. Préparez une présentation sur un aspect de cette région que vous trouvez intéressant.

Savez-vous que l'Hexagone (la France métropolitaine en Europe) est seulement une partie de la République française? Quelles autres parties pouvez-vous nommer?

En effet, la République française **comprend:**

- la France métropolitaine
- quatre départements d'outre-mer (les DOM)
- plusieurs collectivités d'outre-mer (les COM)
- la Nouvelle-Calédonie
- les **Terres australes** et antarctiques françaises

La France a colonisé les quatre DOM—la Guadeloupe, la Martinique, la Guyane et La Réunion—au 17e **siècle.** Depuis 1946, ils **font partie de** la France, **tout comme** Hawaii fait partie des États-Unis.

Fort-de-France, **chef-lieu** de la Martinique

L'Île du Diable, **célèbre bagne** de la Guyane, fermé en 1945

Saint-Denis, chef-lieu de La Réunion

---

d'outre-mer *overseas*   **En effet** *In fact*   **comprend** *includes*   **Terres australes** *Southern Lands*   **siècle** *century*   **font partie de** *are part of*   **tout comme** *just as*   **chef-lieu** *administrative center*   **L'Île du Diable** *Devil's Island*   **célèbre bagne** *famous penal colony*

LA GUADELOUPE
NOMBRE D'HABITANTS: 453 000
(les Guadeloupéens)
CHEF-LIEU (*ADMINISTRATIVE CENTER*): Basse-Terre

LA MARTINIQUE
NOMBRE D'HABITANTS: 399 000
(les Martiniquais)
CHEF-LIEU: Fort-de-France
Visit it live on Google Earth!

Les collectivités d'outre-mer — la Polynésie française, Wallis-et-Futuna, Mayotte et Saint-Pierre-et-Miquelon — sont des territoires de la France, **pareils** aux territoires américains de Puerto Rico et Guam.

L'ancien territoire de la Nouvelle-Calédonie a **un statut particulier** comme «pays d'outre-mer **au sein de** la République».

La France possède aussi les Terres australes et antarctiques françaises (TAAF), composées de plusieurs îles dans l'Océan indien et d'une partie du continent antarctique.

La biodiversité en Nouvelle-Calédonie

❀ Qu'en savez-vous?

Servez-vous des renseignements et des photos sur ces pages et aussi de la carte du monde au début du livre *(the world map in the front of the book)* pour répondre à ces questions. Devinez *(Guess)* si nécessaire.

1. Les _départements d'outre-mer (DOM)_ font partie de la France, tout comme Hawaii fait partie des États-Unis. Les _C. OM._ sont des territoires de la France, pareils aux territoires américains de Puerto Rico et Guam.

2. La _martinique_ et la _guadaloup_ sont deux îles dans la mer *(sea)* des Caraïbes. La majorité des habitants de ces deux départements sont des descendants d'esclaves africains emmenés *(African slaves brought)* dans ces îles pour travailler dans les plantations.

3. La _Guyane_ est en Amérique du sud. Au 19e siècle, la France envoyait *(used to send)* ses prisonniers politiques au bagne de cette région.

4. _Saint-Pierre-et-Miquelon_ est composé d'un groupe d'îles près de Terre-Neuve *(Newfoundland)*. Au printemps, on peut voir la migration des baleines *(whales)* de ses côtes *(coasts)*.

5. La _Réunion_ est située dans l'océan Indien près de Madagascar. C'est le département d'outre-mer le plus peuplé, avec une société multi-ethnique: des Africains, des Européens, des Indiens, des Chinois et des Malgaches *(inhabitants of Madagascar)*.

6. La _nouvelle-calédonie_ a un statut particulier. En 2014, ses habitants vont voter sur l'indépendance. Cette région a une biodiversité extraordinaire avec une très grande variété de plantes, de reptiles, d'oiseaux *(birds)*, d'insectes, de poissons et d'autres animaux.

Les Terres australes et antarctiques françaises

pareils *similar* **L'ancien** *The former* **un statut particulier** *a unique status* **au sein de** *within*

Talking about vacation

Les vacances

Luc, un jeune Parisien, va passer ses vacances en Guadeloupe. Et vous? Où aimez-vous passer vos vacances?

dans un pays étranger ou exotique | sur une île tropicale ou **à la mer** | dans une grande ville | à la montagne

Qu'est-ce qu'on peut faire dans chaque **endroit**?

admirer **les paysages** *(m)* | visiter des sites *(m)* historiques et touristiques | profiter des activités culturelles

Vocabulaire supplémentaire

faire du tuba *to go snorkeling*
faire de la plongée sous-marine *to go scuba diving*
faire de la planche à voile *to go windsurfing*

bronzer ou **courir** le long des plages | **goûter** la cuisine locale **assis** sur la terrasse d'un restaurant | faire des randonnées *(f)*

CD 4-2

Luc parle à son ami Alain de ses prochaines vacances en Guadeloupe.

LUC: Je vais bientôt partir en vacances.
ALAIN: Et tu vas où?
LUC: Je vais aller en Guadeloupe.
ALAIN: La Guadeloupe? Quelle chance! Tu pars quand?
LUC: Je vais partir le 20 juillet et je **compte** passer trois semaines **là-bas.**
ALAIN: Génial! J'espère que **ça te plaira**!

à la mer *at the coast, by the sea*   **un endroit** *a place*   **les paysages** *(m) scenery, landscapes*   **bronzer** *to tan*   **courir** *to run*
goûter *to taste*   **assis(e)** *seated*   **compter** *to plan on, to count on*   **là-bas** *over there*   **ça te plaira** *you'll like it*

A. Où? Où fait-on les choses suivantes?

EXEMPLE

On nage à la mer.

dans un pays étranger
à la mer
à la montagne
dans une grande ville
sur une île tropicale

1.    **2.**    **3.**

4.    **5.**    **6.**

B. Voyages. Imaginez qu'un(e) ami(e) a passé ses vacances dans les endroits suivants. Préparez une conversation dans laquelle vous parlez de l'endroit où il/elle est allé(e) et de ce qu'il/elle a fait, comme dans l'exemple.

    EXEMPLE   en Espagne
           —**Alors, tu as passé tes vacances dans un pays étranger?**
           —**Oui, je suis allé(e) en Espagne.**
           —**Qu'est-ce que tu as fait en Espagne?**
           —**J'ai visité des sites historiques et touristiques.**

1. à New York   **3.** en France
2. à Tahiti   **4.** dans les Alpes

C. Entretien. Interviewez votre partenaire.

1. Préférerais-tu visiter une île tropicale ou visiter une grande ville? aller à la mer ou à la montagne? faire une randonnée ou faire du ski? faire de l'exercice à l'hôtel ou courir le long des plages? goûter la cuisine locale ou manger un hamburger? dîner sur la terrasse d'un restaurant élégant ou faire un pique-nique? bronzer ou nager? visiter des sites touristiques ou profiter des activités culturelles?

2. Où est-ce que tu aimerais passer tes prochaines vacances? Qu'est-ce qu'on peut faire dans cette région? Où est-ce que tu as passé tes meilleures vacances? Pourquoi as-tu trouvé ces vacances agréables? Qu'est-ce que tu as fait?

D. Conversation. Avec un(e) partenaire, relisez la conversation entre Luc et Alain à la page précédente. Ensuite, imaginez que vous allez faire le voyage de vos rêves *(dreams)* et changez la conversation pour dire où vous allez, avec qui, quand et combien de temps vous comptez rester.

You can find a list of the new words from the vocabulary and grammar sections of this ***Compétence*** on page 380 and a recording of this list on track 4-3 of your *Text Audio CD.*
CD 4-3

Pour vérifier

1. What do most verbs have as the stem in the future tense? Which verbs have irregular stems? What are their stems? What other verb form has the same stem as the future?

2. What endings do you use to form the future tense in French?

3. What verb tense is used in clauses with **quand** referring to the future in French? What tense is used in English in such clauses? How do you say *When I finish, I'll go home?*

✳ Note *de grammaire*

The future/conditional stem always ends with **-r.** Do you remember these irregular ones?

aller	ir-
avoir	aur-
être	ser-
faire	fer-
devoir	devr-
vouloir	voudr-
venir	viendr-
revenir	reviendr-
devenir	deviendr-
voir	verr-
pouvoir	pourr-
mourir	mourr-
courir	courr-

Note these forms in the future:

il y a	il y aura
il faut	il faudra
il pleut	il pleuvra

✳ Note *de grammaire*

As in the conditional, verbs like **se lever, payer,** and **appeler** have spelling changes in *all* forms of the future (**je me lèverai, je paierai, j'appellerai**). Those like **préférer** do not (**je préférerai**).

 To download a podcast on Future Tense, go to **academic.cengage.com/french.**

✳ Note *de prononciation*

As in the conditional forms, an unaccented **e** is usually not pronounced in future tense forms if you can drop it without bringing together three pronounced consonants (**j'habiterai, nous inviterons**).

Le futur

You have used **aller** + *infinitive* to say what someone *is going* to do. You can use the future tense to say what someone *will* do. Form the future tense by adding the boldfaced endings below to the same stem you use for the conditional.

PARLER	ÊTRE	VENIR
je parler**ai**	je ser**ai**	je viendr**ai**
tu parler**as**	tu ser**as**	tu viendr**as**
il/elle/on parler**a**	il/elle/on ser**a**	il/elle/on viendr**a**
nous parler**ons**	nous ser**ons**	nous viendr**ons**
vous parler**ez**	vous ser**ez**	vous viendr**ez**
ils/elles parler**ont**	ils/elles ser**ont**	ils/elles viendr**ont**

The future is generally used in French as it is in English. However, one difference is its use in clauses with **quand** referring to the future. English has the present in such clauses.

> **quand** + future → future

Quand j'**arriverai** en Guadeloupe, je **prendrai** un taxi pour aller à l'hôtel.
*When I **arrive** in Guadeloupe, I'**ll take** a taxi to go to the hotel.*

As in English, use the future tense to say what will happen if another event occurs. Use the present tense in the clause with **si.**

> **si** + present → result in future

Si je **peux** visiter la Martinique, je **serai** vraiment content!
*If I **can** visit Martinique, I **will be** really happy!*

A. Boule de cristal. Vous pouvez voir l'avenir *(the future)* dans une boule de cristal. Comment sera la vie des personnes suivantes dans cinq ans?

> **EXEMPLE** Moi, je… (être riche)
> **Je serai riche. / Je ne serai pas riche.**

1. Moi, je (j')…
habiter ici
avoir mon diplôme
devoir travailler
aller souvent en France

2. Mon meilleur ami
(Ma meilleure amie)…
venir souvent me voir
réussir dans la vie
sortir souvent avec moi
faire souvent des voyages

3. La personne de mes rêves
et moi, nous…
se marier
avoir des enfants
acheter une maison
faire beaucoup de voyages
ensemble

4. Tous les membres de ma famille…
s'entendre bien
se rendre souvent visite
se voir souvent
voyager souvent ensemble

5. *[à un(e) autre étudiant(e)]*
Toi, tu… finir tes études
trouver un bon travail
apprendre beaucoup
avoir beaucoup de problèmes

6. *[au professeur]* Vous…
travailler toujours *(still)* ici
avoir toujours cours à 7 heures du matin
pouvoir prendre votre retraite *(retirement)*
être heureux (heureuse)

B. Quand. Utilisez un élément de chaque groupe pour créer deux phrases logiques pour chaque sujet.

EXEMPLE Je me reposerai quand je finirai mes études.

1. Je…

3. Mon meilleur ami (Ma meilleure amie)…

2. Dans ma famille, nous…

4. Mes amis…

être content(e)(s)	avoir un diplôme
se reposer	avoir plus de temps libre
être moins stressé(e)(s)	sortir ce week-end
avoir plus d'argent	trouver un bon travail
faire de l'exercice	pouvoir dormir plus
s'amuser	être en vacances
???	???

quand

C. Si… Complétez logiquement ces phrases.

EXEMPLE S'il pleut ce week-end, je **resterai à la maison.**

1. S'il fait beau ce week-end, je (j')…
2. S'il fait mauvais ce week-end, je (j')…
3. Si je sors avec des amis ce week-end, nous…
4. Si je peux partir en vacances cette année, je (j')…
5. Si un jour je peux visiter la France, je (j')…
6. Si mes amis et moi décidons de visiter une autre ville, nous…

D. Entretien. Pensez à un voyage (réel ou imaginaire) que vous ferez pendant les prochaines vacances. Votre partenaire vous posera des questions au sujet de ce voyage. Après, changez de rôles.

1. Où iras-tu? Comment est-ce que tu voyageras?
2. Quand est-ce que tu partiras? Quand est-ce que tu reviendras?
3. Qui fera le voyage avec toi? Qu'est-ce que chacun *(each one)* devra apporter *(to bring)*?
4. Où descendrez-vous?
5. Qu'est-ce que vous ferez pendant le voyage? Qu'est-ce que vous verrez d'intéressant? Quels sites touristiques est-ce que vous visiterez?

Stratégies et Lecture

French has other compound tenses which, like the **passé composé,** are formed with the auxiliary verb **avoir** or **être** and a past participle (**dansé, mangé, vu,** etc.). To translate these tenses, change the auxiliary verb *have* in English to the same tense as in French (imperfect, future, conditional): *They had (will have, would have) arrived.*

In the **passé composé,** where the auxiliary verb is in the *present* tense, translate it as the simple past or as *has/have + past participle.*

J'**ai** commencé.	Elle **est** rentrée.
I began. / I have begun.	*She returned. / She has returned.*

If the auxiliary verb is in the *imperfect,* translate it as *had + past participle.*

J'**avais** déjà commencé.	Il n'**était** pas encore rentré.
*I **had** already begun.*	*He **hadn't** returned yet.*

If the auxiliary verb is in the *conditional,* translate it as *would have + past participle.*

J'**aurais** déjà commencé.	Nous ne **serions** pas encore rentrés.
*I **would have** already begun.*	*We **wouldn't have** returned yet.*

If it is in the *future,* translate it as *will have + past participle.*

J'**aurai** déjà commencé.	Tu ne **seras** pas encore rentré(e).
*I **will have** already begun.*	*You **will not have** returned yet.*

A. Et vous? Traduisez les phrases suivantes en anglais.

1. J'ai déjà visité la Guadeloupe.
2. L'année dernière, j'y suis resté un mois.
3. Avant de partir en vacances, j'avais réservé une chambre d'hôtel.
4. J'ai visité la Martinique aussi. J'y étais déjà allé(e) deux fois avant.
5. Si j'avais eu assez d'argent, j'aurais passé mes vacances en Europe.
6. Mes vacances auraient été plus agréables s'il n'avait pas plu tout le temps.
7. Quand j'aurai fini mes études, je ferai un long voyage.
8. Je visiterai la France quand j'aurai fini mes quatre semestres de français.

B. Le temps des verbes. Dans le texte qui suit, traduisez tous les verbes *en italique.*

Lecture: Quelle aventure!

Luc, un jeune Parisien qui passe ses vacances en Guadeloupe, raconte ses aventures dans un mail à son ami Alain.

Salut Alain:

Je passe des vacances formidables ici en Guadeloupe! *Je t'aurais écrit* plus tôt si *je n'avais pas été* si occupé. Ici, tout est à mon goût… la cuisine, le paysage, les femmes! En fait, j'ai rencontré une jeune Guadeloupéenne très sympa. Elle s'appelle Micheline et nous passons beaucoup de temps ensemble depuis notre rencontre assez comique au parc naturel.

J'étais allé au parc pour faire l'escalade de la Soufrière, un énorme volcan en repos… mais comme j'allais bientôt le voir, pas si «en repos» que ça! En montant vers le volcan, *j'avais remarqué* qu'il y avait un peu de vapeur qui sortait du cratère, mais *je n'avais pas fait trop attention.* Quand j'étais presque au sommet du volcan, je m'étais assis par terre pour me reposer un peu et c'est là que la comédie a commencé. Là où j'étais assis, la terre était toute chaude, mais vraiment chaude, et je voyais des jets de vapeur qui sortaient du sommet! J'ai pensé que le volcan allait exploser!

J'ai commencé à crier aux autres touristes: «Attention! Attention! Le volcan entre en éruption, il va exploser!» Heureusement, Micheline était parmi le groupe et elle nous a expliqué calmement: «Mais non, mais non… calmez-vous! C'est tout à fait normal. Le volcan est en repos, il n'y a pas de danger!» Si *elle n'avait pas été* avec nous, *on aurait* tous *commencé* à courir, paniqués.

Sur le moment, j'ai eu l'impression d'être complètement ridicule! Mais cette impression n'a pas duré. On a commencé à parler et nous avons continué l'escalade du volcan ensemble. Arrivés au sommet, nous avons trouvé une vue impressionnante… la lave…, les fissures…, l'odeur… C'était un paysage presque irréel. Pendant un instant, j'ai eu l'impression d'être sur une autre planète!

Alors, tout est bien qui finit bien. Si *je n'avais pas fait* cette bêtise, *Micheline et moi n'aurions jamais commencé à parler et je n'aurais pas fait la connaissance* de cette femme extraordinaire. Elle est super sympa et nous sortons ensemble presque tous les soirs!

À bientôt,
Luc

La Soufrière

Compréhension. Répondez aux questions suivantes d'après la lecture.

1. Quel site touristique est-ce que Luc visitait quand il a rencontré Micheline?
2. Qu'est-ce que Luc avait vu avant de commencer à crier que le volcan allait exploser?
3. Qu'est-ce que tous les touristes auraient fait si Micheline n'avait pas été là pour les calmer?
4. Pourquoi est-ce que Luc dit que «tout est bien qui finit bien»?

Preparing for a trip

Les préparatifs

Avant de faire un voyage **à l'étranger,** il faut faire beaucoup de préparatifs *(m)*. Vous devez acheter votre **billet** *(m)* **d'avion** dans une agence de voyages ou votre **billet électronique** sur Internet et avant votre départ, il faut aussi…

vous informer sur des sites Web et **obtenir** des renseignements.

lire des guides *(m)* touristiques.

téléphoner à l'hôtel pour réserver une chambre.

dire à votre famille où vous allez.

demander à **vos voisins** de **donner à manger à** votre chien.

faire vos valises *(f)*.

À votre arrivée, vous devez…

montrer votre passeport *(m)*.

passer la douane.

changer de l'argent ou **des chèques** *(m)* **de voyage.**

Les préparatifs *(m)* Preparations   à l'étranger *in another country, abroad*   un billet d'avion *a plane ticket*   un billet électronique *an e-ticket*   s'informer *to find out information*   obtenir *to obtain*   un(e) voisin(e) *a neighbor*   donner à manger à *to feed*   faire sa valise *to pack one's bag*   des chèques *(m)* de voyage *traveler's checks*

Alain parle à sa femme du mail qu'**il a reçu** de son ami Luc.

CATHERINE: Qu'est-ce que **tu lis**?

ALAIN: C'est un mail que j'ai reçu de Luc. Il **m'**écrit de la Guadeloupe où il passe ses vacances.

CATHERINE: Et **ça lui plaît,** la Guadeloupe?

ALAIN: Ça lui plaît beaucoup.

CATHERINE: La Guadeloupe doit être jolie. J'aimerais bien voir les plages et les paysages tropicaux.

ALAIN: Luc dit qu'il aime beaucoup le paysage, la cuisine et le climat. Il me parle aussi d'une «femme extraordinaire» qu'il a rencontrée là-bas.

A. Avant le départ ou après l'arrivée? Quand on voyage, est-ce qu'il faut faire les choses suivantes **avant le départ** ou **après l'arrivée**?

EXEMPLE acheter un billet d'avion
Il faut acheter un billet d'avion avant le départ.

1. passer la douane
2. écrire pour obtenir des renseignements
3. s'informer sur des sites Web
4. acheter des chèques de voyage
5. changer des chèques de voyage
6. réserver une chambre
7. montrer son passeport
8. lire des guides touristiques
9. demander à un ami de donner à manger à son chien
10. faire des préparatifs

B. Mon dernier voyage? Dites si vous avez fait chaque chose de l'activité précédente lors de *(at the time of)* vos dernières vacances.

EXEMPLE acheter un billet d'avion
Je n'ai pas acheté de billet d'avion. J'ai pris ma voiture.

C. Que fait-on? Faites une liste de ce qu'on fait dans chacun des endroits suivants.

1. à l'agence de voyages
2. à l'aéroport
3. à la banque
4. à l'hôtel
5. sur des sites Web

D. Conversations. Avec un(e) partenaire, relisez la conversation entre Alain et Catherine en haut de la page. Ensuite, imaginez que vous recevez un mail d'un(e) ami(e) qui visite une autre région francophone. Parlez avec votre partenaire de vos impressions de cette région et dites pourquoi vous voudriez ou ne voudriez pas y aller.

 You can find a list of the new words from the vocabulary and grammar sections of this *Compétence* on page 380 and a recording of this list on track 4-6 of your *Text Audio CD.*

---

il a reçu (recevoir *to receive)* **tu lis (lire** *to read)* **me (m')** *me, to me* **ça lui plaît (plaire** *to please) does he like it*

Pour vérifier

1. What are the conjugations of **dire, lire,** and **écrire**? What do you need to remember about the **vous** form of **dire**? What are the future and conditional stems of these verbs?

2. Which two of these verbs have similar past participles? What are they? What is the past participle of **lire?**

Communicating with people

Les verbes *dire, lire* et *écrire*

You have already seen the verbs **dire** *(to say, to tell),* **lire** *(to read),* and **écrire** *(to write).* Here are their full conjugations. The verb **décrire** *(to describe)* is conjugated like **écrire.**

DIRE *(to say, to tell)*	LIRE *(to read)*	ÉCRIRE *(to write)*
je **dis**	je **lis**	j' **écris**
tu **dis**	tu **lis**	tu **écris**
il/elle/on **dit**	il/elle/on **lit**	il/elle/on **écrit**
nous **disons**	nous **lisons**	nous **écrivons**
vous **dites**	vous **lisez**	vous **écrivez**
ils/elles **disent**	ils/elles **lisent**	ils/elles **écrivent**
PASSÉ COMPOSÉ: j'**ai dit**	PASSÉ COMPOSÉ: j'**ai lu**	PASSÉ COMPOSÉ: j'**ai écrit**
IMPARFAIT: je **disais**	IMPARFAIT: je **lisais**	IMPARFAIT: j'**écrivais**
CONDITIONNEL: je **dirais**	CONDITIONNEL: je **lirais**	CONDITIONNEL: j'**écrirais**
FUTUR: je **dirai**	FUTUR: je **lirai**	FUTUR: j'**écrirai**

Here are some things you might want to read or write.

un article *an article*
une carte postale *a postcard*
un mail *an e-mail*
une histoire *a story*
un journal (*pl* **des journaux**)
  a newspaper

une lettre *a letter*
un magazine *a magazine*
un poème *a poem*
une rédaction *a composition*
un roman *a novel*

A. En cours de français. Est-ce que ces personnes font souvent les choses indiquées en cours de français?

souvent   quelquefois   rarement   ne… jamais

> **EXEMPLE** je / écrire des poèmes
> **Je n'écris jamais de poèmes en cours de français.**

1. le professeur / écrire au tableau
2. les étudiants / écrire au tableau
3. je / écrire quelque chose dans mon cahier
4. nous / écrire une rédaction
5. les autres étudiants et moi / s'écrire des mails après le cours
6. je / lire le journal
7. le professeur / lire des poèmes à la classe
8. nous / lire des phrases à haute voix *(aloud)*
9. les étudiants / lire des romans en français

Maintenant, dites si ces personnes ont fait ces choses en cours la semaine dernière.

> **EXEMPLE** je / écrire des poèmes
> **Je n'ai pas écrit de poèmes en cours de français la semaine dernière.**

B. Qu'est-ce qu'on dit? Dites si ces personnes font les choses indiquées.

EXEMPLE   je / dire «merci» quand le professeur me rend mes devoirs
Je dis (Je ne dis pas) «merci» quand le professeur me rend mes devoirs.

1. le prof / dire «bonjour» quand il arrive en cours
2. les autres étudiants et moi / se dire «bonjour» en cours
3. les étudiants / dire la vérité *(the truth)* au prof
4. nous / le dire au prof quand nous ne comprenons pas
5. je / dire «au revoir» quand je quitte la classe
6. je / dire «merci» au prof

Maintenant, dites si ces personnes ont dit les choses indiquées au dernier cours.

EXEMPLE   je / dire «merci» quand le professeur me rend mes devoirs.
J'ai dit (Je n'ai pas dit) «merci» quand le professeur m'a rendu mes devoirs.

C. En vacances. Vous faites le voyage de vos rêves avec un(e) ami(e). Avec un(e) partenaire, faites des phrases logiques en utilisant un élément de chaque colonne. Faites au moins deux phrases pour chaque sujet.

EXEMPLE   Je lis des guides touristiques.

| Je… Nous… L'agent de voyages *(The travel agent)*… | dire écrire lire | des cartes postales des mails un mail pour réserver une chambre des sites Web pour obtenir des renseignements des guides touristiques à des voisins de donner à manger aux animaux «au revoir» à nos amis le nom de notre hôtel à ma famille le prix *(price)* du voyage |

D. Entretien. Interviewez votre partenaire.

1. Est-ce que tu écris plus de lettres ou plus de mails? Est-ce que tu as écrit un mail ce matin? À qui? Quand tu voyages, est-ce que tu écris des cartes postales? des mails?
2. Lis-tu le journal tous les jours? Quel journal préfères-tu lire? Le liras-tu ce soir? Est-ce que tu l'as lu ce matin? Quel magazine lis-tu le plus souvent? Est-ce que tu l'as lu ce mois-ci?
3. Lis-tu beaucoup de romans? Lis-tu plus de romans d'aventures ou d'amour? Quel est le dernier roman que tu as lu? Quand est-ce que tu l'as lu?

Pour vérifier

1. What are the direct object pronouns *him, her, it, them*? What are the indirect object pronouns *(to) him / (to) her / (to) them*?

2. How can you often recognize a noun that is an indirect object in French? What types of verbs are frequently followed by indirect objects?

3. Where do you place the object pronoun when there is an infinitive in the same clause? Where does it go otherwise?

4. Where do you place the object pronoun in the **passé composé**? When does the past participle agree with an object?

✳ Note *de grammaire*

In French, a direct object generally follows the verb directly, whereas an indirect object is preceded by a preposition, usually **à**.

J'invite **mes amis** chez moi. (direct object)
Je **les** invite chez moi.

Je téléphone **à mes amis**. (indirect object)
Je **leur** téléphone.

 To download a podcast on Object Pronouns, go to **academic.cengage.com/french.**

Avoiding repetition

*Les pronoms compléments d'objet indirect (**lui, leur**) et reprise des pronoms compléments d'objet direct (**le, la, l', les**)*

In ***Chapitre 5,*** you learned that you can replace the direct object of the verb with the direct object pronouns **le, la, l',** and **les.**

— Tu fais **ta valise** maintenant?   — Tu as acheté **ton billet**?
— Oui, je **la** fais.   — Oui, je **l'**ai acheté.

Replace the indirect object of the verb with the indirect object pronouns **lui** (*[to] him, [to] her*) and **leur** (*[to] them*). Generally, indirect objects in French can only be people or animals, not places or things. You can recognize a noun that is an indirect object because it is usually preceded by the preposition **à** (**à, au, à la, à l', aux**).

Verbs indicating communication or exchanges, such as **parler à, téléphoner à, dire à, écrire à, demander à, rendre visite à,** and **donner à,** are often followed by indirect objects.

— Tu écris **à ta mère**?   — Tu vas rendre visite **à tes parents**?
— Oui, je **lui** écris un mail.   — Oui, je vais **leur** rendre visite
                                                       ce week-end.

DIRECT OBJECT PRONOUNS		INDIRECT OBJECT PRONOUNS	
le (l')	*him, it* (m)	**lui**	*(to) him*
la (l')	*her, it* (f)	**lui**	*(to) her*
les	*them*	**leur**	*(to) them*

Indirect object pronouns follow the same placement rules as direct object pronouns. Generally, place them *immediately* before the verb. They go before the infinitive if there is one in the same clause. If not, they go before the conjugated verb. In the **passé composé,** they go before the auxiliary verb.

— Luc va téléphoner **à Micheline**?   — *Is Luc going to call **Micheline**?*
— Oui, il va **lui** téléphoner.   — *Yes, he's going to call **her**.*

— Il écrit **à son ami**?   — *Is he writing **to his friend**?*
— Oui, il **lui** écrit.   — *Yes, he is writing **(to) him**.*

— Il a parlé **à ses parents**?   — *Has he talked **to his parents**?*
— Non, il ne **leur** a pas parlé.   — *No, he hasn't talked **to them**.*

In negated sentences, place **ne** immediately after the subject and **pas, rien,** or **jamais** immediately after the first verb.

Je ne veux pas **lui** écrire.   *présent*
Je ne **lui** écris jamais.   *futur*
Je ne **lui** ai pas écrit.   *passé*

In the **passé composé,** the past participle agrees with direct object pronouns, but not with indirect objects.

Luc a invité Micheline.   Luc **l'**a invité**e**.
Luc a téléphoné à Micheline.   Luc **lui** a téléphoné.

A. En voyage. Quel genre de voyageur (voyageuse) êtes-vous? Formez des phrases pour parler de vos habitudes en voyage. Utilisez les pronoms **le, la, l', les.**

> **EXEMPLE** J'écris *mes cartes postales* (le premier jour / juste avant de rentrer).
> **Je les écris le premier jour.**

1. Je réserve *mon hôtel* (dans une agence de voyages / sur Internet).
2. Je fais *ma valise* (au dernier moment / à l'avance *[in advance]*).
3. Je lis *le guide touristique* (avant de partir / à l'hôtel au dernier moment).
4. Je visite *les sites touristiques* (avec un guide / sans guide).

Maintenant, utilisez les pronoms **lui** et **leur** pour remplacer les noms compléments d'objet indirect.

5. Je dis (toujours / quelquefois / rarement) *à mes parents* où je vais.
6. J'écris (souvent / quelquefois / rarement) des mails *à mes amis.*
7. (Je téléphone / Je ne téléphone pas) *à mon meilleur ami (à ma meilleure amie).*
8. J'envoie (envoyer *[to send]*) des photos *à mon meilleur ami (à ma meilleure amie).*

B. La prochaine fois. Refaites les phrases de *A. En voyage* pour parler de ce que vous allez faire la prochaine fois que partirez en voyage.

> **EXEMPLE** J'écris *mes cartes postales* (le premier jour / juste avant de rentrer).
> **La prochaine fois, je vais les écrire le premier jour.**

Maintenant, refaites ces mêmes phrases au passé composé pour dire ce que vous avez fait la dernière fois que vous êtes parti(e) en voyage.

> **EXEMPLE** J'écris *mes cartes postales* (le premier jour / juste avant de rentrer).
> **La dernière fois, je les ai écrites le premier jour.**

C. Habitudes de voyage. Parlez de vos voyages en répondant à ces questions. Utilisez **le, la, l', les, lui** ou **leur.**

> **EXEMPLE** Vous demandez de l'argent *à vos parents?*
> **Non, je ne leur demande pas d'argent.**

1. Vous réservez *votre chambre d'hôtel* sur Internet?
2. Vous achetez *votre billet* sur Internet ou dans une agence de voyages?
3. Vous proposez *à vos parents* d'y aller avec vous?
4. Vous invitez *votre meilleur(e) ami(e)?*
5. Vous demandez *à vos voisins* de donner à manger à votre chien ou à votre chat?
6. Vous lisez *le magazine de la compagnie aérienne* dans l'avion?
7. Vous téléphonez *à votre mère* pendant le voyage?
8. Vous écrivez des cartes postales *à vos amis?*
9. Vous passez *les soirées* à l'hôtel?
10. À votre retour *(return)*, vous parlez du voyage *à vos parents?*
11. Vous montrez *vos photos du voyage* à vos amis?
12. Vous mettez *vos photos* sur Internet?
13. Vous décrivez le voyage *à vos amis?*

Buying your ticket

À l'agence de voyages

Note culturelle

Les salariés en France ont jusqu'à sept semaines de vacances chaque année. La majorité des Français organisent leurs vacances bien à l'avance, mais de plus en plus d'entre eux *(of them)* font des projets de vacances de dernière minute à cause des imprévus *(unforseen events)* de la vie moderne et grâce aux *(thanks to)* services disponibles *(available)* sur Internet. La majorité des vacanciers français restent en France où ils aiment aller (en ordre de préférence) à la mer, à la campagne, en ville et à la montagne. Combien de semaines de vacances a-t-on généralement dans votre région? Quelles sont les destinations préférées des vacanciers?

Pour voyager à l'étranger, il faut avoir…

un passeport
des chèques de voyage
un billet d'avion avec
un itinéraire
une carte de crédit
une carte bancaire

Il faut aussi **savoir…**

le numéro du **vol**
l'heure de départ
l'heure d'arrivée
**la porte
d'embarquement**
la porte d'arrivée

Aimez-vous préparer vos voyages à l'avance? Il faut lire des guides touristiques pour mieux **connaître…**

l'histoire et la
géographie de la
région et les
gens et leur
culture

le système de
transports *(m)*
en commun

CD 4-7

Avant son voyage, Luc va acheter son billet à l'agence de voyages.

LUC:	Bonjour, monsieur. Je voudrais acheter un billet Paris–Pointe-à-Pitre.
L'AGENT DE VOYAGES:	Très bien, monsieur. Vous voulez un billet aller-retour ou un aller simple?
LUC:	Un billet aller-retour.
L'AGENT DE VOYAGES:	À quelle date est-ce que vous voulez partir?
LUC:	Le 20 juillet.
L'AGENT DE VOYAGES:	Quand est-ce que vous voudriez rentrer?
LUC:	Le 12 août.
L'AGENT DE VOYAGES:	Vous voulez un billet de première classe ou de classe touriste?
LUC:	De classe touriste.
L'AGENT DE VOYAGES:	Très bien. Il y a un vol le 20 juillet, départ Paris-Orly à 15h15, arrivée à Pointe-à-Pitre à 17h30. Pour le retour, il y a un vol qui part de Pointe-à-Pitre le 12 août à 20h15 et qui arrive à Paris-Orly à 10h15 le 13 août. **Ça vous convient?**
LUC:	Oui, c'est parfait. Combien coûte le billet?
L'AGENT DE VOYAGES:	C'est 759 euros.
LUC:	Bon. Alors, faites ma réservation. Voilà ma carte de crédit.

---

une carte bancaire *a bank/debit card*   **savoir** *to know*   **un vol** *a flight*   **la porte d'embarquement** *the departure gate*
la porte d'arrivée *the arrival gate*   **connaître** *to know, to be familiar with, to be acquainted with*   **les transports** *(m)*
en commun *public transportation*   **Ça vous convient?** *Is that good for you?*

A. Le voyage de Luc. Lisez l'itinéraire de Luc et répondez à ces questions.

1. Est-ce que Luc a acheté un billet aller-retour ou un aller simple?
2. Est-ce que Luc voyagera en première classe ou en classe touriste?
3. Quelle est la date de son départ? de son retour? De quel aéroport partira-t-il?
4. Il devra arriver à l'aéroport combien d'heures avant le départ?
5. À quelle heure est son départ de Paris? À quelle heure est son arrivée à Pointe-à-Pitre?
6. Est-ce qu'un repas sera servi en route?
7. Quelle est la date de son retour à Paris? C'est quel jour de la semaine?

> ## ITINÉRAIRE
> À l'intention de: Moreau/Luc
>
> **Aller:** Mardi 20 juillet:
> Départ de Paris-Orly   15h15
> Air France-Vol 624   Classe touriste
> Arrivée à Pointe-à-Pitre   17h30
> • Un repas et une collation seront servis en vol.
>
> **Retour:** Jeudi 12 août:
> Départ de Pointe-à-Pitre   20h15
> Air France-Vol 625   Classe touriste
> Arrivée à Paris-Orly   10h15
> • Un repas et une collation seront servis en vol.
>   Prix du billet aller-retour: 759€.
>
> Prévoyez d'arriver à l'aéroport deux heures avant l'heure de départ et n'oubliez pas de reconfirmer votre retour 72 heures avant le départ.
>
> BON VOYAGE!

B. Et vous? Choisissez la phrase qui vous décrit le mieux quand vous voyagez.

1. **a.** Je préfère voyager en première classe.
   b. Je préfère voyager en classe touriste.
   c. Ça dépend de qui va payer.

2. **a.** J'arrive à l'aéroport bien en avance.
   b. J'arrive à l'aéroport au dernier moment.
   c. Je manque *(miss)* quelquefois mon vol.

3. **a.** Je préfère préparer mes voyages bien à l'avance.
   b. Je prépare tout quelques jours avant de partir.
   c. Je préfère voyager à l'imprévu *(unexpectedly)*.

4. **a.** Pendant le voyage, je préfère tout payer par carte de crédit.
   b. Je préfère tout payer par carte bancaire ou en espèces *(in cash)*.
   c. Pendant le voyage, je préfère tout payer en chèques de voyage.

5. **a.** Dans une grande ville comme Paris, j'utilise les moyens de transport en commun.
   b. Je prends toujours un taxi ou je loue une voiture.
   c. Je ne sors pas de l'hôtel.

6. **a.** J'aime lire un guide pour connaître l'histoire et la culture d'une région.
   b. J'aime mieux m'informer sur des sites Web pour connaître la région.
   c. Je préfère tout découvrir *(discover)* pendant le voyage.

C. Conversation. Avec un(e) partenaire, relisez la conversation entre Luc et l'agent de voyages à la page précédente. Ensuite, imaginez que vous êtes dans une agence de voyages d'une ville francophone et que vous achetez un billet pour rentrer chez vous. Votre partenaire jouera le rôle de l'agent de voyages.

CD 4-8 You can find a list of the new words from the vocabulary and grammar sections of this *Compétence* on page 381 and a recording of this list on track 4-8 of your *Text Audio CD*.

1. What is the conjugation of **savoir**? of **connaître**?

2. Do you use **savoir** or **connaître** when *to know* is followed by a verb? by a question word, **si, que,** or **ce que**? to say that one knows a language? if *to know* is followed by a noun that indicates a fact or information? by a noun that indicates that someone is familiar with a person, place or thing?

Saying what people know

Les verbes savoir et connaître

Both **savoir** and **connaître** mean *to know*. The verb **reconnaître** *(to recognize)* has the same conjugation as **connaître**.

SAVOIR (to know [how])	CONNAÎTRE (to know, to be familiar with, to be acquainted with)
je **sais** nous **savons** tu **sais** vous **savez** il/elle/on **sait** ils/elles **savent** PASSÉ COMPOSÉ: j'**ai su** *(I found out)* IMPARFAIT: je **savais** *(I knew)* CONDITIONNEL: je **saurais** FUTUR: je **saurai**	je **connais** nous **connaissons** tu **connais** vous **connaissez** il/elle/on **connaît** ils/elles **connaissent** PASSÉ COMPOSÉ: j'**ai connu** *(I met)* IMPARFAIT: je **connaissais** *(I knew)* CONDITIONNEL: je **connaîtrais** FUTUR: je **connaîtrai**

Use **savoir** to say you *know* . . .

FACTS OR INFORMATION:

Est-ce que tu **sais** la réponse?
Nous ne **savons** pas où ils sont.

A LANGUAGE:

Je **sais** le français.
Je ne **sais** pas l'allemand.

HOW TO DO SOMETHING:

Je **sais** nager.
Je ne **sais** pas danser.

Use **connaître** to say you *know (of)* or *are familiar* or *acquainted with* . . .

PEOPLE:

Vous **connaissez** mon amie Micheline?
Je la **connais** bien.

PLACES:

Est-ce que tu **connais** bien la Guadeloupe?
Qui **connaît** ce quartier?

THINGS:

Je ne **connais** pas bien l'histoire de Guadeloupe.
Tu **connais** ce film?

Use **savoir** when *to know* is followed by a verb, a question word (**qui, où**…), or by **si, que,** or **ce que,** or to say that one knows a language. When *to know* is followed by a noun, use **savoir** to say one *knows a fact or information,* and **connaître** to say one is *familiar with a person, place, or thing.*

A. Quel pays? Luc vous parle des gens qu'il connaît et des pays où ils habitent. Quels pays est-ce que ces personnes connaissent bien? Quelles langues savent-ils parler?

> **EXEMPLE** J'habite à Paris.
> **Je connais bien la France. Je sais parler français.**

la France	l'Allemagne	???	le Canada
l'Espagne	les États-Unis	le Sénégal	

1. Mon amie Sophie habite à Berlin. Elle…
2. Mes cousins habitent à Barcelone. Ils…
3. Mes parents et moi habitons à Paris. Nous…
4. Mon frère habite à Dakar. Il…
5. *[au professeur]* Et vous, vous habitez à *[votre ville]*. Alors, vous… ?

B. Qui sait faire ça? Dites qui sait faire les choses suivantes dans votre famille. Dites **Personne ne sait...** pour dire *No one knows how to . . .*

Connaissez-vous la Guadeloupe?
Savez-vous parler français?

> **EXEMPLE** nager
> **Tout le monde sait nager dans ma famille.**
> **Moi, je sais nager mais les autres ne savent pas nager.**
> **Personne ne sait nager dans ma famille.**

1. bien faire la cuisine
2. faire du ski
3. bien danser
4. jouer au tennis
5. bien chanter
6. parler français

Maintenant demandez aux personnes de votre classe si elles savent faire ces choses.

> **EXEMPLE** nager
> — **Marc, tu sais nager?**
> — **Oui, je sais nager.**
> **Non, je ne sais pas nager.**

C. Et vous? Complétez ces phrases avec **je sais / je ne sais pas** ou avec **je connais / je ne connais pas** pour parler de vos connaissances.

1. _____ bien le campus. _____ où se trouve *(is located)* la bibliothèque et d'autres endroits importants.

2. En cours, d'habitude, _____ répondre aux questions du prof. _____ très bien le français. _____ bien les conjugaisons des verbes que nous avons étudiés. _____ qu'il est très important de bien apprendre toutes les conjugaisons.

3. _____ le nom de tous mes camarades de classe. _____ bien ces étudiants. _____ ce qu'ils vont tous faire après les cours aujourd'hui.

4. _____ bien la bibliothèque. _____ où se trouvent tous les livres en français.

5. _____ utiliser Internet pour trouver comment dire ce que je veux en français. _____ des sites Web avec de bons dictionnaires.

D. Les voyages et la géographie. Complétez chaque question avec la forme correcte de **connaître** ou de **savoir** et posez-la à votre partenaire.

1. _____-tu une bonne agence de voyages? Est-ce que tu _____ combien coûte un billet d'ici à Paris? _____-tu s'il y a un vol direct d'ici à Paris? _____-tu combien de temps prend un vol d'ici à Paris?

2. Combien de langues est-ce que tu _____ parler? Est-ce que tu _____ l'allemand? _____-tu un peu l'Europe? _____-tu quelle ville est la capitale de la Belgique?

3. _____-tu la Guadeloupe? Est-ce que tu _____ quelle ville est le chef-lieu *(administrative center)* de la Guadeloupe? _____-tu bien l'histoire et la géographie de la Guadeloupe? _____-tu en quelle année Christophe Colomb est arrivé en Guadeloupe?

Indicating who does what to whom

Les pronoms **me, te, nous** et **vous**

The pronouns **me** *(me, to me)*, **te** *(you, to you)*, **nous** *(us, to us)*, and **vous** *(you, to you)* are used as both direct and indirect objects.

me (m')	*me, to me*	Tu ne **m'**attends pas?
te (t')	*you, to you* (familiar)	Nous **t'**avons attendu(e) une heure.
nous	*us, to us*	Tu peux venir **nous** chercher?
vous	*you, to you* (plural / formal)	Je **vous** téléphonerai plus tard.

To download a podcast on Object Pronouns, go to **academic.cengage.com/french.**

All object pronouns go immediately before an infinitive if there is one in the same clause, otherwise they go before the conjugated verb. In the **passé composé,** they go before the auxiliary verb.

> Je vais **te** voir demain.   Il ne **nous** connaît pas bien.   Je **vous** ai vu(e)(s).

In the **passé composé,** the past participle agrees with preceding *direct* objects, but not with *indirect* objects.

> Il **nous** a **vus** mais il ne **nous** a pas **parlé.**

The expression **il faut** followed by an infinitive generally means *it is necessary* or *one must.*

> Il faut arriver une heure à l'avance.
> *It is necessary to arrive (One must arrive) one hour in advance.*

Use **il faut** with the indirect object pronouns **me, te, nous, vous, lui,** and **leur** to say that someone needs something or needs to do something.

> Il me faut aller au consulat. Il me faut un passeport.
> *I need to go to the consulate. I need a passport.*

A. Que voulez-vous? Dites la même chose en utilisant l'expression **il me faut, il te faut, il lui faut, il nous faut, il vous faut** ou **il leur faut.**

> **EXEMPLE**   J'ai besoin d'un passeport.
>   **Il me faut un passeport.**

1. Tu as besoin d'une carte de crédit.
2. Nous avons besoin d'un guide.
3. Vous avez besoin d'un billet.
4. J'ai besoin d'un nouveau bikini.
5. Tu as besoin d'une pièce d'identité *(identification).*
6. Vous avez besoin d'une réservation.
7. Il a besoin d'un passeport.
8. Ils ont besoin d'une carte d'embarquement *(boarding pass).*

Maintenant, expliquez pourquoi chacun a besoin de ces choses.

EXEMPLE   J'ai besoin d'un passeport.
Il me faut un passeport pour faire un voyage à l'étranger.

changer un chèque de voyage		avoir une chambre d'hôtel
faire un voyage à l'étranger		payer le voyage
monter dans l'avion	préparer un itinéraire	aller à la plage

B. Meilleurs amis. Demandez à votre partenaire si son meilleur ami (sa meilleure amie) fait les choses suivantes. Utilisez le pronom **te (t')** dans vos questions.

EXEMPLE   téléphoner souvent
—**Il/Elle te téléphone souvent?**
—**Non, il/elle ne me téléphone pas souvent.**
Oui, il/elle me téléphone souvent.

1. parler tous les jours
2. retrouver souvent en ville
3. écouter toujours
4. comprendre bien

5. rendre toujours visite le week-end
6. embêter *(to annoy)* quelquefois
7. donner de l'argent
8. demander beaucoup de services *(favors)*

C. Je te promets! Un jeune homme dit à sa fiancée qu'il fait et qu'il va faire tout ce qu'elle veut. Elle lui pose les questions suivantes. Comment répond-il?

EXEMPLE   Tu m'aimes vraiment beaucoup?
Oui, je t'aime vraiment beaucoup.

1. Tu m'adores?
2. Tu me trouves laide?
3. Tu me comprends?
4. Tu m'écoutes quand je te parle?
5. Tu veux me voir tous les jours?

6. Tu vas venir me voir demain?
7. Tu vas me donner ta photo?
8. Tu vas m'aider avec mon travail?
9. Tu vas m'abandonner?
10. Tu vas m'aimer pour toujours?

D. Professeurs et étudiants. Dites au professeur trois choses que les autres étudiants et vous faites pour lui et trois choses que le professeur fait pour vous. Faites deux listes sur une feuille de papier.

EXEMPLES   **Nous vous écoutons...**
Vous nous donnez trop de devoirs...

E. Entretien. Interviewez votre partenaire.

1. Est-ce que tes amis t'invitent souvent à partir en voyage avec eux *(them)?*
2. As-tu des amis qui te téléphonent d'un autre pays de temps en temps?
3. De tous les endroits où tu as passé tes vacances, quelle ville est-ce que tu me recommandes de visiter? Pourquoi?

Deciding where to go on a trip

Luc visite la Guadeloupe. Et vous? Quels continents et pays aimeriez-vous visiter?

l'Afrique *(f)*: **le Maroc,** l'Algérie *(f)*, l'Égypte *(f)*, le Sénégal, la Côte d'Ivoire

l'Asie *(f)* et **le Moyen-Orient:** la Chine, Israël *(m)*, le Japon, le Viêt Nam

l'Amérique *(f)* du Nord ou l'Amérique centrale: **les Antilles** *(f)*, le Canada, les États-Unis *(m)*, le Mexique

l'Amérique *(f)* du Sud: l'Argentine *(f)*, le Brésil, le Pérou, la Colombie, le Chili, la Guyane

l'Océanie *(f)*: l'Australie *(f)*, la Nouvelle-Calédonie, la Polynésie française

L'Arcade du Cinquantenaire, Bruxelles

l'Europe *(f)*: l'Allemagne *(f)*, la Belgique, l'Espagne *(f)*, la France, **le Royaume-Uni,** l'Italie *(f)*, la Russie, la Suisse

Vocabulaire supplémentaire

EN AFRIQUE	**l'Afrique** *(f)* **du Sud**
	la Tunisie
EN ASIE	**la Corée**
	l'Inde *(f)*
	l'Indonésie *(f)*
	l'Iran *(m)*
	l'Irak *(m)*
	la Turquie
EN EUROPE	**le Danemark**
	la Grèce
	la Norvège
	la Pologne
	le Portugal
	la République tchèque
	la Suède *(Sweden)*

---

le Maroc *Morocco*   **le Moyen-Orient** *the Middle East*   **les Antilles** *(f pl) the West Indies*   **le Royaume-Uni** *the United Kingdom*

Luc et Micheline parlent des voyages qu'ils ont faits.

MICHELINE: Pourquoi es-tu venu tout seul en Guadeloupe? Tu aimes voyager?
LUC: Oui, j'adore ça!
MICHELINE: Quels pays étrangers as-tu visités?
LUC: J'ai visité les États-Unis, la Chine et le Canada. Et toi? Tu aimes voyager à l'étranger?
MICHELINE: Je n'ai jamais quitté la Guadeloupe, mais j'aimerais bien visiter l'Afrique un jour.
LUC: Où aimerais-tu aller en Afrique?
MICHELINE: Moi, j'aimerais surtout visiter le Sénégal et la Côte d'Ivoire.

A. Quel continent? Où se trouvent *(are located)* ces pays?

en Amérique du Nord	en Afrique	en Amérique du Sud
en Océanie	en Asie	en Europe

EXEMPLE la Chine
La Chine se trouve en Asie.

1. les États-Unis
2. l'Algérie
3. le Japon
4. l'Australie
5. l'Allemagne
6. le Sénégal
7. la Guyane
8. le Maroc

B. Quels pays? Dites quels pays vous aimeriez visiter dans la région indiquée.

EXEMPLE en Europe
En Europe, j'aimerais visiter la France, l'Espagne...

1. en Asie et au Moyen-Orient
2. en Amérique du Nord et du Sud
3. en Océanie
4. en Afrique
5. en Europe

Marrakech, Maroc

C. Associations. Travaillez avec un(e) partenaire pour trouver l'endroit de chaque groupe qui ne va pas avec les autres. Expliquez pourquoi.

EXEMPLE l'Allemagne, les États-Unis, la France, la Suisse
les États-Unis: Tous les autres sont en Europe.

1. le Canada, l'Argentine, l'Espagne, le Pérou, le Mexique
2. l'Australie, la Polynésie française, la Martinique, le Sénégal
3. la France, les États-Unis, l'Australie, le Royaume-Uni
4. le Sénégal, l'Égypte, le Brésil, l'Algérie, le Maroc
5. la France, la Belgique, le Sénégal, la Suisse, le Mexique

D. Conversation. Avec un(e) partenaire, relisez la conversation entre Micheline et Luc en haut de la page. Ensuite, changez la conversation pour parler des régions et pays que vous avez visités et de ceux que vous aimeriez visiter.

You can find a list of the new words from the vocabulary and grammar sections of this **Compétence** on page 381 and a recording of this list on track 4-10 of your *Text Audio CD.*

Saying where you are going

Les expressions géographiques

Pour vérifier

1. With which one of the following do you generally not use a definite article when it is the subject or direct object of a verb: cities, states, provinces, countries, or continents? Would you use **le, la, l'**, or **les** before the following place names:
_____ Italie, _____ Antilles, _____ Ohio, _____ Japon, _____ France?

2. Which countries, states or provinces are generally feminine? masculine?

3. How do you say *to* or *in* with a city? with a feminine country? with a masculine country beginning with a vowel sound? with a masculine country beginning with a consonant? with plural countries?

❋ Notes de grammaire

A. The following places are exceptions to the rule that countries and states ending in **-e** are feminine: **le Royaume-Uni, le Mexique, le Delaware, le Maine, le New Hampshire, le Nouveau-Mexique, le Rhode Island, le Tennessee.**
B. You also say **dans le** with masculine states **(dans le Vermont). C.** You say **(dans) l'état de New York** and **(dans) l'état de Washington** to clarify that you are talking about the states rather than the cities with the same names.

When a place name is used as the subject or object of a verb, you generally need to use the definite article with continents, countries, states, and provinces, but not with cities. Most continents, countries, states, and provinces ending in **-e** are feminine, whereas most others are masculine. **Le Mexique** and **le Royaume-Uni** are exceptions.

J'adore l'Europe. **La** France est très belle. Nous allons visiter Londres, Paris et Nice. J'aimerais aussi voir **les** États-Unis: **la** Californie, **le** Texas et **la** Floride.

To say *to* or *in* with a geographical location, the preposition you use varies.

to / in		
à	with cities	**à** Paris
aux	with any plural country or region	**aux** États-Unis
en	with any feminine country or region and with any masculine one beginning with a vowel	**en** France
		en Ontario
au	with any masculine country or region beginning with a consonant	**au** Canada

A. C'est connu! D'abord, mettez la forme convenable de l'article défini devant le nom de chaque pays. Ensuite, demandez à votre partenaire quel pays est connu *(known)* pour les choses indiquées.

_____aux_____ Royaume-Uni ✔ _____en_____ Égypte _____en_____ Suisse

_____en_____ Colombie _____aux_____ États-Unis _____en_____ France

_____au_____ Mexique _____en_____ Italie _____au_____ Brésil

EXEMPLE —**Quel pays est connu pour le café?**
—**La Colombie.**

Quel pays est connu pour... ?

1. le fromage et le vin **3.** le chocolat **5.** les spaghetti **7.** la musique rock
2. le carnaval **4.** le thé **6.** les pyramides **8.** le sphinx

B. Leçon de géographie. Votre ami(e) n'est pas très fort(e) en géographie et il/elle vous pose des questions. Répondez-lui. D'abord, donnez la préposition convenable pour dire *to / in* avec chaque pays. Ensuite, jouez les deux rôles avec votre partenaire.

EXEMPLE Londres (_____ Royaume-Uni, _____ Canada)
—**Londres se trouve *(is located)* au Royaume-Uni ou au Canada?**
—**Londres se trouve au Royaume-Uni.**

1. Tokyo (_____ Chine, _____ Japon)

2. Mexico (_____ Mexique, _____ Pérou)

3. Moscou (_____ Italie, _____ Russie)

4. Berlin (_____ Espagne, _____ Allemagne)

5. Hanoi (_____ Viêt Nam, _____ Brésil)

6. Alger (_____ Algérie, _____ Maroc)

7. Le Caire (_____ Maroc, _____ Égypte)

8. Dakar (_____ Sénégal, _____ Côte d'Ivoire)

9. La Nouvelle-Orléans (_____ États-Unis, _____ France)

10. Abidjan (_____ Côte d'Ivoire, _____ Sénégal)

C. C'est où? Devinez où dans le monde francophone se trouvent *(are located)*
ces sites touristiques.

EXEMPLE Le palais de Versailles
**Le palais de Versailles se
trouve à Versailles en France.**

le Palais de Versailles

Dakar (Sénégal)	Québec (Canada)	Papeete (Polynésie française)
Fès (Maroc)	Bruxelles (Belgique)	Versailles (France)

1.

la Grand-Place

4.

le Marché de Papeete

2.

le Château Frontenac

5.

la Grande Mosquée

3.

la Médina

Reprise

Making travel plans and preparing for a trip

Dans le **Chapitre 9,** vous avez appris à parler des vacances. Maintenant vous allez réviser ce que vous avez appris.

A. Qu'est-ce qu'on fait? Après son voyage en Guadeloupe, Luc décide d'aller visiter l'Afrique francophone avec Micheline. Dites ce qu'ils pourraient faire dans les endroits suivants: dans une grande ville, à la mer, à la montagne.

> **EXEMPLE**   dans une grande ville
> **Dans une grande ville, ils pourraient profiter des activités culturelles**…

B. Destinations. Donnez l'article défini qui correspond aux pays suivants.

_____ Égypte	_____ Maroc
_____ États-Unis	_____ Algérie
_____ Sénégal	_____ Côte d'Ivoire
_____ Japon	_____ Brésil

Luc et Micheline visiteront tous les pays africains de la liste précédente. Quels pays visiteront-ils?

> Ils visiteront…

Maintenant, complétez les phrases suivantes avec le nom du pays logique. N'oubliez pas d'utiliser la préposition correcte: **en, au** ou **aux.**

> D'abord, Luc et Micheline iront au Caire…
>
> Après l'Égypte, ils prendront l'avion pour Alger…
>
> D'Algérie, ils prendront l'autocar pour aller à Fès…
>
> De Fès, ils iront à Abidjan…
>
> Finalement, avant de rentrer chez Luc à Paris, ils passeront quelques jours à Dakar…

C. En Égypte. Micheline parle avec une amie de son itinéraire pour le voyage en Égypte avec Luc. D'abord, mettez le verbe de chaque phrase au futur. Ensuite, mettez les phrases dans l'ordre logique.

_____ On arrive au Caire après plus de 14 heures en avion.

_____ Quelqu'un de l'hôtel vient nous chercher à l'aéroport à notre arrivée. L'hôtel coûte très cher et Luc paie tout.

_____ Le premier soir, nous restons à l'hôtel et nous nous reposons. Le lendemain, un guide nous montre les pyramides et nous visitons le sphinx aussi.

_____ D'abord, notre avion part de Guadeloupe à 3 heures de l'après-midi.

_____ Nous sommes en première classe dans l'avion.

_____ Après notre séjour au Caire, nous allons à Alexandrie où nous passons trois jours.

_____ L'après-midi de notre arrivée, nous prenons un guide privé pour visiter Le Caire.

D. Un bon guide. Quand Luc et Micheline visitent les pyramides avec un groupe de touristes, ils ont un bon guide qui est très bien informé. Complétez les phrases suivantes avec la forme convenable du verbe **savoir** ou **connaître**.

1. Le guide _____ parler arabe et plusieurs langues européennes.
2. Après cinq minutes, il _____ le nom de tous les touristes qui font l'excursion.
3. Il _____ très bien la culture égyptienne.
4. Il _____ très bien les pyramides aussi.
5. Il _____ répondre à toutes nos questions.

E. Et vous? Quelles sont vos habitudes quand vous partez en voyage? Répondez aux questions avec un pronom complément d'objet direct ou indirect.

D'habitude quand vous voyagez...
1. Faites-vous *vos préparatifs* bien à l'avance?
2. Invitez-vous quelquefois *votre meilleur(e) ami(e)* à voyager avec vous?

La prochaine fois que vous partirez en voyage...
3. Allez-vous dire *à vos parents* où vous allez?
4. Allez-vous faire *votre valise* bien à l'avance?

La dernière fois que vous êtes parti(e) en voyage...
5. Vous avez montré *vos photos du voyage* à votre famille après?
6. Vous avez téléphoné *à vos amis* pendant le voyage?

F. Correspondance. Luc correspond par mail avec Micheline après leur retour à Paris et en Guadeloupe. Dans le paragraphe suivant, il parle à son ami, Alain, de ses relations avec elle. Complétez le paragraphe avec la forme correcte des verbes entre parenthèses.

Micheline et moi, nous _____ (s'écrire) des mails. Je lui _____ (écrire) tous les jours mais récemment elle m'_____ (écrire) moins. Normalement, nous _____ (se dire) tout, mais maintenant, quand je _____ (lire) ses mails, je suis certain qu'il y a quelque chose qu'elle ne me _____ (dire) pas. Je lui _____ (dire) que je l'aime mais elle ne me _____ (dire) jamais qu'elle m'aime.

Maintenant, Alain lui pose des questions sur ses relations avec Micheline. Complétez ses questions avec la forme correcte du verbe indiqué. Ensuite, imaginez les réponses de Luc d'après le paragraphe précédent.

1. Est-ce que Micheline t'_____ (écrire) tous les jours?
2. Est-ce que tu lui _____ (écrire) aussi?
3. Est-ce qu'elle te _____ (dire) qu'elle t'aime?

G. Des reproches. Luc commence à faire des reproches à Micheline. Il pense qu'elle va l'oublier. Qu'est-ce qu'il dit? Utilisez le pronom **me**.

> **EXEMPLE** ne pas aimer
> **Tu ne m'aimes pas.**

1. ne pas demander mon opinion
2. ne pas écrire tous les jours
3. ne jamais téléphoner
4. ne pas parler de tes projets
5. parler très peu de tes amis en Guadeloupe
6. quitter pour un autre

Pour rassurer Luc, Micheline dit qu'elle va ou ne va pas faire chacune de ces choses. Qu'est-ce qu'elle dit?

> **EXEMPLE** **Je vais t'aimer!**

Lecture et Composition

Ma grand-mère m'a appris à ne pas compter sur les yeux des autres pour dormir

Je suis restée avec grand-mère moins longtemps qu'avec maman. Maman était en meilleure santé, elle ne buvait pas, mais grand-mère a plus fait pour moi que maman. Elle m'a beaucoup appris. Et surtout à ne pas compter sur les yeux des autres pour dormir.

Elle m'**a enseigné** le travail de la terre, à organiser un jardin, à planter des légumes. À reconnaître aussi les plantes qui soignent, celles qui sont bonnes pour **le ventre**, pour **la toux**, pour **les blessures.**

[Quand **j'ai très mal,** ma grand-mère m'avait donné **un mouchoir.** Alors je prends ce mouchoir—ce que l'on appelle un madras chez nous ici—et je serre **ma tête** avec ce madras et je me sens très forte.]

La nuit venue, quand grand-mère **était d'attaque, debout** sur ses deux pieds, la tête bien fraîche, elle s'asseyait dans sa berceuse et me lançait: *Yékrik!* Je répondais: *Yékrak!* et allais m'installer **sur ses genoux.** Ma petite main dans **la sienne, j'enfouissais** ma tête entre ses deux **seins.** Alors grand-mère me faisait voyager dans **un monde étrange, celui** des contes… J'aimais beaucoup les contes où les **enfants orphelins, pauvres, à force de lutter contre la misère,** de marcher, de marcher, de marcher, **d'employer la ruse comme Compère Lapin,** finissaient, une fois grands, par devenir riches et respectés par tous.

a enseigné *taught*   **le ventre** *belly*   **la toux** *cough*   **les blessures** *injuries*   **j'ai très mal** *I hurt very badly*   **un mouchoir** *a handkerchief*   **ma tête** *my head*   **était d'attaque, debout** *was feeling fit, standing*   **Yékrik! Yékrak!** *a cry used to begin a story*   **sur ses genoux** *on her lap*   **la sienne** *hers*   **j'enfouissais** *I buried*   **tête** *head*   **seins** *breasts*   **un monde étrange, celui** *a strange world, the one*   **enfants orphelins, pauvres** *orphaned children, poor*   **à force de lutter contre la misère** *by fighting poverty*   **d'employer la ruse comme Compère Lapin** *using trickery like Compère Lapin* (equivalent of Brer Rabbit)

Lecture

❀ **Pour mieux lire:** *Understanding words with multiple meanings*

You are going to read an extract from a work by Dany Bébel-Gisler (1935–2003) whose stories depict the culture of the Antilles. As you will find in this reading, words often have more than one meaning. Learning to be flexible about the meanings of words will help you read more easily. Consider the multiple meanings of these words.

apprendre	*to learn*	*to teach*
compter	*to count, to plan*	**compter sur** *to depend on, to count on*
la terre	*the ground*	*the earth*
serrer	*to squeeze*	*to wrap around*
une berceuse	*a lullaby*	*a rocking chair*
soigner	*to care for*	*to cure*
frais (fraîche)	*cool*	*fresh*
finir	*to finish*	**finir par** *to end up*

Quel sens? Traduisez les phrases suivantes. Choisissez selon le contexte le sens le plus logique pour les mots en italique. Voir la liste ci-dessus. *(See the above list.)*

1. Ma grand-mère *m'a appris* à ne pas trop *compter* sur les autres.
2. Elle m'a appris le travail de *la terre,* à reconnaître les plantes qui *soignent* les maladies.
3. Je *serre* ma tête *(head)* avec ce madras [a type of Caribbean scarf].
4. Ma grand-mère avait la tête *fraîche,* elle s'asseyait *(used to sit)* dans sa *berceuse.*
5. Ils *finissaient par* devenir riches.

Compréhension

1. Avec qui est-ce que la petite fille aimait passer son temps? Pourquoi?
2. Qu'est-ce qu'elle a appris de sa grand-mère?
3. Quelle sorte de contes est-ce qu'elle aimait?

Composition

⚙ **Pour mieux écrire:** *Revising what you write*

Editing and revising what you write is an important final step in the writing process. Once you finish a composition, reread it and make sure you have an introductory and a concluding sentence and that your sentences and paragraphs are clear and well organized. Then, check each sentence against this checklist:

Are the verbs in the proper form for the subject and the tense?
Do all of your adjectives agree (masculine, feminine, singular, plural) with the nouns they modify?

Are all the words spelled correctly (including accents) and do the nouns have the correct article (**un, une, le, du, de,** …), possessive adjective (**mon, ton, ses,** …), … ? Did you use the correct forms of the prepositions **de** (**du, de la,** …) and **à** (**au, à la,** …)?

Révisons! Lisez ce paragraphe. D'abord, trouvez une bonne phrase pour commencer le paragraphe et une autre pour le terminer. Ensuite, trouvez les 16 erreurs *(errors)* dans le paragraphe et corrigez-les.

Philippe préfère voyagé à l'étranger, mais Marie préfère reste dans son propre *(own)* pays. Quand ils voyage ensemble, Philippe passe très peu du temps au hôtel mais Marie aime passer toutes les soirées dans son chambre. Philippe préfère visiter une grand ville et profiter de les activités culturelles. Marie préfère les activités de plein air et elle aime passer sa vacances à la montange ou à la mère. L'année prochain, ils visiteront Nice ou Philippe iront au musées et Marie passera sa temps à la plage.

If you have access to SYSTÈME-D software, you will find the following phrases, vocabulary, grammar, and dictionary aids there.
Phrases: Planning a vacation
Vocabulary: Traveling; Calendar
Grammar: Future tense

Un itinéraire

Imaginez que votre classe de français va faire un voyage d'une semaine dans un pays francophone. Écrivez une description détaillée du voyage que la classe fera ensemble. Dans la description, donnez les renseignements suivants.

- où vous irez, quand vous partirez et quand vous reviendrez
- comment vous voyagerez et combien coûtera le voyage par personne
- où vous descendrez et où vous prendrez les repas
- ce que vous ferez chaque jour de la semaine

N'oubliez pas de relire votre composition et de la réviser si nécessaire.

Comparaisons culturelles

Le créole

Le français est la langue officielle des Antilles françaises. La population locale parle aussi créole. Par définition une langue créole est une langue formée d'une combinaison de plusieurs langues. Le créole antillais est **un mélange de** français avec des langues **indigènes** et africaines, avec des mots **provenant de** l'espagnol, du portugais, de l'anglais et du hindi.

Le créole, c'est plus qu'une langue, c'est «**également une façon de vivre,** et l'histoire d'un peuple, **évoquant à la fois** l'Afrique, **l'esclavage,** mais aussi la danse, la musique, les îles, la fête... »[1]

---

un mélange de *a mixture of*   **indigènes** *indigenous*   **provenant de** *derived from*   **également une façon de vivre** *equally a way of life*   **évoquant à la fois** *evoking at the same time*   **l'esclavage** *slavery*

[1] http://www.webcaraibes.com/guadeloupe/culture.htm

Voilà quelques expressions créoles avec leurs équivalents français. Prononcez chacune et indiquez où vous remarquez une similarité avec la prononciation de la version française.

Bonjou	*Bonjour*
Sa ki là?	*Qui est là?*
Doudou	*Chérie* (Darling)
Resté là, mwen ka vini	*Reste là, j'arrive*
Mwen là	*Ça va, je suis là*
Ki laj ou?	*Quel âge as-tu?*
Mwen aimé ou doudou	*Chérie je t'aime*
Ba mwen	*Donne-moi*
Ou ka comprendre?	*Tu comprends?*
Es ou tann' sa mwen di ou?	*Tu entends ce que je te dis?*
Mi bel plési!	*Quel plaisir!*
Tanzantan	*De temps en temps*
An ti sèk	*Un verre de rhum sec*
I bon (memm)	*C'est bon*
Vini là	*Viens ici*
Boug mwen	*Mon ami*
Pani problem	*Pas de problème*
Méssyé zé dam	*Messieurs et Mesdames*
Bonswa	*Bonsoir*

Visit **academic.cengage.com/french** for YouTube video cultural correlations, cultural information and activities.

Compréhension

1. Quelle est la langue officielle des Antilles françaises? Quelle autre langue est-ce que la population locale parle aussi?

2. Quelle est la définition d'une langue créole? Le créole antillais est un mélange de quelles langues?

3. Pensez à l'histoire des îles caraïbes, une histoire de colonisation, de plantations et d'esclavage. Comment est-ce que cette histoire explique le développement de la langue créole?

4. Regardez la liste des expressions créoles et leurs équivalents français. Pouvez-vous déterminer comment on dit les mots suivants en créole?
je/moi/mon   tu/toi/ton bon

5. Est-ce qu'il y a une langue officielle dans votre pays? Est-ce qu'il devrait y en avoir une? *(Should there be one?)* Pourquoi ou pourquoi pas?

Résumé de grammaire

The future tense (*Le futur*)

Use the future tense to say what someone *will* do. Form it by adding the bold-faced endings below to the same stem that you used for the conditional. For most verbs, it is the infinitive, but drop the final **e** of infinitives ending with **-re**.

Je **prendrai** des vacances en été.

Tu resteras ici?

Tu partiras tout seul?

Mes parents voyageront avec moi.

VISITER	CONNAÎTRE	FINIR
je visiter**ai**	je connaîtr**ai**	je finir**ai**
tu visiter**as**	tu connaîtr**as**	tu finir**as**
il/elle/on visiter**a**	il/elle/on connaîtr**a**	il/elle/on finir**a**
nous visiter**ons**	nous connaîtr**ons**	nous finir**ons**
vous visiter**ez**	vous connaîtr**ez**	vous finir**ez**
ils/elles visiter**ont**	ils/elles connaîtr**ont**	ils/elles finir**ont**

The following verbs have irregular stems.

J'irai en Europe.

Combien de temps **serez-vous** en Europe?

On reviendra après trois semaines.

-r-		-vr- / -dr-		-rr-	
aller:	ir-	devoir:	devr-	voir:	verr-
avoir:	aur-	vouloir:	voudr-	pouvoir:	pourr-
être:	ser-	venir:	viendr-	mourir:	mourr-
faire:	fer-	devenir:	deviendr-	courir	courr-
savoir:	saur-	revenir:	reviendr-		
		obtenir	obtiendr-		

S'il **peut,** mon frère **ira** en vacances avec nous.

Il décidera quand **on saura** la date exacte de notre départ.

As in English, use the future tense in *if / then* sentences to say what will happen if something else occurs. Use the present tense in the clause with **si**. Unlike English, use the future in French in clauses with **quand** referring to the future. English has the present in such clauses.

The verbs *dire, lire,* and *écrire*

The verbs **dire, lire,** and **écrire** are irregular in the present tense and the **passé composé (j'ai dit, j'ai lu, j'ai écrit).** As with other verbs, use the stem for **nous** in the present tense to form the imperfect **(je disais, je lisais, j'écrivais).** Obtain the future / conditional stem by dropping the final **e** of the infinitive **(je dirai, je lirai, j'écrirai).**

Est-ce que **tu lis** ton mail quand tu voyages?

J'écris à mes amis et je leur montre des photos de mon voyage.

Mes parents disent que la Méditerranée est très jolie.

DIRE	LIRE	ÉCRIRE
je dis	je lis	j' écris
tu dis	tu lis	tu écris
il/elle/on dit	il/elle/on lit	il/elle/on écrit
nous disons	nous lisons	nous écrivons
vous dites	vous lisez	vous écrivez
ils/elles disent	ils/elles lisent	ils/elles écrivent

The verbs *savoir* and *connaître*

Savoir and **connaître** both mean *to know*. Use **savoir** when *to know* is followed by a verb, a question word (**qui, où…**), or by **si, que,** or **ce que,** or to say that one knows a language. When *to know* is followed by a noun, use **savoir** to say one *knows a fact or information,* and **connaître** to say one is *familiar with a person, place, or thing.*

SAVOIR	CONNAÎTRE
je sais	je connais
tu sais	tu connais
il/elle/on sait	il/elle/on connaît
nous savons	nous connaissons
vous savez	vous connaissez
ils/elles savent	ils/elles connaissent
P. C.: j'ai su *(I found out)*	j'ai connu *(I met)*
IMPARFAIT: je savais *(I knew)*	je connaissais *(I knew)*
CONDITIONNEL: je saurais	je connaîtrais
FUTUR: je saurai	je connaîtrai

Quelles langues **sais-tu?**
Je sais parler français mais **mes parents savent** l'allemand.

Savez-vous si vous allez visiter l'Allemagne?
On ira à Berlin, où **mes parents connaissent** beaucoup de gens.

Je ne connais pas du tout l'Europe. Est-ce que **tu connais** bien l'histoire de la région?

Direct and Indirect object pronouns

Direct object pronouns replace nouns that are the direct object of the verb. Indirect object pronouns replace nouns that are the indirect object of the verb. Generally, indirect objects are people or animals, not things, and they follow the preposition **à.** They often are used with verbs indicating communication or exchanges (**parler à, téléphoner à, dire à, écrire à, demander à, rendre visite à, donner à**).

DIRECT OBJECT PRONOUNS				INDIRECT OBJECT PRONOUNS			
me (m')	*me*	**nous**	*us*	**me (m')**	*(to) me*	**nous**	*(to) us*
te (t')	*you*	**vous**	*you*	**te (t')**	*(to) you*	**vous**	*(to) you*
le (l')	*him, it*	**les**	*them*	**lui**	*(to) him*	**leur**	*(to) them*
la (l')	*her, it*			**lui**	*(to) her*		

Est-ce que tu **m'**écriras si je **te** donne mon adresse mail?

Mon frère habite à Paris. Je vais **te** donner son numéro de téléphone et tu pourras **lui** téléphoner quand tu seras en France.

Both direct and indirect object pronouns have the same placement rules. They go immediately before the infinitive if there is one in the same clause. If not, they go before the conjugated verb. In the **passé composé,** they go before the auxiliary verb. The past participle agrees with direct object pronouns, but not with indirect objects.

Les amis de mes parents **nous** ont demandé de **leur** rendre visite. Mes parents ne **les** ont pas vus depuis vingt ans, la dernière fois qu'ils **leur** ont rendu visite.

Geographical expressions

Use the definite article with names of continents, countries, states, and provinces used as the subject or object of a verb, but not with cities. Most continents, countries, states, and provinces ending in **e** are feminine, whereas most others are masculine.

To say *to* or *in* with a geographical location, use…

Je voudrais visiter **les** États-Unis, **le** Canada et **la** Colombie.

à	with cities
aux	with any plural country or region
en	with any feminine country or region and with any masculine one beginning with a vowel sound
au	with any masculine country or region beginning with a consonant

Pendant notre voyage, on ira **à** Berlin **en** Allemagne, **à** Copenhague **au** Danemark, **à** Amsterdam **aux** Pays-Bas et **à** Paris et **à** Nice **en** France.

Vocabulaire

COMPÉTENCE 1 — Track 3

Talking about vacation

NOMS MASCULINS

un endroit	*a place*
un Parisien	*a Parisian*
le paysage	*the landscape, scenery*
un site	*a site, a spot*

NOMS FÉMININS

une île	*an island*
la mer	*the sea*
une Parisienne	*a Parisian*
une terrasse	*a terrace*

EXPRESSIONS VERBALES

admirer	*to admire*
bronzer	*to tan*
compter	*to count on, to plan on*
courir	*to run*
goûter	*to taste*
profiter de	*to take advantage of*

ADJECTIFS

assis(e)	*seated*
exotique	*exotic*
historique	*historic*
local(e) (*mpl* **locaux**)	*local*
touristique	*touristic*
tropical(e) (*mpl* **tropicaux**)	*tropical*

DIVERS

Ça te plaira.	*You'll like it.*
là-bas	*over there*
le long de	*along*

COMPÉTENCE 2 — Track 6

Preparing for a trip

NOMS MASCULINS

un article	*an article*
un billet (électronique)	*an (e-)ticket*
un chèque de voyage	*a travelers' check*
le climat	*the climate*
un départ	*a departure*
un guide	*a guidebook, a guide*
un magazine	*a magazine*
un passeport	*a passport*
un poème	*a poem*
des préparatifs	*preparations*
un roman	*a novel*
un site Web	*a website*
un voisin	*a neighbor*

NOMS FÉMININS

une agence de voyages	*a travel agency*
une arrivée	*an arrival*
une carte postale	*a postcard*
la douane	*customs*
une histoire	*a story*
une lettre	*a letter*
une rédaction	*a composition*
une valise	*a suitcase*
une voisine	*a neighbor*

EXPRESSIONS VERBALES

changer	*to change, to exchange*
décrire	*to describe*
dire	*to say, to tell*
donner à manger à	*to feed*
écrire	*to write*
faire sa valise	*to pack your bag*
s'informer	*to find out information*
lire	*to read*
obtenir	*to obtain*
passer	*to pass (through)*
recevoir	*to receive*
réserver	*to reserve*

DIVERS

à l'étranger	*in another country, abroad*
Ça lui plaît?	*Does he/she like it?*
extraordinaire	*extraordinary, great*
leur	*(to) them*
lui	*(to) him, (to) her*
me (m')	*(to) me*
sur Internet	*on the Internet*

Buying your ticket

NOMS MASCULINS

un agent de voyages	*a travel agent*
un aller simple	*a one-way ticket*
un billet aller-retour	*a round-trip ticket*
les gens	*the people*
un itinéraire	*an itinerary*
le retour	*the return*
le système de transports en commun	*the public transportation system*
un vol	*a flight*

NOMS FÉMININS

une carte bancaire	*a bank card, a debit card*
une carte de crédit	*a credit card*
la classe touriste	*tourist class, coach*
la culture	*the culture*
la géographie	*the geography*
l'heure d'arrivée	*the arrival time*
l'heure de départ	*the departure time*
la porte d'arrivée	*the arrival gate*
la porte d'embarquement	*the departure gate*
la première classe	*first class*

EXPRESSIONS VERBALES

connaître	*to know, to be familiar with, to be acquainted with*
faire une réservation	*to make a reservation*
reconnaître	*to recognize*
savoir	*to know*

DIVERS

à l'avance	*in advance*
Ça te/vous convient?	*Does that work for you?*
il me (te/nous/vous/lui/leur) faut	*I (you/we/you/he [she]/they) need*
me	*(to) me*
nous	*(to) us*
te	*(to) you*
vous	*(to) you*

Deciding where to go on a trip

NOMS MASCULINS

le Brésil	*Brazil*
le Canada	*Canada*
le Chili	*Chile*
un continent	*a continent*
les États-Unis	*the United States*
Israël	*Israel*
le Japon	*Japan*
le Maroc	*Morocco*
le Mexique	*Mexico*
le Moyen-Orient	*the Middle East*
l'Ontario	*Ontario*
le Pérou	*Peru*
le Royaume-Uni	*the United Kingdom*
le Sénégal	*Senegal*
le Texas	*Texas*
le Viêt Nam	*Vietnam*

NOMS FÉMININS

l'Afrique	*Africa*
l'Algérie	*Algeria*
l'Allemagne	*Germany*
l'Amérique centrale	*Central America*
l'Amérique du Nord	*North America*
l'Amérique du Sud	*South America*
les Antilles	*the West Indies*
l'Argentine	*Argentina*
l'Asie	*Asia*
l'Australie	*Australia*
la Belgique	*Belgium*
la Californie	*California*
la Chine	*China*
la Colombie	*Colombia*
la Côte d'Ivoire	*Ivory Coast*
l'Égypte	*Egypt*
l'Espagne	*Spain*
l'Europe	*Europe*
la Floride	*Florida*
la France	*France*
la Guyane	*French Guiana*
l'Italie	*Italy*
la Nouvelle-Calédonie	*New Caledonia*
l'Océanie	*Oceania*
la Polynésie française	*French Polynesia*
la Russie	*Russia*
la Suisse	*Switzerland*

DIVERS

adorer	*to adore, to love*

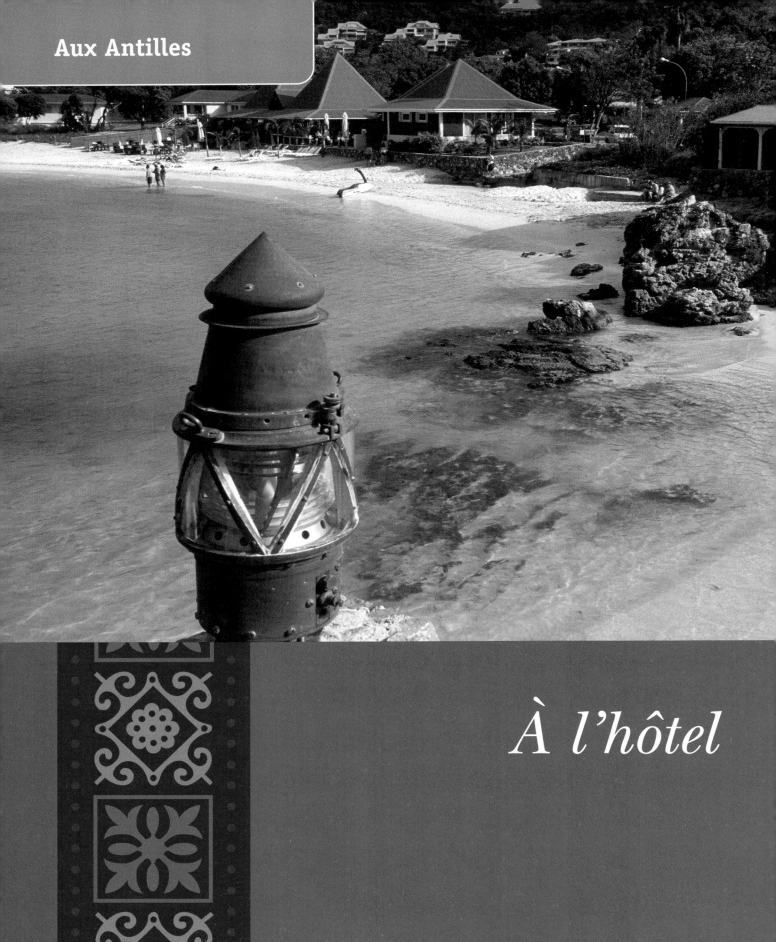

À l'hôtel

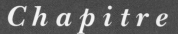

iLrn iLrn Heinle Learning Center

academic.cengage.com/french/horizons

Système-D

Audio　　iRadio

LES ANTILLES

Aux Antilles, on parle français aussi en Haïti. Faites des recherches sur l'histoire, la géographie, l'économie et la culture de cette région sur Internet.

Avez-vous déjà visité une île aux Caraïbes? Voudriez-vous visiter les Antilles? Les Antilles françaises **comprennent** la Martinique et la Guadeloupe et son **archipel** (Marie-Galante, les Saintes, Saint-Martin, Saint-Barthélemy, la Désirade et Petite-Terre). La Guadeloupe et la Martinique sont **à la fois** départements d'outre-mer et régions de France. Cette situation donne à leurs **citoyens** tous les **droits** et les responsabilités des citoyens français. Ces îles offrent donc aux visiteurs **un monde** caraïbe **à la française.**

Quatre-vingt-dix pour cent des habitants de la Martinique et de la Guadeloupe sont des descendants d'**esclaves** africains. Cet héritage est évident dans la culture créole.

La mer des Caraïbes

La célèbre Fête des cuisinières en Guadeloupe

La montagne Pelée, en Martinique

comprennent *include*   **archipel** *archipelago*   **à la fois** *at the same time*   **citoyens** *citizens*   **droits** *rights*
un monde *a world*   **à la française** *French-style*   **esclaves** *slaves*

LA GUADELOUPE
NOMBRE D'HABITANTS: 453 000
  (les Guadeloupéens)
CHEF-LIEU (ADMINISTRATIVE
  CENTER): Basse-Terre

LA MARTINIQUE
NOMBRE D'HABITANTS: 399 000
  (les Martiniquais)
CHEF-LIEU: Fort-de-France
Visit it live on Google Earth!

Depuis le temps de ses premiers habitants, on appelle la Martinique «l'île aux **fleurs**», et la beauté de ses paysages et **la chaleur** de son peuple sont **renommées**. Fort-de-France, **le chef-lieu,** est une ville pleine d'activité. Saint-Pierre, l'**ancien** chef-lieu de la Martinique, a été **détruit** par une éruption de la montagne Pelée en 1902. **Au milieu de** la ville **vivante** d'aujourd'hui, on peut voir des ruines de l'ancienne ville.

La Guadeloupe est composée de deux îles, Grande-Terre et Basse-Terre. Grande-Terre est plutôt **plate** et **sèche** et **recouverte de champs** de canne à sucre. Pointe-à-Pitre, la plus grande ville de la Guadeloupe, **se trouve** sur Grande-Terre.

Basse-Terre est **couverte de** montagnes volcaniques et de forêts tropicales. La Soufrière, un volcan actif, domine la partie sud de l'île et une grande partie de l'île, le Parc national de la Guadeloupe, est protégée. Basse-Terre, le chef-lieu de la Guadeloupe, se trouve sur l'île de Basse-Terre.

Grande-Terre

Pointe-à-Pitre

L'île de Basse-Terre

❀ Qu'en savez-vous?

Voici quelques dates importantes de l'histoire des Antilles françaises. Devinez quelle est la date de chacun des événements suivants.

1648   1848   1902   1493   1946   1502

1. Christophe Colomb a découvert la Guadeloupe au cours de son deuxième voyage en Amérique. —1493
2. Christophe Colon a débarqué brièvement en Martinique au cours de son quatrième voyage en Amérique. 1502
3. Les premiers colons (colonists) français sont arrivés aux Saintes, dans l'archipel de la Guadeloupe. 1648
4. La France a aboli l'esclavage (slavery) presque vingt ans avant les États-Unis. 1848
5. Près de 30 000 personnes sont mortes dans la ville de Saint-Pierre après l'éruption de la montagne Pelée en Martinique. 1902 Seulement un habitant de la ville de Saint-Pierre a survécu (survived), un prisonnier protégé par les murs de la prison.
6. La Guadeloupe, la Martinique, la Guyane et La Réunion sont devenues des départments français. 1946

---

fleurs *flowers*   **la chaleur** *the warmth*   **renommées** *renowned*   **le chef-lieu** *the administrative center*   **ancien** *former*
détruit *destroyed*   **Au milieu de** *In the midst of*   **vivante** *living*   **plate** *flat*   **sèche** *dry*   **recouverte de champs** *covered with fields*   **se trouve** *is located*   **couverte de** *covered with*

Deciding where to stay

Le logement

Quand vous êtes en vacances, est-ce que vous aimez mieux descendre dans... ?

un hôtel (de luxe) **une auberge de jeunesse** un chalet de ski **une station estivale**

Préférez-vous avoir une chambre... ?

à deux lits ou avec un grand lit avec ou sans salle de bains et **W.-C.** avec douche

Comment préférez-vous **régler la note**?

en espèces *(f)* en chèques de voyage par carte de crédit

CD 4-11

Luc a quitté la Guadeloupe pour aller passer quelques jours en Martinique. Il arrive à la réception d'un hôtel.

Luc:	Bonjour, monsieur.
L'hôtelier:	Bonjour, monsieur.
Luc:	Avez-vous une chambre pour ce soir?
L'hôtelier:	Eh bien... nous avons une chambre avec salle de bains et W.-C. privés.
Luc:	C'est combien la nuit?
L'hôtelier:	108 euros, monsieur.
Luc:	Vous avez quelque chose de moins cher?
L'hôtelier:	Voyons... nous avons une chambre avec douche et **lavabo** à 88 euros, si vous préférez.
Luc:	Je préfère une chambre calme.
L'hôtelier:	Alors, **il vaut mieux** prendre la chambre avec douche. C'est **côté cour** et il y a moins de **bruit**.

---

une auberge de jeunesse *a youth hostel*   **une station estivale** *a summer resort*   **régler la note** *to pay the bill*   **en espèces** *(f) in cash*   **un lavabo** *a sink*   **il vaut mieux** *it's better*   **côté cour** *on the courtyard side*   **le bruit** *noise*

LUC:	Bon, d'accord. Le petit déjeuner est **compris**?
L'HÔTELIER:	Non, monsieur. Il y a un supplément de 6 euros. Il est servi entre sept heures et neuf heures dans la salle à manger.
LUC:	Eh bien, je vais prendre la chambre avec douche. Vous préférez que je vous paie maintenant?
L'HÔTELIER:	Non, monsieur. Vous pouvez régler la note à votre départ. Voici **la clé.** C'est la chambre 210. C'est au bout du couloir.
LUC:	Y a-t-il un restaurant dans le quartier?
L'HÔTELIER:	Je vous recommande Le Tropical.
LUC:	Est-ce qu'il faut réserver?
L'HÔTELIER:	Oui, il vaut mieux.
LUC:	Merci, monsieur.
L'HÔTELIER:	**Bon séjour.**

A. Préférences. Indiquez vos préférences.

1. Quand je pars en vacances, je préfère *visiter un autre pays / rester dans mon propre* (my own) *pays.*
2. J'aime mieux *visiter une grande ville / aller à la montagne / aller à la mer / ???.*
3. Comme activités en vacances, j'aime *nager / goûter la cuisine locale / ???.*
4. Je préfère descendre dans *un hôtel pas cher / un hôtel de luxe / une auberge de jeunesse / une station estivale / ???. (Ça dépend de qui va payer!)*
5. À mon avis, *il vaut mieux réserver une chambre d'hôtel à l'avance / on peut toujours trouver un hôtel à son arrivée.*
6. Je préfère une chambre *avec douche / avec salle de bains. (Je préfère la chambre la moins chère.)*
7. Quand je descends dans un hôtel, je préfère prendre mon petit déjeuner *dans ma chambre / dans le restaurant de l'hôtel / dans un autre restaurant / dans un fast-food / ???. (Je ne prends pas de petit déjeuner.)*
8. Je préfère régler la note *en espèces / en chèques de voyage / par carte de crédit.*

B. Réponses. Votre meilleur(e) ami(e) et vous allez passer six jours dans un petit hôtel en Martinique. Répondez aux questions de l'hôtelier selon vos besoins et vos goûts.

1. Vous voulez une chambre pour une seule personne?
2. C'est pour combien de nuits?
3. Vous voulez une chambre à deux lits ou avec un grand lit?
4. Vous préférez une chambre avec ou sans salle de bains?
5. Nous avons une chambre à 75 euros. Vous préférez régler la note maintenant ou à votre départ?
6. Il y a un supplément de 6 euros pour le petit déjeuner. Vous allez prendre le petit déjeuner à l'hôtel?
7. Comment voulez-vous payer?
8. C'est à quel nom?

C. Conversation. Avec un(e) partenaire, relisez à haute voix la conversation entre Luc et l'hôtelier. Ensuite, imaginez que vous allez visiter la Martinique ensemble. Parlez de quelle sorte de chambres vous voulez et comment vous allez payer.

You can find a list of the new words from CD 4-12 the vocabulary and grammar section of this ***Compétence*** on page 418 and a recording of this list on track 4-12 of your *Text Audio CD.*

---

compris(e) *included*   **la clé** *the key*   **Bon séjour** *Enjoy your stay*

Pour vérifier

1. What are two ways to say *it is necessary*? How do you say *it's not necessary*? What does **il ne faut pas** mean? How do you say *it's better*? *it's important*? *it's good*? *it's bad*?

2. When offering general advice, what form of the verb do you use following these impersonal expressions? How do you negate an infinitive?

Giving general advice

Les expressions impersonnelles et l'infinitif

The following expressions can be used to give advice and state opinions. When making generalizations, follow them with an infinitive.

Notice that although **il faut** means *it is necessary*, **il ne faut pas** means *one should not* or *one must not*. Use **il n'est pas nécessaire** to say *it's not necessary*.

Il faut	Il faut payer un supplément pour le petit déjeuner.
Il ne faut pas	Il ne faut pas faire trop de bruit.
Il vaut mieux	Il vaut mieux réserver à l'avance.
Il est nécessaire (de)	Il est nécessaire de réserver.
Il n'est pas nécessaire (de)	Il n'est pas nécessaire de téléphoner à l'avance.
Il est essentiel (de)	Il est essentiel de régler la note.
Il est important (de)	Il est important de ne pas perdre la clé.
Il est bon (de)	Il est bon de choisir une chambre calme.
Il est mauvais (de)	Il est mauvais de faire trop de bruit.
C'est bien (de)...	C'est bien de profiter de la piscine.

Notes de grammaire

1. Note that the expressions that have **être** (**Il est important / essentiel / bon...**) require the preposition **de** before an infinitive. Remember that **de** elides before a vowel sound.

2. **C'est bien...** is less formal than **Il est bon...** and is more likely to be used when talking with a friend. You will also hear **C'est important / essentiel / bon...** in less formal conversation.

3. Remember to place both parts of a negative expression before the infinitive when negating an infinitive: **Il est important de ne pas perdre la clé.**

A. Préparatifs Un ami fait les préparatifs pour un voyage que vous allez faire ensemble. Utilisez un élément de chaque colonne pour lui expliquer ce qu'il faut faire.

EXEMPLE **Il vaut mieux réserver une chambre à l'avance.**

Il faut	réserver une chambre à l'avance
Il vaut mieux	obtenir les passeports bien à l'avance
Il est bon de	oublier les billets
Il n'est pas bon de	savoir le numéro et l'heure de départ du vol
Il est important de	tout payer par carte de crédit
Il n'est pas important de	choisir une chambre côté rue
Il ne faut pas	choisir une chambre côté cour
	faire beaucoup de bruit dans l'hôtel

B. Qu'est-ce qu'il faut faire? Qu'est-ce qu'il faut faire dans les situations suivantes quand on voyage?

EXEMPLE Si on est fatigué?
Il faut rentrer à l'hôtel.

rentrer à l'hôtel		se coucher
téléphoner à l'ambassade *(embassy)*		téléphoner à des amis
acheter un plan *(map)* de la ville		changer d'hôtel
aller à la banque		acheter un guide touristique
	aller au restaurant	

1. Si on perd son passeport?
2. Si on veut visiter la ville?
3. Si on a faim?
4. Si l'hôtel est trop bruyant *(noisy)*?
5. Si on cherche une liste de bons restaurants et de sites touristiques?
6. Si on a sommeil?
7. Si on se sent un peu seul *(lonely)*?
8. Si on a besoin de changer de l'argent?

C. Étiquette en France. Pour chaque paire, dites s'il faut faire les choses suivantes quand on est invité à dîner chez des Français. L'un des conseils de chaque paire est quelque chose qu'il ne faut pas faire. Completez chaque phrase avec:

il faut	il ne faut pas	il vaut mieux

1. _____ offrir des fleurs ou un autre cadeau à votre hôtesse en arrivant.
   _____ apporter *(bring)* de chrysanthèmes.
2. _____ apporter une bouteille de vin pour le dîner.
   _____ laisser votre hôte choisir le vin.
3. _____ serrer *(shake)* la main des autres invités en arrivant.
   _____ mettre les mains dans les poches *(pockets)*.
4. _____ garder *(to keep)* les deux mains sur la table pendant qu'on mange.
   _____ mettre une main sur les genoux *(lap, knees)*.
5. _____ manger des frites avec les mains.
   _____ manger un fruit avec une fourchette et un couteau *(fork and knife)*.
6. _____ parler de cuisine, d'art, de musique, de films ou de l'actualité *(current events)*.
   _____ parler d'argent ou demander où les autres travaillent.
7. _____ annoncer que vous allez aux toilettes.
   _____ quitter la table discrètement et seulement si nécessaire.

D. Chez vous. Un groupe de Martiniquais va venir visiter votre région. Donnez-leur des conseils.

EXEMPLE Il est essentiel d'aller **au City Arts Museum.**

1. Il vaut mieux venir au mois de (d')...
2. Il ne faut pas venir au mois de (d')...
3. Il est important d'apporter *(to bring)*...
4. Il est essentiel de ne pas oublier...
5. Il est bon de descendre à l'hôtel...
6. Il est bon de goûter la cuisine locale au restaurant...
7. Il n'est pas bon de manger au restaurant...
8. Il est essentiel de voir...

Que faut-il faire pour préparer un voyage en Martinique?

Stratégies et Compréhension auditive

When you cannot understand everything you hear, use what you can understand, as well as non-verbal cues such as circumstances, tone of voice, and written materials such as ads or signs to anticipate what someone will say. Read the two hotel ads at the bottom of this page and on the next page and list five things you learned about each hotel from its ad.

A. Quel hôtel? On parle de l'hôtel de l'Anse Bleue ou de l'hôtel Bakoua?

CD 4-13

B. Le ton de la voix. Écoutez le début de ces conversations dans un hôtel. Pour chacune, écoutez le ton de la voix *(tone of voice)* pour deviner la suite *(what follows)*, **a** ou **b**.

CD 4-14

1. **a.** C'est bien. Nous allons prendre la chambre.
   b. Est-ce que vous avez quelque chose de moins cher?
2. **a.** Nous préférons une chambre avec salle de bains.
   b. Bon, c'est bien. Je vais prendre cette chambre.
3. **a.** Voici votre clé, monsieur. Vous avez la chambre numéro 385.
   b. Je regrette, mais nous n'avons pas de réservation à votre nom.

Compréhension auditive: À la réception

CD 4-15

Deux touristes arrivent dans un hôtel. Écoutez cette conversation pour déterminer le prix de leur chambre.

À l'hôtel. Écoutez la conversation une seconde fois et répondez à ces questions.

1. Pourquoi est-ce que les touristes ne veulent pas la première chambre?
2. Combien coûte le petit déjeuner? Où est-ce qu'il est servi?
3. Quel est le numéro de leur chambre?

Bienvenue dans l'univers enchanté du Bakoua

Charme suranné des splendeurs coloniales... Ici le temps semble s'être arrêté. A la Pointe du Bout, face à l'une des plus belles baies du monde : une oasis de confort et de volupté pour votre plus grand plaisir.

- Un hôtel Sofitel Coralia 4 étoiles du Groupe Accor.
- 132 chambres grand confort climatisées avec terrasse ou balcon.
  - 6 suites de luxe de style colonial.
  - 2 restaurants proposant une cuisine raffinée créole et internationale.
  - 2 bars face à la piscine ou sur la plage.

INFORMATIONS - RÉSERVATIONS

Tél. : 0596 66 02 02 • Fax : 0596 66 00 41

SOFITEL BAKOUA CORALIA
LA POINTE DU BOUT
97229 LES TROIS ILETS

Going to the doctor

✳ **Note** *culturelle*

Voici quelques statistiques intéressantes sur les pratiques de santé des Français: Les Français consultent leur médecin en moyenne sept fois par an et dépensent à peu près *(spend more or less)* 10% de leur PIB *(GNP)* pour les soins médicaux *(medical care)*. 76% de leurs dépenses médicales sont remboursées par la Sécurité sociale. La majorité des Français traitent quelquefois leurs maladies eux-mêmes *(themselves)* et achètent des médicaments en vente libre *(over the counter)*. Est-ce que la situation est semblable dans votre pays?

Chez le médecin

Luc tombe **malade** pendant son séjour en Martinique. Savez-vous communiquer avec le médecin si vous tombez malade **au cours d'**un voyage?

—Où est-ce que vous **avez mal**?

—J'ai mal à la tête et au ventre.

—Quels autres symptômes avez-vous?

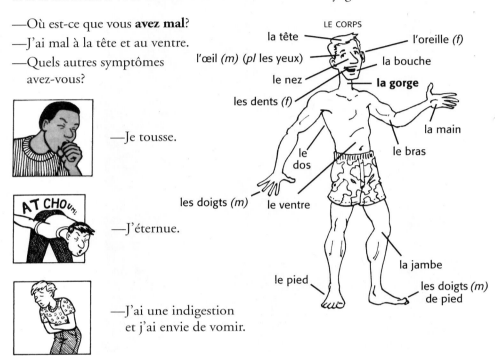

—Je tousse.

—J'éternue.

—J'ai une indigestion et j'ai envie de vomir.

Avez-vous **la grippe**? **un rhume**? un virus? des allergies?
Êtes-vous **enceinte**?

CD 4-16

Luc va chez le médecin.

LE MÉDECIN:	Bonjour, monsieur. **Qu'est-ce qui ne va pas** aujourd'hui?
LUC:	Je ne sais pas exactement. Je me sens mal. Je tousse, j'**ai des frissons** et j'ai mal un peu partout.
LE MÉDECIN:	Vous avez mal à la gorge?
LUC:	Oui, très.
LE MÉDECIN:	Eh bien, vous avez tout simplement la grippe.
LUC:	Qu'est-ce que je dois faire?
LE MÉDECIN:	Je vais vous donner **une ordonnance.** Il faut que vous preniez ces médicaments trois fois par jour. Il est important que vous finissiez tous ces médicaments. N'oubliez pas de boire beaucoup de liquides, mais il ne faut pas que vous buviez d'alcool et il est essentiel que vous restiez au lit.

---

le médecin *the doctor*   **malade** *sick*   **au cours de** *in the course of, during, while on*   **avoir mal (à)...** *one's . . . hurts*   **la gorge** *the throat*   **la grippe** *the flu*   **un rhume** *a cold*   **enceinte** *pregnant*   **Qu'est-ce qui ne va pas** *What's wrong*   **avoir des frissons** *to have the shivers*   **une ordonnance** *a prescription*

A. J'ai mal partout! Un hypocondriaque va voir son médecin. Selon lui *(According to him)*, il a mal partout, de la tête jusqu'aux pieds. De quoi se plaint-il? *(What does he complain about?)*

EXEMPLE **Mon Dieu, docteur! J'ai mal à la tête, j'ai mal aux yeux, j'ai mal au nez...**

B. Associations. Quelle partie(s) du corps associez-vous aux verbes suivants?

EXEMPLE écrire **la main et les doigts**

1. parler   **4.** lire   **7.** écouter   **10.** faire du jogging
2. fumer   **5.** boire   **8.** voir   **11.** toucher
3. se brosser   **6.** manger   **9.** éternuer   **12.** embrasser

C. Qu'est-ce qui ne va pas? Quels symptômes ont-ils?

EXEMPLE **Il a mal aux yeux.**

 1.  2.

3.  4. 5.

D. Des symptômes. Nommez autant de symptômes que possible pour chaque situation.

EXEMPLE Quand on a la grippe, **on a mal partout. On a des frissons et...**

1. Quand on a un rhume...
2. Quand on a des allergies...
3. Quand on a un virus intestinal...
4. Quand on est enceinte...

E. Entretien. Interviewez votre partenaire.

1. La dernière fois que tu as été malade, est-ce que tu avais mal à la tête? à la gorge? Est-ce que tu avais des frissons? Est-ce que tu es allé(e) chez le médecin? Qu'est-ce que tu avais? *(What was wrong?)* Est-ce que tu as pris des médicaments?
2. Est-ce que tu as des allergies? Quels symptômes as-tu? Pendant quels mois as-tu ces symptômes? Est-ce que tu prends des médicaments? Est-ce que tu vas chez le médecin pour une ordonnance ou est-ce que tu achètes des médicaments sans ordonnance?

F. Conversation. Avec un(e) partenaire, relisez à haute voix la conversation entre Luc et le médecin. Ensuite, imaginez que vous êtes malade et créez une conversation entre le médecin et vous.

Vocabulaire supplémentaire

un antibiotique *an antibiotic*
un antihistaminique *an antihistamine*
une aspirine *an aspirin*
le cou *the neck*
l'épaule *(f) the shoulder*
le genou *the knee*
des pastilles *(f)* **contre la toux** *cough drops*
la poitrine *the chest*
du sirop *cough syrup*
avoir de la fièvre *to have a fever*
avoir le nez bouché *to have a stuffy nose*
avoir le nez qui coule *to have a runny nose*
se brûler/se casser/se couper le doigt *to burn / break/cut your finger*
se fouler la cheville *to sprain your ankle*
faire une piqûre *to give a shot*
prendre sa température *to take your temperature*

You can find a list of the new words from CD 4-17 the vocabulary and grammar sections of this ***Compétence*** on page 418 and a recording of this list on track 4-17 of your *Text Audio CD.*

Pour vérifier

1. When do you use the subjunctive?
2. What do you use as the subjunctive stem for all verb forms except **nous** and **vous**? What endings do you use?
3. For most verbs, the **nous** and **vous** forms of the subjunctive look just like what other verb tense?

Note de grammaire

The **de** in expressions like **il est important de** is replaced by **que** in these structures. Remember that verbs ending in **-ier**, like **étudier** and **oublier**, will have two **i**'s in the **nous** and **vous** forms of the subjunctive, just as they did in the **imparfait: nous oubliions, vous étudiiez.**

 To download a podcast on the subjunctive, go to **academic.cengage.com/french.**

Giving advice to someone in particular

Les expressions impersonnelles et les verbes réguliers au subjonctif

You know you can use impersonal expressions like **il faut** and **il est important de** followed by an infinitive to give general advice or state opinions. When talking to or about a particular person, you can use these same expressions followed by **que** and a second clause with a conjugated verb.

Il est important **de bien manger.**   Il est important **que tu manges mieux.**
*It's important **to eat well.***   *It's important **that you eat better.***

When giving advice to a particular person, the verb in the second clause is in a form called the subjunctive. You have used verbs in the indicative mode to say what happens. The subjunctive is another verb mode. The subjunctive is generally used in the second clause of a sentence, when the first clause expresses a feeling, attitude, or opinion about what should or might be done, rather than simply stating what is happening. The present subjunctive may imply either present or future actions.

Il faut que	Il faut que tu restes au lit.
Il ne faut pas que	Il ne faut pas que tu sortes du lit.
Il vaut mieux que	Il vaut mieux que tu ne travailles pas.
Il est nécessaire que	Il est nécessaire que tu prennes ces médicaments.
Il n'est pas nécessaire que	Il n'est pas nécessaire que tu prennes de l'aspirine.
Il est essentiel que	Il est essentiel que tu finisses tous tes médicaments.
Il est important que	Il est important que tu te reposes.
Il est bon que	Il est bon que tu te sentes mieux.
Il est mauvais que	Il est mauvais que tu boives de l'alcool.
C'est bien que	C'est bien que tu ne fumes plus.

For most verbs, the subjunctive is formed as follows:

- For **nous** and **vous,** the subjunctive looks like the imperfect.
- For the other forms, find the stem of the subjunctive by dropping the **-ent** ending of the **ils/elles** form of the present indicative and use the endings: **-e, -es, -e, -ent.**

	PARLER	FINIR	RENDRE
que je (j')	parl**e**	finiss**e**	rend**e**
que tu	parl**es**	finiss**es**	rend**es**
qu'il/elle/on	parl**e**	finiss**e**	rend**e**
que nous	parl**ions**	finiss**ions**	rend**ions**
que vous	parl**iez**	finiss**iez**	rend**iez**
qu'ils/elles	parl**ent**	finiss**ent**	rend**ent**

Most irregular verbs follow the same rule.

connaître	que je connaiss**e**	que nous connaiss**ions**
dire	que je dis**e**	que nous dis**ions**
dormir	que je dorm**e**	que nous dorm**ions**
écrire	que j'écriv**e**	que nous écriv**ions**
lire	que je lis**e**	que nous lis**ions**
partir	que je part**e**	que nous part**ions**
sortir	que je sort**e**	que nous sort**ions**

These verbs follow the same rule, but have a different stem for the **nous** and **vous** forms.

acheter	que j'achèt**e**	que nous achet**ions**
boire	que je boiv**e**	que nous buv**ions**
devoir	que je doiv**e**	que nous dev**ions**
payer	que je pai**e**	que nous pay**ions**
prendre	que je prenn**e**	que nous pren**ions**
venir	que je vienn**e**	que nous ven**ions**

A. Conseils. Selon les circonstances indiquées, dites **s'il faut** ou **s'il ne faut pas** que ces personnes fassent ces choses.

> **EXEMPLE**   Je suis fatigué(e). Alors... je (se reposer, sortir)
> **Il faut que je me repose. Il ne faut pas que je sorte.**

1. J'ai la grippe. Alors... je (se reposer, rendre visite à ma famille, acheter des médicaments, prendre de l'aspirine, boire beaucoup d'eau)
2. *(à votre professeur)* Vous avez la grippe aussi? Alors... vous (boire beaucoup de liquides, venir en cours, sortir, finir tous vos médicaments, fumer)
3. *(à un[e] camarade de classe)* Il y a un examen de français bientôt. Alors... tu (écrire tous les exercices dans le cahier, le dire au professeur si tu ne comprends pas, connaître bien les conjugaisons, sortir tous les soirs)
4. Les autres étudiants et moi voulons réussir au cours de français. Alors... nous (partir avant la fin du cours, écouter bien en cours, perdre notre temps en cours, prendre des notes, dormir en cours)
5. Mon meilleur ami veut réussir à ses examens. Alors... il (finir tous ses devoirs, obéir à ses professeurs, attendre ses professeurs s'ils arrivent en retard, regarder les examens des autres)
6. Mes amies s'ennuient. Alors... elles (trouver de nouveaux passe-temps, s'amuser plus, rester toujours à la maison, partir en voyage, sortir plus, apprendre quelque chose de nouveau, venir me voir)

B. Encore des conseils. Complétez ces phrases logiquement.

1. Vous êtes enceinte? Alors, il faut que vous... Il ne faut pas que vous...
2. Votre ami a la grippe? Il vaut mieux qu'il... Il est important qu'il...
3. Vos enfants ont un virus intestinal? Il est essentiel qu'ils... Il ne faut pas qu'ils...
4. Vous voulez rester en forme? Il est bon que vous... Il est mauvais que vous...

Pour vérifier

1. What are seven verbs that are irregular in the subjunctive?

2. Which four of these verbs have a different stem for the **nous** and **vous** forms?

3. What are the conjugations of these seven verbs in the subjunctive?

4. What is the subjunctive of **il y a**? of **il pleut**?

Giving advice

Les verbes irréguliers au subjonctif

The following seven verbs are irregular in the subjunctive. Note that **être, avoir, aller,** and **vouloir** have a different stem for the **nous** and **vous** forms. All except **être** and **avoir** have the regular subjunctive endings.

	ÊTRE	AVOIR	ALLER	VOULOIR
	soi- / soy-	*ai- / ay-*	*aill- / all-*	*veuill- / voul-*
que je (j')	sois	aie	aille	veuille
que tu	sois	aies	ailles	veuilles
qu'il/elle/on	soit	ait	aille	veuille
que nous	soyons	ayons	allions	voulions
que vous	soyez	ayez	alliez	vouliez
qu'ils/elles	soient	aient	aillent	veuillent

	FAIRE	POUVOIR	SAVOIR
	fass-	*puiss-*	*sach-*
que je	fasse	puisse	sache
que tu	fasses	puisses	saches
qu'il/elle/on	fasse	puisse	sache
que nous	fassions	puissions	sachions
que vous	fassiez	puissiez	sachiez
qu'ils/elles	fassent	puissent	sachent

The subjunctive of **il y a** is **qu'il y ait** and the subjunctive of **il pleut** is **qu'il pleuve**.

A. Réactions. Une amie vous parle des habitudes de sa famille. Réagissez *(React)* à ce qu'elle dit avec **c'est bien que...** ou **ce n'est pas bien que...**

EXEMPLE   Je ne fume plus.
     C'est bien que tu ne fumes plus.

1. Je veux améliorer ma santé.
2. Je vais souvent au club de gym.
3. Mes enfants font très attention à leur santé.
4. Mon mari n'est pas en forme.
5. Il a souvent mal à la tête.
6. Le médecin ne sait pas pourquoi.
7. Mon mari ne veut pas arrêter de fumer.
8. Nous sommes stressés.
9. Nous avons beaucoup de problèmes.
10. Nous ne pouvons pas bien dormir la nuit.
11. Nous ne savons pas contrôler le stress.
12. Nous voulons apprendre à faire du yoga.
13. Nous faisons des promenades ensemble.
14. Nous allons au club de gym ensemble aussi.

B. La grossesse. Une femme enceinte parle avec son médecin. Lui dit-il de faire ou de ne pas faire les choses indiquées à droite?

> **EXEMPLES** **Il faut que vous mangiez bien.**
> **Il ne faut pas que vous fumiez.**

> manger bien
> fumer
> se reposer assez
> avoir beaucoup de stress
> faire attention à votre santé
> être très agitée
> boire de l'alcool
> savoir contrôler le stress
> grossir beaucoup
> prendre des vitamines

C. Conseils. Vous êtes conseiller (conseillère) familial(e). Expliquez à des parents s'il faut ou s'il ne faut pas que leurs enfants fassent ces choses.

> **EXEMPLE** dormir assez
> **Il faut qu'ils dorment assez.**

1. faire de l'exercice
2. aller toujours en cours
3. manger toujours dans un fast-food
4. avoir des responsabilités à la maison
5. savoir que vous les aimez
6. pouvoir faire tout ce qu'ils veulent
7. vouloir réussir à l'école
8. être toujours sages

D. Préparatifs. Une amie va bientôt partir en vacances. Dites-lui ce qu'il faut qu'elle fasse, selon les illustrations.

> **EXEMPLE** **Il faut que tu t'informes sur des sites Web.**

> s'informer sur des sites Web
> changer de l'argent
> faire ta valise
> passer la douane
> dire à tes parents où tu vas
> lire des guides
> téléphoner à l'hôtel pour
>   réserver une chambre

1.
2.
3.
4.
5.
6.

E. L'ange et le diable. Vous vous trouvez dans les situations suivantes. Imaginez ce que l'ange *(angel)* et le diable *(devil)* vous disent de faire. Utilisez **Il faut que… / Il ne faut pas que…**

> **EXEMPLE** Mes amis m'ont invité à sortir ce soir, mais j'ai un examen de français demain.
> Le diable: **Il faut que tu sortes!**
> L'ange: **Il ne faut pas que tu sortes! Il faut que tu prépares ton examen!**

1. Je devrais aller en cours, mais je suis fatigué(e) et je voudrais rentrer.
2. J'aime fumer, mais le médecin m'a dit d'arrêter de fumer.
3. J'ai envie d'aller au cinéma, mais j'ai des devoirs à faire.
4. J'ai acheté un cadeau *(gift)* pour une amie, mais maintenant je voudrais le garder *(to keep it)*.
5. Ma mère veut que je l'aide à la maison samedi, mais je voudrais sortir.
6. Ma sœur veut qu'on sorte ensemble ce soir, mais je préfère sortir avec mon meilleur ami.

Running errands on a trip

Note *culturelle*

En France, les cabines téléphoniques n'acceptent pas les pièces de monnaie! Pour passer un appel local dans une cabine téléphonique, vous devez avoir une carte téléphonique. Vous pouvez acheter ces cartes (pour une valeur de 5 euros, 10 euros et 15 euros) dans les bureaux de poste, dans les cafés, dans les tabacs *(tobacco shops)* et dans les kiosques à journaux. Pour un appel international, vous pouvez utiliser votre carte de crédit internationale. Quand est-ce que vous utilisez une carte téléphonique chez vous?

Notes *de grammaire*

1. Envoyer is a **-yer** spelling change verb, like s'ennuyer (j'envoie, tu envoies, il/elle/on envoie, nous envoyons, vous envoyez, ils/elles envoient). The stem for the future and conditional is **enverr-**.

2. Remember that nouns ending in **-eau**, like **cadeau**, form their plurals with **-x (des cadeaux)**.

Note *de vocabulaire*

The post office is referred to as **le bureau de poste**, **la Poste**, or **les PTT**.

Des courses en voyage

Ces touristes ont beaucoup de choses à faire aujourd'hui. Où vont-ils aller?

Il faut qu'il/qu'elle aille...

au **distributeur de billets** pour **retirer** de l'argent

à la banque pour changer des chèques de voyage

à la pharmacie pour acheter de l'aspirine *(f)*

chez le marchand de **cadeaux** pour acheter un cadeau pour un ami

au kiosque pour acheter le journal et une carte téléphonique

au bureau de poste pour **envoyer** des cartes postales et acheter **des timbres** *(m)*

CD 4-18

Luc quitte la Martinique pour retourner en Guadeloupe. Il parle au téléphone avec Micheline.

MICHELINE: Je suis contente que tu reviennes bientôt de Martinique. Quand penses-tu arriver en Guadeloupe?

LUC: Je prends l'avion vendredi matin.

MICHELINE: Voudrais-tu que j'**aille** te **chercher** à l'aéroport?

LUC: Non, non, je ne veux pas que tu perdes ton temps à l'aéroport si l'avion arrive **en retard. J'aimerais autant** prendre **la navette.**

MICHELINE: Mais non, j'insiste! L'avion arrive à quelle heure?

LUC: À 10 heures.

MICHELINE: Alors, je viendrai te chercher devant la porte principale de l'aéroport vers dix heures et quart. Et si tu n'as pas d'autres projets, nous pouvons passer la journée à Pointe-à-Pitre.

LUC: Bonne idée! J'aimerais faire un tour de la ville.

MICHELINE: Parfait. À demain, alors.

LUC: Oui, au revoir, à demain.

---

un distributeur de billets *an ATM machine* **retirer** *to withdraw* **un cadeau** *a gift* **envoyer** *to send* **un timbre** *a stamp*
aller / venir chercher *to go / come pick up* **en retard** *late* **J'aimerais autant** *I would just as soon* **la navette** *the shuttle*

A. Où faut-il aller? Dites où il faut que les personnes suivantes aillent.

EXEMPLE   Notre vol va partir dans deux heures.
Il faut que nous allions à l'aéroport.

1. Vous voulez changer des chèques de voyage?
2. Tu as perdu la clé de ta chambre?
3. Tes amis ont besoin d'acheter une carte téléphonique?
4. J'ai besoin de retirer de l'argent.
5. Nous voulons envoyer des cartes postales.
6. Luc veut acheter de l'aspirine.
7. Micheline a besoin d'acheter des timbres.
8. Luc veut acheter un cadeau pour Micheline.

> à la banque
> à un restaurant
> au distributeur de billets
> à la pharmacie
> au bureau de poste
> à la réception de l'hôtel
> chez le marchand de cadeaux
> au kiosque
> à l'aéroport

B. Des courses. Où dit-on les choses suivantes?

EXEMPLE   C'est combien pour envoyer cette carte postale en Belgique?
au bureau de poste

1. Une carte téléphonique de dix euros, s'il vous plaît.
2. Qu'est-ce que vous recommandez pour les allergies? J'éternue beaucoup.
3. Je voudrais changer des dollars, s'il vous plaît.
4. C'est combien pour ces paniers *(baskets)* traditionnels? Je cherche un cadeau pour ma femme.
5. Avez-vous des magazines africains?
6. Trois timbres à 54 centimes, s'il vous plaît.

C. Une journée chargée. Pourquoi est-ce que Luc est proba-blement allé aux endroits indiqués?

EXEMPLE   Luc est allé au marché pour **acheter des fruits.**

1. Luc est allé au bureau de poste pour...
2. Il est allé à la pharmacie pour...
3. Il a cherché un distributeur de billets pour...
4. Il est allé à la banque pour...
5. Il est allé au restaurant pour...
6. Il est allé au kiosque pour...
7. Il est allé à l'agence de voyages pour...
8. Il est allé chez le marchand de cadeaux pour...

D. Conversation. Avec un(e) partenaire, relisez à haute voix la conversation entre Luc et Micheline à la page précédente. Ensuite, imaginez qu'un(e) ami(e) va venir vous rendre visite. Votre partenaire va jouer le rôle de votre ami(e). Créez une conversation dans laquelle vous parlez de quel jour votre ami(e) va arriver, où vous allez vous retrouver et ce que vous allez faire ensemble au cours de son séjour.

CD 4-19   You can find a list of the new words from the vocabulary and grammar sections of this ***Compétence*** on page 419 and a recording of this list on track 4-19 of your *Text Audio CD*.

Expressing wishes and emotions

Les expressions d'émotion et de volonté et le subjonctif

 To download a podcast on when to use the subjunctive, go to **academic.cengage.com/french.**

The indicative mood is used to talk about reality. The subjunctive mood conveys subjectivity: feelings, desires, opinions, requests, doubts, and fears.

You know that you use the subjunctive to give advice and state opinions to someone in particular after impersonal expressions like **il faut que** and **il vaut mieux que.** You also use the subjunctive in a second clause beginning with **que** when:

- the verb in the first clause "triggers" the subjunctive in the second clause by expressing feelings, desires, doubts, fears, opinions, or requests.
- the subject of the first clause is not the same as the subject of the second clause.

Verbal expressions such as those that follow will "trigger" the subjunctive in the second clause.

FEELINGS	DESIRES
être content(e) que *to be glad that*	vouloir que *to want that*
être heureux (heureuse) que *to be happy that*	préférer que *to prefer that*
être furieux (furieuse) que *to be furious that*	aimer mieux que *to prefer that*
être surpris(e) que *to be surprised that*	souhaiter que *to wish that*
être étonné(e) que *to be astonished that*	**DOUBTS AND FEARS**
être triste que *to be sad that*	
être désolé(e) que *to be sorry that*	douter que *to doubt that*
regretter que *to regret that*	avoir peur que *to be afraid that*
OPINIONS	**REQUESTS / DEMANDS**
accepter que *to accept that*	insister que *to insist that*
c'est dommage que *it's too bad that*	
il est bon / mauvais, etc., que *it's good / bad, etc., that*	

Je suis désolé que votre chambre n'ait pas de vue sur la mer.

Je préfère que la chambre soit au premier étage.

J'ai peur que le quartier de l'hôtel ne soit pas calme.

C'est dommage que votre lit ne soit pas confortable.

J'insiste que nous changions d'hôtel.

Remember that the present subjunctive expresses either the present or the future.

Je doute qu'elle soit ici.	*I doubt she **is / will be** here.*
Je doute qu'il arrive demain.	*I doubt he **will arrive** tomorrow.*

A. Quel hôtel? Vous allez faire un voyage. Quelle sorte d'hôtel préférez-vous? Donnez votre réaction comme indiqué.

EXEMPLE l'hôtel / être près des sites touristiques
Je préfère que l'hôtel soit près des sites touristiques.

1. l'hôtel / avoir une piscine
2. le réceptionniste / parler anglais
3. l'hôtel / accepter les cartes de crédit
4. la chambre / être grande

> Je veux absolument que...
> Je préfère que...
> Il n'est pas important que...

5. la chambre / avoir une salle de bains privée
6. on / (ne pas) pouvoir fumer dans la chambre
7. l'hôtel / (ne pas) être cher
8. on / pouvoir acheter de beaux cadeaux dans la boutique

B. Réactions. Vous êtes parti(e) en voyage organisé en Martinique et vous partagez votre chambre d'hôtel avec un(e) autre touriste. Donnez votre réaction à ce qu'il/elle vous dit.

> **EXEMPLE**   Je parle français couramment *(fluently)*.
> **Je suis content(e) que vous parliez français couramment.**

1. Notre hôtel est tout près de la mer.
2. Il y a deux grands lits.
3. Les lits sont très confortables.
4. Je fume dans la chambre.
5. Je ne dors pas bien la nuit.
6. Je tousse toute la nuit.
7. L'hôtel n'accepte pas les cartes de crédit.
8. Il n'y a pas de distributeur de billets à l'hôtel.
9. Je n'ai pas assez d'argent pour payer ma part de la chambre.

> Je (ne) suis (pas) content(e) que...
> Je suis furieux (furieuse) que...
> Je suis triste que...
> Je suis désolé(e) que...
> Je regrette que...

C. Tu m'accompagnes? Une amie de Micheline est en vacances avec sa famille. Qu'est-ce qu'elle veut que ces personnes fassent avec elle?

> **EXEMPLE**   **Elle veut que son fils joue au tennis avec elle.**

son fils

1. sa fille

2. son fils

3. son mari

4. ses enfants

5. son amie

D. Réactions. Votre partenaire et vous pensez peut-être partir en voyage ensemble. Posez ces questions à votre partenaire pour parler de ses habitudes quand il/elle est en vacances. Réagissez chaque fois à sa réponse.

> **EXEMPLE**   **—Tu passes beaucoup de temps à l'hôtel?**
> **—Non, je ne passe pas beaucoup de temps à l'hôtel.**
> **—Je suis content(e) que tu ne passes pas beaucoup de temps à l'hôtel.**

1. Tu préfères aller à la plage ou à la montagne?
2. Tu descends dans un hôtel de luxe ou dans un hôtel moins cher?
3. Tu sors souvent le soir ou tu restes à l'hôtel?
4. Tu fumes?
5. Tu dînes dans un restaurant ou dans ta chambre?

E. Un voyage en Afrique. Luc persuade Micheline de faire un voyage avec lui en Afrique. Qu'est-ce qu'il lui dit? Commencez chaque phrase avec **j'aimerais que...** ou **je ne voudrais pas que...**.

> **EXEMPLE** aller en vacances avec moi / me dire non
> **J'aimerais que tu ailles en vacances avec moi.**
> **Je ne voudrais pas que tu me dises non.**

1. rater *(lose out on)* cette occasion de voir l'Afrique / faire ce voyage avec moi
2. être timide / dire ce que tu veux
3. visiter plusieurs pays africains avec moi / rentrer tout de suite en Guadeloupe
4. pouvoir rester au moins un mois en Afrique avec moi / prendre moins de quatre semaines de vacances
5. sortir seule la nuit / être avec moi
6. avoir peur / se sentir à l'aise *(at ease)*
7. s'amuser / s'ennuyer
8. se souvenir de ce voyage / oublier notre voyage en Afrique

F. Ce qu'en disent les femmes. Pour faire bonne impression sur Micheline, Luc lit des articles sur ce que les Françaises veulent chez les hommes. Voici le résultat de plusieurs sondages *(polls)* qu'il a trouvés. Complétez les phrases avec les verbes logiques entre parenthèses au subjonctif.

1. (faire, être, avoir)
   Pour la majorité des femmes, il est plus important qu'un homme _____ un bon sens de l'humour et qu'il les _____ rire *(laugh)*. Il est moins important qu'il _____ sexy.

2. (être, montrer, avoir, accepter, payer)
   Les femmes veulent qu'un homme _____ moderne et convaincu *(convinced)* des valeurs du féminisme, et qu'il _____ l'égalité sociale, politique et économique de la femme. Mais elles veulent aussi qu'il _____ des valeurs traditionnelles. Elles veulent encore qu'il _____ le chemin *(way)* et qu'il _____ l'addition au restaurant.

3. (être, avoir)
   Pour 37% (pour cent) des femmes, il faut absolument que leur partenaire _____ fidèle mais 9% acceptent sans problèmes qu'il _____ d'autres partenaires.

4. (se séparer, rester)
   Si un couple avec un jeune enfant ne s'entend plus, 19% des femmes pensent qu'il est nécessaire que le couple _____ ensemble mais 73% disent qu'il vaut mieux que le couple _____.

5. (être, avoir)
   La moitié *(half)* des Françaises veulent que leur partenaire _____ une dimension spirituelle mais pour l'autre moitié il n'est pas important qu'il _____ religieux.

G. Un couple heureux. Regardez les sondages *(polls)* aux pages 294–295 et travaillez avec un(e) camarade de classe pour compléter les phrases suivantes. Quel groupe peut faire le plus grande nombre de phrases logiques?

> Il est très important qu'un couple / qu'une femme / qu'un homme...
>
> Il est assez important qu'un couple / qu'une femme / qu'un homme...
>
> Il n'est pas important qu'un couple / qu'une femme / qu'un homme...

H. Politique en Guadeloupe.
Voici le résultat d'un sondage fait en Guadeloupe il y a quelques années sur le statut *(status)* de département d'outre-mer de l'île. Complétez les phrases avec la forme correcte des verbes entre parenthèses au subjonctif.

1. 5% (pour cent) des Guadeloupéens préfèrent que la Guadeloupe _____ (être) indépendante.

2. 18% veulent que la Guadeloupe _____ (faire) partie de la France sans changement de son statut actuel de DOM.

3. 52% veulent garder le statut de DOM, mais ils voudraient que la Guadeloupe _____ (pouvoir) créer plus de ses propres lois *(own laws)* décidées par les assemblées locales.

4. 21% souhaitent que la Guadeloupe _____ (avoir) un statut d'autonomie où presque toutes les lois seraient décidées par des assemblées locales.

5. Certains indépendantistes voudraient que le créole _____ (devenir) une langue officielle à côté du français.

6. Beaucoup de Guadeloupéens regrettent que le gouvernement national _____ (choisir) rarement des Antillais pour représenter la France dans les organisations régionales de la Caraïbe ou en Amérique latine.

I. Discours politiques.
Voici quelques citations du président français pendant sa campagne électorale. Choisissez l'expression en italique logique pour indiquer s'il était pour ou contre chaque idée mentionnée et mettez le verbe entre parenthèses au subjonctif.

> **EXEMPLE** *Je veux / Je ne veux pas* que la France _____ (rester) ouverte, accueillante *(welcoming)*, généreuse.
> **Je veux que la France reste ouverte, accueillante, généreuse.**

1. *Il faut / Il ne faut pas* que l'immigration _____ (être) ressentie comme une menace *(taken as a threat)* sur son identité.

2. *Je souhaite / Je ne souhaite pas* qu'on ne _____ (pouvoir) pas vivre en France sans respecter sa culture et ses valeurs.

3. *J'accepte / Je n'accepte pas* qu'on _____ (vouloir) habiter en France sans respecter et sans aimer la France.

4. *J'accepte / Je n'accepte pas* qu'on _____ (faire) des enseignants *(teachers)* les boucs émissaires *(scapegoats)* d'un désastre dont la politique est seule responsable.

5. *Je vous propose / Je ne vous propose pas* que chaque famille _____ (avoir) le choix de l'établissement scolaire de son enfant.

6. *Je veux / Je ne veux pas* que l'impôt *(taxes)* _____ (pouvoir) prendre plus de 50% du revenu.

7. Je veux être le Président d'une France réunie... Cette unité, *je veux / je ne veux pas* qu'elle _____ (être) comme une renaissance.

8. *Il faut / Il ne faut pas* que je _____ (être) à la fois très fort et en même temps très sensible *(sensitive)*.

9. *Je souhaite / Je ne souhaite pas* que la femme _____ (avoir) la liberté de travailler et d'élever *(rear)* ses enfants.

10. *Je veux / Je ne veux pas* qu'il y _____ (avoir) de travailleurs pauvres qui ne peuvent pas vivre du fruit de leur travail.

11. *Je veux / Je ne veux pas* que demain _____ (ressembler) à hier.

Pour vérifier

1. Do you use the infinitive or the subjunctive when people have feelings about what *others* should or might do? when they have feelings about what *they themselves* should or might do?

2. When do you use the infinitive after impersonal expressions such as **il faut**? When do you use the subjunctive?

Saying who you want to do something

Le subjonctif ou l'infinitif?

You know to use the subjunctive in a second clause when the first clause expresses feelings, desires, doubts, fears, requests, or opinions about what someone else does, might do, or should do. In this case, the subjunctive is used only when there are different subjects in the main and dependent clauses. When there is no change of subject, you normally use the infinitive.

FEELINGS ABOUT SOMEONE ELSE	FEELINGS ABOUT ONESELF
Je veux que tu le fasses.	Je veux le faire.
I want you to do it.	*I want to do it.*
Nous préférons qu'il soit à l'heure.	Nous préférons être à l'heure.
We prefer that he be on time.	*We prefer to be on time.*

Use **de** before an infinitive after the verb **regretter** and when the expression includes the verb **être.**

| Je regrette **de** partir demain. | Elle est contente **de** venir. |

Remember to use an infinitive after expressions such as **il faut** or **il est important de** to talk about people in general, rather than someone specific.

TALKING ABOUT SOMEONE SPECIFIC	TALKING ABOUT PEOPLE IN GENERAL
Il faut que nous le fassions.	Il faut le faire.
We have to do it.	*It has to be done.*
Il est important qu'il y aille.	Il est important **d'**y aller.
It's important for him to go there.	*It's important to go there.*

A. De bons conseils. Dites s'il faut, s'il vaut mieux ou s'il ne faut pas faire ces choses quand on voyage à l'étranger.

> **EXEMPLE** prendre la photo d'un tableau avec un flash dans un musée
> **Il ne faut pas prendre la photo d'un tableau avec un flash dans un musée.**

1. arriver à l'aéroport bien à l'avance
2. oublier son passeport
3. passer la sécurité
4. fumer dans l'avion
5. montrer son passeport à la douane
6. réserver une chambre avant de partir
7. faire beaucoup de bruit à l'hôtel
8. savoir parler un peu la langue

Maintenant, imaginez que vous donnez ces mêmes conseils à un groupe de jeunes qui partent en voyage.

> **EXEMPLE** prendre la photo d'un tableau avec un flash dans un musée
> **Il ne faut pas que vous preniez la photo d'un tableau avec un flash dans un musée.**

B. Des courses.
Micheline et sa sœur se préparent pour aller voir leur oncle qui habite dans une autre ville. Micheline préfère faire ce qu'on peut faire à la maison et elle veut que sa sœur aille faire les courses. Que dit-elle à sa sœur de faire?

> **EXEMPLE** faire le ménage / faire des courses
> **Je voudrais que tu fasses des courses.**
> **Moi, je préfère faire le ménage.**

1. aller retirer de l'argent au distributeur de billets / faire les valises
2. acheter une carte téléphonique au kiosque / téléphoner à l'oncle Jean
3. écrire un mail à l'oncle Jean / envoyer ces lettres
4. téléphoner à l'hôtel / aller à la pharmacie
5. acheter de la nourriture pour chien (*dog food*) / donner à manger au chien
6. écrire des mails pour obtenir des renseignements sur la région / acheter des chèques de voyage à la banque

C. Préférences.
Choisissez les mots entre parenthèses qui décrivent le mieux vos préférences quand vous voyagez. Conjuguez le verbe au subjonctif ou utilisez l'infinitif comme il convient.

1. Pour un long voyage, je préfère... (prendre l'avion, prendre le train, prendre ma voiture, ???)
2. Je préfère que mon vol... (être le matin, être l'après-midi, être le soir)
3. Pendant le vol, j'aime... (lire, voir le film, écouter de la musique, dormir, parler avec d'autres passagers, ???)
4. Je n'aime pas que les autres passagers près de moi... (parler tout le temps, avoir un petit bébé, se lever tout le temps, ???)
5. Je préfère que l'hôtel... (être agréable et de luxe, être grand mais pas trop cher)
6. Je préfère que ma chambre d'hôtel... (avoir un grand lit, avoir un petit lit)
7. Généralement, j'aime... (dîner dans ma chambre d'hôtel, manger au restaurant de l'hôtel, sortir dîner dans un autre restaurant)
8. À l'hôtel, je préfère... (payer en chèques de voyage, payer par carte de crédit, payer en espèces)

D. Entretien.
Interviewez votre partenaire sur un voyage qu'il/elle voudrait faire.

1. Où est-ce que tu voudrais faire un voyage? Quand est-ce que tu voudrais le faire? Est-ce que tu aimerais que ta famille ou que tes amis voyagent avec toi?
2. Est-ce que tu préfères que ton hôtel soit un hôtel de luxe ou pas cher? Est-il important qu'il y ait une piscine? Aimes-tu nager dans la piscine d'un hôtel?
3. As-tu peur de prendre l'avion? Aimes-tu parler avec les personnes à côté de toi dans l'avion ou préfères-tu dormir?

Giving directions

✳ **Note** *culturelle*

Sur le plan de Pointe-à-Pitre, vous pouvez voir le musée Schœlcher. Victor Schœlcher, homme politique français, était à la tête du mouvement pour l'abolition de l'esclavage *(slavery)* dans les colonies françaises. En 1848, il a réussi à faire accomplir son but *(goal)* et par le décret d'abolition de l'esclavage du 27 avril 1848, l'esclavage a été aboli. Que savez-vous de l'histoire de l'abolition de l'esclavage?

Les indications

Luc et Micheline visitent Pointe-à-Pitre. Ils sont à l'office de tourisme. Voilà un plan du centre-ville. Qu'est-ce qu'il y a dans le quartier?

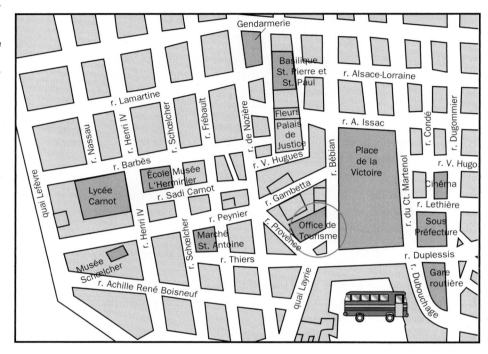

L'employé à l'office de tourisme va **expliquer** à Luc et à Micheline comment arriver au musée Schœlcher. Voilà quelques expressions **utiles** pour **indiquer le chemin.**

Prenez la rue...	**Traversez la place...**
Continuez **tout droit jusqu'à...**	C'est dans la rue...
Tournez à droite.	sur le boulevard...
Tournez à gauche.	sur l'avenue...
Descendez la rue...	sur la place...
Montez la rue...	C'est **au coin de** la rue.

---

expliquer *to explain*   **utile** *useful*   **indiquer le chemin** *to give directions, to show the way*   **tout droit jusqu'à...** *straight ahead until / as far as . . .*   **traverser** *to cross, to go across*   **la place** *the square*   **au coin de** *on the corner of*

Micheline demande à l'office de tourisme comment aller au musée Schœlcher.

MICHELINE: S'il vous plaît, monsieur, pourriez-vous m'expliquer comment aller au musée Schœlcher?

L'EMPLOYÉ: Bien sûr, mademoiselle, il n'y a rien de plus simple. C'est tout près. Montez la rue Provence jusqu'à la rue Peynier. Tournez à gauche...

MICHELINE: À gauche dans la rue Peynier?

L'EMPLOYÉ: Oui, c'est ça. Continuez tout droit et le musée Schœlcher est sur votre gauche, juste après la rue Henri IV.

MICHELINE: Je vous remercie, monsieur.

L'EMPLOYÉ: Je vous en prie, mademoiselle.

A. Où allez-vous?
Imaginez que vous êtes à l'office de tourisme avec Luc et Micheline. D'abord, complétez les explications suivantes en traduisant les mots entre parenthèses. Ensuite regardez le plan à la page précédente et dites où vous arrivez.

1. _____ *(Go up)* la rue Provence _____ *(as far as)* la rue Peynier. _____ *(Turn left)*. _____ *(Continue straight ahead)* et il est sur votre gauche, juste après la rue Henri IV.

2. _____ *(Cross)* la place de la Victoire et prenez la rue Lethière. _____ *(Continue straight ahead)* jusqu'à la rue Condé et _____ *(turn left)*. Il est sur votre _____ *(right)* entre la rue Victor Hugo et la rue Lethière.

3. _____ *(Go up)* la rue Bébian _____ *(as far as)* la rue Alsace-Lorraine. _____ *(Turn left)*. Elle est juste devant vous.

4. _____ *(Go up)* la rue Provence, _____ *(turn left)* dans la rue Peynier. _____ *(Continue straight ahead)* et il est sur votre gauche, entre la rue Frébault et la rue Schœlcher.

B. Conversation.
D'abord, avec un(e) partenaire, relisez à haute voix la conversation entre Micheline et l'employé de l'office de tourisme. Ensuite, votre partenaire va vous demander comment aller chez vous en partant de *(leaving from)* l'université. Expliquez-lui comment y aller. Il/Elle va créer un plan selon vos indications.

Vocabulaire supplémentaire
au feu *at the light*
au stop *at the stop sign*
Prenez l'autoroute 35. *Take freeway 35.*
Prenez la sortie 7. *Take exit 7.*
vers le nord / le sud / l'est / l'ouest *toward the north / the south / the east / the west*

CD 4-21 You can find a list of the new words from the vocabulary and grammar sections of this *Compétence* on page 419 and a recording of this list on track 4-21 of your *Text Audio CD.*

Pour vérifier

1. How do you form the imperative of most verbs? Which verbs drop the final **s** in the **tu** form of the imperative? Which two verbs are irregular in the imperative and what are their forms?

2. Where do you place **y, en,** and object and reflexive pronouns in affirmative commands? What happens to **me** and **te** in an affirmative command? Where do you place **y, en,** and object and reflexive pronouns in negative commands?

3. When do you reattach the **s** to a **tu** form command?

Telling how to go somewhere

Reprise de l'impératif et les pronoms avec l'impératif

You use the **impératif** (command) form of the verb to give directions. As you have seen, the imperative of most verbs is the **tu, vous,** or **nous** form of the verb without the subject pronoun.

Descends cette rue!	*Go down this street!*
Traversez la place!	*Cross the square!*
Allons à la banque!	*Let's go to the bank!*

Remember to drop the final **s** of **-er** verbs and of **aller,** but not of other verbs, in **tu** form commands.

	Tourne à gauche!	*Turn left!*	Va en ville!	*Go to town!*
BUT:	Prend**s** la navette!	*Take the shuttle!*	Fai**s** ta valise!	*Pack your bag!*

Review the irregular command forms of **être** and **avoir.**

Sois calme!	*Be calm!*	Aie de la patience!	*Have patience!*
Soyons gentils!	*Let's be nice!*	Ayons confiance!	*Let's have confidence!*
Soyez à l'heure!	*Be on time!*	Ayez pitié!	*Have pity!*

In negative commands, reflexive pronouns, direct and indirect object pronouns, **y,** and **en** are placed before the verb.

Ne te perds pas!	*Don't get lost!*
Ne les prends pas!	*Don't take them!*
N'y va pas!	*Don't go there!*

In affirmative commands, pronouns are attached to the end of the verb with a hyphen.

Attends-le à l'aéroport.	*Wait for him at the airport.*
Dis-lui que nous arriverons bientôt.	*Tell her that we will arrive soon.*

When **me** and **te** are attached to the end of the verb, they become **moi** and **toi.**

Attendez-moi!	*Wait for me!*	Lève-toi!	*Get up!*

When **y** or **en** follows a **tu** form command, the final **s** is reattached to the end of the verb and it is pronounced in liaison.

Va**s**‿y!	*Go ahead!*	Mange**s**‿y!	*Eat there!*
Achète**s**‿en!	*Buy some!*	Mange**s**‿en!	*Eat some!*

A. Le chemin. Consultez le plan à la page 406 et expliquez comment aller...

• de l'office de tourisme à la gendarmerie *(police station)*
• de la gendarmerie au musée Schœlcher
• du musée Schœlcher à la sous-préfecture *(administrative building)*

B. Un drôle de touriste. Votre nouvel ami, un extra-terrestre, descend dans un hôtel. Dites-lui ce qu'il faut et ce qu'il ne faut pas faire.

> **EXEMPLE** Je m'habille avant de prendre une douche?
> **Non, ne t'habille pas avant de prendre une douche.**
> **Habille-toi après.**

1. Je me couche par terre?
2. Je m'habille dans le jardin?
3. Je me brosse les mains?
4. Je me lave à la réception?
5. Je me lève à minuit?
6. Je me couche à midi?
7. Je me déshabille dans le couloir?
8. Je me brosse les dents avec l'eau de la piscine?

C. Luc est amoureux. Luc est tombé amoureux de Micheline et il ne veut pas qu'elle l'oublie quand il sera de retour en France. Vous êtes son ami(e). Répondez à ses questions. Dites-lui de faire ou de ne pas faire chaque chose.

> **EXEMPLE** —Est-ce que je devrais lui écrire des mails de France?
> **—Oui, écris-lui des mails.**
> **Non, ne lui écris pas de mails. Téléphone-lui.**

1. Est-ce que je devrais l'inviter à venir me voir l'été prochain?
2. Je devrais lui téléphoner deux fois par jour?
3. Est-ce que je devrais lui dire que je suis amoureux d'elle?
4. Est-ce que je devrais lui envoyer des fleurs *(flowers)*?
5. Est-ce que je devrais l'oublier?
6. Je ferais mieux de la quitter pour toujours?
7. Est-ce que je devrais l'embrasser avant de partir?

D. Micheline aussi! Micheline aussi est amoureuse de Luc. Est-ce qu'elle lui dirait de faire les choses indiquées dans *C. Luc est amoureux*?

> **EXEMPLE** **Écris-moi des mails. / Ne m'écris pas de mails. Téléphone-moi.**

E. Conseils. Un touriste pose des questions. Répondez à ses questions. Utilisez l'impératif et le pronom convenable.

> **EXEMPLE** —Quand est-ce que je devrais confirmer mon vol?
> **—Confirmez-le 72 heures avant votre départ.**

1. Quand est-ce que je devrais régler la note de la chambre?
2. Comment est-ce que je peux régler la note?
3. Où est-ce que je peux prendre le petit déjeuner?
4. Où est-ce que je peux changer mes chèques de voyage?
5. Où est-ce que je peux acheter des timbres?
6. Où est-ce que je peux acheter un plan de la ville?
7. Comment est-ce que je peux aller à l'aéroport?
8. Où est-ce que je peux acheter de l'aspirine?

Reprise

Being on a trip

Dans le **Chapitre 10,** vous avez appris à obtenir une chambre d'hôtel, à demander et à suivre des indications, à parler avec un médecin si vous êtes malade, à faire des recommandations, à exprimer vos désirs et à donner votre réaction à ce qui se passe. Maintenant vous allez réviser ce que vous avez appris.

A. À l'étranger. Dites ce qu'il vaut mieux faire si on part à l'étranger.

> **EXEMPLE**   apporter *(to bring)* beaucoup de choses ou apporter une seule valise?
> **Il vaut mieux apporter une seule valise.**

1. chercher un hôtel à l'arrivée ou réserver une chambre à l'avance?
2. faire les valises à l'avance ou faire les valises au dernier moment?
3. arriver à l'aéroport juste avant le départ ou être à l'aéroport au moins deux heures avant le départ?
4. se souvenir de prendre les passeports ou oublier les passeports à la maison?
5. envoyer des cartes postales pendant le voyage ou envoyer les cartes postales après le retour?

Deux de vos amis partent à l'étranger pour la première fois. Dites-leur ce qu'il vaut mieux qu'ils fassent. Utilisez les phrases précédentes.

> **EXEMPLE**   **Il vaut mieux que vous apportiez une seule valise.**

B. Des préparatifs. Vous faites les préparatifs pour un voyage avec un(e) ami(e). Dites à votre ami(e) ce que vous préférez faire et ce que vous préférez qu'il/elle fasse.

> **EXEMPLE**   aller à la banque pour acheter des chèques de voyage / aller à l'agence de voyages pour acheter les billets
> **Je préfère aller à l'agence de voyages pour acheter les billets et je préfère que tu ailles à la banque pour acheter des chèques de voyage.**

1. choisir l'hôtel / choisir le vol
2. faire les réservations d'hôtel / louer une voiture
3. lire le guide touristique / chercher des renseignements sur le Web
4. être assis(e) côté hublot *(window)* / être assis(e) côté couloir *(aisle)*
5. dormir dans le lit / dormir sur le canapé
6. acheter des timbres au bureau de poste / changer des chèques de voyage
7. payer le voyage / ne rien payer

C. En voyage. Votre ami(e) vous demande les choses suivantes pendant votre voyage. Répondez en utilisant l'impératif avec un pronom complément d'objet direct.

> **EXEMPLE**   Je mets le réveil *(set the alarm)* pour six heures ou pour huit heures?
> **Ne le mets pas pour six heures. Mets-le pour huit heures.**

1. J'apporte *(I bring)* mon passeport avec moi ou je le laisse à l'hôtel?
2. Je paie l'hôtel avec ma carte de crédit ou avec ta carte de crédit?
3. Je fais le lit ou je le laisse pour la femme de chambre *(maid)*?
4. Je prends la clé avec moi ou je la laisse à la réception?
5. J'appelle le taxi une heure ou deux heures avant le vol?
6. J'écris ces cartes postales avant de partir ou je les écris dans l'avion?

D. Une réservation perdue. Vous êtes dans les situations suivantes pendant votre voyage. Décrivez vos réactions.

EXEMPLE   Votre avion est en retard.
Je suis furieux (furieuse) que mon avion soit en retard.

Je suis content(e) que...   Il est bon que...
Je ne suis pas content(e) que...   C'est dommage que...
Je regrette que...   Il n'est pas important que...
Je suis furieux (furieuse) que...

1. On ne peut pas trouver votre réservation d'hôtel.
2. Il n'y a pas de chambres disponibles *(available)*.
3. Il n'y a pas de télé dans la chambre d'hôtel.
4. L'hôtel a un grand restaurant.
5. Les repas à l'hôtel sont excellents.
6. Votre ami(e) veut passer toute la journée dans la chambre d'hôtel.
7. Il fait très mauvais et il pleut tous les jours.
8. Il n'y a pas assez d'eau chaude le matin.

E. On cherche un hôtel. On a perdu votre réservation d'hôtel, alors vous cherchez un autre hôtel. Avec un(e) partenaire, préparez une conversation avec le (la) réceptionniste dans laquelle vous discutez les choses suivantes.

- *say that you are looking for a room and for how many nights*
- *explain what sort of room you are looking for, including the number of beds and the sort of bathroom you need*
- *discuss the price, including breakfast, and ask where and at what time breakfast is served* **(est servi)**

F. Pourriez-vous m'indiquer le chemin? Regardez le plan de Pointe-à-Pitre à la page 406. Vous êtes à la gare routière dans la rue Dubouchage. (Cherchez le petit autobus.) Vous désirez aller au marché St. Antoine. Votre partenaire va vous dire comment y aller. Ensuite, changez de rôles. Cette fois, votre partenaire voudrait aller de la gare routière au lycée Carnot.

G. Chez le médecin. Vous tombez malade pendant votre voyage. Avec un(e) partenaire, préparez la conversation suivante avec un médecin.

- *The doctor greets you and asks what is wrong.*
- *You say that you are coughing, sneezing, and you have a sore throat and a headache.*
- *The doctor says you have the flu and gives you a prescription for medicine. He/She says that it is important that you take it every morning and gives you other advice on what else to do.*

Lecture et Composition

Tiken Jah Fakoly

Lecture

⚙ Pour mieux lire: *Using recent events*

Social justice is a common theme in many songs by artists from francophone Africa and the Antilles, such as the Ivoirian Tiken Jah Fakoly and the Martiniquais Yannis Ouda. In their song *Y en a marre*, they sing about how people are fed up with the injustice they encounter in regions of Africa.

Knowledge of some of the recent history of political problems in Africa should help you guess the meaning some of the unfamiliar words in the lyrics. Before reading the lyrics, do this activity to make your reading easier.

Injustices sociales. Utilisez ce que vous savez des injustices sociales dans le monde *(world)* pour deviner le sens des mots en italique dans les paroles *(lyrics)* de la chanson. Utilisez aussi les mots suivants que vous avez déjà vus.

> *opprimé(e):* oppression (*déprimé[e]* → dépression)
> *détourné(e):* tourner
> *affamé(e):* faim
> *mondialisation:* monde

Y en a marre
(Refrain)

On en a marre

L'Afrique en a marre marre marre

On en a marre

Le peuple en a marre marre marre

Des journalistes assassinés

Parce que des présidents assassins

Des généraux aux commandes

Des populations *opprimées*

Des aides aux pays *détournées*

Des populations *affamées*

Les fonds du pays **dilapidés**

Les droits de l'homme ignorés

(Refrain)

Après l'abolition de *l'esclavage*

Ils ont créé la colonisation

Lorsque l'on a trouvé la solution

Ils ont créé la coopération

Comme on dénonce cette situation

Ils ont créé la *mondialisation*

Et sans expliquer la mondialisation

C'est Babylone qui nous exploite

(Refrain)

Faut qu'on arrête de cautionner

Ça, la vie de nos frères ne compte pas pour cette bande de **vanpayas**

Stoppons **les guerres, gardons la foi**

Faya sur tous les chefs d'État qui nous envoient **tuer** nos brothers

Ils ne nous respectent pas c'est la même chose pour leurs **lois**

Ils ne regardent même pas quand le peuple réclame ses droits

Ils ne partagent surtout pas l'argent c'est pas qu'y en a pas

Ils ne font rien pour nos sisters qui se vendent pour vivre dans ce monde-là

(Refrain)

Des présidents assassins

On veut plus

Des généraux aux commandes

On n'en veut plus

Des *enfants militaires*

On veut plus

Des *orphelins de guerre*

On n'en veut plus

(Refrain)

L'Afrique en a marre

De toutes ces machinations

Mon peuple en a marre

De toutes ces manipulations

L'Afrique en a marre

De toutes ces exploitations

Mon peuple en a marre

De toute cette oppression

L'Afrique en a marre

On en a marre. *We're fed up.* **les fonds dilapidés** *misappropriated funds* **lorsque** *when* **vanpayas** *[vampires]* **les guerres** *wars* **gardons la foi** *let's keep the faith* **faya** *[fire]* **tuer** *to kill* **lois** *laws*

Compréhension

Complétez les phrases suivantes avec des mots trouvés dans la chanson. Il y a plusieurs possibilités pour chacune.

1. Il est injuste que _____ soient _____.

2. Il est triste qu'il y ait _____.

3. Le peuple veut que les chefs d'État _____.

4. Le peuple ne veut pas que les chefs d'État _____.

Composition

> ### ⚙ Pour mieux écrire: *Softening or hardening your tone*

When making suggestions, criticizing or trying to persuade someone to do something in French, you sound more forceful or more gentle by using the subjunctive, the imperative or the conditional to harden or soften you tone. Generally, using the imperative will sound more demanding and the conditional will sound more polite. Expressions that are followed by the subjunctive can range from soft to harsh.

Organisez-vous. Vous allez décrire une situation dont vous avez marre *(with which you are fed up)* et suggérer des changements. Avant d'écrire votre rédaction, considérez les phrases suivantes et mettez-les en ordre du plus doux *(soft)* au plus sévère.

1. Faites-le! / Pourriez-vous le faire? / Il faut que vous le fassiez.
2. Vous devriez être plus réalistes. / Soyez plus réalistes! / Il vaut mieux être plus réalistes.
3. Il faut que ça change. / Je préfère que ça change. / Je préférerais que ça change.
4. Je ne veux pas que ça continue. / Je regrette que ça continue. / Je suis furieux (furieuse) que ça continue.
5. Il est essentiel qu'on dise ce qu'on pense. / Il vaut mieux qu'on dise ce qu'on pense. / Il est important qu'on dise ce qu'on pense.
6. J'insiste que tout le monde sache la vérité *(the truth)*. / Je voudrais que tout le monde sache la vérité. / Je veux que tout le monde sache la vérité.

If you have access to SYSTÈME-D software, you will find the following phrases, vocabulary, grammar, and dictionary aids there.

Phrases: Disapproving; Expressing an opinion
Vocabulary: Problems
Grammar: Imperative; Impersonal **il**; Subjunctive

J'en ai marre!

Vous en avez marre d'une situation ou d'un problème particulier. Donnez autant de *(as many)* détails que possible à son sujet et expliquez clairement pourquoi vous voulez une fin ou une solution à ce problème. Cette situation peut être quelque chose de votre vie personnelle, une situation politique ou une injustice sociale comme dans la chanson *Y en a marre* à la page précédente. Ensuite, suggérez ce qu'il faut faire, à votre avis, pour améliorer la situation.

Comparaisons culturelles

La musique francophone: les influences africaines et antillaises

Le Français moyen écoute au moins 2 heures de musique par jour et la diversité **croissante** de la société française est reflétée dans sa musique. La chanson française traditionnelle reste la musique préférée de la plupart des Français, mais la musique africaine et antillaise est de plus en plus populaire. Ces dernières années, cette musique représente une plus grande **part** de la musique exportée par la France chaque année.

Music

Sahel Afro-Beat Maloya Rumba Mandingue

Aujourd'hui, des artistes viennent en France de partout dans le monde francophone pour **enregistrer** leurs chansons. C'est en partie dû à la **loi** Toubon, **promulguée** en 1994 pour protéger le **patrimoine** linguistique du français contre l'extension de l'anglais. Cette loi **exige** qu'au moins 40% de la musique jouée à la radio en France soit en français.

Dans la musique francophone d'Afrique, on trouve cinq genres d'influence régionale importants.

Angélique Kidjo

la rumba
Pays francophones d'origine: la République démocratique du Congo, le Congo
Instruments typiques: **les tambours, les trompes,** les flûtes et les xylophones
Artistes: Papa Wemba, Zao, Tabu Ley Rochereau, Wendo Kolosay

la musique Sahel
Pays francophones d'origine: le Sénégal, le Burkina Faso, la Mauritanie, le Mali, le Niger
Instruments typiques: les luths et les tambours
Artistes: Youssou N'Dour, Wasis Diop, Ismaël Lô, Ali Farka Touré

l'afrobeat
Pays francophones d'origine: le Togo, le Bénin, le Cameroun, la République centrafricaine
Instruments typiques: la percussion
Artistes: Angélique Kidjo, Francis Bebey, Lapiro Mbanga, Sally Nyolo

la musique Mandingue
Pays francophones d'origine: le Sénégal, la Côte d'Ivoire, la Guinée
Instruments typiques: **la kora, le balafon,** la percussion
Artistes: Amadou & Mariam, Tiken Jah Fakoly, Alpha Blondy, Salif Keïta

la musique Maloya
Pays francophones d'origine: Madagascar, l'Île Maurice, La Réunion, les Seychelles et les Comores
Instruments typiques: **la cithare** et l'accordéon
Artistes: René Lacaille, Danyel Waro, Abou Chihabi

croissante *growing* **part** *share* **enregistrer** *to record* **loi** *law* **promulguée** *passed* **patrimoine** *heritage* **exige** *requires* **les tambours** *drums* **les trompes** *horns* **la kora** *the kora (a 21 string harp lute)* **le balafon** *the balaphone (an instrument similar to the xylophone)* **la cithare** *the zither*

Youssou N'Dour

Quand on pense à la musique antillaise, le reggae et le zouk **viennent d'abord à l'esprit.** Le reggae, né en Jamaïque pendant les années 60, est devenu populaire chez les Français. Dans un sondage sur les genres de musique les plus appréciés en France, 38% des jeunes hommes (de 15 à 24 ans) ont mentionné le reggae.

Le zouk, né en Guadeloupe et en Martinique dans les années 80, est chanté en français ou en créole et le verbe *zouker* est devenu un synonyme de *danser* dans la région. Comme beaucoup de musique aux Caraïbes, cette musique montre des influences de la rumba africaine. Le succès du reggae et des artistes du zouk antillais, comme Tanya St.-Val, Kaysha, Malavoi, Jocelyne Béroard, Sonia Dersion, Zouk Machine et surtout du groupe Kassav', a servi d'inspiration pour une renaissance de la musique populaire en Afrique. L'interaction artistique entre les Antilles et l'Afrique est signe des **liens** culturels forts entre leurs peuples.

Tabu Ley Rochereau

Compréhension

1. Qu'est-ce que la loi Toubon exige? Pourquoi est-ce que cette loi a changé la musique qu'on entend en France? Qu'est-ce que vous pensez de cette loi?

2. Quels sont cinq genres de musique africaine qui ont influencé la musique francophone? Dans quelle région d'Afrique est-ce que chacun trouve ses origines? Est-ce que la musique africaine a influencé la musique de votre pays? Quels genres de musique?

3. Quels sont deux genres de musique antillaise populaires en France? Dans lequel de ces genres est-ce qu'on trouve souvent des chansons en créole? Qui est Kassav'? Est-ce qu'on écoute ces genres de musique dans votre région?

Visit **academic.cengage.com/french** for YouTube video cultural correlations, cultural information and activities.

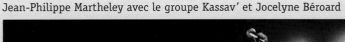
Jean-Philippe Martheley avec le groupe Kassav' et Jocelyne Béroard

---

viennent d'abord à l'esprit *first come to one's mind*   **liens** *ties*

Résumé de grammaire

Impersonal expressions and the infinitive

Use an infinitive after the following expressions to state general advice and opinions. Notice that **il faut** means *it is necessary*, **il ne faut pas** means *one should / must not,* and **il n'est pas nécessaire** means *it's not necessary.*

Pour préparer un voyage à l'étranger, **il faut obtenir** des passeports. **Il vaut mieux réserver** une chambre à l'avance. **Il ne faut pas attendre** le dernier moment.

> Il faut... / Il ne faut pas...
> Il est nécessaire de... / Il n'est pas nécessaire de...
> Il vaut mieux...
> Il est essentiel / important / bon / mauvais de...
> C'est bien de...

The subjunctive *(Le subjonctif)*

The indicative mood expresses reality. The subjunctive mood conveys subjectivity; that is, feelings, desires, doubts, fears, opinions, and requests about what happens or might happen. The present subjunctive may imply either present or future actions.

The subjunctive is used in a second clause preceded by **que:**

S'il est malade, il faut **qu'il téléphone** au médecin.
J'ai peur **qu'il soit** très malade.

Je suis content **qu'il aille** chez le médecin.

* to give advice for someone in particular after impersonal expressions like those listed above. (In expressions like **il est bon de, que** replaces **de.)**
* when the verb in the first clause "triggers" the subjunctive in the second clause by expressing feelings, desires, doubts, fears, opinions, or requests; provided that the subject of the first clause is not the same as the subject of the second clause. (See page 400 for a list of such "trigger" verbs.)

For most verbs, form the subjunctive as follows.

* For **nous** and **vous,** the subjunctive looks like the imperfect.
* For the other forms, drop the **-ent** ending of the **ils/elles** form of the present indicative and add the endings: **-e, -es, -e, -ent.**

Le médecin veut **qu'il reste au lit** et **qu'il finisse** tous ses médicaments. Il vaut mieux **qu'il ne rende pas visite** à ses amis.

	PARLER	FINIR	RENDRE
que je	parle	finisse	rende
que tu	parles	finisses	rendes
qu'il/elle/on	parle	finisse	rende
que nous	parlions	finissions	rendions
que vous	parliez	finissiez	rendiez
qu'ils/elles	parlent	finissent	rendent

Most irregular verbs follow the same pattern.

Il ne veut pas **que je dise** à ses parents qu'il est malade. Il faut **qu'il dorme** beaucoup. Il ne faut pas **qu'il sorte** ce soir.

connaître	que je connaisse	que nous connaissions
dire	que je dise	que nous disions
dormir	que je dorme	que nous dormions
écrire	que j'écrive	que nous écrivions
lire	que je lise	que nous lisions
partir	que je parte	que nous partions
sortir	que je sorte	que nous sortions

These verbs follow the same pattern, but have a different stem for the **nous** and **vous** forms.

acheter	que j'achèt**e**	que nous achet**ions**
boire	que je boiv**e**	que nous buv**ions**
devoir	que je doiv**e**	que nous dev**ions**
payer	que je pai**e**	que nous pay**ions**
prendre	que je prenn**e**	que nous pren**ions**
venir	que je vienn**e**	que nous ven**ions**

Il faut **que nous achetions** ces médicaments à la pharmacie.
Il veut **que tu viennes** le voir.

Only seven verbs are irregular in the subjunctive: **avoir, être, aller, faire, vouloir, savoir,** and **pouvoir.** Memorize their conjugations from the charts on page 396. The subjunctive of **il y a** is **qu'il y ait** and the subjunctive of **il pleut** is **qu'il pleuve.**

Je regrette **qu'il soit** malade mais je suis content **qu'il aille** voir le médecin.

The subjunctive or the infinitive?

The subjunctive is used when there are different subjects in the main and dependent clauses. When there is no change of subject, you normally use the infinitive. Use **de** before an infinitive after the verb **regretter** and when the expression includes the verb **être.** Also remember to use an infinitive after expressions such as **il faut** or **il est important de** to talk about what should be done as a general rule, rather than what specific people should do.

Je ne veux pas **changer** mes chèques de voyage. Je préfère **que tu changes** tes chèques de voyage.

Commands and using pronouns with commands

The imperative (command form) of most verbs is the **tu, nous,** or **vous** form of the verb without the subject pronoun. Remember to drop the final **s** of -**er** verbs and of **aller,** but not of other verbs, in **tu** form commands.

Être and **avoir** have irregular command forms: **sois, soyons, soyez** and **aie, ayons, ayez.** In negative commands, reflexive and object pronouns, **y,** and **en** are placed before the verb.

In affirmative commands, pronouns are attached to the end of the verb with a hyphen, and **me** and **te** become **moi** and **toi.** When **y** or **en** follows a **tu** form command, the final **s** is reattached to the end of the verb.

Prends la rue Provence, **va** jusqu'à la rue Thiers et **tourne** à gauche.
Prenons la rue Provence.
Prenez la rue Provence.

Sois à l'heure.
Aie de la patience.

Ne lui achète pas de cadeau dans la boutique de l'aéroport.
Achète-lui un cadeau au marché.

Réveille-toi tôt et **vas-y** le matin.

Vocabulaire

CD 4

COMPÉTENCE 1 Track 12

Deciding where to stay

NOMS MASCULINS

un bruit	a noise
un chalet de ski	a ski lodge
un hôtelier	a hotel manager
un lavabo	a washbasin, a sink
le logement	lodging
un supplément	an extra charge, a supplement

NOMS FÉMININS

une auberge de jeunesse	a youth hostel
une clé	a key
une hôtelière	a hotel manager
la réception	the front desk
une station estivale	a summer resort

EXPRESSIONS VERBALES

C'est bien de...	It's good to . . .
Il est bon de...	It's good to . . .
Il est essentiel de...	It's essential to . . .
Il est important de...	It's important to . . .
Il est mauvais de...	It's bad to . . .
Il est nécessaire de...	It's necessary to . . .
Il n'est pas nécessaire de...	It's not necessary to . . .
Il faut...	One must . . ., It's necessary to . . .
Il ne faut pas...	One shouldn't . . ., One must not . . .
Il vaut mieux...	It's better to . . .
recommander	to recommend

ADJECTIFS

calme	calm
compris(e)	included
privé(e)	private
servi(e)	served

DIVERS

bon séjour	enjoy your stay
côté cour	on the courtyard side
de luxe	deluxe
en espèces	in cash
régler la note	to pay the bill

COMPÉTENCE 2 Track 17

Going to the doctor

NOMS MASCULINS

les frissons	the shivers
un liquide	a liquid
un médecin	a doctor
un médicament	a medecine, a medication
un rhume	a cold
un symptôme	a symptom
un virus	a virus

NOMS FÉMININS

une allergie	an allergy
la grippe	the flu
une indigestion	indigestion
une ordonnance	a prescription

LES PARTIES DU CORPS

la bouche	the mouth
le bras	the arm
le corps	the body
les dents (f)	the teeth
les doigts (m)	the fingers
les doigts de pied	the toes
le dos	the back
la gorge	the throat
la jambe	the leg
la main	the hand
le nez	the nose
l'œil (m) (pl les yeux)	the eye
l'oreille (f)	the ear
le pied	the foot
la tête	the head
le ventre	the stomach

EXPRESSIONS VERBALES

avoir des frissons	to have the shivers
avoir mal à...	one's . . . hurt(s)
communiquer	to communicate
éternuer	to sneeze
tomber malade	to get sick
tousser	to cough
vomir	to vomit, to throw up

DIVERS

au cours de	in the course of, during, while on
enceinte	pregnant
exactement	exactly
Qu'est-ce qui ne va pas?	What's wrong?
tout simplement	quite simply

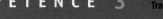
Running errands on a trip

NOMS MASCULINS

un aéroport	an airport
un bureau de poste	a post office
un cadeau (*pl* des cadeaux)	a present
un distributeur de billets	an ATM machine
un kiosque	a kiosk
un marchand de cadeaux	a gift shop
un timbre	a stamp

NOMS FÉMININS

de l'aspirine	aspirin
une banque	a bank
une carte téléphonique	a telephone card
une navette	a shuttle
une pharmacie	a pharmacy

EXPRESSIONS VERBALES

accepter que...	to accept that . . .
aller / venir chercher quelqu'un	to go / come pick someone up
c'est dommage que...	it's too bad that . . .
douter que...	to doubt that . . .
envoyer	to send
être content(e) que...	to be happy that . . .
être désolé(e) que...	to be sorry that . . .
être étonné(e) que...	to be astonished that . . .
être furieux (furieuse) que...	to be furious that . . .
être heureux (heureuse) que...	to be happy that . . .
être surpris(e) que...	to be surprised that . . .
être triste que...	to be sad that . . .
insister que...	to insist that . . .
j'aimerais autant...	I would just as soon . . .
regretter que...	to regret that . . .
retirer de l'argent	to withdraw money
souhaiter que...	to wish that . . .

DIVERS

en retard	late
principal(e) (*mpl* principaux)	principal, main

Giving directions

NOMS MASCULINS

un employé	an employee
l'office de tourisme	the Tourist Office
un plan	a map

NOMS FÉMININS

une employée	an employee
une expression	an expression
les indications	directions
une place	a (town) square, a plaza

EXPRESSIONS VERBALES

avoir pitié (de)	to have pity (on)
continuer (tout droit)	to continue (straight ahead)
descendre la rue...	to go down . . . Street
expliquer	to explain
indiquer le chemin	to give directions, to show the way
monter la rue...	to go up . . . Street
prendre la rue...	to take . . . Street
remercier	to thank
tourner (à droite / à gauche)	to turn (right / left)
traverser	to cross, to go across

EXPRESSIONS PRÉPOSITIONNELLES

au coin de	on the corner of
dans la rue...	on . . . Street
jusqu'à	until, up to, as far as
sur l'avenue / le boulevard / la place...	on . . . Avenue / Boulevard / Square

DIVERS

juste	just
tout droit	straight (ahead)
utile	useful

Tes vacances avec moi

SONIA DERSION

Dans sa chanson *Tes vacances avec moi*, Sonia Dersion invite un ami à passer ses vacances avec elle. Quelles sont les activités qu'on peut faire en couple en vacances?

Tes vacances avec moi. Voilà quelques phrases qu'on entend dans la chanson de Sonia Dersion, *Tes vacances avec moi*. En vous servant des mots que vous reconnaissez et de ce que vous pouvez deviner, trouvez l'équivalent de ces phrases en anglais.

1. serre-moi dans tes bras
2. le soleil tape si fort
3. tu m'emmènes avec toi
4. je m'évade
5. je garde la cadence
6. mon cœur bat si vite
7. j'évite les garçons
8. je te suivrais
9. ça m'est égal

a. *my heart beats so fast*
b. *it's all the same to me*
c. *hold me in your arms*
d. *I avoid boys*
e. *the sun's so strong*
f. *you take me with you*
g. *I keep the beat*
h. *I get away from it all*
i. *I would follow you*

Bien que *(Although)* née en Guadeloupe, Sonia Dersion a passé toute sa jeunesse en Bretagne. Pourtant, le rythme des Antilles est évident dans sa musique.

You can access these songs at the iTunes playlist on **academic.cengage.com/french/horizons.**

Plus rien ne m'étonne

TIKEN JAH FAKOLY

Dans ses chansons, Tiken Jah Fakoly parle souvent de l'injustice, de l'oppression, de la colonisation, de la mondialisation *(globalization)* et des droits de l'homme *(human rights)*. Actuellement *(Currently)*, il vit *(lives)* en exil au Mali.

A. Paroles. Voici quelques nouveaux mots utilisés dans les paroles *(lyrics)* de la chanson *Plus rien ne m'étonne*. Est-ce que vous pouvez imaginer de quoi *(about what)* Tiken Jah Fakoly pourrait parler en utilisant ces mots dans le contexte de la colonisation ou de la mondialisation?

L'Ivoirien Tiken Jah Fakoly, chanteur de musique reggae, dit qu'il fait de la musique pour «éveiller *(to awaken)* les consciences».

l'uranium
l'aluminium
les gisements *(mineral deposits)*
le blé *(wheat)*
l'or *(gold)*

B. Régions. Les endroits suivants sont mentionnés dans la chanson. Qu'est-ce que vous savez de l'histoire récente de ces endroits?

la Thétchénie	l'Afghanistan	Haïti	l'Irak
l'Arménie	le Pakistan	Bangui	le Kurdistan

Tiken Jah Fakoly mentionne aussi ces groupes ethniques. Informez-vous sur ces peuples sur Internet.

les Maldingues   les Wollofs   les Mossi   les Soussous

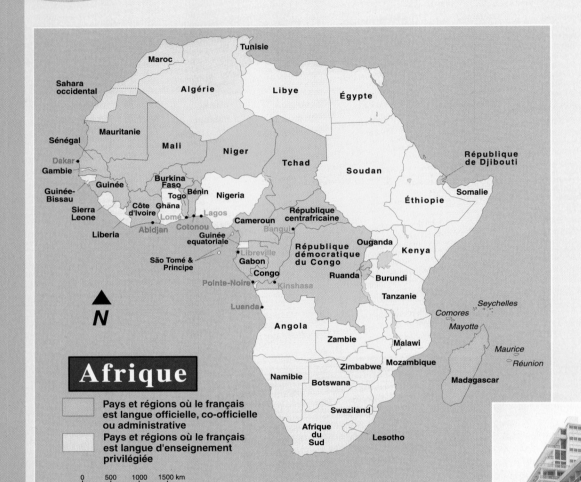

Afrique

Pays et régions où le français est langue officielle, co-officielle ou administrative

Pays et régions où le français est langue d'enseignement privilégiée

0   500   1000   1500 km

LE FRANÇAIS est une langue importante dans 22 pays d'Afrique, et plus de 200 millions d'habitants de ce continent parlent français. La colonisation de l'Afrique par la France est en grande partie à l'origine de la francophonie en Afrique.

Aujourd'hui en Afrique, on trouve le moderne juxtaposé au traditionnel.

Allons visiter quelques pays francophones africains!

La Côte d'Ivoire est un pays fascinant par sa diversité géographique et culturelle. Dans ce seul pays, vous pouvez voir des régions géographiques très variées. Le long de **la côte,** il y a des plages et **des falaises.** Au centre, il y a la jungle et des forêts tropicales. Dans le nord, il y a la savane.

Il y a plus de 60 **tribus** différentes en Côte d'Ivoire, **chacune** avec ses **propres** traditions.

Abidjan, la plus grande ville ivoirienne, est une belle ville moderne. On l'appellait **autrefois** le «Paris de l'Afrique».

---

la côte *the coast*   **des falaises** *cliffs*   **tribus** *tribes*   **chacune** *each one*   **propres** *own*
autrefois *in the past*

Avec plus de 500 tribus différentes, la République démocratique du Congo, **anciennement** le Zaïre, est un pays de diversité et de contradictions où les différences ethniques provoquent souvent une instabilité sociale. Kinshasa, la capitale, est la plus grande ville d'Afrique subsaharienne.

70% de la population du pays habite dans des régions rurales où les traditions remontent à plus de mille ans.

---

anciennement *formerly*

Le Maroc, aussi appelé «le pays du soleil couchant» *(al-Maghrib al-aqsa),* est l'état le plus occidental de l'Afrique du Nord.

Par sa situation entre la Méditerranée, l'Atlantique et le Sahara, le Maroc **appartient à la fois** au monde méditerranéen, occidental et berbère. Composé de montagnes, de déserts, de plages, de **côtes escarpées** et de forêts, et **doté de** villes fascinantes (la capitale, Rabat, Casablanca et Marrakech) et de sites archéologiques (Fès, Salé), le Maroc est un des plus beaux pays du monde.

Encore plus **attirante** que la beauté de ses paysages, la culture marocaine est très riche **car** elle reflète l'histoire et les traditions du peuple marocain, **tant d'**origine arabe que berbère et saharienne.

---

appartient à la fois *belongs at the same time*   **côtes escarpées** *rocky coasts*   **doté de** *endowed with*   **attirante** *attractive*
car *because*   **tant de** *as much*

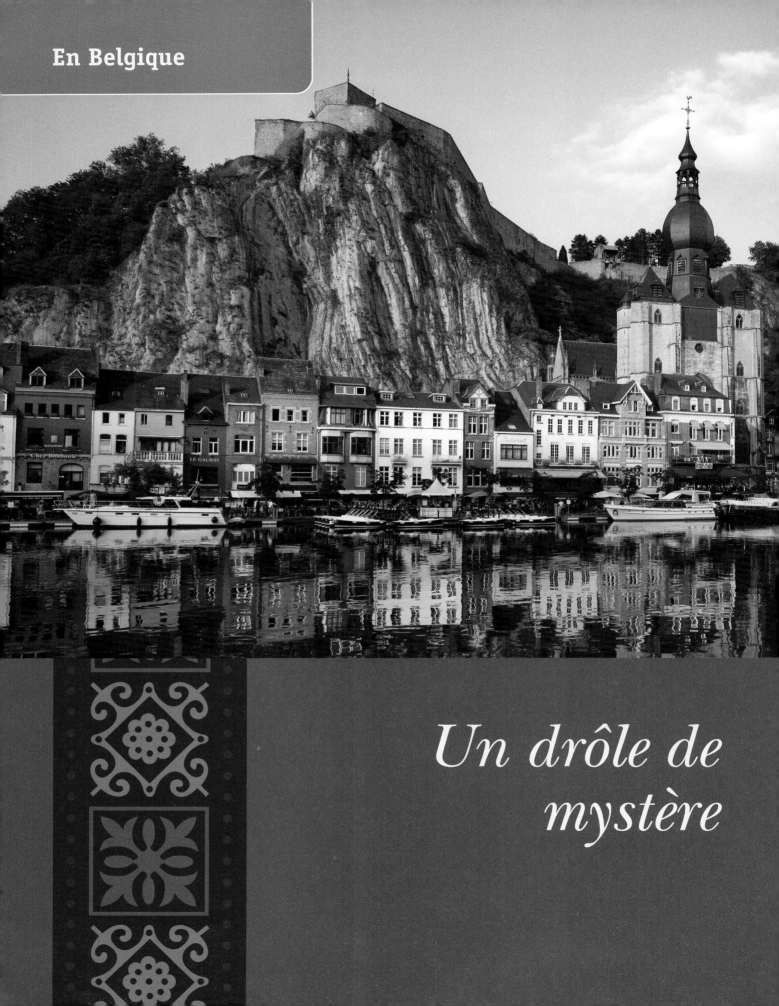

Un drôle de mystère

Quelqu'un a été assassiné et c'est à vous, le détective, de trouver le criminel. En même temps, vous allez faire une révision de ce que vous avez appris dans *Horizons*. Si vous avez des difficultés en faisant un exercice, référez-vous aux pages indiquées en marge *(in the margin)*.

Les personnages

Un mystère dans les Ardennes

Épilogue

LA BELGIQUE

 En Europe, on parle français en France, en Belgique, en Suisse, au Luxembourg et à Monaco. Choisissez une de ces régions et faites des recherches à son sujet sur Internet. Préparez une présentation sur un aspect de cette région que vous trouvez intéressant.

Avez-vous visité l'Europe? Connaissez-vous la Belgique? Voudriez-vous y aller?

La Belgique a **une frontière** commune avec la France **au sud, les Pays-Bas au nord** et l'Allemagne et le Luxembourg **à l'est.** Du point de vue culturel, la Belgique est **un mélange de** cultures latines, celtiques et germaniques, et cette diversité culturelle est reflétée dans la division culturelle et linguistique du pays.

En Belgique, il y a trois langues officielles: le français, **le flamand** (un dialecte **néerlandais**) et l'allemand.

Dans la Région flamande, au nord du pays, on parle flamand.

Dans la Région **wallonne,** au sud, on parle français.

Bruxelles, la capitale belge, est une ville bilingue.

La Grand-Place, à Bruxelles, est charmante.

Anvers est la plus grande ville de la Région flamande.

Liège est la plus grande ville wallonne.

---

une frontière *a border*   **au sud** *to the south*   **les Pays-Bas au nord** *the Netherlands to the north*   **à l'est** *to the east*
un mélange de *a mixture of*   **le flamand** *Flemish*   **néerlandais** *Dutch*   **wallonne** *Walloon (French-speaking Belgian)*

La Belgique (le Royaume de Belgique)
Nombre d'habitants: 10 511 000 (les Belges)
Capitale: Bruxelles

 Visit it live on Google Earth!

L'opposition linguistique entre les Flamands et les Wallons est souvent reflétée dans une opposition politique. Pour dissiper cet antagonisme, un effort de décentralisation a donné plus de **pouvoir** aux trois régions: la Région flamande, la Région wallonne et la Région de Bruxelles.

La Belgique, un des membres fondateurs de l'Union européenne, est **le siège** du Conseil de l'Union européenne et aussi le siège européen de **l'OTAN.**

Le bâtiment Justus Lipsius, siège du Conseil de l'Union européenne à Bruxelles.

✿ Qu'en savez-vous?

1. La culture belge est un mélange de cultures _____, _____ et _____.
2. Les trois langues officielles de la Belgique sont _____, _____ et _____.
3. La Belgique est divisée en trois régions: la Région _____ au nord, la Région _____ au sud et la Région de _____ (la capitale).
4. Il y a souvent une opposition politique entre les _____ et les _____.
5. La Belgique est un des membres fondateurs de l'_____.
6. La Belgique est le siège du Conseil de l'_____ et aussi le siège européen de l'_____.

pouvoir *power*   **le siège** *headquarters*   **l'OTAN** *NATO*

Les personnages

Dans ce chapitre, vous allez **résoudre** l'énigme d'un crime. C'est **un meurtre** qui **a lieu** dans un vieux château de la forêt des Ardennes, dans **le sud** de la Belgique. En résolvant le mystère, vous allez aussi réviser ce que vous avez appris dans ce livre. D'abord, faisons la connaissance des personnages de l'histoire.

Regardez les personnages suivants. Comment sont-ils?

François Fédor, millionnaire excentrique

Laurent Lavare, **le comptable** de François Fédor

Valérie Veutoux, l'ex-femme de François Fédor

Bernard Boncorps, le neveu de François Fédor

Nathalie Lanana, la petite amie de Bernard Boncorps

le/la domestique

le détective

Il y a encore un dernier petit détail. Le/La domestique sera joué(e) par votre professeur. Et le détective, qui est-ce? Oui, **vous avez deviné juste** (comme un bon détective); c'est vous!

---

résoudre *to resolve* **un meurtre** *a murder* **a lieu** *takes place* **le sud** *the south* **le comptable** *the accountant*
vous avez deviné juste *you guessed right*

A. Descriptions. Choisissez quatre adjectifs pour décrire chacun des personnages.

• Pour réviser l'accord des adjectifs, voir les pages 34, 40 et 48.

riche	bête	???	intelligent
???	paresseux	(mal)heureux	???
malhonnête *(dishonest)*	laid	désagréable	sportif
blond	sexy	matérialiste	
beau	suspect	froid	frivole
???	méchant	hostile	sérieux
âgé	sympathique	grand	intéressant
???	irresponsable	petit	snob

B. Explications. Avec un(e) partenaire, devinez qui va être la victime et qui va commettre le crime. Imaginez une explication. Utilisez un dictionnaire si nécessaire.

• Pour réviser le futur immédiat, voir la page 158.

C. Stratégies. Vous avez appris plusieurs stratégies pour lire plus facilement en français. Avant de lire *Un mystère dans les Ardennes*, révisez les stratégies suivantes.

a. Utilisez les mots apparentés et le contexte pour donner le sens de ces phrases.

   1. L'aptitude de François Fédor à faire fortune était sans égal. Et on pouvait dire la même chose de son aptitude à se faire des ennemis.
   2. Dans le village, où il n'allait jamais, on l'appelait le vieux Midas parce qu'on disait que tout ce qu'il touchait se transformait en or.

b. Utilisez les mots entre parenthèses pour deviner le sens des mots en italique.

   1. (jeune) On disait que François Fédor avait fait fortune en Afrique pendant sa *jeunesse*.
   2. (attendre) Cette *attente* avait duré presque deux jours.

c. Vous avez appris à reconnaître la signification des temps composés. Comparez ces phrases.

Je l'**ai** fait.	*I **have** done it.*	Il **est** parti.	*He **has** left.*
Je l'**avais** fait.	*I **had** done it.*	Il **était** parti.	*He **had** left.*
Je l'**aurai** fait.	*I **will have** done it.*	Il **sera** parti.	*He **will have** left.*
Je l'**aurais** fait.	*I **would have** done it.*	Il **serait** parti.	*He **would have** left.*

Donnez le sens des expressions en italique dans les phrases suivantes.

1. François Fédor *avait toujours fait* ce qu'il voulait et il *avait toujours négligé* (négliger *to neglect*) les membres de sa famille.
2. Ils acceptaient son argent chaque mois sans poser de questions et ils *n'auraient jamais pensé* que François Fédor puisse choisir un acte de charité plus méritoire *(deserving)*.
3. Si M. Lavare, le comptable, *n'avait pas été* là, on *n'aurait pas dit* quatre mots durant tout le dîner.

Maintenant, utilisez ces stratégies pour lire le dossier *(file)* sur ce cas aux pages suivantes.

Un mystère dans les Ardennes

CD 4-22

Certains l'admiraient, d'autres le détestaient. Il avait toujours fait ce qu'il voulait et **personne ne discutait** ce qu'il faisait. François Fédor habitait dans un vieux château **au fond de** la forêt des Ardennes. Dans le village, où il n'allait jamais, on l'appelait le vieux Midas parce qu'on disait que tout ce qu'il touchait se transformait en or. Personne ne savait exactement d'où venait sa fortune, mais on disait qu'il avait fait fortune en Afrique pendant sa jeunesse.

Son aptitude à faire fortune était sans égal. Et on pouvait dire la même chose de son aptitude à se faire des ennemis. François Fédor avait toujours négligé les membres de sa famille et il n'avait jamais pris le temps de se faire des amis. Quand je dis qu'il avait négligé les membres de sa famille, je ne veux pas donner l'impression qu'il ne partageait pas sa richesse avec **eux;** au contraire, ils ne **manquaient de** rien. Comme dans **un trou** noir, chaque mois, François Fédor **versait** une petite fortune sur **les comptes en banque** de son neveu Bernard Boncorps et de son ex-femme Valérie Veutoux. Il payait cet argent depuis vingt ans sans avoir **le moindre** contact avec l'un ou l'autre. En fait, il n'avait jamais rencontré son neveu, qui **vivait** une vie de play-boy à Monaco **grâce à** son vieil oncle. Et eux non plus, ils n'avaient jamais essayé de venir le voir. Ils acceptaient son argent chaque mois sans poser de questions et ils n'auraient jamais pensé que François Fédor puisse choisir un jour un acte de charité plus **méritoire.**

C'était donc avec grande surprise que son neveu et son ex-femme avaient reçu un coup de téléphone de Laurent Lavare, le comptable de François Fédor, quelques semaines **auparavant.** Ils étaient **priés de se rendre** chez le vieux Midas le dernier jour du mois **courant** avant midi. Chacun se demandait ce que le vieux Fédor pouvait bien vouloir après tout ce temps. Mais M. Lavare avait refusé de leur donner plus de détails. Quand ils étaient arrivés au grand château sombre, Valérie Veutoux, Bernard Boncorps et sa petite amie Nathalie Lanana s'étaient sentis un peu **mal à l'aise.** Après avoir passé deux journées entières dans le château sans voir leur hôte, les invités avaient senti leur **malaise** se transformer en panique. Mais que pouvaient-ils faire sinon accepter **les caprices** de leur **bienfaiteur** et chercher une manière de passer le temps? Quand Bernard n'était pas avec Nathalie, il jouait au billard pendant qu'elle nageait dans la piscine. Valérie Veutoux restait toute la journée dans sa chambre. Cette attente avait duré presque deux jours quand le/la domestique les avait enfin informés qu'ils verraient M. Fédor au dîner à huit heures, dans la salle à manger.

Accompagné de son comptable, François Fédor les attendait, assis à table, quand ils étaient descendus. Sans dire un mot, le vieil hôte leur avait indiqué d'un geste

---

personne ne discutait *no one questioned*   **au fond de** *deep in*   **eux** *them*   **manquaient de** *lacked*   **un trou** *a hole*   **versait** *poured, deposited*   **les comptes en banque** *the bank accounts*   **le moindre** *the least*   **vivait** *lived*   **grâce à** *thanks to*   **méritoire** *deserving*   **auparavant** *beforehand*   **priés de se rendre** *requested to appear*   **courant** *current*   **mal à l'aise** *ill at ease*   **malaise** *uneasiness*   **les caprices** *the whims*   **bienfaiteur** *benefactor*

de la main où chacun devait **s'asseoir,** à l'autre bout de la table. Le/La domestique avait servi un excellent dîner mais les invités, qui n'avaient pas l'habitude d'apprécier ce qu'on leur donnait, **n'**avaient fait **aucun** compliment. Ils étaient trop curieux de connaître la raison de cette réunion soudaine et **inattendue.** Si M. Lavare, le comptable, n'avait pas été là, on n'aurait pas dit quatre mots durant tout le dîner.

Le repas fini, François Fédor s'était retiré à la bibliothèque et il avait demandé au/à la domestique de faire entrer son neveu et son ex-femme l'un après l'autre pour boire un cognac avec lui... Il avait quelque chose d'important à leur dire. Ils avaient eu avec M. Fédor une conférence d'une demi-heure chacun, puis le/la domestique les avait raccompagnés à leur chambre et leur avait **souhaité** une bonne nuit. Devinaient-ils la scène qui les attendrait le lendemain matin en sortant de leur chambre? Savaient-ils qu'un détective voudrait leur parler et qu'ils seraient **soupçonnés** d'un meurtre? Au moins une personne présente cette nuit-là le savait. Mais qui était-ce?

Quand ils s'étaient levés, ils avaient appris que tôt le matin, le/la domestique avait téléphoné à la police pour dire que François Fédor avait été victime d'un meurtre au cours de la nuit. Qui avait **commis** ce crime? Quel était **le mobile** du meurtre? Pourquoi est-ce que François Fédor leur avait demandé de venir? Qu'est-ce qu'il leur avait dit dans la bibliothèque? Qu'est-ce que M. Lavare savait? Et le/la domestique? Qu'est-ce qui s'était passé ce soir-là?

C'est à vous de résoudre le mystère. Qu'est-ce que le célèbre inspecteur Maigret aurait fait à votre place? Vous allez sans doute vouloir poser beaucoup de questions et prendre des notes.

D. Détails. Lisez le texte *Un mystère dans les Ardennes* et répondez aux questions suivantes.

1. Où est-ce que François Fédor habitait?
2. D'où venait sa fortune?
3. Avait-il beaucoup d'amis?
4. Qui profitait aussi de son argent?
5. Qui a téléphoné à Bernard Boncorps et à Valérie Veutoux pour les inviter au château?
6. Combien de temps ont-ils dû attendre avant de voir François Fédor?
7. À votre avis *(opinion),* qu'est-ce que François Fédor a dit à Bernard Boncorps et à Valérie Veutoux dans la bibliothèque?

Un château de la forêt des Ardennes

---

s'asseoir *to sit*   **ne... aucun** *no, not any*   **inattendue** *unexpected*   **souhaité** *wished*   **soupçonnés** *suspected*
commis *committed*   **le mobile** *the motive*

• Pour réviser l'imparfait, voir la page 232.

• Pour réviser comment dire l'heure, voir la page 16.

CD 4-23

E. Vous êtes le détective. Pour commencer votre enquête *(investigation)*, écoutez la déclaration de chacun des personnages qui a passé la nuit au château. En les écoutant, notez les réponses aux questions qui suivent sur une autre feuille de papier.

Bernard Boncorps   Valérie Veutoux   Laurent Lavare   le/la domestique

1. Qu'est-ce que chaque personne a fait après le dîner?
2. À quelle heure est-ce que chacun s'est couché?
3. Qu'est-ce que chacun a entendu dans le couloir pendant la nuit?

Écoutez une fois de plus les déclarations de Valérie Veutoux, de Laurent Lavare et de Bernard Boncorps et notez qui faisait chaque chose à l'heure indiquée.

EXEMPLE   être déjà au lit
À dix heures et demie, Valérie Veutoux était déjà au lit.

1. avoir mal à la tête travailler sur l'ordinateur être au village

2. prendre un verre au café lire parler au téléphone

3. jouer aux cartes dormir

F. Il a disparu. Le corps de François Fédor a disparu *(disappeared)*. Vous devez bien examiner le lieu *(place)* du crime. Observez bien tous les indices *(clues)*. Voici la chambre de François Fédor avant le dîner et le lendemain du crime. Quelles différences y a-t-il?

• Pour réviser les prépositions, voir la page 118.

• Pour réviser les meubles, voir les pages 114 et 120.

avant le dîner

le lendemain du crime

Regardez encore une fois les deux dessins. Demandez au/à la domestique si chaque chose qui se trouve *(is located)* dans la chambre le lendemain du crime et qui n'était pas là la nuit précédente appartenait *(belonged)* à François Fédor. Dites à qui pourraient appartenir les choses qui n'étaient pas à lui.

• Pour réviser comment exprimer la possession, voir les pages 122 et 124.

> **EXEMPLE** — **Est-ce que c'était son ordinateur?**
> — **Non, ce n'était pas l'ordinateur de M. Fédor.**
> — **Alors, c'est peut-être l'ordinateur de M. Lavare.**

• Pour réviser les prépositions, voir la page 118.

CD 4-24

G. Dans quelle chambre?
Tout le monde a dormi le long du même couloir hier soir. Écoutez le/la domestique pour déterminer qui a dormi dans chaque chambre.

EXEMPLE **Mme Veutoux était au bout du couloir, en face de la salle de bains.**

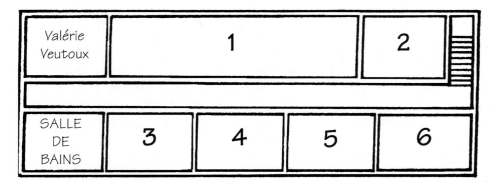

• Pour réviser les pronoms compléments d'objet direct et indirect, voir les pages 202, 360 et 366.

CD 4-25

H. Relations.
Utilisez le pronom **le** ou le pronom **lui** avec les verbes suivants à l'imparfait pour interroger le/la domestique sur ses relations avec M. Fédor. Écoutez ses réponses.

EXEMPLE connaître M. Fédor depuis longtemps
— **Est-ce que vous le connaissiez depuis longtemps?**
— **Je le connaissais depuis 15 ans.**

1. aimer bien M. Fédor
2. parler à M. Fédor de sa famille
3. emprunter *(to borrow)* quelquefois de l'argent à M. Fédor
4. réveiller M. Fédor à la même heure tous les jours
5. trouver M. Fédor sévère

CD 4-26

Maintenant demandez au/à la domestique si M. Fédor faisait les choses suivantes. Écoutez ses réponses.

EXEMPLE vous irriter quelquefois
— **Est-ce que M. Fédor vous irritait quelquefois?**
— **Oui, il m'irritait quelquefois. Ce n'était pas un homme facile.**

1. vous dire tout   2. vous payer bien   3. vous parler de sa vie privée

• Pour réviser le subjonctif, voir les pages 394–395, 396 et 400.

I. Je ne veux pas que...
Dites aux suspects ce qu'ils doivent et ne doivent pas faire.

EXEMPLE **Je ne veux pas que vous partiez d'ici.**

Il faut que... Il ne faut pas que... Je veux que... Je ne veux pas que... Il vaut mieux que...	partir d'ici dire tout ce que vous savez être calmes avoir peur toucher aux affaires *(things)* de M. Fédor faire une déposition parler à la presse m'obéir être patients

J. Savoir ou connaître? Votre enquête *(investigation)* progresse. Dites si vous savez ou si vous connaissez les choses ou les personnes suivantes en utilisant le verbe **savoir** ou le verbe **connaître**.

• Pour réviser **savoir** et **connaître**, voir la page 364.

1. la date du crime
2. le/la domestique de M. Fédor
3. l'heure approximative du crime
4. le château de M. Fédor
5. tous les amis de M. Fédor
6. tous les détails de la vie de M. Fédor
7. des mobiles *(motives)* possibles
8. l'identité de l'assassin

K. Il faut penser comme le/la criminel(le). Pour attraper le/la criminel(le), il faut penser comme lui/elle. Si vous étiez le/la criminel(le), est-ce que vous feriez les choses suivantes? Utilisez le conditionnel.

• Pour réviser le conditionnel, voir les pages 330–331.

Si j'étais le/la criminel(le),...

EXEMPLE   faire quelque chose d'inhabituel
Si j'étais le/la criminel(le), je ne ferais rien d'inhabituel.

1. être calme
2. parler beaucoup du crime
3. savoir tous les détails du crime
4. obéir à la police
5. s'intéresser beaucoup à l'enquête
6. dire la vérité *(truth)*
7. avoir envie de partir
8. devenir de plus en plus nerveux (nerveuse)
9. accuser quelqu'un d'autre
10. ???

L. Une matinée typique. Voici comment François Fédor passait ses matinées. Décrivez sa journée typique. Utilisez l'imparfait.

• Pour réviser les verbes réfléchis, voir les pages 264–265, 272, 280 et 282.

• Pour réviser l'imparfait, voir la page 232.

• Pour réviser comment dire l'heure, voir la page 16.

1.

2.

3.

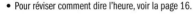

4.

5.

6.

• Pour réviser le passé composé et l'imparfait, voir les pages 238, 240 et 244.

M. Accusations. Dans le château Fédor, chacun des suspects vient vous expliquer pourquoi il/elle soupçonne *(suspects)* les autres. Complétez les paragraphes suivants en mettant les verbes entre parenthèses au passé composé ou à l'imparfait.

BERNARD BONCORPS

Je crois que c'est Laurent Lavare, le comptable de mon oncle qui le (l') __1__ (assassiner). Je (J') __2__ (entendre) dire récemment qu'il __3__ (avoir) des problèmes financiers. Certains disent qu'il __4__ (emprunter *to borrow*) des millions d'euros à mon oncle sans le lui dire. En fait, un ami suisse qui travaille à la banque de mon oncle me (m') __5__ (dire) qu'il y __6__ (avoir) très peu d'argent sur son compte. Je pense que mon oncle __7__ (apprendre) ce qui __8__ (se passer) et je suis certain qu'il __9__ (dire) à M. Lavare qu'il __10__ (aller) le dénoncer à la police.

VALÉRIE VEUTOUX

Il faut que vous sachiez que Bernard Boncorps __11__ (être) furieux contre son oncle. François Fédor __12__ (penser) que son neveu __13__ (faire) des études de droit à l'université de Nice. En vérité, Bernard __14__ (passer) tout son temps sur les plages et dans les casinos de Monaco. Quand son oncle __15__ (comprendre) la situation, il __16__ (se fâcher *to get angry*) et il __17__ (dire) à son neveu qu'il __18__ (vouloir) qu'il vienne finir ses études en Belgique, à l'université de Liège. Quand sa sœur, la mère de Bernard, __19__ (mourir), elle lui __20__ (demander) de se charger de l'éducation de son neveu. Bernard __21__ (ne pas comprendre) pourquoi son oncle, qu'il n'avait jamais vu, __22__ (s'intéresser) après tout ce temps à ce qu'il __23__ (faire). Bernard __24__ (ne pas vouloir) abandonner sa vie de play-boy sur la Côte d'Azur et il __25__ (avoir) peur que sa petite amie, Nathalie Lanana, refuse de venir ici avec lui. Et puis, il faut ajouter aussi que Bernard __26__ (avoir) des dettes énormes dans les casinos. Il __27__ (ne pas pouvoir) payer ses dettes avec l'argent que son oncle lui __28__ (donner) chaque mois. Bernard __29__ (ne pas vouloir) attendre la mort naturelle de son oncle pour hériter de sa part de la fortune.

LAURENT LAVARE

Je suis presque certain que Valérie Veutoux __30__ (assassiner) François Fédor. Récemment, elle __31__ (faire) la connaissance de Jean Jigaulaux, un jeune homme de 25 ans, et elle __32__ (tomber) amoureuse de lui. Ils __33__ (sortir) quelques mois ensemble, puis il lui __34__ (demander) de l'épouser *(to marry)*. La vieille Veutoux __35__ (ne pas comprendre) qu'il ne __36__ (vouloir) que *(only)* son argent et le jeune Jigaulaux __37__ (ne pas savoir) qu'elle ne recevrait plus un centime de François Fédor si elle __38__ (se remarier). La vaniteuse Valérie Veutoux __39__ (sans doute comprendre) qu'elle n'aurait jamais le joli Jigaulaux tant que *(as long as)* François Fédor __40__ (être) en vie et elle __41__ (se débarrasser *to get rid*) de lui.

Répondez aux questions suivantes au sujet des suspects. Utilisez un pronom dans chaque réponse pour remplacer les mots en italique.

• Pour réviser les pronoms compléments d'objet direct et indirect, **y** et **en,** voir les pages 152, 202, 324, 360 et 366.

Laurent Lavare

1. Qui a accusé *Laurent Lavare* du crime?
2. D'après son accusateur, est-ce que Laurent Lavare avait *des problèmes financiers*?
3. Disait-il *à François Fédor* qu'il lui empruntait de l'argent?
4. Combien empruntait-il *à François Fédor*?
5. D'après le banquier, ami de Bernard Boncorps, combien *d'argent* y avait-il sur le compte de son oncle?

Bernard Boncorps

1. Est-ce que Bernard Boncorps rendait souvent visite *à son oncle*?
2. Combien de fois est-ce que Bernard avait vu *son oncle*?
3. Est-ce que Bernard voulait aller *à Liège* pour finir ses études?
4. Combien de temps passait-il *sur les plages et dans les casinos*?
5. Est-ce qu'il avait *des dettes*?
6. Est-ce que Bernard avait assez *d'argent* pour payer *ses dettes*?

Valérie Veutoux

1. Qui pense que Valérie Veutoux a assassiné *François Fédor*?
2. Après combien de temps est-ce que Jean Jigaulaux a demandé *à Valérie Veutoux* de l'épouser?
3. Pourquoi est-ce que le jeune Jigaulaux aimait *la vieille Veutoux*?

N. Qui est-ce? Que savons-nous des suspects? Complétez les phrases suivantes avec **il est** ou **c'est**. Ensuite, dites si vous pensez que chaque phrase décrit plutôt Laurent Lavare ou Bernard Boncorps.

• Pour réviser l'usage de **c'est** et **il/elle est,** voir les pages 34 et 48.

EXEMPLE C'est quelqu'un qui travaille beaucoup.
C'est Laurent Lavare.

1. _____ le neveu de François Fédor.
2. _____ comptable.
3. _____ suisse.
4. _____ jeune.
5. _____ un play-boy.
6. _____ peut-être l'assassin.

O. Le dîner. Complétez le paragraphe suivant avec l'article défini (**le, la, l', les**), l'article indéfini (**un, une, des**), le partitif (**du, de la, de l'**) ou **de.**

• Pour réviser les produits alimentaires, voir les pages 88, 304–305, 314–315 et 322.

• Pour réviser les articles, voir les pages 46, 52, 310 et 320.

___1___ soir où M. Fédor est mort, M. Fédor et M. Lavare sont descendus vers sept heures et demie et ils ont pris ___2___ vin blanc avant de dîner. Pendant le repas, M. Fédor n'avait pas très faim; il a mangé ___3___ soupe et un peu ___4___ pain. Ensuite, il a pris ___5___ poulet et un peu ___6___ riz. Il n'a pas pris ___7___ légumes ni ___8___ tarte aux pommes. Il a pris un peu ___9___ fromage à la fin du repas. Normalement, il mangeait beaucoup. Il aimait bien ___10___ viande et ___11___ pommes de terre mais il ne prenait pas beaucoup ___12___ choses sucrées. Je pense qu'il n'avait pas ___13___ appétit ce soir-là, parce que ses problèmes le préoccupaient. Il n'a pas bu ___14___ vin rouge avec son repas, seulement ___15___ eau minérale et il a pris ___16___ café quand j'ai servi ___17___ dessert. Après ___18___ dîner, M. Fédor s'est retiré à ___19___ bibliothèque où il a bu un verre ___20___ cognac. Il est resté assis dans ___21___ fauteuil près de ___22___ porte pendant ___23___ heure après avoir parlé avec M. Boncorps et Mme Veutoux, puis il est monté se coucher.

Maintenant, dites si François Fédor a mangé ou a bu les choses suivantes le soir de son meurtre.

EXEMPLE **Il n'a pas mangé de pâté. Il a mangé de la soupe.**

• Pour réviser les pronoms relatifs, voir la page 286.

P. Les gens du village. Vous demandez aux gens du village ce qu'ils savaient au sujet de François Fédor. Faites des phrases en utilisant un élément de chaque colonne.

François Fédor était un homme...	qui... que (qu')... dont...	ne parlait pas beaucoup. avait un passé mystérieux. avait une personnalité un peu bizarre. beaucoup de gens trouvaient difficile. n'avait pas beaucoup d'amis. je ne connaissais pas bien. faisait toujours ce qu'il voulait. tout le monde avait un peu peur.

• Pour réviser le passé composé et l'imparfait, voir les pages 238, 240 et 244.

Q. Valérie se marie. Vous avez demandé à des collègues d'observer les activités de chacun des suspects. Celui qui suit *(The one who is following)* Valérie Veutoux a rapporté ces photos prises le lendemain du crime. Vous lui demandez de vous raconter la journée de Valérie Veutoux mais ses notes sont en désordre. D'abord, remettez ses notes dans l'ordre; ensuite, racontez la journée de Valérie Veutoux en mettant les verbes au passé composé ou à l'imparfait.

EXEMPLE **Mme Veutoux est sortie de sa chambre à 8h20 du matin. Elle est descendue...**

- M. Jigaulaux *arrive* ici quelques heures après. Il *retrouve* Mme Veutoux dans la forêt à midi et ils *s'embrassent* passionnément.

- Comme M. Jigaulaux *est* fatigué, il *prend* une chambre à l'hôtel du village, où il *passe* l'après-midi.

- Mme Veutoux *sort* de sa chambre à 8h20 du matin. Elle *descend* au rez-de-chaussée et elle *téléphone* à M. Jigaulaux au Luxembourg. Ensuite, elle *téléphone* à une agence de voyages à Bruxelles.

- Ils *quittent* le restaurant à 20h50. À ce moment-là, un chien m'*attaque* dans les rosiers derrière lesquels je m'étais caché et je les *perds* de vue.

- À 17h00, M. Jigaulaux et Mme Veutoux *se retrouvent* devant l'hôtel, ils *montent* dans la voiture de M. Jigaulaux et *vont* dans le village voisin où ils *se marient* en secret à 18h20.

- Après la cérémonie, ils *dînent* au restaurant du village. À part le serveur, ils *sont* seuls dans le restaurant.

- Pendant le dîner, je les *observe* de l'extérieur. M. Jigaulaux ne *parle* pas beaucoup mais Mme Veutoux lui *explique* quelque chose.

R. Réactions. Valérie Veutoux est furieuse. Imaginez sa réaction quand vous lui dites les choses suivantes.

• Pour réviser le subjonctif, voir les pages 394–395, 396 et 400.

> Il est bon que…   C'est dommage que…
> Il est nécessaire que…   Il est ridicule que…
> Il est impossible que…   Il est essentiel que…

EXEMPLE   Vous ne pouvez pas partir pour quelques jours.
Il est ridicule que je ne puisse pas partir.

1. Oui, madame, vous êtes suspecte.
2. Nous ne savons pas où se trouve *(is located)* le corps de la victime.
3. M. Lavare dit que vous aviez des raisons d'assassiner M. Fédor.
4. Nous savons que vous avez retrouvé M. Jigaulaux dans la forêt.
5. Nous avons des photos de M. Jigaulaux avec vous.
6. Je veux lui parler demain.
7. Il pourra partir après l'interrogatoire.
8. Vous devez tout nous expliquer.

S. Deux billets pour Tahiti. Pendant l'enquête, vous apprenez que François Fédor enregistrait *(recorded)* toutes les conversations téléphoniques chez lui. Vous découvrez que Valérie Veutoux a téléphoné à une agence de voyages à Bruxelles le lendemain du crime. Écoutez la conversation entre Valérie Veutoux et l'agent de voyages. Sur une autre feuille de papier, complétez les détails qui manquent sur l'itinéraire de Valérie ci-dessous.

CD 4-27

• Pour réviser comment acheter un billet d'avion, voir la page 362.

ITINÉRAIRE

À l'intention de: *(Nom)* **et de** *(Nom)*

ALLER   **Air France—Vol** *(Numéro)*
(Date)
Départ de Bruxelles *(Heure)*   **Boeing 747**
                                      Première classe/Vol direct

(Date)
Arrivée à Tahiti *(Heure)*

                              Prix du billet: *(Prix)*
                              Total des deux billets: *(Prix)*

Prévoyez d'arriver à l'aéroport deux heures avant l'heure de départ.

BON VOYAGE!

On parle français à Tahiti.

• Pour réviser le futur, voir la page 352.

T. Une conversation téléphonique.
Voici une transcription de la conversation téléphonique entre Valérie Veutoux et son amant *(lover)*, Jean Jigaulaux, le lendemain du crime. La première partie a été effacée *(erased)* accidentellement. Complétez ce qui reste en mettant les verbes entre parenthèses au futur ou à l'impératif.

• Pour réviser l'impératif, voir les pages 154 et 408.

— ... Après cela, François ne ___1___ (faire) plus obstacle à notre bonheur *(happiness)*. Nous ___2___ (pouvoir) nous marier quand tu ___3___ (vouloir).

— Je ___4___ (venir) aujourd'hui et nous ___5___ (se marier) ce soir. Je vais partir tout de suite et j'___6___ (arriver) un peu avant midi.

— À deux kilomètres d'ici, il y a une vieille école abandonnée. ___7___ (Tourner) à gauche juste après cette école et ___8___ (entrer) dans la forêt. Là, personne ne nous ___9___ (voir). Je t'___10___ (attendre) à cet endroit à midi.

— On ___11___ (être) heureux ensemble.

— Après-demain, nous ___12___ (partir) pour Tahiti et nous ___13___ (commencer) notre nouvelle vie ensemble.

• Pour réviser les chiffres, voir les pages 10, 90 et 110.

U. Le compte en banque.
Quand vous comparez les relevés de compte *(bank statements)* de François Fédor, vous remarquez que quelqu'un avait retiré presque tout son argent ces derniers mois. Combien d'argent est-ce qu'il y avait aux dates suivantes de l'année dernière et de cette année?

• Pour réviser les dates, voir la page 160.

EXEMPLE   **30/9**   20 789 067 euros
Le 30 septembre de l'année dernière, il y avait 20 789 067 euros sur son compte.

1. 15/10   16 136 978 euros
2. 10/11   12 194 456 euros
3. 24/12   8 714 387 euros
4. 1/1 1   1 000 090 euros
5. 15/2   90 506 euros
6. 4/3   11 871 euros

• Pour réviser comment poser une question, voir les pages 42, 84 et 86.

V. Une vidéo révélatrice.
Vous venez de découvrir qu'une caméra de sécurité cachée dans le couloir filmait chaque personne qui entrait dans la chambre de François Fédor. Entre 20h et 8h du matin, la caméra a enregistré une seule personne qui est entrée dans la chambre de la victime. La caméra s'est arrêtée à 8h30 le lendemain matin. Préparez cinq questions que vous voudriez poser à Valérie Veutoux.

pourquoi	combien de temps	que
???	comment	quand
à quelle heure	??? qui	où

W. La dernière volonté de François. Vous avez interrogé Valérie Veutoux et elle a répondu que François Fédor n'était pas fâché *(upset)* qu'elle ait un amant, mais, qu'au contraire, il l'avait encouragée à l'épouser *(to marry him)*. Elle vous raconte ce que François Fédor lui a dit. Est-ce qu'il voulait qu'elle fasse les choses suivantes ou est-ce qu'il voulait les faire lui-même *(himself)*?

• Pour réviser l'usage de l'infinitif ou du subjonctif, voir la page 404.

> **EXEMPLES** se marier avec Jean Jigaulaux
> **Il voulait que je me marie avec Jean Jigaulaux.**
>
> nous offrir un cadeau de mariage
> **Il voulait nous offrir un cadeau de mariage.**

1. tout savoir sur Jean Jigaulaux
2. dire à Jean Jigaulaux de venir ici
3. se marier tout de suite
4. nous offrir un voyage de noces *(honeymoon trip)*
5. téléphoner pour réserver le billet pour Tahiti le lendemain
6. partir pour Tahiti cette semaine
7. être heureuse
8. venir dans sa chambre après le dîner pour prendre l'argent pour payer le voyage

CD 4-28

X. Que faisait le/la domestique? Reformulez les questions suivantes avec l'inversion et posez-les au/à la domestique. Ensuite, écoutez ses réponses.

• Pour réviser l'inversion, voir la page 86.

1. À quelle heure est-ce que vous vous êtes levé(e) le lendemain du crime?
2. Qu'est-ce que vous avez fait après?
3. Est-ce que les autres invités dormaient encore dans le château?
4. Quand est-ce que vous avez découvert *(discover)* que François Fédor était mort?
5. Est-ce que vous avez été surpris(e)?
6. Pourquoi est-ce que vous n'avez pas crié *(scream)*?
7. Est-ce que vous avez réveillé quelqu'un pour vous aider?
8. Vous avez téléphoné à la police à 8h12. À quelle heure est-ce que vous êtes entré(e) dans la chambre?
9. Combien de portes est-ce qu'il y a pour entrer dans la chambre de la victime?
10. Pourquoi est-ce que vous ne dites pas la vérité *(truth)*?
11. Ne faites pas l'innocent(e)! Comment est-ce que vous saviez que François Fédor était mort sans entrer dans sa chambre?
12. Pourquoi est-ce que vous n'êtes pas sur la vidéo de sécurité?
13. Pourquoi est-ce que la vidéo s'arrête à 8h30?
14. Alors, est-ce que vous voulez dire que François Fédor n'est pas mort?

• Pour réviser le passé composé et l'imparfait, voir les pages 238, 240 et 244.

Y. Une confession. Le/La domestique confesse que François Fédor n'est pas mort. En lisant sa confession, mettez les verbes entre parenthèses au passé composé ou à l'imparfait.

Je __1__ (ne pas vouloir) le faire mais c' __2__ (être) la seule manière! C' __3__ (être) la seule manière de sauver le château. M. Fédor m' __4__ (expliquer) que M. Lavare venait de l'informer *(had just told him)* qu'il avait tout perdu. Il avait tout investi dans une société qui avait fait faillite *(had gone bankrupt)*. Il __5__ (devoir) vendre le château pour payer les créanciers *(creditors)*. «Mais, non», je lui __6__ (dire). Il __7__ (savoir) que je (j') __8__ (adorer) ce château et que je ferais tout pour ne pas le perdre. Je __9__ (naître) pas loin d'ici. Quand je (j') __10__ (être) jeune, je (j') __11__ (rêver) d'habiter ici un jour et je (j') __12__ (inventer) des histoires fantastiques qui __13__ (avoir) lieu *(to take place)* ici. Mais toutes ces histoires-là __14__ (finir) toujours bien. Puis, M. Fédor __15__ (suggérer) qu'il y __16__ (avoir) peut-être un moyen de garder le château et que, si on __17__ (réussir), il me le donnerait. Le château serait à moi pour toujours. C'est alors qu'il me (m') __18__ (révéler) son plan. Il prendrait une assurance vie de 10 000 000 d'euros et j'en serais le/la bénéficiaire.

M. Fédor __19__ (ne jamais le dire), mais je (j') __20__ (avoir) l'impression que c' __21__ (être) M. Lavare qui avait inventé ce plan. Je sais que M. Lavare avait dit à M. Fédor que Mme Veutoux avait pris ce M. Jigaulaux comme amant. Cela __22__ (rendre) M. Fédor furieux. Chaque fois que M. Fédor __23__ (parler) de son ex-femme avec M. Lavare, l'un __24__ (devenir) tout rouge et l'autre tout pâle. La vérité, c'est que c' __25__ (être) elle qui avait quitté M. Fédor il y a 15 ans et pas le contraire, comme tout le monde le disait. Il __26__ (ne jamais lui pardonner) et il __27__ (toujours vouloir) contrôler sa vie. Il __28__ (ne pas être) obligé de lui donner cet argent depuis le divorce, mais M. Lavare l'avait persuadé de continuer à lui en donner beaucoup. Il __29__ (dire) à M. Fédor que si Mme Veutoux __30__ (dépendre) de lui financièrement, il pourrait contrôler sa vie. M. Fédor me (m') __31__ (dire) que M. Lavare inviterait M. Boncorps et Mme Veutoux à la maison. M. Fédor expliquerait à son neveu qu'il __32__ (ne plus pouvoir) lui donner d'argent. Mais il dirait à Mme Veutoux qu'il __33__ (vouloir) qu'elle soit heureuse et qu'il __34__ (avoir) l'intention de lui offrir un voyage à Tahiti pour sa lune de miel *(honeymoon)* si elle __35__ (se marier) tout de suite.

D'après le plan, tout le monde penserait que Mme Veutoux avait assassiné M. Fédor et qu'elle était partie pour Tahiti. On la verrait sur la vidéo entrer dans sa chambre la nuit du meurtre et on penserait qu'elle l'avait assassiné pour pouvoir se marier avec son jeune amant. Mais en réalité, on assassinerait Mme Veutoux et on laisserait son corps au fond de la forêt. M. Fédor s'habillerait comme elle et il partirait pour Tahiti à sa place. À l'aéroport de Bruxelles, on verrait Mme Veutoux partir pour Tahiti et personne ne saurait que c' __36__ (être) elle la vraie victime. On accuserait Mme Veutoux de s'être échappée *(of having escaped)* après le meurtre de M. Fédor et on ne la reverrait plus. M. Fédor me laisserait le château et après quelques mois, je mettrais les 10 000 000 d'euros d'assurance sur un compte secret pour M. Fédor.

À ce moment-là, pendant la confession, un policier __37__ (entrer) et il __38__ (annoncer) que des chasseurs (hunters) avaient trouvé le corps d'une femme morte dans la forêt et qu'ils avaient donné la description de Mme Veutoux.

Épilogue

CD 4-29

Vous pensez probablement avoir compris le mystère du meurtre de François Fédor. Vous pensez que le/la domestique va être **arrêté(e)** et que le vieux Midas est parti vivre sur une île tropicale. Mais êtes-vous certain(e) d'avoir trouvé les vrais criminels? Ah! Les voilà **en croisière** quelque part dans l'océan Pacifique. Écoutons un peu leur conversation.

— Quel coup! Tu es **un** vrai **génie,** mon chéri. Qui aurait pensé que nous pourrions réussir! Tout le monde pense que je suis morte et que François est l'assassin. Après toutes ces années, nous allons enfin pouvoir vivre ensemble **sans nous préoccuper de** ce vieux tyran. Je me souviens de la première fois que je t'ai vu quand tu as commencé à travailler pour lui! Quel coup de foudre! Et le pauvre François! Il n'avait aucune idée que je l'ai quitté parce que nous étions amants.

— Je trouve toujours **incroyable** qu'il ait investi toute sa fortune dans cette société qui n'existait pas. Il avait tellement confiance en moi! Ha ha ha!

— Mais pourquoi pas? Le vrai vieux Midas, c'était toi. Tu avais multiplié dix fois sa fortune. Sans toi, cet imbécile aurait perdu tout son argent longtemps avant! Mais maintenant, toute cette fortune est à nous! S'il avait su que tous ces **créanciers** que tu payais n'étaient personne d'autre que moi, son ex-femme! Ha ha ha! Qu'est-ce que tu as fait de son corps?

— Il était vraiment surpris quand, **au lieu de l'amener à** l'aéroport de Bruxelles, nous sommes allés au fond des Ardennes! Quand je lui ai expliqué que toi et moi, nous étions amants depuis le début, j'ai pensé pendant un moment que je n'aurais pas besoin de l'assassiner. Le pauvre, **il a failli avoir** une attaque! Et il était très comique, habillé comme toi.

— Quel dommage que nous n'ayons pas de photos! J'aurais aimé voir ça! Ha ha ha! Mais qu'est-ce qu'on dira si on trouve son corps?

— On pensera sans doute que c'est le/la domestique qui l'a assassiné pour ces 10 000 000 d'euros d'assurance!

— Mais il y a un dernier détail que je ne comprends pas. Comment est-ce que tu as persuadé ton jeune associé de jouer le rôle de Jean Jigaulaux? Il a si bien joué! Pendant un moment, j'ai vraiment eu l'impression que j'allais me marier avec lui.

— Ce jeune homme était tellement ambitieux qu'il aurait fait **n'importe quoi** pour avoir ma clientèle. Je lui ai promis de lui laisser tous mes clients, mais il ne savait pas que je n'en avais qu'un seul, et que c'était François Fédor.

— Ça, c'est trop! Tu es cruel... vicieux! C'est pour ça que je t'aime! Ha ha ha!

Naturellement Valérie Veutoux et Laurent Lavare ont dû changer de noms. Si on vous les présente aujourd'hui, vous ferez la connaissance d'Anabelle Atout et de son mari Richard!

---

arrêté(e) *arrested*   **en croisière** *on a cruise*   **un génie** *a genius*   **sans nous préoccuper de** *without worrying about*
incroyable *unbelievable*   **créanciers** *creditors*   **au lieu de l'amener à** *instead of taking him to*   **il a failli avoir** *he almost had*
n'importe quoi *anything*

L'alphabet phonétique

Voyelles

[a] madame   [i] qui   [œ] sœur

[e] thé   [o] eau   [u] vous

[ɛ] être   [ɔ] porte   [y] sur

[ə] que   [ø] peu

Semi-voyelles

[j] bien   [ɥ] puis   [w] oui

Voyelles nasales

[ɑ̃] quand   [ɛ̃] vin   [ɔ̃] non

Consonnes

[b] bleu   [l] lire   [s] sur

[d] dormir   [m] marron   [ʃ] chat

[f] faire   [n] nouveau   [t] triste

[g] gris   [ɲ] enseigner [v] vers

[ʒ] jaune   [p] parler   [z] rose

[k] quand   [ʀ] rester

Tableau des verbes

Verbes auxiliaires

VERBE INFINITIF	INDICATIF PRÉSENT	PASSÉ COMPOSÉ	IMPARFAIT	FUTUR	CONDITIONNEL PRÉSENT	SUBJONCTIF PRÉSENT	IMPÉRATIF
avoir	ai	ai eu	avais	aurai	aurais	aie	
to have	as	as eu	avais	auras	aurais	aies	aie
	a	a eu	avait	aura	aurait	ait	
	avons	avons eu	avions	aurons	aurions	ayons	ayons
	avez	avez eu	aviez	aurez	auriez	ayez	ayez
	ont	ont eu	avaient	auront	auraient	aient	
être	suis	ai été	étais	serai	serais	sois	
to be	es	as été	étais	seras	serais	sois	sois
	est	a été	était	sera	serait	soit	
	sommes	avons été	étions	serons	serions	soyons	soyons
	êtes	avez été	étiez	serez	seriez	soyez	soyez
	sont	ont été	étaient	seront	seraient	soient	

Verbes réguliers

VERBE INFINITIF	INDICATIF PRÉSENT	PASSÉ COMPOSÉ	IMPARFAIT	FUTUR	CONDITIONNEL PRÉSENT	SUBJONCTIF PRÉSENT	IMPÉRATIF
-er verbs							
parler	parle	ai parlé	parlais	parlerai	parlerais	parle	
to talk,	parles	as parlé	parlais	parleras	parlerais	parles	parle
to speak	parle	a parlé	parlait	parlera	parlerait	parle	
	parlons	avons parlé	parlions	parlerons	parlerions	parlions	parlons
	parlez	avez parlé	parliez	parlerez	parleriez	parliez	parlez
	parlent	ont parlé	parlaient	parleront	parleraient	parlent	
-ir verbs							
finir	finis	ai fini	finissais	finirai	finirais	finisse	
to finish	finis	as fini	finissais	finiras	finirais	finisses	finis
	finit	a fini	finissait	finira	finirait	finisse	
	finissons	avons fini	finissions	finirons	finirions	finissions	finissons
	finissez	avez fini	finissiez	finirez	finiriez	finissiez	finissez
	finissent	ont fini	finissaient	finiront	finiraient	finissent	
-re verbs							
vendre	vends	ai vendu	vendais	vendrai	vendrais	vende	
to sell	vends	as vendu	vendais	vendras	vendrais	vendes	vends
	vend	a vendu	vendait	vendra	vendrait	vende	
	vendons	avons vendu	vendions	vendrons	vendrions	vendions	vendons
	vendez	avez vendu	vendiez	vendrez	vendriez	vendiez	vendez
	vendent	ont vendu	vendaient	vendront	vendraient	vendent	

Verbes réfléchis

VERBE INFINITIF	PRÉSENT	PASSÉ COMPOSÉ	IMPARFAIT	FUTUR	CONDITIONNEL PRÉSENT	SUBJONCTIF PRÉSENT	IMPÉRATIF
		INDICATIF					
se laver	me lave	me suis lavé(e)	me lavais	me laverai	me laverais	me lave	
to wash	te laves	t'es lavé(e)	te lavais	te laveras	te laverais	te laves	lave-toi
oneself	se lave	s'est lavé(e)	se lavait	se lavera	se laverait	se lave	
	nous lavons	nous sommes lavé(e)s	nous lavions	nous laverons	nous laverions	nous lavions	lavons-nous
	vous lavez	vous êtes lavé(e)(s)	vous laviez	vous laverez	vous laveriez	vous laviez	lavez-vous
	se lavent	se sont lavé(e)s	se lavaient	se laveront	se laveraient	se lavent	

Verbes à changements orthographiques

VERBE INFINITIF	PRÉSENT	PASSÉ COMPOSÉ	IMPARFAIT	FUTUR	CONDITIONNEL PRÉSENT	SUBJONCTIF PRÉSENT	IMPÉRATIF
		INDICATIF					
préférer	préfère	ai préféré	préférais	préférerai	préférerais	préfère	
to prefer	préfères	as préféré	préférais	préféreras	préférerais	préfères	préfère
	préfère	a préféré	préférait	préférera	préférerait	préfère	
	préférons	avons préféré	préférions	préférerons	préférerions	préférions	préférons
	préférez	avez préféré	préfériez	préférerez	préféreriez	préfériez	préférez
	préfèrent	ont préféré	préféraient	préféreront	préféreraient	préfèrent	
acheter	achète	ai acheté	achetais	achèterai	achèterais	achète	
to buy	achètes	as acheté	achetais	achèteras	achèterais	achètes	achète
	achète	a acheté	achetait	achètera	achèterait	achète	
	achetons	avons acheté	achetions	achèterons	achèterions	achetions	achetons
	achetez	avez acheté	achetiez	achèterez	achèteriez	achetiez	achetez
	achètent	ont acheté	achetaient	achèteront	achèteraient	achètent	
appeler	appelle	ai appelé	appelais	appellerai	appellerais	appelle	
to call	appelles	as appelé	appelais	appelleras	appellerais	appelles	appelle
	appelle	a appelé	appelait	appellera	appellerait	appelle	
	appelons	avons appelé	appelions	appellerons	appellerions	appelions	appelons
	appelez	avez appelé	appeliez	appellerez	appelleriez	appeliez	appelez
	appellent	ont appelé	appelaient	appelleront	appelleraient	appellent	
essayer	essaie	ai essayé	essayais	essaierai	essaierais	essaie	
to try	essaies	as essayé	essayais	essaieras	essaierais	essaies	essaie
	essaie	a essayé	essayait	essaiera	essaierait	essaie	
	essayons	avons essayé	essayions	essaierons	essaierions	essayions	essayons
	essayez	avez essayé	essayiez	essaierez	essaieriez	essayiez	essayez
	essaient	ont essayé	essayaient	essaieront	essaieraient	essaient	
manger	mange	ai mangé	mangeais	mangerai	mangerais	mange	
to eat	manges	as mangé	mangeais	mangeras	mangerais	manges	mange
	mange	a mangé	mangeait	mangera	mangerait	mange	
	mangeons	avons mangé	mangions	mangerons	mangerions	mangions	mangeons
	mangez	avez mangé	mangiez	mangerez	mangeriez	mangiez	mangez
	mangent	ont mangé	mangeaient	mangeront	mangeraient	mangent	
commencer	commence	ai commencé	commençais	commencerai	commencerais	commence	
to begin	commences	as commencé	commençais	commenceras	commencerais	commences	commence
	commence	a commencé	commençait	commencera	commencerait	commence	
	commençons	avons commencé	commencions	commencerons	commencerions	commencions	commençons
	commencez	avez commencé	commenciez	commencerez	commenceriez	commenciez	commencez
	commencent	ont commencé	commençaient	commenceront	commenceraient	commencent	

Verbes irréguliers

VERBE INFINITIF	PRÉSENT	INDICATIF — PASSÉ COMPOSÉ	IMPARFAIT	FUTUR	CONDITIONNEL PRÉSENT	SUBJONCTIF PRÉSENT	IMPÉRATIF
aller	vais	suis allé(e)	allais	irai	irais	aille	
to go	vas	es allé(e)	allais	iras	irais	ailles	va
	va	est allé(e)	allait	ira	irait	aille	
	allons	sommes allé(e)s	allions	irons	irions	allions	allons
	allez	êtes allé(e)(s)	alliez	irez	iriez	alliez	allez
	vont	sont allé(e)s	allaient	iront	iraient	aillent	
s'asseoir	m'assieds	me suis assis(e)	m'asseyais	m'assiérai	m'assiérais	m'asseye	
to sit	t'assieds	t'es assis(e)	t'asseyais	t'assiéras	t'assiérais	t'asseyes	assieds-toi
(down)	s'assied	s'est assis(e)	s'asseyait	s'assiéra	s'assiérait	s'asseye	
	nous asseyons	nous sommes assis(es)	nous asseyions	nous assiérons	nous assiérions	nous asseyions	asseyons-nous
	vous asseyez	vous êtes assis(es)	vous asseyiez	vous assiérez	vous assiériez	vous asseyiez	asseyez-vous
	s'asseyent	se sont assis(es)	s'asseyaient	s'assiéront	s'assiéraient	s'asseyent	
battre	bats	ai battu	battais	battrai	battrais	batte	
to beat	bats	as battu	battais	battras	battrais	battes	bats
	bat	a battu	battait	battra	battrait	batte	
	battons	avons battu	battions	battrons	battrions	battions	battons
	battez	avez battu	battiez	battrez	battriez	battiez	battez
	battent	ont battu	battaient	battront	battraient	battent	
boire	bois	ai bu	buvais	boirai	boirais	boive	
to drink	bois	as bu	buvais	boiras	boirais	boives	bois
	boit	a bu	buvait	boira	boirait	boive	
	buvons	avons bu	buvions	boirons	boirions	buvions	buvons
	buvez	avez bu	buviez	boirez	boiriez	buviez	buvez
	boivent	ont bu	buvaient	boiront	boiraient	boivent	
conduire	conduis	ai conduit	conduisais	conduirai	conduirais	conduise	
to drive	conduis	as conduit	conduisais	conduiras	conduirais	conduises	conduis
	conduit	a conduit	conduisait	conduira	conduirait	conduise	
	conduisons	avons conduit	conduisions	conduirons	conduirions	conduisions	conduisons
	conduisez	avez conduit	conduisiez	conduirez	conduiriez	conduisiez	conduisez
	conduisent	ont conduit	conduisaient	conduiront	conduiraient	conduisent	
connaître	connais	ai connu	connaissais	connaîtrai	connaîtrais	connaisse	
to be	connais	as connu	connaissais	connaîtras	connaîtrais	connaisses	connais
acquainted	connaît	a connu	connaissait	connaîtra	connaîtrait	connaisse	
with,	connaissons	avons connu	connaissions	connaîtrons	connaîtrions	connaissions	connaissons
to know	connaissez	avez connu	connaissiez	connaîtrez	connaîtriez	connaissiez	connaissez
	connaissent	ont connu	connaissaient	connaîtront	connaîtraient	connaissent	
courir	cours	ai couru	courais	courrai	courrais	coure	
to run	cours	as couru	courais	courras	courrais	coures	cours
	court	a couru	courait	courra	courrait	coure	
	courons	avons couru	courions	courrons	courrions	courions	courons
	courez	avez couru	couriez	courrez	courriez	couriez	courez
	courent	ont couru	couraient	courront	courraient	courent	
croire	crois	ai cru	croyais	croirai	croirais	croie	
to believe	crois	as cru	croyais	croiras	croirais	croies	crois
	croit	a cru	croyait	croira	croirait	croie	
	croyons	avons cru	croyions	croirons	croirions	croyions	croyons
	croyez	avez cru	croyiez	croirez	croiriez	croyiez	croyez
	croient	ont cru	croyaient	croiront	croiraient	croient	

Verbes irréguliers (suite)

VERBE INFINITIF	PRÉSENT	PASSÉ COMPOSÉ	IMPARFAIT	FUTUR	CONDITIONNEL PRÉSENT	SUBJONCTIF PRÉSENT	IMPÉRATIF
devoir	dois	ai dû	devais	devrai	devrais	doive	
must,	dois	as dû	devais	devras	devrais	doives	
to have to,	doit	a dû	devait	devra	devrait	doive	
to owe	devons	avons dû	devions	devrons	devrions	devions	
	devez	avez dû	deviez	devrez	devriez	deviez	
	doivent	ont dû	devaient	devront	devraient	doivent	
dire	dis	ai dit	disais	dirai	dirais	dise	
to say,	dis	as dit	disais	diras	dirais	dises	dis
to tell	dit	a dit	disait	dira	dirait	dise	
	disons	avons dit	disions	dirons	dirions	disions	disons
	dites	avez dit	disiez	direz	diriez	disiez	dites
	disent	ont dit	disaient	diront	diraient	disent	
dormir	dors	ai dormi	dormais	dormirai	dormirais	dorme	
to sleep	dors	as dormi	dormais	dormiras	dormirais	dormes	dors
	dort	a dormi	dormait	dormira	dormirait	dorme	
	dormons	avons dormi	dormions	dormirons	dormirions	dormions	dormons
	dormez	avez dormi	dormiez	dormirez	dormiriez	dormiez	dormez
	dorment	ont dormi	dormaient	dormiront	dormiraient	dorment	
écrire	écris	ai écrit	écrivais	écrirai	écrirais	écrive	
to write	écris	as écrit	écrivais	écriras	écrirais	écrives	écris
	écrit	a écrit	écrivait	écrira	écrirait	écrive	
	écrivons	avons écrit	écrivions	écrirons	écririons	écrivions	écrivons
	écrivez	avez écrit	écriviez	écrirez	écririez	écriviez	écrivez
	écrivent	ont écrit	écrivaient	écriront	écriraient	écrivent	
envoyer	envoie	ai envoyé	envoyais	enverrai	enverrais	envoie	
to send	envoies	as envoyé	envoyais	enverras	enverrais	envoies	envoie
	envoie	a envoyé	envoyait	enverra	enverrait	envoie	
	envoyons	avons envoyé	envoyions	enverrons	enverrions	envoyions	envoyons
	envoyez	avez envoyé	envoyiez	enverrez	enverriez	envoyiez	envoyez
	envoient	ont envoyé	envoyaient	enverront	enverraient	envoient	
faire	fais	ai fait	faisais	ferai	ferais	fasse	
to do,	fais	as fait	faisais	feras	ferais	fasses	fais
to make	fait	a fait	faisait	fera	ferait	fasse	
	faisons	avons fait	faisions	ferons	ferions	fassions	faisons
	faites	avez fait	faisiez	ferez	feriez	fassiez	faites
	font	ont fait	faisaient	feront	feraient	fassent	
falloir	faut	a fallu	fallait	faudra	faudrait	faille	
to be necessary							
lire	lis	ai lu	lisais	lirai	lirais	lise	
to read	lis	as lu	lisais	liras	lirais	lises	lis
	lit	a lu	lisait	lira	lirait	lise	
	lisons	avons lu	lisions	lirons	lirions	lisions	lisons
	lisez	avez lu	lisiez	lirez	liriez	lisiez	lisez
	lisent	ont lu	lisaient	liront	liraient	lisent	
mettre	mets	ai mis	mettais	mettrai	mettrais	mette	
to put (on),	mets	as mis	mettais	mettras	mettrais	mettes	mets
to place,	met	a mis	mettait	mettra	mettrait	mette	
to set	mettons	avons mis	mettions	mettrons	mettrions	mettions	mettons
	mettez	avez mis	mettiez	mettrez	mettriez	mettiez	mettez
	mettent	ont mis	mettaient	mettront	mettraient	mettent	

Verbes irréguliers (suite)

VERBE INFINITIF	INDICATIF PRÉSENT	PASSÉ COMPOSÉ	IMPARFAIT	FUTUR	CONDITIONNEL PRÉSENT	SUBJONCTIF PRÉSENT	IMPÉRATIF
obtenir *to obtain*	obtiens	ai obtenu	obtenais	obtiendrai	obtiendrais	obtienne	
	obtiens	as obtenu	obtenais	obtiendras	obtiendrais	obtiennes	obtiens
	obtient	a obtenu	obtenait	obtiendra	obtiendrait	obtienne	
	obtenons	avons obtenu	obtenions	obtiendrons	obtiendrions	obtenions	obtenons
	obtenez	avez obtenu	obteniez	obtiendrez	obtiendriez	obteniez	obtenez
	obtiennent	ont obtenu	obtenaient	obtiendront	obtiendraient	obtiennent	
ouvrir *to open*	ouvre	ai ouvert	ouvrais	ouvrirai	ouvrirais	ouvre	
	ouvres	as ouvert	ouvrais	ouvriras	ouvrirais	ouvres	ouvre
	ouvre	a ouvert	ouvrait	ouvrira	ouvrirait	ouvre	
	ouvrons	avons ouvert	ouvrions	ouvrirons	ouvririons	ouvrions	ouvrons
	ouvrez	avez ouvert	ouvriez	ouvrirez	ouvririez	ouvriez	ouvrez
	ouvrent	ont ouvert	ouvraient	ouvriront	ouvriraient	ouvrent	
partir *to leave*	pars	suis parti(e)	partais	partirai	partirais	parte	
	pars	es parti(e)	partais	partiras	partirais	partes	pars
	part	est parti(e)	partait	partira	partirait	parte	
	partons	sommes parti(e)s	partions	partirons	partirions	partions	partons
	partez	êtes parti(e)(s)	partiez	partirez	partiriez	partiez	partez
	partent	sont parti(e)s	partaient	partiront	partiraient	partent	
pleuvoir *to rain*	pleut	a plu	pleuvait	pleuvra	pleuvrait	pleuve	
pouvoir *to be able, can*	peux	ai pu	pouvais	pourrai	pourrais	puisse	
	peux	as pu	pouvais	pourras	pourrais	puisses	
	peut	a pu	pouvait	pourra	pourrait	puisse	
	pouvons	avons pu	pouvions	pourrons	pourrions	puissions	
	pouvez	avez pu	pouviez	pourrez	pourriez	puissiez	
	peuvent	ont pu	pouvaient	pourront	pourraient	puissent	
prendre *to take*	prends	ai pris	prenais	prendrai	prendrais	prenne	
	prends	as pris	prenais	prendras	prendrais	prennes	prends
	prend	a pris	prenait	prendra	prendrait	prenne	
	prenons	avons pris	prenions	prendrons	prendrions	prenions	prenons
	prenez	avez pris	preniez	prendrez	prendriez	preniez	prenez
	prennent	ont pris	prenaient	prendront	prendraient	prennent	
recevoir *to receive*	reçois	ai reçu	recevais	recevrai	recevrais	reçoive	
	reçois	as reçu	recevais	recevras	recevrais	reçoives	reçois
	reçoit	a reçu	recevait	recevra	recevrait	reçoive	
	recevons	avons reçu	recevions	recevrons	recevrions	recevions	recevons
	recevez	avez reçu	receviez	recevrez	recevriez	receviez	recevez
	reçoivent	ont reçu	recevaient	recevront	recevraient	reçoivent	
rire *to laugh*	ris	ai ri	riais	rirai	rirais	rie	
	ris	as ri	riais	riras	rirais	ries	ris
	rit	a ri	riait	rira	rirait	rie	
	rions	avons ri	riions	rirons	ririons	riions	rions
	riez	avez ri	riiez	rirez	ririez	riiez	riez
	rient	ont ri	riaient	riront	riraient	rient	
savoir *to know*	sais	ai su	savais	saurai	saurais	sache	
	sais	as su	savais	sauras	saurais	saches	sache
	sait	a su	savait	saura	saurait	sache	
	savons	avons su	savions	saurons	saurions	sachions	sachons
	savez	avez su	saviez	saurez	sauriez	sachiez	sachez
	savent	ont su	savaient	sauront	sauraient	sachent	

Verbes irréguliers (suite)

VERBE INFINITIF	PRÉSENT	INDICATIF PASSÉ COMPOSÉ	IMPARFAIT	FUTUR	CONDITIONNEL PRÉSENT	SUBJONCTIF PRÉSENT	IMPÉRATIF
sortir	sors	suis sorti(e)	sortais	sortirai	sortirais	sorte	
to go out	sors	es sorti(e)	sortais	sortiras	sortirais	sortes	sors
	sort	est sorti(e)	sortait	sortira	sortirait	sorte	
	sortons	sommes sorti(e)s	sortions	sortirons	sortirions	sortions	sortons
	sortez	êtes sorti(e)(s)	sortiez	sortirez	sortiriez	sortiez	sortez
	sortent	sont sorti(e)s	sortaient	sortiront	sortiraient	sortent	
suivre	suis	ai suivi	suivais	suivrai	suivrais	suive	
to follow	suis	as suivi	suivais	suivras	suivrais	suives	suis
	suit	a suivi	suivait	suivra	suivrait	suive	
	suivons	avons suivi	suivions	suivrons	suivrions	suivions	suivons
	suivez	avez suivi	suiviez	suivrez	suivriez	suiviez	suivez
	suivent	ont suivi	suivaient	suivront	suivraient	suivent	
venir	viens	suis venu(e)	venais	viendrai	viendrais	vienne	
to come	viens	es venu(e)	venais	viendras	viendrais	viennes	viens
	vient	est venu(e)	venait	viendra	viendrait	vienne	
	venons	sommes venu(e)s	venions	viendrons	viendrions	venions	venons
	venez	êtes venu(e)(s)	veniez	viendrez	viendriez	veniez	venez
	viennent	sont venu(e)s	venaient	viendront	viendraient	viennent	
vivre	vis	ai vécu	vivais	vivrai	vivrais	vive	
to live	vis	as vécu	vivais	vivras	vivrais	vives	vis
	vit	a vécu	vivait	vivra	vivrait	vive	
	vivons	avons vécu	vivions	vivrons	vivrions	vivions	vivons
	vivez	avez vécu	viviez	vivrez	vivriez	viviez	vivez
	vivent	ont vécu	vivaient	vivront	vivraient	vivent	
voir	vois	ai vu	voyais	verrai	verrais	voie	
to see	vois	as vu	voyais	verras	verrais	voies	vois
	voit	a vu	voyait	verra	verrait	voie	
	voyons	avons vu	voyions	verrons	verrions	voyions	voyons
	voyez	avez vu	voyiez	verrez	verriez	voyiez	voyez
	voient	ont vu	voyaient	verront	verraient	voient	
vouloir	veux	ai voulu	voulais	voudrai	voudrais	veuille	
to want,	veux	as voulu	voulais	voudras	voudrais	veuilles	veuille
to wish	veut	a voulu	voulait	voudra	voudrait	veuille	
	voulons	avons voulu	voulions	voudrons	voudrions	voulions	veuillons
	voulez	avez voulu	vouliez	voudrez	voudriez	vouliez	veuillez
	veulent	ont voulu	voulaient	voudront	voudraient	veuillent	

This list contains words appearing in **Horizons,** except for absolute cognates. The definitions of active vocabulary words are followed by the number of the chapter where they are first presented. A (P) refers to the **Chapitre préliminaire.** When several translations, separated by commas, are listed before a chapter number, they are all considered active. Since verbs are sometimes introduced lexically in the infinitive before the conjugation of the present indicative is presented, consult the **Index** to find out the chapter where a conjugation is introduced. An (m), (f), or (pl) following a noun indicates that it is masculine, feminine, or plural. *Inv* means that a word is invariable. An asterisk before a word beginning with an **h** indicates that the **h** is aspirate.

A

à to, at, in (P); **À bientôt.** See you soon. (P); **à cause de** due to, because of; **À ce soir.** See you tonight/this evening. (2); **à côté (de)** next to (3); **À demain.** See you tomorrow. (P); **à la campagne** in the country (3); **à la française** French-style; **à la maison** at home (P); **à la page...** on page . . . (P); **à l'avance** in advance (9); **à l'étranger** abroad (9); **à l'heure** on time (4); **à peu près** about; **à pied** on foot (4); **À quelle heure?** At what time? (P); **à suivre** to be continued (6); **À tout à l'heure.** See you in a little while. (P); **au café** at the café (2); **au centre-ville** downtown (3); **au coin (de)** on the corner (of) (10); **au cours de** in the course of, during, while on (10); **au-dessus de** above; **au premier étage** on the second floor (3); **Au revoir.** Good-bye. (P); **à votre avis** in your opinion (8); **café au lait** coffee with milk (2); **j'habite à** *(+ city)* I live in *(+ city)* (P)
abandonner to abandon, to leave
abattre to strike down
abbaye *(f)* abbey
abolir to abolish
abonnement *(m)* subscription
abonner: s'abonner à to subscribe to
abord: d'abord first (2)
abrégé(e) abbreviated
abricot *(m)* apricot
abriter to shelter
absolu(e) absolute
absolument absolutely
académique academic
Acadie *(f)* Acadia
accent *(m)* accent (P); **sans accent** without an accent (P)
acceptation *(f)* acceptance
accepter (que) to accept (7)
accès *(m)* access
accessoire *(m)* accessory
accidentellement accidentally
accompagner to accompany
accomplir to accomplish
accord *(m)* agreement; **D'accord!** Okay! Agreed! (2); **se mettre d'accord** to come to an agreement
accordéon *(m)* accordion
accorder: s'accorder to grant each other
accrocher to hang
accueil *(m)* welcome, reception
accueillant(e) welcoming
achat *(m)* purchase
acheter to buy (4)

acier *(m)* steel
acteur *(m)* actor (6)
actif (active) active, working
Action *(f)* **de Grâce: jour** *(m)* **d'Action de Grâce** Thanksgiving Day
activité *(f)* activity (2)
actrice *(f)* actress (6)
actuellement currently
adapter: s'adapter to adapt
addition *(f)* check, bill
adepte *(mf)* one who believes in
adhésion *(f)* joining
adjectif *(m)* adjective (1)
adjoint(e) assistant
admettre to admit
administratif(-ive): centre administratif *(m)* administration building
admirer to admire (9)
adopter to adopt
adorer to love, to adore (9)
adresse *(f)* address (3); **adresse** *(f)* **mail** e-mail address (3)
adresser to address; **s'adresser à** to go and see, to speak to
aérien(ne) aerial
aérobic *(f)* aerobics (8)
aéronautique aeronautical, space
aéroport *(m)* airport (10)
affaire *(f)* thing, belonging, business; **avoir affaire à** to deal with; **femme d'affaires** businesswoman (5); **homme d'affaires** businessman (5)
affichage: affichage public *(m)* signage
affiche *(f)* poster (3)
affiché(e) posted
affinité *(f)* affinity
africain(e) African
Afrique *(f)* Africa (9); **Afrique du Sud** *(f)* South Africa
âge *(m)* age; **Quel âge a... ?** How old is . . . ? (4)
âgé(e) old (4)
agence *(f)* **de voyages** travel agency (9)
agent *(m)* agent; **agent** *(m)* **de police** policeman; **agent** *(m)* **de voyages** travel agent (9)
aggraver to worsen
agir to act, to take action
agité(e) agitated
agneau *(m)* lamb
agréable pleasant (1)
agricole agricultural
aider to help (5)
aïe ouch
aigle *(m)* eagle
aigu(ë) acute, shrill

aiguille *(f)* needle; **travaux** *(mpl)* **d'aiguille** needlework
ail *(m)* garlic
aile *(f)* wing
ailleurs elsewhere; **par ailleurs** furthermore
aimable kind, amiable
aimer to like (2), to love (7); **Aimeriez-vous... ?** Would you like. . . ? (8); **aimer mieux** to like better, to prefer (2); **Est-ce que tu aimes / vous aimez... ?** Do you like. . . ? (1); **J'aime...** I like . . . (1); **J'aimerais...** I would like . . . ; **J'aimerais autant...** I would just as soon... (10); **s'aimer** to love each other (7)
aîné(e) oldest *(child)*
ainsi thus; **ainsi que** as well as
air *(m)* air, look, appearance; **avoir l'air** (+ *adjective*) to look / to seem (+ *adjective*) (4); **de plein air** outdoor (4)
aise *(f)* ease; **mal à l'aise** ill at ease
aisé(e): classe aisée *(f)* upper class
ajouter to add
alcool *(m)* alcohol (8)
alcoolisé(e) alcoholic
Algérie *(f)* Algeria (9)
algérien(ne) Algerian
aliment *(m)* food
alimentaire food
Allemagne *(f)* Germany (9)
allemand *(m)* German (1)
allemand(e) German
aller (à) to go (to) (2); **aller à la chasse** to go hunting; **aller à la pêche** to go fishing; **aller à pied** to walk, to go on foot (4); **aller très bien à quelqu'un** to look very good on someone; **aller voir** to go see, to visit *(a person)* (4); **aller-retour** *(m)* round-trip ticket (9); **Allez au tableau.** Go to the board. (P); **billet aller simple** *(m)* one-way ticket (9); **Ça va.** It's going fine. (P); **Comment allez-vous?** How are you? (P); **Comment ça va?** How's it going? (P); **Comment vas-tu?** How are you? *(informal)*; **je vais** I go, I am going (1); **On va... ?** Shall we go . . . ? (2); **Qu'est-ce qui ne va pas?** What's wrong? (10); **s'en aller** to go away; **tu vas/vous allez** you go, you are going (2)
allergie *(f)* allergy (10)
allié(e) allied
allô hello *(on the telephone)* (6)
allumer to light
allumette *(f)* match
alors so, then, therefore (1)
alpinisme *(m)* mountain climbing; **faire de l'alpinisme** to go mountain climbing
amande *(f)* almond

amant(e) *(mf)* lover
ambassade *(f)* embassy
ambassadeur(-drice) *(mf)* ambassador
ambitieux(-ieuse) ambitious
améliorer to improve (8)
aménagé(e) fitted out
amener to take, to bring
américain(e) American (P); **à l'américaine** American style (8)
amérindien(ne) Native American
Amérique *(f)* America (9); **Amérique centrale** *(f)* Central America (9); **Amérique** *(f)* **du Nord** North America (9); **Amérique** *(f)* **du Sud** South America (9)
ami(e) *(mf)* friend (P); **petit ami** *(m)* boyfriend (2); **petite amie** *(f)* girlfriend (2)
amitié *(f)* friendship
amour *(m)* love (6); **film** *(m)* **d'amour** romantic movie (6); **le grand amour** *(m)* true love (7)
amoureux(-euse) in love (6); **tomber amoureux(-euse) de** to fall in love with (6); **vie amoureuse** *(f)* love life
amovible detachable
amphithéâtre *(m)* lecture hall (1)
amusant(e) fun (1)
amuser to amuse; **s'amuser** to have fun (7)
an *(m)* year (5); **avoir... ans** to be . . . years old (4); **jour** *(m)* **de l'an** *(m)* New Year's Day
ananas *(m)* pineapple
ancêtre *(mf)* ancestor
anchois *(m)* anchovy
ancien(ne) former, old, ancient
anciennement formerly
andouille *(f)* sausage of chitterlings
âne *(m)* donkey
ange *(m)* angel
angine *(f)* tonsillitis
anglais *(m)* English (P)
anglais(e) English
Angleterre *(f)* England; **Nouvelle-Angleterre** *(f)* New England
anglophone English-speaking
angoisse *(f)* anguish
angoisser to agonize, to worry; **angoissé(e)** anguished
animal *(m)* *(pl* **animaux)** animal (3)
animé(e) animated; **dessin animé** *(m)* cartoon
année *(f)* year (4); **les années** *(fpl)* **trente** the thirties
anniversaire *(m)* birthday (4); **anniversaire** *(m)* **de mariage** wedding anniversary
annonce *(f)* advertisement, announcement
annuaire *(m)* telephone book
annuel(le) annual
annuler to annul, to cancel; **annulé(e)** canceled
anorak *(m)* ski jacket, anorak (5)
Antarctique *(m)* Antarctica
anticiper to anticipate
antillais(e) West Indian
Antilles *(fpl)* West Indies (9)
anxiété *(f)* anxiety
août *(m)* August (4)
apercevoir to see, to notice
apéritif *(m)* before-dinner drink (8)
apparaître to appear
appareil *(m)* apparatus, appliance
apparencé *(f)* appearance
apparenté(e) related
appartement *(m)* apartment (3)
appartenir (à) to belong (to)
appeler to call; **Comment s'appelle... ?** What is . . .'s name? (4); **Comment t'appelles-tu?** What's your name? *(informal);* **Comment vous appelez-vous?** What's your name?

(formal) (P); **Il/Elle s'appelle...** His/Her name is . . . (4); **Je m'appelle...** My name is . . . (P); **s'appeler** to be named, to be called (7); **Tu t'appelles comment?** What's your name? *(informal)* (P)
appétit *(m)* appetite
applaudir to applaud
appoint *(m)* exact amount needed
apporter to bring
apprécier to appreciate (6)
apprendre to learn (4); **Apprenez...** Learn. . . (P)
approcher: s'approcher (de) to approach
approprié(e) appropriate
approuver to approve
approximatif(-ive) approximate
après after, afterward (P); **d'après** according to
après-demain the day after tomorrow
après-midi *(m)* afternoon (P); **cet après-midi** this afternoon (4); **Il est une heure de l'après-midi.** It's one o'clock in the afternoon. (P); **l'après-midi** in the afternoon, afternoons (P)
arabe *(m)* Arabic
arachide *(f)* groundnut, peanut
arbre *(m)* tree (1)
arc *(m)* arch, bow; **tir** *(m)* **à l'arc** archery
archange *(m)* archangel
archéologique archeological
archipel *(m)* archipelago
ardent(e) ardent, fervent
argent *(m)* money, silver (2)
Argentine *(f)* Argentina (9)
aristocratie *(f)* aristocracy
armée *(f)* army
arrêt *(m)* stop; **arrêt** *(m)* **d'autobus** bus stop (3)
arrêter to stop; **s'arrêter** to stop (7)
arrivée *(f)* arrival (9); **porte** *(f)* **d'arrivée** arrival gate (9)
arriver to arrive (3), to happen
arrondi(e) rounded
arrondissement *(m)* district
art *(m)* art; **les beaux-arts** the fine arts (1)
article *(m)* article (9)
artificiel(le) artificial
artisanat *(m)* crafts
artiste *(mf)* artist, performer
ascenseur *(m)* elevator (3)
Asie *(f)* Asia (9)
aspect physique *(m)* physical appearance (7)
asperge *(f)* asparagus
aspirant(e) *(mf)* candidate
aspirine *(f)* aspirin (10)
assassin *(m)* murderer, assassin
assassiner to murder, to assassinate
assaut *(m)* assault, attack
assemblage *(m)* assembly, gathering
assemblée *(f)* assembly
asseoir: Asseyez-vous. Sit down.; **s'asseoir** to sit (down)
assez fairly, rather (P); **assez (de)** enough (1)
assiette *(f)* plate
assis(e) seated (9)
assister à to attend
associatif(-ive) in the community
associer to associate; **associé(e)** associated
Assomption *(f)* the Assumption
assurance *(f)* insurance
assuré(e) provided, assured
astronomie *(f)* astronomy
astucieux(-euse) astute
atelier *(m)* workshop
Atlantique *(m)* Atlantic
attaché(e) attached
attaque *(f)* attack; **attaque** *(f)* **d'apoplexie** stroke

attendre to wait (for) (7); **s'attendre à** to expect to
attente *(f)* waiting
attention: faire attention (à) to pay attention (to), to watch out (for) (8)
attirant(e) attractive
attirer to attract
attraper to catch
attribuer assign, allocate
aube *(f)* dawn
auberge *(f)* inn; **auberge** *(f)* **de jeunesse** youth hostel (10)
aubergine *(f)* eggplant
auburn *(inv)* auburn (4)
aucun(e): ne... aucun(e) no, none, not one
audace *(f)* boldness
audacieux(-euse) audacious, bold
au-delà beyond
au-dessus above
auditif(-ive) auditory
aujourd'hui today (P)
aumenter to augment, to raise
auparavant beforehand
auquel (à laquelle, auxquels, auxquelles) to which
aussi too, also (P); **aussi... que** as . . . as (1)
aussitôt que as soon as
austral(e) southern
Australie *(f)* Australia (9)
autant (de)... (que) as much . . . (as), as many . . . (as); **J'aimerais autant...** I would just as soon... (10)
authenticité *(f)* authenticity
autobus *(m)* bus (4); **arrêt** *(m)* **d'autobus** bus stop (3); **en autobus** by bus (4)
autocar *(m)* bus (4); **en autocar** by bus (4)
automatique automatic
automne *(m)* autumn, fall (5); **en automne** in autumn (5)
autonomie *(f)* autonomy
autoportrait *(m)* self-portrait (P)
autorisé(e) authorized
autoritaire authoritarian
autour de around
autre other (P); **dans un autre cours** in another class (P); **quelquefois... d'autres fois** sometimes . . . other times (7); **Qu'est-ce que je peux vous proposer d'autre?** What else can I get you? (8)
autrefois formerly, in the past
Autriche *(f)* Austria
auxiliaire *(m)* auxiliary
avaler to swallow, to gulp
avance *(f)* advance; **à l'avance** in advance (9); **en avance** early
avancer to advance
avant before (P); **avant de partir** before leaving; **avant tout** above all
avantage *(m)* advantage
avec with (P); **Avec plaisir!** With pleasure! (6)
avenir *(m)* future
aventure *(f)* adventure; **film** *(m)* **d'aventures** adventure movie
avenue *(f)* avenue (10)
avion *(m)* airplane (4); **billet d'avion électronique** e-ticket (9); **en avion** by airplane (4)
avis *(m)* opinion; **à votre avis** in your opinion (8)
avocat(e) *(mf)* lawyer
avoir to have (3); **avoir... ans** to be . . . years old (4); **avoir besoin de** to need (4); **avoir chaud** to be hot (4); **avoir cours** to have class (6); **avoir de la fièvre** to have fever; **avoir du mal à...** to have difficulty . . . , to have a hard time. . . ; **avoir envie de** to feel like, to desire (4); **avoir faim** to be hungry (4); **j'ai faim** I'm

hungry (2); **avoir froid** to be cold (4); **avoir *honte** to be ashamed; **avoir l'air** (+ *adjective*) to look / to seem (+ *adjective*) (4); **avoir le nez bouché** to have a stopped-up nose; **avoir le nez qui coule** to have a runny nose; **avoir les cheveux/les yeux...** to have . . . hair/eyes (4); **avoir lieu** to take place; **avoir l'intention de** to plan on, to intend to (4); **avoir mal (à)** one's . . . hurts, to ache (10); **avoir peur (de)** to be afraid (of), to fear (4); **avoir pitié (de)** to have pity (on / for) (10); **avoir raison** to be right (4); **avoir soif** to be thirsty (4); **j'ai soif** I'm thirsty (2); **avoir sommeil** to be sleepy (4); **avoir tort** to be wrong (4); **il y a** there is, there are (1), ago (5); **Quel âge a... ?** How old is . . . ? (4)

avouer to admit
avril *(m)* April (4)
ayant having

B

baby-sitter *(mf)* babysitter
baccalauréat (bac) *(m) a comprehensive examination at the end of secondary school*
bachelier(-ière) *(mf) someone having passed the baccalauréat*
bacon *(m)* bacon (8)
bagages *(mpl)* baggage (9)
bagne *(m)* penal colony
bague *(f)* ring
baguette *(f)* loaf of French bread (8)
baie *(f)* bay
baigner: se baigner to bathe, to go swimming
bain *(m)* bath (7); **bain** *(m)* **de soleil** sunbath (4); **maillot** *(m)* **de bain** swimsuit (5); **salle** *(f)* **de bains** bathroom (3)
baiser *(m)* kiss
baisser to lower
bal *(m)* dance (6)
bambou *(m)* bamboo
banane *(f)* banana (8)
bancaire: carte *(f)* **bancaire** bank card (9)
banlieue *(f)* suburbs (3)
banque *(f)* bank (10)
banquette *(f)* bench, seat
banquier *(m)* banker
barbe *(f)* beard (4)
barrer to cross out
barricadé(e) barricaded
bas *(m)* bottom
bas(se) low; **table basse** *(f)* coffee table
base *(f)* base; **de base** basic
basé(e) sur based on (6)
base-ball *(m)* baseball (2)
basilique *(f)* basilica
basket *(m)* basketball (1)
baskets *(fpl)* tennis shoes (5)
basque *(m)* Basque
bataille *(f)* battle
bateau *(m)* boat (4); **en bateau** by boat (4); **faire du bateau** to go boating (5)
bâtiment *(m)* building (1)
batterie *(f)* drums (2)
battre to beat; **se battre** to fight
bavette *(f)* undercut
beau (bel, belle, *pl* **beaux, belles)** beautiful, handsome (1); **beau-frère** *(m)* brother-in-law; **beau-père** *(m)* father-in-law (4); **beaux-arts** *(mpl)* fine arts (1); **beaux-parents** *(mpl)* stepparents, in-laws; **belle-mère** *(f)* mother-in-law (4); **belle-sœur** *(f)* sister-in-law; **Il fait beau.** The weather's nice. (5)
beaucoup a lot (P); **beaucoup de** a lot of (1)
beauté *(f)* beauty (7)
bébé *(m)* baby

beige beige (3)
beignet *(m)* fritter
belge Belgian
Belgique *(f)* Belgium (9)
bénéficiaire *(mf)* beneficiary
bénéfique beneficial
bénévole benefit, benevolent, voluntary
bénir to bless
berbère Berber
berceuse *(f)* lullaby
besoin *(m)* need; **avoir besoin de** to need (4)
bête *(f)* beast (6), animal
bête stupid, dumb (1)
beurre *(m)* butter (8)
beurré(e) buttered
bibliothèque *(f)* library (1), bookcase
bien well (P), very; **bien d'autres** many others; **bien que** although; **Bien sûr!** Of course! (5); **c'est bien de...** it's good to... (10); **Je voudrais bien.** Sure, I'd like to. (2)
bien-être *(m)* well-being
bienfaiteur *(m)*, **bienfaitrice** *(f)* benefactor
biens *(mpl)* goods
bientôt soon (P); **À bientôt.** See you soon. (P)
bienvenu(e) welcome
bière *(f)* beer (2)
bifteck *(m)* steak (8); **bifteck hâché** *(m)* ground meat
bijoux *(mpl)* jewelry
bikini *(m)* bikini (5)
bilingue bilingual
billard *(m)* billiards
billet *(m)* ticket (9), bill; **distributeur** *(m)* **de billets** ATM machine (10); **billet d'avion électronique** e-ticket (9)
biologie *(f)* biology (1)
bios: produits bios *(mpl)* organic products (8)
biscotte *(f)* melba toast
bise *(f)* kiss
bistro(t) *(m)* restaurant, pub (6)
blanc(he) white (3); **vin blanc** *(m)* white wine (2)
blanquette *(f)* stew *(usually veal)*
bleu(e) blue (3)
blond(e) blond (4)
blouson *(m)* windbreaker, jacket
bœuf *(m)* beef (8); **bœuf bourguignon** *(m)* beef burgundy
bohème bohemian
boire to drink (4)
bois *(m)* wood, woods
boisson *(f)* drink (2)
boîte *(f)* box, can (8); **boîte** *(f)* **de nuit** nightclub (1)
bol *(m)* bowl
bombardement *(m)* bombing
bon(ne) good (1); **Bonne année!** Happy New Year!; **Bon anniversaire!** Happy birthday!; **Bonne idée!** Good idea! (4); **Bonne journée!** Have a good day!; **Bon séjour!** Enjoy your stay! (10); **Bon week-end!** Have a good weekend!
bonbon *(m)* candy
bonheur *(m)* happiness (7)
Bonjour! Hello! Good morning! (P)
bonne *(f)* maid, nanny
Bonsoir! Good evening! (P)
bord *(m)* edge; **à bord** on board; **au bord de** at the edge of; **bord** *(m)* **de la mer** seaside
bordé(e) bordered
bordure: en bordure de along the edge of
botte *(f)* boot (5)
bouche *(f)* mouth (10)
bouché(e) stopped-up; **cidre bouché** *(m)* bottled cider
boucherie *(f)* butcher's shop (8)

boucle *(f)* **d'oreille** earring
boudin *(m)* blood sausage
boue *(f)* mud
boueux(-euse) muddy
bouger to move
bouillabaisse *(f)* fish soup
bouillir to boil
boulangerie *(f)* bakery (8)
boule *(f)* ball
boulevard *(m)* boulevard (10)
boulot *(m)* work *(familiar)*
boum *(f)* party, bash (6)
bourgeoisie: haute bourgeoisie *(f)* upper-middle class
bout *(m)* end (3); **au bout (de)** at the end (of) (3)
bouteille *(f)* bottle (8)
boutique *(f)* shop
bouton *(m)* button, pimple
branché(e) up with things
brancher: se brancher sur to get into
bras *(m)* arm (10)
brasier *(m)* inferno
bref(-ève) brief
Brésil *(m)* Brazil (9)
Bretagne *(f)* Brittany
breton *(m)* Breton
brevet *(m)* certificate, diploma
bricolage *(m)* handiwork
bricoler to do handiwork (2)
brioche *(f)* brioche *(a type of soft bread)*
brise *(f)* breeze
briser to break
britannique British
brochette *(f)* skewer
brocolis *(mpl)* broccoli
bronchite *(f)* bronchitis
bronzer to tan (9)
brosser to brush; **se brosser** to brush (7)
brouillard *(m)* fog, mist, haze
bruit *(m)* noise (10)
brûler to burn; **se brûler la main** to burn your hand
brun(e) *(with hair)* brown, brunette, dark-haired (4)
Bruxelles Brussels
bulletin *(m)* report, bulletin
bureau *(m)* desk (3), office (1); **bureau** *(m)* **de poste** post office (10); **bureau** *(m)* **de tabac** tobacco shop
bus *(m)* bus (4)
but *(m)* goal

C

ça that (P); **Ça fait combien?** How much is it? (2); **Ça fait... euros.** That's . . . euros. (2); **Ça me plaît!** I like it! (3); **Ça lui plaît?** Does he like it? (9); **Ça s'écrit comment?** How is that written? (P); **Ça te/vous dit?** How does that sound to you? (4); **Ça te/vous plaît!** You like it! (3); **Ça va.** It's going fine. (P); **C'est ça!** That's right!; **comme ci comme ça** so-so (2); **Comment ça va?** How's it going? (P); **Qu'est-ce que ça veut dire?** What does that mean? (P)
cabine *(f)* **d'essayage** fitting room (5)
cacao *(m)* cocoa
cacher to hide; **se cacher** to hide oneself, to be hidden
cadien(ne) Cajun (4)
cadeau *(m)* gift (10); **marchand** *(m)* **de cadeaux** gift shop (10)
cadre *(m)* executive
café *(m)* café (1), coffee (2); **café** *(m)* **au lait** coffee with milk (2)

cahier *(m)* notebook (P)
calcul *(m)* calculation
calculer to calculate
Californie *(f)* California (9)
câlin(e) cuddly
calme calm (4)
calmement calmly
calmer: se calmer to calm down
calvaire *(m)* Calvary
camarade *(mf)* pal; **camarade** *(mf)* **de chambre** roommate (P); **camarade** *(mf)* **de classe** classmate
camerounais(e) Cameroonian
campagne *(f)* country (3), campaign; **à la campagne** in the country (3)
camping *(m)* camping, campground (5); **faire du camping** to go camping (5)
camper to camp
campeur *(m)* camper
campus *(m)* campus (1)
Canada *(m)* Canada (9)
canadien(ne) Canadian (P)
canapé *(m)* couch (3), open-faced sandwich
canard *(m)* duck (8)
candidat(e) *(mf)* candidate, applicant
canne à sucre *(f)* sugar cane
canton *(m)* canton, district
capacité *(f)* capacity, ability
capitale *(f)* capital
caprice *(m)* whim
car *(m)* bus (4)
car because
caractère *(m)* character; **en caractères gras** boldfaced
caractériser to characterize
caractéristique *(f)* characteristic
carafe *(f)* carafe *(a decanter)* (8)
caraïbe Caribbean; **mer** *(f)* **des Caraïbes** Caribbean Sea
cardiaque cardiac, of the heart
carie *(f)* cavity
carotte *(f)* carrot (8)
carré(e) square; **Vieux Carré** *(m)* French Quarter (4)
carrière *(f)* career
carte *(f)* menu (8), card, map; **carte** *(f)* **bancaire** bank card (9); **carte** *(f)* **de crédit** credit card (9); **carte** *(f)* **d'identité** identity card; **carte** *(f)* **postale** postcard (9); **carte** *(f)* **téléphonique** telephone card (10)
cas *(m)* case; **dans tous les cas** in any case
case *(f)* box
casier: casier postal *(m)* mailbox
casquette *(f)* cap
casse-cou *(inv)* *(mf)* daredevil
casse-pieds *(inv)* *(mf)* nuisance
casser to break; **se casser la jambe** to break one's leg
cassette *(f)* cassette
catastrophe *(f)* disaster
catégorie *(f)* category
cathédrale *(f)* cathedral
catholique *(mf)* Catholic (1)
cauchemar *(m)* nightmare
cause *(f)* cause; **à cause de** because of
causer to cause
CD *(m)* CD (P); **lecteur** *(m)* **CD** CD player (3)
ce (cet, cette) this, that (3); **ce que** what, that which; **ce qui** what, that which (7); **ces** these, those (3); **ce semestre** this semester (P); **ce soir** tonight, this evening (2); **ce sont** they are, those are (1); **c'est** it's (P), he is, she is, that is, this is (1); **c'est-à-dire** in other words; **Qu'est-ce que c'est?** What is it? (2); **Qui est-ce?** Who is it? (2)

céder to give up
ceinture *(f)* belt
cela that (7); **depuis cela** since then (7)
célèbre famous (4)
célébrer to celebrate
célébrité *(f)* celebrity
céleri *(m)* celery
célibataire single, unmarried (1)
celte Celtic
celtique Celtic
celui (celle) the one
cendre *(f)* ash; **mercredi** *(m)* **des Cendres** Ash Wednesday
cendrier *(m)* ashtray
censure *(f)* censorship
cent *(m)* one hundred (2)
centaine *(f)* about one hundred
centime *(m)* centime *(one hundredth part of a euro)* (2)
central(e) *(mpl* **centraux)** central; **Amérique** *(f)* **centrale** Central America
centre *(m)* center; **centre administratif** *(m)* administration building; **centre commercial** *(m)* shopping center, mall (4); **centre** *(m)* **d'étudiants** student center
centre-ville *(m)* downtown (3)
cercle *(m)* circle
céréales *(fpl)* cereal (8)
céréalier(-ière) cereal
cérémonie *(f)* ceremony
cerise *(f)* cherry (8)
certain(e) certain; **certains** some, certain people
certainement certainly
certes true, indeed, of course
certificat *(m)* certificate
cervelle *(f)* brain
cesser to cease
ceux (celles) those (ones) (8)
chacun(e) each one
chagrin *(m)* sorrow
chaîne *(f)* chain; **chaîne hi-fi** *(f)* stereo (2)
chaise *(f)* chair (3)
chalet de ski *(m)* a ski lodge (10)
chaleur *(f)* warmth
chaleureux(-euse) warm-hearted
chambre *(f)* bedroom (3); **camarade** *(mf)* **de chambre** roommate (P); **chambre** *(f)* **d'hôte** bed and breakfast
champ *(m)* field; **champ** *(m)* **de bataille** battlefield
champignon *(m)* mushroom
chance *(f)* luck
changement *(m)* change
changer to change (6); **changer de l'argent** to exchange money (9)
chanson *(f)* song
chanter to sing (2)
chanteur(-euse) *(mf)* singer
chapeau *(m)* hat
chapelle *(f)* chapel
chaperon: *(m)* hood; **le Petit Chaperon rouge** Little Red Riding Hood
chapitre *(m)* chapter
chaque each, every (3)
charbon *(m)* coal
charcuterie *(f)* delicatessen, deli meats, cold cuts (8)
charger to charge, to load; **chargé(e) (de)** busy, in charge (of); **se charger de** to take charge of
charité *(f)* charity
charmant(e) charming
chasse *(f)* hunt, hunting; **aller à la chasse** to go hunting
chasser to hunt, to make go away

chasseur *(m)* hunter
chat *(m)* cat (3)
châtain *(light to medium)* brown *(hair)* (4)
château *(m)* castle
chaud(e) hot (2); **avoir chaud** to be hot (4); **chocolat chaud** *(m)* hot chocolate (2); **Il fait chaud.** It's hot. (5)
chauffant(e) heating
chauffé(e) heated
chauffeur *(m)* driver
chaume *(m)* thatch
chaussette *(f)* sock
chausson *(m)* **aux pommes** apple turnover
chaussure *(f)* shoe (5)
chef *(m)* head, boss, chief
chef-d'œuvre *(m)* masterpiece
chemin *(m)* road; **chemin** *(m)* **de fer** railroad; **indiquer le chemin** to give directions, to show the way (10)
chemise *(f)* shirt (5); **chemise** *(f)* **de nuit** nightgown
chemisier *(m)* blouse (5)
chêne *(m)* oak
chèque *(m)* check (9); **chèque** *(m)* **de voyage** traveler's check (9)
cher(-ère) expensive (3), dear
chercher to look for (3), to seek; **aller / venir chercher quelqu'un** to go / to come get someone (10)
chercheur(-euse) *(mf)* researcher
chéri(e) *(mf)* honey, darling
cheval *(m)* horse; **faire du cheval** to go horseback riding
chevet: livre *(m)* **de chevet** bedside book
cheveux *(mpl)* hair (4)
cheville *(f)* ankle; **se fouler la cheville** to sprain one's ankle
chèvre *(m)* goat cheese
chez... at / in / to / by . . . 's house/place (2); in *(a person)* (7)
chien *(m)* dog (3)
chiffre *(m)* number, numeral (P)
Chili *(m)* Chile (9)
chimie *(f)* chemistry (1)
chimique chemical
Chine *(f)* China (9)
chinois *(m)* Chinese
chirurgie *(f)* surgery
choc *(m)* shock, impact
chocolat *(m)* chocolate (2); **gâteau au chocolat** *(m)* chocolate cake (8); **pain au chocolat** *(m)* chocolate-filled croissant (8)
choisir (de faire) to choose (to do) (8)
choix *(m)* choice (8)
choquer to shock
chose *(f)* thing (3); **quelque chose** something (2)
chou *(m)* cabbage; **choux** *(mpl)* **de Bruxelles** Brussels sprouts
chouette neat, great
chou-fleur *(m)* cauliflower
chrétien(ne) Christian
chrysanthème *(m)* chrysanthemum
ci: ce (cet, cette)...-ci this. . . (5); **ce mois-ci** this month (4); **ces...-ci** these. . . (5); **ci-dessous** below; **ci-dessus** above; **comme ci comme ça** so-so (2)
ciao bye *(informal)*
cible *(f)* target
ciel *(m)* sky
cinéaste *(mf)* filmmaker
cinéclub *(m)* cinema club (2)
cinéma *(m)* cinema, movie theater (1); **aller au cinéma** to go to the movies (2)
cinématographique film

cinq five (P)

cinquante fifty (2)

cinquième fifth (3)

circonstance *(f)* circumstance

circuit *(m)* circuit, course

circulation *(f)* traffic

circuler to circulate

cité universitaire *(f)* residence halls complex

citoyen(ne) *(mf)* citizen

citoyenneté *(f)* citizenship

citron *(m)* lemon (2); **citron vert** *(m)* lime; **thé** *(m)* **au citron** tea with lemon (2)

civet *(m)* stew

civique civic

clair(e) light, clear; **bleu clair** light blue

clairement clearly

classe *(f)* class (1); **classe aisée** *(f)* upper class; **classe** *(f)* **touriste** tourist class, coach (9); **première classe** *(f)* first class (9); **salle** *(f)* **de classe** classroom (1)

classique classical (1), classic (2)

clavier *(m)* keyboard

clé *(f)* key (10)

client(e) *(mf)* customer

climat *(m)* climate (9)

climatisé(e) air-conditioned

clinique *(f)* clinic

cloche *(f)* bell

clos(e) closed

clôture *(f)* closure, closing date

club *(m)* club; **club** *(m)* **de gym** gym, fitness club (1); **club** *(m)* **de sport** sports club

coca *(m)* cola (2); **coca** *(m)* **light** diet cola (2)

cocotier *(m)* coconut tree

cocotte *(f)* casserole, primper

code *(m)* code; **code** *(m)* **de fonctionnement** responsibility; **code postal** *(m)* zip code (3)

cœur *(m)* heart; **au cœur de** in the heart of

coiffure *(f)* hair style

coin *(m)* corner (3); **au coin (de)** on the corner (of) (10); **café** *(m)* **du coin** neighborhood café; **dans le coin (de)** in the corner (of) (3)

colère *(f)* anger; **en colère** angry

colis *(m)* package

collaborateur(-trice) *(mf)* colleague

collant *(m)* pantyhose

collation *(f)* snack

collectionner to collect

collectivité *(f)* community

collège *(m)* secondary school

collègue *(mf)* colleague

coller to glue

collier *(m)* necklace

colocataire *(mf)* housemate, co-renter (P)

Colombie *(f)* Columbia (9)

colonie *(f)* colony

colonisateur(-trice) *(mf)* colonizer

coloniser to colonize

colonne *(f)* column

combattre to fight, to combat

combien (de) how much, how many (3); **Ça fait combien? / C'est combien?** How much is it? (2); **combien de** how many, how much (3); **Combien font... et... / moins... ?** How much is . . . plus . . . / minus . . . ? (P); **Pendant combien de temps?** For how long? (5); **Vous êtes combien?** How many are there (of you)? (4)

combinaison *(f)* slip

combiner to combine

comédie *(f)* comedy (6); **comédie musicale** *(f)* musical

comédien(ne) *(mf)* actor

comique comical

commander to order (2), to command

comme like, as (1), since (7), for (8); **comme ci comme ça** so-so (2); **comme tu vois** as you see (1)

commencement *(m)* beginning

commencer (à) to begin (to), to start (2); **Le cours de français commence...** The French class starts . . . (P)

comment how (P); **Ça s'écrit comment?** How do you write that? (P); **Comment? What?** (P); **Comment allez-vous?** How are you? (P); **Comment ça va?** How's it going? (P); **Comment dit-on... en français?** How do you say . . . in French? (P); **Comment est-il/elle (sont-ils/elles)... ?** What is he/she (are they) . . . like? (1); **Comment s'appelle...** What is . . . 's name? (4); **Comment vas-tu?** How are you? *(informal)*; **Comment vous appelez-vous?** What's your name? *(formal)* (P); **Tu t'appelles comment? / Comment t'appelles-tu?** What's your name? *(informal)* (P)

commerçant(e) *(mf)* shopkeeper, merchant (8)

commerce *(m)* business (1)

commercial: centre commercial *(m)* shopping center, mall (4)

commettre to commit

commode *(f)* dresser, chest of drawers (3)

commode convenient (3)

commodité *(f)* convenience, comfort

commun(e) common

communauté *(f)* community

commune *(f)* parish

communiquer to communicate (10)

compagnie *(f)* company; **en compagnie de** accompanied by

comparaison *(f)* comparison

comparer to compare (6)

compatibilité *(f)* compatibility (7)

compétence *(f)* skill, competency

complément d'objet direct / indirect *(m)* direct / indirect object

complémentaire complementary

complet(-ète) complete (8); **en phrases complètes** *(f)* in complete sentences (P); **pain complet** *(m)* wholegrain bread (8)

complètement completely

compléter to complete

complexe complex, complicated

compliqué(e) complicated

comporter: se comporter to behave

composer to compose; **composé(e) de** composed of; **se composer de** to be made up of

compote *(f)* stewed fruit

compotier *(m)* fruit bowl

compréhension *(f)* understanding (7)

comprenant including

comprendre to understand (4), to include (8); **compris(e)** included (10); **Je comprends.** I understand. (P); **Vous comprenez?** Do you understand? (P)

comptabilité *(f)* accounting (1)

comptable *(mf)* accountant

compte *(m)* **en banque** bank account

compter to count (2), to plan (9); **Comptez de... à...** Count from . . . to . . . (P)

concentrer: se concentrer sur to concentrate on

concerner to concern

concert *(m)* concert (1); **de concert avec** along with

concevoir to conceive

concombre *(m)* cucumber

concours *(m)* competition, competitive entrance examination

concurrent(e) *(mf)* competitor

conducteur(-trice) *(mf)* driver

conduire to drive

conduite *(f)* conduct

confection *(f)* making

confiance *(f)* confidence; **avoir confiance** to have confidence (4)

confidence *(f)* secret

confier à to confide in, to entrust to

confirmer to confirm

confit *(m)* **de canard** conserve of duck

confiture *(f)* jam, jelly (8)

conflit *(m)* conflict

confondre to confuse; **confondu(e)** combined

confort *(m)* comfort

confortable comfortable (3)

confus(e) confused

conjugal(e) *(mpl* **conjugaux)** married, conjugal

conjuguer to conjugate

connaissance *(f)* acquaintance, knowledge; **faire la connaissance de** to meet (7)

connaître to know, to get to know, to be familiar / acquainted with (4); **Connaissez-vous... ?** Do you know . . . ? (6); **faire connaître** to inform

connu(e) known

conquérant(e) *(mf)* conqueror

conquête *(f)* conquest

consacrer to devote; **consacré(e) à** devoted to

conseil *(m)* a piece of advice (8), council, committee

conseiller(-ère) *(mf)* counselor, adviser

conséquence *(f)* consequence; **en conséquence** as a consequence

conséquent: par conséquent consequently

conservateur(-trice) conservative (7)

conserver to keep

conserves *(fpl)* canned goods (8)

considérer to consider; **considéré(e)** considered; **se considérer** to consider oneself

consommation *(f)* consumption, drink

consonne *(f)* consonant

constamment constantly

constituer to make up

construire to construct, to build

consulat *(m)* consulate

consulter to consult

conte *(m)* story (6); **conte** *(m)* **de fée** fairy tale (6)

contemporain(e) contemporary

contenir to contain

content(e) happy, glad (8)

conteur(-euse) *(mf)* storyteller

contexte *(m)* context

continent *(m)* continent (9)

continuer to continue (10)

contraire *(m)* contrary; **au contraire** on the contrary

contraste *(m)* contrast

contrat *(m)* contract

contre against; **par contre** on the other hand

contrepoids *(m)* counterbalance

contribuer to contribute

contrôle *(m)* control

contrôler to control (8)

convenable appropriate, suitable

convenir to be suitable; **Ça vous convient?** Does that work for you? (9)

convivialité *(f)* friendliness

convoité(e) coveted

cool: assez cool pretty cool (P)

copain *(m)* *(male)* friend, pal (6)

copieux(-euse) copious, large (8)

copine *(f)* *(female)* friend, pal (6)

coq au vin *(m)* chicken in wine sauce

coquillage *(m)* shellfish

coquilles St-Jacques *(fpl)* scallops

corporel(le) of the body
corps *(m)* body (7)
correspondant(e) corresponding
correspondre (à) to correspond (to)
Corse *(f)* Corsica
corse *(m)* Corsican *(language)*
costume *(m)* man's suit (5)
côte *(f)* coast; **côte** *(f)* **de porc** pork chop (8)
côté *(m)* side (3); **à côté (de)** next to (3); **côté cour** on the courtyard side (10); **de l'autre côté (de)** on the other side (of) (3)
Côte d'Ivoire *(f)* Ivory Coast (9)
coton *(m)* cotton
cou *(m)* neck
couchant setting
coucher: se coucher to go to bed (7); **chambre à coucher** *(f)* bedroom
coulée *(f)* flow
couler to run *(liquids)*
couleur *(f)* color (3); **De quelle couleur est/sont... ?** What color is/are . . . ? (3)
coulis *(m)* purée
couloir *(m)* hall, corridor (3)
coup *(m)* stroke, blow; **coup** *(m)* **de foudre** love at first sight (7); **coup** *(m)* **d'état** coup; **coup** *(m)* **de téléphone** telephone call; **tout à coup** all of a sudden (6); **tout d'un coup** all at once (6)
coupe *(f)* dessert dish
couper to cut; **se couper le doigt** to cut one's finger
cour *(f)* court, courtyard; **côté cour** on the courtyard side (10)
couramment fluently
courant(e) present, current, common
courber l'échine to bend one's back
courgette *(f)* zucchini
courir to run (9)
courrier *(m)* mail; **courrier électronique** *(m)* e-mail
cours *(m)* class (P), course; **au cours de** in the course of, during, while on (10); **avoir cours** to have class (6); **cours** *(m)* **de français** French class (P); **dans un autre cours** in another class (P); **suivre un cours** to take a course
course *(f)* errand (5), race; **faire des courses** to run errands (5); **faire les courses** to go grocery shopping
court *(m)* **de tennis** tennis court
court(e) short (4); **court métrage** *(m)* short film
cousin(e) *(mf)* cousin (4)
coûter to cost (5)
coutume *(f)* custom
couture *(f)* sewing, dressmaking; *****haute couture** *(f)* designer fashion
couvert(e) de covered with
couverture *(f)* blanket, cover (3)
couvrir to cover
cravate *(f)* tie (5)
crayon *(m)* pencil (P)
créancier(-ière) *(mf)* creditor
créateur(-trice) *(mf)* creator
crèche *(f)* *(government-sponsored)* day care
crédit: carte *(f)* **de crédit** credit card (9)
créer to create
crème *(f)* cream (8)
créole Creole
crevette *(f)* shrimp (8)
crier to shout
criminel(le) *(mf)* criminal
crise *(f)* crisis; **crise cardiaque** *(f)* heart attack
critique *(f)* criticism
croc *(m)* fang
croire (à) (que) to believe (in) (that) (10); **je crois** I think

croissant *(m)* croissant (8)
croque-madame *(m)* toasted ham-and-cheese sandwich with an egg on top
croque-monsieur *(m)* toasted ham-and-cheese sandwich
cru(e) raw
crudités *(fpl)* raw vegetables (8)
cruel(le) cruel (6)
cuiller *(f)* spoon
cuillerée *(f)* spoonful
cuir *(m)* leather
cuire to cook
cuisine *(f)* kitchen (3), cuisine, cooking (4); **faire la cuisine** to cook (5)
cuisinière *(f)* stove
cuisson *(f)* cooking
cuivre *(m)* copper
cultiver to cultivate (7)
culture *(f)* culture (9), cultivation
culturel(le) cultural (4)
curieux(-euse) curious, odd
curiosité *(f)* curiosity
cyclisme *(m)* cycling

D

dactylographie *(f)* typing
dame *(f)* lady
Danemark *(m)* Denmark
dangereux(-euse) dangerous
dans in (P); **dans la rue...** on . . . street (10)
danse *(f)* dance
danser to dance (2)
danseur(-euse) *(mf)* dancer
date *(f)* date (4); **Quelle est la date aujourd'hui?** What is the date today? (4)
dater de to date from
daurade *(f)* sea bream
davantage more
de from, of (P), about (1); **de la, de l'** some (8); **de luxe** deluxe (10); **de rien** you're welcome (P); **parler de** to talk about
débarquement *(m)* landing
débrouiller: se débrouiller to get by
début *(m)* beginning (6)
débutant(e) *(mf)* beginner
décédé(e) dead; deceased (4)
décembre *(m)* December (4)
décennie *(f)* decade
déchets *(mpl)* trash, rubbish
décidément decidedly, for sure
décider to decide (6); **se décider** to make up one's mind
décision *(f)* decision (7); **prendre une décision** to make a decision (7)
décompresser to let off steam
décorer to decorate
découper to cut out
découverte *(f)* discovery
découvrir to discover
décrire to describe (9)
décrocher to unhook, to get, to land
défaire: défaire sa valise to unpack
défendre to defend, to forbid; **défendu(e)** forbidden; **se défendre** to defend oneself
défi *(m)* challenge
défilé *(m)* parade
défini(e) definite
définir to define
degré *(m)* degree
dégustation *(f)* sampling
dehors outside; **en dehors de** outside of
déjà already (5)
déjeuner *(m)* lunch; **petit déjeuner** *(m)* breakfast (5)
déjeuner to have lunch (2)

délicieux(-euse) delicious (6)
délivrance *(f)* issue, delivery
déluge *(m)* flood
demain tomorrow (P); **À demain!** See you tomorrow! (P)
demande *(f)* request
demander to ask (for) (2); **se demander** to wonder
demeurer to remain
demi *(m)* draft beer (2)
demi(e) half (P); **demi-heure** *(f)* half hour (7); **Il est deux heures et demie.** It's half past two. (P); **un kilo et demi** a kilo and a half (8)
démocratie *(f)* democracy
démocratique democratic
dénoncer to denounce, to turn in
dent *(f)* tooth (7)
dentaire dental
départ *(m)* departure (9)
département *(m)* department *(a French administrative region)*
dépasser to go beyond
dépaysement *(m)* change of scenery
dépêcher: se dépêcher to hurry
dépendre (de) to depend (on) (5); **Ça dépend.** That depends.
dépense *(f)* expense
déplier to unfold
déposer to deposit
déprime *(f)* depression
déprimé(e) depressed
depuis since, for (7), from; **depuis cela** since then (7); **depuis que** since
député *(m)* deputy
dérivé(e) derived
dernier(-ère) last (5)
derrière behind (3)
des some (1)
dés *(mpl)* dice
dès since, right after; **dès que** as soon as
désagréable unpleasant (1)
descendre (de) to go down, to get off (5); **descendre dans / à** to stay at (a hotel) (5)
déshabiller to undress; **se déshabiller** to get undressed (7)
désir *(m)* desire
désirer to desire; **Vous désirez?** What would you like?, May I help you? (2)
désireux (désireuse) desirous
désolé(e) sorry (10)
désordre: en désordre in disorder (3)
désormais henceforth, from now on
dessert *(m)* dessert (8)
dessin *(m)* drawing; **dessin animé** *(m)* cartoon
dessinateur *(m)* artist
dessiner to draw
dessous: ci-dessous below
dessus: au dessus de above
destin *(m)* destiny
détaillé(e) detailed
détendre: se détendre to relax
détenir to hold, to possess
détente *(f)* relaxation
détenteur(-trice) *(mf)* holder
déterminer to determine
détester to hate (7); **se détester** to hate each other (7)
détruit(e) destroyed
dette *(f)* debt
deux two (P); **deux-tiers** two-thirds
deuxième second (3)
devant in front of (3)
devanture *(f)* shop window
développement *(m)* development
développer to develop

devenir to become (4)

deviner to guess

devinette *(f)* riddle

devise *(f)* currency

devoir must, to have to, to owe (6); **il/elle doit** he/she must (3)

devoirs *(mpl)* homework (P)

diabète *(m)* diabetes

diable *(m)* devil

diamant *(m)* diamond

diarrhée *(f)* diarrhea

dictature *(f)* dictatorship

dictée *(f)* dictation

dictionnaire *(m)* dictionary

dieu *(m)* god

différemment differently

différent(e) different

difficile difficult (P)

difficulté *(f)* difficulty

digérer to digest

dignité *(f)* dignity

digue *(f)* causeway

dimanche *(m)* Sunday (P)

diminuer to diminish

dinde *(f)* turkey

dîner *(m)* dinner (8)

dîner to have dinner, to dine (2)

diplôme *(m)* diploma, degree

diplômé(e) *(mf)* graduate

dire to say, to tell (6); **Ça te/vous dit?** How does that sound to you? (4); **Comment dit-on... en français?** How do you say . . . in French? (P); **On dit que...** They say that . . . (4); **Qu'est-ce que ça veut dire?** What does that mean? (P)

directement directly

directeur(-trice) *(mf)* director

diriger to direct, to conduct

discothèque *(f)* dance club

discuter to discuss

disparaître to disappear; **disparu(e)** having disappeared

disponible available

disposer de to have available

disposition: à la disposition de available to

disputer to dispute; **se disputer (avec)** to argue (with) (7)

disque *(m)* record; **disque compact** *(m)* compact disc

dissiper to dissipate

distinguer to distinguish; **distingué(e)** distinguished

distraction *(f)* entertainment (5)

distribué(e) distributed

distributeur *(m)* **de billets** ATM machine (10)

divers(e) diverse, different

diversité *(f)* diversity

diviser to divide; **se diviser (en)** to divide (into)

divorcer to divorce; **divorcé(e)** divorced (1)

dix ten (P); **dix-huit** eighteen (P); **dix-huitième** eighteenth (3); **dix-neuf** nineteen (P); **dix-sept** seventeen (P)

dixième tenth (3)

doctorat *(m)* doctorate

documentaire *(m)* documentary

dodo *(m)* bedtime *(familiar)*

doigt *(m)* finger (10); **doigt** *(m)* **de pied** toe (10)

dollar *(m)* dollar (3)

dolmen *(m)* dolmen *(an ancient megalithic structure)*

domaine *(m)* domain, field

domestique *(mf)* servant

domestique domestic, household; **tâche domestique** *(f)* household chore

domicile *(m)* place of residence

dominer to dominate

dommage: C'est dommage! It's a shame! It's a pity! (7)

donc so, therefore, thus, then (7)

donner to give (2); **donner à manger à** to feed (9); **donner lieu à** to give rise to; **Donnez-moi...** Give me . . . (P)

dont of which, among which, whose (7)

dormir to sleep (2)

dos *(m)* back (10)

dossier *(m)* file

doté(e) endowed

douane *(f)* customs (9)

douanier(-ière) customs

doublé(e) doubled, dubbed

douche *(f)* shower (7)

douleur *(f)* pain, ache

douloureux(-euse) painful

doute *(m)* doubt; **sans doute** without doubt, probably (8)

douter to doubt (10)

doux (douce) sweet, soft, gentle (6)

douzaine *(f)* dozen (8)

douze twelve (P)

dramatique dramatic

dramaturge *(m)* playwright

drame *(m)* drama

drap *(m)* sheet

dresser to set up

droit *(m)* law *(field of study)*, right *(legal)*; **droits** *(mpl)* **de l'homme** human rights; **tout droit** straight (10)

droite *(f)* right *(direction):* **à droite (de)** to the right (of) (3)

du (de la, de l', des) some (8)

dû (due, dus, dues) à due to

duc *(m)* duke

duché *(m)* dukedom, duchy

dur(e) hard; **œuf dur** *(m)* hard-boiled egg (8)

durant during

durée *(f)* duration

durer to last

DVD *(m)* DVD (2); **lecteur** *(m)* **DVD** DVD player (3)

dynamique active (1)

E

eau *(f)* water (2)

écailler to open *(shellfish)*

échange *(m)* exchange

échanger to exchange

échapper to escape; **s'échapper** to escape

écharpe *(f)* winter scarf

échelle *(f)* ladder

échouer to fail

éclair *(m)* éclair *(a pastry)*

éclairage *(m)* lighting

éclaircie *(f)* sunny spell

éclairé(e) lighted

école *(f)* school (6)

écolo(giste) *(mf)* environmentalist

économie *(f)* economy; **faire des économies** to save money

économique economic; **sciences économiques** *(fpl)* economics

écossais(e) plaid

écossé(e) shelled

écoute: être à l'écoute de to be listening to

écouter to listen (to) (2); **Écoutez...** Listen to . . . (P)

écran *(m)* screen

écrevisse *(f)* crawfish

écrire to write (2); **Ça s'écrit comment?** How do you write that? (P); **écrit(e)** written; **Écrivez...** Write . . . (P)

écrivain *(m)* writer

éditer to edit

éduquer to educate

effectuer to carry out

effet *(m)* effect; **effets personnels** personal belongings (10); **effets spéciaux** special effects (6)

efforcer: s'efforcer (de) to endeavor

égal(e) *(mpl* **égaux)** equal; **Ça m'est égal.** It's all the same to me.

également also, as well, equally, likewise

égalité *(f)* equality

égard *(m)* respect

église *(f)* church (4)

égoïste selfish

Égypte *(f)* Egypt (9)

élection *(f)* election

électricité *(f)* electricity

électrique electrical

électronique electronic; **billet** *(m)* **d'avion électronique** e-ticket (9); **courrier** *(m)* **électronique** e-mail

élément *(m)* element

élevage *(m)* raising livestock

élève *(mf)* pupil, student

élevé(e) high, elevated

elle she, it (1), her; **elles** they (1), them; **elle-même** herself

éloigner to remove, to make go away

embarquement *(m)* boarding; **porte** *(f)* **d'embarquement** departure gate (9)

embêtant(e) annoying (3)

embrasser to kiss (7); **s'embrasser** to kiss each other, to embrace each other (7)

émincé(e) thinly sliced

emmener to take

emploi *(m)* employment, use; **emploi** *(m)* **du temps** schedule

employé(e) *(mf)* employee (10)

employer to use; **s'employer** to be used

emporter to carry away

emprisonner to imprison (6)

emprunter (à) to borrow (from)

en some, any, about it/them, of it/them (8); **Je vous/t'en prie.** You're welcome.; **s'en aller** to go away

en in (P); **de temps en temps** from time to time (4); **en avance** early; **en avion** by plane (4); **en désordre** in disorder (3); **en face (de)** across from, facing (3); **en ligne** online (7); **en même temps** at the same time; **en ordre** in order (3); **en plus** furthermore (8); **en retard** late (10); **en solde** on sale (5); **en tout temps** at all times; **en vacances** on vacation (4); **être en train de...** to be in the process of . . . ; **partir en voyage** to leave on a trip (5); **partir en week-end** to go away for the weekend (5); **payer en espèces** to pay cash (10)

enceinte pregnant (10)

enchaîné(e) chained up

Enchanté(e). Delighted to meet you.

enchanter to enchant

encore still (4), again, more (8); **ne... pas encore** not yet (5)

encourager to encourage

endormir: s'endormir to fall asleep (7)

endroit *(m)* place (9)

énergie *(f)* energy

énergique energetic

énerver to irritate

enfance *(f)* childhood

enfant *(mf)* child (4)

enfanter to give birth to

enfer *(m)* hell

enfin finally (7)
enflé(e) swollen
engager to hire
ennemi(e) *(mf)* enemy
ennui *(m)* trouble
ennuyer to bore; **s'ennuyer (de)** to get bored (with), to be bored (with) (7)
ennuyeux(-euse) boring (1)
énorme enormous
enquête *(f)* investigation, survey
enregistrer to record
enrichir to enrich
enseignement *(m)* teaching, education; **enseignement supérieur** higher education
enseigner to teach
ensemble *(m)* whole group
ensemble together (2)
ensuite then, afterwards (4)
entendre to hear (7); **s'entendre bien/mal (avec)** to get along well/badly (with) (7)
enthousiasme *(m)* enthusiasm
entier(-ère) entire, whole; **à part entière** complete
entouré(e) (de) surrounded (by)
entre between (3), among
entrée *(f)* appetizer (8), entry ticket, entrance, entry; **entrée au cinéma** *(f)* cinema attendance
entreprise *(f)* firm, enterprise
entrer (dans) to enter, to go in (5)
entretien *(m)* conversation, interview, maintenance
envahir to invade
enveloppe *(f)* envelope
envers towards
envie: avoir envie de to feel like, to desire (4)
environ around, about (4)
environnement *(m)* environment
environs *(mpl)* surrounding area
envoyer to send (10)
épais(se) thick
épaisseur *(f)* thickness
épanouir: s'épanouir to flourish
épaule *(f)* shoulder
épée *(f)* sword
épicerie *(f)* grocer's shop (8)
épicier(-ière) *(mf)* grocer
épinards *(mpl)* spinach
époque *(f)* time period; **à cette époque-là** at that time, in those days
épouser to marry; **s'épouser** to get married
épouvante: film *(m)* **d'épouvante** horror movie (6)
époux (épouse) *(mf)* spouse
épreuve *(f)* test
épuisé(e) exhausted
équilibré(e) balanced
équipe *(f)* team
équipé(e) equipped
équipée *(f)* venture
équipement *(m)* equipment
escalade *(f)* (rock) climbing
escale *(f)* stopover
escalier *(m)* stairs, staircase (3)
escargot *(m)* snail (8)
escarpé(e) steep
esclavage *(m)* slavery
esclave *(mf)* slave
espace *(m)* space
Espagne *(f)* Spain (9)
espagnol *(m)* Spanish (P)
espagnol(e) Spanish
espèce *(f)* species; **Espèce de... !** You . . . !; **payer en espèces** to pay cash (10)
espérer to hope (3)

espiègle mischievous
espion(ne) *(mf)* spy
espionnage *(m)* spying
espoir *(m)* hope; **meilleur jeune espoir** *(m)* best new actor
esprit *(m)* mind, spirit (7)
essayage: cabine *(f)* **d'essayage** fitting room (5)
essayer to try on (5); **essayer (de faire)** to try (to do)
essentiel(le) essential
essoufflé(e) to be out of breath
est *(m)* east
est-ce que *(question marker)* (1)
estimer to estimate, to reckon
estival(e): station estivale *(f)* a summer resort (10)
et and (P)
établir to establish; **s'établir** to establish oneself, to settle
établissement *(m)* establishment
étage *(m)* floor (3); **à l'étage** on the same floor, down the hall; **À quel étage?** On what floor? (3); **au premier étage** on the second floor (3)
étagère *(f)* shelf, bookcase (3)
étain *(m)* tin
étape *(f)* stopping place, step
état *(m)* state (3), condition
États-Unis *(mpl)* United States (3)
été *(m)* summer (5); **en été** in summer (5)
étendre: s'étendre to extend; **étendu(e)** stretched out
éternuer to sneeze (10)
ethnique ethnic
étoile *(f)* star
étonner to surprise, to amaze; **étonné(e)** surprised, amazed (10)
étouffant(e) stifling
étouffement *(m)* suffocation
étranger(-ère) foreign (1); **à l'étranger** abroad (9)
être to be (1); **c'est** it's (P), he is, she is, this is, that is (1); **C'est quel jour aujourd'hui?** What day is today? (P); **Comment est / sont... ?** What is / are . . . like? (1); **être à** to belong to; **je suis** I'm (P); **le français est...** French is . . . (P); **Nous sommes six.** There are six of us. (4); **Quelle est la date aujourd'hui?** What is the date today? (4); **tu es/vous êtes** you are (P)
être humain *(m)* human being
étroit(e) tight
étude: études *(fpl)* studies (1)
étudiant(e) *(mf)* student (P)
étudier to study (1)
euro *(m)* euro (2)
Europe *(f)* Europe (9)
européen(ne) European
eux them, they; **eux-mêmes** themselves
évader: s'évader to escape
évasion *(f)* escape
événement *(m)* event
évidemment of course, obviously
éviter to avoid (8)
exactement exactly (10)
examen *(m)* test, exam (P)
excentrique eccentric
excessivement excessively
exclamer: s'exclamer to exclaim, to cry out
excuser to excuse, to forgive; **Excusez-moi.** Excuse me. (P); **s'excuser** to apologize
exécutif(-ive) executive
exemple *(m)* example; **par exemple** for example (2)
exercer to exert

exercice *(m)* exercise (P); **faire de l'exercice** to exercise (2)
exiger to require
exister to exist
exotique exotic (9)
expérience *(f)* experience, experiment
explication *(f)* explanation
expliquer to explain (10)
explorateur(-trice) *(mf)* explorer
exploser to explode
exposé(e) exposed
exposition *(f)* exhibit (4)
expression *(f)* expression (10)
expresso *(m)* espresso (2)
exprimer to express
expulser to throw out
extérieur *(m)* outside, exterior
extinction *(f)* extinguishing
extra(ordinaire) great, terrific (4); **extra-scolaire** extracurricular
extrait *(m)* excerpt
extra(ordinaire) great (4)
extraverti(e) outgoing, extroverted (1)

F

fac *(f)* university, campus (2)
face *(f)* face; **en face (de)** across from, facing (3); **face à** across from, confronted with; **faire face à** to face
facile easy (P)
facilement easily (7)
faciliter to facilitate, to make easy
façon *(f)* way
facture *(f)* bill
faculté (fac) *(f)* university, campus (2)
faillir: j'ai failli tomber I almost fell
faim *(f)* hunger; **avoir faim** to be hungry (4); **j'ai faim** I'm hungry (2)
faire to do, to make (2); **Ça fait... euros.** That's . . . euros. (2); **Ça ne se fait pas!** That is not done!; **faire attention (à)** to pay attention (to), to watch out (for) (8); **faire connaître** to inform; **faire de l'aérobic** to do aerobics (8); **faire de l'alpinisme** to go mountain climbing; **faire de la marche à pied** to go walking; **faire de la musculation** to do weight training, to do bodybuilding (8); **faire de la musique** to play music (2); **faire de la planche à voile** to go windsurfing; **faire de la plongée sous-marine** to go scuba diving; **faire de la varappe** to go rock climbing; **faire de l'exercice** to exercise (2); **faire des courses** to run errands (5); **faire des économies** to save up (money); **faire des projets** to make plans (4); **faire du bateau** to go boating (5); **faire du camping** to go camping (5); **faire du cheval** to go horseback riding (5); **faire du jardinage** to garden (5); **faire du jogging** to jog (2); **faire du patin (à glace)** to go (ice-)skating; **faire du roller** to go rollerblading (6); **faire du shopping** to go shopping (2); **faire du skateboard(ing)** to skateboard (6); **faire du ski** to go skiing (2); **faire du sport** to play sports (2); **faire du tuba** to go snorkeling; **faire du vélo** to go bike-riding (2); **faire du VTT** to go all-terrain biking (5); **faire face à** to face; **faire la connaissance de** to meet (7); **faire la cuisine** to cook (5); **faire la fête** to party; **faire la lessive** to do laundry (5); **faire la vaisselle** to do the dishes (5); **faire le ménage** to do housework (5); **faire les courses** to go grocery shopping; **faire mal** to hurt; **faire noir** to be dark; **faire sa toilette** to wash up (7); **faire sa valise** to pack one's

bags (9); **faire une promenade** to go for a walk (5); **faire une randonnée** to go for a hike (8); **faire une réservation** to make a reservation (9); **faire un tour** to take a tour, to go for a ride (4); **faire un voyage** to take a trip (5); **Faites les devoirs dans le cahier.** Do the homework in the workbook. (P); **Il fait beau / chaud / du soleil / du vent / frais / froid / mauvais.** It's nice / hot / sunny / windy / cool / cold / bad. (5); **Il fait bon / du brouillard.** It's nice / foggy.; **Il va faire beau...** It's going to be nice. . . (5); **Je fais du 42.** I wear a 42. (5); **Je ne fais pas de musique / de sport.** I don't play music / sports. (2); **Quelle taille faites-vous?** What size do you wear? (5); **Quel temps fait-il?** What's the weather like? (5); **Quel temps va-t-il faire?** What's the weather going to be like? (5); **Qu'est-ce que vous faites/tu fais?** What are you doing? What do you do? (2)
faisan *(m)* pheasant
falaise *(f)* cliff
falloir: il faut... it is necessary . . . , one must . . . , one needs . . . (8); **il me/te/nous/vous faut** I/you/we/you need (9); **il ne faut pas** one shouldn't, one must not . . . (10)
fameux(-euse) famous
familial(e) *(mpl* **familiaux)** family
familiariser: se familiariser (avec) to get to know
familier(-ère) familiar, informal
familièrement colloquially
famille *(f)* family (P); **nom** *(m)* **de famille** family name, surname (3)
famine *(f)* famine, starvation
fantastique fantastic; **film fantastique** *(m)* fantasy movie
farci(e) stuffed
farine *(f)* flour
fascinant(e) fascinating
fasciner to fascinate
fast-food *(m)* fast food restaurant (1)
fatigant(e) tiring
fatigué(e) tired (6)
faut *See* **falloir.**
faute *(f)* lack, mistake, fault
fauteuil *(m)* armchair (3)
faux (fausse) false
favoriser to favor, to further
féculents *(mpl)* carbohydrates
fédéral(e) *(mpl* **fédéraux)** federal
fée *(f)* fairy; **conte** *(m)* **de fée** fairy tale (6)
femme *(f)* woman (1), wife (2); **ex-femme** *(f)* ex-wife; **femme au foyer** homemaker; **femme d'affaires** businesswoman (5)
fenêtre *(f)* window (3)
fenouil *(m)* fennel
fer *(m)* iron; **chemin** *(m)* **de fer** railroad
férié(e): jour férié *(m)* holiday
ferme *(f)* farm
fermer to close (2); **Fermez votre livre.** Close your book. (P)
féroce ferocious (6)
festival *(m)* festival (4)
fête *(f)* holiday, celebration (4), party (P); **faire la fête** to party; **fête des mères** *(f)* Mother's Day; **fête des pères** *(f)* Father's Day; **fête du travail** *(f)* Labor Day; **fête nationale** *(f)* national holiday
fêter to celebrate
feu *(m)* fire; **prendre feu** to catch fire
feuille *(f)* **de papier** sheet of paper (P)
feuilleté(e) flaky (pastry)
février *(m)* February (4)
fiancé(e) engaged (1)

fiancer: se fiancer to get engaged (7)
ficelle *(f)* string
fiche *(f)* form
fidélité *(f)* faithfulness
fier(-ère) proud
fièvre *(m)* fever; **avoir de la fièvre** to have fever
figure *(f)* face (7)
filière *(f)* career path
fille *(f)* girl; daughter (4); **fille unique** *(f)* only child
film *(m)* movie (1)
filmer to film
fils *(m)* son (4); **fils unique** *(m)* only child
fin *(f)* end
fin(e) fine
finalement finally (6)
financier(-ère) financial
financièrement financially
finir (de faire) to finish (doing) (8); **finir par faire** to end up doing; **Le cours de français finit...** French class ends . . . (P)
fixe fixed (8)
fixer to set, to fix
flamand *(m)* Flemish (language)
fleur *(f)* flower
fleuri(e) with a floral pattern
fleuriste *(mf)* florist
fleuve *(m)* river
flore *(f)* flora
Floride *(f)* Florida (9)
foie *(m)* liver
fois *(f)* time, occasion (5); **à la fois** at the same time; **d'autres fois** other times (7); **Il était une fois...** Once upon a time . . . (6)
folk *(m)* folk music
folklore *(m)* folklore (4)
foncé(e) dark; **bleu foncé** dark blue
fonction *(f)* function; **en fonction de** according to; **voiture** *(f)* **de fonction** company car
fonctionner to function, to work
fond *(m)* bottom, back, background; **dans le fond** really, basically
fondateur: père *(m)* **fondateur** founding father
fonder to found; **fondé(e)** founded
fonderie *(f)* foundry
fondre to melt
fontaine *(f)* fountain
football *(m)* soccer (1); **football américain** football (1)
force *(f)* force, strength
forcément necessarily, inevitably
forcer to force
forêt *(f)* forest
forger to forge, to mold
formation *(f)* education
forme *(f)* shape; **en forme** in shape (8)
former to form, to educate
formidable great (7)
formulaire *(m)* form
formule *(f)* formula, expression
fort(e) strong (8)
fort very
fortifié(e) fortified
fou (folle) crazy
foudre: coup *(m)* **de foudre** love at first sight (7)
foulard *(m)* dress scarf
fouler: se fouler la cheville to sprain one's ankle
four (à micro-ondes) *(m)* (microwave) oven
fourchette *(f)* fork
fournir to furnish
fourrure *(f)* fur
foyer *(m)* home; **femme au foyer** homemaker; **foyer** *(m)* **des étudiants** student center

fragmenté(e) fragmented
frais (fraîche) fresh (8); **Il fait frais.** It's cool. (5)
fraise *(f)* strawberry (8)
framboise *(f)* raspberry
franc *(m)* franc
français *(m)* French (P); **cours** *(m)* **de français** French class (P)
français(e) French (1); **à la française** French-style
France *(f)* France (1)
franchir to cross
francophone French-speaking
francophonie *(f)* French-speaking world
frapper to strike
fraternité *(f)* brotherhood
frénésie *(f)* frenzy
fréquemment frequently
fréquenter to frequent, to hang out at
frère *(m)* brother (1); **beau-frère** *(m)* brother-in-law; **demi-frère** *(m)* stepbrother, halfbrother
frigo *(m)* refrigerator
frire to fry
frisé(e) curly
frisée *(f)* curly endive
frisson *(m)* shiver (10)
frites *(fpl)* French fries (2); **steak-frites** *(m)* steak and fries (8)
frivole frivolous
froid(e) cold (4); **avoir froid** to be cold (4); **Il fait froid.** It's cold. (5)
fromage *(m)* cheese (2)
frontière *(f)* border (10)
fruit *(m)* fruit (8); **fruits** *(mpl)* **de mer** shellfish (8); **jus** *(m)* **de fruit** fruit juice (2)
fruitier(-ière) fruit
fuir to flee, to run away
fumé(e) smoked (8)
fumée *(f)* smoke
fumer to smoke (3)
fumeur(-euse) *(mf)* smoker; **section (non-)fumeur** *(f)* (non-)smoking section
funérailles *(fpl)* funeral
furieux(-euse) furious (10)
futur *(m)* future (tense)

G

gagner to win (2), to gain; **gagner de l'argent** to earn money, to make money
gai(e) gay, lively
gaieté *(f)* cheerfulness
gant *(m)* glove
garage *(m)* garage
garantir to guarantee
garçon *(m)* boy (4), waiter (2)
garder to keep
gare *(f)* train station
garni(e) served with vegetables
garniture *(f)* garnish
gaspiller to waste
gâté(e) spoiled (6)
gâteau *(m)* cake (8)
gauche *(f)* left; **à gauche (de)** to the left (of) (3)
gaulois(e) from Gaul *(ancient name for the region of modern France)*
gaz: gaz naturel *(m)* natural gas
géant(e) giant
gelé(e) frozen
gêné(e) embarrassed
généalogie *(f)* genealogy
général(e) *(mpl* **généraux)** general; **en général** in general (2)
généralement generally (7)
génial(e) *(mpl* **géniaux)** great (4)
genou *(m)* knee

genre *(m)* gender, kind, type, genre
gens *(mpl)* people (1)
gentil(le) nice (1)
géographie *(f)* geography (9)
géographique geographical
géographiquement geographically
géologie *(f)* geology
germer to sprout
geste *(m)* gesture
gestion *(f)* management
gilet *(m)* vest
glace *(f)* ice cream (8), ice; **glace à la vanille** vanilla ice cream (8)
glacier *(m)* ice cream shop
glisser to glide
global(e) *(mpl* **globaux)** global
gloire *(f)* glory
goéland *(m)* seagull
golf *(m)* golf (2)
gommage *(m)* rubbing out
gorge *(f)* throat (10); **soutien-gorge** *(m)* bra
gorille *(m)* gorilla
gosse *(mf)* kid
goulu(e) gluttonous
gousse *(f)* clove
goût *(m)* taste
goûter to taste (9)
goutte *(f)* drop
gouvernement *(m)* government
gouverner to govern
grâce *(f)* grace; **jour** *(m)* **d'Action de grâce** Thanksgiving
grâce à thanks to, because of
gracieux(-euse) gracious (6)
grammaire *(f)* grammar
gramme *(m)* gram (8)
grand(e) big, large, tall (1); **grande surface** *(f)* superstore (8); **le grand amour** *(m)* true love (7)
grand-chose: ne... pas grand-chose not much, not a lot
Grande-Bretagne *(f)* Great Britain
grandir to grow up, to grow, to get taller (8)
grand-mère *(f)* grandmother (4)
grand-père *(m)* grandfather (4)
grands-parents *(mpl)* grandparents (4)
gras(se) *(f)* fatty; **en caractères gras** boldfaced; **matière grasse** *(f)* fat (8)
gratuit(e) free (of charge)
gratuitement without charge
grave serious, grave
Grèce *(f)* Greece
grenade *(f)* pomegranate
grille *(f)* bars
grillé(e) grilled (8); **pain grillé(e)** toast (8)
grippe *(f)* flu (10)
gris(e) gray (3)
gros(se) big, fat (1)
grossir to get fatter (8)
groupe *(m)* group (6); **en groupe** in a group
grouper to group
gruyère *(m)* Swiss cheese
guérir to cure, to heal
guerre *(f)* war
guichet *(m)* ticket window; **guichet automatique** *(m)* automatic teller machine
guide *(m)* guide, guidebook (9)
guitare *(f)* guitar (2)
Guyane *(f)* (French) Guiana (10)
gym: club *(m)* **de gym** gym, fitness club (1)
gymnase *(m)* gym

H

habiller to dress; **s'habiller** to get dressed (7)
habitant(e) *(mf)* inhabitant

habiter to live (2); **j'habite à** (+ *city*) I live in (+ *city*) (P); **Vous habitez... ?** Do you live. . . ? (P)
habitude *(f)* habit; **d'habitude** usually (2)
habitué(e) à used to, accustomed to
habituel(le) customary, usual
*****haché(e)** chopped (up)
*****haine** *(f)* hatred
Haïti *(m)* Haiti
*****hamburger** *(m)* hamburger (8)
*****handicapé(e)** handicapped
*****Hanoukka** *(f)* Hanukkah
*****haricots verts** *(mpl)* green beans (8)
harmonie *(f)* harmony
*****hasard: par hasard** by chance
*****haut: dans les hauts** high above; **(tout) en haut** at the (very) top
*****haut(e)** high; **haute couture** *(f)* high fashion; **haut talon** *(m)* high heel
hébergement *(m)* accommodation
hébreu *(m)* Hebrew
*****hein?** huh?
helvétique Helvetic (Swiss)
herbe *(f)* grass
héritage *(m)* inheritance, heritage
hériter to inherit
hésiter to hesitate
heure *(f)* hour (P); **à l'heure** on time (4); **À tout à l'heure.** See you in a little while. (P); **heure officielle** military time, 24-hour clock; **Il est... heure(s).** It's . . . o'clock. (P); **Quelle heure est-il?** What time is it? (P); **tout à l'heure** in a little while (P), a little while ago
heureusement luckily
heureux(-euse) happy (7)
hier yesterday (5)
hi-fi: chaîne hi-fi *(f)* stereo (2)
histoire *(f)* history (1); story (9)
historique historical (9)
historiquement historically
hiver *(m)* winter (5); **en hiver** in winter (5)
*****hockey** *(m)* hockey (2)
*****homard** *(m)* lobster (8)
homme *(m)* man (1); **homme** *(m)* **d'affaires** businessman (5)
homogène homogeneous
honnête honest
honnêteté *(f)* honesty
honneur *(f)* honor
hôpital *(m)* hospital
horaire *(m)* schedule
horreur *(f)* horror
horrible horrible (6)
*****hors de** outside of
*****hors-d'œuvre** *(m)* (inv) hors d'oeuvre, appetizer (8)
hôte *(m)* host; **chambre** *(f)* **d'hôte** bed and breakfast
hôtel *(m)* hotel (5)
hôtelier(-ère) *(mf)* hotel manager (10)
hôtesse *(f)* hostess
huile *(f)* oil
*****huit** eight (P); **huit jours** one week
*****huitième** eighth (3)
huître *(f)* oyster (8)
humain(e) human; **sciences humaines** *(fpl)* social sciences (1)
humanité *(f)* humanity
humer to breathe in
humeur *(f)* mood; **de bonne humeur** in a good mood
humour *(m)* humor; **sens** *(m)* **de l'humour** sense of humor (7)
hypermarché *(m)* superstore
hypertension *(f)* high blood pressure

I

ici here (P); **par ici** this way (5)
idéaliste idealistic (1)
idée *(f)* idea (4)
identifier to identify
identité *(f)* identity; **carte** *(f)* **/ pièce** *(f)* **d'identité** identity card
igname *(f)* yam
il he (1), it (P); **il faut...** it is necessary . . . , one must . . . (8); **il ne faut pas** one should not, one must not (10); **ils** they (1); **il y a** there is, there are (1), ago (5); **Qu'est-ce qu'il y a?** What's the matter?; **s'il vous plaît** please (P)
île *(f)* island (9)
imaginaire imaginary
imaginer to imagine
immédiatement immediately
immeuble *(m)* apartment building (3)
immigré(e) *(mf)* immigrant
immobilier(-ère) real estate
imparfait *(m)* imperfect
impatient(e) impatient (4)
impératif *(m)* imperative
imperméable *(m)* raincoat (5)
impoli(e) impolite
importance *(f)* importance (7)
important(e) important (5)
importer to be important; **n'importe où** (just) anywhere; **n'importe quel(le)** (just) any; **n'importe qui** (just) anyone; **n'importe quoi** (just) anything
imposer to impose, to lay down
impressionnant(e) impressive
imprimé(e) printed
inaccessibilité *(f)* inaccessibility
inactif(-ive) inactive, non-working
inattendu(e) unexpected
inciter à to make one feel
inclure to include; **inclus(e)** included
inconditionnel(le) *(mf)* devotee
inconstitutionnel(le) unconstitutional
inconvénient *(m)* disadvantage
incroyable incredible
Inde *(f)* India
indécision *(f)* indecision (7)
indéfini indefinite
indépendant(e) independent
indicatif régional *(m)* area code
indications *(fpl)* directions (10)
indifférence *(f)* indifference (7)
indigène native
indigestion *(f)* indigestion (10)
indiquer to show, to indicate (3); **indiqué(e)** indicated; **indiquer le chemin** to give directions, to show the way (10)
indispensable essential
individu *(m)* individual
Indochine *(f)* Indochina
industrie *(f)* industry
inégalé(e) unequaled
inégalité *(f)* inequality
inférieur(e) inferior, lower
infidélité *(f)* unfaithfulness (7)
infinitif *(m)* infinitive
infirmier(-ère) *(mf)* nurse
influencer to influence; **s'influencer** to influence each other
informatique *(f)* computer science (1)
informer to inform; **s'informer** to find out information (9)
infusion *(f)* herbal tea
ingénieur *(m)* engineer
innover to innovate
inquiétant(e) disturbing
inscription *(f)* registration

inscrire to register; **s'inscrire** to register (3)
insensibilité *(f)* insensitivity (7)
insister to insist (10)
instabilité *(f)* instability
installation *(f)* arrangements
installer: s'installer (à / dans) to settle (in), to move (into) (7), to set up business
instant *(m)* instant; **Un instant!** Just a moment!
institut *(m)* institute
instituteur(-trice) *(mf)* elementary school teacher
instrument *(m)* **de musique** musical instrument
insulter to insult
insupportable unbearable, intolerable
intellectuel(le) intellectual (1)
intelligent(e) intelligent (1)
intention: avoir l'intention de to plan on, to intend to (4)
interdire to forbid; **interdit(e)** forbidden
intéressant(e) interesting (P)
intéresser to interest; **s'intéresser à** to be interested in (7)
intérêt *(m)* interest
intérieur *(m)* inside
intermédiaire intermediate
Internet *(m)* Internet; **sur Internet** on the Internet (9)
interprète *(mf)* interpreter
interprété(e) interpreted
interrogatif(-ive) interrogative, question
interroger to question
interrompre to interrupt
intitulé(e) titled, called
introduire to introduce
introverti(e) introverted
investir to invest
invitation *(f)* invitation (6)
invité(e) *(mf)* guest
inviter (à) to invite (to) (2)
iPod *(m)* iPod (3)
irresponsable irresponsible
irriter to irritate
isolé(e) isolated
Israël *(m)* Israel (9)
issu(e): être issu(e) de to come from
Italie *(f)* Italy (9)
italien(ne) Italian
italique: en italique in italics
itinéraire *(m)* itinerary (9)
ivoirien(ne) from Côte d'Ivoire

J
jadis formerly
jalousie *(f)* jealousy (7)
jaloux(-ouse) jealous (7)
jamais: ne... jamais never (2)
jambe *(f)* leg (10); **se casser la jambe** to break your leg
jambon *(m)* ham (2); **sandwich** *(m)* **au jambon** ham sandwich (2)
janvier *(m)* January (4)
Japon *(m)* Japan (9)
japonais *(m)* Japanese
jardin *(m)* garden (5), yard
jardinage *(m)* gardening; **faire du jardinage** to garden (5)
jardiner to garden
jaune yellow (3)
jazz *(m)* jazz (1)
je (j') I (P)
jean *(m)* jeans (5)
jet *(m)* stream
jeu *(m)* game; **jeu** *(m)* **de société** board game; **jeu** *(m)* **vidéo** video game (2)

jeudi *(m)* Thursday (P)
jeune young (1); **jeunes** *(pl)* young people
jeunesse *(f)* youth (7); **auberge** *(f)* **de jeunesse** youth hostel (10)
jogging: faire du jogging to jog (2)
joie *(f)* joy
joindre: se joindre à to join
joli(e) pretty (1)
jouer to act *(in movies and theater)* (6); **jouer à** to play *(a sport or game)* (2); **jouer de** to play *(an instrument)* (2)
jour *(m)* day (P); **C'est quel jour, aujourd'hui?** What day is today? (P); **huit jours** one week; **jour** *(m)* **de l'an** New Year's Day; **jour J** *(m)* D-day; **quinze jours** two weeks; **tous les jours** every day (P)
journal *(m)* newspaper (5), journal
journaliste *(mf)* journalist
journée *(f)* day (2), daytime; **Bonne journée!** Have a good day!; **journée continue** nine-to-five schedule; **toute la journée** the whole day (2)
joyeux(-euse) happy; **Joyeux Noël!** Merry Christmas!
juif(-ive) *(mf)* Jew
juillet *(m)* July (4)
juin *(m)* June (4)
jumeau (jumelle) twin (1)
jupe *(f)* skirt (5)
jus (de fruit) *(m)* (fruit) juice (2)
jusqu'à until, up to (2)
jusque until
juste just (10), fair, **juste là** right there
justement precisely, exactly; as a matter of fact (3)
justifier to justify

K
kilo *(m)* kilo(gram) *(2.2 pounds)* (8)
kilomètre *(m)* kilometer *(.6 miles)*
kiosque *(m)* kiosk

L
la the (1), her, it (5)
là there (8); **à ce moment-là** at that time; **ce...-là** that. . . ; **là-bas** over there (8)
laboratoire: laboratoire *(m)* **de langues / d'informatique** language / computer laboratory (1)
lac *(m)* lake
laid(e) ugly (1)
laïque lay, secular, civil
laisser to leave (behind) (3), to let; **laisser tomber** to drop
lait *(m)* milk (8); **café au lait** coffee with milk (2)
laitier(-ère) milk, dairy
laitue *(f)* lettuce (8)
lampe *(f)* lamp (3); **lampe** *(f)* **de poche** flashlight
langouste *(f)* spiny lobster
langoustines *(fpl)* scampi
langue *(f)* language (1); tongue
lapin *(m)* rabbit
laqué(e) lacquered, with a gloss finish
lardon *(m)* piece of bacon
large wide
largement widely
lavabo *(m)* washbasin, sink (10)
laver to wash; **se laver** to wash (up) (7)
lave-vaisselle *(m)* dishwasher
le the (1), him, it (5); **le lundi** on Mondays (P); **le matin** in the morning, mornings (P); **le week-end** on the weekend, weekends (P)
leçon *(f)* lesson

lecteur (lectrice) *(mf)* reader; **lecteur** *(m)* **CD** CD player (3); **lecteur** *(m)* **DVD** DVD player (3); **lecteur MP3** *(m)* MP3 player (3)
lecture *(f)* reading
léger(-ère) light (8)
légume *(m)* vegetable (8)
lendemain *(m)* the next day (5)
lentement slowly (8)
lequel (laquelle, lesquels, lesquelles) which, which one(s) (6)
les the (1); them (5);
lessive *(f)* laundry (5)
lettre *(f)* letter; **lettres** *(fpl)* study of literature
leur (to, for) them (9)
leur their (3)
levant *(m)* east, sunrise
lever: se lever to get up (7)
lèvre *(f)* lip
liaison *(f)* linking, link
libéral(e) *(mpl* **libéraux)** liberal (7)
libérer: se libérer to free oneself
liberté *(f)* freedom
librairie *(f)* bookstore (1)
libre free (2); **temps libre** *(m)* free time (4)
licence *(f)* *three-year university degree*
licencié(e) *(mf)* *someone with the licence degree*
lien *(m)* link
lié(e) linked
lier to connect, to link
lieu *(m)* place; **avoir lieu** to take place
light: coca *(m)* **light** diet cola (2)
ligne *(f)* figure; line; **en ligne** online (7)
limande *(f)* dab
limité(e) limited
limiter to limit, to border; **se limiter à** to limit oneself to
linguistique linguistic
liquide *(m)* liquid (10)
lire to read (2); **Lisez...** Read . . . (P)
liste *(f)* list
lit *(m)* bed (3); **rester au lit** to stay in bed (2)
litre *(m)* liter *(approximately one quart)* (8)
littéraire literary
littérature *(f)* literature (1)
living *(m)* living room
livre *(m)* book (P)
livre *(f)* pound, half-kilo (8)
livrer: se livrer à to participate in
local(e) *(mpl* **locaux)** local (9)
locataire *(mf)* renter
location *(f)* rental; **voiture** *(f)* **de location** rental car (5)
logement *(m)* lodging (3)
loger to lodge
logique logical
logiquement logically
loi *(f)* law
loin (de) far (from) (3); **au loin** in the distance; **de loin** by far
loisir *(m)* leisure activity
Londres London
long: le long de along (9); **au long de** along
long(ue) long (4)
longtemps a long time (5)
longueur *(f)* length
lors de at the time of
lorsque when
loterie *(f)* lottery
loto *(m)* lotto, bingo
louer to rent (4)
Louisiane *(f)* Louisiana
loup *(m)* wolf
lourd(e) heavy
loyer *(m)* rent (3)
lui him (6), (to, for) him (9); **lui-même** himse

lundi *(m)* Monday (P)
lune *(f)* moon; **lune** *(f)* **de miel** honeymoon
lunettes *(fpl)* glasses (4); **lunettes** *(fpl)* **de soleil** sunglasses (5)
lutte *(f)* struggle, fight
lutter to struggle, to fight
luxe *(m)* luxury; **de luxe** deluxe (10)
luxembourgeois *(m)* Luxemburgian *(native language of Luxembourg)*
luxembourgeois(e) from Luxembourg
lycée *(m)* French secondary school (6)
lycéen(ne) *(mf)* high school student (6)

M
macérer to soak
madame (Mme) *(f)* madam (Mrs.) (P)
mademoiselle (Mlle) *(f)* miss (P)
magasin *(m)* store, shop (4)
magazine *(m)* magazine (9)
magnétoscope *(m)* video cassette recorder
magnifique magnificent
mai *(m)* May (4)
maigre skinny (8)
maigrir to get thinner, to slim down (8)
mail *(m)* e-mail (2)
maillot *(m)* **de bain** swimsuit (5)
main *(f)* hand (7)
maintenant now (P)
maintenir to maintain
maire *(m)* mayor
mairie *(f)* town hall
mais but (P)
maïs *(m)* corn
maison *(f)* house (1); **à la maison** (at) home (P); **maison** *(f)* **d'édition** publishing company
maître *(m)* master
maîtrise *(f)* master's degree
majoré(e) with a surcharge
majoritaire *(adj)* majority
majorité *(f)* majority
mal *(m)* bad, evil; **avoir mal à... ** one's. . . hurts (10); **faire mal (à)** to hurt
mal badly (P); **mal à l'aise** ill at ease; **pas mal** not bad(ly) (P)
malade *(mf)* sick person
malade ill, sick (10)
maladie *(f)* illness
malaise *(f)* discomfort
malgache from Madagascar
malgré in spite of
malheureusement unfortunately
malheureux(-euse) unhappy
malhonnête dishonest
maman *(f)* mama, mom
mamie *(f)* granny, grandma (7)
Manche *(f)* English Channel
mandarine *(f)* tangerine
mandat *(m)* money order
manger to eat (2); **donner à manger à** to feed (9); **salle** *(f)* **à manger** dining room (3)
mangue *(f)* mango
manière *(f)* manner, way
manifestation *(f)* demonstration; **manifestation sportive** *(f)* sports event
manifester: se manifester to be reflected
manoir *(m)* manor, country house
manquer to miss, to lack
manteau *(m)* overcoat (5)
manuel *(m)* textbook
manufacturier(-ère) manufacturing
manuscrit *(m)* manuscript
maquillage *(m)* make-up
maquiller: se maquiller to put on make-up (7)
marais *(m)* swamp

marchand(e) *(mf)* merchant, shopkeeper (6); **marchand** *(m)* **de cadeaux** gift shop (10)
marche à pied *(f)* walking; **faire de la marche à pied** to go walking
marché *(m)* market (8)
marcher to walk (8), to work
mardi *(m)* Tuesday (P); **Mardi gras** *(m)* Fat Tuesday
maréchal *(m)* marshall
marée *(f)* tide
marge *(f)* margin
mari *(m)* husband (2); **ex-mari** *(m)* ex-husband
mariage *(m)* marriage (7)
marié(e) married (1)
marier: se marier (avec) to get married (to) (7)
marinier(-ère): moules marinières *(f)* mussels cooked with onions and white wine
marketing *(m)* marketing (1)
Maroc *(m)* Morocco (9)
marocain(e) Moroccan
marquer to mark
marron *(inv)* brown (3)
mars *(m)* March (4)
martiniquais(e) from Martinique
masse *(f)* **d'eau** body of water
massif *(m)* group of mountains, clump
match *(m)* match, game (1)
matelas *(m)* mattress
matérialiste materialistic
matériel(le) material
matériellement materially
maternel(le) maternal; **école maternelle** *(f)* kindergarten
mathématiques *(fpl)* mathematics (1)
maths *(fpl)* math (1)
matière *(f)* matter; **matières grasses** fat (8)
matin *(m)* morning (P); **À huit heures du matin.** At eight o'clock in the morning. (P); **le matin** mornings, in the morning (P)
matinée *(f)* morning (2)
matrimonial(e) *(mpl* **matrimoniaux***)* marriage
mauvais(e) bad (1); **Il fait mauvais.** The weather's bad. (5)
me (to, for) me (9), myself (7); **Ça me plaît!** I like it! (3); **il me faut...** I need. . . (9)
méchant(e) mean (1)
mécontent(e) displeased
médaille *(f)* medal
médecin *(m)* doctor, physician (10)
médicament *(m)* medication, medicine, drugs (10)
médiocre mediocre (6)
Méditerranée: (mer) Méditerranée *(f)* Mediterranean (Sea)
méditerranéen(ne) Mediterranean
méfiance *(f)* mistrust
meilleur(e) best (1), better
mélange *(m)* mixture
membre *(m)* member
même same (1), even; **moi-même** myself; **quand même** all the same
mémoire *(f)* memory
menacer to threaten
ménage *(m)* housework (5), household
ménager(-ère) household
mener to lead
menhir *(m)* menhir *(an ancient megalithic structure)*
menthe *(f)* mint
mentionner to mention
mentir to lie
menu *(m)* menu (8)
mépris *(m)* scorn
mer *(f)* sea (9); **bord** *(m)* **de la mer** seaside; **fruits** *(mpl)* **de mer** shellfish (8)

merci (bien) thank you, thanks (P)
mercredi *(m)* Wednesday (P)
mère *(f)* mother (4)
méritoire deserving
merveille *(f)* marvel, wonder
merveilleux(-euse) marvelous
messager(-ère) *(mf)* messenger (6)
messieurs (MM.) gentlemen, sirs
mesurer to measure
métier *(m)* occupation
métrage: court métrage *(m)* short film
mètre *(m)* meter
métrique metric
métro *(m)* subway (4); **en métro** by subway (4)
metteur *(m)* **en scène** director
mettre to put (on), to place (5); **mettre à part** to set aside; **mettre en scène** to present; **mettre en valeur** to emphasize; **mettre la table** to set the table; **se mettre d'accord** to come to an agreement
meublé(e) furnished
meubles *(mpl)* furniture, furnishings (3)
meurtre *(m)* murder
meurtrier *(m)* murderer
meurtrière *(f)* murderess
Mexico Mexico City
Mexique *(m)* Mexico (9)
mi- mid-, half-; **cheveux mi-longs** *(mpl)* shoulder-length hair (4)
micro-ondes *(m)* microwave oven
midi *(m)* noon (P)
mie: pain *(m)* **de mie** soft sandwich bread
mieux (que) better (than) (2); **aimer mieux** to prefer (2); **il vaut mieux** it's better (10); **le mieux** the best (7)
milieu *(m)* middle, milieu, environment; **au milieu (de)** in the middle (of)
militaire military
mille one thousand (3)
mille-feuille *(f)* mille-feuille *(a layered pastry)*
millénaire *(m)* millennium
million: un million (de) *(m)* one million (3)
mince thin (1)
minéral(e) *(mpl* **minéraux***)*: **eau minérale** *(f)* mineral water (2)
minier(-ère): exploitation minière *(f)* mining
ministère *(m)* ministry, department
ministre *(m)* minister, secretary
minoritaire minority
minorité *(f)* minority
minuit *(m)* midnight (P)
minute *(f)* minute (5)
miroir *(m)* mirror
mise *(f)* putting; **mise** *(f)* **en bouteille** bottling; **mise** *(f)* **en place** establishment; **mise** *(f)* **en relief** highlighting, accentuating
misère *(f)* misery
mobile *(m)* motive
mobilier *(m)* furnishings
mode *(f)* fashion, *(m)* type
modèle *(m)* model
moderne modern (1)
moi me (P); **chez moi** at my house (2); **Donnez-moi...** Give me . . . (P); **Excusez-moi.** Excuse me. (P); **moi-même** myself
moindre: le moindre the least
moins minus (P); **au moins** at least; **de moins en moins** fewer and fewer, less and less; **Il est trois heures moins le quart.** It's a quarter to three. (P); **le moins** the least; **moins de** fewer, less (8); **moins... que** less . . . than (1)
mois *(m)* month (3); **ce mois-ci** this month (4); **par mois** per month (3)
moitié *(f)* half

moment *(m)* moment; **à ce moment-là** at that time; **au dernier moment** at the last minute
mon (ma, mes) my (3); **ma famille** my family (P); **mes amis** my friends (1)
monarchie *(f)* monarchy
monde *(m)* world, crowd; **faire le tour du monde** to take a trip around the world; **Tiers-Monde** *(m)* Third World; **tout le monde** everybody, everyone (6)
mondial(e) *(mpl* **mondiaux)** world(-wide)
monétaire monetary
monnaie *(f)* change (2), currency
monoparental(e) *(mpl* **monoparentaux)** single parent
monotonie *(f)* monotony
monsieur (M.) *(m)* mister (Mr.), sir (P), man
monstre *(m)* monster (6)
mont *(m)* mount
montagne *(f)* mountain (5); **aller à la montagne** to go to the mountains (5)
montagneux(-euse) mountainous
monter (dans) to go up; to get on/in (5), to set up, to climb
montre *(f)* watch (5)
montrer to show (3)
morceau *(m)* piece (8)
moribond(e) moribund, dying
mort *(f)* death
mort(e) dead (5)
mosaïque *(f)* mosaic
mosquée *(f)* mosque
mot *(m)* word (P)
moule *(f)* mussel (8)
moulin *(m)* mill
mourant(e) dying
mourir to die (5)
moustache *(f)* mustache (4)
moutarde *(f)* mustard
mouton *(m)* sheep
mouvement *(m)* movement
moyen *(m)* means; **moyen** *(m)* **de transport** means of transportation (4)
moyen(ne) medium; **de taille moyenne** medium-sized (4); **Moyen-Orient** *(m)* Middle East (9)
moyenne *(f)* average; **en moyenne** on average
MP3: lecteur *(m)* **MP3** MP3 player (3)
MST *(f)* STD
muet(te) silent
multiplier to multiply
mur *(m)* wall (3)
musculation: faire de la musculation to do weight training, to do bodybuilding (8)
musée *(m)* museum (4)
musical(e) *(mpl* **musicaux): comédie musicale** *(f)* musical
musicien(ne) *(mf)* musician
musicien(ne) musical
musique *(f)* music (1); **musique zydeco** zydeco music (4)
musulman(e) Muslim
myrtille *(f)* blueberry
mystère *(m)* mystery

N

nager to swim (2)
naissance *(f)* birth
naître to be born (5); **être né(e)** to be born (5)
natal(e) native
nationalité *(f)* nationality (3)
nature *(f)* nature (7); **grandeur nature** *(f)* life-sized; **nature morte** *(f)* still life; **omelette nature** *(f)* plain omelet
naturel(le) natural
naturellement naturally

nausée *(f)* nausea
nautique: faire du ski nautique *(m)* to go water-skiing (5)
navette *(f)* shuttle (10)
ne: je ne travaille pas I don't work (P); **ne... aucun(e)** none, not one; **ne... jamais** never (2); **ne... ni... ni...** neither . . . nor; **ne... nulle** part nowhere; **ne... pas (du tout)** not (at all) (1); **ne... pas encore** not yet (5); **ne... personne** nobody, no one; **ne... plus** no more, no longer (8); **ne... que** only; **ne... rien** nothing (5); **ne... rien que** nothing but; **n'est-ce pas?** right? (1); **n'importe où** (just) anywhere
né(e) born (5); **être né(e)** to be born (5)
nécessaire necessary (10)
nécessiteux *(mpl)* needy
néerlandais(e) Dutch
néfaste harmful
négliger to neglect
négocier to negociate
neige *(f)* snow (5)
neiger to snow (5)
nerf *(m)* nerve; **maladie** *(f)* **des nerfs** nervous disorder; **nerfs à vif** nerves on edge
nerveux(-euse) nervous
n'est-ce pas? right? (1)
Net: surfer le Net to surf the Net (2)
neuf nine (P)
neuf (neuve) brand-new
neutralité *(f)* neutrality
neutre neutral
neveu *(m)* *(pl* **neveux)** nephew (4)
neuvième ninth (3)
nez *(m)* nose (10); **avoir le nez bouché** to have a stopped-up nose
ni: ne... ni... ni... neither . . . nor
niçois(e) from Nice
nièce *(f)* niece (4)
niveau *(m)* level
Noël *(m)* Christmas
noir(e) black (3); **Il faisait noir.** It was dark.
noisette *(inv)* hazel *(with eyes)* (4)
nom *(m)* name (3); **au nom de** in the name of; **nom de famille** family name, surname (3)
nombre *(m)* number
nombreux(-euse) numerous
nommé(e) named
nommer to name
non no (P); **non?** right? (1); **non plus** neither (3)
non-pratiquant(e) *(mf)* non-churchgoer
nord *(m)* north; **Amérique** *(f)* **du Nord** North America (9)
normal(e) *(mpl* **normaux)** normal
normalement normally
Norvège *(f)* Norway
note *(f)* grade, note; **régler la note** to pay the bill (10)
noter to note, to notice
notre *(pl* **nos)** our (3)
nourrir to feed, to nourish, to nurture (8); **se nourrir** to feed oneself, to nourish oneself, to nurture oneself (8)
nourriture *(f)* food, nourishment
nous we (1); (to, for) us (9), ourselves (7); **avec nous** with us (2); **Nous sommes six.** There are six of us. (4)
nouveau (nouvel, nouvelle) new (1); **de nouveau** again, anew; **Nouvelle-Angleterre** *(f)* New England; **Nouvelle-Calédonie** *(f)* New Caledonia (9); **La Nouvelle-Orléans** *(f)* New Orleans (4)
novembre *(m)* November (4)
noyau *(m)* pit

nu(e) naked; **pieds nus** barefoot
nuage *(m)* cloud
nuageux(-euse) cloudy
nucléaire nuclear
nuisible harmful
nuit *(f)* night (5); **boîte** *(f)* **de nuit** nightclub (1)
nul(le) (en) no good (at), really bad (at); **ne... nulle part** nowhere
numéro *(m)* number (3), issue
numéroté(e) numbered

O

obéir (à) to obey (8)
objectif *(m)* objective
objet *(m)* object
obligatoire obligatory, required
obligeance *(f)* kindness
obliger to force, to make; **obligé(e)** obliged, forced
observer to observe
obtenir to get, to obtain
occasion: d'occasion second-hand
occidental(e) *(mpl* **occidentaux)** western
occitan *(m)* Occitan
occupé(e) busy
occuper to occupy; **s'occuper de** to take care of
océan *(m)* ocean
Océanie *(f)* Oceania (9)
octobre *(m)* October (4)
œil *(pl* **yeux)** *(m)* eye (10); **avoir les yeux...** to have . . . eyes (4)
œuf *(m)* egg (8); **œuf dur** *(m)* hard-boiled egg (8)
œuvre *(f)* work
office *(m)* **de tourisme** tourist office (10)
officiel(le) official
officiellement officially
offrir to offer; **offrant** offering
oignon *(m)* onion (8); **soupe** *(f)* **à l'oignon** onion soup (8)
oiseau *(m)* bird
ombre *(f)* shadow, shade
omelette *(f)* omelet (8)
on one, they, we, people, you (4); **Comment dit-on... en français?** How do you say . . . in French? (P); **On... ?** Shall we . . . ?, How about. . . ? (4); **On dit que...** They say that . . . (4); **On va... ?** Shall we go. . . ? (2)
oncle *(m)* uncle (4)
Ontario *(m)* Ontario (9)
onze eleven (P)
opposer to oppose; **s'opposer** to confront each other
oppresseur *(m)* oppressor
opprimé(e) oppressed
opter to opt
optimiste optimistic (1)
or *(m)* gold
orage *(m)* storm
orange *(f)* orange (8); **jus** *(m)* **d'orange** orange juice (2)
orange *(inv)* orange (3)
Orangina *(m)* Orangina *(an orange drink)* (2)
oratoire *(m)* oratory, small chapel
orchestre *(m)* orchestra, band (4)
ordinateur *(m)* computer (2)
ordonnance *(f)* prescription (10)
ordre *(m)* order; **en ordre** in order (3)
oreille *(f)* ear (10)
oreiller *(m)* pillow
oreillons *(mpl)* mumps
organiser to organize; **s'organiser** to get organized
organisme *(m)* organism, body

originaire de coming from
origine *(f)* origin; **d'origine...** of. . . origin (7)
orner to decorate
orthographique spelling
os *(m)* bone
ou or (P)
où where (1); **d'où** from where (1); **n'importe où** (just) anywhere
oublier to forget (8)
ouest *(m)* west
oui yes (P)
outre-mer overseas
ouvert(e) open
ouverture *(f)* opening
ouvrir to open; **Ouvrez...** Open . . . (P)

P

pacifique pacific, peaceful
page *(f)* page (P)
paiement *(m)* payment
pain *(m)* bread (8); **pain au chocolat** *(m)* croissant with chocolate filling (8); **pain complet** *(m)* wholegrain bread (8); **pain grillé** *(m)* toast (8)
pair: jeune fille au pair au pair, nanny
paisible peaceful, calm
paix *(f)* peace; **Corps** *(m)* **de la Paix** Peace Corps
palais *(m)* palace (6)
pâle pale
palme *(f)* palm leaf
pamplemousse *(m)* grapefruit
panique *(f)* panic
panoramique panoramic
pantalon *(m)* pants (5)
papa *(m)* dad, papa
papier *(m)* paper; **feuille** *(f)* **de papier** sheet of paper (P)
pâque juive *(f)* Passover
Pâques *(fpl)* Easter
paquet *(m)* package, bag (8)
par per (3), by; **par ailleurs** furthermore; **par conséquent** consequently; **par contre** on the other hand; **par exemple** for example (2); **par *hasard** by chance; **par ici** this way (5); **par la fenêtre** through the window; **par mois** per month (3); **par terre** on the ground / floor (3)
paradis *(m)* paradise, heaven
paraître to appear
parapluie *(m)* umbrella (5)
parc *(m)* park (1); **parc naturel** natural park, nature reserve
parce que because (P)
parcourir to skim, to glance through
Pardon. Excuse me. (P)
pardonner to forgive, to pardon
pareil(le) (à) similar (to)
parent *(m)* parent (4), relative (5); **chez mes parents** at my parents' house (3)
parenté *(f)* relationship
parenthèses *(fpl)* parentheses
paresseux(-euse) lazy (1)
parfait(e) perfect (7)
parfaitement perfectly (7)
parfois sometimes
parfum *(m)* perfume
Parisien(ne) *(mf)* Parisian (9)
parking *(m)* parking lot (1), parking garage
parlementaire parlementary
parler to talk, to speak (2); **je parle** I speak (P); **se parler** to talk to each other (7); **Vous parlez... ?** Do you speak. . . ? (P)
parmi among
paroisse *(f)* parish

parole *(f)* word, lyric
part: à part... besides . . . ; **à part entière** complete; **mettre à part** to set aside; **ne... nulle part** nowhere; **quelque part** somewhere
partager to share (3), to divide up; **partagé(e)** shared, divided (3)
partenaire *(mf)* partner (7)
parti (politique) *(m)* (political) party
participer (à) to participate (in)
particulier(-ère) particular, private; **en particulier** especially
partie part *(f)*; **en grande partie** mostly, in large part; **en partie** partially; **faire partie de** to be a part of
partir (de... pour) to leave (from . . . for), to go away (4); **à partir de** starting from; **partir en voyage** to leave on a trip (5)
partout everywhere (3)
pas not (P); **je ne comprends pas** I don't understand (P); **ne... pas (du tout)** not (at all) (1); **ne... pas encore** not yet (5); **Pas de problème!** No problem! (3); **pas plus** no more (4)
passant(e) *(mf)* passerby
passé *(m)* past (6)
passeport *(m)* passport (9)
passer to spend, to pass (2); **passer chez** to go by . . .'s house (2); **passer le temps / la matinée** to spend one's time / the morning (2); **passer un film** to show a movie (6); **Qu'est-ce qui s'est passé?** What happened? (7); **s'en passer** to do without; **se passer** to happen (7)
passe-temps *(m)* pastime (2)
passion *(f)* passion (7)
pastèque *(f)* watermelon
pâte *(f)* paste, dough
pâté *(m)* pâté, meat spread (8)
patience *(f)* patience; **avoir de la patience** to have patience (4)
patient(e) *(mf)* patient
patient(e) patient (6)
patin *(m)* skate; **patin** *(m)* **à glace** ice-skate, iceskating; **patin** *(m)* **à roulettes** roller skate, roller skating
pâtisserie *(f)* pastry shop, pastry
patrie *(f)* homeland
patrimoine *(m)* patrimony, heritage
patron(ne) *(mf)* owner, boss
pâturage *(m)* pasture
pauvre poor
pavé *(m)* thick slice (8)
pavé(e) paved
payant(e) not free
payer to pay (2)
pays *(m)* country (3)
paysage *(m)* landscape (9)
Pays-Bas *(mpl)* Netherlands
peau *(f)* skin
pêche *(f)* peach (8), fishing; **aller à la pêche** to go fishing
peigner: se peigner to comb one's hair (7)
peintre *(m)* painter
peinture *(f)* painting
pèlerin *(m)* pilgrim
pendant during, for (5); **pendant que** while
pensée *(f)* thought
penser to think (2); **penser à** think about; **je pense que** I think that (P)
pension *(f)* room and board
perçu(e) perceived
perdre to lose, to waste (time) (7); **perdu(e)** lost; **se perdre** to get lost (7)
père *(m)* father (4); **le père Noël** Santa Claus
perfectionnement *(m)* perfecting
perfectionner to perfect

période *(f)* period
permettre (de) to permit, to allow; **permis(e)** permitted, allowed
Pérou *(m)* Peru (9)
perpétuel(le) perpetual
personnage *(m)* character
personnalisé(e) personalized (8)
personnalité *(f)* personality (1)
personne *(f)* person (6); **ne... personne** nobody, no one
personnel(le) personal; **effets personnels** *(mpl)* personal belongings (3)
persuader to persuade
perte: à perte de vue as far as you can see
pessimiste pessimistic (1)
petit(e) small, little, short (1); **petit ami** *(m)* boyfriend (2); **petit à petit** little by little (6); **petit déjeuner** *(m)* breakfast (5); **petite amie** *(f)* girlfriend (2); **petite annonce** *(f)* classified ad; **petits pois** *(mpl)* peas (8)
petite-fille *(f)* granddaughter (7)
petit-fils *(m)* grandson (7)
petits-enfants *(mpl)* grandchildren
pétrole *(m)* oil
pétrolier(-ière): industries pétrolières *(f)* oil industry
peu little (P); **à peu près** approximately, about
peuple *(m)* people
peur *(f)* fear; **avoir peur (de)** to be afraid (of), to fear (4); **faire peur à** to frighten
peut-être perhaps, maybe (3)
pharmacie *(f)* pharmacy (10)
pharmacien(ne) *(mf)* pharmacist
philosophe *(mf)* philosopher
philosophie *(f)* philosophy (1)
photo *(f)* photo
phrase *(f)* sentence (P)
physiologique physiological
physique *(f)* physics (1)
physique physical; **aspect physique** *(m)* physical appearance (7)
piano *(m)* piano (2)
pièce *(f)* room (3); **pièce** *(f)* **de théâtre** play (4); **pièce** *(f)* **d'identité** identity card
pied *(m)* foot (10); **aller à pied** to walk, to go on foot (4); **doigt** *(m)* **de pied** toe (10); **pieds nus** barefoot
pin *(m)* pine
pique-nique *(m)* picnic
pire worse
piscine *(f)* swimming pool (4)
piste *(f)* trail, lead
pitié *(f)* pity; **avoir pitié (de)** to have pity (on / for) (10)
pizza *(f)* pizza (8)
placard *(m)* closet (3)
place *(f)* square, place, plaza (10); **à sa place** in its place (3)
plage *(f)* beach (4)
plaine *(f)* plain
plaire to please (9); **Ça me plaît!** I like it! (3); **Ça t'a plu?** Did you like it? (6); **Ça te plaira!** You'll like it! (9); **Ça te plaît!** You like it! (3); **s'il vous plaît** please (P)
plaisant(e) pleasant
plaisir *(m)* pleasure; **Avec plaisir!** It would be a pleasure! (6); **faire plaisir à** to please
plan *(m)* map, level; **plan** *(m)* **d'eau** stretch of water
planche *(f)* **à voile** windsurfing; **faire de la planche à voile** to windsurf
plante *(f)* plant (3)
planter to plant
plastique *(m)* plastic; **sac** *(m)* **en plastique** plastic bag

plat *(m)* dish (8); **plat préparé** *(m)* ready-to-serve dish (8)

plat(e) flat; **œuf au plat** *(m)* fried egg

plateau *(m)* tray

platine *(m)* platinum; **platine laser** *(f)* CD player

plein(e) full; **de plein air** outdoor (4); **plein de** full of, a lot of

pleur *(m)* sobbing

pleurer to cry

pleuvoir to rain (5)

plongée sous-marine *(f)* scuba diving

plonger to dive, to plunge

pluie *(f)* rain (5)

plupart: la plupart *(f)* the most part; **la plupart de** *(f)* the majority of (7); **la plupart du temps** most of the time (7)

plus plus; **À plus tard!** See you later! (2); **de plus** in addition; **de plus en plus** more and more (8); **en plus** besides, furthermore (8); **ne... plus** no more, no longer (8); **non plus** neither (3); **pas plus** no more (4); **plus de** more (8); **plus... que** more . . . than (1); **plus tard** later (4)

plusieurs several (8)

plutôt rather (1); instead (4); **plutôt que** rather than

poche *(f)* pocket; **lampe** *(f)* **de poche** flashlight

poêle *(f)* frying pan

poêlée (de) *(f)* frying pan full (of)

poème *(m)* poem (9)

poésie *(f)* poetry

poète *(m)* poet

poids *(m)* weight

poing *(m)* fist

point *(m)* point; **au point de** to be about to; **point** *(m)* **de vue** viewpoint

poire *(f)* pear (8)

poireau *(m)* leek

pois: petits pois *(mpl)* peas (8)

poisson *(m)* fish (8); **poissons** *(mpl)* **d'avril** April Fool's Day

poissonnerie *(f)* fish shop (8)

poitrine *(f)* chest

poivre *(m)* pepper (8)

poivron *(m)* (bell) pepper

poli(e) polite

police *(f)* police, policy

policier(-ère) detective, police

politesse *(f)* politeness

politique *(f)* politics (7), policy

politique political; **homme politique** *(m)* politician

polo *(m)* knit shirt (5)

Pologne *(f)* Poland

Polynésie française *(f)* French Polynesia (9)

pomme *(f)* apple (8); **pomme** *(f)* **de terre** potato (8)

pommier *(m)* apple tree

populaire popular, pop (1)

porc *(m)* pork (8); **côte** *(f)* **de porc** pork chop (8)

portable *(m)* cell phone, laptop (3)

porte *(f)* door (3); **porte** *(f)* **d'arrivée** arrival gate (9); **porte** *(f)* **d'embarquement** departure gate (9)

portefeuille *(m)* wallet (5)

porte-parole de *(m, inv)* spokesperson for

porter to wear, to carry

portugais *(m)* Portuguese

poser to place; **poser une question** to ask a question (3)

posséder to possess, to own

possibilité *(f)* possibility (4)

postal(e) *(mpl* **postaux): carte postale** *(f)* post-card (9); **code postal** *(m)* zip code (3)

poste *(f)* post office; **bureau** *(m)* **de poste** post office (10)

poste *(m)* position

pot *(m)* jar (8)

poubelle *(f)* trash can

poudre *(f)* powder

poulet *(m)* chicken (8)

poumon *(m)* lung

pour for (P), in order to (1); **pour cent** percent; **pour que** so that

pourcentage *(m)* percentage

pourquoi why (2)

poursuite *(f)* pursuit, chase

poursuivre to pursue

pourtant however (8)

pousser to push

poussière *(f)* dust

pouvoir *(m)* power

pouvoir to be able, can, may (6); **Je peux vous aider?** Can I help you? (5); **on peut** one can (4)

pratique *(f)* practice

pratique practical

pratiquement practically

pratiquer to practice, to play *(a sport),* to do

préavis *(m)* (previous) notice

précédent(e) preceding

précipitamment hurriedly

préciser to specify

préféré(e) favorite (3)

préférence *(f)* preference; **de préférence** preferably

préférer to prefer (2); **je préfère** I prefer (1)

premier(-ère) first (1); **Premier ministre** Prime Minister

prendre to take (4); **prendre contact** to get in touch; **prendre du poids** to put on weight; **prendre feu** to catch fire; **prendre possession de** to take possession of; **prendre son petit déjeuner** to have one's breakfast (5); **prendre un bain** to take a bath (7); **prendre un bain de soleil** to sunbathe (4); **prendre une décision** to make a decision (7); **prendre une douche** to take a shower (7); **prendre un verre** to have a drink (2); **Prenez une feuille de papier et un crayon ou un stylo.** Take out a piece of paper and a pencil or a pen. (P)

prénom *(m)* first name (3)

préoccuper to worry; **se préoccuper (de)** to worry (about)

préparatifs *(mpl)* preparations (9)

préparatoire preparatory

préparer to prepare (2); **plat préparé** ready-to-serve dish (8); **préparer les cours** to prepare for class, to study (2); **Préparez l'examen.** Prepare / Study for the exam. (P)

près (de) near (1), nearly; **à peu près** approximately, about

présentation *(f)* introduction

présenter to introduce, to present; **Je vous/te présente...** I would like to introduce . . . to you.; **se présenter** to arise, to introduce oneself

préservatif *(m)* condom

préserver to preserve

présider (à) to preside

presque almost, nearly (2)

presse *(f)* press

pressé(e) hurried

pression *(f)* pressure

prestigieux(-euse) prestigious

prêt(e) ready (4)

prétendre to claim

prêter to loan, to lend (9)

preuve *(f)* proof

prévisions météo *(fpl)* weather forecast

prévu(e) planned, foreseen

prier to beg, to request, to pray; **Je vous en prie.** You're welcome.

prière *(f)* prayer

primaire: école primaire *(f)* elementary school

primeur *(m)* produce

principal(e) *(mpl* **principaux)** main (8); **à titre principal** mainly

principauté *(f)* principality

principe *(m)* principle

printemps *(m)* spring (5); **au printemps** in spring (5)

prise *(f)* electrical outlet; **prise** *(f)* **en charge** taking up

prisé(e) sought after

privé(e) private (10)

privilégié(e) privileged, favored

prix *(m)* price; **à prix fixe** with a set price (8)

probablement probably

problème *(m)* problem; **pas de problème** no problem (3)

prochain(e) next (4); **le prochain cours** the next class (P)

proche (de) near (to)

production *(f)* **cinématographique** cinematic production

produire to produce

produit *(m)* product (8); **produits bios** *(mpl)* organic products (8)

professeur *(m)* professor (P)

profession *(f)* profession (7)

professionnel(le) professional (7)

profil *(m)* profile

profiter de to take advantage of (9)

profond(e) deep

programme *(m)* program

programmeur(-euse) *(mf)* computer programmer

progrès *(m)* progress

projecteur *(m)* projector

projet *(m)* plan (4); **faire des projets** to make plans (4)

promenade *(f)* walk (5); **faire une promenade** to take a walk (5)

promener: se promener to go walking (7)

promettre (de) to promise (6)

promouvoir to promote

promulguer des lois to create laws

pronom *(m)* pronoun

prononcer to pronounce

prononciation *(f)* pronunciation

proposer to offer, to suggest, to propose; **Qu'est-ce que je peux vous proposer d'autre?** What else can I get you? (8); **se proposer de** to intend

propre clean (3), own

propriétaire *(mf)* owner

propriété *(f)* property

prospérité *(f)* prosperity

protectorat *(m)* protectorate

protéger to protect; **protégé(e) par** protected by

protéines *(fpl)* protein

protestant(e) *(mf)* Protestant

provençal *(m)* Provençal

provenir de to come from

province *(f)* province (3)

provisions *(fpl)* supplies, groceries

proximité: à proximité de in the vicinity of

prune *(f)* plum

pruneau *(m)* prune

psychologie *(f)* psychology (1)

psychologique psychological
public(-que) public; **santé publique** *(f)* public health
publicité *(f)* advertising, advertisement
publier to publish
puis then (4)
puisque since
puissant(e) powerful
pull *(m)* pullover sweater (5)
punir to punish
purée *(f)* mashed potatoes
pureté *(f)* purity
pyjama *(m)* pajamas

Q

quai *(m)* quay, wharf
qualité *(f)* quality
quand when (2); **quand même** all the same
quantité *(f)* quantity
quarante forty (2)
quart *(m)* quarter; **Il est deux heures et quart.** It's a quarter past two. (P)
quartier *(m)* neighborhood (1)
quatorze fourteen (P)
quatre four (P)
quatre-vingt-dix ninety (2)
quatre-vingts eighty (2)
quatrième fourth (3)
que that (P), than, as (1), what (2), which, whom (7); **ce que** what, that which; **ne... que** only; **ne... rien que** nothing but; **que ce soit** whether it be; **qu'est-ce que** what (1); **Qu'est-ce que ça veut dire?** What does that mean? (P); **Qu'est-ce que c'est?** What is it? (2)
quel(le) which, what (3); **À quelle heure?** At what time? (P); **C'est quel jour aujourd'hui?** What day is it today? (P); **n'importe quel(le)...** (just) any . . . ; **Quel âge a... ?** How old is . . . ? (4)
quelconque any
quelque some; **quelque chose** something (2); **quelque part** somewhere; **quelques** a few, several (5); **quelqu'un** someone, somebody (6); **quelques-uns** a few
quelquefois sometimes (2)
quelques-un(e)s *(mf)* a few
question *(f)* question (P)
qui who (2), that, which, who (7); **ce qui** what (7); **Qu'est-ce qui ne va pas?** What's wrong? (10); **Qu'est-ce qui s'est passé?** What happened? (6); **Qui est-ce?** Who is it? (2)
quinze fifteen (P); **quinze jours** two weeks
quinzième fifteenth
quitter to leave (4); **se quitter** to leave each other (7)
quoi what; **n'importe quoi** (just) anything
quoique although
quotidien(ne) daily (7)

R

raccompagner to (re)accompany
raccrocher to hang up
racisme *(m)* racism
raconter to tell, to recount (7)
radio *(f)* radio (2), X-ray
rafale *(f)* blast, gust
raffinerie *(f)* refinery
raie *(f)* skate (fish), rayfish (8)
raisin *(m)* grape(s) (8); **raisins secs** *(mpl)* raisins
raison *(f)* reason; **avoir raison** to be right (4)
raisonnable reasonable
ralenti *(m)* slow motion
ralentir to slow down

ramadan *(m)* Ramadan
randonnée *(f)* hike (8); **faire une randonnée** to go for a hike (8)
rangé(e) orderly, put away, in its place (3)
ranger to arrange, to order (7)
rapide rapid (8)
rappeler to remind
rapport *(m)* relationship, report
rapporter to bring back; **se rapporter à** to be related to
rapprochement *(m)* drawing together
rapprocher: se rapprocher de to get closer to
rarement rarely (2)
raser: se raser to shave (7)
rasoir *(m)* razor
rassembler: se rassembler to gather
rassis(e) stale
rassurant(e) reassuring
rater to miss
ratifier to ratify
ravigote *(f)* vinaigrette
rayé(e) striped
réagir (à) to react (to)
réalisateur *(m)* producer
réalisation *(f)* carrying out
réaliser to accomplish
réaliste realistic (1)
réalité *(f)* reality
réapparaître to reappear
récemment recently (5)
réception *(f)* front desk (10), receiving
recette *(f)* recipe, receipt
recevoir to receive (9)
recherche *(f)* research
rechercher to seek; **recherché(e)** sought
réciproque reciprocal
recommander to recommend (10); **recommandé(e)** recommended
récompenser to recompense
réconcilier: se réconcilier to make up with each other (7)
reconfirmer to reconfirm
reconnaître to recognize (7); **se reconnaître** to recognize each other (7)
reconstruire to reconstruct
recopier to copy
recoucher: se recoucher to go back to bed (7)
recouvert(e) covered
recréer to recreate
récrire to rewrite
rédacteur(-trice) *(mf)* **en chef** editor-in-chief
rédaction *(f)* composition (9)
redéfinir to redefine
réduire to reduce
réel(le) real
référer: se référer à to refer to
refermer to close back up
réfléchi(e) reflexive
réfléchir (à) to think (about), to reflect (on) (8)
reflet *(m)* reflection
refléter to reflect
réflexion *(f)* reflection, thought
réfrigérateur *(m)* refrigerator
réfugier: se réfugier to take refuge
regagner to regain
regard *(m)* look
regarder to look at, to watch (2); **se regarder** to look at each other (7)
régime *(m)* diet; regime; **être au régime** to be on a diet
région *(f)* region (4)
régional(e) *(mpl* **régionaux)** regional (4)
régir to govern
règle *(f)* rule
règlement *(m)* payment

réglementé(e) regulated
régler to adjust; **régler la note** to pay the bill (10)
regretter to regret (6)
regrouper to regroup
régulier(-ière) regular
régulièrement regularly (8)
rein *(m)* kidney; **reins** *(mpl)* lower back
reine *(f)* queen
rejeter to reject
rejoindre to join
relais *(m)* inn
relation *(f)* relationship (7)
relativement relatively
relier to connect
religieuse *(f)* cream puff
religieux(-euse) religious
religion *(f)* religion (7)
relire to reread
remarquable remarkable
remarquer to notice
remède *(m)* remedy, cure
remercier (de) to thank (for) (10)
remettre to put back; **remettre en cause** to call into question
remonter to go back (up)
remplacer to replace
remporter to win
rencontre *(f)* meeting, encounter (7)
rencontrer to meet for the first time or by chance, to run into (1); **se rencontrer** to run into each other (7)
rendez-vous *(m)* date, appointment; **Rendez-vous à...** Let's meet at . . .
rendormir: se rendormir to fall back asleep
rendre (quelque chose à quelqu'un) to return, to give something back to someone (7); **rendre** (+ *adjective*) to make (+ *adjective*); **rendre visite à** to visit *(someone)* (7); **se rendre (à / chez)** to go (to)
renommée *(f)* fame
renommé(e) renowned
rénové(e) renovated
renseignement *(m)* a piece of information (3)
renseigner to inform
rentrée *(f)* return
rentrer to return, to come / go back (home) (2)
repartir to start again, to leave again
repas *(m)* meal (6)
répéter to repeat (2); **Répétez, s'il vous plaît.** Repeat, please. (P); **se répéter** to be repeated
répondre (à) to answer (6); **Répondez à la question.** Answer the question. (P)
réponse *(f)* answer (P)
reposant(e) restful
reposer to set down; **se reposer** to rest (7)
représentant(e) *(mf)* representative
représenter to represent
reproche *(m)* reproach
république *(f)* republic
requis(e) required
réseau *(m)* network
réservation *(f)* reservation (9); **faire une réservation** to make a reservation (9)
réserve: sous réserve de subject to
réserver to reserve (9)
résidence *(f)* dormitory, residence hall (1); **résidence secondaire** *(f)* second home
résoudre to solve
respecter to respect
respirer to breathe
responsabilité *(f)* responsiblity
ressemblance *(f)* similarity
ressembler à to look like, to resemble
ressentir to feel

ressortir: faire ressortir to make stand out

restaurant *(m)* restaurant (1); **dîner au restaurant** to dine out (2); **restau-u** *(m)* university cafeteria (6)

reste *(m)* rest (7); **le reste (de)** the rest (of) (7)

rester to stay (2); **rester au lit** to stay in bed (2)

résultat *(m)* result

résumé *(m)* summary

retard *(m)* delay; **en retard** late (10)

retirer to take out, to withdraw (10)

retour *(m)* return (9); **(billet) aller-retour** *(m)* round-trip ticket (9)

retourner to return (5); **se retourner** to turn around

retravailler to rework

rétrécir to shrink

retrouver to meet (4), to find (again); **se retrouver** to meet (each other), to find each other again (7)

réunion *(f)* meeting

réunir: se réunir to meet

réussir (à) to succeed (in) (8)

revanche: en revanche on the other hand

rêve *(m)* dream

réveil *(m)* alarm clock (7), awakening

réveiller to wake up; **se réveiller** to wake up (7)

réveillon *(m)* **du jour de l'an** New Year's Eve

révélateur(-trice) revealing

révéler to reveal; **se révéler** to turn out to be

revendre to resell, to sell back (7)

revenir to come back (4)

revenu *(m)* income; **Revenu National Brut (R.N.B)** *(m)* gross national product (GNP)

rêver (de) to dream (about) (7)

rêveur(-euse) dreamy

réviser to review

révision *(f)* review

revoir to see again; **Au revoir.** Good-bye. (P)

révolte *(f)* revolt

revue *(f)* magazine

rez-de-chaussée *(m)* ground floor (3)

rhum *(m)* rum

rhume *(m)* cold (10)

riche rich (2)

richesse *(f)* wealth

ride *(f)* wrinkle

rideau *(m)* curtain (3)

ridicule ridiculous

rien: de rien you're welcome (P); **ne... rien** nothing (5); **ne... rien de spécial** nothing special (5) ; **ne... rien que** nothing but; **rien du tout** nothing at all (6)

rigoureux(-euse) rigorous, harsh

rillettes *(fpl)* potted pork or goose

rire *(m)* laugh, laughter,

rire to laugh

rive *(f)* bank

rivière *(f)* river

riz *(m)* rice (8)

robe *(f)* dress (5)

rocher *(m)* rock, boulder

rocheux(-euse) rocky

rock *(m)* rock music (1)

roi *(m)* king

rôle *(m)* role

roller: faire du roller to go rollerblading (6)

romain(e) Roman

roman *(m)* novel (9)

romanche *(m)* Romansh

romancier *(m)* novelist

romantique romantic

rond *(m)* circle

rosbif *(m)* roast beef (8)

rose pink (3)

rosier *(m)* rosebush

rôti(e) roasted; **rôti** *(m)* **de porc** pork roast

roue *(f)* wheel

rouge red (3); **vin rouge** *(m)* red wine (2)

rougeole *(f)* measles

rougir to turn red, to blush

roulette: patin *(m)* **à roulettes** roller skate

route *(f)* route, way

routine *(f)* routine (7)

roux (rousse) red *(hair)* (4)

royaume *(m)* kingdom; **Royaume-Uni** *(m)* United Kingdom (9)

rue *(f)* street (3); **dans la rue...** on . . . street (10)

ruine *(f)* ruin

ruminer to ponder

rupture *(f)* breaking up

rural(e) *(mpl* **ruraux)** rural

russe *(m)* Russian

Russie *(f)* Russia (9)

S

sable *(m)* sand

sac *(m)* purse (5)

sage good, well-behaved (4)

saharien(ne) Saharan

sain(e) healthy (8)

Saint-Valentin *(f)* Valentine's Day

saison *(f)* season (5)

salade *(f)* salad (8); **salade** *(f)* **de tomates** tomato salad (8)

salaire *(m)* salary

sale dirty (3)

salé(e) salted

salle *(f)* room; **salle** *(f)* **à manger** dining room (3); **salle** *(f)* **de bains** bathroom (3); **salle** *(f)* **de classe** classroom (1)

salon *(m)* living room (3)

saluer to greet

Salut! Hi! (P), Bye!

salutation *(f)* greeting

samedi *(m)* Saturday (P)

sandale *(f)* sandal (5)

sandwich *(m)* sandwich (2)

sang *(m)* blood

sanglier *(m)* wild boar

sanitaires *(mpl)* bathroom

sans without (P)

santé *(f)* health (8)

satisfaisant(e) satisfying

satisfait(e) satisfied

sauce *(f)* sauce, gravy, dip

saucière *(f)* sauceboat

saucisse *(f)* sausage (8)

saucisson *(m)* salami (8)

sauf except (2)

saumon *(m)* salmon (8)

sauvage wild

sauvegardé(e) preserved

sauver to save; **sauvé(e)** saved

savane *(f)* savanna

savoir to know (how) (9); **Je ne sais pas.** I don't know. (P); **Savez-vous... ?** Do you know (how to). . . ? (8)

savon *(m)* soap

scénario *(m)* screenplay

scène *(f)* stage, scene, skit

sceptique skeptical

science *(f)* science (1); **film** *(m)* **de science-fiction** science fiction movie; **sciences économiques** *(fpl)* economics; **sciences humaines** *(fpl)* social sciences (1); **sciences politiques** *(fpl)* political science, government (1)

scientifique scientific

scolaire school; **extra-scolaire** extracurricular

sculpteur *(m)* sculptor

se herself, himself, itself, oneself, themselves (7); **Il/Elle se trouve...** It is located. . .

séance *(f)* showing (6)

sec (sèche) dry

second(e) second

secondaire secondary

seconde *(f)* second (5)

secrétaire *(mf)* secretary

secteur *(m)* sector, area

section (non-)fumeur *(f)* (non-)smoking section

sécurité *(f)* security, safety

séduire to seduce

séduisant(e) seductive

sein *(m)* breast; **au sein de** within

seize sixteen (P)

seizième sixteenth

séjour *(m)* stay (7)

séjourner to stay

sel *(m)* salt (8)

self-service *(m)* self-service restaurant (8)

selon according to

semaine *(f)* week (P); **en semaine** weekdays

semblable similar

sembler to seem

semestre *(m)* semester (P)

Sénégal *(m)* Senegal (9)

sénégalais(e) Senegalese

sens *(m)* meaning, sense; **sens** *(m)* **de l'humour** sense of humor (7)

sensible sensitive

sensuel(le) sensual

sensualité *(f)* sensuality

sentiment *(m)* feeling (7)

sentimental(e) *(mpl* **sentimentaux)** sentimental, emotional (7)

sentir: se sentir to feel (8)

séparé(e) separated

sept seven (P)

septembre *(m)* September (4)

septième seventh (3)

série *(f)* series, category

sérieusement seriously

sérieux(-euse) serious

serveur *(m)* waiter (8)

serveuse *(f)* waitress (8)

service *(m)* service (8)

serviette *(f)* towel

servir to serve (4); **servi(e)** served (10); **se servir de** to use

seul(e) alone (P), only (1), single, lonely

seulement only (8)

sévère strict

sexualité *(f)* sexuality

sexuel(le) sexual

sexy *(inv)* sexy (2)

shopping: faire du shopping to go shopping (2)

short *(m)* shorts (5)

si if (5), yes (8); **s'il vous plaît** please (P)

SIDA *(m)* AIDS

siècle *(m)* century

siège *(m)* seat

sieste *(f)* nap

sigle *(m)* set of initials

signaler to draw attention to

signifier to mean, to signify

similaire (à) similar (to)

similarité *(f)* similarity

simple simple; **billet aller simple** *(m)* one-way ticket (9)

simplement simply (10)

singe *(m)* monkey

sinon if not, otherwise

sinusite *(f)* sinusitis
site *(m)* site (9)
situer: se situer to be situated; **situé(e)** situated
six six (P)
sixième sixth (3)
skateboard(ing): faire du skateboard(ing) to skateboard (6)
ski *(m)* skiing (2); **chalet de ski** *(m)* a ski lodge (10); **faire du ski** to go skiing (2); **faire du ski nautique** to go (water-)skiing (5)
skier to ski
slip *(m)* briefs, panties
sociabilité *(f)* socializing
social(e) *(mpl* **sociaux)** social
société *(f)* company, society; **jeu** *(m)* **de société** board game
sociologie *(f)* sociology
sœur *(f)* sister (1); **belle-sœur** *(f)* sister-in-law; **demi-sœur** *(f)* stepsister, half-sister
soi oneself
soif: avoir soif to be thirsty (4); **j'ai soif** I'm thirsty (2)
soin *(m)* care
soir *(m)* evening (P); **à huit heures du soir** at eight in the evening (P); **ce soir** tonight, this evening (2); **le soir** evenings, in the evening (P)
soirée *(f)* evening (4), party (6)
soixante sixty (2)
soixante-dix seventy (2)
soja *(m)* soya
sol *(m)* ground
soldat *(m)* soldier
solde: en solde on sale (5)
sole *(f)* sole (fish)
soleil *(m)* sun; **Il fait du soleil.** It's sunny. (5); **lunettes** *(fpl)* **de soleil** sunglasses (5); **prendre un bain de soleil** to sunbathe (4)
solitaire lonely
solitude *(f)* loneliness
sombre dark, gloomy
somme *(f)* sum
sommeil *(m)* sleep; **avoir sommeil** to be sleepy (4)
son *(m)* sound
son (sa, ses) her, his, its (3)
sondage *(m)* poll
sonner to ring (7)
sorcière *(f)* witch
sorte *(f)* kind, sort; **en sorte que** so that
sortie *(f)* outing (6), exit
sortir (de) to go out (2); to leave (6); to take out
souci *(m)* care
soudain suddenly (6)
soudain(e) sudden
soudainement suddenly
souffrance *(f)* suffering
souffrir to suffer
souhait *(m)* wish
souhaiter (que) to wish (that) (10)
soumettre: se soumettre à to submit to
soupçonner to suspect
soupe *(f)* soup (8); **soupe** *(f)* **à l'oignon** onion soup (8)
souper to have supper
sourire *(m)* smile
sous under (3); **sous réserve de** subject to
sous-estimer to underestimate
sous-marin(e) underwater; **plongée sous-marine** *(f)* scuba diving
sous-sol *(m)* basement (3)
sous-titres *(mpl)* subtitles
sous-vêtements *(mpl)* underwear
soutenir: se soutenir to support one another; **soutenu(e)** supported

soutien-gorge *(m)* bra
souvenir *(m)* memory
souvenir: se souvenir (de) to remember (7)
souvent often (1)
souveraineté *(f)* sovereignty
spécial(e) *(mpl* **spéciaux)** special; **effets spéciaux** *(mpl)* special effects (6); **ne... rien de spécial** nothing special (5)
spécialisation *(f)* specialization, major
spécialisé(e) specialized
spécialiser: se spécialiser en to specialize in
spécialité *(f)* specialty (4)
spectacle *(m)* show
spectaculaire spectacular
spectateur(-trice) *(mf)* spectator, viewer
spiritualité *(f)* spirituality (7)
sport *(m)* sport (1); **faire du sport** to play sports (5)
sportif(-ive) athletic (1)
stabilité *(f)* stability
stade *(m)* stadium (1)
stage *(m)* internship
standard *(m)* switchboard
station *(f)* station; **station estivale** *(f)* summer resort (10); **station-service** *(f)* service station
statut *(m)* statute, status
steak-frites *(m)* steak and fries (8)
stimuler to stimulate
stratégie *(f)* strategy
stress *(m)* stress (8)
stressé(e) stressed (out) (8)
style *(m)* style
stylo *(m)* pen (P)
subventions *(fpl)* subsidies
succès *(m)* success
succursale *(f)* branch office
sucer to suck
sucre *(m)* sugar (8)
sucré(e) sweet, sugary
sud *(m)* south; **Amérique** *(f)* **du Sud** South America (9)
Suède *(f)* Sweden
suffire: il suffit de... it's enough to . . . **Suffit!** That's enough!
suffisant(e) sufficient
suggérer to suggest (6)
Suisse *(f)* Switzerland (9)
suisse Swiss
suite: toute de suite right away (6)
suivant(e) following (3)
suivre to follow (7); **à suivre** to be continued (6); **suivre un cours** to take a course
sujet *(m)* subject
super great (P)
superficie *(f)* area
supérieur(e) superior, higher
supermarché *(m)* supermarket
supplément *(m)* extra charge (10)
supplémentaire supplementary
supporter to bear, to tolerate, to put up with (7)
supposer to suppose, to presume
suprématie *(f)* supremacy
sur on (1); **sept jours sur sept** seven days out of seven
sûr(e) sure; **Bien sûr!** Of course! (5)
sûrement surely
surface: grande surface *(f)* superstore (8)
surfer le Net to surf the Net (2)
surgelé(e) frozen (8)
surgir to arise, to come up; to appear suddenly, to surge, to begin to grow
surimpression *(f)* **d'images** double exposure
surpasser to surpass
surprenant(e) surprising
surprendre to surprise; **surpris(e)** surprised (10)

surtout especially, above all (8)
survêtement *(m)* jogging suit (5)
symbiose *(f)* symbiosis
sympathique (sympa) nice (1)
symptôme *(m)* symptom (10)
synagogue *(f)* synagogue
synonyme synonymous
systématiquement systematically
système *(m)* system (9); **système** *(m)* **de transports en commun** public transportation system (9)

T

tabac *(m)* tobacco (8); **bureau** *(m)* **de tabac** tobacco shop
table *(f)* table (3); **table basse** *(f)* coffee table
tableau *(m)* board (P); painting, picture (3), act, scene; **tableau** *(m)* **d'affichage** bulletin board
tâche *(f)* task; **tâche domestique** household chore
taille *(f)* size (4); **de taille moyenne** medium-sized, of medium height (4); **Quelle taille faites-vous?** What size do you wear? (5)
tailleur *(m)* woman's suit
taire: se taire to be silent
talon *(m)* heel; *haut talon *(m)* high heel
tandis que whereas, while
tant (de) so much, so many; **tant que** as long as
tante *(f)* aunt (4)
tapis *(m)* rug (3)
tapisserie *(f)* tapestry
tard late (4); **plus tard** later (4)
tarte *(f)* pie (8); **tarte** *(f)* **aux pommes** apple pie (8)
tartelette *(f)* **(aux fraises)** (strawberry) tart (8)
tartine *(f)* bread and butter (with jam) (8)
tas *(m)* pile; **un tas de** a bunch of
tasse *(f)* cup
taxi *(m)* taxi (4); **en taxi** by taxi (4)
te (to, for) you (9), yourself (7); **Ça te dit?** How does that sound to you? (4); **Ça te plaît?** Do you like it? (3); **Je te présente...** I would like to introduce . . . to you.; **s'il te plaît** please; **Te voilà!** There you are!
technique technical (1)
technologie *(f)* technology
technologique technological
tee-shirt *(m)* T-shirt (5)
teinturerie *(f)* dry cleaner's
tel(le): tel(le) que such as (9); **un(e) tel(le)** such a (7)
télé *(f)* TV (2)
télécopie *(f)* fax
téléphone *(m)* telephone (2); **au téléphone** on the telephone (2); **numéro** *(m)* **de téléphone** telephone number (3)
téléphoner (à) to phone (3); **se téléphoner** to telephone each other (7)
téléphonique: appareil *(m)* **téléphonique** telephone; **carte** *(f)* **téléphonique** telephone card (10)
télévision (télé) *(f)* television (2)
tellement so much, so (6)
témoignage *(m)* testimony, evidence
température *(f)* temperature
temple *(m)* temple, Protestant church
temps *(m)* time (2), weather (5); **de temps en temps** from time to time (4); **emploi** *(m)* **du temps** schedule; **en même temps** at the same time; **en tout temps** at all times, at any time; **Pendant combien de temps?** For how long? (5); **Quel temps fait-il?** What's the weather like? (5); **temps libre** *(m)* free time (4); **temps verbal** *(m)* tense

tendance *(f)* tendency
tendre tender
tendresse *(f)* tenderness
tenir to hold; **Ah tiens!** Hey!; **tenir à** to value; **tenir la maison** to keep house
tennis *(m)* tennis (1); **court** *(m)* **de tennis** tennis court
tentation *(f)* temptation
tenter to attempt
terme *(m)* term; **mettre terme à** to put an end to
terminaison *(f)* ending
terminer to finish
terrain: sur le terrain on site
terrasse *(f)* terrace (9)
terre *(f)* earth; **par terre** on the ground / floor (3); **pomme** *(f)* **de terre** potato (8)
territoire *(m)* territory, lands, grounds
tertiaire: activités tertiaires *(fpl)* service industries
test *(m)* test (7)
tête *(f)* head (10); **prendre la tête** to take charge
Texas *(m)* Texas (9)
thé *(m)* tea (2)
théâtre *(m)* theater (1), drama (1)
thon *(m)* tuna (8)
tiers *(m)* third; **Tiers-Monde** *(m)* Third World
timbre *(m)* stamp (10)
timide shy, timid (1)
tiroir *(m)* drawer
tisser to weave; **se tisser** to be woven
titre *(m)* title; **à titre exclusif** exclusively; **à titre principal** mainly
titulaire *(mf)* holder
toi you (P); **chez toi** at your house (2)
toilette: toilettes *(fpl)* toilet, restroom (3); **faire sa toilette** to wash up (7)
toit *(m)* roof
tomate *(f)* tomato (8)
tombe *(f)* grave
tomber to fall (5); **tomber amoureux(-euse) (de)** to fall in love (with) (6); **tomber malade** to get sick (10)
ton *(m)* tone
ton (ta, tes) your (3); **tes amis** your friends (1); **ton université** your university (1)
tort: avoir tort to be wrong (4)
tôt early (4)
totalité: la totalité de all of
toucher to touch
toujours always (2), still
tour *(m)* tour, ride (4); **faire un tour** to take a tour, to go for a ride (4)
tour *(f)* tower
tourisme *(m)* tourism; **office** *(m)* **de tourisme** tourist office (10)
touriste *(mf)* tourist; **classe touriste** *(f)* tourist class, coach (9)
touristique tourist (9)
tournée *(f)* tour
tourner to turn (10), to stir, to film; **se tourner (vers)** to turn (toward); **tourné(e)** filmed
tourte *(f)* pie
Toussaint *(f)* All Saints' Day
tousser to cough (10)
tout (toute, tous, toutes) everything, all (3), whole; **ne... pas du tout** not at all (1); **rien du tout** nothing at all (6); **tous (toutes) les deux** both; **tous les jours** every day (P); **tous les soirs** every evening; **tout à coup** all of a sudden (6); **tout à fait** completely; **tout à l'heure** in a little while (P), a while ago; **tout de suite** right away (6); **tout droit** straight (10); **tout d'un coup** all at once (6); **toute la journée** the whole day (2); **tout en** while; **toutes sortes de...** all kinds of . . .;

tout le monde everybody, everyone (6); **tout près (de)** right by, very near (3); **tout simplement** quite simply (10)
toutefois however
traditionnel(le) traditional (8)
traditionnellement traditionally
traducteur(-trice) *(mf)* translator
traduire to translate
train *(m)* train (4); **en train** by train (4); **être en train de...** to be in the process of. . .
traîneau *(m)* sled
traîner to hang around
trait *(m)* trait (7)
traité *(m)* treaty
traitement *(m)* treatment
tranche *(f)* slice (8)
tranquille tranquil, calm
transformer: se transformer en to change into
transmettre to transmit; to pass on
transpercer to pierce
transport *(m)* transportation; **moyen** *(m)* **de transport** means of transportation (4); **système** *(m)* **de transports en commun** public transportation system (9)
travail *(m)* *(pl* **travaux)** work (6); **fête** *(f)* **du travail** Labor Day; **travaux** *(mpl)* **d'aiguille** needlework
travailler to work, to study (2); **je travaille** I work (P); **Tu travailles? / Vous travaillez?** Do you work? (P)
travailleur(-euse) *(mf)* worker
travers: à travers across
traversée *(f)* crossing
traverser to cross, to go across (10)
treize thirteen (P)
trembler to tremble
trentaine *(f)* thirties
trente thirty (P)
très very (P)
tribu *(f)* tribe
triste sad (10)
trois three (P)
troisième third (3); **troisième âge** *(m)* age of retirement
trompette *(f)* trumpet
trop too, too much (3); **trop de** too much, too many (6)
tropical(e) *(mpl* **tropicaux)** tropical (9)
trou *(m)* hole
trouver to find (4); **Il/Elle se trouve...** It is located. . .
truc *(m)* thing (1); **Ce n'est pas mon truc.** That's not my thing. (1)
truite *(f)* trout
tu you (P)
tuba: faire du tuba: to go snorkeling
tuberculose *(f)* tuberculosis
tuer to kill
Tunisie *(f)* Tunisia
tunisien(ne) Tunisian
Turquie *(f)* Turkey
typique typical (2)
typiquement typically
tyran *(m)* tyrant

U

un(e) one, a (1)
uni(e) (à) close (to), united, solid-colored; **Nations unies** *(fpl)* United Nations; **Royaume-Uni** *(m)* United Kingdom (9)
unique only, single, unique
uniquement only
unité *(f)* unity, unit
universitaire university (1)
université *(f)* university (P)

urgence *(f)* emergency
usage *(m)* use
usine *(f)* factory
utile useful (10)
utiliser to use, to utilize

V

vacances *(fpl)* vacation (4); **en vacances** on vacation (4)
vacancier *(m)* vacationer
vache *(f)* cow
vague *(f)* wave
vaincu(e) defeated
vaisselle *(f)* dishes; **faire la vaisselle** to wash dishes (5); **lave-vaisselle** *(m)* dishwasher
valeur *(f)* value; **mettre en valeur** to emphasize
valise *(f)* suitcase (9); **faire sa valise** to pack one's bag (9)
vallée *(f)* valley
valoir to be worth; **il vaut mieux (que)...** it's better (that) . . . (10)
valse *(f)* waltz
valser to waltz
vanille *(f)* vanilla (8)
vanité *(f)* vanity (7)
vaniteux(-euse) vain
varappe *(f)* rock climbing; **faire de la varappe** to go rock climbing
varicelle *(f)* chicken pox
varié(e) varied
variété *(f)* variety
vaste vast
vaut See **valoir.**
veau *(m)* veal
végétarien(ne) vegetarian
véhicule *(m)* vehicle
veillée *(f)* evening together
veiller to watch over
vélo *(m)* bicycle (2); **à vélo** by bike (4); **faire du vélo** to go bike-riding (2)
vendeur(-euse) *(mf)* salesperson (5)
vendre to sell (7)
vendredi *(m)* Friday (P)
venir to come (4); **venir de** (+ *infinitive*) to have just (+ *past participle*); **Viens voir...** Come see . . . (3)
vent *(m)* wind; **Il fait du vent.** It's windy. (5)
vente *(f)* sale
ventre *(m)* stomach, belly (10)
verbe *(m)* verb
verglaçant(e) icy
verglas: Il y a du verglas. It's icy.
vérifier to check
véritable true, real
vérité *(f)* truth
verre *(m)* glass (2); **prendre un verre** to have a drink (2)
vers *(m)* verse
vers toward(s), about, around (2)
vert(e) green (3)
vestige *(m)* remnant
vêtements *(mpl)* clothes (3); **sous-vêtements** *(mpl)* underwear
vétérinaire *(m)* veterinarian
veuf *(m)* widower (7)
veuve *(f)* widow (7)
vexer to vex, to upset
viande *(f)* meat (8)
vicieux(-euse) vicious
victime *(f)* victim
vidéo *(f)* video (2); **jeu vidéo** *(m)* video game (2)
vidéocassette *(f)* video cassette
vie *(f)* life (6)
vieillir to age, to get old

viennoiserie *(f) baked goods sold at a bakery*
Viêt Nam *(m)* Vietnam (9)
vieux / vieil (vieille) old (1); **Vieux Carré** *(m)* French Quarter (4)
vif(-ive) lively, bright; **bleu vif** bright blue
vigueur: en vigueur in effect; **reprendre vigueur** to take on a new life
village *(m)* village, town
villageois(e) *(mf)* villager
ville *(f)* city (3); **en ville** in town (3)
villégiature *(f)* vacation stay
vin *(m)* wine (2)
vinaigre *(m)* vinegar
vingt twenty (P)
vingtième twentieth
violence *(f)* violence (7)
violet(te) violet (3)
virus *(m)* virus (10)
visa *(m)* visa
visage *(m)* face
visé(e) stamped, approved
visite: rendre visite à to visit *(a person)* (7)
visiter to visit (1)
visiteur(-euse) *(mf)* visitor
vitamine *(f)* vitamin (8)
vite quickly, fast (7)
vitesse *(f)* speed
vivant(e) alive
vivement greatly
vivier *(m)* fish reservoir
vivoir *(m)* living room
vivre to live
vocabulaire *(m)* vocabulary (P)
vocation *(f)* calling

voici here is, here are (2)
voilà there is, there are (2); **Te/Vous voilà!** There you are!
voile *(f)* sailing; **faire de la planche à voile** *(f)* to go windsurfing
voir to see (1); **aller voir** to go see, to visit (4); **comme tu vois** as you see (3); **se voir** to see each other (7), to find oneself; **Voyons!** Let's see! (5)
voire even
voisin(e) *(mf)* neighbor (9)
voiture *(f)* car (3); **en voiture** by car (4); **voiture** *(f)* **de location** rental car (5)
voix *(f)* voice
vol *(m)* flight (9)
volaille *(f)* poultry (8)
volcan *(m)* volcano
voleur *(m)* thief
volley *(m)* volleyball (2)
volonté *(f)* will, wish
volontiers gladly, willingly (8)
vomir to vomit (10)
voter to vote
vôtre: le/la vôtre yours
votre *(pl vos)* your (3); **Ouvrez votre livre.** Open your book. (P)
vouloir to want (6); **Je voudrais (bien)...** I would like . . . (2); **Qu'est-ce que ça veut dire?** What does that mean? (P); **Qu'est-ce que vous voudriez faire?** What would you like to do? (2); **Tu voudrais... ?** Would you like . . . ? (2)
vous you (P), (to, for) you (9), yourself(-selves) (7); **Je vous présente...** I would like to intro-

duce . . . to you.; **s'il vous plaît** please (P); **vous-même** yourself; **Vous voilà!** There you are!
voyage *(m)* trip (4); **agence** *(f)* **de voyages** travel agency (9); **agent** *(m)* **de voyages** travel agent (9); **chèque** *(m)* **de voyage** traveler's check (9); **faire un voyage** to take a trip (5); **partir en voyage** to leave on a trip (5); **voyage** *(m)* **de noces** honeymoon
voyager to travel (2)
voyelle *(f)* vowel
vrai(e) true
vraiment really, truly (2)
VTT: faire du VTT to go all-terrain biking (5)
vue *(f)* view (3); **point** *(m)* **de vue** viewpoint

W

wallon(ne) Walloon
W.-C. *(m)* toilet, restroom (10)
Web: site *(m)* **Web** website (9)
week-end *(m)* weekend (P); **Bon week-end!** Have a good weekend!; **le week-end** on weekends (P)

Y

y there (4); **il y a** there is, there are (1), ago (5)
yaourt *(m)* yogurt (8)
yeux *(mpl)* *(sing* œil*)* eyes (4)
Yom Kippour *(m)* Yom Kippur

Z

zapper to channel surf, to switch back and forth
zéro *(m)* zero (P)
zydeco: musique *(f)* **zydeco** zydeco music (4)

The ***Vocabulaire anglais–français*** includes all words presented in *Horizons* for active use, as well as others that students may need for more personalized expression. The definitions of active vocabulary words are followed by the number of the chapter where they are first presented. A (P) refers to the ***Chapitre préliminaire.*** When several translations, separated by commas, are listed before a chapter number, they are all considered active. Since verbs are sometimes introduced lexically in the infinitive before the conjugation of the present indicative is presented, consult the ***Index*** to find out the chapter where a conjugation is introduced. An *(m), (f)* or *(pl)* following a noun indicates that it is masculine, feminine, or plural. *Inv* means that a word is invariable. An asterisk before a word beginning with an **h** indicates that the **h** is aspirate.

A

a un(e) (P); **a few** quelques (5); **a lot** beaucoup (P)
able: be able pouvoir (6)
about vers (2), environ (4), de (1); **about it/them** en (8); **About what?** À propos de quoi?; **think about** penser à
above au-dessus de; **above all** surtout (8)
abroad à l'étranger (9)
absolutely absolument
Acadia Acadie *(f)*
accent accent *(m)* (P); **without an accent** sans accent (P)
accept accepter (7)
accident accident *(m)*
accompany accompagner
according to selon
account compte *(m)*
accountant comptable *(mf)*
accounting comptabilité *(f)* (1)
accustomed to habitué(e) à
ache douleur *(f)*
ache avoir mal (à) (10)
acquaintance: make the acquaintance of faire la connaissance de (7)
acquainted: be / get acquainted with connaître (4)
across (from) en face (de) (3); **go across** traverser (10)
act jouer *(in movies and theater)* (6); agir
active dynamique (1)
activity activité *(f)* (2)
actor acteur *(m)* (6)
actress actrice *(f)* (6)
actually effectivement, réellement
adapt s'adapter
add ajouter
address adresse *(f)* (3); **e-mail address** adresse *(f)* mail (3)
adjective adjectif *(m)* (1)
administration building centre administratif *(m)*
admire admirer (9)
adopted adopté(e)
adore adorer
adult adulte *(mf)*
advance avance *(f)*; **in advance** à l'avance (9)
advantage avantage *(m)*; **take advantage of** profiter de (9)
adventure aventure *(f)*; **adventure movie** film *(m)* d'aventures
advertisement publicité *(f)*; **classified ad** petite annonce *(f)*

advertising publicité *(f)*
advice conseils *(mpl)* (8); **give a piece of advice** donner un conseil
aerobics: do aerobics faire de l'aérobic (8)
afraid: be afraid (of) avoir peur (de) (4)
Africa Afrique *(f)* (9)
African africain(e)
after après (P); **after having done . . .** après avoir fait... ; **day after tomorrow** après-demain
afternoon après-midi *(m)* (P); **in the afternoon, afternoons** l'après-midi (P); **It's one o'clock in the afternoon.** Il est une heure de l'après-midi. (P); **this afternoon** cet après-midi (4)
afterwards après (P), ensuite (4)
again encore (8), de nouveau
against contre (10)
age âge *(m)* (4)
age vieillir
agency: travel agency agence *(f)* de voyages (9)
agent agent *(m)*; **travel agent** agent *(m)* de voyages (9)
ago il y a (5); **How long ago?** Il y a combien de temps? (5)
agree être d'accord; **Agreed!** D'accord! (2)
agricultural agricole
ahead: straight ahead tout droit (10)
AIDS SIDA *(m)*
air air *(m)*
airplane avion *(m)* (4); **by airplane** en avion (4)
airport aéroport *(m)* (10)
alarm: alarm clock réveil *(m)* (7)
alcohol alcool *(m)* (8)
alcoholic drink boisson alcoolisée *(f)*
algebra algèbre *(f)*
Algeria Algérie *(f)* (9)
alive vivant(e)
all tout (toute, tous, toutes) (3); **above all** surtout (8); **all day** toute la journée (2); **all of a sudden** tout d'un coup (6); **all of the time** tout le temps; **all sorts of** toutes sortes de; **all the better** tant mieux; **not at all** ne... pas du tout (1); **nothing at all** rien du tout (6); **That's all.** C'est tout. (8)
allergy allergie *(f)* (10)
allow permettre (de); **allowed** permis(e)
almost presque (2)
alone seul(e) (P)
along le long de (9); **get along well / badly** s'entendre bien / mal (7)
already déjà (5)
also aussi (P)
although bien que, quoique

always toujours (2)
A.M. du matin (P)
amaze étonner; **amazed** étonné(e) (10)
America Amérique *(f)* (9)
American américain(e) (P); **American style** à l'américaine (8)
among parmi
amusing amusant(e) (1)
an un(e) (1)
ancestor ancêtre *(mf)*
and et (P)
angry fâché(e); **get angry** se fâcher
animal animal *(m)* (*pl* animaux) (3)
animated animé(e)
ankle cheville *(f)*
anniversary *(wedding)* anniversaire *(m)* de mariage
annoying embêtant(e) (3)
another un(e) autre (1); **another glass of . . .** encore un verre de... ; **another thing** autre chose; **one another** se, nous, vous (7)
answer réponse *(f)* (P)
answer répondre (à) (6); **Answer the question.** Répondez à la question. (P)
anthropology anthropologie *(f)*
any du, de la, de l', de, des, en (8)
anymore: not anymore ne... plus (8)
anyone quelqu'un (6); **(just) anyone** n'importe qui; **not . . . anyone** ne... personne
anything quelque chose (2); **(just) anything** n'importe quoi; **not . . . anything** ne... rien (5)
anyway quand même
anywhere: (just) anywhere n'importe où; **not . . . anywhere** nulle part
apartment appartement *(m)* (3); **apartment building** immeuble *(m)* (3)
appear paraître
appearance: physical appearance aspect physique *(m)* (7)
appetite appétit *(m)*
appetizer *hors-d'œuvre *(m)* (8)
apple pomme *(f)* (8); **apple pie** tarte *(f)* aux pommes (8)
appointment rendez-vous *(m)* (6)
appreciate apprécier (6)
appropriate approprié(e), convenable
apricot abricot *(m)*
April avril *(m)* (4); **April Fool's Day** les poissons *(mpl)* d'avril
Arabic arabe *(m)*
architect architecte *(mf)*
architecture architecture *(f)*

Argentina Argentine (f) (9)
argue (with) se disputer (avec) (7)
arm bras (m) (10)
armchair fauteuil (m) (3)
around vers (2), environ (4) autour de
arrange ranger (7)
arranged rangé(e) (3)
arrival arrivée (f) (9); **arrival gate** porte (f) d'arrivée (9)
arrive arriver (3)
art art (m); **fine arts** beaux-arts (mpl) (1)
article article (m) (9)
artist artiste (mf); **graphic** artiste dessinateur (-trice) (mf) de publicité
as comme (P); **as . . . as** aussi... que (1); **as long as** tant que; **as many . . . (as)** autant de... (que); **as much . . . (as)** autant de... (que); **as soon as** aussitôt que; **as you see** comme tu vois (3)
ash cendre (f); **AshWednesday** mercredi (m) des Cendres
ashamed: be ashamed avoir *honte
Asia Asie (f) (9)
ask (for) demander (2); **ask a question** poser une question (3)
asleep: fall asleep s'endormir (7)
asparagus asperge (f)
aspirin aspirine (f) (10)
assembly assemblage (m)
associate associer
astronomy astronomie (f)
at à (P); **at home** à la maison (P); **at my parents' house** chez mes parents (3); **at . . . 's house / place** chez... (2)
athletic sportif(-ive) (1)
ATM machine distributeur de billets (m) (10)
attend assister à
attention attention (f); **pay attention (to)** faire attention (à) (8)
attract attirer
auburn auburn (inv) (4)
August août (m) (4)
aunt tante (f) (4)
Australia Australie (f) (9)
automatic: automatic teller machine distributeur de billets (m) (10)
autumn automne (m) (5); **in autumn** en automne (5)
available disponible
avenue avenue (f) (10)
average moyen(ne) (4)
avoid éviter (8)
awaken se réveiller (7)
awakening réveil (m)
away: go away partir (4), s'en aller; **put away** bien rangé(e) (3); **right away** tout de suite (6)

B

baby bébé (m)
babysitter baby-sitter (mf)
back dos (m) (10)
back: bring back rapporter; **come back** revenir (4); **give back** rendre (7); **go back** rentrer (2), retourner (5); **go back to bed** se recoucher (7); **in the back of** au fond de; **sell back** revendre (7)
bacon bacon (m) (8)
bad mauvais(e) (1); **It's too bad!** C'est dommage! (7); **really bad** nul(le) (7); **The weather's bad.** Il fait mauvais. (5)
badly mal (P), **not badly** pas mal (P)
bag sac (m) (5), paquet (m) (8); **pack one's bag** faire sa valise (9)
baggage bagages (mpl) (9)
bakery boulangerie (f) (8), pâtisserie (f)

balcony balcon (m)
bald chauve
ball balle (f), (inflated) ballon (m)
banana banane (f) (8)
band orchestre (m) (4)
bank banque (f) (10); **bank card** carte bancaire (f) (9)
banker banquier (m)
bar bar (m)
baseball base-ball (m) (2)
based: based on basé(e) sur (6)
basement sous-sol (m) (3)
basketball basket (m) (1)
bath bain (m) (7)
bathe prendre un bain (7), se baigner
bathroom salle (f) de bains (3)
be être (1); **be able** pouvoir (6); **be afraid (of)** avoir peur (de) (4); **be ashamed** avoir *honte; **be bored** s'ennuyer (7); **be born** naître, être né(e) (5); **be familiar with** connaître (4); **be hot** avoir chaud (4); **be hungry** avoir faim (4); **I'm hungry.** J'ai faim. (2); **be interested in** s'intéresser à (7); **be named** s'appeler (7); **be right** avoir raison (4); **be sleepy** avoir sommeil (4); **be thirsty** avoir soif (4); **I'm thirsty.** J'ai soif.(2); **be wrong** avoir tort (4); **be . . . years old** avoir... ans (4); **here is/are** voici (2); **How are you?** Comment allez-vous? (P); **How is it going?** Comment ça va? (P); **I am . . .** Je suis... (P); **isn't it?** n'est-ce pas?, non? (1); **It is located...** Il/Elle se trouve... ; **It's Monday.** C'est lundi. (P); **My name is . . .** Je m'appelle... (P); **That's . . . euros.** Ça fait... euros. (2); **There are six of us.** Nous sommes six. (4); **there is/are** il y a (1), voilà (2); **The weather's nice / bad / cold / cool / hot / sunny / windy.** Il fait beau / mauvais / froid / frais / chaud / du soleil / du vent. (5); **to be continued** à suivre (6); **you are** tu es/vous êtes (P)
beach plage (f) (4)
beans: green beans *haricots verts (mpl) (8)
bear supporter (7)
beard barbe (f) (4)
beast animal (m) (6)
beat battre
beautiful beau (bel, belle, pl beaux, belles) (1)
beauty beauté (7)
because parce que (P); **because of** à cause de
become devenir (4)
bed lit (m) (2); **bed and breakfast** chambre (f) d'hôte; **go back to bed** se recoucher (7); **go to bed** se coucher (7); **stay in bed** rester au lit (2)
bedroom chambre (f) (3)
bedspread couverture (f) (3)
beef bœuf (m) (8); **roast beef** rosbif (m) (8)
beer bière (f) (2); **draft beer** demi (m) (2)
before avant (P); **before (doing)** avant de (faire); **before-dinner drink** apéritif (m) (8)
beforehand auparavant
begin commencer (2); **The French class begins at...** Le cours de français commence à... (P)
beginning début (m); **at the beginning** au début (6)
behaved: well-behaved sage (4)
behind derrière (3)
beige beige (3)
Belgium Belgique (f) (9)
believe (in) croire (à)
bell cloche (f)
belly ventre (m) (10)
belong to appartenir à, être à
belongings effets personnels (mpl) (3), affaires (fpl)

belt ceinture (f)
benefit (work) bénévole
beside à côté de (3)
besides de plus, d'ailleurs
best (le/la) meilleur(e) (adjective) (1), (le) mieux (adverb)
better meilleur(e) (adjective) (1), mieux (adverb) (2); **do better. . .** faire mieux... (8); **it's better, you had better** il vaut mieux (10)
between entre (3)
beverage boisson (f) (2)
bicycle vélo (m) (2)
bicycle-riding: go bicycle-riding faire du vélo (2)
big grand(e) (1), gros(se) (1)
bike vélo (m) (2); **by bike** à vélo (4)
bikini bikini (m) (5)
bilingual bilingue
bill (restaurant) addition (f), (utilities) facture (f); **pay the bill** (at a hotel) régler la note (10)
billiards billard (m)
biology biologie (f) (1)
bird oiseau (m)
birth naissance (f); **date of birth** date (f) de naissance
birthday anniversaire (m) (4)
bizarre bizarre
black noir(e) (3)
blackboard tableau (m) (P)
blanket couverture (f) (3)
bless bénir
blond blond(e) (4)
blood sang (m)
blouse chemisier (m) (5)
blue bleu(e) (3)
blueberry myrtille (f)
blues (music) blues (m)
blush rougir
board tableau (m) (P)
boat bateau (m) (4); **by boat** en bateau (4)
boating: go boating faire du bateau (5)
body corps (m) (7)
bodybuilding: to do bodybuilding faire de la musculation (8)
book livre (m) (P)
bookcase étagère (f) (3)
bookstore librairie (f) (1)
boot botte (f) (5)
border frontière (f)
bored: be / get bored s'ennuyer (7)
boring ennuyeux(-euse) (1)
born né(e) (5); **be born** naître (5); **He/She was born . . .** Il/Elle est né(e)... (5)
borrow emprunter
boss patron(ne) (mf)
both les deux
bottle bouteille (f) (8)
boulevard boulevard (m) (10)
bowl bol (m)
box boîte (f), paquet (m) (8)
boy garçon (m) (4)
boyfriend petit ami (m) (2)
bra soutien-gorge (m)
bracelet bracelet (m)
brave courageux(-euse)
Brazil Brésil (m) (9)
bread pain (m) (8); **bread-and-butter** tartine (f) (8); **loaf of French bread** baguette (f) (8); **wholegrain bread** pain complet (m) (8)
break casser; **break down** (machine) tomber en panne; **break one's arm** se casser le bras
breakfast petit déjeuner (m) (5); **bed and breakfast** chambre (f) d'hôte; **to have / eat one's breakfast** prendre son petit déjeuner (5)

breathe respirer
brief bref (brève)
briefly brièvement
briefs slip (m)
bright (colors) vif(-ive)
bring (a thing) apporter, (a person) amener; **bring back** rapporter
Britain: Great Britain Grande-Bretagne (f)
Brittany Bretagne (f)
broccoli brocolis (mpl)
brother frère (m) (1); **brother-in-law** beau-frère (m)
brown marron (3), brun(e) (4), (hair) châtain (4)
brunette brun(e)
brush (one's teeth) (se) brosser (les dents) (7)
Brussels sprouts choux (mpl) de Bruxelles
build construire
building bâtiment (m) (1); **administration building** centre administratif (m); **apartment building** immeuble (m) (3)
burn (oneself) (se) brûler
bus (in city) autobus (m) (3), (between cities) autocar (m) (4); **bus stop** arrêt (m) d'autobus (3)
business affaires (fpl); **business course** cours (m) de commerce (1)
businessman homme (m) d'affaires (5)
businesswoman femme (f) d'affaires (5)
busy chargé(e), occupé(e)
but mais (P); **nothing but** ne... rien que
butcher's shop boucherie (f) (8)
butter beurre (m) (8); **bread-and-butter** tartine (f) (8)
buy acheter (4)
by par; **by bike / boat / bus / car / plane / taxi** à vélo / en bateau / en autobus (autocar) / en voiture / en avion / en taxi (4); **by chance** par *hasard; **by the way** à propos; **go by . . .'s house** passer chez… (2); **right by** tout près (de) (3)
Bye! Salut!, Ciao!

C
cab taxi (m) (4)
cabbage chou (m)
café café (m) (1)
cafeteria cafétéria (f); **university cafeteria** restau-u (m) (6)
Cajun cadien(ne) (4)
cake gâteau (m) (8); **chocolate cake** gâteau au chocolat (8)
calculator calculatrice (f)
Caledonia: New Caledonia Nouvelle-Calédonie (f) (9)
California Californie (f) (9)
call communication (f); appel (m)
call téléphoner (3), appeler (6); **Who's calling?** Qui est à l'appareil?
calm calme (4), tranquille
calm down se calmer
camera appareil photo (m)
campground camping (m) (5)
camping camping (m) (5); **go camping** faire du camping (5)
campus campus (m) (1); fac(ulté) (f) (2)
can boîte (f) (8)
can (be able) pouvoir (6); **one can** on peut (4)
Canada Canada (m) (9)
Canadian canadien(ne) (P)
canceled annulé(e)
candy bonbon (m)
canned goods conserves (fpl) (8)
cap casquette (f)
capital capitale (f)

car voiture (f) (3); **by car** en voiture (4); **rental car** voiture (f) de location (5)
carafe carafe (f) (8)
carbohydrates féculents (mpl)
card carte (f); **bank card** carte bancaire (f) (9); **credit card** carte (f) de crédit (9); **debit card** carte bancaire (f) (9); **identity card** carte (f) d'identité; **telephone card** carte téléphonique (10)
care: I don't care. Ça m'est égal.; **take care of** s'occuper de, (health) (se) soigner
career carrière (f)
careful soigneux(-euse); **be careful** faire attention (à)
carefully soigneusement
carpenter charpentier (m)
carrot carotte (f) (8)
carry porter (4); **carry away** emporter
cartoon dessin animé (m)
cash: pay cash payer en espèces (10)
cashier caissier(-ère) (mf)
cassette cassette (f); **video cassette** vidéocassette (f); **videocassette player** magnétoscope (m)
castle palais (m) (6), château (m)
cat chat (m) (3)
cathedral cathédrale (f)
Catholic catholique (P)
cauliflower chou-fleur (m)
cause cause (f)
cause causer
CD CD (m) (P), disque compact (m); **CD player** lecteur (m) CD (3); platine laser (f)
celebrate célébrer (6), fêter
celebration fête (f) (4)
celery céleri (m)
cell phone portable (m) (3)
cent centime (m) (2)
center centre (m); **shopping center** centre commercial (m) (4)
centime centime (m) (2)
central central(e) (mpl centraux)
Central America Amérique centrale (f) (9)
century siècle (m)
cereal céréales (fpl) (8)
certain certain(e), sûr(e)
certainly certainement
certificate certificat (m)
chair chaise (f) (3)
chance: by chance par *hasard; **have the chance to** avoir l'occasion de
change monnaie (f) (2); **Here's your change.** Voici votre monnaie. (2)
change changer (de) (6); **change one's mind** changer d'avis
character (disposition) caractère (m), (from a story) personnage (m)
charge: extra charge supplément (m) (10); **in charge of** chargé(e) de, responsable de
charge charger
cheap bon marché
check chèque (m) (9), (restaurant) addition (f); **traveler's check** chèque (m) de voyage (9)
cheese fromage (m) (2); **cheese sandwich** sandwich (m) au fromage (2)
chemistry chimie (f) (1)
cherry cerise (f) (8)
chest poitrine (f); **chest of drawers** commode (f) (3)
chicken poulet (m) (8)
child enfant (mf) (4)
childhood enfance (f)
Chile Chili (m) (9)
chill frisson (m) (10)
China Chine (f) (9)
Chinese chinois(e)

chips chips (fpl)
chocolate chocolat (m) (2); **chocolate cake** gâteau (m) au chocolat (8); **chocolate-filled croissant** pain (m) au chocolat (8)
choice choix (m) (8)
choose (to do) choisir (de faire) (8)
chop: pork chop côte (f) de porc (8)
chore: household chore tâche domestique (f)
Christian chrétien(ne)
Christmas Noël (m); **Merry Christmas!** Joyeux Noël!
church église (f) (4), (Protestant) temple (m)
cinema cinéma (m) (1); **cinema club** cinéclub (m) (2)
circumstance circonstance (f)
city ville (f) (3)
class cours (m) (P), classe (f) (1); **first class** première classe (f) (9); **French class** cours (m) de français (P); **have class** avoir cours (6); **in another class** dans un autre cours (1); **tourist class** classe touriste (f) (9); **What is the homework for the next class?** Quels sont les devoirs pour le prochain cours? (P)
classic classique (m) (2)
classical classique (1)
classmate camarade (mf) de classe
classroom salle (f) de classe (1)
clean propre (3)
climate climat (m) (9)
climb (tree) grimper, (rocks) escalader
climbing: go mountain climbing faire de l'alpinisme; **go rock climbing** faire de la varappe
clinic clinique (f)
clock horloge (f); **alarm clock** réveil (m) (7)
close fermer (2); **Close your book.** Fermez votre livre. (P)
close to (location) près de (1); (a friend) uni(e), proche
closet placard (m) (3)
clothes vêtements (mpl) (3)
cloud nuage (m)
cloudy nuageux(-euse); **It's cloudy.** Il y a des nuages.
club club (m) (5); **cinema club** cinéclub (m) (2); **fitness club** club (m) de gym (1); **nightclub** boîte (f) de nuit (1)
coach classe touriste (f) (9)
coast côte (f); **Ivory Coast** Côte d'Ivoire (f) (9); **from/of the Ivory Coast** ivoirien(ne)
coat manteau (m) (5), pardessus (m)
code: zip code code postal (m) (3)
coffee café (m) (2); **coffee table** table basse (f)
coin pièce (f) de monnaie
Coke coca (m) (2)
cola coca (m) (2); **diet cola** coca light (m) (2)
cold froid(e); **be cold** avoir froid (4); **cold cuts** charcuterie (f) (8); **It's cold.** Il fait froid. (5)
cold rhume (m) (10)
colleague collègue (mf)
collect collectionner
college: go to college étudier à l'université
Colombia Colombie (f) (9)
color couleur (f) (3); **What color is/are . . . ?** De quelle couleur est/sont… ? (3)
comb one's hair se peigner (7)
come venir (4); **come back** revenir (4); **come down** (from) descendre (de) (5); **come get someone** venir chercher quelqu'un (10); **Come see!** Viens voir! (3)
comedy comédie (f) (6)
comfortable confortable (3)
commercial publicité (f)
communicate communiquer (10)
communication communication (f)

compact disc disque compact *(m)*, CD *(m)* (P)
company société *(f)*, compagnie *(f)*, entreprise *(f)*
compare comparer (6)
compatibility compatibilité *(f)* (7)
complain se plaindre
complete complet(-ète) (8); **in complete sentences** en phrases complètes (P)
completely tout à fait
complicated compliqué(e)
composition rédaction *(f)* (9), composition *(f)*
computer ordinateur *(m)* (2); **computer science** informatique *(f)* (1); **computer scientist** informaticien(ne) *(mf)*
concern concerner
concert concert *(m)* (1)
condition condition *(f)*
confidence confiance *(f)*; **have confidence** avoir confiance (4)
confused confus(e)
congratulations félicitations *(fpl)*
connection *(telephone)* communication *(f)*
conservative conservateur(-trice) (7)
conserve conserver
constantly constamment
consulate consulat *(m)*
contact contact *(m)*; **contact lenses** lentilles *(fpl)*
content content(e) (8)
continent continent *(m)* (9)
continue continuer (10)
continued: to be continued à suivre (6)
contrary: on the contrary par contre; au contraire
control contrôler (8)
convenient commode (3)
cook faire la cuisine (5); (faire) cuire
cooking cuisine *(f)* (4)
cool frais (fraîche); **pretty cool** assez cool (P); **The weather's cool.** Il fait frais. (5)
copious copieux(-euse) (8)
co-renter colocataire *(mf)* (P)
corn maïs *(m)*
corner coin *(m)* (3); **on the corner** *(of)* au coin (de) (10)
corridor couloir *(m)* (3)
cost coûter (5)
cotton coton *(m)*
couch canapé *(m)* (3)
cough tousser (10)
count compter (2); **Count from . . . to . . .** Comptez de... à... (P)
country campagne *(f)* (3), pays *(m)* (3); **country music** musique country *(f)*; **in the country** à la campagne (3)
couple couple *(m)*
course cours *(m)* (1); **first course** *(of a meal)* entrée *(f)* (8); **in the course of** au cours de (10); **Of course!** Bien sûr! (5), Évidemment!; **take a course** suivre un cours
court: tennis court court *(m)* de tennis
courtyard cour *(f)*; **on the courtyard side** côté cour (10)
cousin cousin(e) *(mf)* (4)
cover couverture *(f)* (3)
cover couvrir
crab crabe *(m)*
crazy fou (folle)
cream crème *(f)* (8); **ice cream** glace *(f)* (8)
create créer
credit card carte *(f)* de crédit (9)
crime crime *(m)*, criminalité *(f)*
criminal criminel(le) *(mf)*
criticize critiquer
croissant croissant *(m)* (8); **chocolate-filled croissant** pain *(m)* au chocloat (8)

cross traverser (10)
cruel cruel(le) (6)
crustaceans fruits *(mpl)* de mer (8)
cry pleurer
cucumber concombre *(m)*
cuisine cuisine *(f)* (4)
cultiver to cultivate (7)
cultural culturel(le) (4)
culture culture *(f)* (9)
cup tasse *(f)*
cure guérir
curly frisé(e)
current actuel(le)
currently actuellement
curtains rideaux *(mpl)* (3)
custom coutume *(f)*
customs *(border)* douane *(f)* (9)
cut: cold cuts charcuterie *(f)* (8)
cut (one's finger) (se) couper (le doigt); **cut class** sécher un cours
cycling cyclisme *(m)*

D

dad(dy) papa *(m)*
daily quotidien(ne) (7)
dairy laitier(-ère)
dance danse *(f);* bal *(m)* (6)
dance danser (2)
dancer danseur(-euse) *(mf)*
danger danger *(m)*
dangerous dangereux(-euse)
dark foncé(e); **dark-haired** brun(e) (4); **to be dark** *(outside)* faire noir
darling chéri(e)
date date *(f)* (4); rendez-vous *(m)*; **What is the date?** Quelle est la date? (4)
date sortir avec
daughter fille *(f)* (4)
day jour *(m)* (P), journée *(f)* (2); **day after tomorrow** après-demain; **day before yesterday** avant-hier; **every day** tous les jours (P); **Father's Day** fête *(f)* des Pères; **following day** lendemain *(m)* (5); **Have a good day!** Bonne journée!; **Mother's Day** fête des Mères; **next day** lendemain *(m)* (5); **the whole day** toute la journée (2); **What day is today?** C'est quel jour, aujourd'hui? (P)
daycare crèche *(f)*
daytime journée *(f)*
dead mort(e) (5)
death mort *(f)*
debit: debit card carte bancaire *(f)* (9)
deceased décédé(e) (4)
December décembre *(m)* (4)
decide décider (de) (6)
decision décision *(f)*; **make a decision** prendre une décision (7)
degree *(temperature)* degré *(m)*, *(university)* diplôme *(m)*
delay retard *(m)*
delicatessen charcuterie *(f)* (8); **deli meats** charcuterie *(f)* (8)
delicious délicieux(-euse) (6)
delighted ravi(e); **Delighted to meet you.** Enchanté(e).
deluxe de luxe (10)
demand exiger
democracy démocratie *(f)*
democratic démocratique
Denmark Danemark *(m)*
dentist dentiste *(mf)*
department département *(m)*; **department store** grand magasin *(m)*
departure départ *(m)* (9); **departure gate** porte *(f)* d'embarquement (9)

depend (on) dépendre (de) (5); **That depends.** Ça dépend.
deposit déposer
depressed déprimé(e)
depressing déprimant(e)
depression déprime *(f)*
descend descendre (5)
describe décrire (9)
description description *(f)*
designer fashion *haute couture *(f)*
desire avoir envie de (4), désirer (2)
desk bureau *(m)* (3); **front desk** réception *(f)* (10)
despite malgré
dessert dessert *(m)* (8)
destroy détruire
detest (each other) (se) détester (7)
develop (se) développer
dictatorship dictature *(f)*
dictionary dictionnaire *(m)*
die mourir (5)
diet régime *(m)*; **be on a diet** être au régime; **diet cola** coca *(m)* light (2)
different différent(e)
differently différemment
difficult difficile (P)
difficulty difficulté *(f)*
digest digérer
dine (out) dîner (au restaurant) (2)
dining: dining hall restaurant universitaire *(m)*, restau-u (6); **dining room** salle à manger *(f)* (3)
dinner dîner *(m)* (8); **before-dinner drink** apéritif *(m)* (10); **have dinner** dîner (2)
diploma diplôme *(m)*
direct diriger
direct direct(e)
directions indications *(fpl)* (10); **give directions** indiquer le chemin (10)
directly directement
dirty sale (3)
disadvantage inconvénient *(m)*
disappointed déçu(e)
disc: compact disc disque compact *(m)*, CD *(m)* (P); **compact disc player** lecteur *(m)* CD (3); platine *(f)* laser
discover découvrir
discuss discuter (de)
disguise (oneself) (se) déguiser
dish plat *(m)* (8); **do the dishes** faire la vaisselle (5); **ready-to-serve dish** plat préparé *(m)* (8)
dishwasher lave-vaisselle *(m)*
disorder désordre *(m)* (3); **in disorder** en désordre (3)
diversity diversité *(f)*
divided partagé(e) (3)
diving: scuba diving plongée sous-marine *(f)*
divorce divorcer
divorced divorcé(e) (1)
do faire (2); **do aerobics** faire de l'aérobic (8); **do better...** faire mieux... (8); **do handiwork** bricoler (2); **Do the homework.** Faites les devoirs. (P); **do weight training** faire de la musculation (8); **Do you . . . ?** Est-ce que vous... ? (1); **I do not...** Je ne... pas (P)
doctor médecin *(m)* (10)
doctorate doctorat *(m)*
dog chien *(m)* (3)
dollar dollar *(m)* (3)
domestic domestique
door porte *(f)* (3); **next door** d'à côté
dormitory résidence universitaire *(f)* (1)
doubt doute *(m)*; **without doubt** sans doute (8)
doubt douter (10)
down: go / come down descendre (5)

downtown au centre-ville *(m)* (3)
dozen douzaine *(f)* (8)
draft beer demi *(m)* (2)
drama drame *(m)*; **drama course** cours *(m)* de théâtre (1)
dramatic dramatique
draw dessiner
drawer tiroir *(m)*; **chest of drawers** commode *(f)* (3)
drawing dessin *(m)*
dream rêve *(m)*
dream (about) rêver (de) (7)
dress robe *(f)* (5)
dress habiller; **get dressed** s'habiller (7)
dresser commode *(f)* (3)
drink boisson *(f)* (2); **before-dinner drink** apéritif *(m)* (8); **have a drink** prendre un verre (2)
drink boire (4)
drive conduire; **go for a drive** faire un tour en voiture
drop laisser tomber
drums batterie *(f)* (2)
dry sécher; **dry cleaner's** teinturerie *(f)*
duck canard *(m)* (8)
due to à cause de
dumb bête (1)
during pendant (5), au cours de (10)
DVD DVD *(m)* (2); **DVD player** lecteur *(m)* DVD (3)

E

each chaque (3); **each one** chacun(e); **each other** se, vous, nous (7), l'un(e) l'autre
ear oreille *(f)*
early tôt (4), en avance
earn gagner
earring boucle *(f)* d'oreille
earth terre *(f)*
easily facilement (7)
east est *(m)*; **Middle East** Moyen-Orient *(m)* (9)
Easter Pâques *(fpl)*
easy facile (4)
eat manger (2); **eat one's breakfast** prendre son petit déjeuner (5); **eat dinner** dîner (2); **eat dinner out** dîner au restaurant (2); **eat lunch** déjeuner (2)
eccentric excentrique
ecological écologique
economics sciences économiques *(fpl)*
economy économie *(f)*
editor rédacteur(-trice) *(mf)*
educate éduquer
education éducation *(f)*
effect effet *(m)* (6); **special effects** effets spéciaux *(mpl)* (6)
egg œuf *(m)* (8); **hard-boiled egg** œuf dur *(m)* (8)
eggplant aubergine *(f)*
Egypt Égypte *(f)* (9)
eight *huit (P)
eighteen dix-huit (P)
eighty quatre-vingts (2)
eighth *huitième (3)
either . . . or . . . soit... soit...
elect élire
election élection *(f)*
element élément *(m)*
elementary school école primaire/élémentaire *(f)*
elevated élevé(e)
elevator ascenseur *(m)* (3)
eleven onze (P)
else: What else? Quoi d'autre?; **What else can I get you?** Qu'est-ce que je peux vous proposer d'autre? (8)
elsewhere ailleurs

email mail *(m)* (2), courrier électronique *(m)*; **email address** adresse *(f)* mail (3)
embarrassed gêné(e)
embassy ambassade *(f)*
embrace (each other) (s')embrasser (7)
emotional sentimental(e) *(mpl* sentimentaux) (7)
employee employé(e) *(mf)* (10); **governement employee** fonctionnaire *(mf)*
encounter rencontre *(f)* (7)
end fin *(f)*; **at the end (of)** au bout (de) (3)
end finir (8), (se) terminer; **end up doing** finir par faire; **French class ends…** Le cours de français finit… (P)
energy énergie *(f)*
engaged fiancé(e) (1); **get engaged** se fiancer (7)
engineer ingénieur *(m)*
engineering études *(fpl)* d'ingénieur, génie *(m)*
English anglais *(m)* (P)
English anglais(e)
enjoy: Enjoy your stay! Bon séjour! (10)
enough assez (de) (1)
enter entrer (dans) (5)
enterprise entreprise *(f)*
entertainment distractions *(fpl)* (5)
enthusiastic enthousiaste
entire entier(-ère)
environment environnement *(m)*
equality égalité *(f)*
equals: . . . plus . . . equals . . . ... et... font... (P)
errand course *(f)* (5); **run errands** faire des courses (5)
especially surtout (8)
espresso expresso *(m)* (2)
essential essentiel(le)
establish établir
euro euro *(m)* (2)
Europe Europe *(f)* (9)
European européen(ne)
eve: New Year's Eve party le réveillon *(m)* du jour de l'an
even même; **even though** bien que
evening soir *(m)* (P), soirée *(f)* (4); **At ten o'-clock in the evening.** À dix heures du soir. (P); **Good evening.** Bonsoir. (P); **in the evening, evenings** le soir (P); **See you this evening.** À ce soir. (2)
every tout (toute, tous, toutes) (3), chaque (3); **every day** tous les jours (P); **every evening** tous les soirs
everybody tout le monde (6)
everyone tout le monde (6)
everything tout (3)
everywhere partout (3)
exactly justement (3), exactement (10)
exam examen *(m)* (P)
example exemple *(m)*; **for example** par exemple (2)
excellent excellent(e) (6)
except sauf (2)
exception exception *(f)*; **with the exception of** à l'exception de
exchange money changer de l'argent (9)
exciting passionnant(e)
excuse excuser; **Excuse me.** Excusez-moi, Pardon. (P)
executive cadre *(m)*
exercise exercice *(m)* (P)
exercise faire de l'exercice (2)
exhausted épuisé(e)
exhibit exposition *(f)* (4)
ex-husband ex-mari *(m)*
exotic exotique (9)
expensive cher (chère) (3)
experience expérience *(f)*
explain expliquer

express exprimer
expression expression *(f)* (10)
extra charge supplément *(m)* (10)
extracurricular extra-scolaire
extraordinary extra(ordinaire) (4)
extroverted extraverti(e) (1)
ex-wife ex-femme *(f)*
eye œil *(m)* *(pl* yeux) (10); **to have . . . eyes** avoir les yeux... (4)

F

face figure *(f)* (7), visage *(m)*
facing en face (de) (3)
fact fait *(m)*; **in fact** en fait
fail échouer (à)
fair juste
fairly assez (P)
fairy tale conte *(m)* de fée (6)
fall automne *(m)* (5); **in the fall** en automne (5)
fall tomber (5); **fall asleep** s'endormir (7); **fall in love (with)** tomber amoureux(-euse) (de) (6)
false faux (fausse)
fame renommée *(f)*
familiar: be familiar with connaître (4)
family famille *(f)* (P); **family name** nom *(m)* de famille (3)
famous célèbre (4), fameux(-euse)
far (from) loin (de) (3); **as far as** jusqu'à (10)
farm ferme *(f)*
fashion mode *(f)*; **designer fashion** *haute couture *(f)*
fast vite (7), rapide (8)
fast food restaurant fast-food *(m)* (1)
fat matières grasses *(fpl)* (8)
fat gros(se) (1); **get fatter** grossir (8)
father père *(m)* (4); **father-in-law** beau-père *(m)* (4); **Father's Day** fête *(f)* des Pères
fatty gras(se)
favorite préféré(e) (3)
fear avoir peur (de) (4)
February février *(m)* (4)
feed nourrir (8), donner à manger à (9); **to feed oneself** se nourrir (8)
feel (se) sentir (8); **feel like** avoir envie de (4)
feeling sentiment *(m)* (7)
ferocious féroce (6)
festival festival *(m)* (4)
fever fièvre *(f)*; **have fever** avoir de la fièvre
few: a few quelques (5), quelques-un(e)s
fewer moins de (8); **fewer . . . than** moins de... que
fiancé fiancé *(m)*
fiancée fiancée *(f)*
field champ *(m)*
fifteen quinze (P)
fifth cinquième (3)
fifty cinquante (2)
fight combattre, se battre; **fight (against)** lutter (contre)
fill (in) remplir
film film *(m)* (1)
finally finalement (6), enfin (7)
find trouver (4); **find out information** s'informer (9)
fine: fine arts beaux-arts *(mpl)* (1); **It's going fine.** Ça va. (P)
finger doigt *(m)* (10)
finish (doing) finir (de faire) (8), terminer
firm entreprise *(f)*
first premier(-ère) (1); **at first** au début; **first course** *(of a meal)* entrée *(f)* (8); **first floor** rez-de-chaussée *(m)* (3); **first name** prénom *(m)* (3); **first of all** d'abord (4); **in first class** en première classe (9); **love at first sight** coup *(m)* de foudre (7)

fish poisson *(m)* (8); **fish shop** poissonnerie *(f)* (8)

fishing pêche *(f)*; **go fishing** aller à la pêche

fist poing *(m)*

fitness club club *(m)* de gym (1)

fitting room cabine *(f)* d'essayage (5)

five cinq (P)

fixed: at a fixed price à prix fixe (8)

flashlight lampe *(f)* de poche

flight vol *(m)* (9)

floor étage *(m)* (3); **ground floor** rez-de-chaussée *(m)* (3); **on the floor** par terre (3); **on the second floor** au premier étage (3)

floral à fleurs

Florida Floride *(f)* (9)

florist fleuriste *(mf)*

flower fleur *(f)*

flu grippe *(f)* (10)

fluently couramment

foggy: It's foggy. Il fait du brouillard.

folk music folk *(m)*

folklore folklore *(m)* (4)

follow suivre (7)

following suivant(e) (3)

food aliments *(mpl)*, nourriture *(f)*

foot pied *(m)* (10); **go on foot** aller à pied (4)

football football américain *(m)* (1)

for pour (P), pendant (5), depuis (7), comme (8); **for example** par exemple (2); **For how long?** Pendant combien de temps? (5); **for the last three days** depuis les trois derniers jours; **go away for the weekend** partir en week-end (5); **look for** chercher (3); **watch out for** faire attention à (8)

forbidden: It's forbidden to . . . Il est inderdit de...

foreign étranger(-ère) (1)

foreseen prévu(e)

forest forêt *(f)*

forget oublier (8)

forgive pardonner

fork fourchette *(f)*

former ancien(ne)

formerly autrefois, jadis

forty quarante (2)

fountain fontaine *(f)*

four quatre (P)

fourteen quatorze (P)

fourth quatrième (3)

France France *(f)* (1)

frankly franchement

free libre (2), *(price)* gratuit(e); **free time** temps libre *(m)* (4)

freedom liberté *(f)*

French français *(m)* (P); **French class** cours *(m)* de français (P); **How do you say . . . in French?** Comment dit-on... en français? (P)

French français(e) (1); **French fries** frites *(fpl)* (8); **French Guiana** Guyane *(f)* (9); **French Polynesia** Polynésie française (9); **French Quarter** Vieux Carré *(m)* (4); **French West Indies** Antilles *(fpl)* (9); **loaf of French bread** baguette *(f)* (8)

French-speaking francophone

frequently fréquemment

fresh frais (fraîche) (8)

Friday vendredi *(m)* (P)

friend ami(e) *(mf)* (P), copain *(m)*, copine *(f)* (6)

friendly amical(e) *(mpl* amicaux)

fries: French fries frites *(fpl)* (2); **steak and fries** steak-frites (8) *(m)*

frisbee: to play frisbee jouer au frisbee

from de *(m)*, depuis

front: front desk réception *(f)* (10); **in front of** devant (3)

frozen surgelé(e) (8)

fruit fruit *(m)* (8); **fruit juice** jus *(m)* de fruit (2)

full plein(e)

fun amusant(e) (1); **Does that sound like fun?** Ça te dit? (4); **have fun (doing)** s'amuser (à faire) (7); **make fun of** se moquer de

funny drôle

furious furieux(-euse) (10)

furnishings meubles *(mpl)* (3)

furniture meubles *(mpl)* (3)

furthermore en plus (8)

futon futon *(m)*

future avenir *(m)*

G

gain gagner; **gain weight** prendre du poids

game match *(m)* (1), jeu *(m)* (2); **video game** jeu vidéo *(m)* (2)

garage garage *(m)*

garden jardin *(m)* (5)

garden faire du jardinage (5), jardiner

gardening jardinage *(m)*

gate: arrival gate porte *(f)* d'arrivée (9); **departure gate** porte *(f)* d'embarquement (9)

general: in general en général (2)

generally généralement

generous généreux(-euse)

gentle doux(-ce) (6)

gentleman monsieur *(m)*; **ladies-gentlemen** messieurs-dames

geography géographie *(f)* (9)

geology géologie *(f)*

German allemand *(m)* (1)

German allemand(e)

Germany Allemagne *(f)* (9)

get obtenir (9), recevoir; **get along** s'entendre (7); **get bored** s'ennuyer (7); **get dressed** s'habiller (7); **get engaged** se fiancer (7); **get fatter** grossir (8); **get lost** se perdre (7); **get married (to)** se marier (avec) (7); **get off** descendre (de) (5); **get older** vieillir; **get on** monter (dans) (5); **get ready** se préparer; **get sick** tomber malade (10); **get taller** grandir (8); **get thinner** maigrir (8); **get to know** connaître (4); **get undressed** se déshabiller (7); **get up** se lever (7); **get well** guérir; **go/come get someone** aller/venir chercher quelqu'un (10); **What else can I get you?** Qu'est-ce que je peux vous proposer d'autre? (8)

gift cadeau *(m)* (10); **gift shop** marchand *(m)* de cadeaux (10)

girl (jeune) fille *(f)* (4)

girlfriend petite amie *(f)* (2)

give donner (2); **give (something) back (to someone)** rendre (quelque chose à quelqu'un) (7); **give directions** indiquer le chemin (10); **Give me your sheet of paper.** Donnez-moi votre feuille de papier. (P)

glad content(e)

gladly avec plaisir (6), volontiers (8)

glass verre *(m)* (2); **a glass of** un verre de (2)

glasses lunettes *(fpl)* (4)

global global(e) *(mpl* globaux)

glove gant *(m)*

go aller (2), se rendre (à / chez); **go across** traverser (10); **go all-terrain biking** faire du VTT (5); **go away** partir (4), s'en aller; **go back** rentrer (2), retourner (5); **go bike-riding** faire du vélo (5); **go boating** faire du bateau (5); **go by / past** passer (2); **go camping** faire du camping (5); **go down** descendre (5); **go for a ride** faire un tour (4); **go for a walk** faire une promenade (5); **go get someone** aller chercher quelqu'un (10); **go gro-**cery shopping** faire les courses (7); **go hiking** faire une randonnée (8); **go in** entrer (dans) (5); **go home** rentrer (2); **go jogging** faire du jogging (2); **go on foot** aller à pied (4); **go out** sortir (2); **go rollerblading** faire du roller (6); **go scuba diving** faire de la plongée sous-marine; **go see** aller voir (4); **go shopping** faire du shopping (2); **go skiing** faire du ski (2); **go to bed** se coucher (7); **Go to the board!** Allez au tableau! (P); **go to the movies** aller au cinéma (2); **go up** monter (5); **go walking** se promener (7), faire de la marche à pied; **go water-skiing** faire du ski nautique; **go windsurfing** faire de la planche à voile; **How's it going?** Comment ça va? (P); **It's going fine.** Ça va. (P)

goal but *(m)*

god dieu *(m)*

golf golf *(m)* (2)

good: canned goods conserves *(fpl)* (8)

good bon(ne) (1), sage (4); **Good evening.** Bonsoir. (P); **Good idea!** Bonne idée! (4); **good in/at** fort(e) en; **Good morning.** Bonjour. (P); **Have a good day!** Bonne journée!; **Have a good weekend!** Bon week-end!; **It's good to...** C'est bien de... (10); **One has a good time!** On s'amuse bien!

good-bye au revoir (P)

government gouvernement *(m)*; **government worker** fonctionnaire *(mf)*

gracious gracieux(-euse) (6)

grade note *(f)*

gram gramme *(m)* (8)

grammar grammaire *(f)*

grandchildren petits-enfants *(mpl)*

granddaughter petite-fille *(f)* (7)

grandfather grand-père *(m)* (4)

grandma mamie *(f)* (7)

grandmother grand-mère *(f)* (4)

grandparents grands-parents *(mpl)* (4)

grandson petit-fils *(m)* (7)

granny mamie *(f)* (7)

grape(s) raisin *(m)* (8)

grapefruit pamplemousse *(m)*

graphic artist dessinateur(-trice) *(mf)* (de publicité)

gray gris(e) (3)

great super (P), extra(ordinaire) (4), génial(e) *(mpl* géniaux) (4), formidable (7), magnifique

Great Britain Grande-Bretagne *(f)*

green vert(e) (4); **green beans** *haricots verts *(mpl)* (8)

greet saluer

grilled grillé(e) (8)

grocery: go grocery shopping faire les courses (8); **grocery store** épicerie *(f)* (8)

ground terre *(f)*; **ground floor** rez-de-chaussée *(m)* (3); **on the ground** par terre (3)

ground: ground meat bifteck *haché *(m)*

group groupe *(m)* (6)

grow (up) grandir (8)

guess deviner

Guiana: French Guiana Guyane *(f)* (9)

guide guide *(m)* (9)

guidebook guide *(m)* (9)

guilty coupable

guitar guitare *(f)* (2)

gym club *(m)* de gym (1), gymnase *(m)*

H

hair cheveux *(mpl)* (4); **comb one's hair** se peigner (7); **hair stylist** coiffeur(-euse) *(mf)*

Haiti Haïti *(m)*

half moitié *(f)*
half demi(e) (P); **half-brother** demi-frère *(m)*;
half hour demi-heure *(f)* (7); **half-sister**
demi-sœur *(f)*; **It's half past two.** Il est deux
heures et demie. (P); **a kilo and a half** un
kilo et demi (8)
hall couloir *(m)* (3); **dining hall** restaurant universitaire *(m)*, restau-u *(m)* (6); **lecture hall**
amphithéâtre *(m)* (1); **residence hall** résidence universitaire *(f)* (1)
ham jambon *(m)* (2); **ham sandwich** sandwich
au jambon *(m)* (2)
hamburger *hamburger *(m)* (8)
hand main *(f)* (7); **on the other hand** par contre
handiwork: do handiwork bricoler (2)
handsome beau/bel (belle) (1)
hang up raccrocher
Hanukkah *Hanoukka *(f)*
happen se passer (7), arriver; **What happened?**
Qu'est-ce qui s'est passé? (7)
happiness bonheur *(m)* (7)
happy content(e) (8), heureux(-euse) (7);
Happy Birthday! Bon anniversaire!
hard dur(e); **have a hard time** avoir du mal à
hard-boiled egg œuf dur *(m)* (8)
hardly ne... guère
hard-working travailleur(-euse)
hat chapeau *(m)*
hate (each other) (se) détester (7)
hatred *haine *(f)*
have avoir (3); **have a drink** prendre un verre
(2); **have one's breakfast** prendre son petit
déjeuner (5); **have class** avoir cours (6); **have
difficulty doing** avoir du mal à faire; **have
dinner** dîner (2); **have fun (doing)** s'amuser
(à faire) (7); **have just (done)** venir de
(faire); **have lunch** déjeuner (2); **have to**
devoir (6)
hazel *(eyes)* noisette *(inv)* (4)
he il (1); **he is . . .** c'est..., il est... (1)
head tête *(f)* (10)
health santé *(f)* (8); **health center** infirmerie *(f)*
healthy sain(e) (8)
hear entendre
heart cœur *(m)*
heavy lourd(e)
Hebrew hébreu *(m)*
heels: high heels *hauts talons *(mpl)*
height *hauteur *(f)*, taille *(f)*; **of medium
height** de taille moyenne (4)
hello bonjour (P), *(on the telephone)* allô (6)
help aider (5); **May I help you?** Je peux vous
aider? (5)
henceforth désormais
her la (5); **to her** lui (9); **with her** avec elle
her son (sa, ses) (3)
here ici (P); **here is/are** voici (2)
herself se (7), elle-même
Hi! Salut! (P)
high élevé(e), *haut(e); **high fashion** *haute
couture *(f)* (1); **high heels** *hauts talons *(mpl)*;
high school lycée *(m)* (6); **high school student** lycéen(ne) *(mf)* (6)
hiking: to go hiking faire une randonnée (8)
him le (5); **to him** lui (9); **with him** avec lui
(6)
himself se (7), lui-même
his son (sa, ses) (3)
historic historique (9)
history histoire *(f)* (1)
hobby passe-temps *(m)* (2)
hockey *hockey *(m)* (2)
hold tenir
holiday fête *(f)* (4); **national holiday** fête
nationale *(f)*

home: at home à la maison (P); **come / go
home** rentrer (2)
homework devoirs *(mpl)* (P); **Do the homework.** Faites les devoirs. (P)
honest honnête
honey miel *(m)*, chéri(e)
honeymoon lune *(f)* de miel, voyage *(m)* de
noces
hope espérer (3)
horrible horrible (6), affreux(-euse)
horror movie film *(m)* d'épouvante
hors d'œuvre *hors-d'œuvre *(m)* *(inv)*, entrée
(f) (8)
horse cheval *(m)* *(pl* chevaux); **ride a horse**
monter à cheval
horseback: go horseback riding faire du cheval
hose: panty hose collant *(m)*
hospital hôpital *(m)*
hostel: youth hostel auberge *(f)* de jeunesse
hot chaud(e) (2); **be hot** avoir chaud (4); **hot
chocolate** chocolat chaud *(m)* (2); **The
weather's hot.** Il fait chaud. (5)
hotel hôtel *(m)* (5); **hotel manager** hôtelier
(-ère) *(mf)* (10)
hour heure *(f)* (P); **half hour** demi-heure *(f)* (7)
house maison *(f)* (1); **at / to / in my house**
chez moi (2); **at my parents' house** chez
mes parents (3); **pass by the house of . . .**
passer chez... (2)
household ménage *(m)*; **household chore** tâche
domestique *(f)*
housemate colocataire *(mf)* (P)
housework ménage *(m)* (5)
housing logement *(m)* (3)
how comment (P); **How are you?** Comment
allez-vous? (P); **How does that sound to
you?** Ça te dit? (4); **How do you say . . . ?**
Comment dit-on... ? (P); **how many** combien (de) (3); **How many are there of you?**
Vous êtes combien? (4); **how much** combien
(de) (3); **How much is it?** C'est combien?,
Ça fait combien? (2); **How much is . . . plus
/ minus . . . ?** Combien font... et / moins... ?
(P); **How old is . . . ?** Quel âge a... ? (4);
How's it going? Comment ça va? (P); **How's
the weather?** Quel temps fait-il? (5); **That
takes how long?** Ça prend combien de
temps? (4)
however pourtant (8)
human humain(e)
humor: sense of humor sens *(m)* de l'humour
(7)
hundred: one hundred cent (2)
hunger faim *(f)*
hungry: be hungry avoir faim (4); **I'm hungry.**
J'ai faim. (2)
hunter chasseur *(m)*
hunting chasse *(f)*; **go hunting** aller à la chasse
hurry se dépêcher (de); **hurried** pressé(e)
hurt: one's... hurt(s) avoir mal (à)... (10); **hurt
(someone)** faire mal (à quelqu'un)
husband mari *(m)* (2)

I

I je, j' (P)
ice glace *(f)*; **ice cream** glace *(f)* (8)
ice-skating patin *(m)* à glace; **go ice-skating**
faire du patin à glace
icy: It's icy. Il y a du verglas.
idea idée *(f)* (4)
idealistic idéaliste (1)
identify identifier
identity card carte *(f)* d'identité
if si (5)

ill malade (10)
illness maladie *(f)*
image image *(f)*
immediately immédiatement, tout de suite (7)
impatient impatient(e) (4)
importance importance *(f)* (7)
important important(e) (5)
imprison emprisonner (6)
improve améliorer (8)
impulsive impulsif(-ive)
in dans (P), en (P), chez (+ *a person*) (7); **go in**
entrer (dans) (5); **I live in** (+ *city*) J'habite à
(+ *city*) (P); **in advance** à l'avance (9); **in bed**
au lit (2); **in front of** devant (3); **in love**
amoureux(-euse); **in order to** pour (1); **in
the country** à la campagne (3); **in the
morning** le matin (P); **in your opinion** à
votre avis (8)
include comprendre (8); **included** compris(e)
(10)
indecision indécision *(f)* (7)
indefinite indéfini *(m)*
independent indépendant(e)
India Inde *(f)*
Indies: West Indies Antilles *(fpl)* (9)
indifference indifférence *(f)* (7)
indigestion indigestion *(f)* (10)
Indochina Indochine *(f)*
industry industrie *(f)*
inequality inégalité *(f)*
inexpensive pas cher(-ère) (7)
infidelity infidélité *(f)* (7)
inflexibility inflexibilité *(f)* (7)
influence each other s'influencer
inform (oneself) (s')informer (9)
information renseignements *(mpl)* (3); **find out
information** s'informer (9)
inherit hériter
in-laws beaux-parents *(mpl)*
insensitivity insensibilité *(f)* (7)
inside à l'intérieur
insist insister (10)
instant instant *(m)*
instead plutôt (4)
institution institution *(f)*
instructions instructions *(fpl)*
intellectual intellectuel(le) (1)
intelligent intelligent(e) (1)
intend avoir l'intention de (4)
interested: be interested in s'intéresser à (7)
interesting intéressant(e) (P)
international international(e) *(mpl* internationaux)
Internet Internet *(m)*; **on the Internet** sur
Internet (9)
interpret interpréter
interpreter interprète *(mf)*
introduce présenter; **Let me introduce . . . to
you.** Je vous/te présente...
introverted introverti(e)
investigation enquête *(f)*
invitation invitation *(f)* (6)
invite inviter (à) (3)
iPod iPod *(m)* (3)
Irak Iraq *(m)*
Iran Iran *(m)*
island île *(f)* (9)
Israel Israël *(m)* (9)
it ce (P), il (P), elle (1), le, la (5); **How's it
going?** Comment ça va? (P); **isn't it?** n'est-ce
pas?, non? (1); **it's . . .** c'est... (P); **It's going
fine.** Ça va. (P); **of it** en (8)
Italian italien *(m)*
Italian italien(ne)
Italy Italie *(f)* (9)

itinerary itinéraire *(m)* (9)
its son *(sa, ses)* (3)
Ivory Coast Côte d'Ivoire *(f)* (9); **from/of the Ivory Coast** ivoirien(ne)

J

jacket veste *(f)*, blouson *(m)*; **ski jacket** anorak *(m)* (5); **windbreaker jacket** blouson *(m)*
jam confiture *(f)* (8)
January janvier *(m)* (4)
Japan Japon *(m)* (9)
Japanese japonais *(m)*
Japanese japonais(e)
jar pot *(m)* (8)
jazz jazz *(m)* (1)
jealous jaloux(-ouse) (7)
jealousy jalousie *(f)* (7)
jeans jean *(m)* (5)
jelly confiture *(f)* (8)
jewelry bijoux *(mpl)*
job poste *(m)*, travail *(m)* (6)
jog faire du jogging (2)
jogging jogging *(m)* (2); **go jogging** faire du jogging (2); **jogging suit** survêtement *(m)* (5)
join rejoindre
journal journal *(m)*
journalism journalisme *(m)*
journalist journaliste *(mf)*
judge juge *(m)*
juice jus *(m)* (2)
July juillet *(m)* (4)
June juin *(m)* (4)
just seulement (8), juste (10); **I would just as soon...** J'aimerais autant... (10); **have just (done)** venir de (faire); **just anything** n'importe quoi

K

keep garder
key clé *(f)* (10)
keyboard clavier *(m)*
kidney rein *(m)*
kilo kilo *(m)* (8)
kilometer kilomètre *(m)*
kind genre *(m)*; **all kinds of . . .** toutes sortes de...
kindergarten école maternelle *(f)*
kingdom royaume *(m)*; **United Kingdom** Royaume-Uni *(m)* (9)
kiosk kiosque *(m)* (10)
kiss baiser *(m)*, bise *(f)*
kiss (each other) (s')embrasser (7)
kitchen cuisine *(f)* (3)
knee genou *(m)*
knife couteau *(m)*
knit shirt polo *(m)* (5)
know *(person, place)* connaître (4), *(how, answers)* savoir (9); **get to know** connaître (4); **I don't know.** Je ne sais pas. (P); **known** connu(e); **What do you know about...?** Que savez-vous de...?; **Do you know how to...?** Savez-vous...? (8)
knowledge connaissance *(f)*

L

Labor Day fête du travail *(f)*
laboratory: computer lab laboratoire *(m)* d'informatique (1); **language lab** laboratoire *(m)* de langues (1)
lack of manque de *(m)*
lady dame *(f)*; **ladies-gentlemen** messieurs-dames; **lady's suit** tailleur *(m)*
lake lac *(m)*

lamb agneau *(m)*
lamp lampe *(f)* (3)
landscape paysage *(m)* (9)
language langue *(f)* (1); **language lab** laboratoire *(m)* de langues (1)
laptop portable *(m)* (3)
large grand(e) (1); copieux(-euse) (8)
last durer
last dernier(-ère) (5)
late tard (4), en retard (10); **later** plus tard (4); **See you later.** À tout à l'heure. (P); À plus tard! (2)
laugh rire
laundry linge *(m)*; **do laundry** faire la lessive (5)
law loi *(f)*; *(field)* droit *(m)*
lawyer avocat(e) *(mf)*
lazy paresseux(-euse) (1)
learn apprendre (à) (4); **Learn . . .** Apprenez... (P)
leave quitter (4), partir (de) (4), sortir (de) (6), *(something behind)* laisser (3), s'en aller; **leave each other** se quitter (7)
lecture hall amphithéâtre *(m)* (1)
left gauche *(f)* (3); **to the left (of)** à gauche (de) (3)
leg jambe *(f)* (10)
leisure activity loisir *(m)*
lemon citron *(m)* (2); **tea with lemon** thé *(m)* au citron (2)
lend prêter
lense: contact lenses lentilles *(fpl)*
less moins de (8); **less . . . than** moins... que (1)
let laisser; **Let's see!** Voyons! (5)
letter lettre *(f)* (9)
lettuce laitue *(f)* (8)
level niveau *(m)*
liberal libéral(e) *(mpl* libéraux) (7)
library bibliothèque *(f)* (1)
life vie *(f)* (6)
lift weights faire de la musculation (8); faire des haltères
light *(weight)* léger(-ère) (8), *(color)* clair(e)
like aimer (2); **Did you like it?** Ça t'a plu? (6); **Does he like it?** Ça lui plaît? (9); **Do you like?** Est-ce que vous aimez? (1); **I like . . .** J'aime... (1); **I like it!** Il/Elle me plaît! (5); **I would like . . .** Je voudrais (bien)... (2); **like each other** s'aimer bien (7); **What would you like?** Vous désirez? (2); **You'll like it!** Ça te/vous plaira! (9); **You would like . . .** Tu voudrais..., Vous voudriez... (2) **like** comme (1); **What is / are . . . like?** Comment est / sont... ? (1)
lime citron vert *(m)*
line ligne *(f)*; **online** en ligne (7)
lip lèvre *(f)*
liquid liquide *(m)* (10)
listen (to) écouter (2); **Listen to the question.** Écoutez la question. (P)
liter litre *(m)* (8)
literature littérature *(f)* (1)
little peu de (8); **a little** un peu (P); **little by little** petit à petit (6)
little petit(e) (1)
live habiter (2); **Do you live...?** Vous habitez...? (P); **I live in . . .** *(+ city)* J'habite à... *(+ city)* (P)
liver foie *(m)*
living room salon *(m)* (3)
loaf of French bread baguette *(f)* (8)
loafers mocassins *(mpl)*
loan prêter
lobster *homard *(m)* (8)
local local(e) *(mpl* locaux) (9)

located situé(e); **It is located...** Il/Elle se trouve...
lock fermer à clé
lodge: ski lodge chalet *(m)* de ski (10)
lodging logement *(m)* (3)
lonely seul(e)
long long(ue) (4); **a long time** longtemps (5); **as long as** tant que; **How long?** Combien de temps? (4); **no longer** ne... plus (8)
look (at) regarder (2); **look (+ *adjective*)** avoir l'air (+ *adjectif*) (4); **look at each other** se regarder (7); **look for** chercher (3); **look like** ressembler à; **look very good on someone** aller très bien à quelqu'un
lose perdre (7); **get lost** se perdre (7); **lose weight** perdre du poids
lot: a lot beaucoup (P), **a lot of** beaucoup de (1); **not a lot** pas grand-chose
love amour *(m)* (6); **fall in love (with)** tomber amoureux(-euse) (de) (6); **love at first sight** coup *(m)* de foudre (7); **love story** film *(m)* d'amour (6); **true love** le grand amour (7)
love aimer (7), adorer; **love each other** s'aimer (7)
luck chance *(f)* (5)
lucky: be lucky avoir de la chance (9)
luggage bagages *(mpl)*
lunch déjeuner *(m)* (7); **have lunch** déjeuner (2)
lung poumon *(m)*
luxury luxe *(m)*
lyrics paroles *(fpl)*

M

machine machine *(f)*; **automatic teller machine** distributeur de billets *(m)* (10)
madam (Mrs.) madame (Mme) (P)
magazine magazine *(m)* (9)
magnificent magnifique
mail courrier *(m)*; **e-mail** mail *(m)* (2), courrier électronique *(m)*; **mail carrier** facteur *(m)*, factrice *(f)*
main principal(e) *(mpl* principaux) (8)
major in se spécialiser en
majority: the majority of the time la plupart du temps (7)
make faire (2); **make (+ *adjective*)** rendre (+ **adjectif**); **make a decision** prendre une décision (7); **make money** gagner de l'argent; **make up with each other** se réconcilier (7);
make-up maquillage *(m)*; **put on make-up** se maquiller (7)
mall centre commercial *(m)* (4)
mama maman *(f)*
man homme *(m)* (1); monsieur *(m)*
management gestion *(f)*
mango mangue *(f)*
manual worker ouvrier(-ère) *(mf)*
many beaucoup (de) (1); **how many** combien (de) (3); **How many are there of you?** Vous êtes combien? (4); **so many** tant (de); **too many** trop (de) (6)
map plan *(m)* (10), carte *(f)*
March mars *(m)* (4)
market marché *(m)* (8)
marketing marketing *(m)* (1)
marriage mariage *(m)* (7)
married marié(e) (1); **get married (to)** se marier (avec) (7)
marvelous merveilleux(-euse)
mathematics mathématiques (maths) *(fpl)* (1)
matter: It doesn't matter to me. Ça m'est égal.; **What's the matter?** Qu'est-ce qu'il y a?
May mai *(m)* (3)

may pouvoir (6); **May I help you?** Je peux vous aider? (5)

maybe peut-être (3)

me moi (P), **me** (9); **Give me . . .** Donnez-moi... (P)

meal repas *(m)* (6)

mean: What does that mean? Qu'est-ce que ça veut dire? (P)

mean méchant(e) (1)

means moyen *(m)*; **means of transportation** moyen *(m)* de transport (4)

meat viande *(f)* (8); **ground meat** bifteck *haché *(m)*; **meat spread** pâté *(m)* (8)

medical médical(e) *(mpl* médicaux)

medication médicament *(m)* (10)

medicine *(studies)* médecine *(f)*, *(medication)* médicaments *(mpl)* (10)

medium moyen(ne); **medium-sized** de taille moyenne (4)

meet *(by design)* retrouver (4), *(by chance)* rencontrer (1), faire la connaissance de (7), se réunir; **Let's meet at . . .** Rendez-vous à...; **meet each other** se rencontrer, se retrouver (7)

meeting réunion *(f)*

melon melon *(m)*

member membre *(m)*

memory souvenir *(m)*, mémoire *(f)*

menu *(fixed price)* menu *(m)* (à prix fixe), carte *(f)* (8)

merchant marchand(e) *(mf)* (6)

Merry Christmas! Joyeux Noël!

message message *(m)*

messenger messager(-ère) *(mf)* (6)

Mexico Mexique *(m)* (9)

microwave oven four *(m)* à micro-ondes

middle milieu *(m)*; **in the middle of** au milieu de

Middle East Moyen-Orient *(m)* (9)

midnight minuit *(m)* (P)

milk lait *(m)* (8); **coffee with milk** café *(m)* au lait (2)

milk laitier(-ère)

million: one million un million (de) (3)

millionaire millionnaire *(mf)*

mind esprit *(m)* (7)

mine le mien (la mienne, les miens, les miennes)

mineral water eau minérale *(f)* (2)

minus: How much is . . . minus . . . ? Combien font... moins... ? (P)

minute minute *(f)* (5); **at the last minute** au dernier moment

mirror miroir *(m)*

mischievous espiègle

miss mademoiselle (Mlle) (P)

mistake erreur *(f)*; **make a mistake** se tromper

mister (Mr.) monsieur (M.) (P)

mistrust se méfier de

modern moderne (1)

mom maman *(f)*

moment instant *(m)*, moment *(m)*

Monday lundi *(m)* (P)

money argent *(m)* (2); **save up money** faire des économies

monster monstre *(m)* (6)

month mois *(m)* (3); **per month** par mois (3); **this month** ce mois-ci (4)

mood: in a good/bad mood de bonne/mauvaise humeur

more plus (1), encore (8), plus de (8); **more and more** de plus en plus (8); **more or less** environ (4); **more . . . than** plus... que (1); **no more** ne... plus (8), pas plus (4)

morning matin *(m)* (P); **at eight o'clock in the morning** à huit heures du matin (P); **Good**

morning. Bonjour. (P); **in the morning, mornings** le matin (P); **morning hours** matinée *(f)* (2)

Morocco Maroc *(m)* (9)

mosque mosquée *(f)*

most: most of la plupart de (7), **the most** le (la) plus

mother mère *(f)* (4); **mother-in-law** belle-mère *(f)* (4); **Mother's Day** fête *(f)* des Mères

mountain montagne *(f)* (5); **go mountain climbing** faire de l'alpinisme; **go to the mountains** aller à la montagne (5)

mouth bouche *(f)* (10)

move (into) s'installer (à/dans) (7)

movement mouvement *(m)*

movie film *(m)* (1); **go to the movies** aller au cinéma (2); **movie theater** cinéma *(m)* (1); **romantic movie** film *(m)* d'amour (6); **show a movie** passer un film (6)

MP3 player lecteur *(m)* MP3

Mr. monsieur (M.) (P)

Mrs. madame (Mme) (P)

much beaucoup (de) (1); **as much . . . (as)** autant de... (que); **how much** combien de (3); **How much is it?** C'est combien?, Ça fait combien? (2); **not much** ne... pas grand-chose; **so much** tellement (6), tant; **too much** trop (3)

muscular musclé(e)

museum musée *(m)* (4)

mushroom champignon *(m)*

music musique *(f)* (1); **listen to music** écouter de la musique (2)

musical *(movie)* comédie musicale *(f)*

musical musicien(ne)

musician musicien(ne) *(mf)*

mussel moule *(f)* (8)

must devoir (6); **he/she must** il/elle doit (3); **one/you must . . .** il faut... (8)

mustache moustache *(f)* (4)

my mon (ma, mes) (3); **at / in / to my house** chez moi (2); **my best friend** mon meilleur ami *(m)*, ma meilleure amie *(f)* (1); **my friends** mes amis (1); **My name is . . .** Je m'appelle... (P); **with my family** avec ma famille (P)

myself me (7), moi-même

N

naive naïf(-ïve)

name nom *(m)* (3); **family name** nom *(m)* de famille (3); **first name** prénom *(m)* (3); **His/Her name is . . .** Il/Elle s'appelle... (4); **last name** nom *(m)* de famille (3); **My name is . . .** Je m'appelle... (P); **What is . . . 's name?** Comment s'appelle... ? (4); **What's your name?** Tu t'appelles comment? *(familiar)* (P), Comment vous appelez-vous? *(formal)* (P)

named: be named s'appeler (7)

nap sieste *(f)*; **take a nap** faire la sieste

nationality nationalité *(f)* (3)

native natal(e)

natural naturel(le)

nature nature *(f)* (7)

near près (de) (1)

nearly presque (2)

necessary nécessaire (10); **it is necessary to . . .** Il faut... (8), il est nécessaire (de)...(10); **it will be necessary to . . .** il faudra...

neck cou *(m)*

necklace collier *(m)*

necktie cravate *(f)* (5)

nectarine nectarine *(f)*

need avoir besoin de (4); **I/you/we/you need** Il me/te/nous/vous faut (9); **one needs...** il faut... (8); **What size do you need?** Quelle taille faites-vous? (5)

needy nécessiteux *(mpl)*

neighbor voisin(e) *(mf)* (9)

neighborhood quartier *(m)* (1)

neither non plus (3); **neither . . . nor** ne... ni... ni...

nephew neveu *(pl* neveux) *(m)* (4)

nervous nerveux(-euse); **feel nervous** se sentir mal à l'aise

never ne... jamais (2)

new nouveau / nouvel (nouvelle) (1); neuf (neuve); **Happy New Year!** Bonne année!; **New Caledonia** Nouvelle-Calédonie *(f)* (9); **New Orleans** La Nouvelle-Orléans (4); **New Year's Eve party** le réveillon *(m)* du jour de l'an

news nouvelles *(fpl)*, *(television program)* informations *(fpl)*

newspaper journal *(m)* (5)

next prochain(e) (4), ensuite (4); **next to** à côté (de) (3); **the next class** le prochain cours (P); **the next day** le lendemain *(m)* (6)

nice sympathique (sympa) (1), gentil(le) (1); **The weather's nice.** Il fait beau. (5)

niece nièce *(f)* (4)

night nuit *(f)* (5); **night stand** table *(f)* de chevet

nightclub boîte *(f)* de nuit (1); **to go to a nightclub** aller en boîte (2)

nightgown chemise *(f)* de nuit

nine neuf *(m)* (P)

nineteen dix-neuf (P)

ninety quatre-vingt-dix (2)

ninth neuvième (3)

no non (P); **no longer** ne... plus (8); **no more** ne... plus (8), pas plus (4); **no one** ne... personne; **No problem!** Pas de problème! (3)

nobody ne... personne

noise bruit *(m)* (10)

none ne... aucun(e)

non-smoking section section non-fumeur *(f)*

noon midi *(m)* (P)

nor: neither . . . nor ne... ni... ni

normal normal(e) *(mpl* normaux)

normally normalement

north nord *(m)*; **North America** Amérique du Nord *(f)* (9)

Norway Norvège *(f)*

nose nez *(m)* (10)

not ne... pas (P); **I do not work.** Je ne travaille pas. (P); **not... anymore** ne... plus (8); **not at all** ne... pas du tout (1); **not bad** pas mal (P); **not one** ne... aucun(e); **not yet** ne... pas encore (5); **Why not?** Pourquoi pas? (2)

notebook cahier *(m)* (1)

nothing ne... rien (5); **nothing at all** rien du tout (6); **nothing but** ne... rien que; **nothing special** ne... rien de spécial (5)

notice remarquer

noun nom *(m)* (3)

nourish nourrir (8); **nourish oneself** se nourrir (8)

nourishment nourriture *(f)*

novel roman *(m)* (9)

November novembre *(m)* (4)

now maintenant (P)

nowadays de nos jours

nowhere nulle part

number chiffre *(m)* (P), numéro *(m)* (3), nombre *(m)*; **telephone number** numéro *(m)* de téléphone (3)

numeral chiffre *(m)* (P)

numerous nombreux(-euse)
nurse infirmier(-ière) *(mf)*
nurture nourrir (8); **nurture oneself** se nourrir (8)

O

obey obéir (à) (8)
object objet *(m)*
observe observer
obtain obtenir (9)
obvious évident(e)
obviously évidemment
ocean océan *(m)*
Oceania Océanie *(f)* (9)
o'clock: It's . . . o'clock. Il est... heure(s). (P)
October octobre *(m)* (4)
of de (1); **Of course!** Bien sûr! (5); Évidemment!; **of it/them** en (8)
off: get off descendre (de) (5)
offer proposer (8), offrir
office bureau *(m)* (1); **post office** bureau *(m)* de poste (10); **tourist office** office *(m)* de tourisme (10)
official time l'heure officielle *(f)* (6)
often souvent (1)
oil huile *(f)*
okay d'accord (2); **It's going okay.** Ça va.
old vieux/vieil (vieille) (1), âgé(e) (4); **be . . . years old** avoir... ans (4); **get older** vieillir; **How old is . . . ?** Quel âge a... ? (4); **oldest** aîné(e)
omelet omelette *(f)* (8)
on sur (1); **online** en ligne (7); **get on** monter dans (5); **on foot** à pied (4); **on Mondays** le lundi (P); **on page . . .** à la page... (P); **on sale** en solde (5); **on . . . street** dans la rue... (10); **on the corner (of)** au coin (de) (10); **on the courtyard side** côté cour (10); **on the ground/floor** par terre (3); **on the Internet** sur Internet (9); **on the weekend** le week-end (P); **on time** à l'heure (4); **On what floor?** À quel étage? (3); **put on** mettre (5); **try on** essayer (5)
once une fois (6); **all at once** tout d'un coup (6); **once more** encore une fois; **once upon a time** il était une fois (6)
one un(e) (P); on (4); **no one** ne... personne; **not one** ne... aucun(e); **one another** se, nous vous (7)
oneself se (7)
one-way ticket aller simple *(m)* (9)
onion oignon *(m)* (8); **onion soup** soupe *(f)* à l'oignon (8)
only uniquement (6); seulement (8), ne... que; **only child** fille unique *(f)*, fils unique *(m)*
Ontario Ontario (9)
open ouvrir; **Open your book.** Ouvrez votre livre. (P)
opening time l'heure d'ouverture *(f)* (6)
opinion avis *(m)*; **in your opinion** à votre avis (8)
opportunity: have the opportunity to avoir l'occasion de
opposite contraire *(m)*
optimistic optimiste (1)
or ou (P)
orange orange *(f)* (8); **orange juice** jus *(m)* d'orange (2)
orange orange (3)
Orangina Orangina *(m)* (2)
orchestra orchestre *(m)* (4)
order commander (2), ranger (7)
order ordre *(m)*; **in order** en ordre (3); **in order to** pour (1)
orderly bien rangé(e) (3)

organic products produits bios *(mpl)* (8)
organization organisation *(f)*
origin origine *(f)*; **of. . . origin** d'origine... (7)
Orléans: New Orleans La Nouvelle-Orléans (4)
other autre (1); **each other** se, nous vous (7); **on the other hand** par contre; **on the other side (of)** de l'autre côté (de); **sometimes . . . other times** quelquefois... d'autres fois (7)
ought to devoir (6)
our notre (nos) (3)
ourselves nous (7); nous-mêmes
out: dine out dîner au restaurant (2); **go out** sortir (2); **Take out a sheet of paper.** Prenez une feuille de papier. (P); **watch out (for)** faire attention (à) (8)
outdoor de plein air (4)
outdoors en plein air
outgoing extraverti(e) (1)
outing sortie *(f)* (6)
outside à l'extérieur, dehors, en plein air; **outside of** *hors de
oven four *(m)*; **microwave oven** four *(m)* à micro-ondes
over (par-)dessus; **invite friends over** inviter des amis à la maison (2); **over there** là-bas (8)
overcast: The sky is overcast. Le ciel est couvert.
overcoat manteau *(m)* (5), pardessus *(m)*
owe devoir (6)
own propre
oyster huître *(f)* (8)

P

pack one's bag faire sa valise *(f)* (9)
package paquet *(m)* (8), colis *(m)*
page page *(f)* (P)
pain douleur *(f)*
paint peindre
painter peintre *(mf)*
painting tableau *(m)* (3), peinture *(f)*
pajamas pyjama *(m)*
pal copain *(m)*, copine *(f)* (6)
palace palais *(m)* (6)
pale pâle
panties slip *(m)*; **panty hose** collant *(m)*
pants pantalon *(m)* (5)
papa papa *(m)* (4)
paper papier *(m)*; **sheet of paper** feuille *(f)* de papier (P)
parade défilé *(m)*
pardon me pardon (P)
parents parents *(mpl)* (3); **at my parents' house** chez mes parents (3)
Parisian Parisien(ne) *(mf)* (9)
park parc *(m)* (1)
parking lot parking *(m)* (1)
part partie *(f)*
participate (in) participer (à)
particular: in particular en particulier
partner partenaire *(mf)* (7)
part-time à temps partiel
party *(social)* fête *(f)* (1), boum *(f)* (6), *(political)* parti *(m)*
pass passer (2), *(exam)* réussir à (8); **pass by the house of . . .** passer chez... (2)
passenger passager(-ère) *(mf)*
passerby passant(e) *(mf)*
passion passion *(f)* (7)
Passover la pâque juive *(f)*
passport passeport *(m)* (9)
past passé *(m)*; **in the past** au passé, autrefois
past passé(e) (6); **It's a quarter past two.** Il est deux heures et quart. (P)
pasta pâtes *(fpl)*

pastime passe-temps *(m)* (2)
pastry pâtisserie *(f)*; **pastry shop** pâtisserie *(f)*
pâté pâté *(m)* (8)
patience patience *(f)* (4); **to have patience** avoir de la patience (4)
patient patient(e) *(mf)*
patient patient(e) (6)
pay (for) payer (2); **pay attention (to)** faire attention (à) (8); **pay the bill** régler la note (10)
peace paix *(f)*
peaceful tranquille
peach pêche *(f)* (8)
peanut cacahouète *(f)*
pear poire *(f)* (8)
peas petits pois *(mpl)* (8)
pen stylo *(m)* (P)
pencil crayon *(m)* (P)
people gens *(mpl)* (1), on (4); **poor people** les pauvres *(mpl)*; **some people** certains *(mpl)*; **young people** les jeunes *(mpl)*
pepper poivre *(m)* (8)
per par (3)
percent pour cent
perfect perfectionner
perfect parfait(e) (7)
perfectly parfaitement (7)
performer artiste *(mf)*
perhaps peut-être (3)
period période *(f)*, époque *(f)*
permit permettre (de); **permitted** permis(e)
person personne *(f)* (6)
personal personnel(le) (3); **personal service** service personnalisé *(m)* (8)
personality personnalité *(f)* (1)
personally personnellement
Peru Pérou *(m)* (9)
pessimistic pessimiste (1)
pharmacist pharmacien(ne) *(mf)*
pharmacy pharmacie *(f)* (10)
philosophy philosophie *(f)* (1)
phone téléphone *(m)* (2); **on the phone** au téléphone (2)
phone téléphoner (à) (3); **phone each other** se téléphoner (7)
photo photo *(f)* (4)
physical appearance aspect physique *(m)* (7)
physics physique *(f)* (1)
piano piano *(m)* (2)
picnic pique-nique *(m)*
picture tableau *(m)* (3)
pie tarte *(f)* (8); **apple pie** tarte *(f)* aux pommes (8)
piece morceau *(m)* (8); **piece of advice** conseil *(m)* (8)
pierced percé(e)
pineapple ananas *(m)*
pink rose (3)
pity pitié *(f)*; **have pity (for / on)** avoir pitié (de) (10); **what a pity** c'est dommage (7)
pizza pizza *(f)* (8)
place endroit *(m)* (9), place *(f)*; **at/to/ in . . . 's place** chez... (2); **in it's place** à sa place (3); **take place** avoir lieu
place mettre
plaid écossais(e)
plan projet *(m)* (4); **make plans** faire des projets (4)
plan organiser; **plan on doing** avoir l'intention de faire (4), compter faire (9); **planned** prévu(e)
plane avion *(m)* (4); **by plane** en avion (4)
plant plante *(f)* (3)
plastic plastique *(m)*; **plastic bag** sac *(m)* en plastique
plate assiette *(f)*

play *(theater)* pièce *(f)* (4)
play (a sport) jouer (à un sport) (2), faire (du sport) (5); **play music** faire de la musique (2); **play (the piano)** jouer (du piano) (2)
player: CD player lecteur *(m)* CD (3); platine laser *(f)*; **DVD player** lecteur *(m)* DVD (3); **MP3 player** lecteur *(m)* MP3 (3)
plaza place *(f)* (10)
pleasant agréable (1)
please plaire à
please s'il vous plaît *(formal)* (P), s'il te plaît *(familiar)*
pleased content(e) (8)
pleasure plaisir *(m)*; **It would be a pleasure!** Avec plaisir! (6)
plum prune *(f)*
plumber plombier *(m)*
plus: How much is . . . plus . . . ? Combien font... et... ? (P)
P.M. de l'après-midi, du soir (P)
poem poème *(m)* (9)
point out signaler
Poland Pologne *(f)*
police police *(f)*
policeman agent *(m)* de police
polite poli(e)
political politique (1); **political science** sciences politiques *(fpl)* (1)
politics politique *(f)* (7)
poll sondage *(m)*
pollution pollution *(f)*
Polynesia: French Polynesia Polynésie française *(f)* (9)
pool billard *(m)*; **swimming pool** piscine *(f)* (4)
poor pauvre
pop music musique populaire *(f)* (1)
popular populaire (1)
population population *(f)*
pork porc *(m)* (8); **pork chop** côte *(f)* de porc (8); **pork roast** rôti *(m)* de porc
portrait: self-portrait autoportrait *(m)* (P)
Portuguese portugais *(m)*
possibility possibilité *(f)* (4)
possible possible
post office bureau *(m)* de poste (10)
postcard carte postale *(f)* (9)
poster affiche *(f)* (3)
potato pomme *(f)* de terre (8)
poultry volaille *(f)* (8)
pound livre *(f)* (8)
poverty pauvreté *(f)*
powerful puissant(e)
preach prêcher
precisely justement (3)
prefer préférer (2), aimer mieux (2); **I prefer . . .** Je préfère... (1)
preferable préférable
pregnant enceinte (10)
preparations préparatifs *(mpl)* (9)
prepare préparer (2); **Prepare for the exam.** Préparez l'examen. (P)
prepared: prepared dish plat préparé *(m)* (8)
preschool école maternelle *(f)*
prescription ordonnance *(f)* (10)
present cadeau *(m)* (10)
pretty joli(e) (1), beau/bel (belle) (1); **pretty cool** assez cool (P)
prevent empêcher
price prix *(m)*; **at a set price** à prix fixe (8)
principal principal(e) *(mpl* principaux) (10)
private privé(e) (10)
probable probable
probably sans doute (8); probablement
problem problème *(m)*; **No problem!** Pas de problème! (3)

process: be in the process of doing être en train de faire
product produit *(m)* (8); **organic products** produits bios *(mpl)* (8)
profession profession *(f)* (7), métier *(m)*
professional professionnel(le) (7)
professor professeur *(m)* (P)
program programme *(m)*
programmer programmeur(-euse) *(mf)*
progress progrès *(m)*; **make progress** faire des progrès
promise promettre (de) (6)
pronunciation prononciation *(f)*
protect (oneself) (against) (se) protéger (contre)
protein protéines *(fpl)*
proud fier(-ère)
province province *(f)* (3)
prune pruneau *(m)*
psychology psychologie *(f)* (1)
public: public transportation transports en commun *(mpl)* (7)
publishing company maison *(f)* d'édition
pullover (sweater) pull *(m)* (5)
punish punir
purple violet(te) (3)
purpose: on purpose exprès
purse sac *(m)* (5)
put (on) mettre (5); **put away** bien rangé(e) (3); **put on make-up** se maquiller (7); **put on weight** prendre du poids; **put up with** supporter (7)

Q
qualify qualifier
quarter quart *(m)* (P); **It's a quarter past two.** Il est deux heures et quart. (P)
question question *(f)* (P); **ask a question** poser une question (3)
quick rapide (8)
quickly vite (7)
quiet tranquille; **be quiet** se taire
quite assez, plutôt; **quite a bit** pas mal de; **quite simply** tout simplement (10)

R
rabbit lapin *(m)*
radio radio *(f)* (2)
rain pluie *(f)* (5)
rain pleuvoir (5); **It's raining. It rains.** Il pleut. (5)
raincoat imperméable *(m)* (5)
raisin raisin sec *(m)*
Ramadan ramadan *(m)*
rapid rapide (8)
rarely rarement (2)
raspberry framboise *(f)*
rather plutôt (1), assez (1)
raw vegetables crudités *(fpl)* (8)
rayfish raie *(f)* (8)
reach atteindre
react (to) réagir (à)
read lire (2); **Read . . .** Lisez... (P)
ready (to) prêt(e) (à) (4); **get ready** se préparer; **ready-to-serve dish** plat préparé *(m)* (8)
real réel(le), véritable
realistic réaliste (1)
realize se rendre compte
really vraiment (2)
reason raison *(f)*; **the reason why I . . .** la raison pour laquelle je...
reasonable raisonnable
receive recevoir (9)
recent récent(e)
recently récemment (5)

recognize (each other) (se) reconnaître (7); **recognize** reconnaître (7)
recommend recommander (10)
reconfirm reconfirmer
record disque *(m)*, *(sports)* record *(m)*
record enregistrer
recorder: video cassette recorder magnétoscope *(m)*
recount raconter (7)
recycle recycler
red rouge (3), *(hair)* roux (rousse) (4); **red wine** vin rouge *(m)* (2); **turn red** rougir
reflect (on) réfléchir (à) (8)
refrigerator réfrigérateur *(m)*
refuse refuser (de)
region région *(f)* (4)
regional régional(e) *(mpl* régionaux) (4)
register s'inscrire (3)
regret regretter (6)
regularly régulièrement (8)
relationship relation *(f)* (7), rapport *(m)*
relatives parents *(mpl)* (5)
relax se reposer (7), se détendre; **relaxed** décontracté(e)
religion religion *(f)* (7)
religious religieux(-euse)
remain rester
remarried remarié(e)
remember se souvenir (de) (7)
rent loyer *(m)* (3)
rent louer (4)
rental car voiture *(f)* de location (5)
repeat répéter (2); **Please repeat.** Répétez s'il vous plaît. (P)
replace remplacer
require exiger, demander; **required** requis(e), obligatoire
research recherche *(f)*; **do research** faire des recherches
resell revendre
resemble ressembler à
reservation réservation *(f)* (9); **make a reservation** faire une réservation (9)
reserve: nature reserve parc naturel *(m)*
reserve réserver (9)
residence hall résidence universitaire *(f)* (1)
resort: summer resort station estivale *(f)* (10)
resources ressources *(fpl)*
respond répondre (6)
rest: the rest (of) le reste (de) (7)
rest se reposer (7); **rested** reposé(e)
restaurant restaurant *(m)* (1); **fast food restaurant** fast-food *(m)* (1); **university restaurant** restau-u *(m)* (6)
restful reposant(e)
restroom toilettes *(fpl)* (3), W.-C. *(mpl)* (10)
retired retraité(e)
return retour *(m)* (9)
return rentrer (2), retourner (5), **return something to someone** rendre quelque chose à quelqu'un (7)
review *(for a test)* réviser
rice riz *(m)* (8)
rich riche (2)
ride: go for a ride faire un tour en voiture (à vélo) (4)
right *(direction)* droite *(f)*, *(legal)* droit *(m)*; **to the right of** à droite de (3)
right correct(e); **be right** avoir raison (4), **right away** tout de suite (6); **right by** tout près (de) (3); **right there** juste là; **right?** n'est-ce pas?, non? (1)
ring bague *(f)*
ring sonner (7)

river fleuve (m), rivière (f)

road chemin (m), route (f)

roast: roast beef rosbif (m) (8); pork roast rôti (m) de porc

rock: rock music rock (m) (1); go rock climbing faire de la varappe; hard rock *hard rock (m)

rollerblade faire du roller (6)

rollerblading roller (m); go rollerblading faire du roller (6)

romantic romantique; romantic movie film (m) d'amour (6)

room pièce (f) (3), salle (f); classroom salle (f) de classe (1); dining room salle à manger (f) (3); fitting room cabine (f) d'essayage (5); living room salon (m) (3)

roommate camarade (mf) de chambre (P)

round-trip ticket (billet) aller-retour (m) (9)

routine routine (f) (7)

row rang (m)

rug tapis (m) (3)

run courir (9); run errands faire des courses (5); run into (each other) (se) rencontrer (1)

Russia Russie (f) (9)

Russian russe (m)

S

sack sac (m) (5), paquet (m) (8)

sad triste

safety sécurité (f)

sailing: go sailing faire de la voile

salad salade (f) (8)

salami saucisson (m) (8)

sale: on sale en solde (5)

salesclerk vendeur(-euse) (mf) (5)

salmon saumon (m) (8)

salt sel (m) (8)

same même (1); all the same quand même

sandal sandale (f) (5)

sandwich sandwich (m) (2); bread-and-butter sandwich tartine (f) (8); cheese sandwich sandwich au fromage (m) (2)

Santa Claus le père Noël

satisfied satisfait(e)

Saturday samedi (m) (P)

sauce sauce (f)

sausage saucisse (f) (8)

save sauver; save up money faire des économies

saxophone saxophone (m)

say dire (6); How do you say . . . in French? Comment dit-on... en français? (P); They say that . . . On dit que... (4)

scallops coquilles St-Jacques (fpl)

scarf (winter) écharpe (f), (dressy) foulard (m)

scenery paysage (m) (9)

schedule (classes) emploi (m) du temps, (train) horaire (f)

school école (f) (6); high school lycée (m) (6)

science science (f) (1); computer science informatique (f) (1); political science sciences politiques (fpl) (1); science fiction science-fiction (fpl); social sciences sciences humaines (fpl) (1)

scientist scientifique (mf); computer scientist informaticien(ne) (mf)

scuba diving plongée sous-marine (f)

sculpture sculpture (f)

sea mer (f) (9)

season saison (f) (5)

seat place (f), siège (m)

seated assis(e) (9)

second seconde (f) (5)

second deuxième (3), second(e); in second class en classe touriste (9)

secretary secrétaire (mf)

section section (f)

security sécurité (f)

see voir (1); as you see comme tu vois (3); Let's see! Voyons! (5); see each other se voir (7); See you in a little while. À tout à l'heure. (P); See you later! À plus tard! (2); See you soon. À bientôt. (P); See you tomorrow. À demain. (P)

seem avoir l'air... (4), sembler; It seems to me that . . . Il me semble que...

self: myself moi-même; self-portrait autoportrait (m) (P); self-service restaurant self-service (m) (8)

sell vendre (7); sell back revendre (7)

semester semestre (m) (P)

send envoyer (10)

Senegal Sénégal (m) (9)

sense of humor sens (m) de l'humour (7)

sensitive sensible

sentence phrase (f) (P); in complete sentences en phrases complètes (P)

sentimental sentimental(e) (mpl sentimentaux) (7)

separate séparer; separated séparé(e)

separately séparément

September septembre (m) (4)

serious sérieux(-euse), grave

serve servir (4); served servi(e) (10)

server serveur (m), serveuse (f) (8)

service service (m) (8); service station station-service (f)

set mettre (8); set the table mettre la table; with a set price à prix fixe (8)

settle (in) s'installer (à/dans) (7)

seven sept (P)

seventeen dix-sept (P)

seventh septième (3)

seventy soixante-dix (2)

several plusieurs (8)

sexy sexy (2)

shall: Shall we go . . . ? On va... ? (2); What shall we do? Qu'est-ce qu'on fait?

shame *honte (f); It's a shame! C'est dommage! (7)

shape forme (f); in shape en forme (8)

share partager (3)

shared partagé(e) (3)

shave se raser (7)

she elle (1); she is . . . c'est..., elle est... (1)

sheet of paper feuille (f) de papier (P)

shelf étagère (f) (3)

shellfish fruits (mpl) de mer (8)

shirt chemise (f) (5); knit shirt polo (m) (5)

shiver frisson (m) (10)

shock choquer

shoe chaussure (f) (5); tennis shoes baskets (fpl) (5)

shop magasin (m) (4); butcher's shop boucherie (f) (8); fish shop poissonnerie (f) (8); gift shop marchand (m) de cadeaux (10); pastry shop pâtisserie (f); tobacco shop bureau (m) de tabac

shopkeeper marchand(e) (mf) (6), commerçant(e) (mf) (8)

shopping: go grocery shopping faire les courses; go shopping faire du shopping (2); shopping center centre commercial (m) (4)

short petit(e) (1), court(e) (4)

shorts short (m) (5)

shot piqûre (f); give a shot faire une piqûre

should devoir (6); one shouldn't . . . il ne faut pas (10)

shoulder épaule (f); shoulder-length hair cheveux mi-longs (mpl) (4)

show montrer (3), indiquer (3); show a movie passer un film (6)

show time séance (f) (6)

shower douche (f) (7)

shrimp crevette (f) (8)

shy timide (1)

shuttle navette (f) (10)

sick malade (10); get sick tomber malade (10)

side côté (m); on the courtyard side côté cour (10); on the other side (of) de l'autre côté (de)

sight vue (f); love at first sight coup (m) de foudre (7)

silver argent (m) (2)

similar to semblable à, pareil(le) à

simply simplement (10); quite simply tout simplement (10)

since depuis, comme (7), depuis que; since that depuis cela (7)

sincere sincère

sing chanter (2)

singer chanteur(-euse) (mf)

single célibataire (1), seul(e)

sink (bathroom) lavabo (m) (10), (kitchen) évier (m)

sir monsieur (M.) (P)

sister sœur (f) (1); sister-in-law belle-sœur (f)

sit (down) s'asseoir; Sit down! Asseyez-vous!

site site (m) (9)

situation situation (f)

six six (P)

sixteen seize (P)

sixth sixième (3)

sixty soixante (2)

size taille (f) (4); medium-sized de taille moyenne (4)

skate (fish) raie (f) (8); patin (m)

skateboard faire du skateboard (6)

skating patin (m); go (ice-)skating faire du patin (à glace)

skeptical sceptique

ski ski (m) (2); ski jacket anorak (m) (5); ski lodge chalet (m) de ski (10); ski faire du ski (2); water-ski faire du ski nautique (5)

skiing ski (m) (2); water-skiing ski nautique (m) (5)

skin peau (f)

skinny maigre

skirt jupe (f) (5)

sleep dormir (2)

sleepy: be sleepy avoir sommeil (4)

slice tranche (f), pavé (m) (8)

slightly légèrement

slim down maigrir (8)

slip combinaison (f)

slow lent(e); slow motion ralenti (m)

slowly lentement (8)

small petit(e) (1)

smell sentir

smoke fumée (f) (8)

smoke fumer (3); smoked fumé(e) (8)

smoking section section fumeur (f)

snack collation (f)

snail escargot (m) (8)

sneeze éternuer (10)

snob snob

snorkeling: go snorkeling faire du tuba

snow neige (f) (5)

snow neiger (5)

so alors (1), tellement (6), donc (7); so many, so much tant (de); tellement (de); so-so comme ci comme ça (2); so that afin que

soap savon (m)

soccer football (m) (1)

social social(e) (mpl sociaux); social sciences sciences humaines (fpl) (1); social worker assistant(e) social(e) (mf)

society société *(f)*
sociology sociologie *(f)*
sock chaussette *(f)*
sofa canapé *(m)* (3)
soft doux(-ce) (6)
software logiciel *(m)*
sole sole *(f)*
solid-colored uni(e)
solution solution *(f)*
some des (1), du, de la, de l', en (8), quelques (5), certain(e)s
somebody quelqu'un (6)
someone quelqu'un (6)
something quelque chose (2)
sometimes quelquefois (2), parfois
somewhere quelque part
son fils *(m)* (4)
song chanson *(f)*
soon bientôt (P); **as soon as** aussitôt que; **I would just as soon...** j'aimerais autant... (10); **See you soon.** À bientôt. (P)
sorry désolé(e) (10); **be sorry** être désolé(e) (10), regretter (6)
sort: all sorts of toutes sortes de
sound: How does that sound to you? Ça te dit? (4)
soup soupe *(f)* (8); **onion soup** soupe *(f)* à l'oignon (8)
south sud *(m)*; **South Africa** Afrique *(f)* du Sud; **South America** Amérique *(f)* du Sud (9)
space espace *(m)*
Spain Espagne *(f)* (9)
Spanish espagnol *(m)* (P)
Spanish espagnol(e)
speak parler (2); **Do you speak...?** Vous parlez...? (P); **I speak...** Je parle... (P); **speak to each other** se parler (7)
special spécial(e) *(mpl* spéciaux) (6)
specialty spécialité *(f)* (4)
speech discours *(m)*
speed vitesse *(f)*
spend *(time)* passer (2), *(money)* dépenser
spider araignée *(f)*
spinach épinards *(mpl)*
spirituality spiritualité *(f)* (7)
spite: in spite of malgré
split partagé(e) (3)
spoiled gâté(e) (6)
spoon cuillère *(f)*
sport sport *(m)* (1); **play sports** faire du sport (2); **sports club** club *(m)* de gym (1)
spot site *(m)* (9)
sprain one's ankle se fouler la cheville
spring printemps *(m)* (5); **in spring** au printemps (5)
square *(town)* place *(f)* (10)
stadium stade *(m)* (1)
staircase escalier *(m)* (3)
stairs escalier *(m)* (3)
stamp timbre *(m)* (10)
stand: I can't stand... J'ai horreur de..., Je ne supporte pas... (7)
star étoile *(f)*
start commencer (2); **French class starts...** Le cours de français commence... (P)
state état *(m)* (3); **United States** États-Unis (3) *(mpl)*
station: radio station station *(f)* de radio; **service station** station-service *(f)*; **subway station** station *(f)* de métro; **train station** gare *(f)*
stay séjour *(m)* (7); **Enjoy your stay!** Bon séjour! (10)
stay rester (2), *(at a hotel)* descendre (à) (5)

steak bifteck *(m)* (8); **steak and fries** steak-frites *(m)* (8)
steal voler
stepbrother demi-frère *(m)*
stepfather beau-père *(m)* (4)
stepmother belle-mère *(f)* (4)
stepparents beaux-parents *(mpl)*
stepsister demi-sœur *(f)*
stereo chaîne hi-fi *(f)* (2)
still encore (4), toujours
stomach ventre *(m)* (10)
stop: bus stop arrêt *(m)* d'autobus (3)
stop (s')arrêter (7); **stop by the house of...** passer chez... (2); **stopped up** bouché(e)
store magasin *(m)* (4); **bookstore** librairie *(f)* (1)
storm orage *(m)*
story histoire *(f)* (9); conte *(m)* (6)
stove cuisinière *(f)*
straight tout droit (10)
straightened up bien rangé(e) (3)
strange bizarre
strawberry fraise *(f)* (8)
street rue *(f)* (3); **on...Street** dans la rue... (10)
strength force *(f)*
stress stress *(m)* (8)
stressed (out) stressé(e) (8)
strict sévère
striped rayé(e)
strong fort(e) (8)
struggle (against) lutter (contre)
student étudiant(e) *(mf)* (P); **high school student** lycéen(ne) *(mf)* (6); **student center** centre *(m)* d'étudiants
studies études *(fpl)* (1)
study étudier (1), préparer les cours (2); **I study...** J'étudie... (1); **Study for the exam.** Préparez l'examen. (P); **What are you studying?** Qu'est-ce que vous étudiez? (1)
stupid bête (1), stupide
style style *(m)*; **American style** à l'américaine (8)
stylist: hair stylist coiffeur(-euse) *(mf)*
suburbs banlieue *(f)* (3); **in the suburbs** en banlieue (3)
subway métro *(m)* (4); **by subway** en métro (4)
succeed (in) réussir (à) (8)
such as tel(le) que (7)
sudden: all of a sudden tout à coup (6)
suddenly soudain, tout d'un coup (6), soudainement
suffer souffrir
sufficiently suffisamment
sugar sucre *(m)* (8)
suggest suggérer (6)
suggestion suggestion *(f)*
suit *(man's)* costume *(m)* (5), *(woman's)* tailleur *(m)*; **jogging suit** survêtement *(m)* (5)
suitcase valise *(f)* (9)
summer été *(m)* (5); **in summer** en été (5);
summer resort station estivale *(f)* (10)
sun soleil *(m)*
sunbathe prendre un bain de soleil (4)
Sunday dimanche *(m)*
sunglasses lunettes *(f)* de soleil (5)
sunny: It's sunny. Il fait du soleil. (5)
superior supérieur(e)
supermarket supermarché *(m)* (8)
superstore grande surface *(f)* (8)
supplement supplément *(m)* (10)
supplies provisions *(fpl)*
sure sûr(e), certain(e)
surely sûrement
surf *(water)* faire du surf, *(Internet)* surfer; **surf the Net** surfer le Net (2)
surprise étonner, surprendre; **surprised** étonné(e), surpris(e) (10)

surrounded (by) entouré(e) (de)
swallow avaler
sweater: pullover sweater pull *(m)* (5)
sweatshirt sweat *(m)*
sweatsuit survêtement *(m)* (5)
Sweden Suède *(f)*
sweet doux(-ce) (6)
sweets bonbons *(mpl)*
swim nager (4), se baigner
swimming pool piscine *(f)* (4)
swimsuit maillot *(m)* de bain (5)
Switzerland Suisse *(f)* (9)
swollen enflé(e)
sword épée *(f)*
symptom symptôme *(m)* (10)
synagogue synagogue *(f)*
system: public transportation system système *(m)* de transports en commun (9)

T
table table *(f)* (3)
take prendre (4), *(something along)* apporter, *(a person)* emmener; **take a course** suivre un cours; **take advantage of** profiter de (9); **take a tour** faire un tour (4); **take a trip** faire un voyage (5); **take a walk** faire une promenade (5); **Take out a sheet of paper.** Prenez une feuille de papier. (P); **take place** avoir lieu
tale: fairy tale conte *(m)* de fée (6)
talent talent *(m)*
talented doué(e)
talk parler (2); **talk to each other** se parler (7)
tall grand(e) (1)
tan bronzer (9); **tanned** bronzé(e)
tangerine mandarine *(f)*
tart tartelette *(f)* (8)
taste goûter (9)
taxi taxi *(m)* (4); **by taxi** en taxi (4)
tea (with lemon) thé (au citron) *(m)* (2)
teacher *(elementary school)* instituteur(-trice) *(mf)*; *(secondary school)* professeur *(m)*
team équipe *(f)*
technical technique (1)
technician technicien(ne) *(mf)*
technology technologie *(f)*
tee shirt tee-shirt *(m)* (5)
telephone téléphone *(m)* (2); **talk on the telephone** parler au téléphone (2); **telephone card** carte téléphonique *(f)* (10); **telephone number** numéro *(m)* de téléphone (3)
telephone téléphoner (à) (3); **telephone each other** se téléphoner (7)
television télévision (télé) *(f)* (2)
tell dire (6), raconter (7)
teller: automatic teller machine distributeur de billets (10)
temperature température *(f)*
temple temple *(m)*
ten dix (P)
tennis tennis *(m)* (1); **tennis court** court *(m)* de tennis; **tennis shoes** baskets *(fpl)* (5)
tenth dixième (3)
terrace terrasse *(f)* (9)
test examen *(m)* (P), test *(m)* (7), contrôle *(m)*
Texas Texas *(m)* (9)
than: more...than plus... que (1)
thank (for) remercier (de) (10); **thank you** merci (bien) (P)
thanks merci (bien) (P)
Thanksgiving jour *(m)* d'Action de grâce
that ça (P), cela (7), ce (cet, cette) (...-là) (3), que (P), qui (7); **I think that...** je pense que... (P); **that is...** c'est... (1)
the le (la, l', les) (1)

theater théâtre *(for live performances)* (m) (1); **movie theater** cinéma (m) (1)
theft vol (m)
their leur(s) (1)
them les (5); **of them** en (8); **to them** leur (9); **with them** avec eux, avec elles
themselves se (7), eux-mêmes *(mpl)*, elles-mêmes *(fpl)*
then alors (1), ensuite, puis (4), donc (7)
there là (8), y (4); **over there** là-bas (8); **right there** juste là; **there is, there are** il y a (1), voilà (2); **There are six of us.** Nous sommes six. (4); **There you are!** Te/Vous voilà.
therefore donc (7)
these ces (…-ci) (3); **these are . . .** ce sont… (1)
they ils, elles, ce (1), on (4)
thick gros(se)
thickness épaisseur *(f)*
thief voleur (m)
thin mince (1); **get thinner** maigrir (8)
thing(s) chose(s) *(f)* (3), truc (m) (1), affaires *(fpl)*; **That's not my thing.** Ce n'est pas mon truc. (1)
think (about) penser (à) (7), réfléchir (à) (8); **I think that . . .** Je pense que… (P); **What do you think (about it)?** Qu'en penses-tu?, Qu'en pensez-vous?
third troisième (3); **Third World** Tiers-Monde (m)
thirsty: be thirsty avoir soif (4); **I'm thirsty.** J'ai soif. (2)
thirteen treize (P)
thirty trente (P)
this ce (cet, cette) (…-ci) (3); **this evening** ce soir (2); **this is . . .** c'est… (1); **this month** ce mois-ci (4); **this semester** ce semestre (P); **this way** par ici (5) **those** ces (…-là) (3); **those are . . .** ce sont… (1); **those (ones)** ceux (celles) (8)
thousand: one thousand mille (3)
three trois (P)
throat gorge *(f)* (10); **have a sore throat** avoir mal à la gorge
through par; **through the window** par la fenêtre
throw jeter; **throw up** vomir (10)
thumb pouce (m)
Thursday jeudi (m) (P)
thus donc (7)
ticket billet (m) (9), ticket (m); **e-ticket** billet électronique (9); **one-way ticket** aller simple (9); **round-trip ticket** billet aller-retour (m); **ticket window** guichet (m)
tide marée *(f)*
tie cravate *(f)* (5)
tight étroit(e)
till: a quarter till moins le quart (P)
time *(clock)* heure *(f)* (P), temps (m) (2), *(occasion)* fois *(f)* (5); **a long time** longtemps (5); **at that time** à ce moment-là; **At what time?** À quelle heure? (P); **free time** temps libre (m) (4); **from time to time** de temps en temps (4); **have a hard time** avoir du mal à; **most of the time** la plupart du temps (7); **official time** heure officielle *(f)* (6); **Once upon a time…** Il était une fois… (6); **One has a good time.** On s'amuse bien.; **on time** à l'heure (4); **opening time** l'heure d'ouverture *(f)* (6); **show time** séance *(f)* (6); **sometimes . . . other times** quelquefois… d'autres fois (7); **time period** époque *(f)*; **What time is it?** Quelle heure est-il? (P)
timid timide (1)
tip pourboire (m)
tired fatigué(e) (6)

tiring fatiguant(e)
title titre (m)
to à (P); **to go to a club** aller en boîte (2); **to . . .'s house/place** chez… (2)
toast pain grillé (m) (8)
toasted grillé(e) (8)
tobacco tabac (m) (7); **tobacco shop** bureau (m) de tabac
today aujourd'hui (P)
toe doigt (m) de pied (10)
together ensemble (2)
toilet toilettes *(fpl)* (3), W.-C. *(mpl)* (10)
tolerate supporter (7)
tomato tomate *(f)* (8)
tomorrow demain (P); **day after tomorrow** après-demain; **tomorrow morning** demain matin (4)
tonight ce soir (2); **See you tonight.** À ce soir. (2)
too aussi (P), trop (3); **That's too bad!** C'est dommage! (7); **too many** trop (de) (8); **too much** trop (de) (6)
tooth dent *(f)* (7)
tour tour (m); **take a tour** faire un tour (4)
tourism tourisme (m)
tourist touriste *(mf)*; **tourist class** classe touriste *(f)* (9); **tourist office** office (m) de tourisme (10)
touristic touristique (9)
toward(s) vers (2)
towel serviette *(f)*
town ville *(f)* (3); **in town** en ville (3)
toy jouet (m)
traditional traditionnel(le) (8)
traffic circulation *(f)*
train train (m) (4); **by train** en train (4); **train station** gare *(f)*
training: do weight training faire de la mascu(lation) (8); faire des haltères
trait trait (m) (7)
translate traduire
translation traduction *(f)*
transportation transport; **means of transportation** moyen (m) de transport (4); **public transportation** transports *(mpl)* en commun (9)
travel: travel agency agence *(f)* de voyages (9); **travel agent** agent (m) de voyages (9)
travel voyager (2)
traveler's check chèque (m) de voyage (9)
treatment traitement (m)
tree arbre (m) (1)
trimester trimestre (m)
trip voyage (m) (4); **take a trip** faire un voyage (5)
tropical tropical(e) *(mpl* tropicaux) (9)
trouble difficulté *(f)*; **have trouble** avoir des difficultés, avoir du mal (à)
trout truite *(f)*
truck camion (m), *(pick-up)* camionnette *(f)*
true vrai(e) (8); **true love** le grand amour (7)
truly vraiment (2)
trumpet trompette *(f)*
truth vérité *(f)*
try (on) essayer (5)
T-shirt tee-shirt (m) (5)
Tuesday mardi (m) (P)
tuna thon (m) (8)
Tunisia Tunisie *(f)*
Turkey Turquie *(f)*
turkey dinde *(f)*
turn tourner (10); **turn in (something to someone)** rendre (quelque chose à quelqu'un) (7); **turn on** mettre; **turn red** rougir

turnover: apple turnover chausson aux pommes (m)
TV télé *(f)* (2)
twelve douze (P)
twenty vingt (P)
twin jumeau (jumelle) (1)
two deux (P)
type genre (m)
typical typique (2)
typically typiquement

U

ugly laid(e) (1)
umbrella parapluie (m) (5)
unbearable insupportable
unbelievable incroyable
uncle oncle (m) (4)
under sous (3)
understand comprendre (4); **Do you understand?** Vous comprenez? (P); **I understand.** Je comprends. (P); **No, I don't understand.** Non, je ne comprends pas. (P)
understanding compréhension *(f)* (7)
underwear sous-vêtements *(mpl)*
undressed: get undressed se déshabiller (7)
unfaithfulness infidélité *(f)* (7)
unfortunately malheureusement
unhappy malheureux(-euse)
uniquely uniquement (6)
united uni(e); **United Kingdom** Royaume-Uni (m) (9); **United States** États-Unis *(mpl)* (3)
university université *(f)* (P); **fac(ulté)** *(f)* (2); **university restaurant** restau-u (m) (6)
university universitaire (1)
unless à moins que
unlikely peu probable
unmarried célibataire (1)
unpack défaire sa valise
unpleasant désagréable (1)
until jusqu'à (2)
up: get up se lever (7); **go up** monter (5); **straightened up** rangé(e) (3); **up to** jusqu'à (2); **wake up** se réveiller (7); ; **wash up** faire sa toilette (7)
us nous (9)
use utiliser (6), employer
used to habitué(e) à
useful utile (10)
usually d'habitude (2)
utilize utiliser (6)

V

vacation vacances *(fpl)* (4); **on vacation** en vacances
vaccination vaccination *(f)*
Valentine's Day Saint-Valentin *(f)*
vanilla ice cream glace *(f)* à la vanille (8)
vanity vanité *(f)* (7)
variety variété *(f)*
VCR magnétoscope (m)
veal veau (m)
vegetable légume (m) (8); **raw vegetables** crudités *(fpl)* (8); **vegetable soup** soupe *(f)* de légumes
vegetarian végétarien(ne)
very très (8); **very near** tout près (de) (3)
vest gilet (m)
veterinarian vétérinaire *(mf)*
video vidéo *(f)*; **video cassette** vidéocassette *(f)*; **video cassette recorder** magnétoscope (m); **video game** jeu vidéo (m) (2)
Vietnam Viêt Nam (m) (9)
view vue *(f)* (3)
vinegar vinaigre (m)

violence violence *(f)* (6)
violent violent(e)
violet violet(te) (3)
virus virus *(m)* (10)
visa visa *(m)*
visit visite *(f)*; **medical visit** consultation *(f)*
visit *(place)* visiter (1), *(someone)* rendre visite à (7); **go visit** *(a person)* aller voir (4)
vitamin vitamine *(f)* (8)
vocabulary vocabulaire *(m)* (P)
voice voix *(f)*
volleyball volley *(m)* (2)
volunteer *(work)* bénévole
vomit vomir (10)
vote voter

W

wait (for) attendre (7)
waiter garçon *(m)* (2), serveur *(m)* (8)
waitress serveuse *(f)* (8)
wake up (se) réveiller (7)
walk promenade *(f)* (5); **go for / take a walk** faire une promenade (5)
walk aller à pied (4), marcher (8)
walking marche *(f)* à pied; **go walking** se promener (7), faire de la marche à pied
wall mur *(m)* (3)
wallet portefeuille *(m)* (5)
want vouloir (6), avoir envie de (4)
war guerre *(f)*
warmth chaleur *(f)*
wash (se) laver (7); **wash clothes** faire la lessive (5); **wash up** faire sa toilette (7)
washbasin lavabo *(m)* (10)
waste gaspiller; **waste time** perdre du temps
watch montre *(f)* (5)
watch regarder (2); **watch out (for)** faire attention (à) (8); **watch over** veiller
water eau *(f)* (2)
watermelon pastèque *(f)*
water-skiing ski nautique *(m)* (5)
way façon *(f)* (6); **show the way** indiquer le chemin (10); **this way** par ici (5)
we nous (1), on (4); **Shall we go . . . ?** On va... ? (2); **What shall we do?** Qu'est-ce qu'on fait?
weak faible
weakness faiblesse *(f)*
wear porter (4); **I wear a 42.** Je fais du 42. (5); **What size do you wear?** Quelle taille faites-vous? (5)
weather temps *(m)* (5); **The weather's bad / cold / cool / hot / nice / sunny / windy.** Il fait mauvais / froid / frais / chaud / beau / du soleil / du vent. (5); **What's the weather like?** Quel temps fait-il? (5)
Website site *(m)* Web (9)
wedding mariage *(m)*; **wedding anniversary** anniversaire *(m)* de mariage
Wednesday mercredi *(m)* (P)
week semaine *(f)* (P); **in one/two week(s)** dans huit/quinze jours

weekend week-end *(m)* (P); **Have a good weekend!** Bon week-end!; **on weekends** le week-end (P)
weigh peser
weight poids *(m)*; **do weight training** faire de la musculation (8), faire des haltères; **gain weight** prendre du poids; **lose weight** perdre du poids; **put on weight** prendre du poids
welcome bienvenue *(f)*, **You're welcome.** De rien. (P); Je vous en prie. (2) Je t'en prie.
well bien (P); **get well** guérir; **well-behaved** sage (4)
west ouest *(m)*; **West Indies** Antilles *(fpl)* (9)
what qu'est-ce que (1), que (2), comment (P), quel(le) (3), ce que (5), ce qui (7), quoi; **What day is today?** C'est quel jour, aujourd'hui? (P); **What does that mean in English?** Qu'est-ce que ça veut dire en anglais? (P); **What is / are . . . like?** Comment est / sont... ? (1); **What is . . . 's name?** Comment s'appelle... ? (4); **What is your name?** Tu t'appelles comment? *(familiar)* (P); Comment vous appelez-vous? *(formal)* (P); **What luck!** Quelle chance! (5); **What's the weather like?** Quel temps fait-il? (5); **What time is it?** Quelle heure est-il? (P)
when quand (2)
where où (1); **from where** d'où (1)
whereas tandis que
which quel(le) (3); que, qui (7); **about/of which** dont (7); **which one** lequel (laquelle) (6)
while tandis que, pendant que; **See you in a little while.** À tout à l'heure. (P); **while on** au cours de (10)
white blanc(he) (3); **white wine** vin blanc *(m)* (2)
who qui (1)
whom qui (2), que (7)
whole tout (toute); **the whole day** toute la journée (2)
wholegrain bread pain complet *(m)* (8)
whose dont (7)
why pourquoi (2)
widespread répandu(e)
widow veuve *(f)* (7)
widower veuf *(m)* (7)
wife femme *(f)* (2)
win gagner (2)
wind vent *(m)*
windbreaker blouson *(m)*
window fenêtre *(f)* (3); **ticket window** guichet *(m)*
windsurfing: go windsurfing faire de la planche à voile
windy: It's windy. Il fait du vent. (5)
wine vin *(m)* (2)
winter hiver *(m)* (5); **in winter** en hiver (5)
wish souhaiter (10)
with avec (P); chez (+ *person*) (7); **coffee with milk** café au lait *(m)* (2)

withdraw retirer (10)
without sans (P); **without doing it** sans le faire
woman femme *(f)* (1); **woman's suit** tailleur *(m)*
wonder se demander
wonderful merveilleux(-euse)
word mot *(m)* (P); *(lyrics)* paroles *(fpl)*
work travail *(m)*
work travailler (2); **Does that work for you?** Ça te/vous convient? (9); **Do you work?** Tu travailles? / Vous travaillez? **I work . . .** Je travaille... (P)
workbook cahier *(m)* (P)
worker *(manual)* ouvrier(-ère) *(mf)*
world monde *(m)*; **Third World** Tiers-Monde *(m)*
world-(wide) mondial(e) *(mpl* mondiaux)
worry (about) (se) préoccuper (de)
worse pire
would: I would like to . . . Je voudrais (bien)... (2); **What would you like to do?** Qu'est-ce que vous voudriez faire... (2); **You would like . . .** Tu voudrais... (2)
write écrire (2); **How is that written?** Ça s'écrit comment? (P); **Write the answer.** Écrivez la réponse. (P)
writer écrivain *(m)*
wrong: be wrong avoir tort (4); **What's wrong?** Qu'est-ce qui ne va pas? (10)

Y

yard jardin *(m)*
year année *(f)* (4), an *(m)* (5); **be . . . years old** avoir... ans (4); **Happy New Year!** Bonne année!; **New Year's Eve** le réveillon *(m)* du jour de l'an
yellow jaune (3)
yes oui (P), si (8)
yesterday hier (5)
yet pourtant, déjà; **not yet** ne... pas encore (5)
yogurt yaourt *(m)* (8)
you tu, vous (P), te (9); **And you?** Et toi?, Et vous? (P); **See you tomorrow!** À demain! (P); **Thank you!** Merci! (P); **There you are!** Te / Vous voilà!; **with you** avec toi, avec vous
young jeune (1)
your ton (ta, tes) (3); votre (vos) (3); **Open your book.** Ouvrez votre livre. (P); **What is your name?** Tu t'appelles comment? *(familiar)* (P); Comment vous appelez-vous? *(formal)* (P); **your friends** tes amis (1)
yourself te, vous (7); toi-même, vous-même(s)
youth jeunesse *(f)* (7); **youth hostel** auberge *(f)* de jeunesse (10)

Z

zero zéro (P), nul(le)
zip code code postal *(m)* (3)
zucchini courgette *(f)*
zydeco music: musique zydeco *(f)* zydeco (4)

Indice

Credits

Text/Realia Credits

p. 83: Le Trapèze; **p. 94:** Courtesy of Aux Trois Obus; **p. 132:** Adapté de Kate Macrae, *Les couleurs et leurs effets sur la nature humaine*, www.sylkacoordination.com; **p. 168:** Bruce Daigrepont, Cœur des Cajuns, Bayou Pon Pon, ASCAP-Happy Valley Music, BMI from Cœur des Cajuns on Rounder Records (#6026); **p. 229:** CommeauCinema.com; **pp. 290–292:** Eugène Ionesco, *Conte no. 4* © Éditions Gallimard, 1985 www.gallimard.fr; **pp. 308–309:** Courtesy of restaurant Maraîchers; **p. 336:** Jacques Prévert, "Déjeuner du matin" in *Paroles* © Éditions Gallimard © Fatras, succession Jacques Prévert pour les droits audio, électroniques et Internet; **p. 374:** Dany Bébel-Gisler, *À la recherche d'une odeur de grand-mère* © Éditions Jasor, 2000; **pp. 390–391:** Courtesy of Trois-Îlets Magazine; **p. 412:** Y EN A MARRE Copyright 2002 Sony/ATV Music Publishing France. All rights administered by Sony/ATV Music Publishing, 8 Music Square West, Nashville, TN 37203. All rights reserved. Used by permission.

Photo Credits

pp. 2–3: ©Walter Bibikow/Jon Arnold Images/Photolibrary; **p. 4 left:** ©Directphoto.org/Alamy; **p. 4 bottom center:** ©travelstock44/Alamy; **p. 4 right:** ©AP Photo/Jacques Brinon; **p. 5 top right:** ©Trevor Pearson/Alamy; **p. 5 center:** ©G P Bowater/Alamy; **p. 5 bottom:** ©Mychele Daniau/AFP/Getty Images; **p. 17:** ©Owen Franken/CORBIS; **p. 23:** ©Rick Strange/Index Stock Imagery; **p. 24:** ©John Angerson/Alamy; **pp. 28–29:** ©Art Kowalsky/Alamy; **p. 30 left:** ©Charles & Josette Lenars/CORBIS; **p. 30 top right:** ©Mike Harrington/Alamy; **p. 30 bottom right:** ©Walter Bibikow/Photolibrary; **p. 31 left:** ©D. Bretzfolder/PhotoEdit; **p. 31 right:** ©Sylvain Grandadam/Robert Harding Picture Library Ltd/Photolibrary; **p. 54 left:** ©Eric Ryan/Getty Images; **p. 54 right:** ©Michel Spingler/AFP/Getty Images; **p. 56:** ©Directphoto.org/Alamy; **p. 59 top:** ©Trevor Payne/Alamy; **p. 59 bottom:** ©Directphoto.org/Alamy; **pp. 64–65:** ©Gavin Hellier/Robert Harding Picture Library Ltd./Photolibrary; **p. 66 left:** ©Walter Rawlings/Robert Harding World Imagery/Getty Images; **p. 66 top right:** ©JTB Photo Communications Inc/Photolibrary; **p. 66 bottom right:** ©Hideo Haga/HAGA/The Image Works; **p. 67 top left:** ©JUPITERIMAGES/Agence Images/Alamy; **p. 67 top right:** ©Philippe Hays/Alamy; **p. 67 center:** ©Daniel Thierry/Photononstop/Photolibrary; **p. 67 bottom:** ©Bill Bachmann/Alamy; **p. 72:** ©Stockdisc/PhotoLibrary; **p. 73 top:** ©Esther Marshall/Heinle; **p. 77:** ©Directphoto.org/Alamy; **p. 78:** ©Danita Delimont/Alamy; **p. 90:** ©AbleStock/Index Stock Imagery; **p. 96 top left:** ©Maria Taglienti/Index Stock Imagery; **p. 96 top right:** ©Beryl Goldberg; **p. 97 top left:** ©IPA/The Image Works; **p. 97 top right:** ©Nicholas Raducnu/Heinle; **p. 102 top:** Courtesy of Martin Hallier, Kiemsa; **p. 102 bottom:** ©Werner Dieterich/F1 Online Digital Stock Photo Agency/Photolibrary; **p. 103 top:** ©Christopher Hunt/Getty Images; **p. 103 bottom:** ©Michael Dwyer/Alamy; **pp. 104–105:** ©Paul Nevin/Photolibrary; **p. 106 top:** ©David Whitten/Index Stock Imagery; **p. 106 bottom:** ©Philippe Henry/Photolibrary; **p. 107 top left:** ©Keith Levit Photography/Index Open; **p. 107 top right:** ©Yoshio Tomii/SuperStock; **p. 107 bottom:** ©Walter Bibikow/Photolibrary; **p. 125:** ©Ulrike Welsch; **p. 132:** ©Andreas von Einsiedel; Elizabeth Whiting & Associates/CORBIS; **p. 134 top:** ©J. A. Kraulis/Masterfile; **p. 134 bottom left:** ©Ann Ronan Picture Library/HIP/The Image Works; **p. 134 bottom right:** ©The Granger Collection, New York; **p. 135 top:** ©AP Photo/CP, Jacques Boissinot; **p. 135 right:** ©Jane George/AFP/Getty Images; **pp. 140–141:** ©John Coletti/Jon Arnold Images/Photolibrary; **p. 142 left:** ©Neil Rabinowitz/CORBIS; **p. 142 center:** ©Reuters/CORBIS; **p. 142 right:** ©Philip Gould/CORBIS; **p. 143 left:** ©Joe Raedle/Getty Images; **p. 143 right:** ©Nathan Benn/CORBIS; **p. 157:** ©Mark Segal/Index Stock Imagery; **p. 165:** ©Diaphor Agency/Index Stock Imagery; **p. 168:** ©Philip Gould/CORBIS; **p. 170:** *Street Scene, New Orleans* (oil on canvas), Mantelet-Martel, Andre (b.1876) / Waterhouse and Dodd, London, UK/The Bridgeman Art Library; **p. 171:** ©AP Photo/David J. Phillip; **p. 176 top:** ©Paul J. Richards/AFP/Getty Images; **p. 176 bottom:** ©William Albert Allard/National Geographic/Getty Images; **p. 177 top:** ©Marie-Reine Mattera; **p. 177 bottom:** ©Walter Bibikow/Mauritius Die Bildagentur Gmbh/Photolibrary; **pp. 178–179:** ©age fotostock/SuperStock; **p. 180 top:** ©Chris Jones/Photolibrary; **p. 180 center and bottom:** ©Brigitte Merle/Photononstop/Photolibrary; **p. 181 top left:** ©Rhoda Sidney/PhotoEdit; **p. 181 top right:** ©Jon Arnold Images/SuperStock; **p. 181 center:** ©Jacques Kerebel/Photononstop/Photolibrary; **p. 181 bottom:** ©SuperStock; **p. 183:** ©Chris Jones/Photolibrary; **p. 189 top left:** ©George Simhoni/Masterfile; **p. 189 top center:** ©Hornst Von Irmer/Index Stock Imagery; **p. 189 top right:** ©Bill Bachman/The Image Works; **p. 189 bottom left:** ©Bill Bachmann/Photolibrary; **p. 189 bottom center:** ©Photononstop/SuperStock; **p. 189 bottom right:** ©Robert Holmes/CORBIS; **p. 197 left:** ©Sandro Vannini/CORBIS; **p. 197 center:** ©Andrzej Gorzkowski/Alamy; **p. 198:** ©Directphoto.org/Alamy; **p. 203 top left:** ©Bill Bachman/The Image Works; **p. 203 bottom right:** ©Mark Antman/The Image Works; **p. 204 top:** ©Bill Ross/CORBIS; **p. 204 bottom:** ©Robert Holmes/CORBIS; **p. 205:** ©Malatesta Photo/Photographers Direct; **p. 208:** ©Iconotec/Alamy; **p. 209:** ©Paul Thompson; Eye Ubiquitous/CORBIS; **p. 210 top and bottom:** ©Directphoto.org/Alamy; **p. 211 bottom:** ©Image Source/SuperStock; **p. 216 top:** ©Brenda Tharp/CORBIS; **p. 216 bottom:** ©Buddy Mays/CORBIS; **p. 218 bottom:** ©Ray Juno/CORBIS; **pp. 220–221:** ©Brigitte Merle/Photononstop/ Photolibrary; **p. 222 bottom left:** ©Thomas Craig/Index Stock Imagery; **p. 222 bottom right:** ©Kindra Clineff/Index Stock Imagery; **p. 223 top:** ©Directphoto.org/ Alamy; **p. 223 center:** ©Walter Bibikow/Index Stock Imagery; **p. 230 left:** ©Ron Chapple/Thinkstock Images/Jupiter Images; **p. 230 right:** ©Purestock/Alamy; **p. 242:** ©DiScina/Courtesy of Getty Images; **p. 248:** ©UGC/Studio Canal/The Kobal Collection; **p. 250 top:** ©Gaumont/20th Century Fox/The Kobal Collection; **p. 250 bottom:** ©Paris/Panitalia/Titanus/The Kobal Collection; **p. 251:** ©Films 13/TF1 Films/The Kobal Collection; **p. 256 top:** Courtesy of www.soma-riba.com; **p. 256 bottom:** ©Hans-Peter Merten/Mauritius Die Bildagentur Gmbh/Photolibrary; **p. 257 top:** ©BARIL PASCAL/CORBIS SYGMA; **p. 257 bottom:** ©Louise Heusinkveld/Alamy; **p. 258–259:** ©age fotostock/SuperStock; **p. 260 top left:** ©Marc Garanger/CORBIS; **p. 260 top right:** ©Sueter Photography/Alamy; **p. 260 bottom:** ©Hemis/Alamy; **p. 261 top:** ©Vladimir Pcholkin/Taxi/Getty Images; **p. 261 bottom:** ©Alain Nogues/CORBIS SYGMA; **p. 275:** ©Owen Franken/CORBIS; **p. 282:** ©Robert Fried/Alamy; **p. 284 top:** ©Image Source/Corbis; **p. 284 bottom:** ©Olivia Baumgartner/CORBIS SYGMA; **p. 289:** ©Hans-Peter Merten/Mauritius Die Bildagentur Gmbh/Photolibrary; **p. 293:** ©Directphoto.org/Alamy; **p. 294:** ©Photodisc/Getty Images; **pp. 300–301:** ©Nigel Blythe/Cephas Picture Library Ltd/Photolibrary; **p. 302 center:** ©Robert Harding Picture Library Ltd/Alamy; **p. 302 bottom:** ©RESO-DIAPHOR Images/Index Stock Imagery; **p. 303 top left:** ©Prisma/SuperStock; **p. 303 top center:** ©Lee Snider/The Image Works; **p. 303 top right:** ©SCPhotos/Alamy; **p. 303 bottom:** ©Erich Lessing/Art Resource, NY; **p. 313 top:** ©Catherine Karnow/CORBIS; **p. 313 bottom:** ©Thomas Craig/Index Stock Imagery; **p. 315:** ©Esther Marshall/Heinle; **p. 317:** ©David R. Frazier Photolibrary, Inc./Alamy; **p. 328 right:** ©ImageState Royalty-Free/ Alamy; **p. 336:** ©James Leynse/CORBIS; **p. 338 top:** ©Ulrike Welsch; **p. 338 bottom:** ©Stuart Cohen; **p. 344 top:** ©Fabrice Vallon/Cub Sept/Corbis; **p. 344 bottom:** ©Patrick Mac Sean/Photoalto/Photolibrary; **p. 345 top:** ©FRANCIS VERNHET; **p. 345 bottom:** ©Bernd Opitz/Taxi/Getty Images; **pp. 346–347:** ©Chad Ehlers/Photolibrary; **p. 348 left:** ©George Steinmetz/Corbis; **p. 348 top right:** ©Rolf Richardson/Alamy; **p. 348 bottom right:** ©Ben Mangor/SuperStock; **p. 349 top:** ©Peter Fogg/Photolibrary; **p. 349 bottom:** ©Roger Blurn/Photononstop/Photolibrary; **p. 355:** ©Philippe Giraud/Goodlook Pictures/Corbis; **p. 361:** ©Rosine Mazin/Photononstop/Photolibrary; **p. 365:** ©Steve Vidler/ImageState/Jupiter Images; **p. 368 top:** ©Tiziana and Gianni Baldizzone/CORBIS; **p. 368 center:** ©age fotostock/SuperStock; **p. 368 bottom:** ©Phyllis Picardi/Index Stock Imagery; **p. 369:** ©Peter Adams/Jon Arnold Images/Photolibrary; **p. 371 left:** ©Steve Vidler/ImageState/Photolibrary; **p. 371 top right:** ©Steve Vidler/ImageState/Jupiter Images; **p. 371 center right:** ©David R. Frazier/The Image Works; **p. 371 bottom left:** ©Daryl Benson/Masterfile; **p. 371 bottom right:** ©Bernard Desjeux/CORBIS; **p. 374:** ©Alyx Kellington/Index Stock Imagery; **p. 375:** ©Chad Ehlers/Nordicphotos/Photolibrary; **p. 376 top left:** ©AP Photo/Ariana Cubillos; **p. 376 bottom left:** ©Hemis/Alamy; **p. 376 bottom right:** ©Sylvain Grandadam/Riser/Getty Images; **pp. 382–383:** ©Fausto Giaccone/Anzenberger Agency/Jupiter Images; **p. 384 top and bottom:** ©Robert Fried/Alamy; **p. 384 center:** ©JTB Photo Communications, Inc/Photolibrary; **p. 385 top left:** ©Marc Garanger/CORBIS; **p. 385 top right:** ©Robert Fried/Alamy; **p. 385 bottom:** ©Walter Bibikow/Index Stock Imagery; **p. 389:** ©Index Stock Imagery; **p. 395:** ©Warren Morgan/CORBIS; **p. 399:** ©Philip Gould/CORBIS; **p. 402:** ©Yadid Levy/Alamy; **p. 404:** ©ThinkStock LLC/Index Stock Imagery; **p. 407:** ©Stuart Cohen/The Image Works; **p. 412:** ©Eric Vernazobres/Corbis; **p. 414:** ©AP Photo/Jason DeCrow; **p. 415 top:** ©AP Photo/Keystone, Fabrice Coffrini; **p. 415 center and bottom left:** ©Philip Gould/CORBIS; **p. 415 bottom right:** ©Pascal Guyot/AFP/Getty Images; **p. 420 top:** ©Agricole Galleria; **p. 420 bottom:** ©Steve Mason/Photodisc/Getty Images; **p. 421 top:** ©Alain Jocard/AFP/Getty Images; **p. 421 bottom:** ©AP Photo/Brennan Linsley; **p. 422:** ©Carl Purcell/Photo Researchers, Inc.; **p. 423 top left:** ©Bruce Paton/Panos Pictures; **p. 423 top right:** ©David Reed/Panos Pictures; **p. 423 center:** ©Gisele Wulfsohn/Panos Pictures; **p. 423 bottom left:** ©Charles O. Cecil/Alamy; **p. 423 bottom right:** ©Bethune Carmichael/Lonely Planet Images; **p. 424 top:** ©Robert Grossman/CORBIS SYGMA; **p. 424 bottom:** ©Otto Lang/CORBIS; **p. 425 top:** ©Christine Osborne/CORBIS; **p. 425 center left:** ©Chris Lisle/CORBIS; **p. 425 center right:** ©Chinch Gryniewicz; Ecoscene/CORBIS; **p. 425 bottom:** ©Robert van der Hilst/CORBIS; **pp. 426–427:** ©David A. Barnes/Alamy; **p. 428 top:** ©Steve Vidler/SuperStock; **p. 428 center:** ©Morton Beebe/CORBIS; **p. 428 bottom:** ©Kevin Burke/Corbis; **p. 429:** ©Vario images GmbH & Co.KG/Alamy; **p. 441:** ©Keren Su/CORBIS.

*All photographs not credited are the property of Cengage Learning and Heinle Image Resource Bank.